RUBENIANUM

CONCEPT, DESIGN & EXECUTION IN FLEMISH PAINTING (1550-1700)

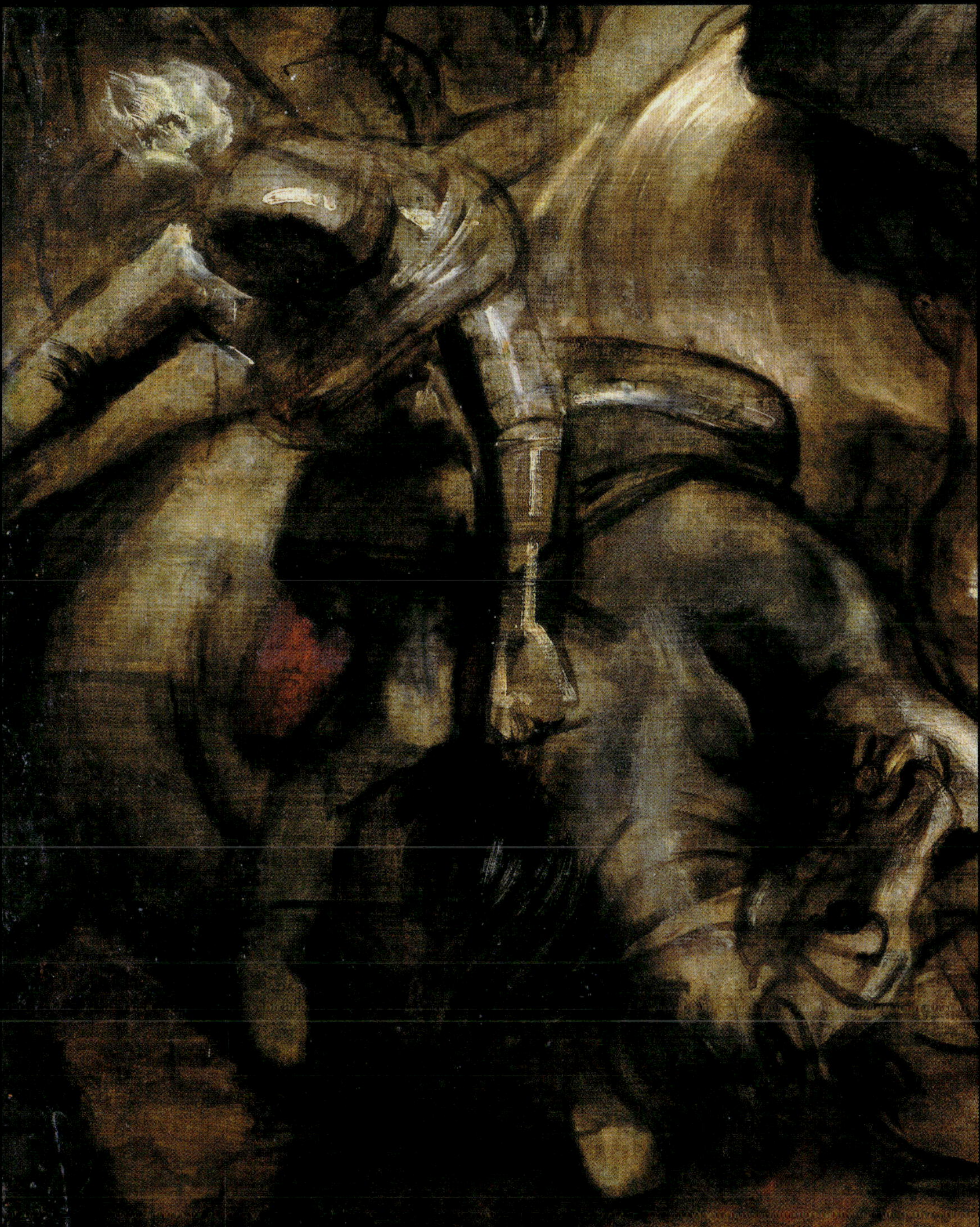

BREPOLS

Concept, Design & Execution in Flemish Painting (1550-1700)

CONCEPT, DESIGN & EXECUTION IN FLEMISH PAINTING (1550-1700)

Edited by Hans Vlieghe, Arnout Balis and Carl Van de Velde

BREPOLS

Copy-editor Hans Devisscher

ISBN 2-503-50731-X
D/2000/0095/86

Printed in the E.U. on acid-free paper

Foreword

To conclude the 6-year project, *Concept-Design-Execution: an Analysis of Creative Processes in Flemish Painting of the sixteenth and seventeenth Century*, funded by the Fonds voor Wetenschappelijk Onderzoek-Vlaanderen, a symposium took place at the Rubenianum, Antwerp, from 21 to 22 November, 1997. It was organized by the three directors of the project, Carl Van de Velde (Vrije Universiteit Brussel), Arnout Balis (Universitaire Faculteiten Sint-Ignatius Antwerpen), and Hans Vlieghe (Katholieke Universiteit Leuven). The practical organization was handled by the Nationaal Centrum voor de Plastische Kunsten van de 16e en de 17e Eeuw and the Wetenschappelijke Onderzoeksgemeenschap Vlaamse Renaissance- en Barokkunst.

The tripartite division of the symposium derives from the structure of the project.
– Part one, *Concept* (chaired by Justus Müller Hofstede), addresses all the elements from the social and intellectual context, which have played a role in the formation of a work of art, such as institutions, working conditions, intellectual make-up of artist or commissioner.
– Part two, *Design* (chaired by Egbert Haverkamp-Begemann), concentrates on specific studio practices which are preparatory to the eventual realization: these include the use of study material (e. g. the accumulated stock of exempla) as well as operational procedures such as sketching and studying the model.
– Part three, *Execution* (chaired by Peter Hecht) centres on the eventual realization on the definitive support and will address the problem of the autograph execution viz. the participation of other hands (studio assistants or specialists in their own field).

The Editors

Contents

Concept, Design and Execution: The Intervention of the Patron

Frans Baudouin

Concept, Design and Execution: As this symposium is devoted to these aspects of the process of realization of Flemish paintings in the period concerned, I presume that you expect that my inaugural lecture will address these stages in the creation of a work of art, showing perhaps how they can be traced successively in one single painting, or in a series, or an otherwise coherent group of paintings. I tried to find an appropriate topic of that sort, but finally decided to present three distinct, relatively short papers in which concept, design and execution will be dealt with separately. Examples of the patron's intervention in the creative process will, however, be provided throughout this lecture, thereby making the patron the 'trait d'union' that connects the three separate accounts.[1]

I

The term 'concept' refers to ideas, convictions, traditions, institutions, as well as the whole cultural atmosphere prevailing in a society to which the artists as well as the patrons belong. In some essays that I have published in the course of some ten or fifteen years, I tried to elucidate the fundamental factors which strongly influenced cultural life and consequently religious painting as well in seventeenth-century Antwerp.[2] This is not the occasion for returning at length to facts that I have already noted. I may recall here the conditions imposed at the capitulation of the city of Antwerp in 1585, in particular, those concerning the re-establishment of Roman Catholicism as the only accepted religion; the order imposed on guilds and brotherhoods to restore the destroyed altars in the churches; the decrees of the Council of Trent and their application to works of art, as propagated by diocesan synods in Mechelen and Antwerp; and lastly, the treatises written by prominent ecclesiastical authors who promoted the creation of a religious art that would embody the spirit of the Counter-Reformation.

Of course, none of these factors had any influence on artistic life in the Northern Provinces. It is common knowledge that after the separation of the two parts of the Netherlands, which became evident around 1600, painting in Holland developed itself in a direction which was very different from that followed in the Southern Provinces. This contrast was mainly the result of different religious circumstances. In the North, Roman Catholics were not allowed to worship publicly or even to have churches. Simultaneously, the Calvinists prohibited what they called 'idolatrous' imagery in their own places of worship. Both circumstances had a dramatic effect on religious painting. Commissions for altarpieces and other paintings for churches became virtually non-existent. Understandably, in 1678 Samuel van Hoogstraeten, Rembrandt's disciple, complained that, as a consequence, 'de beste loopbanen namentlyck de kerken, daerdoor gesloten zijn, en de meeste schilders zich derhalven tot geringe zaeken, jae zelfs tot beuzelingen te schilderen geheelijck begeven'[3] (the best careers, namely the churches, are not available to us, and therefore most painters devote themselves completely to minor things, even trifles).

The effect of this situation in the two separated parts of the Netherlands could hardly be better illustrated than by a comparison of paintings and engravings portraying Dutch and Flemish church interiors. One very instructive comparison, for example, are two early seventeenth-century (probably German) engravings in the Bibliothèque Nationale in Paris showing, respectively, a protestant church, in which no religious imagery is present, and a catholic one filled with altars, statues, sculptured screens etc (Figs. 1–2).[4]

The same contrast can be easily observed when paintings of church interiors by Pieter Jansz. Saenredam (Fig. 6), Emmanuel de Witte and other Dutch artist are compared with pan-

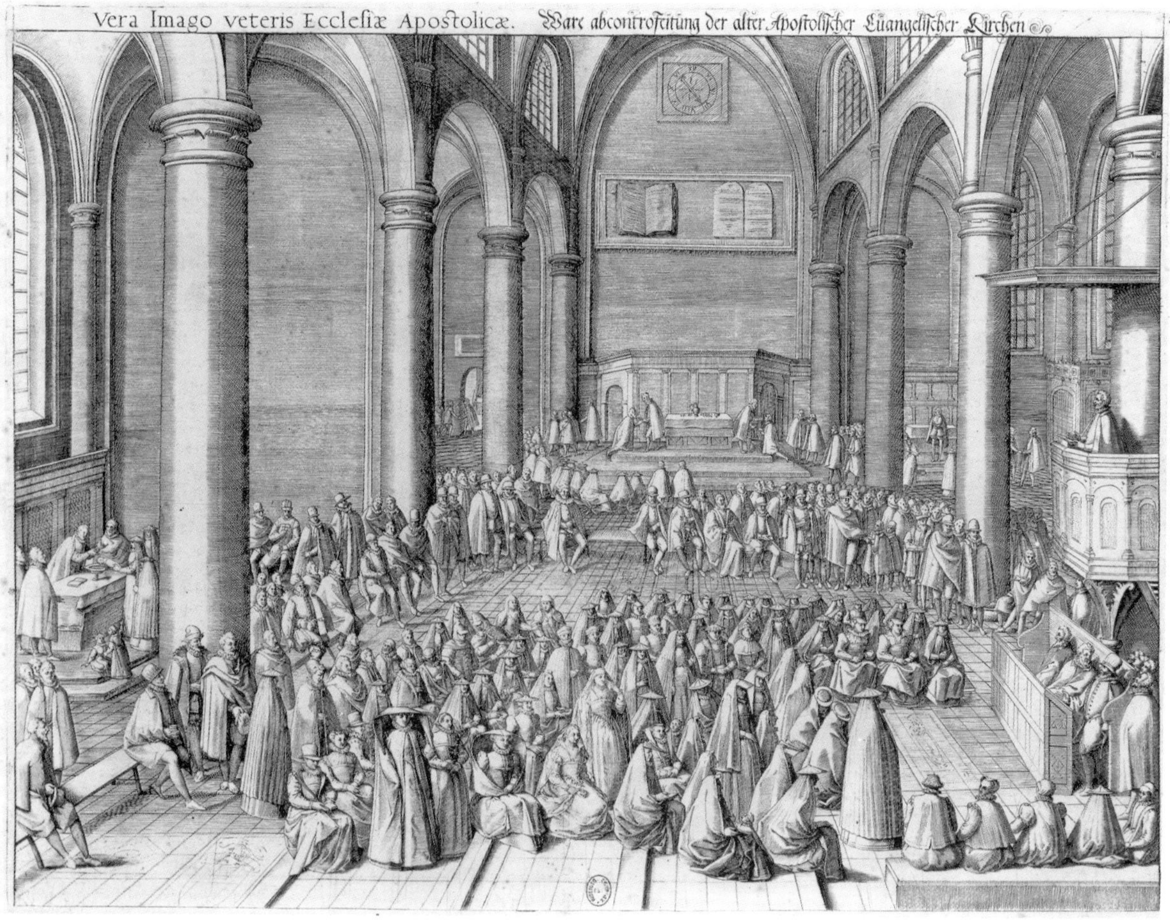

Fig. 1. German?, early seventeenth century, *Vera Imago veteris Ecclesiae apostolicae*, engraving. Paris, Bibliothèque Nationale

els by Hendrik van Steenwyck, Pieter Neeffs (Fig. 3), Willem van Ehrenbergh (Fig. 5) and Anton Gheringh. In this regard, David Freedberg noted: 'No contrast could be more revealing about the different states of visual culture in the North and in the South'.[5]

Of course, this does not mean that religious pictures were no longer painted in Holland. While they were usually not commissioned for churches, they were acquired by merchants and craftsmen for the decoration of their private homes. In accordance with the rather modest dimensions of the interiors in which they lived, the dimensions of these paintings are also rather small. Moreover, the total number of religious paintings that one could find in Dutch houses was less than that of genre scenes, still-lives, landscapes, seascapes and other rather 'secular' genres. Because of the specialized and innovative characteristics of their art, which deviated from the Baroque style that was so pervasive in most parts of Europe, Dutch artists paved the way to new, more 'modern' artistic conceptions.[6] This also explains why Dutch art was admired so much by later generations.

In the Northern Netherlands, group portraits (mostly of militia companies) constituted the only category of paintings for which large-sized canvases were used. To quote E. Haverkamp-Begemann: 'Apart from townhall decorations, these militia pieces, together with group portraits of governors of other city organizations, were the only institutional commissions in Holland in the seventeenth century'.[7] Similarly, Kurt Bauch emphasized: 'Gruppenbildnisse sind ja die eigentliche Monumentalkunst der holländischen Malerei'.[8]

In the Southern Netherlands 'Monumentalkunst' was, however, something very different. Here we observe another 'state of visual culture' (to use Freedberg's term). As Roman Catholicism was the only accepted religion and was strongly supported by the political authorities – a support based on the principle 'cujus

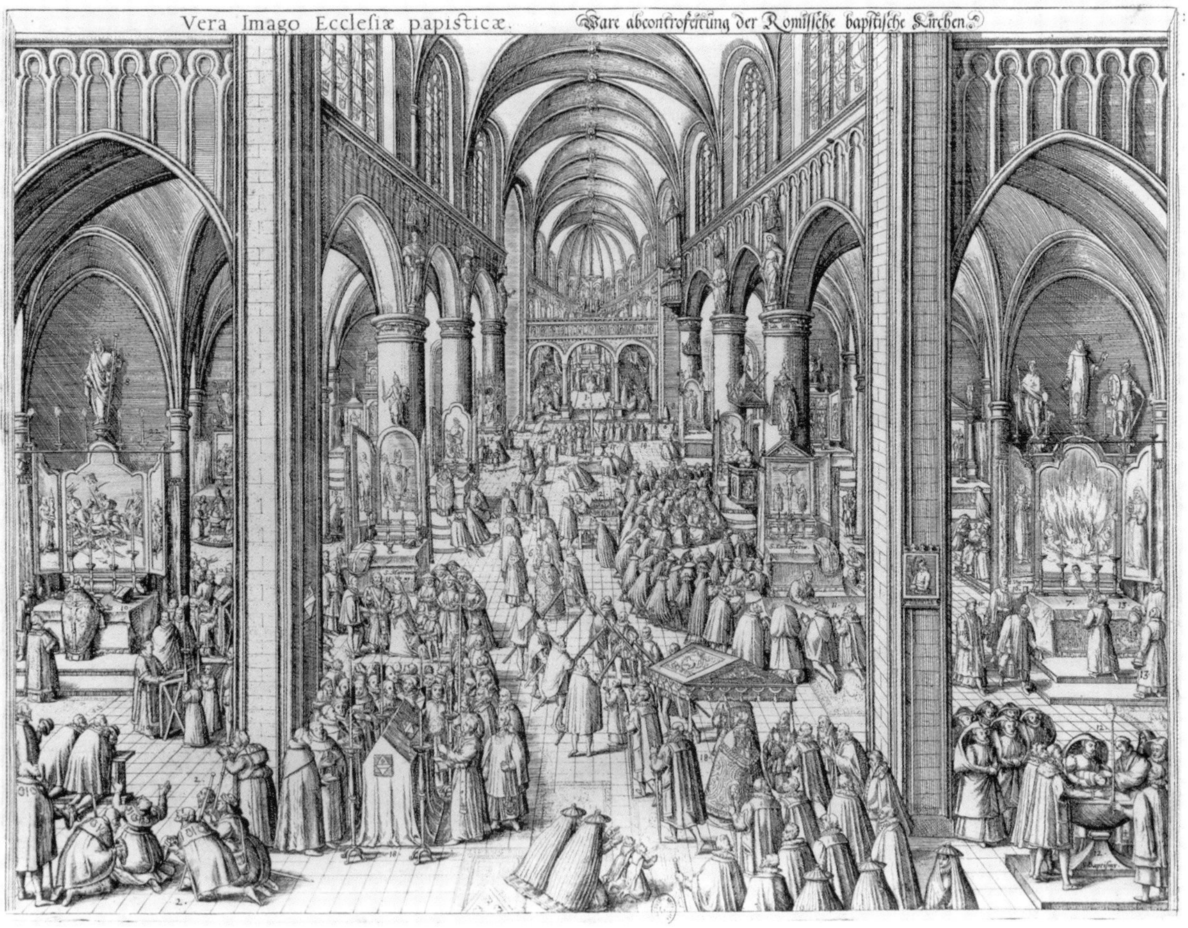

Fig. 2. German?, early seventeenth century, *Vera Imago Ecclesiae papisticae*, engraving. Paris, Bibliothèque Nationale

regio, eius religio' – 'the opportunities for painting altarpieces and every other kind of devotional painting were possibly even more abundant than they had been before'.[9]

To illustrate that contrast, I have argued in earlier essays that, while there was most likely no fundamental difference between a 'kolveniersgilde', a harquebusiers guild in the Northern Provinces and its counterpart in the Southern Netherlands – the only difference I have noted is that in the North they no longer took part in processions, as these were not held anymore – there is a striking disparity in the kind of art works they commissioned. For example, in 1611 the Antwerp Kolveniersgilde commissioned Rubens to paint a triptych, the famous *Descent from the Cross* (Fig. 7), to be placed above their altar in the cathedral. They certainly would have regarded this as the supreme expression of their existence as an important civic organization. In contrast, in Haarlem, Frans Hals painted group portraits of the officers and assistants of the 'Cluveniersdoelen' in 1627 and 1633 (Fig. 8), while in 1642 in Amsterdam, Rembrant painted the group portrait of Banning Cocq's company of 'harquebusiers', his famous so-called *Nightwatch*, currently in the Rijksmuseum (Fig. 9). This huge masterpiece, as well as Hals's militia portraits, were painted for the assembly halls of the 'Kolveniersdoelen' in Amsterdam and Haarlem, respectively, and not for churches.[10]

Today, I would like to complete and correct my earlier arguments with some remarks concerning a genre which deserves more attention than it has received thus far: Flemish seventeenth-century group portraits. We should indeed be aware of the fact that, however undeniable the contrasts are between the well-defined categories of paintings ordered by Dutch and Flemish harquebusiers, respectively, this should not lead to the conclusion that in the seventeenth century the militia groups, as well as other civilian corpses in the Southern

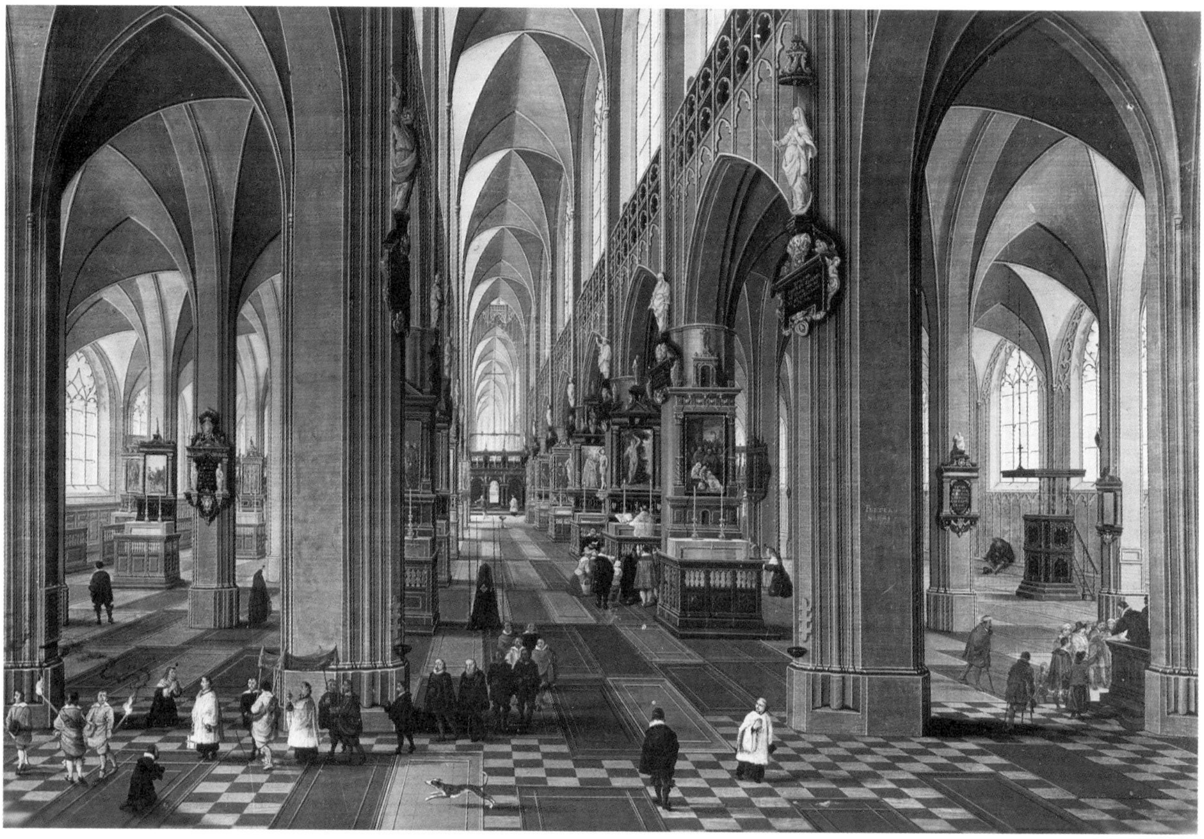
Fig. 3. Peter Neeffs the Elder, *The Interior of Antwerp Cathedral*. Brussels, Royal Museums of Fine Arts of Belgium

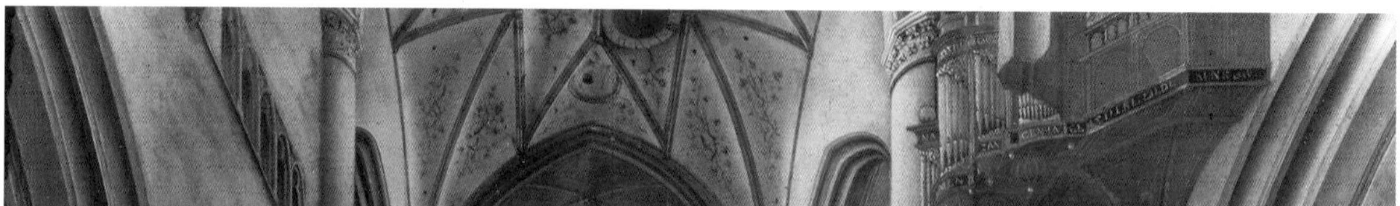
Fig. 4. Isaac van Nickelen, *The Interior of the St Bavo Church in Haarlem*. Brussels, Royal Museums of Fine Arts of Belgium

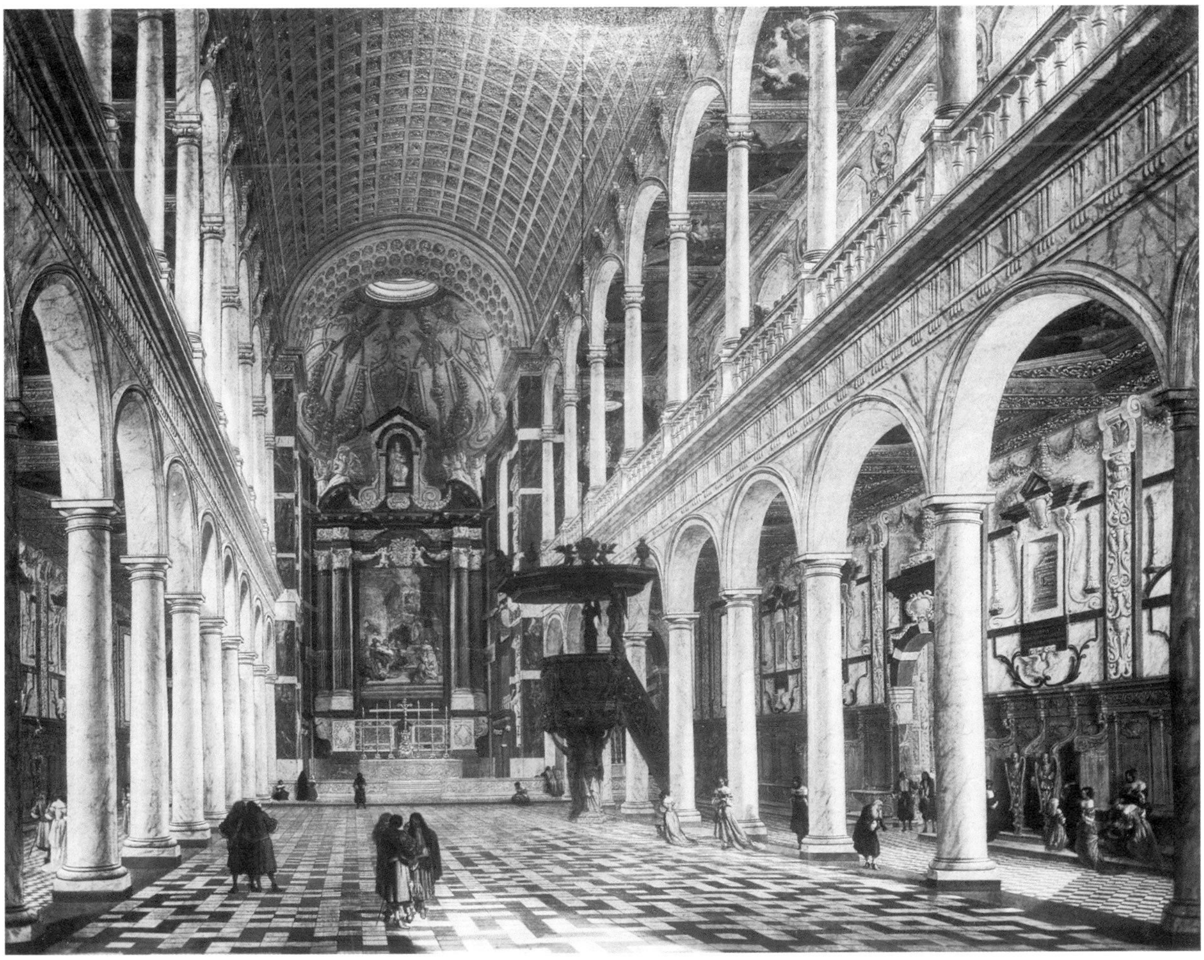

Fig. 5. Willem van Ehrenberg, *The Interior of the Jesuit Church in Antwerp*, 1667. Brussels, Royal Museums of Fine Arts of Belgium

Netherlands, no longer commissioned group portraits.

It is true that such paintings were most likely not as common in the South as in Holland.[11] And as we shall see, when compared with their Dutch counterparts, they exhibit different characteristics, which once again reveal a distinct cultural background.

In an essay on the Reformation and art in the Netherlands, Christian Tümpel drew attention to the fact that in the Northern Provinces group portraiture was steeped in a tradition that, in the early sixteenth century, was already much stronger than in the Southern Provinces. For example, c. 1500 the Great Crossbow guild in Mechelen had an image of their patron, Saint George, included in the middle of a painting of their militia, between two groups of members shown in as if in prayer (Fig. 10; Antwerp, Koninklijk Museum voor Schone Kunsten). And yet, as early as 1529 in Amsterdam, Dirk Jacobsz painted a group portrait of kolveniers (Fig. 11; Amsterdam, Rijksmuseum) without any reference to saints or religious symbols. For Tümpel, this contrast proves that very early on in the North the Reformation provoked 'eine tiefgreifende Säkularisation der traditionellen Volksfrömmigkeit'[12] (a profound secularization of the traditional popular devotion).

In 1556 Peter Pourbus (1524–1584) painted two panels for the Brotherhood of the Holy Blood (of Christ) in Bruges, which were added to a polyptic that already contained (as its central panel) *The Marriage in Cana* by Gerard David, from 1515 (currently in the Louvre). In these wings (Bruges, Kapel van het Heilig Bloed) members of the brotherhood are still portrayed in a manner similar to that seen in the panel of the militia guild in Mechelen, painted more than fifty years earlier.[13]

It would certainly be fascinating to trace other sixteenth-century group portraits in the

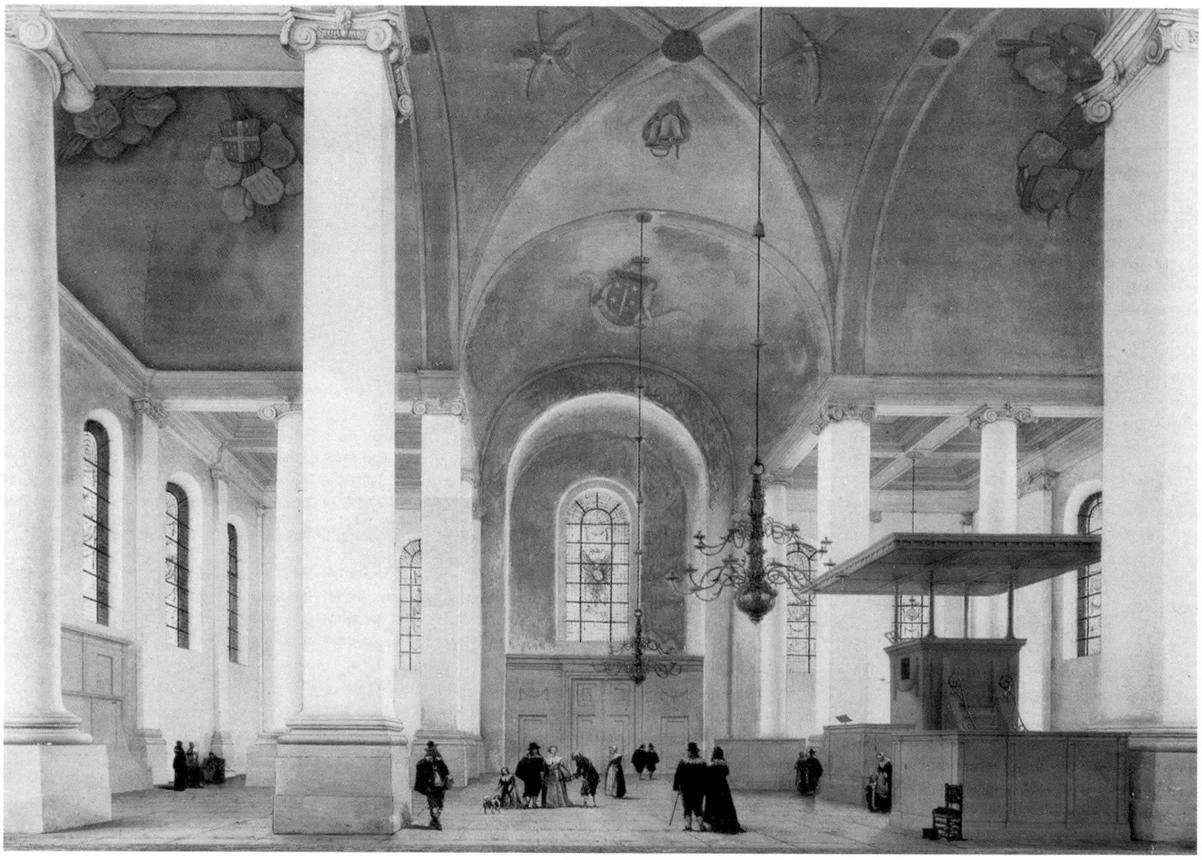

Fig. 6. Pieter Saenredam, *The Interior of the Nieuwe Kerk (New Church) in Haarlem*, 1652. Haarlem, Frans Halsmuseum

Southern Netherlands. But I prefer to leave this to specialists of that period and to restrict my investigations to seventeenth-century examples.

This research has led me to the conclusion that in the seventeenth century three categories of Flemish group portraiture can be distinguished.

First, one that continues a tradition that can be traced back to at least the fifteenth century.

Second, a category in which an allegorical or a historical motif is featured instead of a religious one.

And third, one in which there are no more direct references to religious figures, secular allegories or historical events. In this case, the group portrait recalls 'conversation pieces' that represent a family.

These categories seem to point to a shift in mentality and culture, but as it requires much more historical research I have omitted this subject from my exposé.

My first example illustrating the first category is an oil sketch traditionally attributed to Rubens[14] and dated *c.* 1615–1618 (Fig. 12; Antwerp, Maagdenhuis). This attribution has been contested repeatedly of late, except by Julius Held. I tend to agree with his view that the unfavorable impression one gets from it derives from its poor state of preservation. There is indeed considerable abrasion of the paint surface. The panel has also been cut at the bottom and has suffered from later restorations. The oil sketch originally belonged to the 'Knechtjeshuis' at the Paardenmarkt in Antwerp. The scene represented here is related to the fact that the 'Knechtjeshuis' was the orphanage for boys in Antwerp. Therefore, the title often given to this oil sketch, *Christ invoked for the poor families*, is completely inadequate. In fact, on the left half of the scene – the two halves were separated intentionally – six almoners responsible for the care of the orphans, dressed in their characteristic 'tabbaarden' (gowns, tabberts), and accompanied by two servants, who are discreetly shown in the middle in the background. The almoners present five naked children to Christ, who

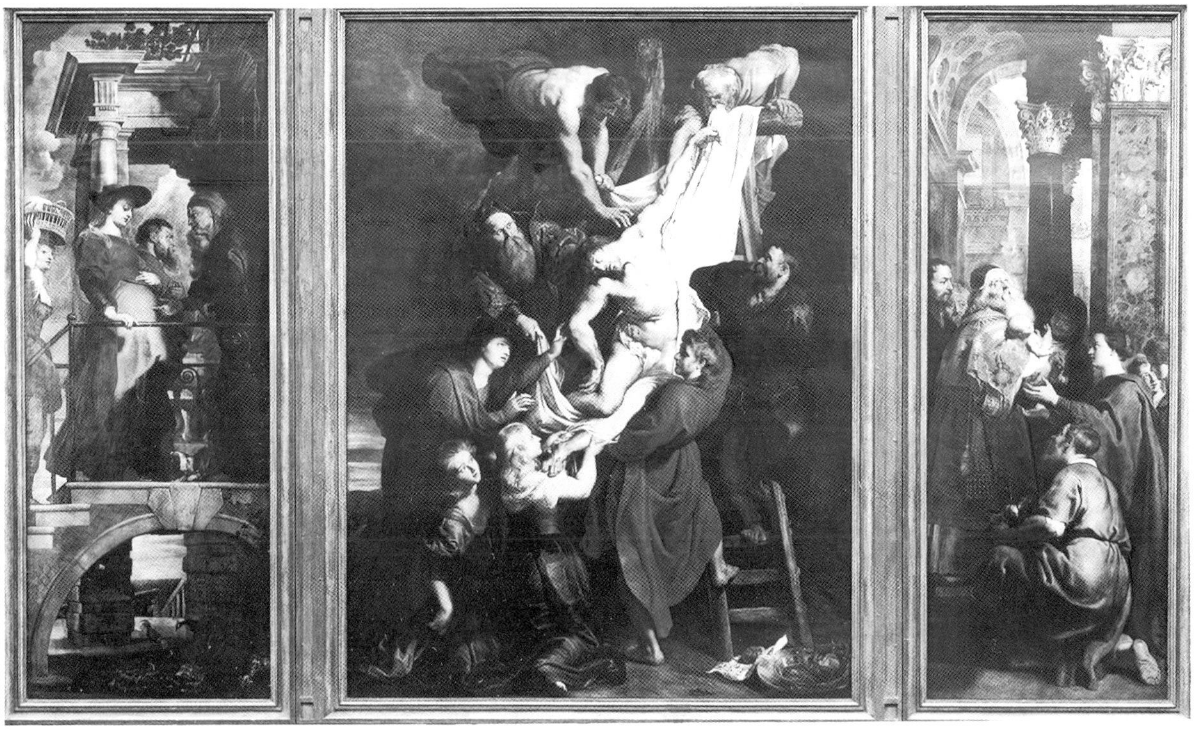

Fig. 7. Peter Paul Rubens, *The Triptych of the Descent from the Cross*, with on the left wing *The Visit of the Virgin to Her Niece Elizabeth*, and on the right one *The Presentation in the Temple*, 1612–1614. Antwerp, Cathedral

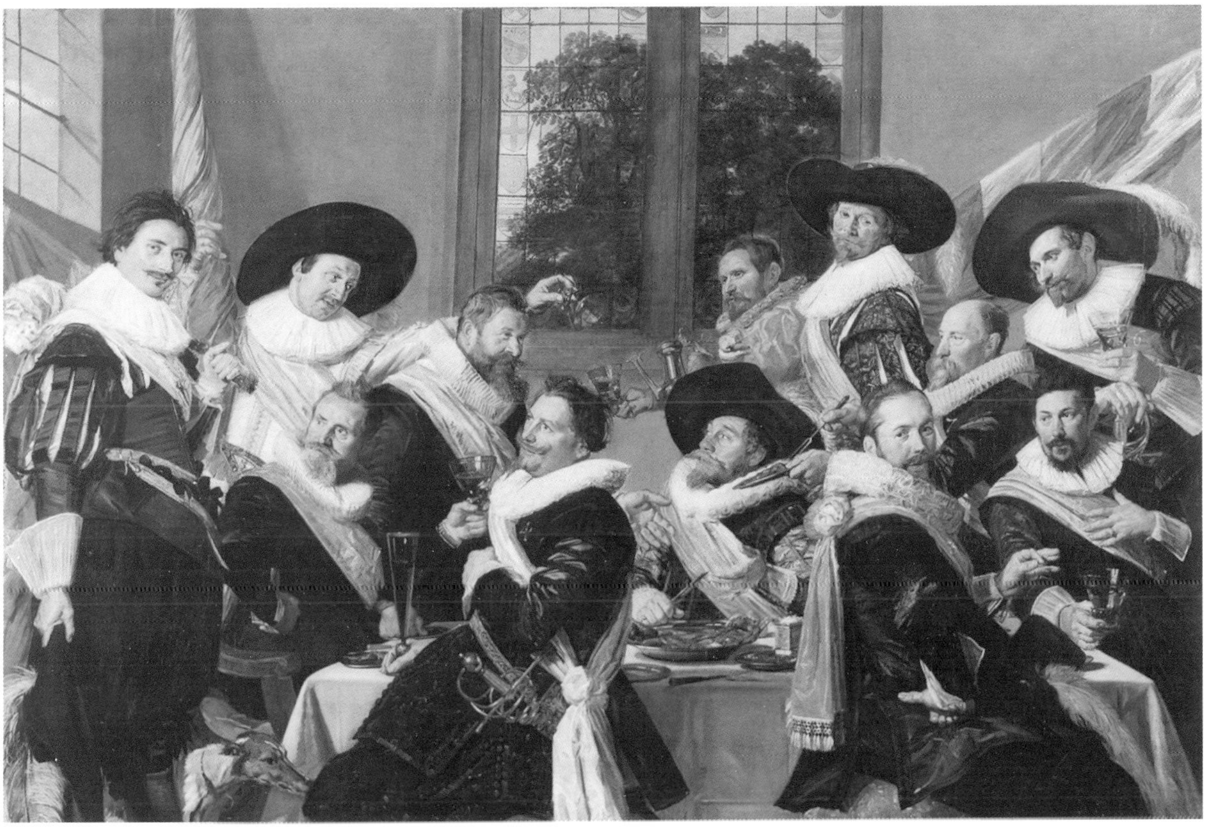

Fig. 8. Frans Hals, *The Assembly of the Officers and Sergeants of the 'Cluveniersdoelen' (Harquebusiers or Civic Guard of St. Adrian) in Haarlem*, 1633. Haarlem, Frans Halsmuseum

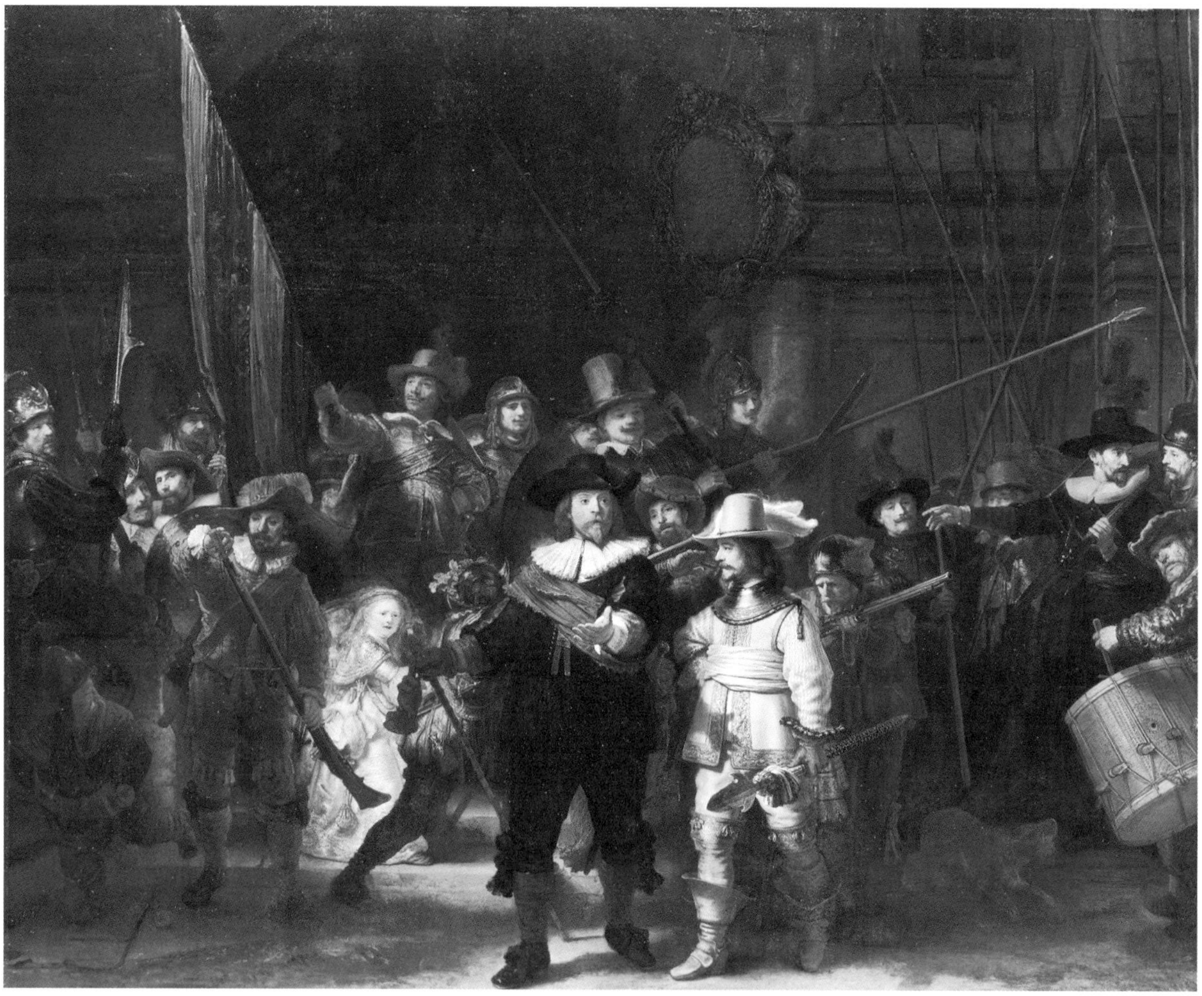

Fig. 9. Rembrandt, *The Nightwatch: the Harquebusiers' Company of Captain Banning Cocq and Lieutenant Willem van Ruytenburch*, 1642. Amsterdam, Rijksmuseum

blesses them. Next to Him is 'Caritas', who is nursing two children and by the gesture of her left arm recommends the orphans to Him. She simultaneously symbolizes the virtue of charity performed by the almoners for the orphans.

This oil sketch is certainly a design for a group portrait, in which a religious theme is included that is related to the function of the sitters. It is not known whether a large painting based on this project has ever been executed.

In the panel *The Assumption of the Virgin in the Presence of the Deans and Members of the Brussels Guild of the Great Arbalet (Voetboog)*, at the Royal Museums of Fine Arts in Brussels (Fig. 13), Gaspar de Crayer (1584–1669) adhered more to the visual tradition in which the religious subject is placed in the middle and the portraits – which are really superb ones! – are distributed equally to the left and the right of it. The sitters are shown in an attitude of prayer or holding a prayer book in their hands. Hans Vlieghe noted that the embroidered coat of arms, which consists of three small arbalets and is present on the gowns of some of these men, was not common before 1620. On the other hand, stylistic characteristics indicate that this group portrait could not have been painted much later.[15]

Vlieghe has also written about another group portrait painted by De Crayer, which can be seen in the same museum. Here, too, a religious motif, *Christ on the cross*, is represented in the middle, separating two small groups, consisting of a priest and the guardians of the beguinage of Brussels. They are also represented in an attitude of prayer, with either a rosary or a prayer book in their hands.[16]

In 1644, Peter Meert (1617–1669), a lesser-known artist also living in Brussels, painted the

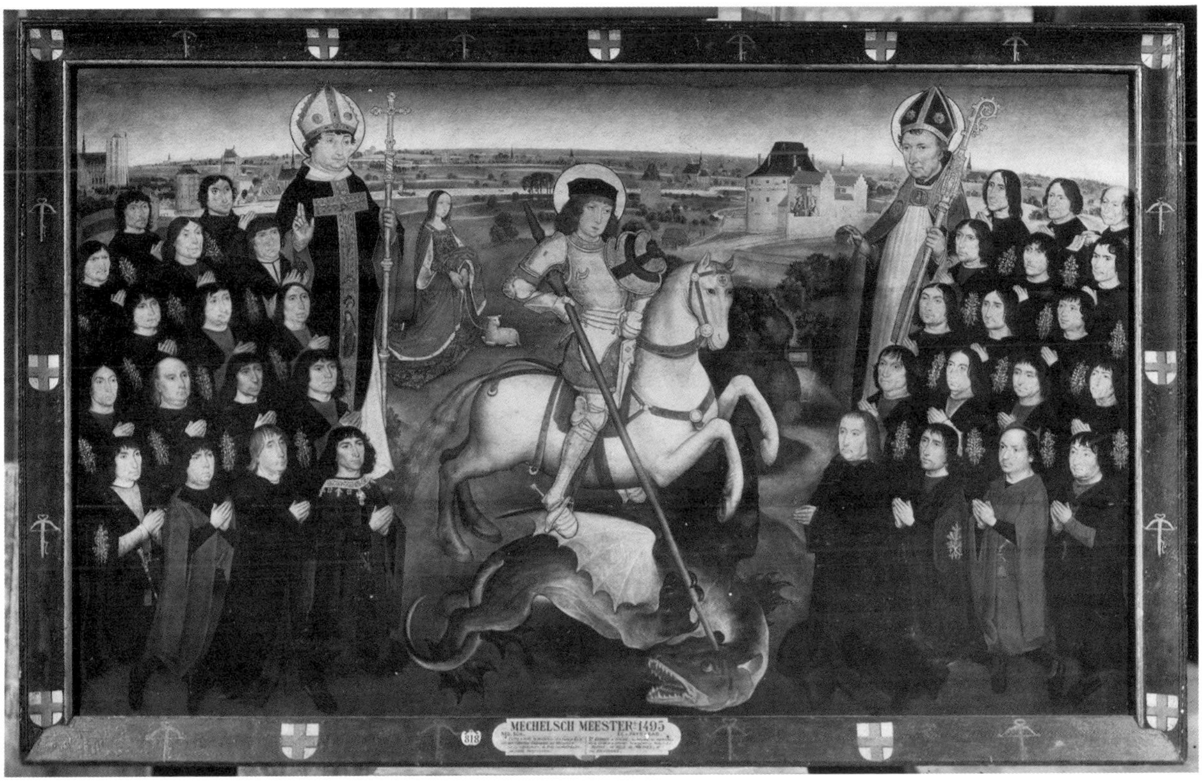

Fig. 10. Unknown Master, Mechelen *c.* 1500, *Group Portrait of Members of the Great Crossbow Guild in Mechelen, with their Patron, St George, and two other Saints.* Antwerp, Koninklijk Museum voor Schone Kunsten

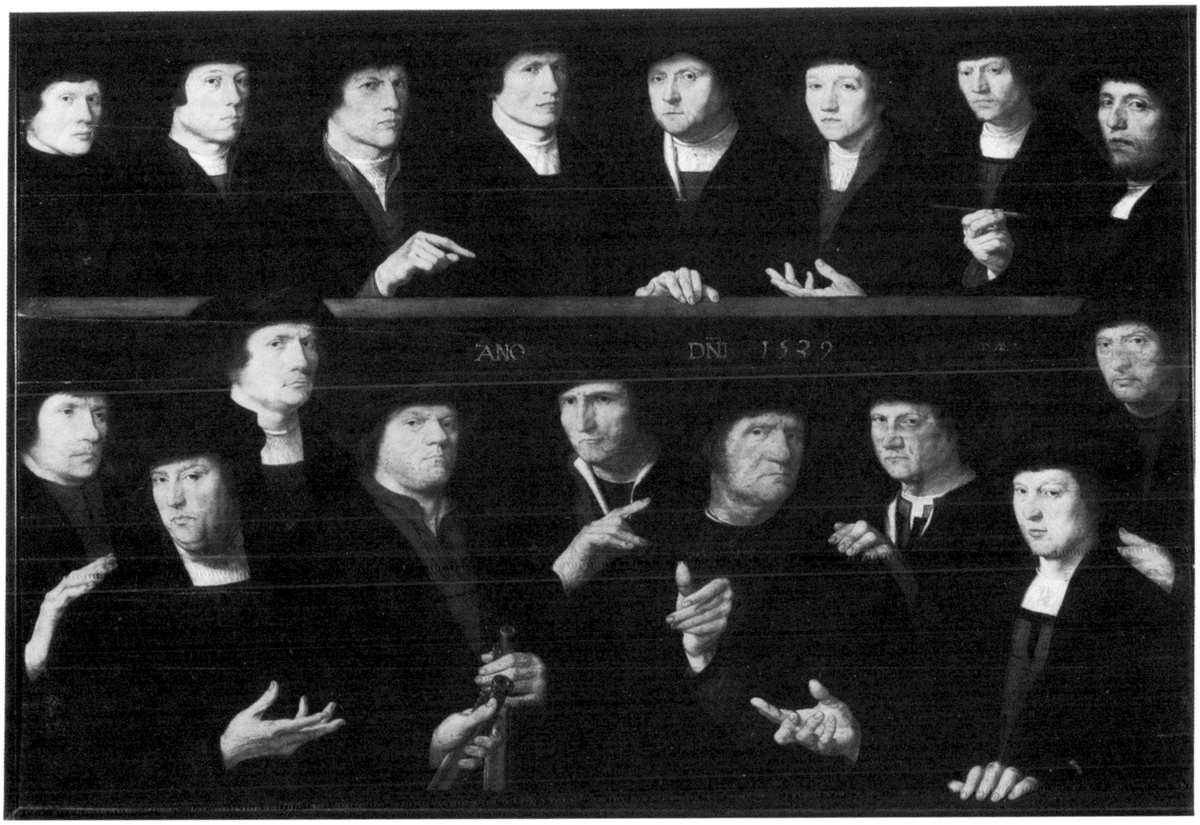

Fig. 11. Dirck Jacobsz, *Group Portrait of Officers of the Guild of Harquebusiers in Amsterdam*, 1529. Amsterdam, Rijksmuseum

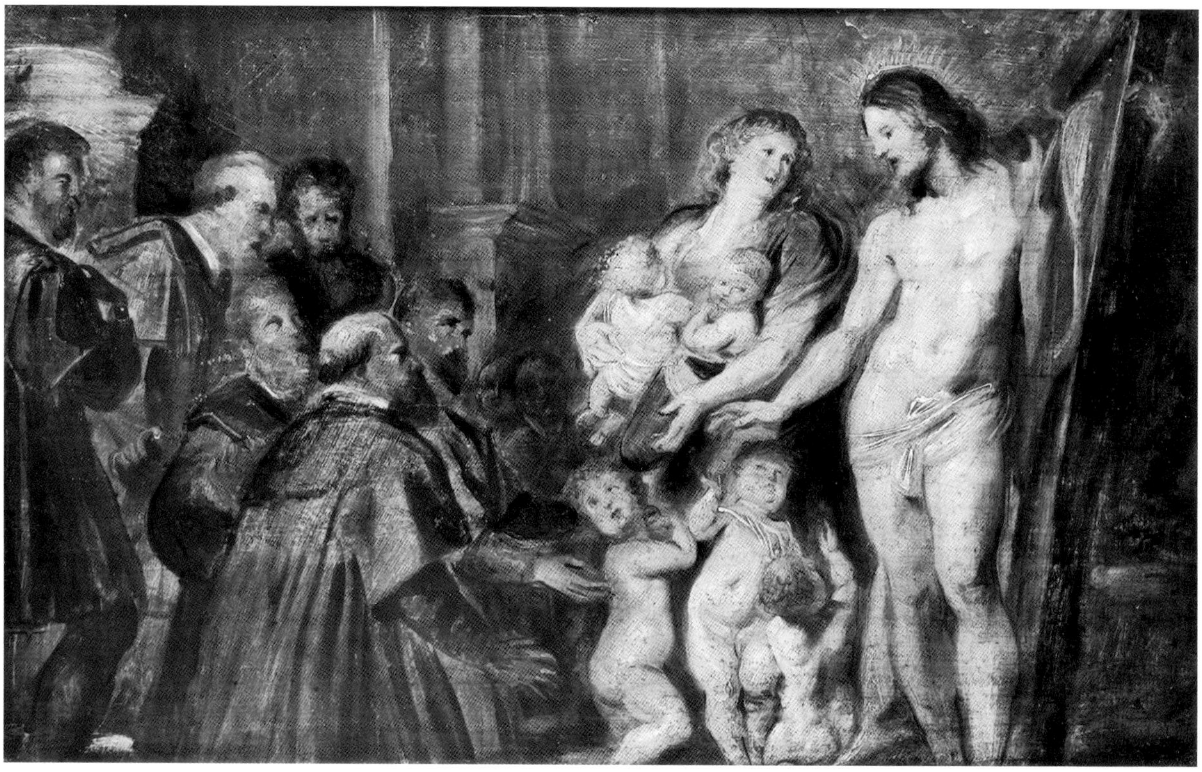

Fig. 12. Attributed to Peter Paul Rubens, *Preparatory oil sketch for a Group Portrait of the Almoners of the Orphanage for boys (Knechtjeshuis) in Antwerp, kneeling before Christ, Caritas standing next to Him*, (*c.* 1615–1620). Antwerp, Maagdenhuis (O.C.M.W.)

group portrait of the so-called masters of the foundlings of that city, together with their treasurer (or better still, paymaster), who is shown on the left behind a table on which the bread that will be given to the children is displayed (Fig. 14). Here, as well, one observes a religious subject in the middle: the Virgin and Child above in the clouds, accompanied by Saint Anne. Striking are the white crosses above the heads of four standing figures and on the dress of one of them. In a well-documented study of this picture, Madame Bonenfant-Feytmans explains that in Brussels such crosses were added to the painting whenever one of the sitters died.[17] Usually, the crosses were removed later on. This painting is an exception in that respect. Before the French Revolution it hung on the back panel of the choir stalls reserved for the masters of the foundlings in the Saint Michael and Saint Gudula church in Brussels. It is now at the museum of the Openbaar Centrum voor Maatschappelijk Werk (Public Centre for Social Work) in the same city.

Four years earlier, in 1640 – just after his return from Italy – Peter van Lint (1609–1690) painted an important group portrait of the deans and members of the Antwerp Carpenter's Guild (Fig. 15).[18] Although this painting is currently hanging on a wall in an appendant building of the Antwerp cathedral, it was not executed for this church, but undoubtedly for the assembly room of the Carpenter's guild house. Once again, a religious subject is represented in the middle, *The Marriage of Mary and Joseph*, which is shown taking place in a church before a priest who is wearing a chasuble of the same kind that was used in the seventeenth century by the Roman Catholic clergy. As, according to the Apocrypha, Jesus's foster father was a carpenter, it does not come as a surprise that a subject was chosen in which he plays a prominent role. The Antwerp carpenters themselves are also portrayed here in a familiar fashion, standing on the same level as Joseph and Mary, on either side of them, as if they were witnesses of this ceremony. Familiar companionship with saints is also characteristic of the devotional literature of this period in the Southern Netherlands. It should be noted that the individuality of the members of the guild seems to have been rendered faithfully and with great care in these beautiful portraits. Their names

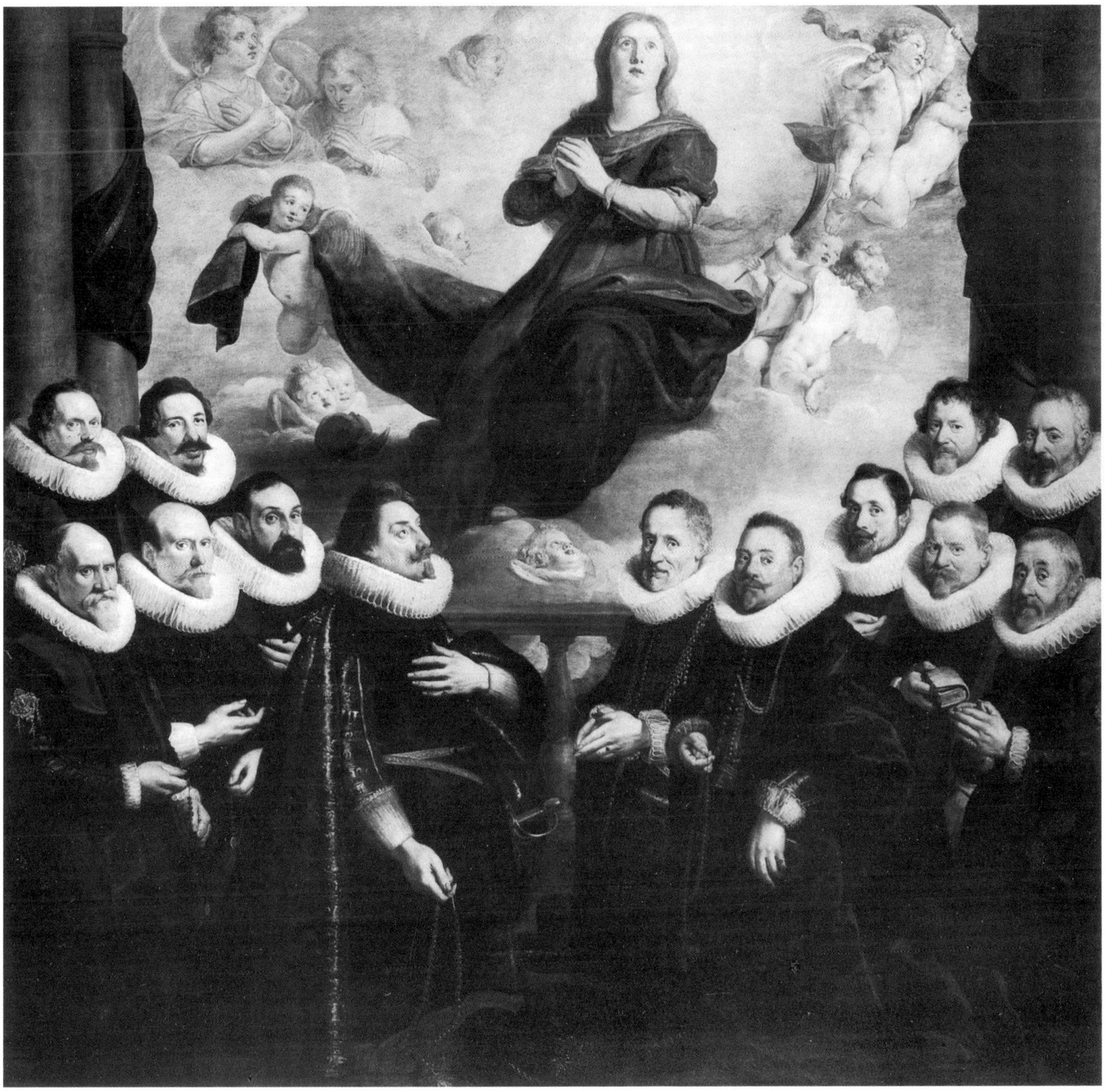

Fig. 13. Gaspar de Crayer, *The Assumption of the Virgin, above the Group Portrait of the Brussels Guild of the Great Arbalet (Grote Voetboog)*, *c.* 1620. Brussels, Royal Museums of Fine Arts of Belgium

are recorded on the pedestals that are used as seats by the allegorical figures representing the three Christian Virtues: on the left, Love with three children; on the right, Hope with the anchor; and next to her, Faith with a helmet on her head and holding two stone tablets of the Old Covenant and the Gospel under her left arm and a candle and a heart with her right arm. To the best of my knowledge, group portraits in which such theological elements were included were not painted in Holland in the seventeenth century.

In the Southern Netherlands we discern a second category of group portraits in which the religious motif is replaced by a 'secular' allegorical figure or a historical personality, placed in the middle or in the right half of the composition.

A beautiful seventeenth-century example is the oil sketch by Antoon Van Dyck in the Ecole Nationale des Beaux-Arts in Paris, which is the modello for a group portrait he painted in 1634–1635.[19] In it, seven Brussels magistrates, burgomasters and aldermen are represented with *Justitia* sitting on a throne in the middle. This large painting hung in the room where the magistrates acted as judges. When the Swedish architect Nicodemus Tessin the

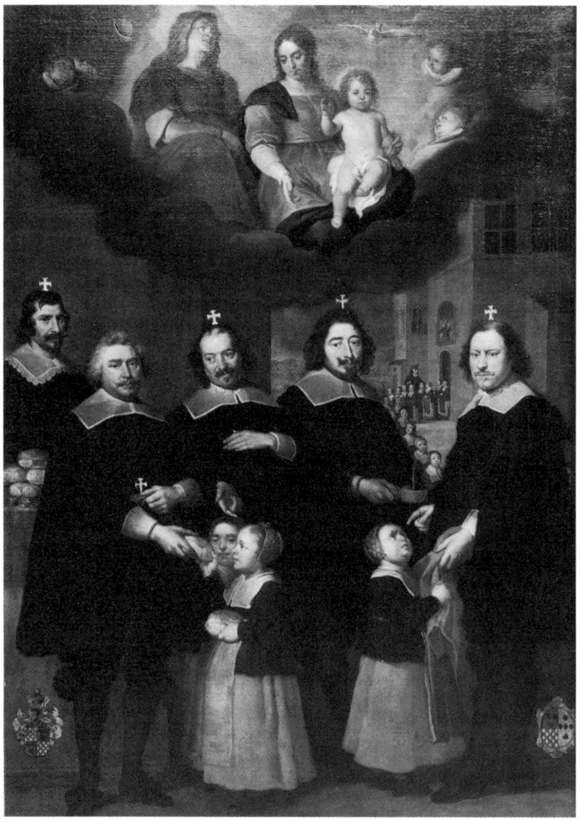

Fig. 14. Peter Meert, *The Guardians of the Foundlings in Brussels, under the protection of the Virgin and Child, accompanied by St Anne*, 1644. Brussels, Museum of the O.C.M.W.

Younger visited the Brussels Town Hall in 1687, he admired it there. In another room, which also contained Rubens's *Judgement of Cambyses*, he noticed a much larger painting by Van Dyck that contained no less than twenty-three full-length portraits of members of the City Council.[20] Both paintings by Van Dyck, as well as that by Rubens and also Roger van der Weyden's *Herkenbald-series*, were destroyed by fire in 1695 during the artillery bombardment of Brussels by the French troops commanded by Maréchal de Villeroy, – a true disaster for the arts in that city.

Van Dyck's group portrait of seven Brussels magistrates was certainly not the first in which Justice was part of the composition. She appears, for example, on a panel painted in 1594 by Maarten de Vos that portrays ten members of the court of Justice of the Brabant 'Munt' (Mint), established in Antwerp (Fig. 16; Antwerp, Rockoxhuis).[21] Seated at her feet are two captive naked figures representing 'Fallacia' (deceit) and 'Vis' (brutal force). Justice is also accompanied by four great legislators of the past. On the left, one sees Moses and Justinianus, the Byzantine emperor, on the right, Numa Pompilius, king of the Romans, and Caius Junius Secundus.

Similar, quasi sophisticated figures (most likely selected by a learned humanist) are not present in Van Dyck's modello for one of his paintings in the town hall in Brussels (Fig. 17). Justice appears here alone, sitting on a throne amidst the magistrates as if she is presiding at their deliberations.

In 1644, Cornelis de Vos (1585–1651) received the commission to paint a group portrait of the former deans and actual members of the board of the guild of the Kolveniers (harquebusiers), the same militia group that had commissioned Rubens's *Descent from the cross* thirty years before (Fig. 18). In an account concerning this group portrait, it is called: 'het stuck van keyser Carel en alle de oude dekens ende den dienenden eedt... staende op de camer in den hoff', or 'the piece of emperor Charles V and all the past and present deans of the guild, that is hanging in the guild house in the garden'. Unfortunately, Cornelis de Vos's large painting also went up in flames during a fire in 1731 that severely damaged the building. Fortunately, an oil sketch, in fact a rather large preparatory 'modello' for it, turned up about ten years ago in England, in Sudely Castle at Whichcombe – Cheltenham. A close examination of records concerning the Kolveniers at the Stadsarchief enabled Nora De Poorter to establish the history of this commission with great accuracy. For those interested in these details, she has published the results of her research in the 1985 yearbook of the Koninklijk Museum voor Schone Kunsten te Antwerpen.

From the document cited above, we know that here Charles V is shown seated on a throne in the middle of the painting. Other records reveal that on 15 June 1524 he granted a privilege to the Antwerp Kolveniers that allowed them to accept twelve 'wepelaers' in their corpse annually. 'Wepelaers' were citizens who, by paying rather high contributions to the guild, freed themselves from several civic duties, while simultaneously providing the guild with special financial resources. The oil sketch portrays the emperor giving that charter to the 'hoofdman' (head) of the guild. Of course, the man represented is not the one who served that

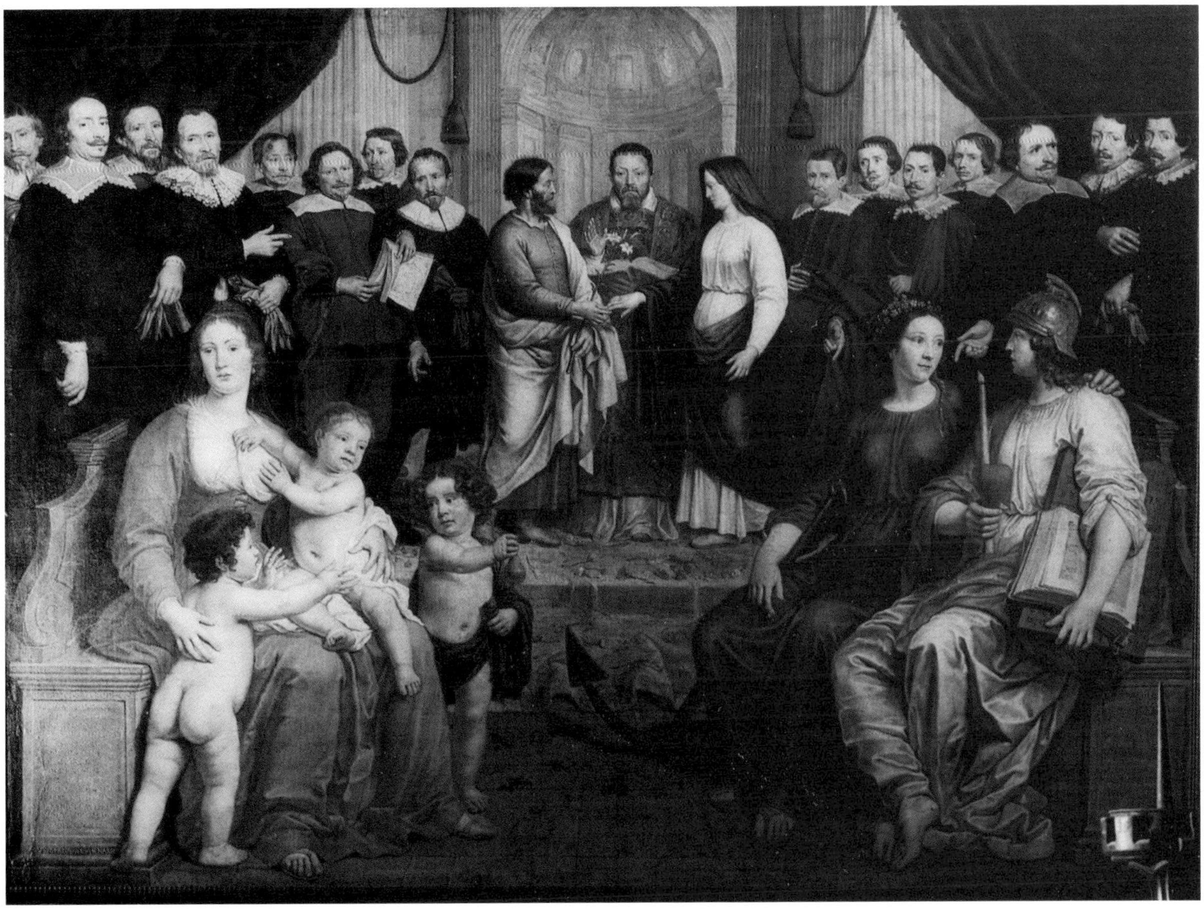

Fig. 15. Peter van Lint, *The Wedding of Joseph and Mary amidst the Deans and Members of the Antwerp Carpenters Guild of Antwerp, and assisted by the three Theological Virtues: Love, Hope and Faith*, 1640. Antwerp, Cathedral

function in 1524, but rather, the man who was in charge in 1644. He is presented to Charles V by Minerva or Bellona, while other harquebusiers (about 30 in all) are also portrayed on either side of the throne.

This painting is an excellent example of the portraiture of an important militia group, in which references to a historical figure and a historical event are included. The event shown here was still of great importance to the corpse during the year in which the picture was painted. In this regard, it should be noted that by painting this group portrait free of charge and by paying an additional 300 guilders, Cornelius de Vos acquired the freedom granted by the emperor's privilege for his son and himself.[23]

Other group portraits belonging to the same category are known, but as the titles traditionally given to them are most likely inaccurate, they still require some investigation in order to establish what they really represent. I will only mention two examples briefly. In a hallway of the Koninklijke Academie voor Schone Kunsten, in the Mutsaertstraat in Antwerp, there is a large group portrait signed by Peter Thys (1624–1677), which is sometimes erroneously entitled *Philip IV giving the charter of the Antwerp Academy of Fine Arts to David Teniers*. This Spanish king is certainly not represented here, nor is the painter David Teniers recognizable. In the Koninklijk Museum voor Schone Kunsten in Antwerp there is a very large canvas (more than 7 meters wide) signed 'HVBERTVS SPORCKMANS PINXIT', which, until 1859, was hanging in the 'schipperskamer', the guild house of the shipmasters. J.F. Van den Branden has reported that he had seen a date behind that signature, which was, however, somewhat damaged.[24] He suggested it reads 1677, which, on the basis of the clothes worn by the gentlemen portrayed, seems rather late. In even the most recent catalogues of the museum, the ruler seated on the throne is identified as Emperor Leopold I, an attribution which is not convincing for various reasons.[25]

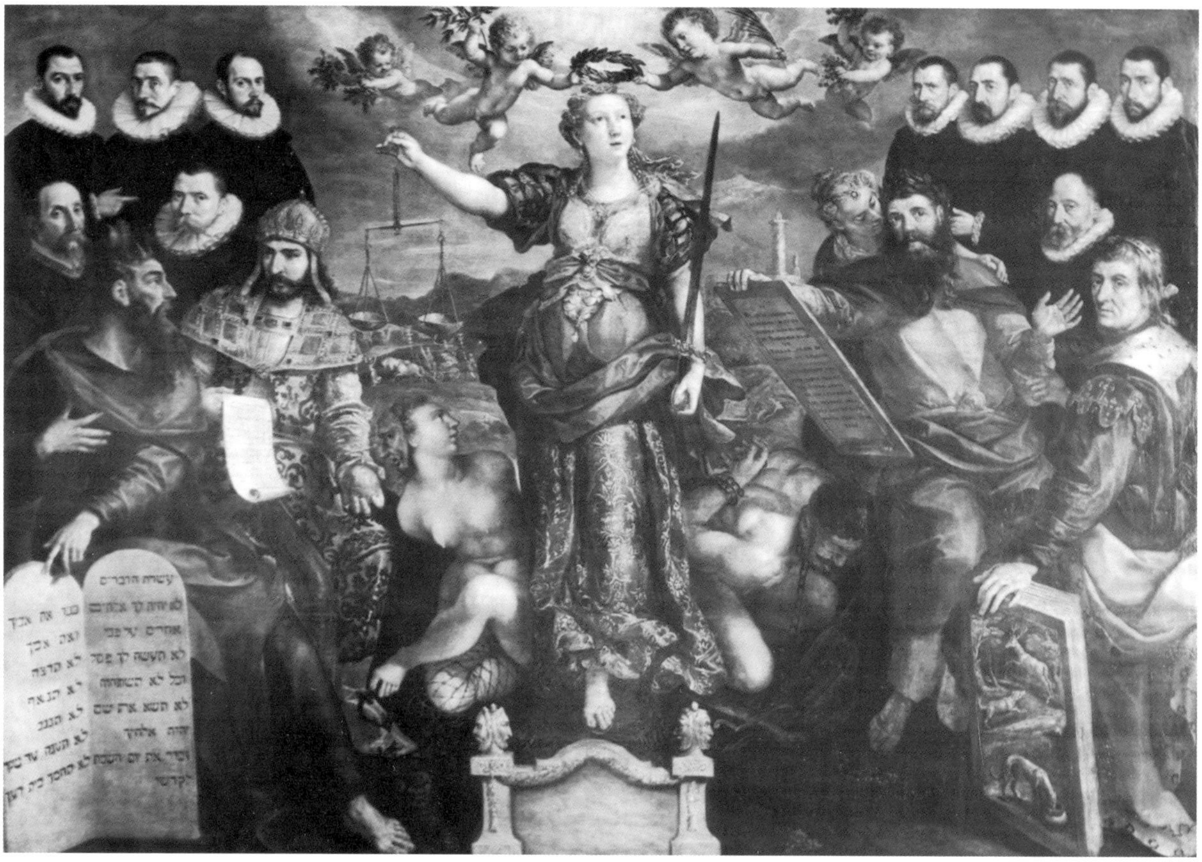

Fig. 16. Maarten de Vos, *Group Portrait of the Members of the Justice Court of the Brabant 'Mint', with Justitia, standing in the middle, accompanied by four great Legislators of the Past*, 1594. Antwerp, Rockoxhuis

There is a third category of group portraits in which neither religious nor allegorical and historical elements play a role. A striking example is a painting by David Teniers the younger (1610–1690), signed and dated 1643, at the Ermitage in St Petersburg (Fig. 19). It represents the guild of the Old Crossbow gathering in the Grote Markt in Antwerp, before the town hall and near their guild house, which is one of the buildings on the right. Altogether, more than forty persons are portrayed.[26] Nora De Poorter has shown that by painting this militia piece and giving it to the guild, Teniers was accepted as a 'wepelaer', and thus freed himself from several civic obligations.[27]

Teniers's painting, which looks somewhat like an enlarged conversation piece, actually generally corresponds with Dutch group portraits. It is true that in the latter the figures are mostly taller, but the way in which they are represented is almost the same. The same characteristics are also apparent in a group portrait by Nicolaas van Eyck (1617–1679) showing the militia of the city of Antwerp (1673; Antwerp, Vleeshuis).[28]

It is perhaps interesting to note that Teniers's picture was painted one year after Rembrandt's *Nightwatch* (of 1642). It was also painted three years after Peter van Lint finished his rather 'traditional' carpenters's piece and two years before Cornelis de Vos started his impressive group portrait of the kolveniers, with Charles V in the middle. Thus, we can see that at that moment the three categories of Flemish group portraiture that I have defined existed almost simultaneously. To avoid any misunderstanding, I would like to conclude this first part of my paper by observing that, for each of these categories, only a few examples could be shown. In fact, it is desirable that a complete scholarly catalogue of Flemish seventeenth century group portraits be compiled.

II

Let us now draw attention to the second theme of this symposium: Design. The question I would like to raise here is whether cases are

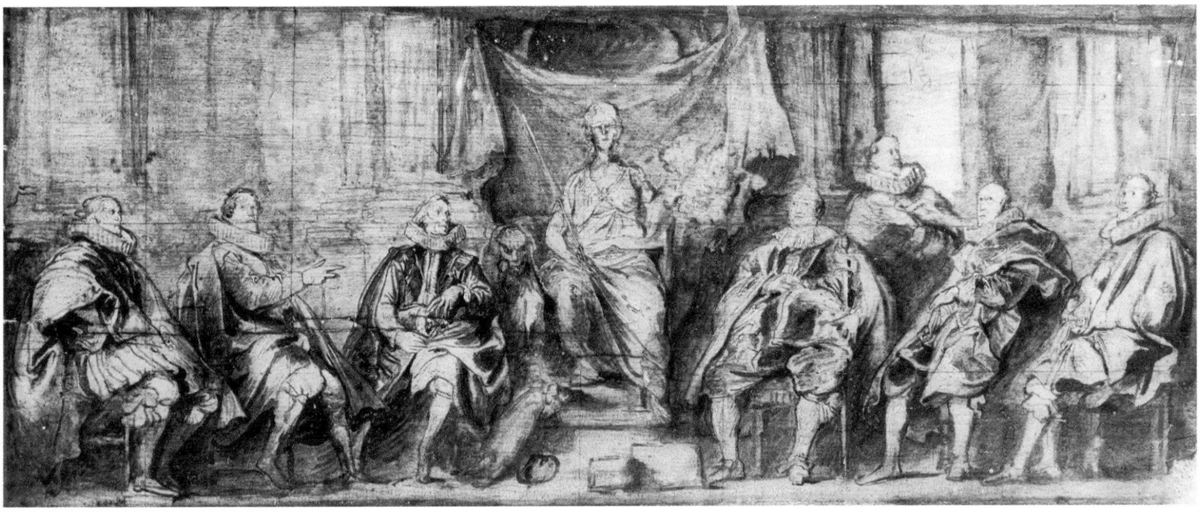

Fig. 17. Anthony van Dyck, *Preparatory oil sketch for a life-size Group Portrait of Seven Aldermen of the City of Brussels with, in the middle, Justitia, sitting on a throne*, 1634. Paris, Ecole Nationale des Beaux-Arts

known which allow us to ascertain a direct intervention of the patron in the elaboration of the design(s).

Rubens's correspondence with Nicolas Claude de Peiresc concerning the Marie de Medicis series informs us about changes that had to be made after the submission of oil sketches and even that some subjects were discarded and replaced by other ones.[29] From the correspondence between Constantijn Huygens and Jacob Jordaens, we learn about the changes the painter was asked to make after he had sent his first designs for the Huis Den Bosch to the Hague.[30]

Unfortunately, for the majority of paintings, particularly private commissions and those intended for churches, comparable sources are generally not available. Iconography and some knowledge about spirituality in the seventeenth century, occasionally make it possible, nevertheless, to detect the intervention of the patron or of his advisors in the elaboration of the design.

I would like to illustrate this briefly with just one example. Specifically, a close examination of the designs for the huge altarpiece Rubens painted shortly before his departure for Madrid in August 1628 for the high altar of the church

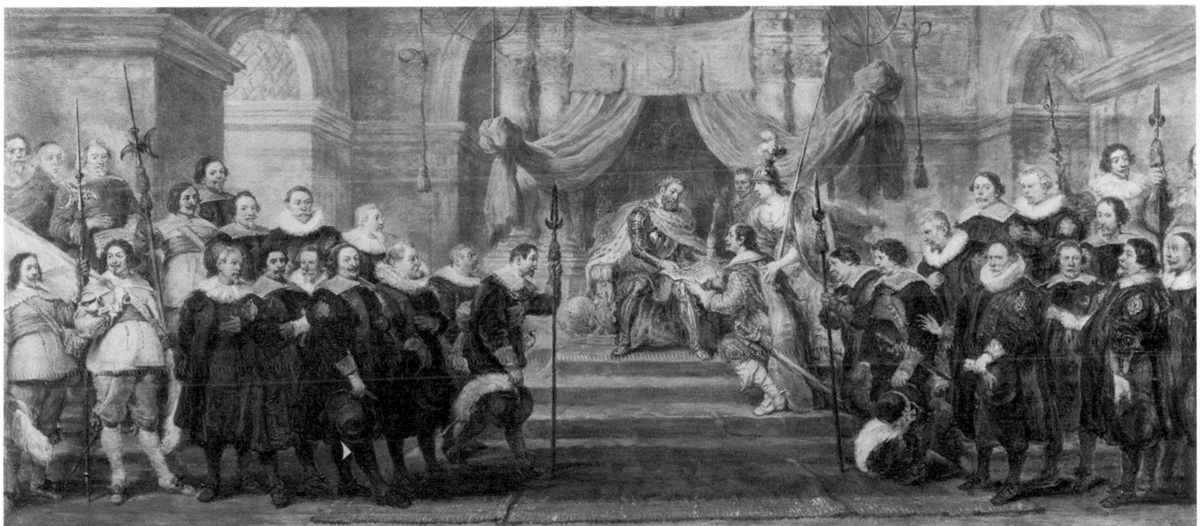

Fig. 18. Cornelis de Vos, *Preparatory oil sketch for a life-size Group Portrait of the former and present Deans of the Kolveniersgilde in Antwerp, with, on the middle the emperor Charles V granting privileges to that Guild*, (1643–1644). Lady Ashcombe, Sudeley Castle, Whinchcombe (Gloucestershire)

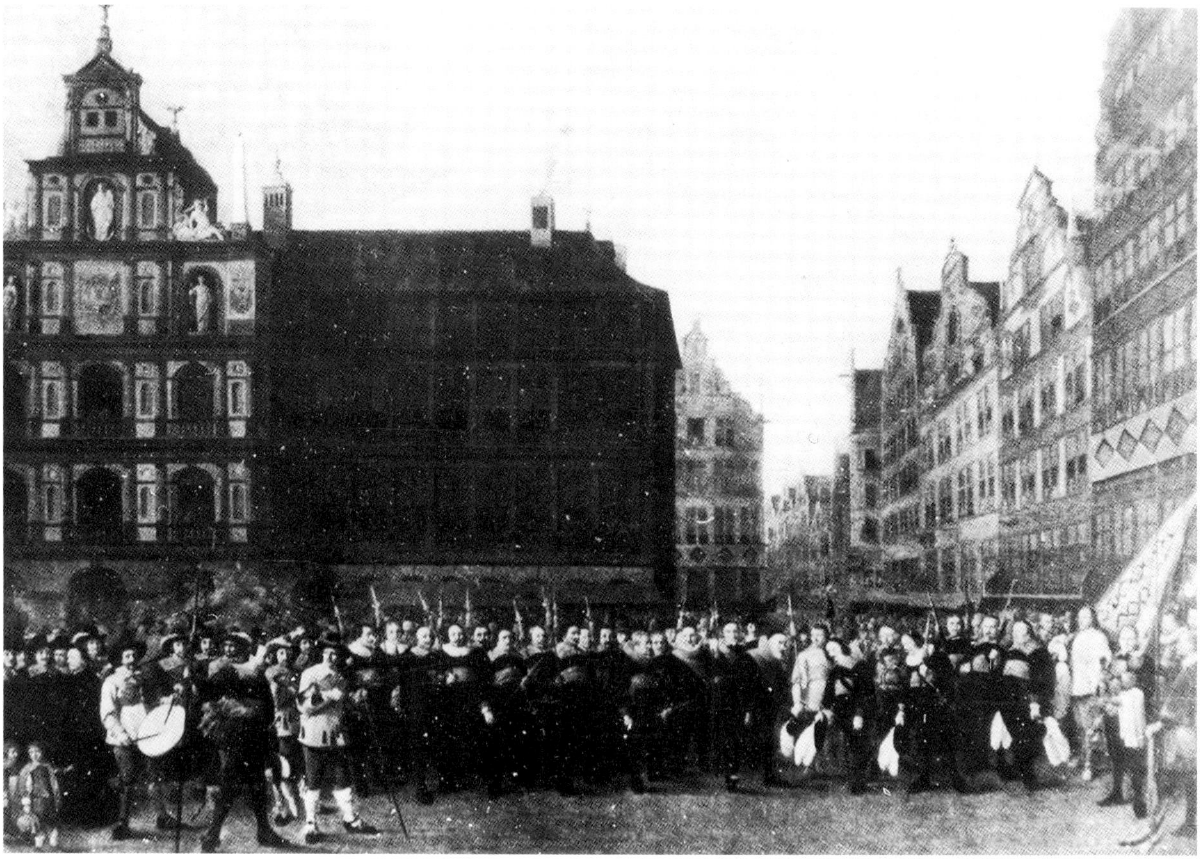

Fig. 19. David Teniers the Younger, *Group Portrait of the Guild of the 'Oude Voetboog' (Old Arbalet) in Antwerp, standing before the Town Hall and next to their guildhouse, on the right*, 1643. St Petersburg, Hermitage

of the Antwerp Augustinian Fathers (Fig. 20) seems to be instructive in this respect.

Rubens started his commission with a drawing, currently in the National Museum in Stockholm (Fig. 21), in which the pose of the Virgin and Child are worked out on paper. On the other side of the same sheet he then drew a few lines in black chalk, strengthened with pen and wash, as his initial idea for the entire composition. The Virgin and Child are represented at the top of a high pedestal, accompanied by the kneeling Saint Catherine and a group of female saints on the left, while in the foreground there are three male saints: Saint Sebastian and Saint George on the left and Saint Augustin on the right.[31]

In the first oil sketch (a 'modello') currently in the Städel in Frankfurt am Main (Fig. 22), a few saints have been added and the figures are now 'brilliantly arranged to create a circular or a rhomboid movement around the Virgin and Child'.[32]

In the second modello (Fig. 23; Berlin, Gemäldegalerie) in which the shape of the finished painting is established, the number of saints was increased again, requiring that the group in the lower left be rethought in order to incorporate the figure of William of Aquitaine with his shield, a saint of the order of Saint Augustine, between Saint George and Saint Sebastian. Somewhat higher, on the left, Mary Magdalene was added next to Saint Catherine of Montefalcone. Another important addition was that of Saint Joseph, standing partly behind the Virgin. As far as I know, this addition has not yet received sufficient attention.[33]

It should not come as a surprise that Saint Joseph was absent from the first designs, as he was not included in any Italian renaissance altarpiece representing a 'sacra conversazione' that Rubens may have remembered when he started on this commission.[34] It should be noted that Saint Joseph must have even been added to the Berlin panel somewhat later than the other saints who are similarly missing from the Frankfurt 'modello'. He is indeed the only figure that is drawn simply in outline with a thin

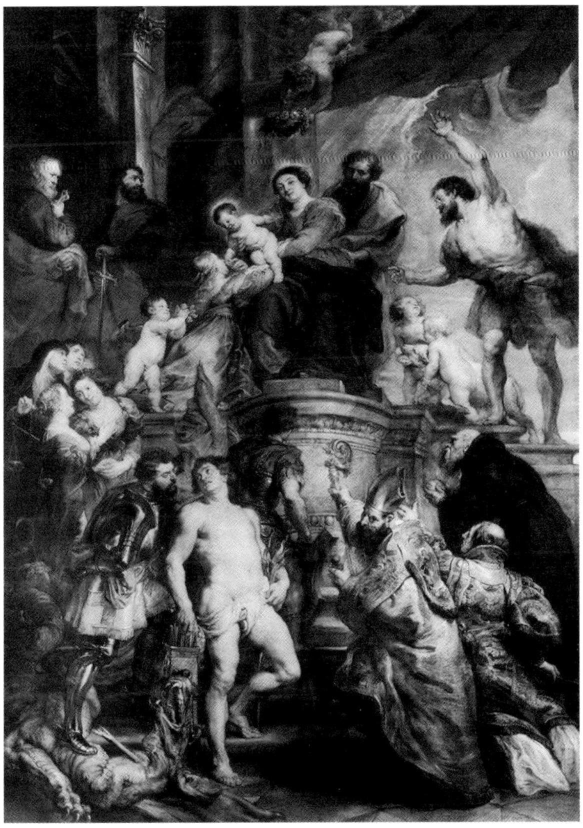

Fig. 20. Peter Paul Rubens, *The Virgin and Child enthroned with saints: Altarpiece*, 1628. Antwerp, St Augustine (temporarily at the Koninklijk Museum voor Schone Kunsten)

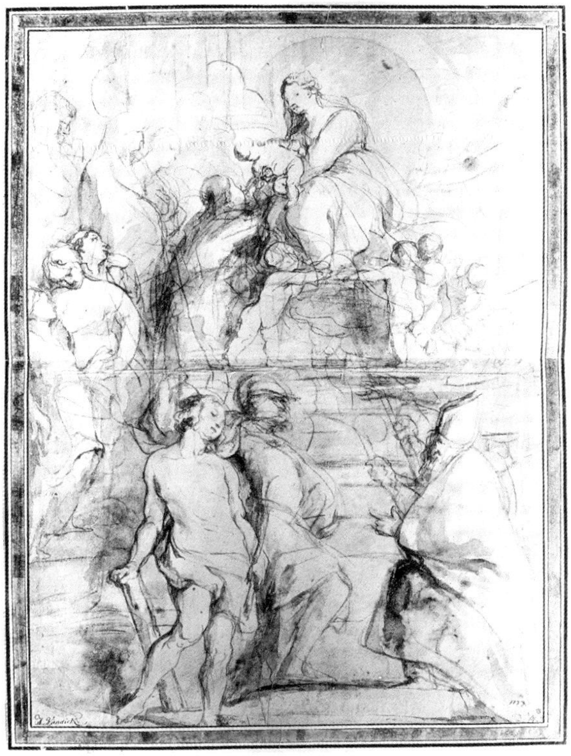

Fig. 21. Peter Paul Rubens, *Prepartory Drawing for The Virgin and Child enthroned adored by saints* (Fig. 20). Stockholm, Nationalmuseum

paint-brush, rather monochrome and without any specific indication of coloring. It thus seems quite probably that Saint Joseph was a 'last-minute' addition to the whole composition. His presence is accentuated in the definite version, the large painting that was intended for the high altar of Saint-Augustine's church and which is now – I hope, only temporarily – on view at the Koninklijk Museum in Antwerp.

There must have been a special reason for giving Saint Joseph such a prominent place in the picture. Unfortunately, the available documents do not provide conclusive information about this. One could postulate that around the same time a confraternity of Saint Joseph was founded at the Saint Augustine's church in Antwerp, which might have insisted upon the presence of their patron saint in the altarpiece. But, this does not seem to have been the case,[35] although such a brotherhood did exist at the Augustinians' church in Brussels as of 1618.[36] Among the first confraternities devoted to Saint Joseph, it was soon to be followed by many others in the Southern Netherlands, including ones in churches of other orders. I cannot dwell on the circumstances that explain why, as of about 1600, the devotion of Jesus's foster father, as well as that of the Holy Family as an example for all Christian families, spread so quickly in the Southern Netherlands.[37] But, we may confidently accept that the Augustinian fathers, by asking Rubens to include Joseph in their huge altarpiece, simply met the growing demands of that rapidly increasing devotion.

III

Execution is the third topic to be dealt with at this symposium.

As far as I know, no Flemish seventeenth century artist encountered the same fate as Caravaggio, whose *Death of the Virgin*, currently in the Louvre, was removed by his patron from the altar in Santa Maria della Scala in Rome, shortly after it had been placed upon it.[38] That does not mean that the relationship between Flemish artists and their patrons was never problematic. When Marie de Medici was

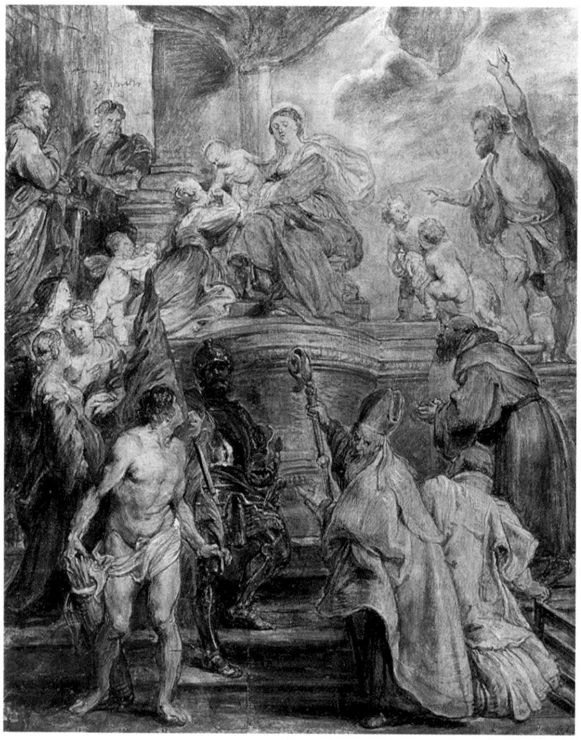

Fig. 22. Peter Paul Rubens, *Oil sketch for The Virgin and Child enthroned adored by saints* (Fig. 20). Frankfurt, Städelsches Kunstinstitut

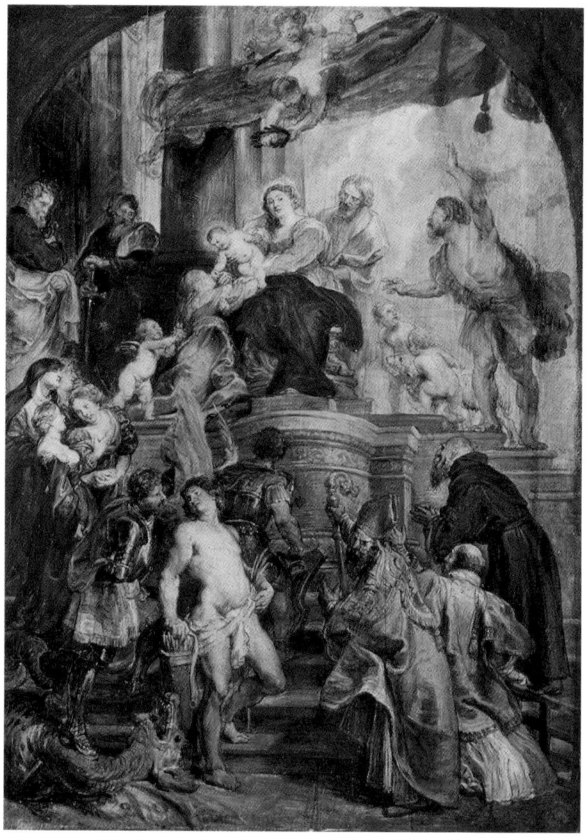

Fig. 23. Peter Paul Rubens, *Modello for The Virgin and Child enthroned adored by saints* (Fig. 20). Berlin, Staatliche Museen, Gemäldegalerie

forced to leave France in 1631, the large paintings of the Henry IV series commissioned from Rubens remained partly unfinished and completely unpaid in the painter's studio. After his death they were still in his estate.[39]

Sometimes a great lapse of time intervened between the presentation and the acceptance of the 'modello', on the one hand, and the final execution of the definite painting on the other. The best-known case is that of Rubens's *Conversion of Saint Bavo* for the high altar of the Cathedral in Gent. On 19 March 1614, the painter wrote to Archduke Albert that the latter, 'thanks to his extremely good memory', certainly would remember having seen a 'dissegno colorito', that he had painted two years before (i.e., in 1612) 'to serve as a model for the triptych of the high altar of the Cathedral of Ghent'. Although the design had been accepted by the Chapter, after the death of bishop Maes, who had ordered the triptych, his successor decided to erect instead 'the most preposterous high altar, without a picture of any sort, but only a statue of St Bavo in a marble niche with some columns'. In spite of the intervention of the Archduke, Bishop F.H. van der Burch went through with his decision. On 29 January 1615, a contract was signed with Robert Colyns de Nole for a monumental altar with a sculpture in marble upon it.[40] The realization of this project was itself the victim of changes. Alterations had to be made in 1622 when Antoon Triest, after he had become the bishop of Gent, decided to place a painting by Rubens upon the altar. In the meantime, however, ten years had elapsed and a triptych was no longer required. Instead, tall panels or canvases, corresponding with the shape of the huge aedicula or portico altars had to be used. Consequently, the 'modello' for the 'tavolla colle porte' that Rubens painted *c.* 1612 was no longer of use. A new composition had to be designed for the painting that was now to be conceived in an upward movement reducing the subject to its most essential elements and covering the surface almost completely with figures (Gent, St.-Baafs kathedraal).[41] Thus, in this case the death of the first patron and the divergent preferences of his successors determined the fate of the commission.

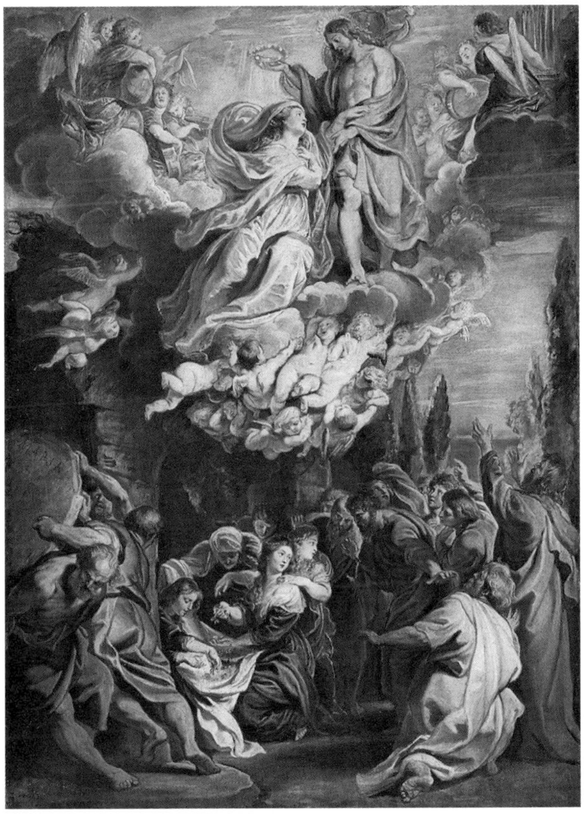

Fig. 24. Peter Paul Rubens, *The Assumption and Coronation of the Virgin*, modello (*c.* 1611). St Petersburg, Ermitage

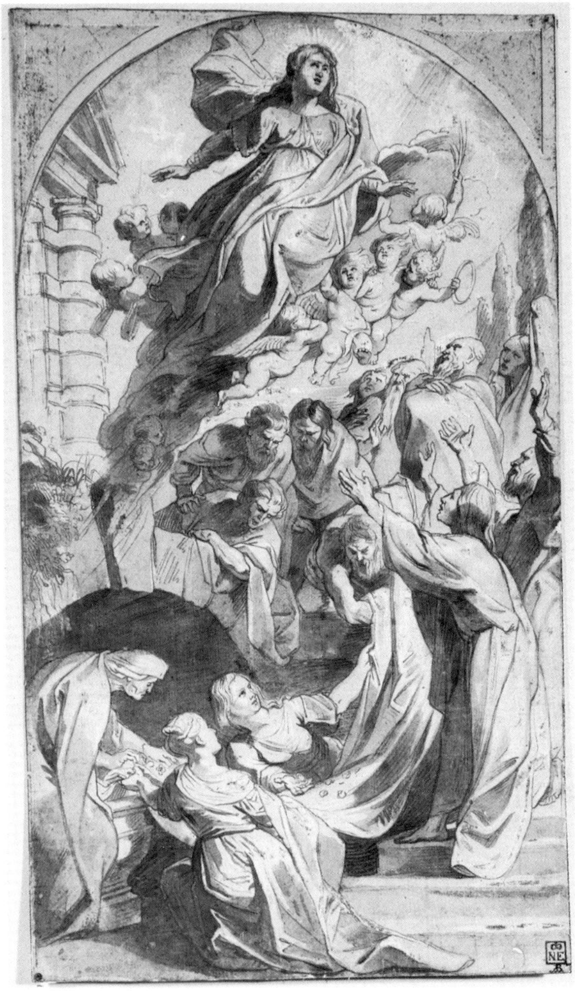

Fig. 25. Circle of Rubens, *The Assumption of the Virgin*, drawing. Budapest, Szepmüvészeti Múzeum, Printroom

The origin of Rubens's *Assumption of the Virgin* for the high altar of the Antwerp Cathedral (Fig. 31) is more complex. In 1972, I had the opportunity to draw attention to an archival source from which we learn that on 22 April 1611 (after Otto van Veen (Venius) had already submitted a design) Rubens presented the canons and the churchwardens of the Antwerp Cathedral with two sketches, depicting two different compositions the Assumption of the Virgin. Considering that the sketches 'gave no rise to objections and were not opposed to the traditions of the Church', the canons liked them, but did not make a choice between the 'two excellent paintings'.[42]

My suggestion that a sketch in the Ermitage (Fig. 24) could safely be identified with one of the two 'modelli' that Rubens submitted in 1611 has been generally accepted.[43] From the same document we learn, however, that Rubens produced a second 'modellum' (as it is called in the text), with a distinct composition of the same subject. As I wrote in 1972, 'It is not altogether improbable that in this case he depicted the Assumption of Mary as he would subsequently consistently draw and paint it: The Holy Virgin seated on a cloud surrounded and supported by a great number of putti, while her glance is directed heavenwards.' I also noted: 'I have looked in vain, among the many sketches of Assumption and Coronations of the Virgin, from Rubens's hand, for a 'modello' with the same stylistic traits as the one in St Petersburg. It is possible that this second modello became in one way or another the victim of time.'

In addition, I put forth the hypothesis that Rubens's second modello might have consisted only of a variation of the upper part of the modello currently in St Petersburg. In support of this, I cited a drawing of the ascending Virgin in the Albertina in Vienna that, as I then supposed, could have been a preliminary study for that second modello.[44] I also mentioned the

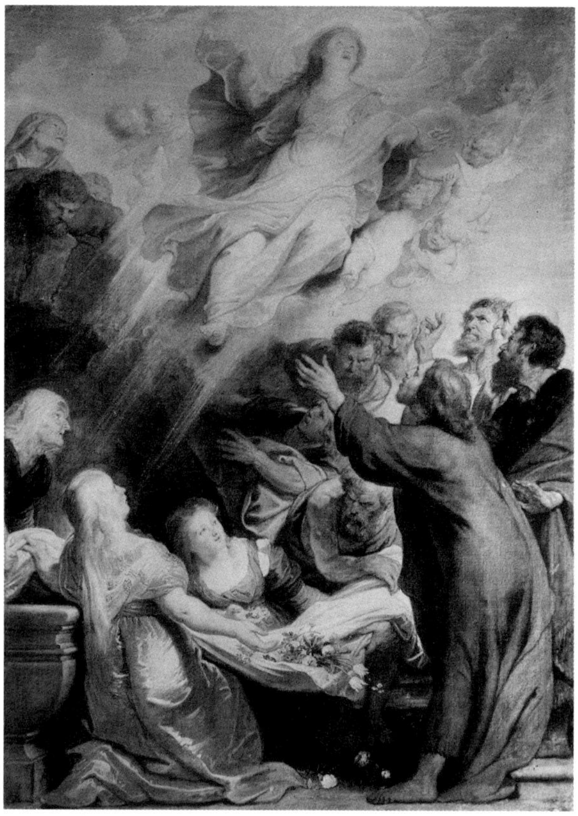

Fig. 26. Peter Paul Rubens (and his studio), *The Assumption of the Virgin*, altarpiece (*c.* 1615). Schleissheim, Neues Schloss

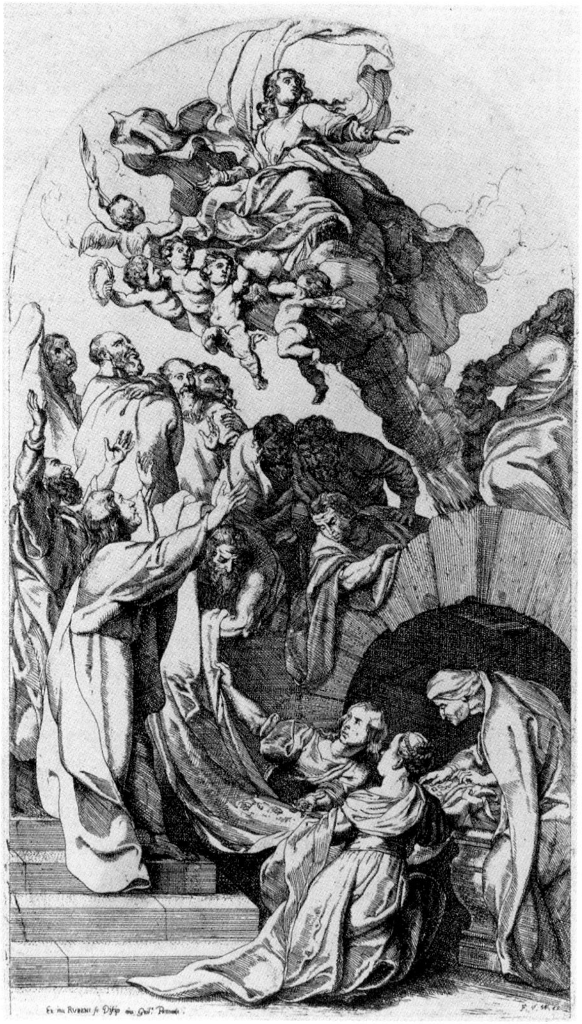

Fig. 27. Willem Panneels, after Rubens, *The Assumption of the Virgin*, engraving. Antwerp, Rubenshuis

well-known painting, *The Assumption of the Virgin* that originally decorated the Houtappel or Rubens's chapel in the Jesuit church of Antwerp and is currently in the Kunsthistorisches Museum in Vienna.[45] Here, the soaring Madonna is similarly depicted as in the drawing in the Albertina, although reversed and somewhat modified, while the lower part of the painting corresponds with that in the 'modello' in St Petersburg.

Today I would like to propose a different hypothesis based upon a drawing that is most likely a copy of the lost second modello by Rubens, or at least a copy of a painting related to that lost oil sketch. I found the drawing in the print room of the National Museum in Budapest (Fig. 25), where it is attributed to Willem Panneels.[46] In my opinion, this attribution is questionable, but is based, nevertheless, on a etching by this disciple of Rubens, showing the same composition in reverse and slightly altered (Fig. 27). The inscription underneath on the left indicates that the composition is Rubens's invention and that the etching is by 'Guillielmo' Panneels; the phrase on the right, 'F. V. W. excudit', refers to the publisher of the print, Franciscus van den Wyngaert.[47]

Instead of the large stone rolled away from the top of the Virgin's tomb that we see in the version in St Petersburg, in the Budapest drawing, we see three women before an arch – marking the entrance to the sepulchre, perhaps – and gathered round the sarcophagus in which the Virgin was buried. In their hands they hold in their hands the winding cloth upon which the flowers were spread that, according to the 'Golden Legend', were discovered in the empty tomb. This shroud is picked up by a bearded man, shown leaning forward and kneeling, who is situated somewhat higher on an elevation reached by a few steps. Two apostles standing

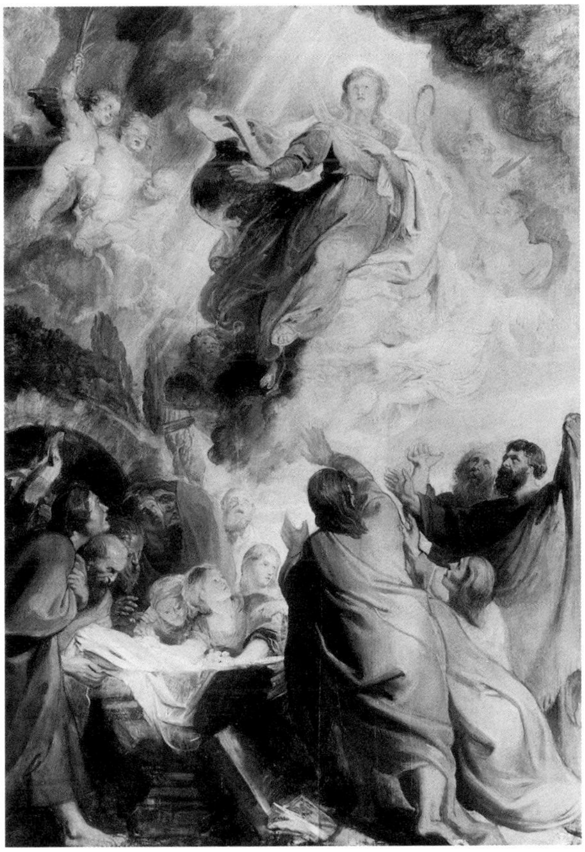

Fig. 28. Peter Paul Rubens (?), *The Assumption of the Virgin*, modello (?) for Fig. 29. Hamburg, Kunsthalle

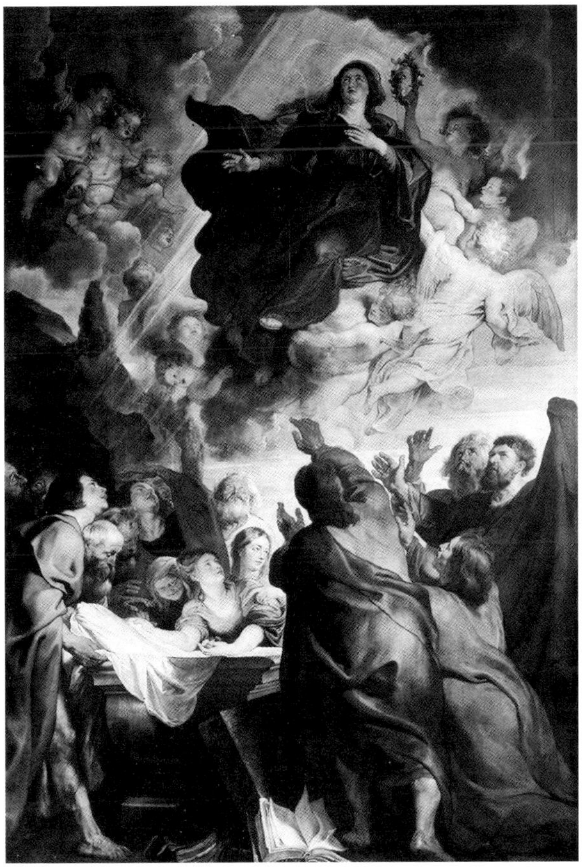

Fig. 29. Peter Paul Rubens, *The Assumption of the Virgin*, altarpiece painted for the Kapellekerk in Brussels (*c.* 1617). Düsseldorf, Kunstmuseum

upon these steps look upwards towards the Virgin, in admiration. On the left, on the same level as the kneeling man, we see three apostles looking down, while on the right five others witness the Ascension of the Virgin, who is accompanied by a cluster of winged putti. On the right side, we note the same kind of cypresses as on the modello in St Petersburg. Most figures also recall those on that oil sketch. The powerful light and shade contrasts, as well as the shape of the folds of the dresses, are also similar. Many other stylistic traits, especially the forceful composition, point to the fact that the oil sketch, of which the drawing in Budapest is most likely a faithful copy, must have been the 'second' modello that Rubens presented, together with the first one, to the chapter and church wardens of the Antwerp Cathedral.

The embossed column on the left, which constitutes the right part of the architectural framing of the gate, seems to foreshadow the portico that Rubens erected some years later on the side of the courtyard of his house that leads into the garden.[48] If we accept that the sheet of paper in Budapest really is a copy of the 'second' modello that Rubens showed on 22 April 1611 to the chapter of the Antwerp cathedral, we must conclude that even a few months after he had acquired the property on which his house and studio were to be build,[49] he already had some ideas in mind about the shape he intended to give to that portico.

In the context of the theme of the Assumption of the Virgin, this gate has, of course, a spiritual meaning. It refers to names given to Maria: 'Porta Paradisi', and, even more appropriate, 'Porta Coeli'. To quote Pamela Askew: 'The Virgin as door, as the entrance through which Christ entered the world, was a common epithet.... It was, moreover, precisely by triumphing over death that the Virgin opened the door of life'.[50]

There is, unfortunately, no time left to examine how this composition can be situated among the numerous Assumptions Rubens

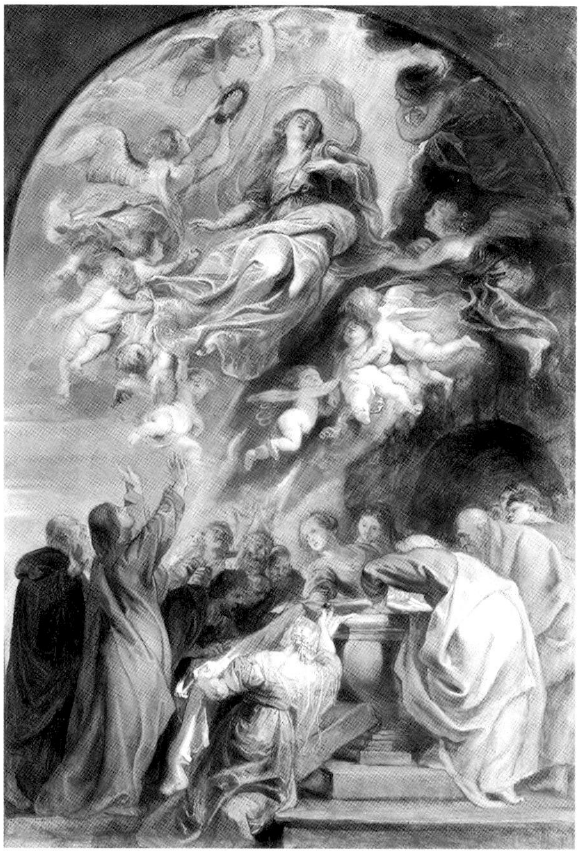

Fig. 30. Peter Paul Rubens, *The Assumption of the Virgin*, modello for the Altarpiece (Fig. 31). The Hague, Mauritshuis

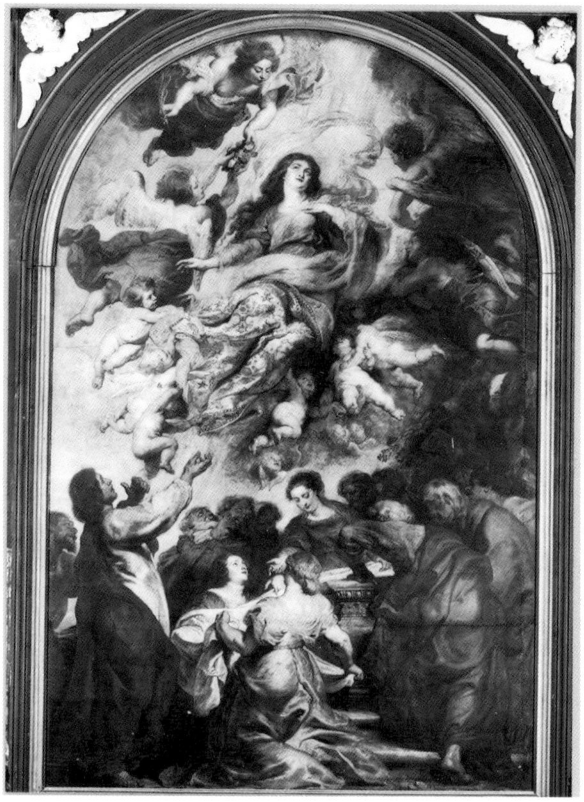

Fig. 31. Peter Paul Rubens, *The Assumption of the Virgin*, altarpiece, 1626. Antwerp, Cathedral

painted between 1611 and 1626, the latter being the year in which the artist finally completed the commission for the high altar of the Antwerp Cathedral, which he had started fifteen years before. I can only briefly mention a few paintings that contain some of the elements that also appear on the drawing in Budapest. For additional information on those pictures, see David Freedberg's volume of the *Corpus Rubenianum Ludwig Burchard*.

To start, a rather small altarpiece in the Neues Schloss Schleissheim (Fig. 26), executed to a great extent by Rubens's assistants, should be mentioned. Freedburg has already studied this painting in relationship with Panneels's engraving (Fig. 27).[51] It now turns out to be a somewhat summary version of Rubens's composition seen in the drawing in Budapest.

Nearly the same pose for the Virgin was used in an oil sketch in Hamburg (Fig. 28), which most authors regard as a copy.[52] Here, too, we find a similar sarcophagus on the left and the same vaulted entrance to the sepulchre on the right. This composition is related to the splendid *Assumption* painted by Rubens in 1616–1618 for the Kapellekerk in Brussels, now in the Kunstmuseum in Düsseldorf (Fig. 29).[53]

It is clear that the modello copied on the sheet of paper in Budapest was not the one chosen by the Antwerp Cathedral chapter. Ultimately, they preferred the modello currently in the Ermitage. This can be deduced from the fact that the lower part of its composition was repeated on the large panel mentioned above and currently in Vienna. As Carl Van de Velde has shown, Rubens must have started the execution of that painting shortly before 1613.[54] It never decorated the high altar in the cathedral, however, but remained in the artist's studio for many years. Later (after 1620), it was moved elsewhere: it was placed above the altar of the Maria- or Houtappelkapel (subsequently called the Rubenskapel).

Different reasons have been given to explain why this altarpiece was not placed above the high altar of the cathedral. Constant financial problems may certainly have been one factor.

But, as Van de Velde has argued, more important was the fact that the new altarpiece would have been overshadowed (both in terms of its size and composition) by the much more monumental works Rubens had painted in the meantime – *The Raising of the Cross* for the high altar of the Saint Walburgis church and, even more annoying, *The Descent from the Cross*, which was placed in the cathedral itself above the altar of the kolveniers. Therefore, new arrangements had to be made with Rubens. Consequently, in 1618 he once again presented two modelli for the altarpiece, which most likely also included designs for the frame.

I do not intend to take a position at present in the discussion of whether the 'modello' at the Mauritshuis in The Hague (Fig. 30), which preceded the final work, is one of the two panels submitted in 1618, or, as most authors believe, a later version that was made only shortly before Rubens started to paint the huge altarpiece in 1625.[55] I only would like to draw attention to the fact that in that beautiful oil sketch we still discover some elements, which, as we can ascertain from the drawing in Budapest, already appeared in the earlier 'second' modello. Consider the figure of the Virgin (although, in the later work she glances upwards to Heaven), as well as (but in reverse), the mouth of the sepulchre, the shape of the sarcophagus, the pose of the kneeling woman in front of it, that of her companion (now placed behind the sarcophagus), and finally the two apostles on the left, of whom only the youngest stretches his arms upwards. It should be noted, however, that these elements were not incorporated in the final work.[56]

I still owe you an explanation about the drawing in Vienna that I once thought was a preparatory study for the 'second' modello presented in 1611.[57] At present, I assume that it was probably drawn one or two years later, when Rubens tried out a reformulation of the Assumption, e.g., in the oil sketch in Buckingham Palace. Here, too, the ascending Virgin is looking upwards towards a sculpted form higher up on top of the altar. In the Maria or Houtappel Chapel it is God the Father, holding the crown in his hand, ready to put it on her head when she arrives in Heaven.[58]

The purpose of the last part of my lecture was to show a few examples of the vicissitudes that, owing to the desiderata of the patrons and the circumstances surrounding their commissions, affected the execution of specific paintings. I hope that I have also demonstrated the importance of copies.

NOTES

1. Together with an increase in attention for the function of the work of art (see e.g. H.W. Janson, *Form follows Function - or does it* [First Gerson Lecture], Maarsen, 1982), the role of the patron is currently an object of growing research (see e.g. the excellent brief survey by A. Boschloo, 'De kunstenaar, de opdrachtgever en de onderzoeker. Een inleiding', in H. Hendrix and J. Stumpel, ed., *Kunstenaars en opdrachtgevers*, Utrecht Renaissance Studies, II, Amsterdam, 1996, pp. 1–6, and the case studies in the same publication by B. Kempers, H.T. van Veen, A. Boschloo, R. Rasch, O. Ottenheym). For Italian examples, see C. Hope, 'Artists, Patrons and Advisors in the Renaissance', in G.F. Lyde and S. Orgel, ed., *Patronage in the Renaissance*, Princeton, 1981, pp. 293–343, and F. Haskell, *Patrons and Painters, A Study of the Relations between Italian Art and Society in Baroque Art*, New York, 1971 (1st ed. 1963).

2. F. Baudouin, '1585: De Val van Antwerpen, ook een belangrijke datum voor de kunstgeschiedenis der Nederlanden', in *Willem van Oranje, 1584–1984, Herdenking door de Koninklijke Academiën van België*, Brussel, 1985, pp. 87–103; F. Baudouin, 'Religion und Malerei nach der Teilung der Niederlande', in A. Buck ed., *Renaissance - Reformation, Gegensätze und Gemeinsamkeiten*, Wolfenbütteler Abhandlungen zur Renaissanceforschung, V, Wiesbaden, 1984, pp. 7–22; F. Baudouin, 'Godsdienst en Kunst in de Zuidelijke Nederlanden, 1500–1700', in [cat. exh.] *Luister van Spanje en de Belgische steden*, Brussel, Paleis voor Schone Kunsten, 1985, pp. 138–170 (also a French edition); F. Baudouin, 'Iconografie en stijlontwikkeling in de godsdienstige schilderkunst te Antwerpen in de zeventiende eeuw', in *Antwerpen in de XVIIe eeuw*, Genootschap voor Antwerpse Geschiedenis, Antwerpen, 1989, pp. 329–364.

3. S. Hoogstraten, *Inleidyngh tot de Hooge Schoole der Schilderkunst*, Rotterdam, 1678, p. 257 (reprint: Doornspijk, 1969).

4. See [cat. exh.] *Luther und die Folgen für die Kunst*, Hamburg, Kunsthalle, 1983, p. 355, nos. 223 and 224.

5. D. Freedberg, 'Painting and the Counter Reformation in the Age of Rubens', in P. Sutton ed., [cat. exh.] *The Age of Rubens*, Boston–Antwerp, 1993–1994, p. 133.

6. In recent years, several authors strongly defended the opinion that this 'deviation' from the Baroque was not so decisive as had generally been accepted up to now. In this respect, they point to the Utrecht and Haarlem schools, *c.* 1590 and in the two first decades of the seventeenth century (the 'Dawn of the Golden Age'), to the important commissions given to baroque painters by Stadhouder Frederik-Hendrik and Amalia van Solms, and also to the symbolic meaning detected by iconologists in apparently realistic paintings. Of course, I acknowledge the importance of these reassessments (see Baudouin 1984 [see note 2], p. 8, and F. Baudouin, 'Aantekeningen over Venus en Adonis – taferelen van Thomas Willeboirts Bosschaert', *Oud Holland*, IC, 1984, pp. 130–144, and more specifically, pp. 139–141, and p. 144 notes 53–56). But, they do not invalidate the opinion that Dutch painting is generally characterized by an originality that makes it different from Baroque art in other European countries. I intend to return to this subject later in a separate article. In the meantime, I agree with G.L. Price's argument that, while there is 'a need for reassessment', this will most likely not 'wish away that Dutch art must still be seen as part of a major cultural transformation in the Northern Netherlands' (G.L. Price, 'By their fruits you shall know them: 'the cultural legacy of the Revolt'', *De Zeventiende Eeuw*, X, 1994, pp. 50–51.

7. E. Haverkamp-Begemann, *Rembrandt: The Night-watch*, Princeton, NJ, 1982, p. 65.

8. K. Bauch, *Rembrandt van Rijn, Die Nachtwache*, Stuttgart, 1957, p. 21.

9. Freedberg 1993–1994 (see note 5), p. 133. W. Braunfels changed the adagium 'cuius regio, eius religio' into 'eius ars', in [cat. exh.] *Um Glauben und Reich: Kurfürst Maximilian I*, (Wittelsbach und Bayern, II, 1), Munich–Zurich, 1980, pp. 133–140.

10. In 1945, Count d'Arschot already wrote about group portraits of members of militia guilds and brotherhoods in the Southern Netherlands: 'Ces peintures ont été peu étudiées jusqu'à présent, et dans leur ensemble et moins encore d'une manière approfondie. Il est souhaitable que ce travail soit un jour entrepris' (Comte d'Arschot, *Le Portrait aux XVIIe et XVIIIe siècle*, L'Art en Belgique, Brussel, 1945, p. 16.

11. Paul Knevel (*Burgers in het geweer, De Schutterijen in Holland, 1550–1700*, Hilversum, 1994, p. 12) mentions that Rembrandt's *Nightwatch* was only one of less than 135 militia paintings in Holland and Zeeland that still exist today. But, there must have been many more that have since been lost due to fire or lack of care. Out of seven militia paintings that hung on the walls of the 'doelen' in Rotterdam, only one survives (p. 312).

12. C. Tümpel, 'Die Reformation und die Kunst der Niederlande', in [cat. exh.] Hamburg 1983 (see note 4), p. 313. The panel in Antwerp: P. Vandenbroeck, *Koninklijk Museum voor Schone Kunsten, Catalogus Schilderkunst 14de en 15de eeuw*, Antwerpen, 1985, pp. 84–90. no. 818, Fig. 37. The painting by Dirk Jacobsz.: *Alle schilderijen van het Rijksmuseum te Amsterdam. Volledige geïllustreerde catalogus*, Amsterdam, 1976, p. 302, no. C402. See also C. Tümpel, 'De Amsterdamse schuttersstukken', in [cat. exh.] *Schutters in Holland, kracht en zenuwen van de stad*, Zwolle–Haarlem, 1988, pp. 74–103.

13. P. Huvenne, [cat. exh.] *Pieter Pourbus, meester-schilder 1524–1584*, Bruges, 1984, pp. 145–153 no. 4.

14. J.S. Held, *The Oil-Sketches of Peter Paul Rubens, A critical catalogue*, I, Princeton, NJ, 1920, pp. 528–529 (as Rubens, dating *c.* 1615–1617); D. Freedberg, *The Life of Christ after the Passion*, Corpus Rubenianum Ludwig Burchard, VII, London, 1984, p. 8, H. Vlieghe, in J. Vanderstock ed., [cat. exh.] *Stad in Vlaanderen, Cultuur en Maatschappij, 1477–1787*, Brussel, 1991, p. 401, no. 130; D. Christiaens, in [cat. exh.] *Maagdenhuismuseum Het Sint Anna drieluik, Restauratie en presentatie van de nieuwe Rubenszaal*, Antwerpen, 1993, pp. 49–50.

15. H. Vlieghe, *Gaspar de Crayer, Sa Vie et ses Œuvres*, Brussels, 1972, I, pp. 102–103, no. A31; II, Fig. 34.

16. Vlieghe 1972 (see note 15), I, pp. 203–204, no. A167; II, Fig. 161.

17. A.-M. Bonenfant-Feytmans, 'Le problème des enfants trouvés à Bruxelles, A propos d'un tableau de Pierre Meert', *Bulletin de la Société Royale d'Archéologie de Bruxelles*, 1950, pp. 1–20; H. Coenen and M. Maistriaux, *Het Kunstpatrimonium van het Openbaar Centrum voor Maatschappelijk Welzijn te Brussel,*

Schilderijen en Tekeningen, Brussel, 1995, p. 62, no. 129 T 3, Fig. facing the title-page. Other group portraits from Brussels belong to this category as well. See e.g. [cat. exh.] 'Trésors des Eglises de Bruxelles', *Annales de la Société Royale d'Archéologie de Bruxelles*, LVI, 1979, pp. 38–39, no. 9 and pp. 98–99, no. 57 (articles by D.Vautier).

18. F. Baudouin, 'De 17de en de 18de eeuw', in W. Aerts ed., *De Onze-Lieve-Vrouwekathedraal van Antwerpen*, Antwerp, 1993, p. 254 (with a colour reproduction); S. Grieten and J. Bungeneers, ed., *De Onze-Lieve-Vrouwekathedraal van Antwerpen*, Inventaris van het Kunstpatrimonium van de Provincie Antwerpen, 3, Turnhout, 1946, p. 417, no. 965, Fig. on p. 416.

19. H. Vey, 'Anton van Dyck's Ölskizzen', in *Bulletin, Koninklijk Museum voor Schone Kunsten, Brussel*, V, 1956, p. 198, Fig. 23; H. Vey and R.A. d'Hulst, [cat. exh.] *Antoon van Dyck, Tekeningen en olieverfschetsen*, Antwerp–Rotterdam, 1960, pp. 166–168, no. 133, Fig. LXXX.

20. 'Im Stadthaus haben wir zwey sehr herrliche Stycke, die sehr gross und sehr schön waren, gesehen. [The first was Rubens's *Cambyses*] ... das andere war dass sehr trefliche stycke van Van Dyck, warinnen er den ganzen Magistrat hatte abgemahlet, die al bestunde in 23 lebensgrossen Contrefaiten. Sonsten war da auch ein anders von ihme van six figuren'. Nicodemus Tessin, 'Studiënresor i Danmark, Tyskland, Holland, Frankrike ock Italia', ed. O. Sirén, Stockholm, 1914, p. 85.

21. J.H.A. de Ridder, *Gerechtigheidstaferelen voor Schepenhuizen in de Zuidelijke Nederlanden in de 14de, 15de en 16de eeuw*, Verhandelingen van de Koninklijke Academie voor Wetenschappen, Letteren en Schone Kunsten van België, XLV, Brussel, 1989, pp. 119–142, no. 23, Fig. 47–52. The author is grateful to Mrs. Hildegard Van de Velde for the photograph of the painting she provided, as well as to the 'Stichting Nicolaas Rockox v.z.w.' for the authorization to reproduce it here.

22. N. De Poorter, 'Rubens "onder de wapenen", De Antwerpse schilders als gildebroers van de kolveniers in de eerste helft van de zeventiende eeuw', in *Jaarboek Koninklijk Museum voor Schone Kunsten Antwerpen*, 1988, pp. 232–249; K. Van der Stighelen, *De portretten van Cornelis de Vos. Een kritische catalogus*, Verhandelingen van de Koninklijke Academie voor Wetenschappen, Letteren en Schone Kunsten van België, LI, Brussels, 1990, pp. 238–240, no. 108, Fig. 108 and 108 a and b.

23. De Poorter 1988 (see note 22), pp. 232–237.

24. F.J. Van den Branden, *Geschiedenis van de Antwerpsche Schilderschool*, Antwerpen, 1883, pp. 924–925.

25. The most recent: [cat. exh.] *America, bruid van de zon, 500 jaar Latijns Amerika en de Lage Landen*, Antwerpen, 1992, pp. 249–250, no. 3 (art. by P. Vandenbroeck). Comparing this with numerous portraits of Leopold I indicates that it is not likely that this emperor was depicted on Sporckman's group portrait (See e.g. portraits of Leopold I in G. Heinz, 'Studiën zur Porträt Malerei an den Höfen der Osterreichischen Erblande', in *Jahrbuch der Kunsthistorischen Sammlungen in Wien*, LIX, 1963, pp. 169–170; *Katalog der Gemäldegalerie, Porträtgalerie zur Geschichte Osterreichs von 1400 bis 1800*, Vienna, 1976, pl. XII (facing p. 208), nos. 128–132 and nos. 213, 215, 229 and 230). The pose of the ruler derives from that of Charles on the front face of the 'Arch of Philip', which was part of the decoration for the Joyous Entry of Cardinal-Infant Ferdinand in Antwerp, 1635 (J.R. Martin, *The decorations for the Pompa Introitus Ferdinandi*, Corpus Rubenianum Ludwig Burchard, XVI, Brussels, 1972, Fig. 24.

26. M. Klinge, [cat. exh.] *David Teniers de Jonge, Schilderijen, Tekeningen*, Antwerpen, 1991, pp 93–97.

27. De Poorter 1988 (see note 22), p. 207.

28. *Koninklijk Museum voor Schone Kunsten, Catalogus Schilderkunst, Oude Meesters*, Antwerp, 1988, p. 134, no. 735 (on loan at the Vleeshuis, Antwerp). A colour reproduction on the cover of *Antwerpen, 1200 jaren Antwerpen, en hun misdaden en straf*, Waar is de tijd, 8, Zwolle, 1997. The painting by Karel E. Biset (1633–1691), representing *The Legend of Wilhelm Tell performed before the Antwerp Guild of Saint Sebastian* (1672–1674; Brussels, Koninklijke Musea voor Schone Kunsten van België, inv. 1476), to a great extent belongs to the same type of portraiture by and large, although a 'historic' motif related to the activities of the guild is still included in the composition.

29. J. Thuillier and J. Foucart, *Le storie di Maria de'Medici di Rubens al Lussemburgo*, Milaan, 1967; J. Thuillier, 'La "Gallerie de Medicis" de Rubens et sa genèse: un document inédit', *Revue de l'Art*, 1969, pp. 52–62. Among the numerous recent publications: R.F. Miller and R.E. Wolf, *Heroic Deeds and Mystic Figures: A new Reading of Rubens's Life of Marie de Medici*, Princeton, NJ, 1989; M.-N. Baudouin-Matuszeck ed., *Marie de Medicis et le Palais du Luxembourg*, Paris, 1991 (especially the articles by the editor (pp. 217–224) and J. Foucart (pp. 224–232).

30. R.-A. d'Hulst, *Jacob Jordaens*, Antwerp, 1982, pp. 232–233; an excellent summary by M. Vandenven, in [cat. exh.] *Jacob Jordaens (1593–1678), I: Schilderijen en Wandtapijten*, Antwerpen, 1993, pp. 252–254; P. van der Ploeg and C. Vermeeren, in [cat. exh.] *Vorstelijk Verzameld*, Den Haag–Zwolle, 1997, pp. 54–55, 156–159, no. 14. Important in this respect is also: I. von zur Mühlen, 'Nachtridentinische Bildauffassungen. Cesare Baronio und Rubens' Gemälde für S. Maria in Vallicella in Rom', *Münchner Jahrbuch der bildenden Kunst*, 3. Folge, XLI, 1990, pp. 23–60.

31. L. Burchard and R.A. d'Hulst, *Rubens Drawings*, Brussels, 1963, pp. 225–227, no. 145, Fig. 145v; J. Held, *Rubens: Selected Drawings*, 2nd ed., Oxford, 1986. p. 136, nos 171 and 172, pl. 169 and 170.

32. C. White, *Peter Paul Rubens, Man and Artist*, New Haven–London, 1987. This author gives an excellent brief survey of the creative phases of Rubens's altarpiece of the St Augustine church in Antwerp (pp. 204–207). E. Hubala, *Peter Paul Rubens, Die Gemälde im Städel*, Frankfurt a. Main, 1990, pp. 16–43; J. Sander and B. Brinkmann, *Die Niederländischen Gemälde van 1800 im Städel*, Frankfurt am Main, 1995, p. 48, Tafel 117.

33. J. Kelch, *Peter Paul Rubens, Kritischer Katalog der Gemälde im Besitz der Gemäldegalerie Berlin*, Berlin–Dahlem, 1978, pp. 45–52. Hubala 1990 (see note 32), p. 30 considers the adding of Saint Joseph (as well as of the head of a female saint near S. Catherine of Montefalco) as the result of the upward surge in the composition. They are 'Oktavierungen einzelner Positionen zugünsten des vollen Klangs der Aufwärtsbewegung'.

34. E.g. Titian's *Pesaro Madonna* (Venice, S. Maria dei Frari), Veronese's *Pala di San Zaccaria* (Venice, Academy) (Hubala 1990 [see note 32), pp. 23–25, Fig. 22–23).

35. There is no trace of such a confraternity in the Antwerp Saint-Augustine's church in: *Verzamelingen der Graf- en Gedenkschriften van de Provincie Antwerpen, Arrondissement Antwerpen*, IV, Antwerp, 1859, pp. 245–285, nor in F. Peeters, *L'Eglise de Saint-Augustin à Anvers*, Antwerp, 1930.

36. S. Axters, *Geschiedenis van de vroomheid in de Nederlanden*, IV: *Na Trente*, Antwerp, 1960, p. 167. The first confraternity of Saint Joseph in the Southern Netherlands was founded in 1604 in the St Peter's Abbey in Ghent.

37. The devotion of Saint Joseph, officially recognized by the Council of Trent (1545–1563), was actively propagated by the Discalced Carmelites, who were following the example of S. Teresa of Avila. In this respect, Rubens's *Saint Joseph holding*

the Infant Christ in his arms (*c.* 1620) should be mentioned, which he painted for the chapel of the 'ermitage' of the Discalced Carmelites in the 'désert' of Marlagne near Namur (H.Vlieghe, *Saints*, Corpus Rubenianum Ludwig Burchard, VIII, Brussels, 1972–1973, II, pp. 102–103. n° 124, Fig. 67 and 68 (copies of the lost painting). For works of art ordered by the Carmelites in the Southern Netherlands and featuring St Joseph, see also C. Emond, *L'iconographie Carmélitaine dans les anciens Pays-Bas*, Mémoires de l'Académie Royale de Belgique, Classe des Beaux-Arts, col. in 8°, 2ième série, t. xii), Brussels, 1961, pp. 109–113; also Axters 1960 (see note 36), 179. Other religious orders also demonstrated a great devotion for Saint Joseph. A side chapel of the Antwerp Jesuits' Church was dedicated to him, and N. Rockox paid for its altarpiece, painted by Rubens, representing *The Holy Family returning from Egypt* (F. Baudouin, *Nicolaas Rockox, friend and patron of Peter Paul Rubens*, 2nd ed., Antwerp, 1984, pp. 24–26, figs.). It should be noted that in 1621, i.e. nearly the same year in which Rubens painted this altarpiece as well as that for Marlagne, pope Gregory XV issued a decree officially establishing a saint's day for Saint Joseph. In 1637 a confraternity of Saint Joseph was founded in the chapel of the cloister of the 'Falcontinnen' (nuns who lived according to the rule of the canons of Saint Augustine) in Antwerp (M.J. Marinus, *De contrareformatie te Antwerpen (1585–1676)*, Verhandelingen van de Koninklijke Academie voor Wetenschappen, Letteren en Schone Kunsten van België, Klasse der Letteren, 57, Brussels, 1995, p. 248, 265). The wealthy merchant Louis de Roomere and his family financed the richly decorated chapel of Saint Joseph, adorned with paintings by Gerard Zegers and Jan Boeckhorst (H. Lahrkamp, in [cat. exh.] *Jan Boeckhorst, 1604–1668*, Antwerp–Munster, 1990, pp. 14–15 (with a reproduction of an engraving showing the interior of the chapel); see also *Graf- en Gedenkschriften* (see note 35), pp. 326–332 (for the works of art in that chapel) and pp. CXIII–CXVIII (for a short history of the cloister by F.H. Mertens). It is obvous that the Antwerp Augustinian Fathers did not want to be left behind in terms of the devotion of Saint Joseph.

38. S. Loire and A. Brejon de Lavergnée, *Caravage, La Mort de la Vierge, une mort sans dignité*, Paris, 1990, see also note 50.

39. J. Muller, *Rubens: The Artist as Collector*, Princeton, NJ, 1989, pp. 144–145, pl. 111–115.

40. For more information on this altar, see M. Casteels, *De beeldhouwers de Nole te Kamerijk, te Utrecht en te Antwerpen*, Verhandelingen van de Koninklijke Academie voor Wetenschappen, Letteren en Schone Kunsten van België, Klasse der Schone Kunsten, 16, Brussel, 1961, pp. 113–119.

41. G.Martin, *The Flemish School circa 1600–circa 1900*, National Gallery Catalogues, London, 1970, pp. 126–133, n° 57 (2nd ed. London, 1986); Vlieghe 1972–1973 (see note 37), pp. 102–107, n° 71, Fig. 122, and pp. 107–109, n° 72, Fig. 123. The translation of the fragments of Rubens's letter is taken from: R.S.Magurn, *The letters of P.P. Rubens*, Cambridge Mass., 1955, pp. 56–57, no. 24. It should be noticed that Rubens, in his letter to Archduke Albert, wrote that he had put 'considerable effort into drawing up the plan for the entire project, just as much for the marble ornamentation as for the picture'. This makes it likely that, besides the magnificent 'modello' for the triptych in the National Gallery, other 'designs' may have existed that included (a) project(s) for the frame of the altarpiece. It should be noted that in the modello for the *Conversion of St Bavo* in the National Gallery – just as in Rubens's *Raising of the Cross*, in the Antwerp Cathedral – a single scene has been worked out across the entire surface of the open triptych. I have already emphasized that this concentration on an unique theme was a striking innovation in Flemish art of the early seventeenth century ('The Elevation of the Cross in Rubens's Work', *Bulletin Koninklijk Instituut voor het Kunstpatrimonium*, XXIV, 1992, p. 16).

42. F. Baudouin, 'Altars and Altarpieces before 1620', in J.R. Martin ed., *Rubens before 1620*, Princeton NJ, 1972, pp. 64–72.

43. Freedberg 1984 (see note 14), pp. 190–194, no. 46, Fig. 129.

44. Freedberg 1984 (see note 14), pp. 147–149 no. 36, Fig. 86.

45. Freedberg 1984 (see note 14), pp. 149–153 no. 37, Fig. 87.

46. Budapest, Szépmüvészeti Muzeum, Print room, inv. 1558; provenance: Esterhazy collection. I am very grateful to Dr. Teréz Gerszi for showing me this drawing and for the autorization to reproduce it here.

47. There is an excellent reproduction in Freedberg 1984 (see note 14), Fig. 103.

48. There is a somewhat similar shape in Rubens's *Ceres*, dating *c.* 1614–1615, in the Ermitage in St Petersburg (R. Oldenbourg, *P.P. Rubens, Des Meisters Gemälde*, Klassiker der Kunst, 5, Stuttgart–Berlin, 1921, p. 83.

49. The agreement concerning the condition of the sale of the estate to Rubens was made in Amsterdam in November 1610; the definite acquisition was registered in Antwerp on 4 January 1611 (A.J.J.Delen, *Het Huis van Pieter Pauwel Rubens, Wat het was, wat het is, en wat het worden kan*, Brussels, 1933, pp. 21–25).

50. P. Askew, *Caravaggio's Death of the Virgin*, Princeton, NJ, 1990, pp. 130–131.

51. Freedberg 1984 (see note 14), pp. 162–163, no. 40, Fig. 104.

52. Held 1980 (see note 14), pp. 512–513, no. 376 (as Rubens).

53. Freedberg 1984 (see note 14), pp. 163–168, no. 41, Fig. 105.

54. C.Van de Velde, 'Rubens' Hemelvaart van Maria in de Kathedraal te Antwerpen', *Jaarboek Koninklijk Museum voor Schone Kunsten Antwerpen*, 1975, pp. 245–277, especially pp. 259–160. See also W.Prohaska, article in *Flämische Malerei im Kunsthistorischen Museum Wien*, Zürich, 1989, pp. 140–142. The author presumes that Rubens, in accordance with the contract made with the 'praefectus' of the Antwerp Profess House, dated 25 March 1620, gave this painting to the Jesuits for the decoration of the altar of the chapel of the Huly Virgin in their church, in compensation for the oil sketches for the 39 ceiling paintings of that church that remained in his possession.

55. Freedberg 1984 (see note 14), pp. 178–180, no. 430, Fig. 120.

56. Freedberg 1984 (see note 14), pp. 172–178, no. 43, Fig. 43.

57. Freedberg 1984 (see note 14), pp. 146–149, no. 36, Fig. 86. I now agree with Freedberg about the date and the purpose of the drawing, p. 148. Rubens's drawing for the engraving by Theodoor Galle in the *Breviarium Romanum* (1614; now in the J.Paul Getty Museum, Malibu) should also be mentioned in this regard (Held 1986 (see note 31), p. 103, no. 84, pl. 79.

58. Freedberg 1894 (see note 14), Fig. 110.

I. Concept

Painters and Patrons in Antwerp in the Sixteenth and Seventeenth Centuries

Carl Van de Velde

Of the three phases in the creative process which this symposium tries to distinguish from each other, 'Concept' is most liable to involve the active participation of both the artist and his client. Whether the former has received detailed instructions from a patron or produces his work for the free market, there is always some way of interaction between him and his audience. In the phases of 'Design' and 'Execution', this may still be the case, but the part of the artist is, generally speaking, more evident. Therefore, when discussing 'Concept' in a particular period and in a particular place, more attention must be devoted to the audience than for the subsequent phases.

It is safe to say that in sixteenth and seventeenth century Antwerp, the public interested in painting belongs mainly to the bourgeoisie. Roughly speaking, paintings are used in three contexts: in churches and other religious buildings, in official buildings, including official festivities, and in private surroundings, houses of individuals or rooms of collectivities such as guilds.

Even in churches, the ecclesiastical authorities limited their direct commissions to the strictly liturgical functions and left a large part of the decoration to individual or collective initiatives by laymen. From an early stage in the building of Our Lady's Church, confraternities and guilds were given the opportunity to have their own chapels or altars, in reward for their participation in supporting the building costs. The Chapter only checked whether religious orthodoxy is respected. In the later sixteenth century, partly because of the rules imposed by the Council of Trent, the religious authorities became more strict.

The result of these separate initiatives could be nothing else but a certain amount of chaos, which was enhanced by a number of dramatic events that took place in the course of the sixteenth century: the fire of 1533, the rage of the Iconoclasts of 1566, the clearing of the church of its altars in 1581. After the restoration of 1585, the Chapter of the Cathedral tried to seize this opportunity to reorganize the decoration of the church and to give it a more harmonious structure. The armed guilds e.g., being more prosperous than most of the professional corporations, were invited to take the most conspicuous places in the church, around the crossing of the nave and the transept. In the same spirit, some years later, a global plan was devised to build sepulchral monuments to the first bishops of Antwerp, Sonnius, Torrentius, Miraeus and Malderus, grouped around the choir.[1]

The furniture of the City Hall, built in 1560–1564, was almost completely destroyed in the fire caused by the insurrection in 1576 of the Spanish garrison, known as the Spanish Fury. An inventory of 1571 shows it to have been rather modest. After the disaster, the City commissioned a few new pictures and some private individuals gave paintings from their own collection. They can be found in an inventory of 1615, which also contains a number of canvasses that had been rescued from the street decorations for the State Entry in 1599 of the Archdukes Albert and Isabella. Especially made to decorate the State Room for the occasion of the peace talks leading up to the Truce of 1609, were Abraham Janssens's *Scaldis and Antverpia* (Antwerp, Koninklijk Museum voor Schone Kunsten) and Rubens's *Adoration of the Magi* (Madrid, Museo del Prado).[2]

The third category, that of the paintings used in a private context, is the largest group. It is difficult to determine with any precision the time when it became fashionable for the well-to-do Antwerp citizens to decorate their houses with paintings. The birth of the Antwerp school of painting has already been linked to the growing economic prosperity of the city by Van Mander in 1604,[3] but there is very little archival evidence available for the early period. Indications of an increasing artistic activity can be found in the growing number of artists, many of them immigrants from outside

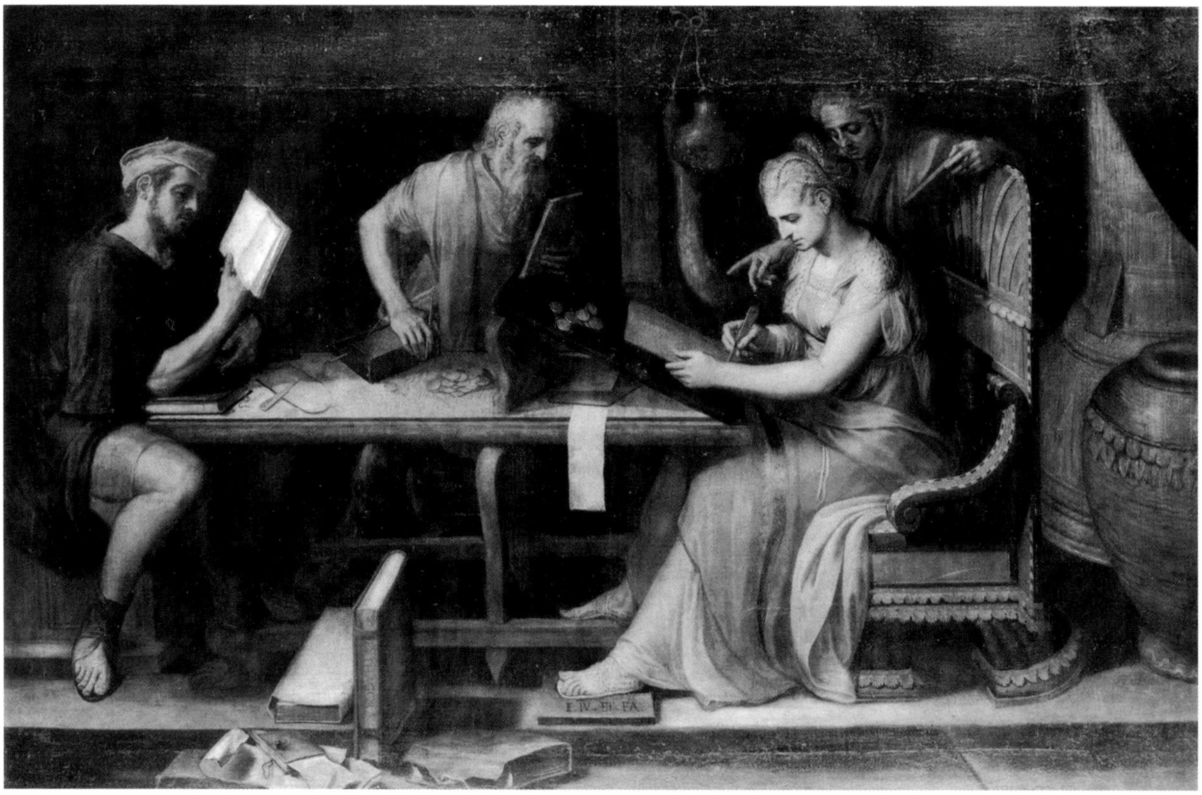

Fig. 1. Frans Floris, *Arithmetica*. New York, R. Feigen

Antwerp, who joined the guild of Saint Luke from the last decades of the fifteenth century onwards, or in the increase of the production of paintings, in the first decades of the sixteenth century, by the so-called Antwerp Mannerists. These small religious pictures, mostly triptychs with scenes from the life or passion of Christ, were meant for private devotion. Some of them can still be identified in private collections in Antwerp in the second half of the sixteenth century, where they will have arrived through inheritance.[4] They were probably made by the same painters who collaborated with the sculptors in the production of the carved wooden altar-pieces and they may have shared the same channels of distribution.[5] These paintings, however, were not items of collection for art lovers, but objects of devotional worship for the pious faithful.

From 1550 onwards, inventories of the movable properties left by deceased citizens are more numerous, in a proportion which cannot be explained only by a better preservation of the archives. Moreover, they contain on average more paintings than the earlier documents. The pictures display a larger range of subjects, and the interest in the artists seems to have increased slightly. Only a very limited number of pictures, however, even in these later sixteenth century inventories, is ascribed to a particular artist.[6]

The answer to the question, in what proportions the pictures of these different categories were painted on commission or for the open market, depends largely upon the specificity of their concept. Most, but probably not all of the paintings for churches have been commissioned, certainly the altarpieces for the church altars and for the guilds and confraternities. They can, moreover, often be recognized in archival documents that allow us to identify both the patrons and the painters. The same applies to the pictures for public buildings or for the street decorations for State Entries and other official festivities. Commissions by individuals have rarely left such traces.

Legally, the right to sell paintings was strictly reserved to the masters of the guild of Saint Luke. This monopoly has been confirmed by the municipal authorities on several occasions. The first regulations of the corporation of the artists in Antwerp were approved in 1382. The

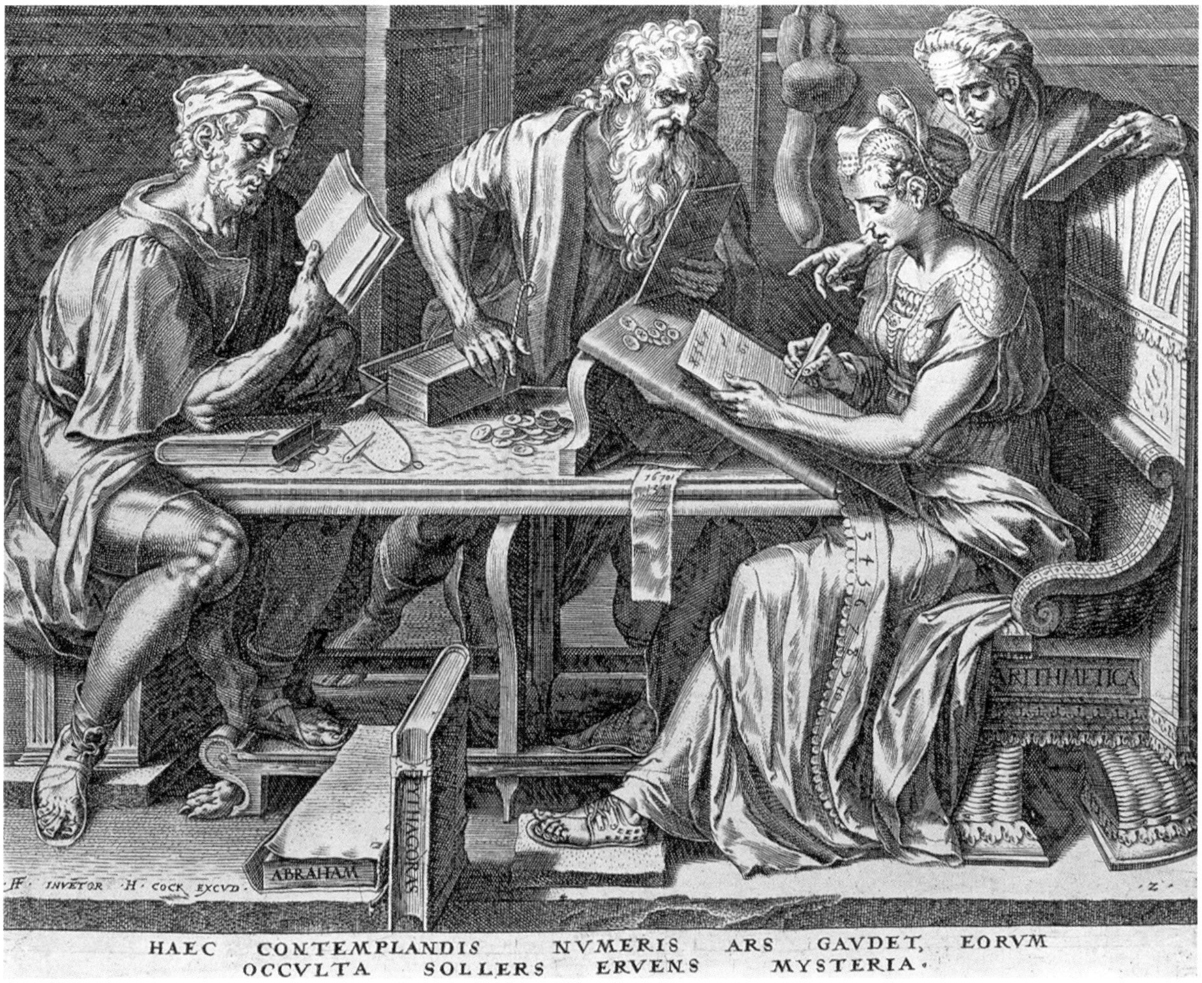

Fig. 2. Cornelis Cort after Frans Floris, *Arithmetica*, engraving

group that then asked for and obtained recognition by the authorities as an independent guild described itself as encompassing goldsmiths, painters, glassmakers, embroiderers, carvers of wooden sculptures and silversmiths.[7] These crafts were all in some way connected to the present and future decoration of the church. Obtaining the monopoly for the members of the guild to make and sell artistic products, in exchange for the observation of rules concerning the materials to be used and working conditions, would secure them a safe future.

When in 1434 the rules were changed for the first time, only the painters and the woodcarvers were specifically mentioned as the crafts united in the guild; the others were simply styled 'those that are attached to them'.[8] This probably indicates that these two disciplines, which together were responsible for the making of the carved wooden retables, had taken the

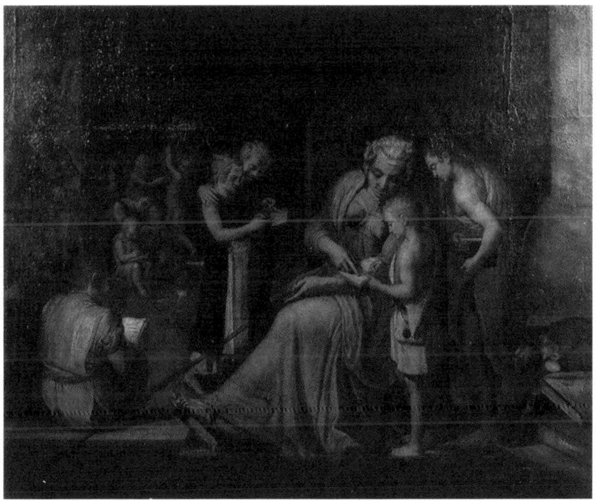
Fig. 3. Frans Floris, *Grammatica*. Private collection

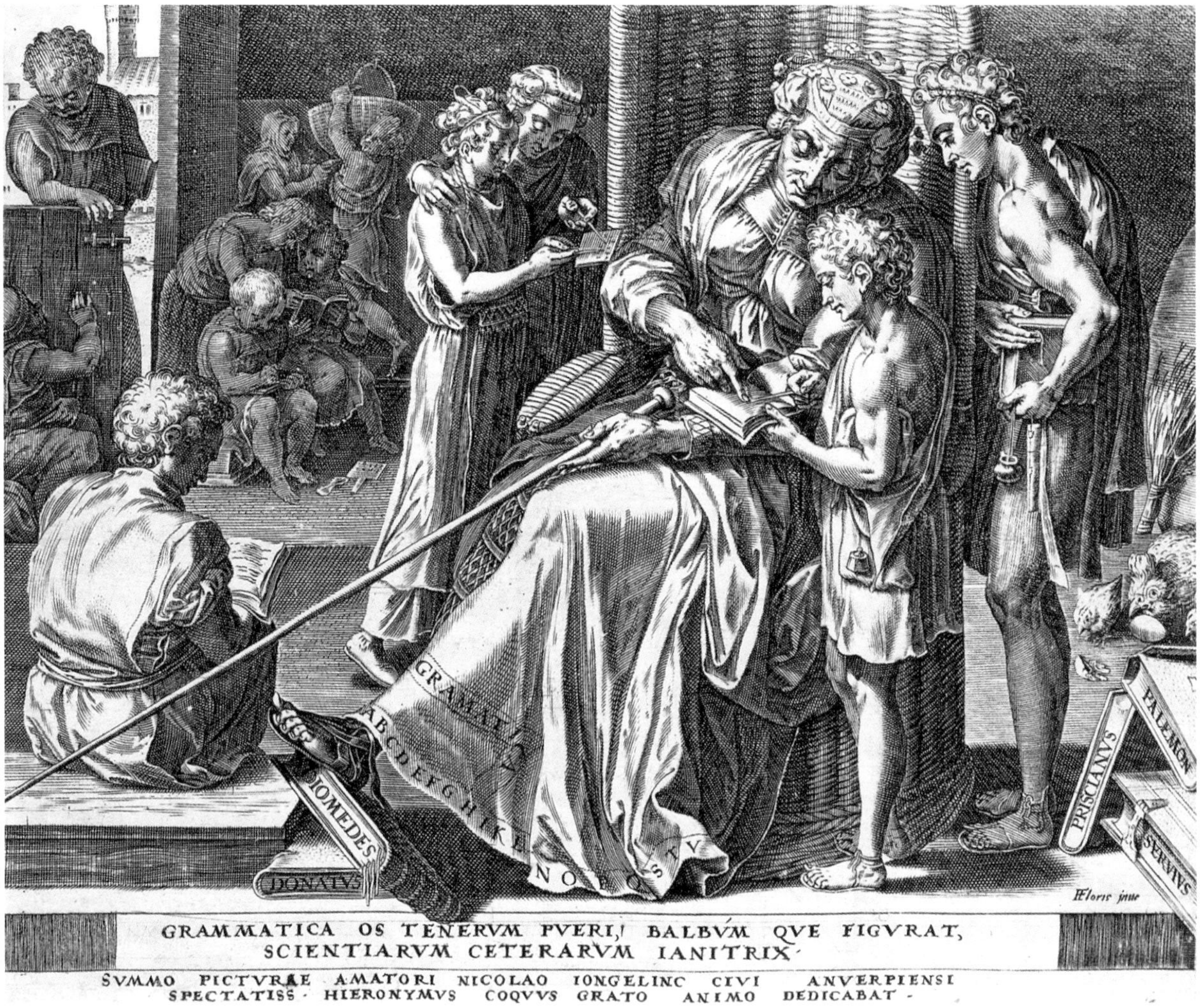

Fig. 4. Cornelis Cort after Frans Floris, *Grammatica*, engraving

leadership of the guild. Since 1442, the year in which they were allowed a chapel in Our Lady's Church, it became known as the guild of Saint Luke. Occasionally, other names have been given to it, such as 'De Violieren' or 'the Guild of the Painters', to indicate that the painters had a leading role in the guild, even if it assembled artists representing many different disciplines, some of them of only limited artistic value. In a document of the beginning of the seventeenth century, no less than twenty-five different possible occupations are listed of 'those that have been since old times and still are members of the guild'.[9] This increase and diversification of the activities of its members has not always improved the cohesion of the guild. The painters were, from the first half of the sixteenth century onwards, the leaders of the guild. The loss of fashion of the carved wooden altarpieces, gradually replaced by painted triptychs, and their final disappearance shortly before the middle of the century have undermined the leading position within the guild of the sculptors in wood. Other groups or 'nations' within the guild, e.g. the window-makers and painters, did not readily accept the domination of the painters and at some times claimed a more or less independent status.

Selling pictures was, in practice, the privilege of the painters. An important exception was the monopoly of the second-hand goods sellers ('oudekleerkopers') to organize the sale of movable goods left after death. These could hold paintings or painter's tools, in particular when the deceased had been an artist. In 1508, the messenger of the guild of Saint Luke obtained the right, through a sentence of the Antwerp magistrate, to schedule such sales. The second-hand goods sellers, however, were not disposed to yield their privilege. As late as 1595, the then messen-

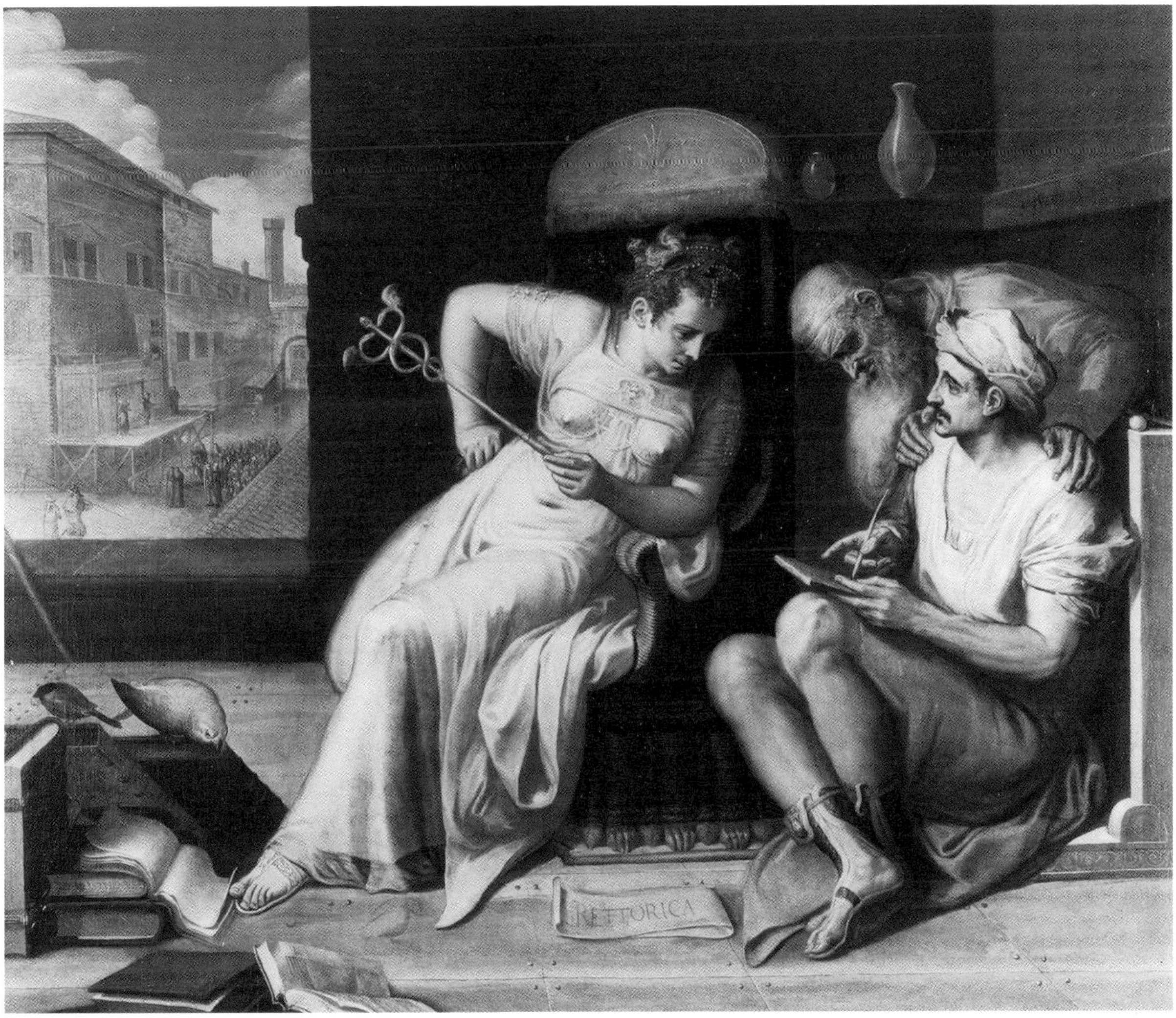

Fig. 5. Frans Floris, *Rhetorica*. Private collection

ger of Saint Luke's guild, Abraham Grapheus, sent a request to the City magistrates, asking for confirmation of the 1508 decision. The second-hand goods sellers replied that their regulations of 1507 and 1538 did not mention any exception to their monopoly in favour of the painters. The authorities did confirm their earlier decision, but again in vain. In 1614, Grapheus's son Abraham the Younger, who had succeeded him as messenger of the guild, complained that his father had never been able to use the rights which the magistrates had repeatedly granted to him, because the second-hand goods sellers had intimidated him and threatened him with law suits.[10] These disputes may have been caused by the growing importance of the art trade in the last decades of the sixteenth century and the eagerness of painters and second-hand good sellers to make a profit out of it.

The earliest instances where members of the guild of Saint Luke are explicitly called 'dealers' in the ledger of the corporation do not concern the trade of paintings, but rather of objects of lesser value, such as popular engravings, ceramics or pigments.[11] In 1588, for the first time, Hans Gabron and Joys van Bimont were both enlisted as masters in the guild with the qualification: 'second-hand goods seller and trading in paintings'. Several of their colleagues followed them in the nineties.[12] This indicates that by the 1580's it was accepted that one could deal in pictures without being a painter oneself, but also that the rule demanding the membership in the guild of Saint Luke in order to be allowed to buy and sell pictures still had to be obeyed.

This rule had been confirmed and strenghtened in 1575. This had become necessary, the

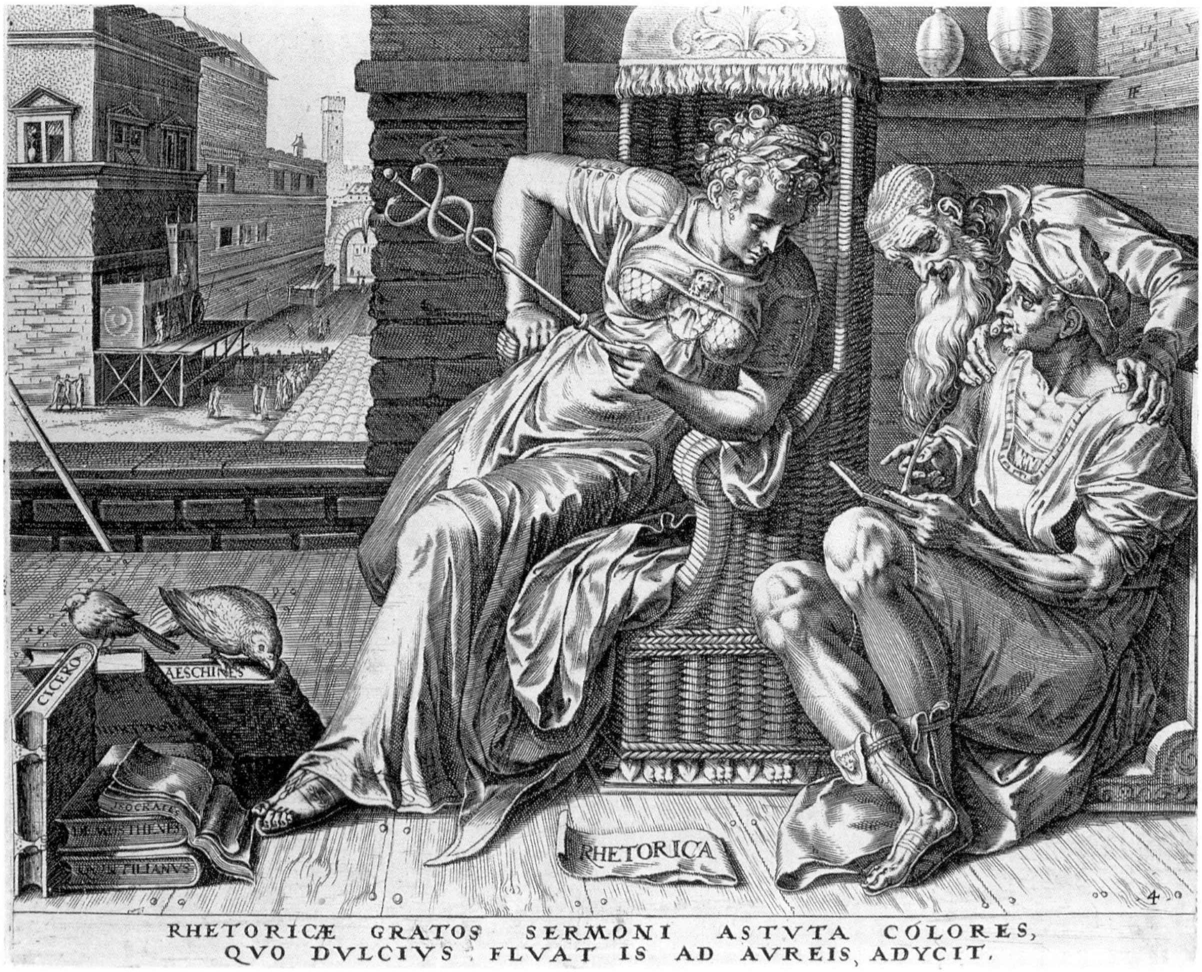

Fig. 6. Cornelis Cort after Frans Floris, *Rhetorica*, engraving

preamble to the regulation explained, because there were people who bought and sold pictures without being citizens and masters in the guild. They put up unlawful workshops, where they made painters, which they withdrew from the regular workshops, to copy pictures of famous masters. By doing so, they not only harmed the rights of the members of the guild, they also committed fraud against their customers, who were convinced they had bought valuable original works.[13] The implication is that masters of the guild could at least provide security regarding the authenticity of the paintings they sold. The popularity of the collecting of painting is also confirmed by the rising number of inventories containing paintings in the last years of the century.[14]

The most remarkable of the sixteenth century collections of paintings in Antwerp is certainly that of Nicolaas Jongelinck (1517–1570). As appears from a widely known document dated 21 February 1566, Jongelinck possessed in his country-house outside Antwerp an important collection of paintings, including twenty-two pictures by Frans Floris, one by Albrecht Durer and sixteen by Pieter Bruegel the Elder.[15] The recent rediscovery of three of the hitherto lost Floris paintings and information about three or four more pieces that are still missing, but not lost, adds to our knowledge of this collection.

It has to be repeated that the 1566 document was not meant to be an inventory of Jongelinck's collection, but only mentioned a few of its most prominent items in order to show that it could indeed be used as a pledge for the enormous debt of 16,000 guilders owed by Jongelinck's partner in business Daniel de Bruyne. Their business included the collecting of taxes, the insuring of ships, the trade of diamonds and probably many other activities.[16]

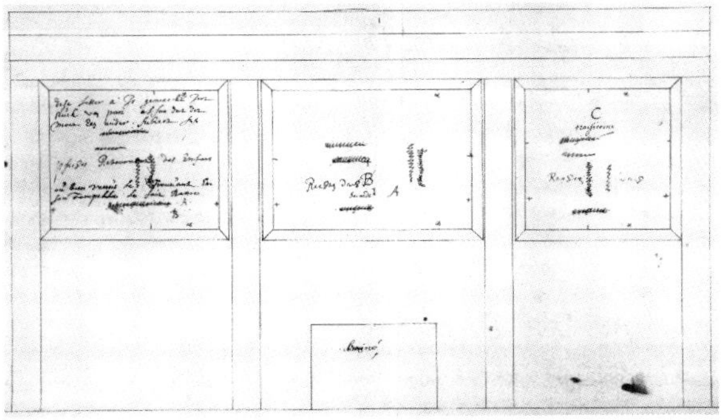

Fig. 7. Anonymous, 1639, Cabinet in the Queen's House, Greenwich: South wall

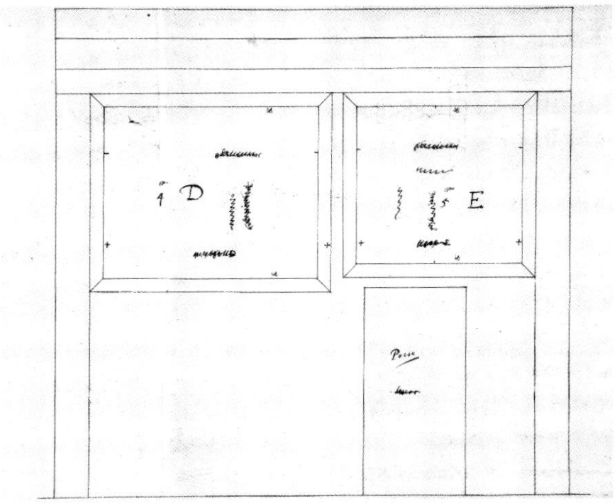

Fig. 8. Anonymous, 1639, Cabinet in the Queen's House, Greenwich: West wall

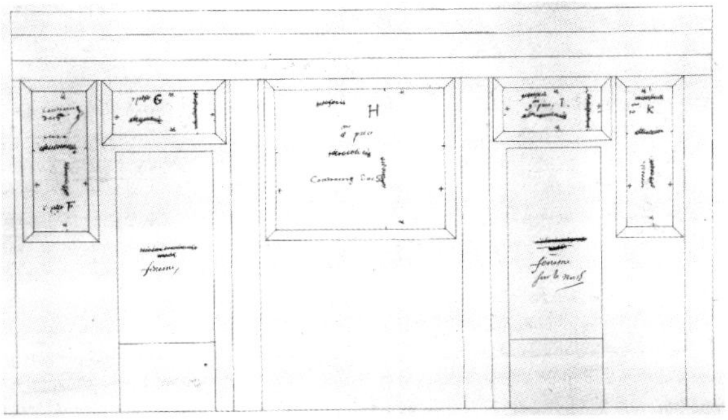

Fig. 9. Anonymous, 1639, Cabinet in the Queen's House, Greenwich: North wall

The fact that in 1594 the City of Antwerp presented to Archduke Ernst of Austria, on the occasion of his State Entry, the six paintings of *The Months* by Bruegel, still is used occasionally to conclude that the debt was not paid and that Jongelinck's collection was confiscated by the City. If this had been the case, the City would not have had to buy these paintings in 1594,[17] nor could the rest of the collection, including the two series by Floris of *The Labours of Hercules* and *The Liberal Arts*, have been for sale in the course of several years following the death of Jongelinck in 1570.[18]

Excepting the missing sixth piece of *The Months*, all the paintings by Bruegel explicitly mentioned in the 1566 document are preserved.[19] The eight unnamed paintings owned by Jongelinck in February 1566, to make a total of sixteen, have not been identified. Paintings dated 1566 or later must be excluded. Considering that most known pictures from Jongelinck's collection all have oblong formats of a size well suited for the decoration of the walls of a room, the most likely candidates to have belonged to Jongelinck among the extant paintings by Bruegel prior to 1566 should be looked for among pieces answering this profile. Complementary evidence is mostly lacking, except maybe in the case of the *Children's Games* (Vienna, Kunsthistorisches Museum), signed and dated 1560, which was sold in 1595 to Archduke Ernst of Austria by the same man who had sold *The Months* to the City of Antwerp the previous year.[20]

Our knowledge of Floris's *Hercules* series remains limited to the one canvas that has emerged and to the ten not very reliable engravings by Cornelis Cort. Until recently, none of the paintings of his second series, *The Liberal Arts*, were known. In a short span of time, three canvasses have come to light: *Arithmetica* (Fig. 1; New York, R. Feigen),[21] *Grammatica* (Fig. 3; private collection)[22] and *Rhetorica* (Fig. 5; private collection).[23] Three more, *Musica*, *Geometria* and *Astrologia* were in 1968 in an Italian private collection, then together with the *Rhetorica*. They have not been seen since. A legal expertise for the Tribunal of Genoa by Prof. Giovanni Vittorio Castelnovi in 1968 described the four pictures as painted in oil on canvasses of 154 x 175 cm. All four had additions of *c.* 6 to 10 cm. above and *c.* 14 to 18 cm. below and were signed and dated 'FF.IV.ET FA. 1557'.[24] This can be confirmed on the recovered *Rhetorica* picture. *Arithmetica* and *Grammatica* have been enlarged above and below as well. An expertise by the laboratory of University College, London (March 1959) on the fabric of the canvas, the composition of the ground and the paint layers on the added

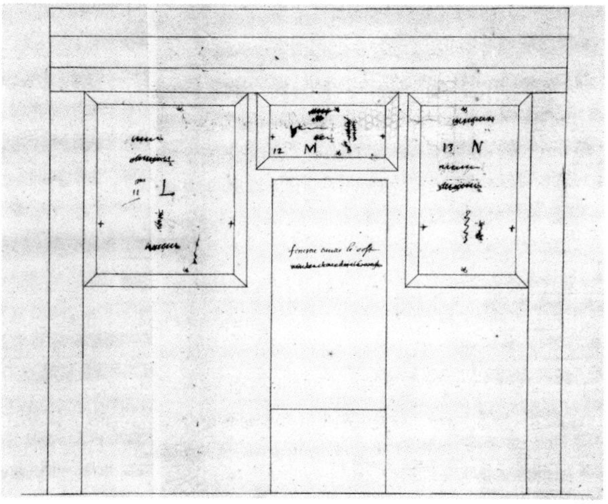

Fig. 10. Anonymous, 1639, Cabinet in the Queen's House, Greenwich: East wall

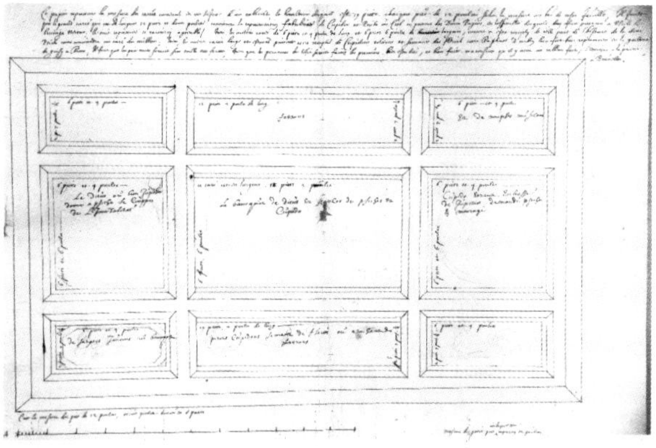

Fig. 12. Balthasar Gerbier, Cabinet in the Queen's House, Greenwich: Ceiling

strips of the *Arithmetica* has shown that these were in all probability made in Italy around 1700.[25] This would suggest the adaptation of the canvasses to a new location at that time. Prof. Castelnovi noticed the presence on the back of the four paintings he had to describe of labels with the inscription 'Gerolamo Balbi, salotto della terasa'. This probably refers to an ancestor of Carlo Balbi (Genoa, 1743–before 1825), who owned paintings by Floris in his Palazzo of the Via San Lorenzo at Genoa in 1780.[26] His collection of paintings descended before 1818 to Goffredo Zoaglio, presumably through his marriage with Carlo's sister Anna and later to his widow, Marchesa Toriglia.[27] Presumably, the series was then still complete. *Arithmetica*, *Grammatica* and *Dialectica* were separated from the rest of the series at some time before 1968.

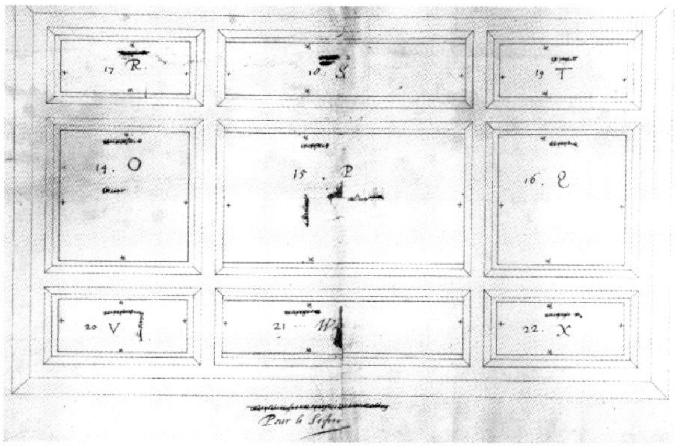

Fig. 11. Anonymous, 1639, Cabinet in the Queen's House, Greenwich: Ceiling

Arithmetica and *Grammatica* are different from the other canvasses in having different sizes and in showing traces of having been manipulated before the series was adapted to its new location in the Palazzo Balbi. The original 127 by 224 cm. size of the *Arithmetica* makes it the largest canvas of the series, exceeding the others in width by almost half a meter. *Grammatica* on the contrary is the smallest piece, being originally only *c.* 1 meter high. The other pieces all measured *c.* 127 x 175 cm. The reason for these discrepancies must probably be found in the disposition of Jongelinck's house. More difficult to explain is at what time *Arithmetica* and *Grammatica* were made smaller at the right edge by folding back a strip. Both show traces there of a vertical fold. Comparison with the corresponding engravings (Figs. 2, 4) shows the changes.

A possible explanation could be that the disposition of the paintings in the 'Room of the Liberal Arts' was changed in 1559, when *The Awakening of the Arts* (Ponce, Museo de Arte),[28] was added to the series. Its measurements, 157 x 238 cm., would not make this impossible. Reducing the width of two of the earlier canvasses could have been necessary to add the eighth piece. In the 1566 documents, the paintings are summed up as 'the eight sleeping arts'. It is striking that Cort's 1565 engraving of *Grammatica* (Fig. 4) omits the jars at the right that disappeared by folding the canvas.

It is a fair assumption that the sequence of the seven Cort engravings, attested by their numbering in the first edition, concurs with that of the paintings in the room: 1. Dialectica, 2. Arithmetica, 3. Grammatica, 4. Rhetorica, 5. Musica, 6. Geometria, 7. Astronomia. This is all

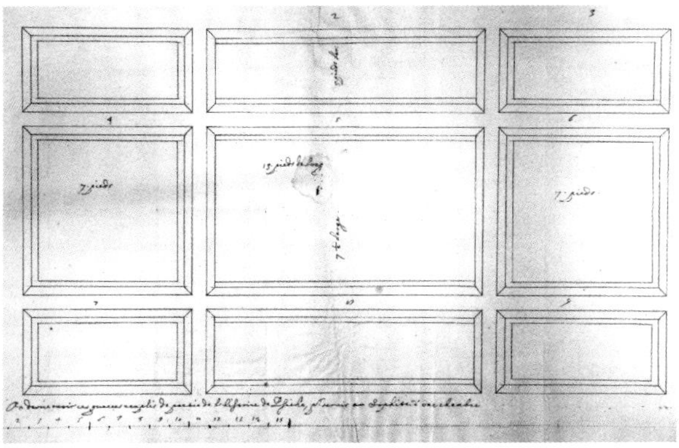

Fig. 13. Balthasar Gerbier, Cabinet in the Queen's House, Greenwich: Idem: Ceiling (second version)

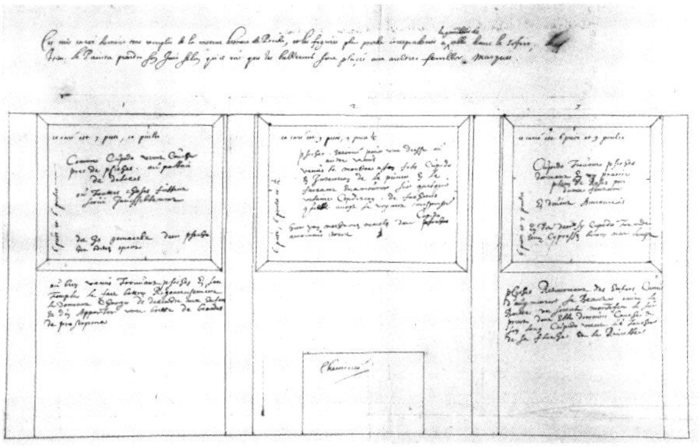

Fig. 14. Balthasar Gerbier, Cabinet in the Queen's House, Greenwich: South wall

the more plausible since this is an unusual sequence, departing in several aspects from tradition. Its most conspicuous novelty is the moving forward into second place of Arithmetica, between Dialectica and Grammatica. This disturbs the universally accepted division of the Arts in the Trivium (Grammatica, Dialectica, Rhetorica) and the Quadrivium (Musica, Arithmetica, Geometria and Astronomia), which was already present in the oldest complete description of the Liberal Arts, Martianus Capella's 4th century A.D. *Wedding of Mercury and Philologia*.[29] In most later descriptions, Musica is moved forward, ahead of the Quadrivium, although Polydorus Vergilius's influential book *De Inventoribus Rerum* discusses Musica prior to Dialectica and inverts Astronomia, Geometria and Arithmetica.[30]

In the present state of our knowledge, it is difficult to assess an interaction between Jongelinck and the artists he entrusted with the decoration of his house. It is unthinkable that the collector would not have been aware of the complexities of their iconography, but we do not know enough about his personality to make any reliable comment on this. He must be regarded as a predecessor of the enlightened collectors of the seventeenth century, the Rockoxes and Van der Geests.

The story of the commission to Jordaens of the *Story of Psyche* for the Cabinet of Henrietta Maria in Queen's House at Greenwich, without his knowing its true destination, has been related several times.[31] Its first phase, the commission (1639–1640) is known through the correspondance about it between the English Court and Balthasar Gerbier, their agent in Brussels, of 1639–1640.[32]

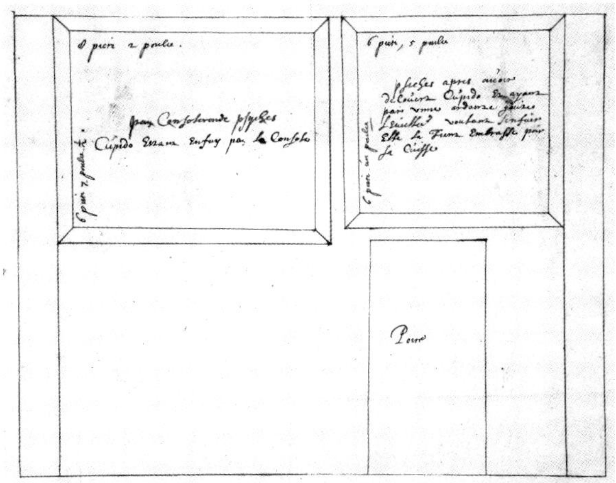

Fig. 15. Balthasar Gerbier, Cabinet in the Queen's House, Greenwich: West wall

The second episode, the legal action undertaken by Jordaens (1641–1642) against the heirs of abbot Alessandro-Cesare Scaglia, who had acted as go-between for Gerbier was described more than sixty years ago by Dora Schlugleit.[33] Although she has duly mentioned the presence in the bundle of 'a series of plans and projects, indicating the subjects to be treated' and gave a transcription of some of the inscriptions on them,[34] a more careful examination of these sheets (Figs. 7–17) reveals some interesting details.

There are eleven drawings among the papers of the 1641–1642 law-suit. They consist of two groups of five and one separate sheet. The first five (Figs. 7–11) give the outlines of the four walls and the ceiling of a room. Each of them

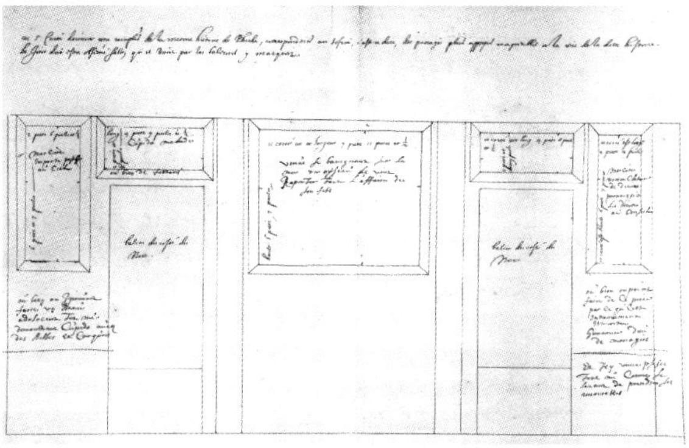

Fig. 16. Balthasar Gerbier, Cabinet in the Queen's House, Greenwich: North wall

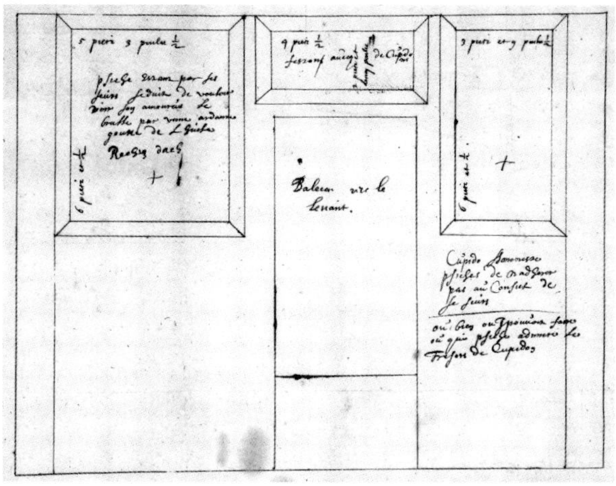

Fig. 17. Balthasar Gerbier, Cabinet in the Queen's House, Greenwich: East wall

shows, against the wall or up the ceiling, squares for paintings, numbered twice, once with the letters of the alphabet, once with arabic numerals. They also show the obstacles in the different walls, indicated by inscriptions in French: 'cheminee' (Fig. 7), 'Porte' (Fig. 8), 'fenetre', 'fenetre sur le nord' (Fig. 9), 'fenetre envers le oost' (Fig. 10), 'Pour le sofito' (Fig. 11). Comparison with autograph letters by Gerbier shows that he is the author of these annotations. In all squares, words have been blotted out, which with a little effort one can read as being the English equivalents of the inscriptions in French, e.g. 'doore' (Fig. 8) or 'window toward the north' (Fig. 9). These cannot be anything but the drawings which Balthasar Gerbier received with a letter from William Murray of 17 October 1639[35] instructing him to contact Jordaens about this commission, but first to replace these drawings by other sheets with inscriptions in French. This is evidently the second group of drawings in the file (Figs. 12, 14–17).

They contain, in Gerbier's handwriting, the same indications as on the first set, complemented by explanatory texts about the commission, such as 'Ces trois carrés doivent estre remplis de la mesme Histoire de Psiche et le figures plus proches correspondents a la grandeur de celles dans le sofite. Item: le peintre prendra son jour selon qu'il voit que les ballecons sont placés aux aultres feuilles marqués' (Fig. 14) or 'Ces 5 carrés doivent estre rempli de la mesme histoire de Psiche, correspondents au sofite, c'est a dire, des passages plus appropriés et agreables à la vue de la dite histoire. Le jour doit estre observé selon qu'il vient sur les balcons y marqués' (Fig. 16). The most explicit comments are given in the drawing of the ceiling: 'Ce papier représente la mesure des carrez contenus en un sofito d'un cabinet la haulteur duquel est 19 pietz, chacque piet de 12 poulces selon la mesure en bas de ceste feuille. Il fault que le grand carré qui est de longueur 12 pietz et deux poulces contienne la représentation fabuleuse de Cupidon et Psiche au Ciel en présence des Dieux payens, en l' assemblée desquels fust presenté a Psiche le bruivage Nectar: le tout representé de racourcy agreable. Item les autres carrez de 6 pietz et 4 poulce de long et 6 pietz et 6 poulce de largeur, auront a estre remply de telle part de l'histoire de la dite psiche come conviendra au carré de milieu. Item les autres carrez longs et estroits pourront estre remplis de Cupidons volants et semant des fleurs comme Raphael d'Urbini les a fort bien representé en la Galerie de Guisy a Rome. Il faut que les peintures soient sur toile tres fortte. Item que les peintures du sofit soient faites les premiers, bien estudiés, et bien faits, et à mesure qu'il y aura un tableau fait, l' envoijer à la pain a Bruxelles' (Fig. 12). This drawing contains below a calibrated line indicating the scale, with the explanation 'Cest la mesure du pied de 12 poulces, et un poulce divise en 8 parts.'

Jordaens received these documents probably towards the end of October or in the beginning of November 1639. He replied to Scaglia that he wanted 6800 florins and that it would take two years to paint the 22 canvasses. Moreover, he would need to have the exact measurements of the canvasses in pieces of rope, with their titles attached to the ropes on pieces

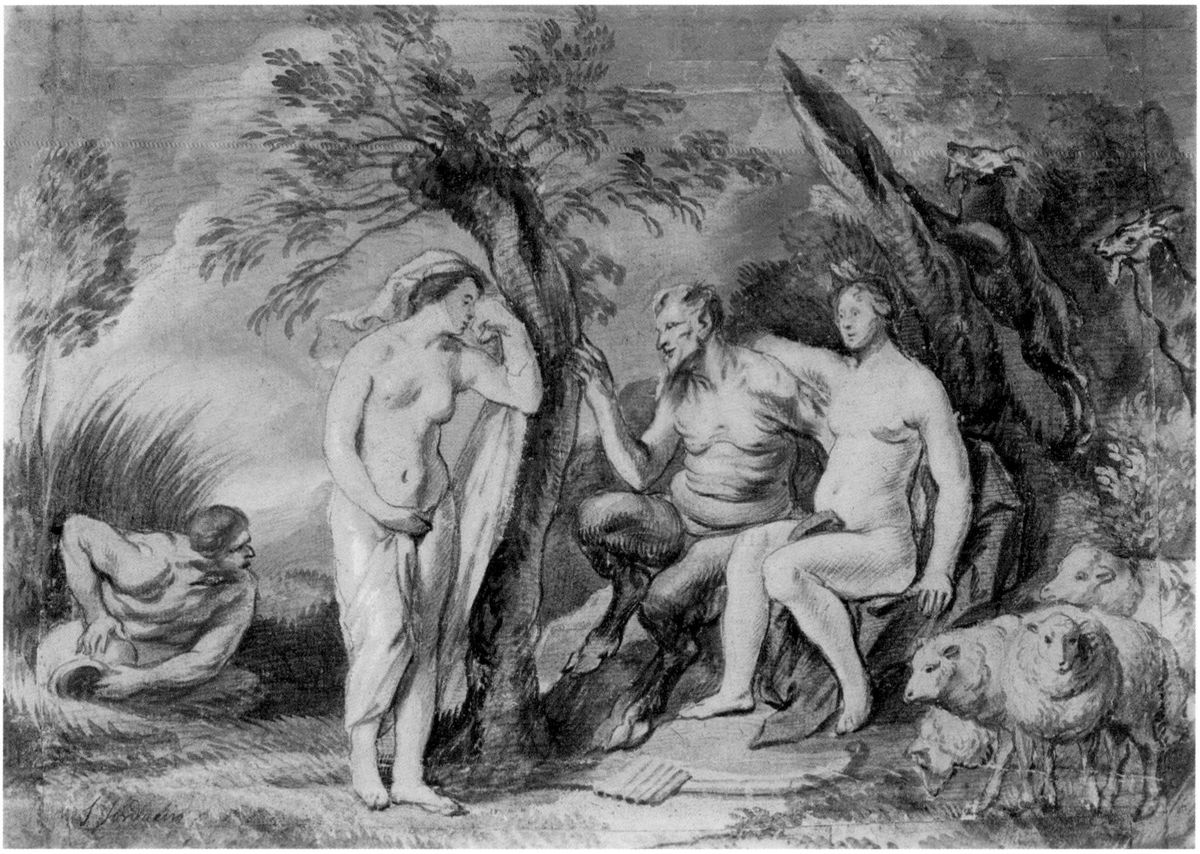

Fig. 18. Jacob Jordaens, *Pan Consoling Psyche*. Antwerp, Stedelijk Prentenkabinet

of parchment, in order to avoid confusion. These informations were transmitted to London before 21 November 1639 by Gerbier. He added the suggestion that Jordaens should be asked to present a design of the work. Gerbier was not enthousiastic about the choice of this artist for such a task, and he repeatedly tried to convince the Court that Rubens would be a much better choice, if not for the whole series, then at least for the ceiling paintings. He was particularly doubtful about Jordaens's ability in mastering the perspective 'di sotto in su', and he repeatedly insisted in London that at least this part of the work should be entrusted to Rubens. He also used Scaglia as an intermediary towards Rubens. On 9 May 1640, he sent him another drawing of the ceiling. When shown this drawing by Scaglia, and it must have been the third version present in the bundle (Fig. 13), Rubens repeated that he would have to charge 2000 patacons, more than Jordaens had asked, and that he suggested that the exterior squares should contain only grotesques and be painted by other hands. For the scenes flanking *The Banquet at the wedding*, he proposed on one side Cupid falling in love with Psyche, on the other her being immortalized by the Gods.

The choice of the subjects was, at least as far as Rubens was concerned, not fixed yet. The drawings sent to Jordaens by Gerbier in October–November 1639 only contained indications concerning the subject of the central scene of the ceiling, which had to be that of Raphael's Farnesina ceiling. The other subjects remained to be determined. Had this to be left to the judgment of the painter? The drawings of the second set have texts written in the squares, mostly in French, some in Dutch, describing subjects of the paintings, sometimes even more than one, as if the choice still had to be made. Most, if not all these inscriptions are in Jordaens's handwriting.

In the first set of drawings, we also recognize Jordaens's handwriting in the indications of the light source 'Rechten dach' (Fig. 7) or 'Contraeren dach' (Fig. 9). It is not clear, however, at what time he could have written this down. It is possible that the first set of the doc-

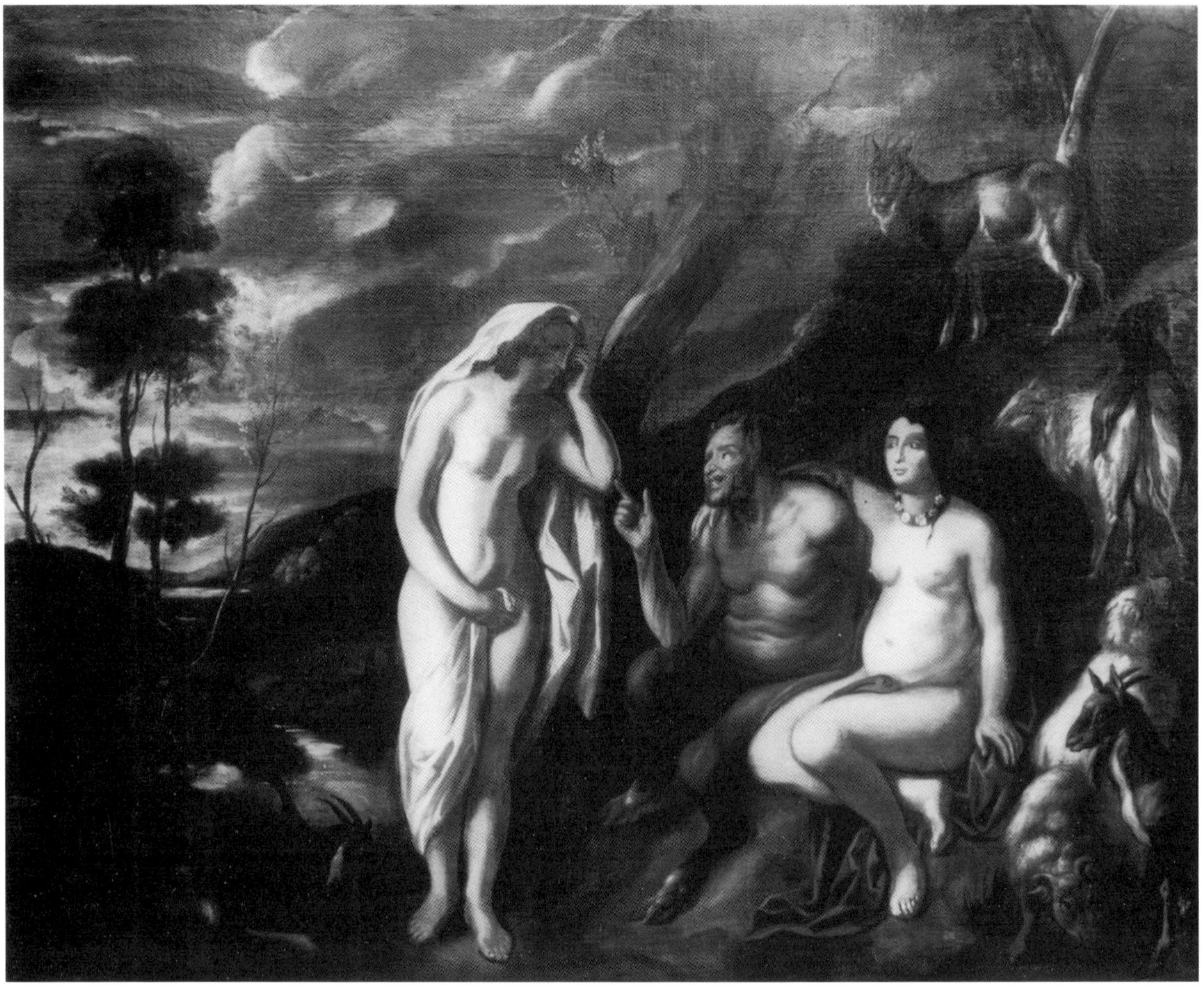

Fig. 19. Jacob Jordaens, *Pan Consoling Psyche*. Private collection

uments was only shown to him in the course of the law suit, but what would have been the point of noting down the direction of the light?

The drawing of the South wall (Fig. 7) also has a comment by Jordaens on the painting on the left: 'Dese letter a is gemaeckt int stuck van Pan alsoo dat dit moet een ander subiect syn'. This refers to the scene of *Pan Consoling Psyche* for which he made a preparatory drawing and which was the first painting to be completed. The drawing is first mentioned in an unpublished letter by Gerbier to Scaglia of 2 February 1640.[36] A Postscriptum to a letter from Gerbier to Charles I of 3 March 1640 confirms that the drawing was sent to London that day.[37] This gives a precise date for the drawing, now in the Stedelijk Prentenkabinet, Antwerpen (Fig. 18):[38] February 1640. From Gerbier's comment in this postscriptum, the impression arises that Jordaens was indeed free to decide 'what he would do'. This quite unusual freedom must probably be explained by the extraordinary circumstances in which the commission was delivered.

The series of paintings was never finished. The eight canvasses that reached England have long since disappeared again, and it is all but certain that the painting of *Pan Consoling Psyche* in a private collection (Fig. 19) is the only remainder of the series.

NOTES

1. C. Van de Velde, "The Sixteenth Century", in W. Aerts ed., *The Cathedral of Our Lady at Antwerp*, Antwerp, 1993, p. 192; F. Baudouin, "The Seventeenth and Eighteenth Century", Ibidem, p. 226; C.J.H.M. Tax and C.M. Tax-Koolen, 'Het verdwenen grafmonument van Franciscus Sonnius in de Onze-Lieve-Vrouwekathedraal te Antwerpen', *Jaarboek Koninklijk Museum voor Schone Kunsten Antwerpen*, 1993, pp. 203–225; S. Grieten and J. Bungeneers, ed., *Inventaris van het Kunstpatrimonium van de Provincie Antwerpen. De Onze-Lieve-Vrouwekathedraal van Antwerpen. Kunstpatrimonium van het Ancien Regime*, Antwerp, 1996, pp. 123–124.

2. C. Van de Genachte, *De Interieur-decoratie van het Antwerps Stadhuis vòòr 1799*, unpublished M.A. diss., V.U.B., Brussels, 1990.

3. 'De vermaerde heerlijcke stadt Antwerpen, door de Coopmanschap in voorspoet wesende, heeft over al tot haer ghewenckt de uytnemenste onser Consten, die veel hun tot haer oock begheuen hebben, om dat de Const gheern is by den rijckdom' (H. Miedema ed., *Karel van Mander, The Lives of the Illustrious Netherlandish and German Painters*, Doornspijk, 1994, I, pp. 134–135; J. Montias, *Le marché de l'art aux Pays-Bas, XVe–XVIIe siècles*, Paris, 1996, p. 25.

4. G. Stappaerts, *Bijdrage tot de studie van schilderijen in privébezit te Antwerpen in de XVIde eeuw*, unpublished M.A. diss., V.U.B., Brussels, 1988, pp. 169–170.

5. L. Jacobs, 'The Marketing and Standardization of South Netherlandish Carved Altarpieces: Limits on the Role of the Patron', *The Art Bulletin*, LXXI, 1989, p. 226.

6. Most of these are contemporary to the inventory (Floris, Adriaen Key, Jacob Grimmer, Antonio Moro), a few older painters are mentioned: Bosch, Metsijs, Gossaert (G. Stappaerts 1988 [see note 4], pp. 11–12, 16, 26, 29, 39–40, 81–82, 116).

7. J.B. Van der Straelen, *Jaerboek der vermaerde en kunstryke gilde van Sint Lucas binnen de Stad Antwerpen*, Antwerpen, 1855, pp. 1–4; C. Huijgens, *Bijdrage tot de geschiedenis van het Antwerpse Sint-Lucasgild in de XVde eeuw*, unpublished M.A. diss., V.U.B, Brussels, 1988, pp. 15–16.

8. 'ende die daer aencleuen' (Van der Straelen 1885 [see note 7], p. 4).

9. Such as the painters (schilders), decorators (stoffeerders), illuminators (verlichters), decorators of mirrors (spiegelstoffeerders), sculptors in wood (houtbeldtsnijders), antique carvers (antijcksnijders), carvers of architecture (metselreysnijders), makers of bows (boogmakers), panelmakers (tafereelmaeckers), makers of glass (gelaesmaeckers), painters on glass (gelaesschrijuers), hammerers of gold (goudtslagers), copperplate cutters (plaetsnijders), woodcarvers (houttefiguersnijders), cutters of letters (lettersteckers), casters of letters (lettergieters), potters (geleyspotbackers), makers of chests (coffermakers), makers of cembalos (clauecimbelmaeckers), makers of boxes (custodimaeckers), printers of books (boeckdruckers), sellers of books (boeckvercoopers), binders of books (boeckbinders), makers of playing cards (quartspelmakers), embroiderers (borduerwerckers)' (Antwerp City Archives, G. & A., 4574, no. 1,2).

10. Antwerp City Archives, P.k., 675, folio 17, 30 verso; P.k., 704, folio 188 recto & verso.

11. E.g. 'Jan Meduwael, beeldvercoopere' (1518), 'Cornelis de Wale gheleyspotvercooper' (1554), 'Merten de Backer heylichvercooper' (1564), 'Jan Bennens pampiervercooper' (1574), 'David Meermaans ververcooper' (1580), etc. (P. Rombouts and T. van Lerius, *De Liggeren en andere historische archieven der Antwerpsche Sint Lucasgilde*, I, Antwerp–The Hague, 1864, *passim*).

12. 'Hans Gabron oucleercooper ende handelt met schilderien'; Joys van Bimont oucleercooper maer handelt met schilderien' (Rombouts and van Lerius 1864 [see note 11], p. 326).

13. Van der Straelen 1885 (see note 7), pp. 63–66.

14. Stappaerts 1888 (see note 8), p. 141.

15. J. Denucé, *De Antwerpsche 'Konstkamers'. Inventarissen van kunstverzamelingen te Antwerpen in de 16e en 17e eeuwen*, Bronnen voor de Geschiedenis van de Vlaamsche Kunst, II, Antwerp, 1932, p. 5; C. Van de Velde, *Frans Floris (1519/20–1570). Leven en Werken*, Verhandelingen van de Koninklijke Vlaamse Academie voor Wetenschappen, Letteren en Schone Kunsten van België, XXX, Brussels, 1975, I, p. 454.

16. I. Buchanan, 'The collection of Niclaes Jongelinck: I. "Bacchus and the Planets" by Jacques Jongelinck', *The Burlington Magazine*, CXXXII, 1990, p. 102.

17. I. Buchanan, 'The collection of Niclaes Jongelinck: II. The "Months" by Pieter Bruegel the Elder', *The Burlington Magazine*, CXXXII, 1990, p. 542.

18. Van de Velde 1975 (see note 15), I, p. 240.

19. H.J. Van Miegroet, '*The twelve months* reconsidered: how a drawing by Pieter Stevens clarifies a Bruegel enigma', *Simiolus*, XVI, 1986, pp. 29–35.

20. Buchanan 1990 (see note 17), *loc. cit.*

21. Canvas, 151 x 224 cm.; prov.: sale New York, Christie's, 11 January 1995, lot 23; lit.: Van de Velde 1975 (see note 15), I, p. 243, no. S94; *The Burlington Magazine*, CXXXVIII, 1996, p. ii, repr.; P. Boccardo, in [cat. exh.] *Van Dyck a Genova*, Genoa, 1997, p. 46, Fig. 33; P. Boccardo, 'Dipinti Fiamminghi del secondo Cinquecento a Genova: Il Ruolo di una Collezione Balbi', in *Pittura Fiamminga in Liguria, Secoli XIV–XVII*, Aosta, 1997, pp. 161–162, 167, repr. in colour.

22. Canvas, 150 x 180 cm.; prov.: sale New York, Christie's, 18 May 1995, lot 32; sale London, Sotheby's, 3 July 1996, lot 212; signed and dated: 'FF.IV.ET.FA.1557'; lit.: Van de Velde 1975 (see note 15), I, p. 243, no. S95.

23. Canvas, 154 x 175 cm.; prov.: private collection, Varezze, 1968; lit.: Van de Velde 1975 (see note 15), I, p. 243, no. S96.

24. '*L'Astrologia, la Musica, la Geometria, la Retorica*, serie di quattro dipinti a olio su tela, ciascuno di cm. 154 x 175. Opere di FRANZ FLORIS; segnate e datate 'FF. IV. ET FA. 1557'. Cornici intagliate e dorate. Nel retro dei telai la scritta 'Gerolamo Balbi, salotto della terasa' indicante l'antico proprietario e l'ubicazione dei quattro quadri nel suo palazzo genovese. Stato di conservazione: le quattro tele presentano (in misura diversa, particolarmente ne 'La Musica') sollevementi e perdite di colore, ma sempre entro la striscie alte cm. 14/18 aggiunte inferiormente alle tele originali e quelle alte cm. 6/10 aggiunte superiormente per aumentare l'altezza dei quattro dipinti, probabil-

mente nel sec. XVIII, allo scopo di addatarli ad una predisposta decorazione parietale di un ambiente; I suddetti danni sono di scarso rilievo non interessando, come si e detto, la pittura originale. Nelle cornici varie scrostature della doratura'.

25. Information from Mrs. A. Guité, New York, for which my sincere thanks.

26. 'Palazzo del Sig. Carlo Balbi, ove si conservano bellissimi quadri Fiamminghi, e singolarmente dell' esimio Francesco Floris' (C.G. Ratti, *Instruzione di quanto puo' vedersi di piu' bello in Genova in Pittura, Scultura ed Architettura ecc.*, 2nd ed., Genoa, 1780, p. 115).

27. 'palazzo ... del quondam Carlo Balbi, ora passato nel marchese Zoaglio. Si conservano in questo bellissimi quadri fiamminghi e singolarmente dell' esimio Francesco Floris' (E. & F. Poleggi, *Descrizione della citta di Genova da un anonimo del 1818*, Genoa, 1974, p. 230; note by E. and F. Poleggi: 'La quadreria fu poi trasportata nel palazzo della marchesa Torriglia ved. Zoagli nella strada Carlo felice (ora via XXV Aprile)'; for the genealogy of the Balbi family, see N. Battilana, *Genealogie delle Famiglie Nobili di Genova*, Bologna, s.d., 1st ed. Genoa, 1825–1833, Balbi, p. 3.

28. Van de Velde 1975 (see note 15), I, pp. 262–265, no. S120; II, Fig. 58.

29. *Martianus Capella and the Seven Liberal Arts. Volume II. The Marriage of Philology and Mercury*, transl. by W.H. Stahl and R. Johson with E.L. Burge, New York, 1977.

30. B. Weiss and L.C. Perez, *Polydore Vergil's De Inventoribus Rerum. An Unabridged Translation and Edition*, Nieuwkoop, 1997.

31. R–A. d'Hulst, *Jacob Jordaens*, Antwerp, 1982, p. 26.

32. N. Sainsbury, *Original unpublished papers illustrative of the life of Sir Peter Paul Rubens*, London, 1859; M. Rooses and C. Ruelens, *Correspondance de Rubens*, VI, Antwerp, 1909, *passim*.

33. D. Schlugleit, 'L'Abbé de Scaglia, Jordaens et l'"Histoire de Psyche" de Greenwich-House', *Revue belge d'archeologie et d'histoire de l'art*, 1937, pp. 139–165.

34. Schlugleit 1937 (see note 33), pp. 162–165.

35. Mentioned in letters from Gerbier to William Murray of 1 December 1639 and 31 May 1640 (Rooses and Ruelens 1909 (see note 32), VI, pp. 245, 296).

36. 'Monsieur, Je vous supplie maintenant de faire demander au Sr. Jordaens s'il veult faire un desseing d'vne des pieces principales de l'histoire de Psiche, dont il vous a plu luy parler il y a quelques temps; s'il dit oui, sçavoir combien il demanderoit pour un tel feit, de l'advertir aussi qu'il auroit a choisir une pièce du sujet dans laquelle il puisse représenter un paysage' (Public Record Office, London, SP 105, 17 Flanders, Gerbier's Entry Book, not paginated).

37. 'The Abat. d'Es. hath given me the draft of Jordaens, with notice of what he will do, I send the same here with, Y. Majesty to peruse the same' (Public Record Office, London, Ibidem).

38. J. Held, in *The Art Bulletin*, LX, 1978, pp. 722–723, Fig. 4; C. Depauw, in [cat. exh.] *Around Rubens, prints and drawings from the Stedelijk Prentenkabinet*, Antwerp, 1991, p. 135; R.A. d'Hulst, in [cat. exh.] *Jacob Jordaens (1593–1678)*, Antwerp, 1993, p. 66, no. B41.

Humanism, Allegorical Invention, and the Personification of the Continents

Elizabeth McGrath

The later sixteenth century in Western Europe, and particularly in the Netherlands, was an age of expansion in many respects, not least in the invention of allegorical figures: those beings, usually female, that personify abstract ideas. It was also the age which attempted to rationalise them and bring them to order – the age of the iconographic handbook, and, it might be added, the age of the learned adviser, for the latter was very much the child of the former.[1] Not that these developments always had an impact on painting. True, elaborate allegorical schemes were given pictorial form on the walls of certain palaces and public buildings of the period, especially in Italy; but pictures – cabinet paintings and easel paintings, the sort of works which increasingly formed the production of artists in late sixteenth-century Flanders – were not, either for scholars or artists, the natural and normal vehicles for erudite argument and ideas. Scholarly input most often belongs to other contexts: book-illustration, of course, and prints, but also the genre of festival decoration and pageantry. Here painting did have a role, in the Netherlands above all, but of a curious sort, on the borderline of theatre – marginal too in the fact that the visual traces of its temporary reality generally survive only in the plates published in commemorative volumes.

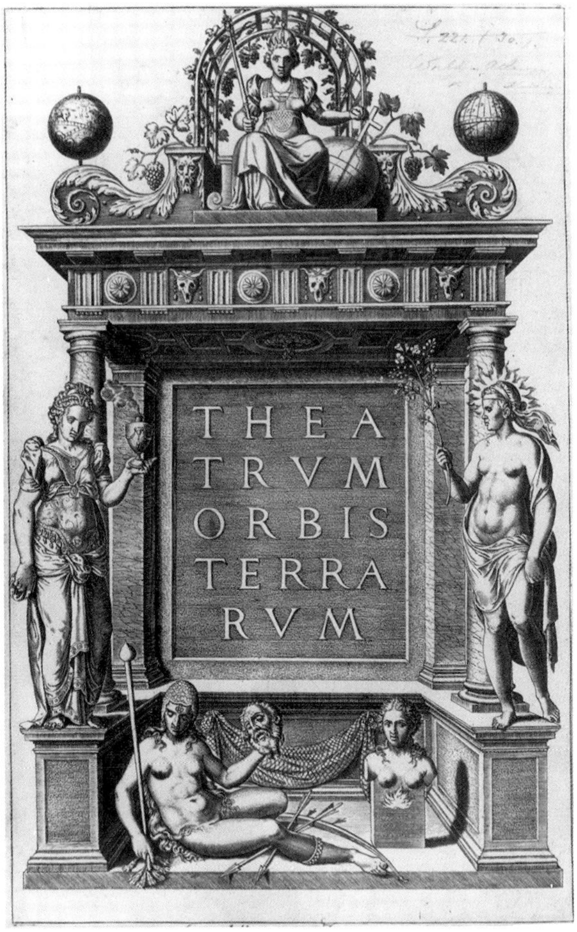

Fig. 1. Titlepage to Abraham Ortelius, *Theatrum Orbis Terrarum* (Antwerp, 1570)

Antwerp has a special part in this story. For the city at this period was a place where artists communicated with humanists to an unusual degree – providing, certainly, more substantial evidence of collaboration than that supposed hotbed of reciprocal interest and influence, late fifteenth-century Florence. There are the friendships, documented in works of art as well as in letters and in the pages of those erudite autograph albums (*alba amicorum*) cherished by learned Northerners:[2] of Hoefnagel and Bruegel with Ortelius;[3] of Van Veen with Ortelius and Lipsius;[4] of Rubens finally with Moretus, Woverius, Gevartius.[5] There are scholars, proferring advice at many levels, from the mere addition of an inscription (done perhaps without seeing the related image) to the detailed specification of a whole subject, as in the case of an exemplary picture commissioned by Lipsius of Van Veen.[6] Indeed in one public sphere the role of the humanist adviser was virtually institutionalised in Antwerp. For the town secretary's duties involved not only making an account of, but organising and composing the inscriptions to the pageantry and triumphal arches which welcomed successive governors and rulers, Habsburg and other. In his preface to the book commemorating the most celebrated of these 'glorious entries', that mounted

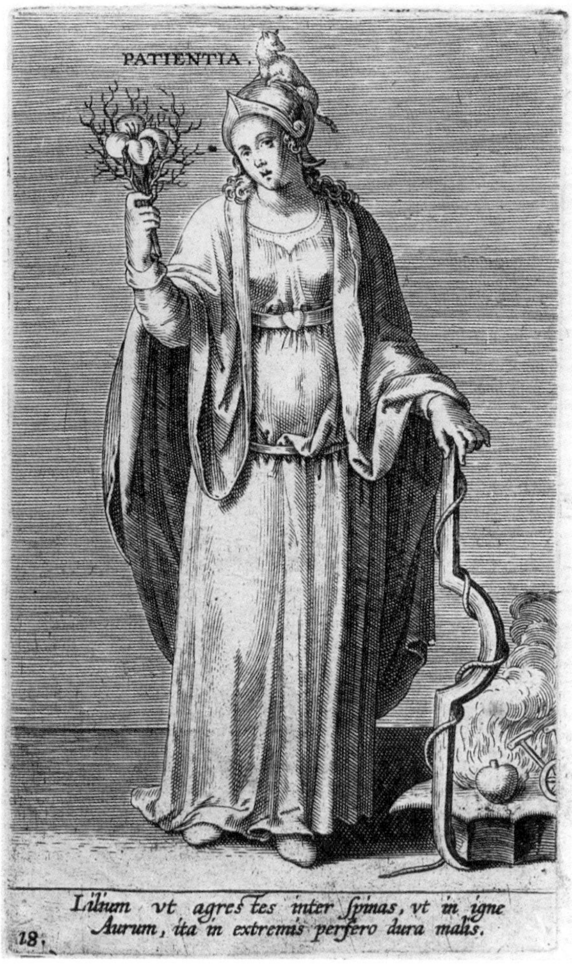

Fig. 2. *Patientia*, from Philips Galle, *Prosopographia*, engraving (*c.* 1600?)

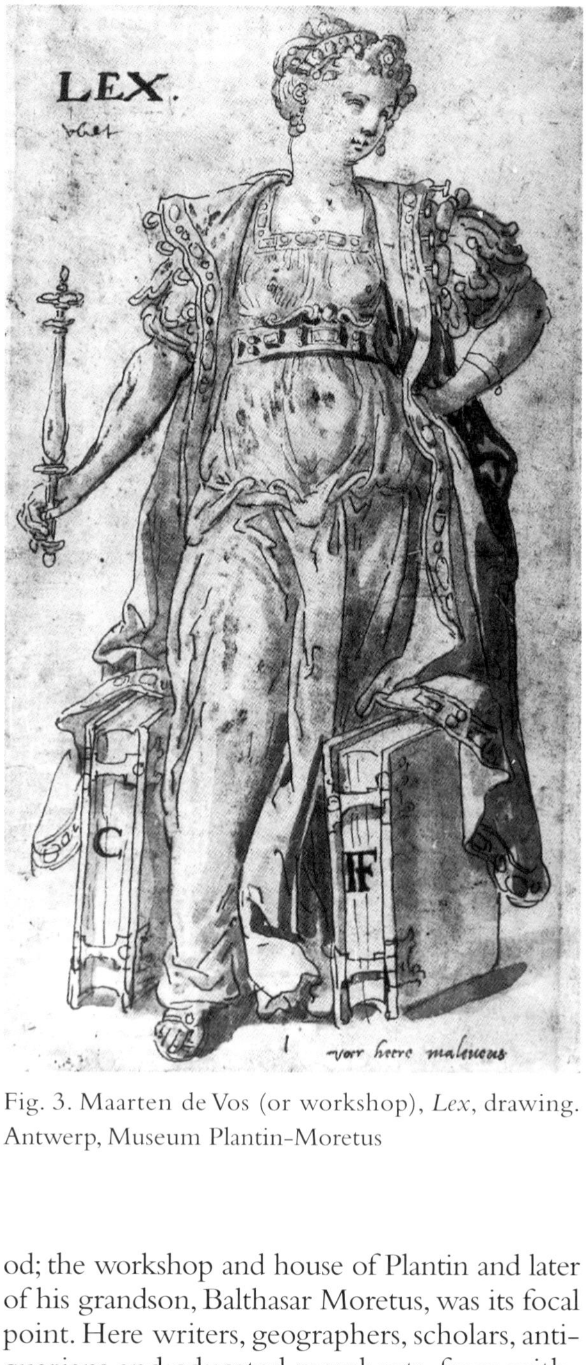

Fig. 3. Maarten de Vos (or workshop), *Lex*, drawing. Antwerp, Museum Plantin-Moretus

by Rubens for the Cardinal-Infante Ferdinand in 1635, Caspar Gevartius presents himself and Rubens firmly as the latest, triumphant duo in a series of humanist/artist associations: Petrus Aegidius and Quintin Massys for the entry of 1520; Cornelius Grapheus and Pieter Coecke for that of 1549; Joannes Bochius and Otto Van Veen for the entries of 1594 and 1599.[7] Still, there is an element of revisionism here, to accomodate earlier events to the desired model, for Rubens undoubtedly had more control over the organisation of the project as a whole than had been the case for earlier artists.[8] Some scholars even drew up their own designs, as in the case of Benito Arias Montano, who not only planned the ill-fated monument to the Duke of Alva, but devised schemes for emblems, and for the titlepage to the Polyglot Bible, that great production of the Plantin press.[9]

Publishing was central to humanist life in Antwerp, as perhaps nowhere else at the period; the workshop and house of Plantin and later of his grandson, Balthasar Moretus, was its focal point. Here writers, geographers, scholars, antiquarians and educated merchants, from within and beyond the city, naturally associated with the artists who were involved, like them, in the production and illustration of books (and the distribution of them).[10] Antwerp humanism took its specific character from these interactions, which involved a commitment to the new as well as the old – modern inventions, the world of the 'new discoveries', as well as the relics of Greece and Rome. In this context Abraham Ortelius becomes almost an emblematic figure: a humanist whose contribution to map-making is now, justly, celebrated over his research on ancient coins, but who found no

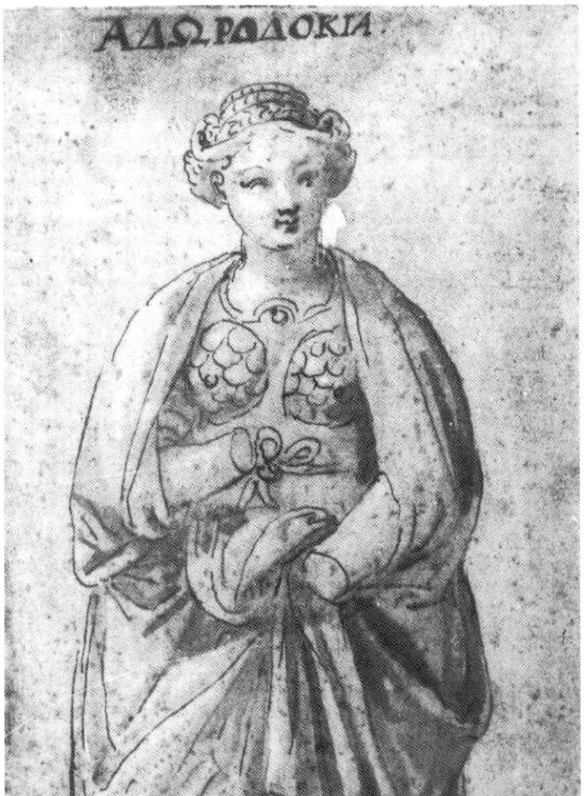

Fig. 4. Maarten de Vos (or workshop), *Adorodokia*, drawing. Antwerp, Museum Plantin-Moretus

contradiction in pursuing both fields with enthusiasm. (Of course he embodies reconciliation – or compromise – in another, still more obvious, way since, like many of his Antwerp friends in this age of religious crisis, he was sympathetic to the 'politiques' and the so-called

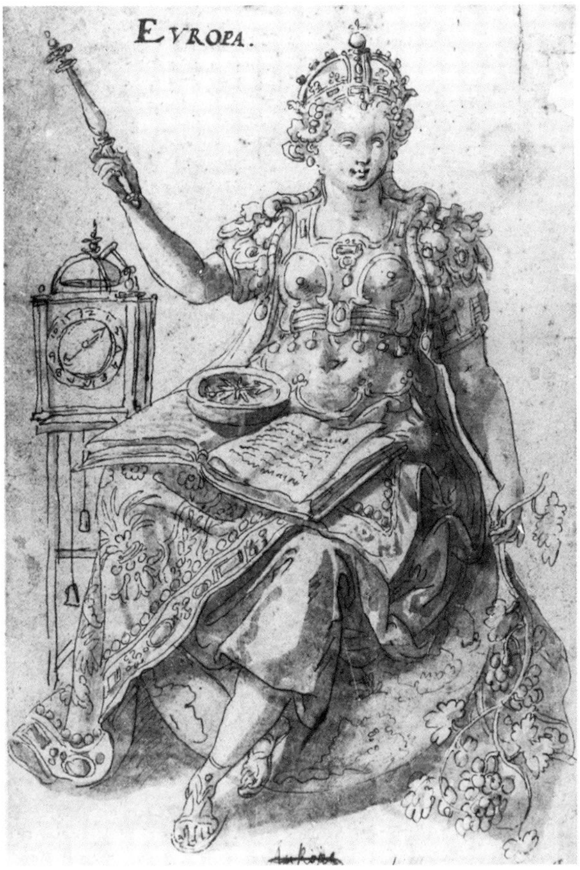

Fig. 5. Maarten de Vos (or workshop), *Europa*, drawing. Antwerp, Museum Plantin-Moretus

Family of Love.)[11] One striking product of this fusion of interests was his re-invention of the image of the world, his presentation of it to the eyes of Europeans, not only in the celebrated series of maps which constitute his *Theatrum orbis terrarum*,[12] but through the tradition of personification. For the extraordinary titlepage he invented for his book (Fig. 1), first published in Antwerp in 1570,[13] and much re-edited, revived the ancient notion of the figuration of the Parts of the World, only to revise it entirely. The relationship of these images to the story of the illustration of the Continents, and particularly to the figure of Africa, for she brought to her modern image the most complex and confusing classical heritage – the effort made by successive artists and writers to reconcile antique allusion and modern reference, symbolism and realism – not only provides a particular and curious case of the influence of humanism on art; it also illustrates the way in which painting might be especially resistant to this influence. In fact Frans Francken the

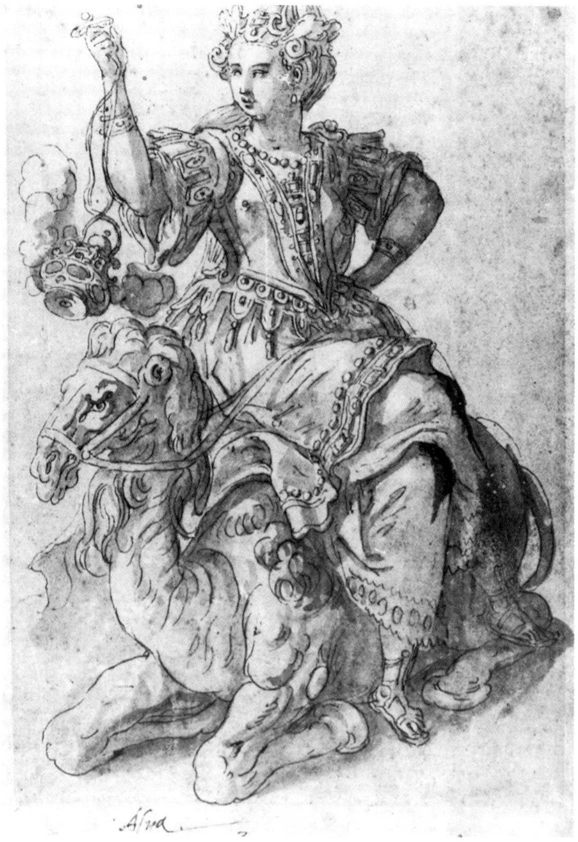

Fig. 6. Maarten de Vos (or workshop), *Asia*, drawing. Antwerp, Museum Plantin-Moretus

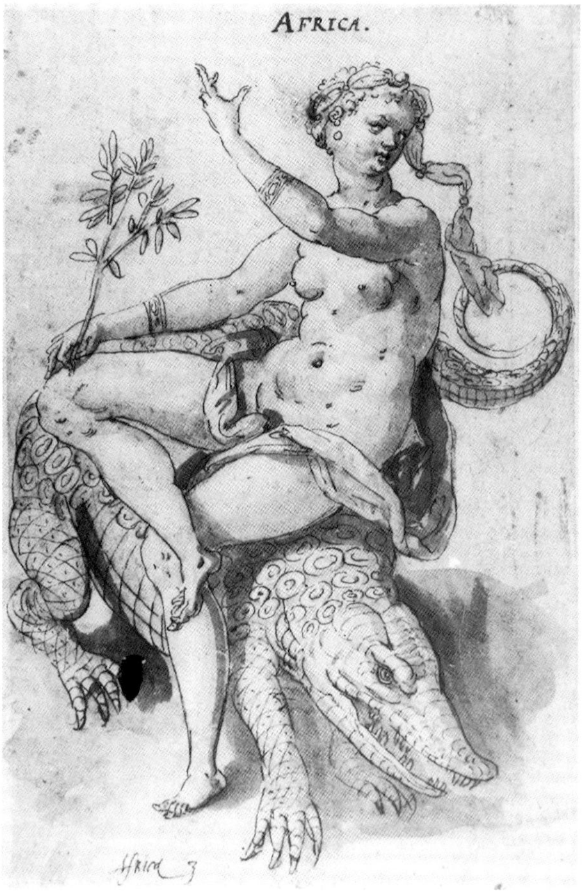

Fig. 7. Maarten de Vos (or workshop), *Africa*, drawing. Antwerp, Museum Plantin-Moretus

Younger was the first Netherlandish artist to introduce the personified Continents into a painted panel (Fig. 28), turning the Theatre of the World into a pictorial theme. In the process, as we shall see, he represented the figures themselves in a more decorous way, modifying their extravagant character, playing down their outlandish attributes – in the case of the animals literally shrinking them. It was no simple matter to translate literary and humanist inventions made for books, print series or pageants into the common currency of painting.

★

Humanists loved, and encouraged the use of, personifications – for their classical aura, for their practical utility as didactic aids, for their evocation, through attitude and still more through emblematic attributes, of concepts, of the world of the mind. Naturally, though, even such symbolically loaded figures were never quite allowed to substitute for words; humanist values could not relax to that extent. They provided a complement, supported by and supportive of texts; if the images themselves looked intriguing, that gave more of an incentive to read the accompanying inscriptions, and absorb their significance. This way of thinking, not entirely unrelated to the theory of the art of memory,[14] itself encouraged the invention of oddities, images more striking than beautiful. Still, meaning was secured, prevented from roaming into free association, by the labels and the texts (whether inscribed or spoken) that the figures were imagined as uttering (abstractions envisioned by Renaissance writers generally pronounce their names and their messages). The humanist impulse, if not compulsion, to make images speak, explain themselves and, ideally, articulate a moral lesson (the hoariest topos of humanist praise of a painting or sculpture is after all that it lacks only a voice) asserts itself constantly in the inscriptions with which scholars accompanied images.[15] And in Flanders this impulse was additionally fuelled by vernacular traditions. Personifications were as normal on the stage of the Rederijkers as they were on titlepages, medals and triumphal arches.

Humanist interest, however, naturally focused on providing allegorical figures with what were judged to be authentic, classical attributes. Essential to this enterprise were two kinds of reference book which were used repeatedly by learned advisers and indeed, increasingly, by artists themselves. First, there were the ancient visual sources presented in the compendia of illustrations of antiquities, especially the reverses of Roman coins which regularly featured personifications. Guillaume Du Choul's *Discours de la religion des anciens romains* (Lyons, 1556), which usefully arranged things iconographically was a notable example. And there were books specifically devoted to coins: by Sebastiano Erizzo, for example, Antonio Agustín, and, in the Netherlands, the artist and scholar Hubert Goltzius, who illustrated his own works.[16] Second, there were the ancient literary testimonies gathered together in handbooks: Vincenzo Cartari's *Imagini degli dei* – which included descriptions of a plethora of near-abstractions on the borderline of the pagan pantheon; and above all Valeriano's *Hieroglyphica*, that impressive encyclopedia of symbolism.[17] Valeriano featured the material in Horapollo's supposed key to the Egyptian hieroglyphs, but included very much more, and had excellent indexes. (This, like the books by Cartari and Du Choul was first published in 1556, something of an *annus mirabilis* for iconography.) These two types of source – visual and literary – provided countless attributes for figures in the later sixteenth century. Both Cartari and Valeriano were used, for example, for the imagery of the entries of 1594 and 1599.[18]

But classical antiquity had its limitations. Not only did it have no prototypes for some obvious Christian virtues; it was hardly equipped to provide for the figuration of concepts and notions which stemmed from the new discoveries, the *Nova Reperta*, whether in the technological or geographical sense.[19] Here ingenuity – and modern sources – had to supply the deficiency; and the books and prints which recorded innovative figures, whether singly, in sets, or in whole decorative programmes – very often festival books such as those of Bochius – came themselves to serve as iconographic models and

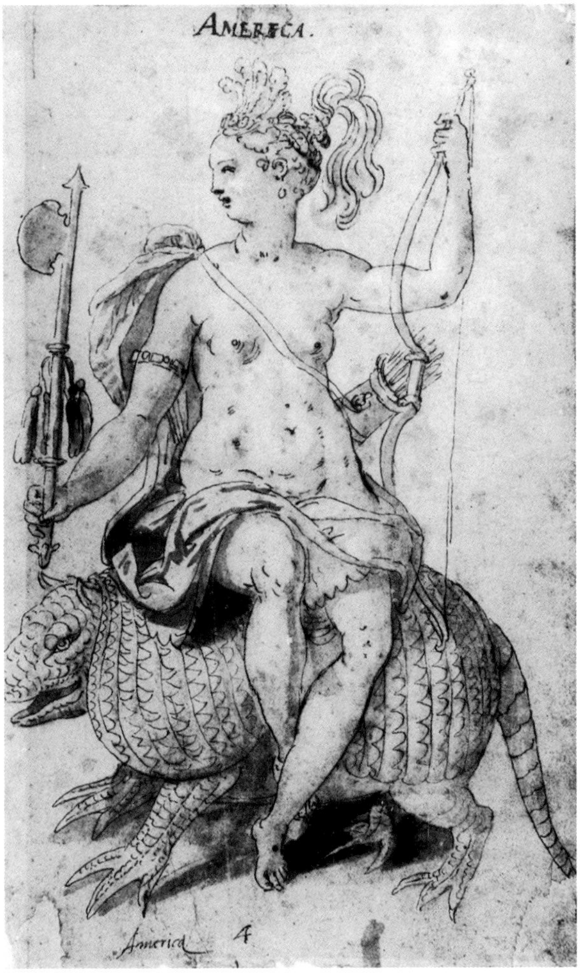

Fig. 8. Maarten de Vos (or workshop), *America*, drawing. Antwerp, Museum Plantin-Moretus

manuals.[20] At the end of the century Ripa's *Iconologia* – first published at Rome in 1593 and then in an expanded, illustrated edition in 1603 – gathered together elements from the various sources, ancient and modern, in an A–Z of personification, designed to facilitate allegorical invention.[21] This gradually came to be used by Netherlandish artists in the seventeenth century, especially, of course, after the publication of the Dutch version in 1644. But in the last decades of the previous century the need for an encyclopedia of symbolic figures was apparently being catered for by the series of engravings which were produced in abundance in the workshops of Antwerp printers. In preparation for the entry of Archduke Ernest to Antwerp in 1594 Philips Galle and the widow of Hieronymus Cock supplied prints which evidently included allegorical figures (they are described as 'gedruckte beeldekens of nymphen'

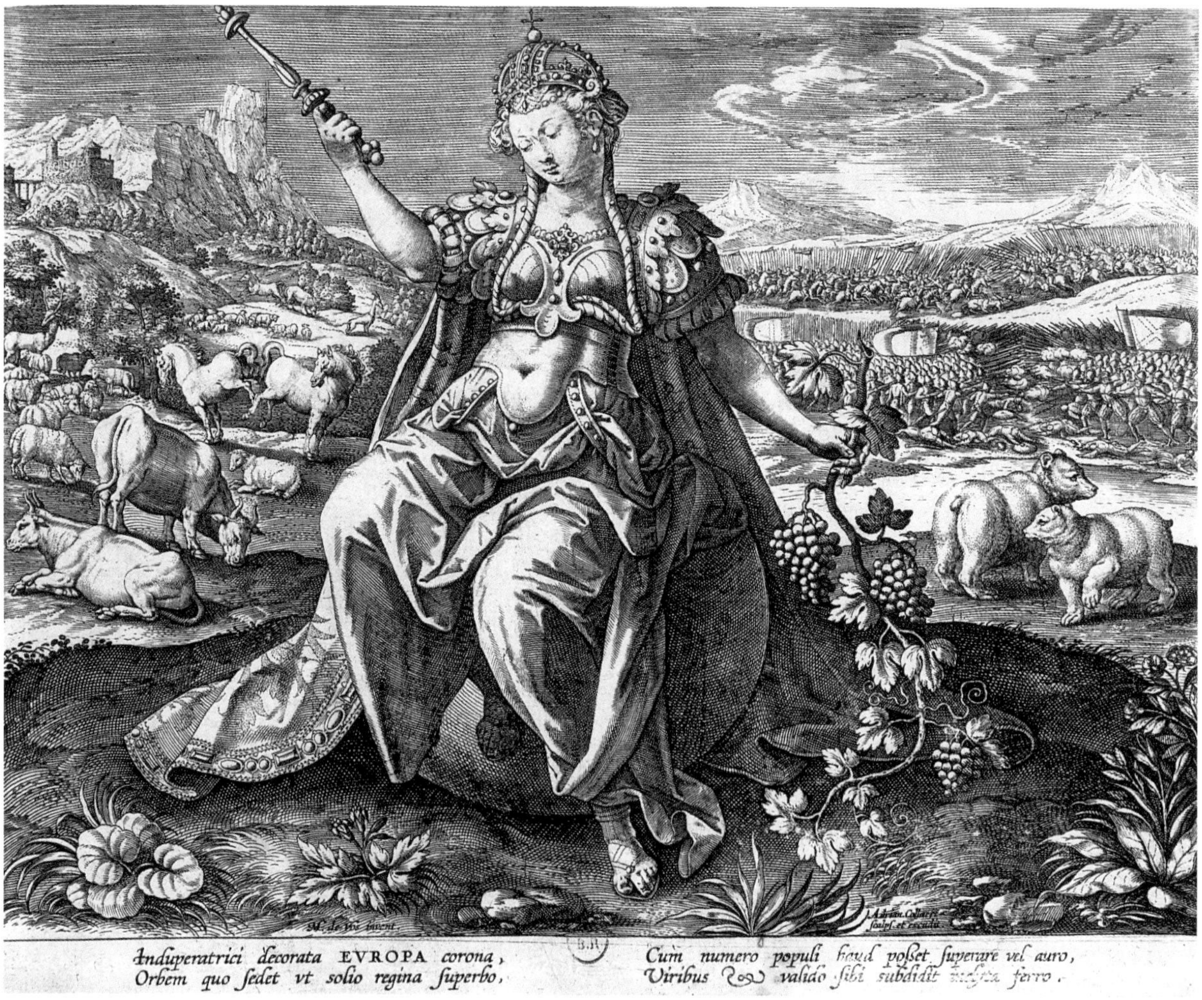

Fig. 9. Adriaen Collaert after Maarten de Vos, *Europa*, engraving (*c.* 1589)

and 'gedruckte figueren' respectively) to serve as models for the characters (both live and painted, it would seem) in the pageants.[22]

It is tempting to associate this episode with the publication by Galle of the series of allegorical prints, engraved by his brother Theodoor and provided with texts by Cornelis Kilian (cf. Figs. 24, 25) which he entitled *Prosopographia*, the drawing of personified characters.[23] This work, the precise date of which is hard to determine, was not quite (as is sometimes implied) a Northern parallel to the *Iconologia* of Ripa, for it aimed not at comprehensiveness, but at supplementing the standard repertory of personifications readily available in prints: the old, familiar septets of Virtues and Vices, Liberal Arts and so on.[24] Interestingly Patience (Fig. 2), a figure especially prominent in Netherlandish allegorical evocations of the religious troubles of the period,[25] heads the list Galle begins to give – evidently he started with the concepts that seemed most relevant. The preface addressed itself not only to artists (and to craftsmen of all kinds), but to pageant designers and Rederijkers (*poetae rhythmici sive rhetores vernaculi*).[26] And the very choice of title suggests a theatrical association – the Greek term *prosopopoiia*, which Galle adapted, is literally the making of masks.[27] Not that there is any clear evidence that this series was used for the figures in the entry of 1594.[28] Rather, the request to the printer's workshop for models for the many personifications needed for the pageantry in 1594 might have alerted Galle, one of the most energetic publishers of the period, to the need for an expansion of the allegorical range. Despite the fact that Galle begins the preface to the *Prosopographia* by addressing painters, he was not perhaps thinking primarily of them, at least not of their normal productions, but of

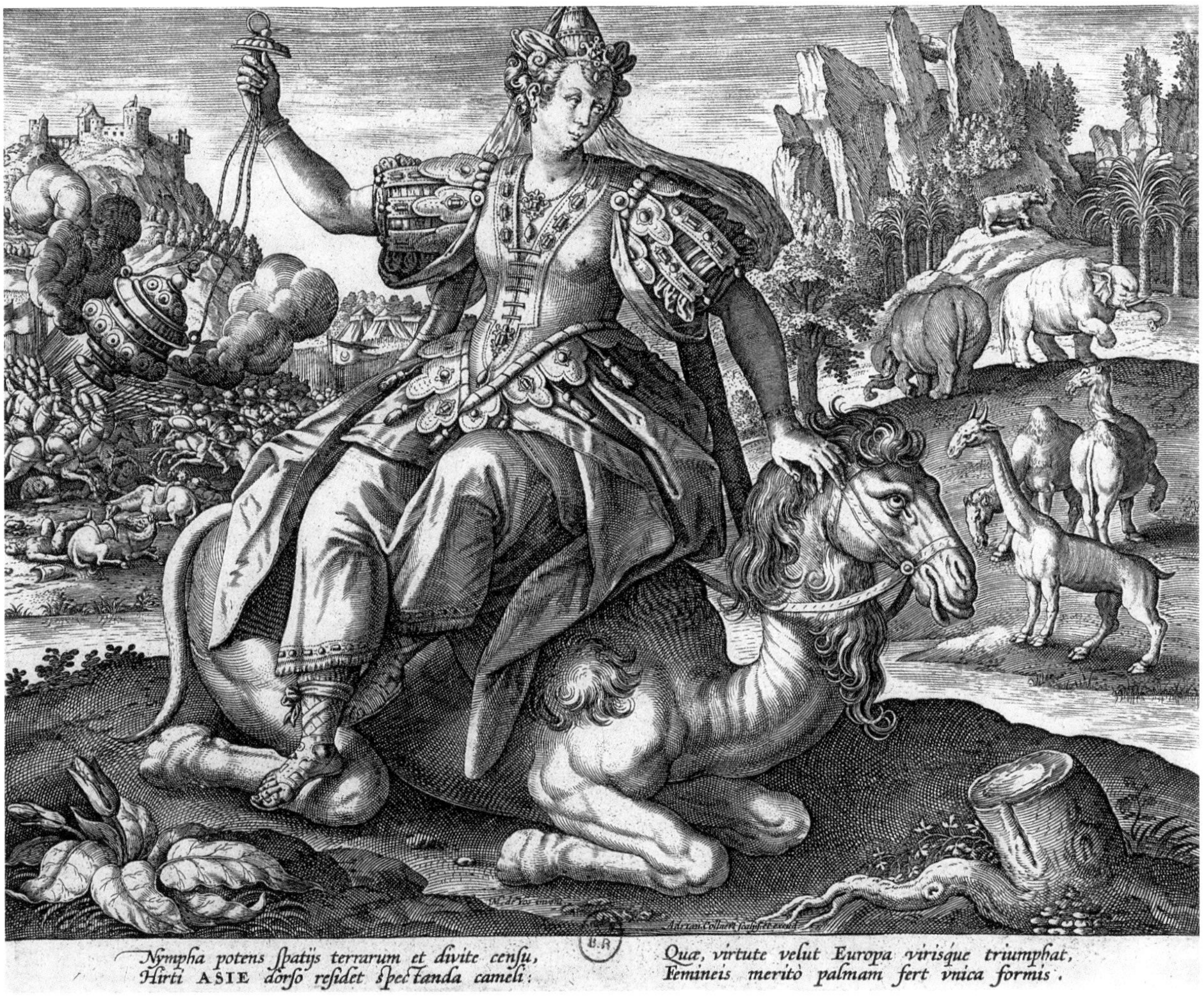

Fig. 10. Adriaen Collaert after Maarten de Vos, *Asia*, engraving (*c.* 1589)

other, more literary and theatrical (and, possibly also, given the reference to his images as 'monochrome',[29] printed) sorts of images. (It is worth recalling too that Ripa's *Iconologia* was initially, in the edition of 1593, addressed to poets, who headed the list even in the illustrated edition of 1603. He certainly envisaged the book's function as helping with the devising of emblems and allegories for pageantry; it was not aimed primarily at painters.)

I suspect that a motive similar to that of Galle lay behind the creation and assembly of a group (or rather several groups) of drawings, now in the Plantin-Moretus Museum and attributed to Maarten de Vos (cf. Figs. 3–8). De Vos was the principal artist charged with the pageantry put on in 1594 by the city of Antwerp (as distinct from the foreign merchants),[30] and these designs, mostly of single figures, labelled and sometimes further inscribed, have been associated with that celebration.[31] A small number of figures display certain correspondences with personifications which featured there. *Lex*, for example, with her books marked for the Code of Justinian and the Pandects (Fig. 3) had a counterpart in the allegorical theatre set up for Archduke Ernest in front of the Town Hall.[32] Most of the others, however, have no particular relationship with anything in the entry, even if they often proclaim themselves as the products of learned invention. *Adorodokia*, Incorruptibility (Fig. 4),[33] for example, has a distinctly humanist aura about her, as much from her lack of hands as from her Greek name. She comes – via Valeriano – from an image of judges without hands in Thebes described by Plutarch.[34] The fact that all of these drawings are not only in more or less the same format, but are for the most part executed in a relatively schematic and routine manner, supports

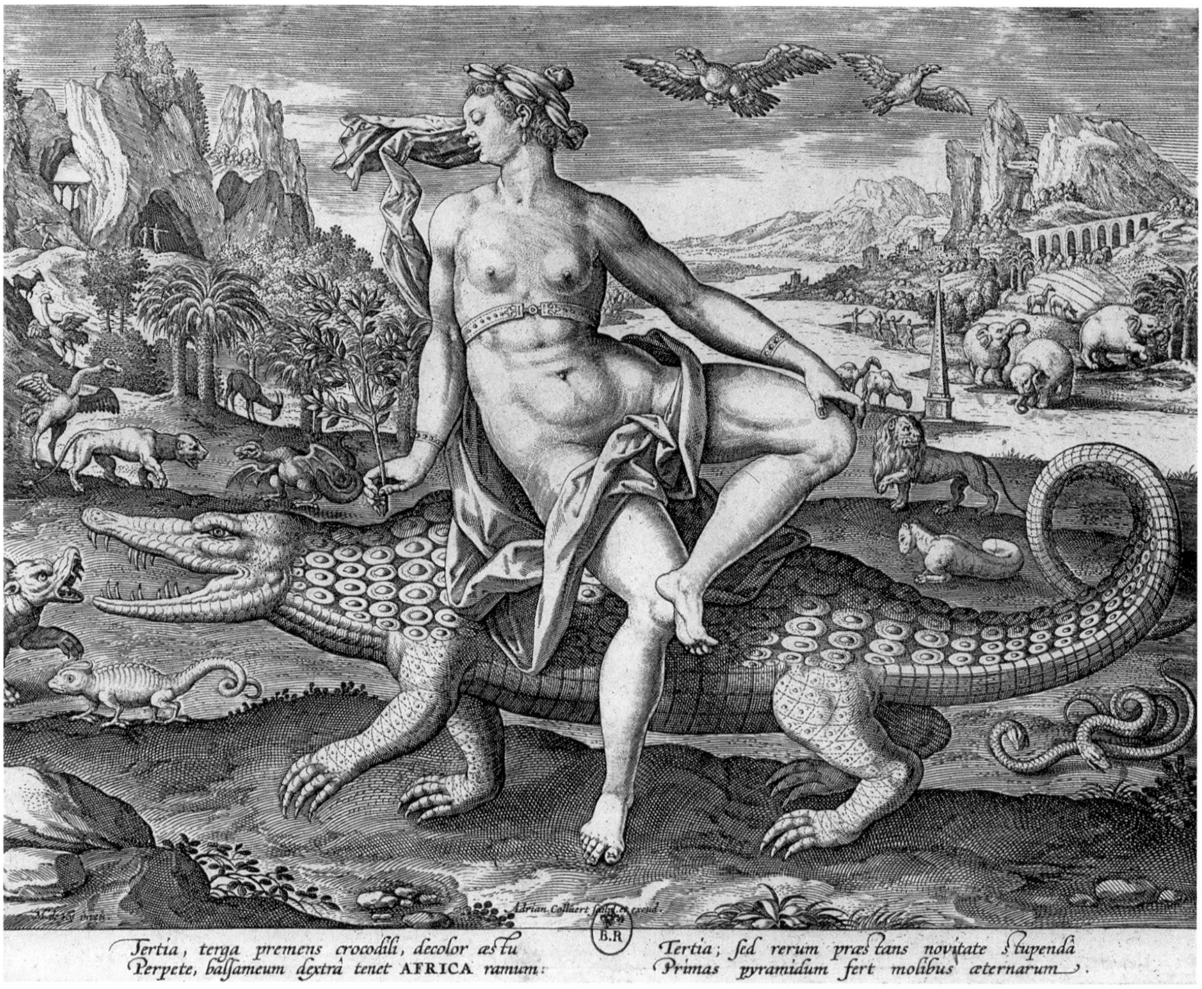

Fig. 11. Adriaen Collaert after Maarten de Vos, *Africa*, engraving (*c.* 1589)

the idea that they were assembled in the De Vos workshop as the artist's own repertory of symbolic figures (a more informal, and private, collection than the series published by Galle), for use in contexts such as pageantry.

Particularly interesting are the figures, numbered 1–4 and evidently a set, illustrating the Continents (Figs. 5, 6, 7, 8).[35] For these relate to a series of prints published by Collaert at the end of the 1580s after designs by De Vos (Figs. 9, 10, 11, 12).[36] 1589 at any rate is the date inscribed by De Vos on one of the two known preliminary drawings for the set, that of *America* (Fig. 13); the drawing for *Asia* (Fig. 14) is dated 1587.[37] Next to these elegant productions the drawings in the Plantin-Moretus Museum look dry and perfunctory. Rather than preceding the inventions of the engravings, as has usually been supposed, it seems likely that they are derivative, an adaptation designed to accomodate the personifications from the prints, in their landscape settings, to the simplified formula of single figures with attributes. (One detail which is perhaps significant is the 'Europeanisation' of Africa's facial features in the Antwerp drawing [Figs. 11, 7].)[38] Such an undertaking might well have been prompted (either at the time, or subsequently) by the experience of the entry of 1594, when the prints were offered as models by Galle and Cock's widow; for, even if the Continents did not feature in the decoration on that occasion, except as a motif embroidered onto the dress of the personification of Spain on the Genoese Arch,[39] their potentiality for use in such contexts was clear, as Habsburg celebrations more and more focused on the imagery of world empire. At Antwerp in 1594 this theme was particularised by the Portuguese merchants into an illustration of the Lusitanian contribution to the Spanish possessions: their arch (Fig. 15) was surmounted by personifica-

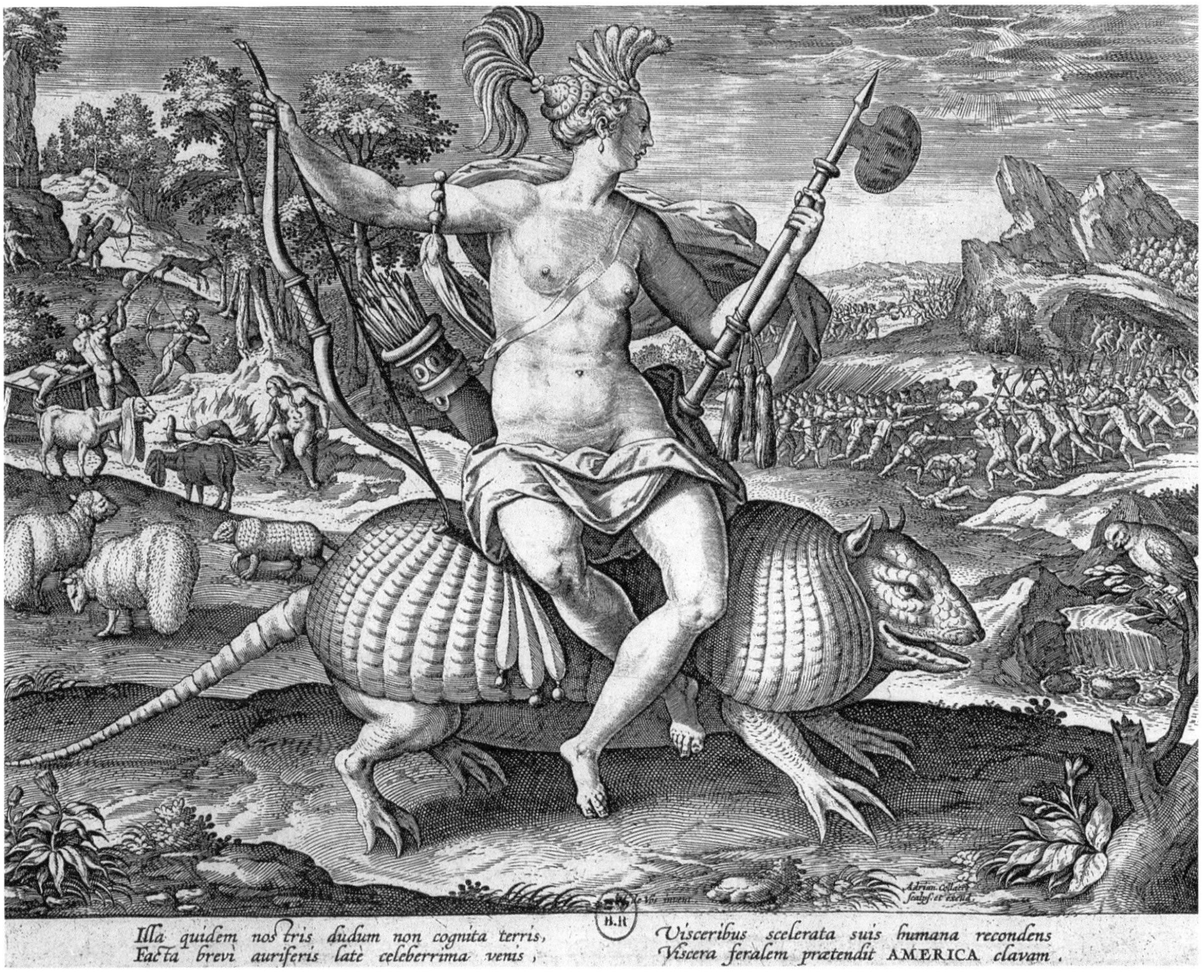

Fig. 12. Adriaen Collaert after Maarten de Vos, *America*, engraving (*c.* 1589)

tions not of the Continents, but of Mauretania, Brasilia, Ethiopia and India.[40] But these near-naked figures on exotic animals were patently adapted from the prints after De Vos, or rather the wilder pair among them (Figs. 11, 12).

Habsburg imperialism was of course epitomised in the figure of Charles V, with his *Plus Ultra* ('Still further'), endlessly varied in emblems and devices. And when Archdukes Albert and Isabella made their entry into Lille in 1600 a theatre in the main square (Fig. 16) showed the Emperor Charles, enthroned in a niche beneath his imperial device and surrounded by images of the Continents based directly on the Collaert prints.[41] In fact the Parts of the World – for that is what they are always called at the period, rather than Continents – had been earlier associated with Charles V in Flemish pageantry. Or rather the three old Parts had been. When he made his entry into Antwerp in 1520 and the Mediterranean was still the focus of Habsburg ambitions, the displays had concluded with a scene of Asia and Africa kneeling before the representative ruler ('Autocrator') as he rescued and embraced Europe, flanked by proleptic trophies of impaled Mohammedan and Ottoman heads.[42] And when the Emperor returned to the city in 1549 to introduce his heir, Philip, the same two figures had joined Europe in presenting themselves as subject to the prince [later Philip II] in a pageant (Fig. 17) which likewise centred on the old world, Asia being dressed in Turkish style and Africa, 'black or dusky', clad in the fashion of the Egyptians.[43] The limited geographical reference was underlined in the following pageant which showed Philip imitating his father by chasing off stage a group of 'Turks, Moors, Arabians, Saracens, Agarenes and Mamluks', all apparently distinctive in their costume, so as to liberate the suppliant provinces of Greece, North Africa and Asia Minor from

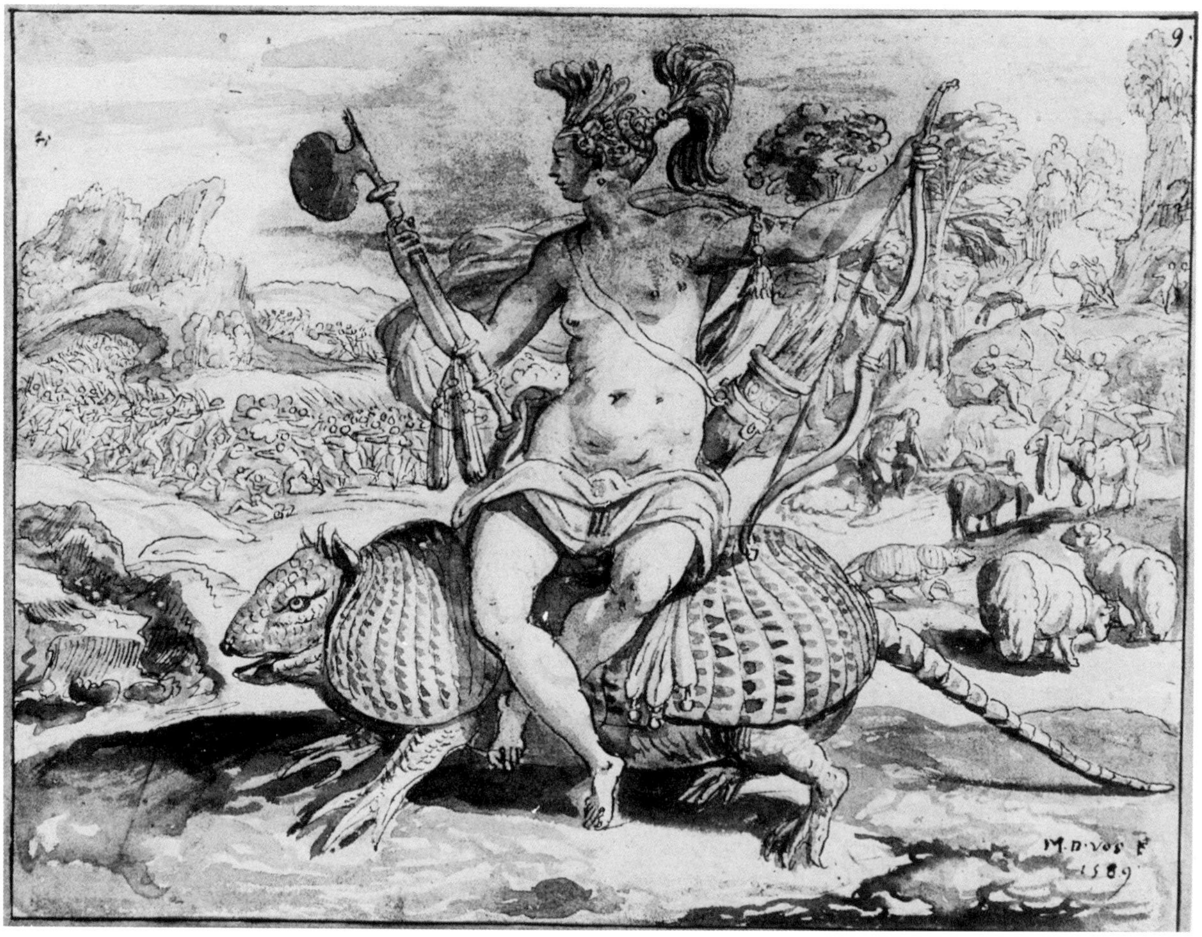

Fig. 13. Maarten de Vos, *America*, drawing (1589). Darmstadt, Hessisches Landesmuseum

their chains and misery (Fig. 18).[44] In fact it was at Antwerp too, and in the context of pageantry, that the Four Parts of the World seem first to have made their appearance as a group. Not that they were immediately assimilated into an imperial allegory; their role in testifying to the global ambitions and power of church and state, a role familiarised in the imagery of Baroque propaganda, came later.[45] Initially they were tributaries to Antwerp and her mercantile ideals, indeed to the notion of the world opened to view as spectacle – those pervasive themes of Antwerp humanism which underlay the whole project of Ortelius. For the Chariot of the Theatre of the World that was invented for the *ommegangen* of 1564 and wheeled out again in 1566 presented four 'triumphal Empresses' transported along with Oceanus to Antwerp by four sea-monsters.[46]

Having arrived, as it were, on the scene, the Four Continents might seem to have slipped with an easy inevitability into a place destined for them among the time-honoured quaternities that formed the medieval macro/microcosmic scheme of things, attaching themselves to the Ages of Man, the Elements, the Seasons, the Four Winds and the Cardinal Points of the earth.[47] All the more so since they displaced, or at least complemented the winds and the cardinal points in modern maps of the world.[48] But their insertion into this picture entails a series of distortions, aptly captured by the contradictory evidence of their most familiar manifestations: on the one hand as apparent equals at the corners of world maps, or in front of an earthly or heavenly power, and on the other hand as evidently distinct in their relative status. Indeed the whole matter of the personification of the parts of the world was beset with confusion and difficulty, involving as it did a Procrustean accomodation of new concepts to old contexts – even, since the image readily presents itself along with the proverbial 'four corners of the globe', a sort of impossibile effort to square the circle...

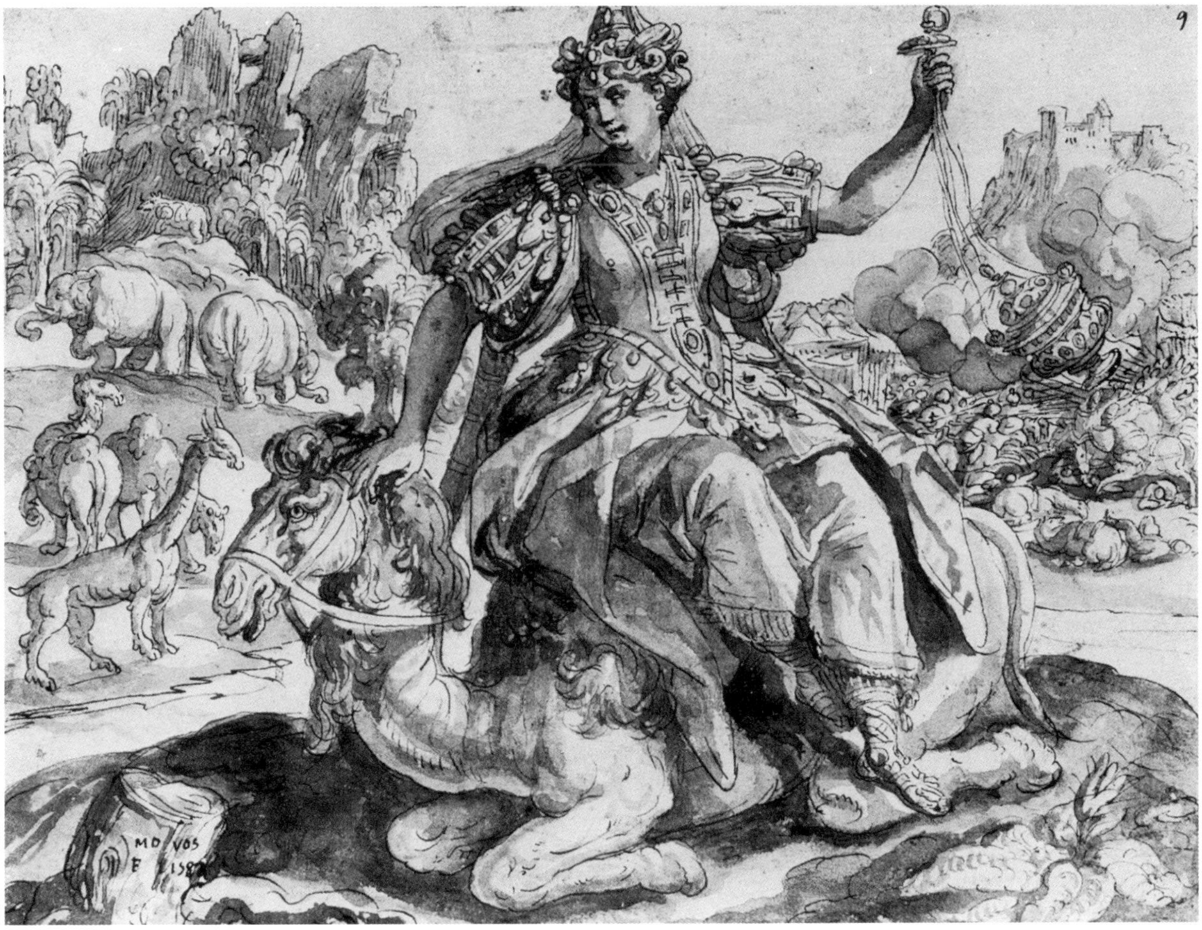

Fig. 14. Maarten de Vos, *Asia*, drawing (1587). Darmstadt, Hessisches Landesmuseum

America was of course a new invention,[49] her appearance and attributes prompted by the 'realistic' details gleaned from geographers and accounts of discoveries. The three 'older' parts of the World were not personified in medieval art;[50] rather they might be represented by the three sons of Noah, or the three Kings in a world centred on Christ and Jerusalem.[51] In formulating them anew as Renaissance figures, in personified abstractions, humanists naturally sought ancient precedents, for ancient geographers had talked of the three parts of the world. Herodotus already uses the names of Europe, Asia and Libya, even if he is puzzled as to why the world was seen as three distinct areas (since he conceived of a single land-mass, and was not sure about the borders).[52] But even though the three had female names, indeed names of mythical women (another thing Herodotus wonders about), the Parts of the World do not appear to have been much needed as ancient concepts. Vaguely defined, they certainly did not have any very specific character in antiquity as personifications.[53] In Roman times, even if Pliny in his *Natural History* talks of the 'three parts of the world', now calling them Europe, Asia and Africa (rather than Libya),[54] geography was thought of in terms of Rome and the imperial provinces. These were the entities that were personified on Roman coins. Thus when Renaissance scholars and artists looked to ancient numismatic sources for iconographic models for the modern 'Continents' they found an Africa and an Asia, but these represented the provinces of these names, areas quite limited in extent. As for Europe, she did not feature at all in this context.[55]

Artists who wanted to represent the three old parts of the world in a suitably ancient manner thus often chose the mythical Europa on her bull. This was alluded to in connection with the figure of Europe which was embraced by the representative of Charles V before a

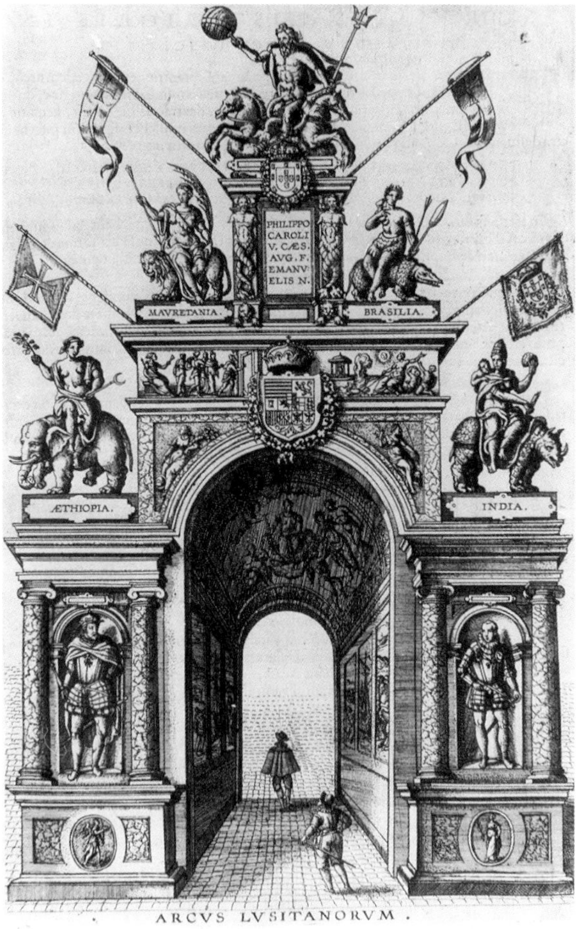

Fig. 15. Pieter van de Borcht, *Portuguese Arch*. From Joannes Bochius, *Descriptio publicae gratulationis, spectaculorum et ludorum, in adventu... Ernesti...* (Antwerp, 1595)

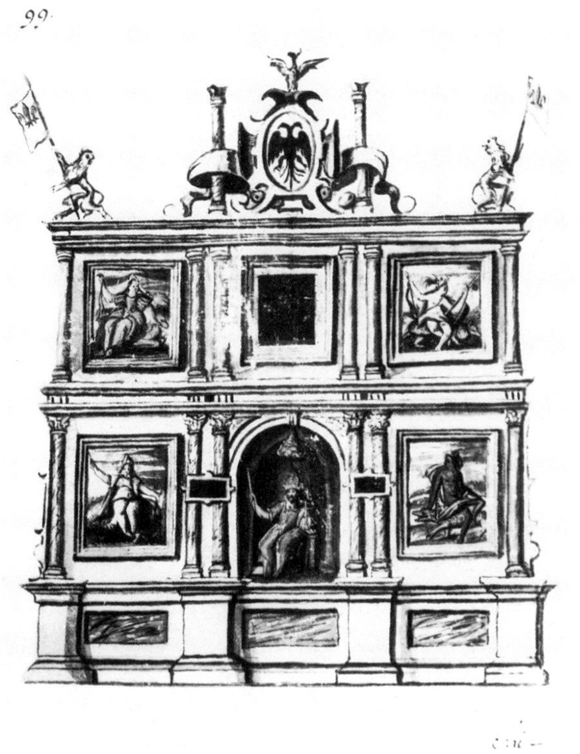

Fig. 16. Theatre with Charles V and the Parts of the World at Lille in 1600. Lille, Bibliothèque municipale, MS 678, fol. 99.

humbled Asia and Africa in the pageant at Antwerp in 1520.[56] And she was represented this way by Abraham de Bruyn on the frontispiece to his book on the costumes of different peoples published by Plantin in 1581 – another sort of manifestation of the 'Theatre of the World' (Fig. 19).[57] Asia the ancient province had been depicted occasionally on coins – for example one (of Hadrian), where she has her foot on the prow of a ship and holds a serpent (or hook) and a rudder – but she had no clear and consistent image.[58] The province of Africa, however, did. In fact Africa was the only Renaissance Part of the World who could claim to be a true heir to a classical iconographic tradition. But since this tradition was of the image of the Roman province, which extended roughly from Egypt to Mauretania (though its borders shifted at different times), it did not very easily match the idea of the 'continent' which was being discovered by Renaissance explorers.

Roman coins, notably of Hadrian, who took a special interest in the province (his birthplace), show Africa (Fig. 20) as a woman in a long dress with cornucopia, scorpion and grain basket of tribute. This is 'Africa fertilis', the bread-basket of ancient Rome. She also wears a very peculiar elephant-head hat.[59] This headdress, which is seen in other ancient contexts, for example a painting from Pompeii which may show Dido, as Aeneas is leaving Africa,[60] was perhaps borrowed from the city of Alexandria, who had in turn taken it on in deference to Alexander.[61] The meaning of all her attributes is not explained in ancient texts, even if it is obvious enough that the scorpion is a dangerous African animal (Pliny called it 'dirum animal Africae').[62] So Valeriano filled the gap, talking of the scorpion as a symbol of the deceitful Carthaginians and the elephant as Africa's animal – though even he couldn't explain why Africa herself had an elephant-head hat. (He discusses it as a trophy of victory in connection with Scipio Africanus.) Perhaps because of this he doesn't

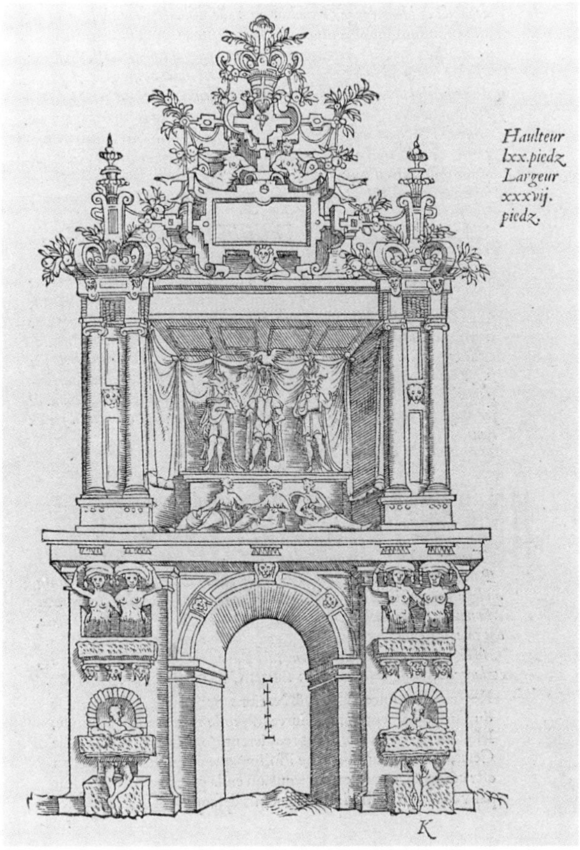

Fig. 17. Theatre in honour of Prince Philip at Antwerp in 1549. From Cornelius Grapheus (Scribonius), *La tresadmirable... entree...* (Antwerp, 1550)

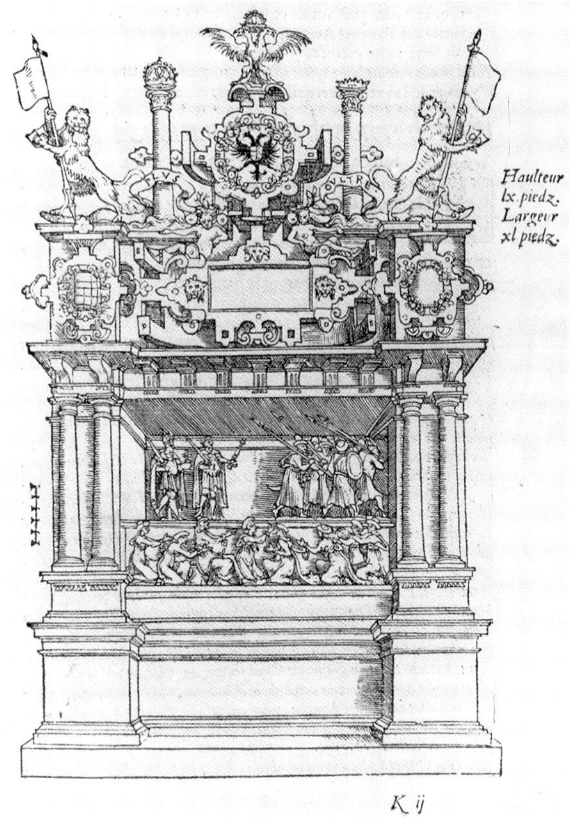

Fig. 18. Theatre showing Charles V and Prince Philip routing infidels, at Antwerp in 1549. From Cornelius Grapheus (Scribonius), *La tresadmirable... entree...* (Antwerp, 1550)

recommend artists to follow the ancient coin for a figure of Africa. Instead, anyone looking up Africa in the index would have come upon a description of the personification in fact illustrated by De Bruyn (Fig. 19): a figure with corn in her hair, leaning on a pillow made of two seas (Ocean and the Mediterranean) and carrying a fan (for the heat) and a pomegranate (for the Carthaginians).[63]

Despite the popularity of De Bruyn's costume book, and the respect accorded Valeriano's *Hieroglyphica*, this image of Africa had no real impact.[64] Of course the Africa it designated was essentially antique, limited in its reference to the area known to the Romans, and therefore antiquated; and this may have been important. But Valeriano's description hardly lent itself to easy visualisation: the pillow of two seas is a particularly intractable feature. Not surprisingly, then, a more accessible *all'antica* figure had a greater influence, even on the personification of modern Africa. This was the representation on the frontispiece to Hubert Goltzius's account of the coins of Augustus (Fig. 21),[65] engraved in 1569 – although the book itself was published only in 1574, at Bruges. Goltzius designed this titlepage himself, and it shows the ancient world, in the form of its three parts, subjected at the foot of the page. On top Caesar receives the globe of the world from the Roman Senate. This is 'pax orbis terrarum', the Roman universal peace that leaves its recipients suitably subdued and pacified: in short, Romanised. Appropriately then, the three adopt the attitudes of captives, sitting, in more or less melancholic poses, in front of a backdrop of their weapons; and, instead of being gracious and dignified figures, clad in long dresses (as generally in the numismatic models for the provinces, even when conquered), they have a peculiarly uncomfortable and dishevelled look. Europa, mural-crowned, sits heavily on her bull, which squirms beneath her, looking as if he is struggling for breath, and apparently too con-

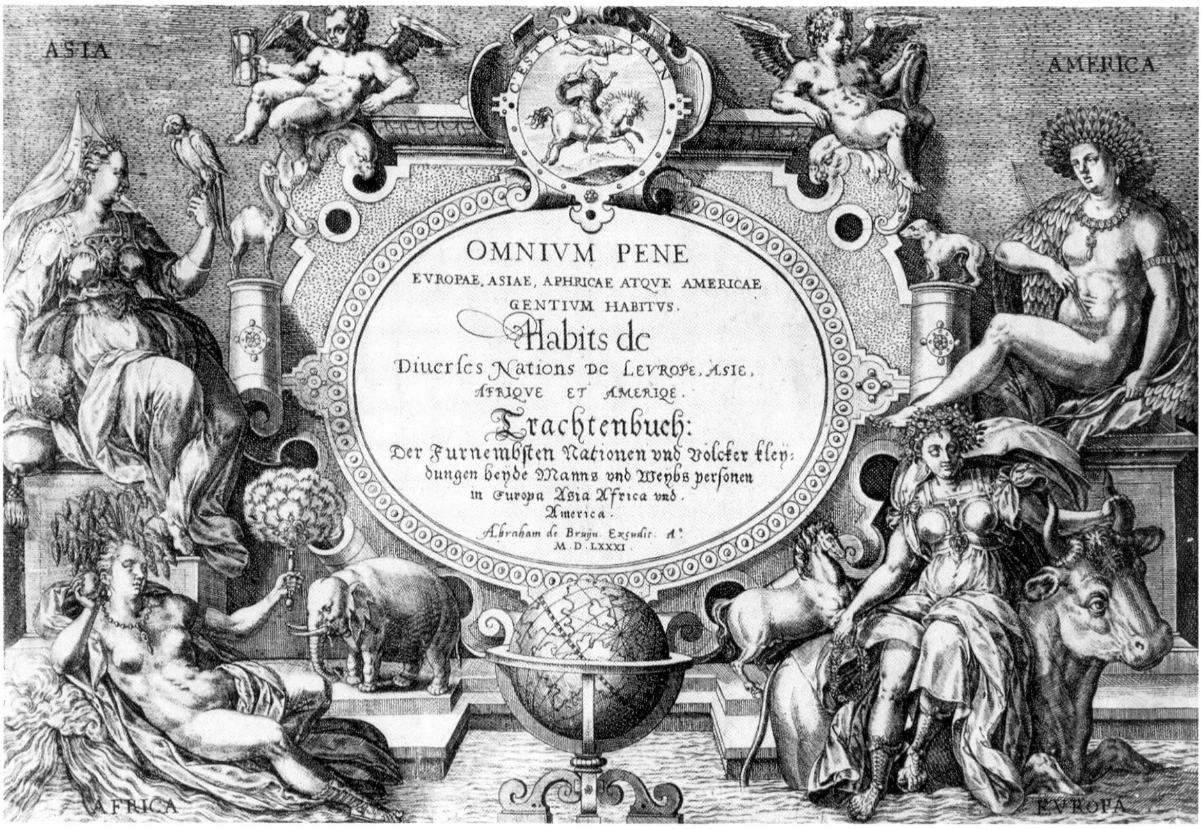

Fig. 19. Titlepage to Abraham de Bruyn, *Omnium pene Europae, Asiae, Aphricae atque Americae gentium habitus* (Antwerp, 1581)

cerned about the nearby crocodile to recall his mythical role as sexual aggressor. Asia, wearing a Phrygian cap, and a quiverful of arrows, is in the middle, sliding off the back of a camel. Africa, near naked except for her elephant-spoil hat,[66] perches thoughtfully on a crocodile, while a sphinx looks the other way.[67]

The fact that Africa is shown with a sphinx and a crocodile indicates that Goltzius, a great student of Roman antiquities, was thinking of the famous sculpture of the Nile in the Vatican, which had just such attributes (along with the sixteen infants who represent the number of cubits he should rise every year in flood; the Vatican statue has three children frolicking on and around the Nile's crocodile.)[68] No doubt it was the notion of putting Europe on her bull that suggested to Goltzius the possibility of giving animal seats to the other two subjected Continents. And with this idea, and the informal, almost mocking character of the motif, came the conceit that enlivens the foreground of this *bas de page*, the aggressive interplay between the animal attributes of Europe and Africa. Both the comical aspect of the personifications themselves, any pretence to classical decorum undermined by the absurdity of their animal-sitting, and their near undress was to be important for the formulation of the imagery of the modern Continents in the Netherlands. Or rather that of the three companions of Europe. For despite the notion of familial 'sisterhood' which would seem to underpin their status as a quaternity – assembled before Church or State; dispersed to the corners of world maps – Asia, Africa and America are generally seen (progressively, in that order) as poorer relations of Europe.

One work was especially important in establishing the paradoxical imagery of the modern Continents as four (un)equals. And this was, itself paradoxically, a work which actually presented the Parts of the World as more than four: the illustrated frontispiece to Ortelius's *Theatrum Orbis Terrarum* of 1570 (Fig. 1).[69] Here wild America was accompanied by the supposed fifth continent, the still unexplored and virginal Magellanica, shown as a bust-length figure with a fire, for Tierra del Fuego, on the socle on which she is set.[70] Like Goltzius's titlepage

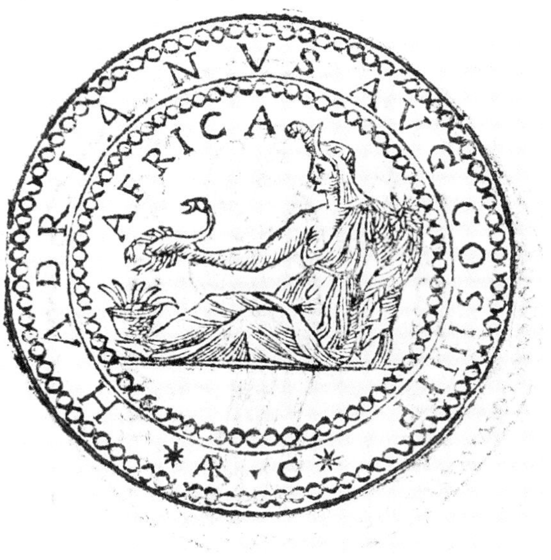

Fig. 20. Coin of Africa. From Antonio Agostini (Agustín), *Dialoghi... intorno alle medaglie...* (Rome, 1592)

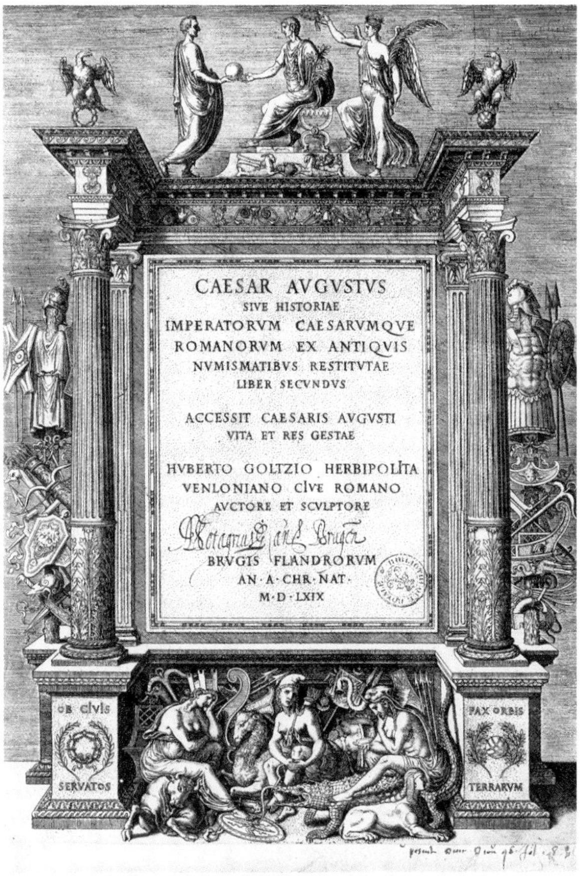

Fig. 21. Titlepage to Hubert Goltzius, *Caesar Augustus sive historiae... ex antiquis numismatibus restitutae liber secundus* (Bruges, 1574)

(Fig. 21), this image was designed by its author, and at virtually the same time. The two men were in fact friends.[71] Ortelius's geographical reading (of Sebastian Münster's *Cosmographia*, for example, and Hans Staden's account of Brazil), reflected in the texts he appended to the various maps,[72] determined the form and the attributes with which he endowed the imaginary characters who introduce his Theatre of the World.[73] Europe is firmly on top, commanding the globe with her Christianised rudder, an empress whose civilised fertility is symbolised in her cultivation of the vine.[74] America, with her Tupinamba paraphanalia and her severed head (token of a cannibalistic feast), is the lowest; Asia, decked with jewels and carrying incense, looks down on her. As for Africa, she gazes straight ahead, no doubt because, being a moor ('Aethiopissa' / 'Moorine' / 'negre' according to the explanatory verses), she is is represented in profile. The flames of the hot sun around her head emphasise her features – which might not be very evident without the commentary. (In coloured versions of the titlepage she was shown as black.) She is also shown nearly naked, hot and uncivilised, with only a sprig of Egyptian balsam as a mitigating attribute.

Ortelius's figures – at least the four principal ones – presented Flemish printmakers with immediate models for a set of Continents, even if not everything about them was easily amenable to their purposes. Marcus Gheeraerts's determinedly decorative quartet of *c.* 1590, each isolated in a plethora of neatly ordered detail (Figs. 22, 23), perversely combines delicacy of attitude with outlandish accompaniments, playing on nudity both as symptom of high art and as symbol of barbarism. He could not, however, accomodate America's severed head. Nor did he represent Africa as a moor.[75] This series was engraved by Philips Galle, whose own *Prosopographia* followed Ortelius still more closely, even emphasising America's cannibalism (Fig. 24), but his allegorical women, neither dainty nor determined, are bland, characterless creatures. Africa (Fig. 25) displays herself with Ortelius's sunny head and sprig of balsam, but there is nothing African, or even distinctive, about her physiognomy.[76]

In his designs for the prints of *c.* 1589 (Figs. 9–12) Maarten de Vos produced something at once more complex and more visually compelling, combining ancient and modern references, and borrowing from the titlepages

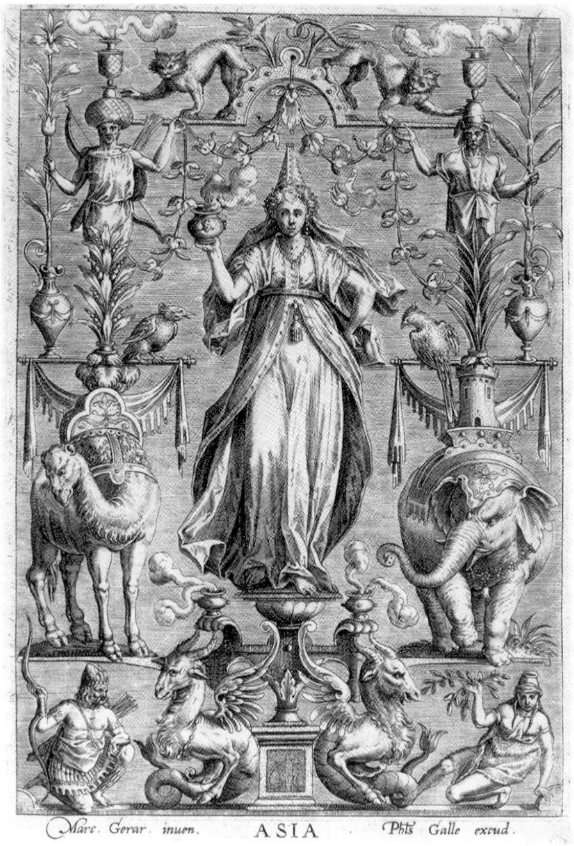

Fig. 22. Marcus Gheeraerts, *Asia*, engraving (*c.* 1590)

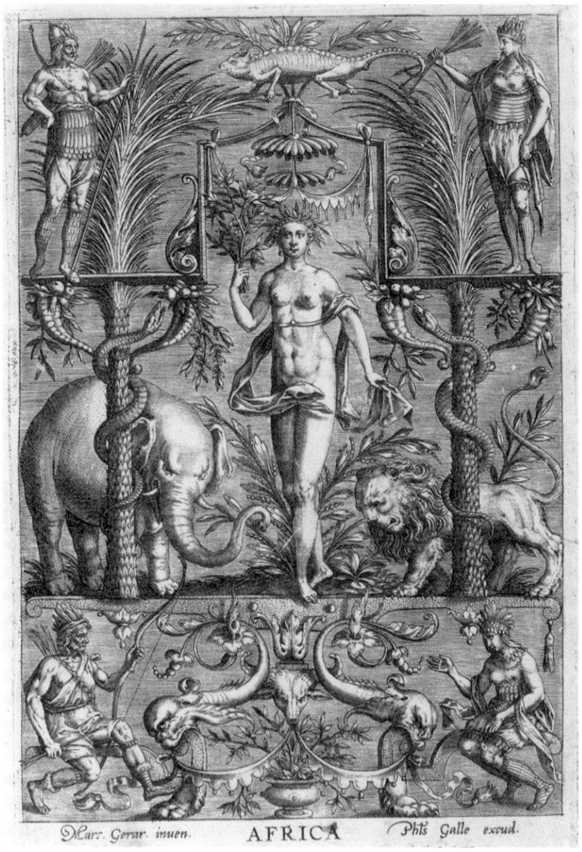

Fig. 23. Marcus Gheeraerts, *Africa*, engraving (*c.* 1590)

of Goltzius and Ortelius alike (Figs. 21, 1). Fundamental to the imagery of this striking series was the adaptation of Goltzius's animal seats, for all the Continents – except, that is, for Europe. Europa's bull may have inaugurated the whole business of animal-sitting, but that situation was evidently judged inappropriate by De Vos to the dignity of his only empress, so that he set Europe instead on the globe, which, like her sceptre and grapes, derived from Ortelius. Asia, sumptuously dressed, is at least on a traditional, if exotic, mount; but Africa is only protected by a thin cloth from the rough back of her crocodile, and the wildest of all, new America, sits almost entirely naked on her tough armadillo. Africa here appears not only with Ortelius's balsam, but with the attribute of moorish features. In the accompanying verses she is described as 'discoloured' by constant heat' ('decolor aestu perpete'), a reference to the old belief (in fact rejected by Ortelius himself, though mentioned by one commentator on his titlepage) that black skin was an effect of hot sun.[77] But the engraving suggests her 'blackness' only in outline, in the profile which she presents as obligingly as does her crocodile.[78] Surrounded by an array of strange beasts, she occupies a landscape marked by evidence of ancient civilisation: an obelisk and aquaduct.[79] At once barbaric and appealing, she has Ortelius's headband elaborated into a puffed and fluttering affair, and is adorned with pearl earring and bracelets, as well as a studded girdle – a variation on the sort of thing worn in art by contemporary mythological Venuses.

De Vos's prints – or sometimes the seated figures extracted from their landscapes – provided diverting marginal motifs for seventeenth-century Netherlandish mapmakers,[80] but were not very serviceable for other sorts of artistic contexts.[81] True, the pageant at Lille in 1600 contrived to use them as the basis for the pictures ranged around the enthroned Charles V (Fig. 16), but only by isolating them one from another, in separate compartments. The ensemble thus hardly visualises the intended message of homage to the world emperor. To present themselves in tribute the Continents at least

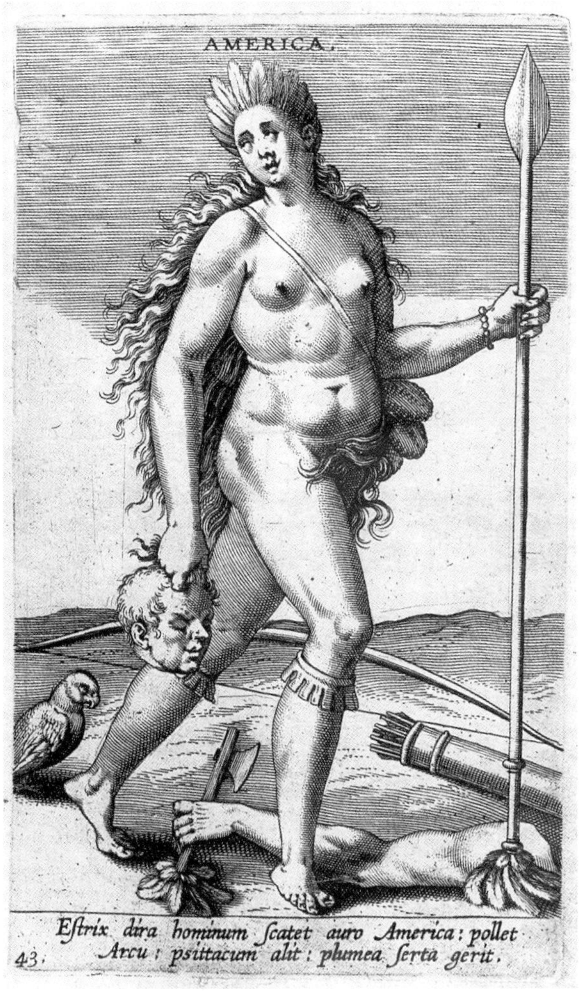

Fig. 24. *America*, from Philips Galle, *Prosopographia*, engraving (*c.* 1600?)

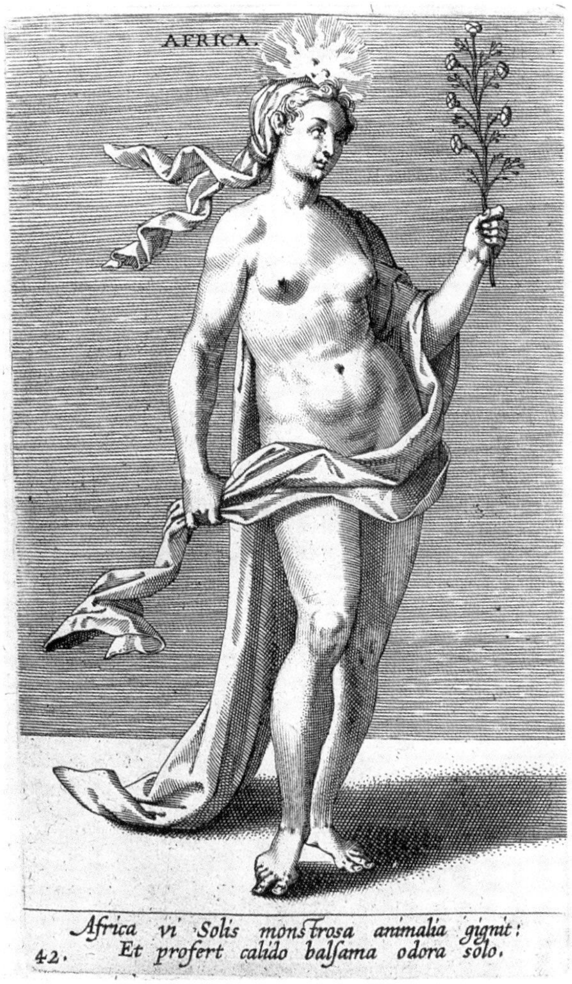

Fig. 25. *Africa*, from Philips Galle, *Prosopographia*, engraving (*c.* 1600?)

ought to be dismounted. In a print of *c.* 1600 (Fig. 26) by Adriaen Collaert after Stradanus, a group based on the inventions of Ortelius (Fig. 1) are kneeling, or getting to their knees, below the arms of Philip III of Spain which are supported by the figures of *Potestas* and *Maiestas* – and observed, somewhat warily, by the reclining Oceanus.[82] Africa's air of distraction is partly the result of the continuing requirement to exhibit her moorish profile, but none of the figures is as yet particularly integrated into an allegorical narrative. More directly involved in the scene were the Continents at the top of Matthias Merian's titlepage to the 1628 edition of Sebastian Münster's *Cosmographia* (Fig. 27).[83] Here they present offerings to the Holy Roman Empire, successor to the Four Monarchies of the Book of Daniel represented in the emperors below. In the process of their accomodation to this context the wilder pair were, for the sake of decorum, given some covering for their nudity, and relegated to the background. The image is important in the present context, since it appears to have been a principal source for the first Flemish painter to portray the personified Parts of the World, in two pictures that not only look theatrical in their disposition, but take up and develop the pageant theme of the homage of the Continents – one in mythological terms and the other with very specific reference to Charles V.

Frans Francken's *Abdication of Charles V* (Fig. 28)[84] has been dated to *c.* 1635, with an eye to the fact that this was the centenary of the emperor's resounding Victory at Tunis. What it explicitly commemorates is, however, an event of 1555, the final, and most famous episode in the Emperor's public life. The inscription on a fictive stone at the lower right runs: 'Emperor

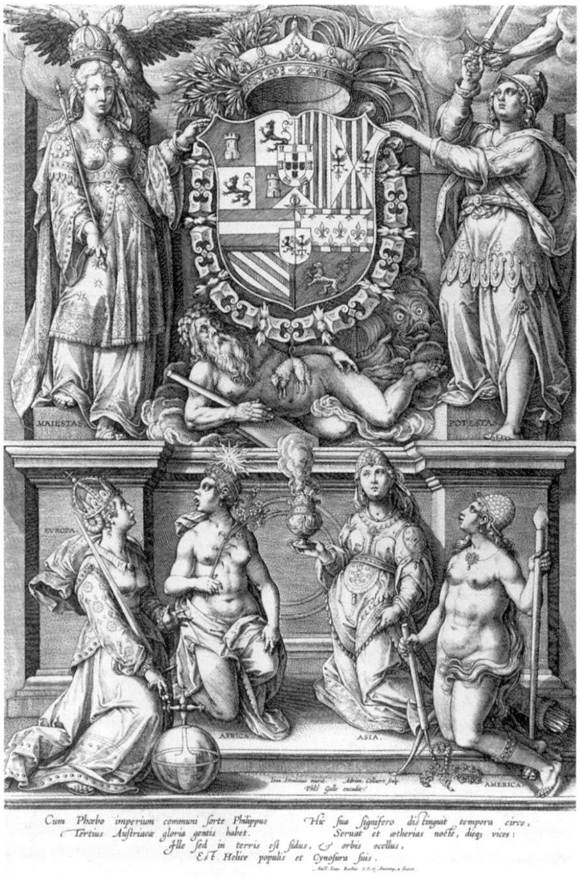

Fig. 26. Adriaen Collaert after Joannes Stradanus, *Allegory in honour of Philip III*, engraving (*c.* 1600)

Charles V's voluntary resignation of the Holy Roman Empire to Ferdinand I, his brother and the heir to his dominions, [and] to his son Philip II King of Spain, made at Brussels in 1555. Frans Francken after the invention of D. Pieter Hannicaert'.[85] Francken had the habit, usual for printmakers, and apparently inaugurated among painters by Frans Floris,[86] to add to his signature a claim that he was the inventor (as well as the 'maker') of many scenes.[87] Here, however, the invention is, uniquely in the artist's work, credited to someone else: Pieter Hannicaert, who has the honorific title of 'Dominus' (*D*), was not (as has sometimes been thought) a fellow artist, but a merchant and town councillor in Antwerp.[88] Presumably then this man was in some sense responsible for the iconography. But not, evidently, all of it. For Francken adapted the scheme of his *Homage of the Earth and Sea to Apollo* (Fig. 29),[89] a painting, dated 1629, which he credited to his own invention.[90] This work is indeed in part a variation on the familiar Francken theme of the mythological sea-triumph – a theme for which the artist, who had close links to the Rederijkers evidently looked to the imagery of Antwerp pageantry.[91] Since the *Homage to Apollo* is a more integrated and successful composition than the *Abdication of Charles V*, it might seem natural to regard it as the later work. But humanist prescriptions, however well-intentioned, have a tendency to cramp a painter's style. And some weight should surely be attached to Francken's claim to have 'invented' the *Homage to Apollo*.[92] Thus it probably did precede the allegory of Charles V, though perhaps not by the six years that is usually supposed;[93] it seems to me that both works might have been produced more or less concurrently.

Seated on clouds against a backdrop of red drapery which is sustained by winged putti (Fig. 29), Apollo receives tributes, on his right, from the assembled sea-deities and, on his left, from creatures of the earth. In the foreground a river-god with an urn, probably intended as Oceanus, indicates a pile of beached fish and shells; this merges into a heap of fruit and vegetables which oddly (and unsteadily) supports the globe of the world. Nearby are the personified Parts of the World, America's knee serving as an additional prop for the globe, which indeed displays the map of her own territory, and the word 'Brasilia' can be deciphered.[94] America offers gold and jewels; Asia a smoking urn of incense; Europe arms and works of artistry (mostly metal); and Africa, behind her, coral and a metal vase (dark-skinned attendants hand her other vessels). It might seem odd that Francken should have put coral in Africa's hand, given that it is such an obvious product of the sea. But the attribute was at least partly conditioned by the corresponding figure in Merian's titlepage of 1628 to Münster's *Cosmographia* (Fig. 27).[95] Francken's Continents go further in the direction of decorum; they are all fully dressed, in long robes, and their conduct is uniformly polite. The attributes they have acquired from other sources are tamed almost beyond recognition. So that it is only reluctantly that America's armadillo, for example, is acknowledged as a probable borrowing from Maarten de Vos (Fig. 12).

Above Apollo is a zodiacal sign which seems to be intended as Cancer.[96] The sign that might have been expected to accompany the sun-god

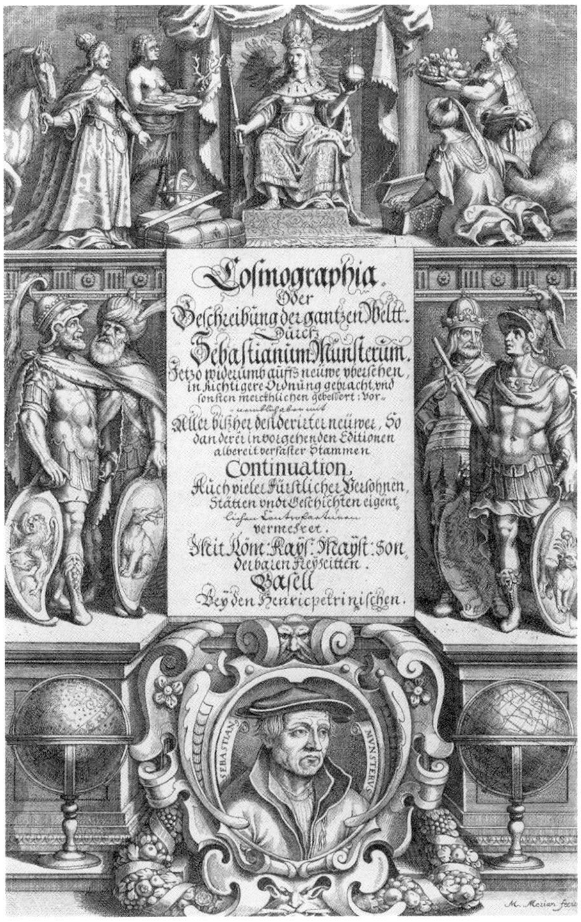

Fig. 27. Matthias Merian, Titlepage to Sebastian Münster *Cosmographia* (Basle, 1628)

is Leo, his 'house' (i.e. the constellation in which he notionally stood at the beginning of time and is 'strongest' in his astrological influence); unless we suppose that Cancer is there as the adjacent sign to show that the Sun is actually *in* Leo (which seems unlikely), the meaning remains mysterious, even if the celestial animal takes up the scaly theme of much in the picture – from armadillo to sea-shell.[97] The idea has been proposed that the painting embodies some allusion to the power of Philip IV, the sun on earth, the monarch whose empire extends worldwide. And although the analogy with the *Abdication of Charles V* (Fig. 28), with its specific portrait reference, might seem to argue against rather than in favour of such a hypothesis, it is notable that Apollo is presented as if on a stage, and in a way which assimilates him to an earthly ruler. In addition, the portrait of a prince dressed in ermine and illuminated by a heavenly light (a work which is placed on the table at the right, on a red cloth) seems to point up the sun-king association.[98]

Whatever the case, the *Abdication of Charles V* (Fig. 28) is explicitly centred on a conventional earthly throne and an earthly emperor. Charles, wearing his imperial robes and the Order of the Golden Fleece, indicates with either hand the documents, somewhat battered (torn, it seems) and lying on the ground, which must represent his titles, now relinquished; his German empire is accepted with a hint of (?modest) hesitancy by his brother Ferdinand, and his Netherlandish, Spanish and Italian dominions are calmly awaited by Philip II. In front of the throne, next to a curious rock and what seems a gratuitous display of sea-shells (irresistable to Francken?), lie the imperial regalia. (The scene in the background, to the left, presumably shows the Emperor's retreat to the Hieronymite monastery at Yuste after his return to Spain.) The throne and canopy were evidently intended to evoke the setting in the Hall of the Golden Fleece at Brussels for the ceremony on 25 October 1555 (cf. Fig. 30).[99] On this occasion Charles in fact resigned only the Netherlands to Philip; the formal transfer to him of Spain and its dependencies in Italy occurred in January 1556, and the legal transfer of the German dominions to Ferdinand had to wait until 1558 and the approval of the Electors. (Possibly Francken meant to suggest something of this in the different reactions he gave to Philip and Ferdinand.) But precise historical circumstances are not obviously relevant to this allegorical image in which the world beyond the seas presents itself as tributary to the man who ruled over an empire more extensive than any before.

From the sea Neptune and his retinue bring marine tributes and trophies (the nymph at the far left seems even to have managed to make a wreath out of shells) along with the components of Charles V's celebrated device: the motto *Plus Ultra*, 'Still further', and its symbolic Columns of Hercules, those two pillars which the hero was fabled to have set up as the limit to the old world: now imperially crowned, and altogether detached from any base, they are ready to be carried ever further over the globe (lodged in Neptune's chariot).

To the right, (just) on dry land and, presumably, as the tributary adjunct to Charles's European realms, America, Asia and Africa offer their treasures, elaborated on those shown in

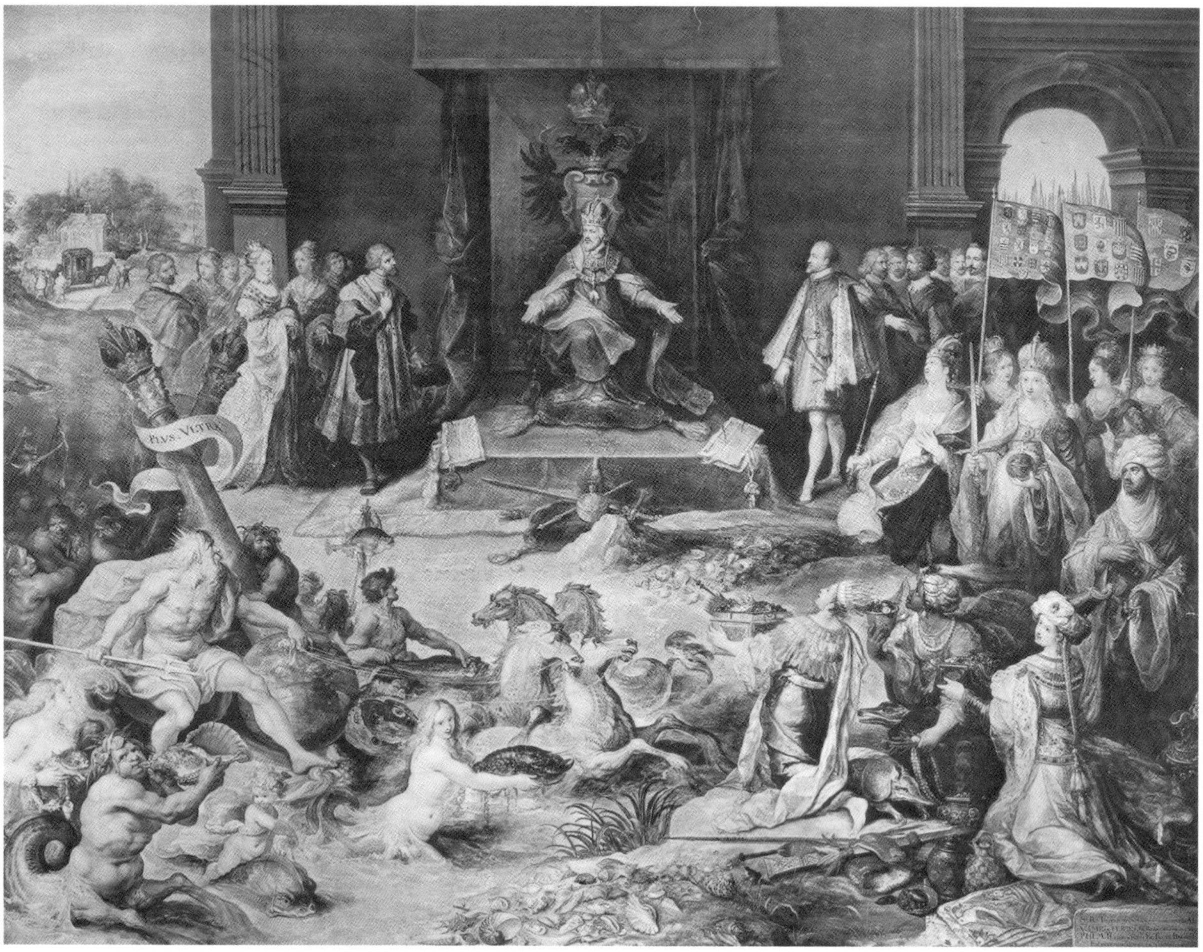

Fig. 28. Frans Francken, *Allegory of the Abdication of Charles V*, painting. Amsterdam, Rijksmuseum

the *Homage to Apollo*, but also concentrated more on riches. As with the massed shells and exotic animals, Francken put his experience in painting *Wunderkammern* to good use – although he does not seem to have felt very confident about Africa's crocodile; this animal (there is no such creature in the *Homage to Apollo*) diminutive as well as domesticated, simply peeps out from behind his mistress; she, holding her coral against strings of pearls, presents a golden bowl stuffed with precious stones. Asia and America bring larger chests of valuables: jewellery in the case of the former, gold and golden crowns that of the latter. 'Exotic' American artefacts lie in the foregound, merging into Asia's produce: Moslem enamelled vases, a Turkish embroidery, and so on.

The activity in the foreground is presided over by a staid figure, wearing a cloak emblazoned with the Habsburg double-eagle and an imperial crown, and carrying a sword and orb; she has been identified as Europe so as to supply the (expected) fourth Continent, with particular reference to the group in the *Homage to Apollo* (Fig. 29).[100] But comparison with that painting surely serves to highlight the difficulties in the analogy. The imperial figure in the Abdication allegory stands next to a similarly crowned woman, bearing a sceptre, who is at least equally equipped to qualify as a figuration of Europe.[101] In fact neither personification need, or even should symbolise Europe; for Europe, at least Habsburg Europe, is already represented in the sum of the countries and provinces depicted behind them: the Habsburg possessions in the Netherlands, Spain and Italy are represented in three women carrying flags with the arms of the various provinces or kingdoms. Iconographically, then, the situation can perhaps be likened to that on the *Weltallschale*, made for Rudolf II by Jonas Silber in 1589, which incorporates, *inter alia*, Africa, Asia and America at the foot, 'supporting' in some sense Europe, who is represented quite separately

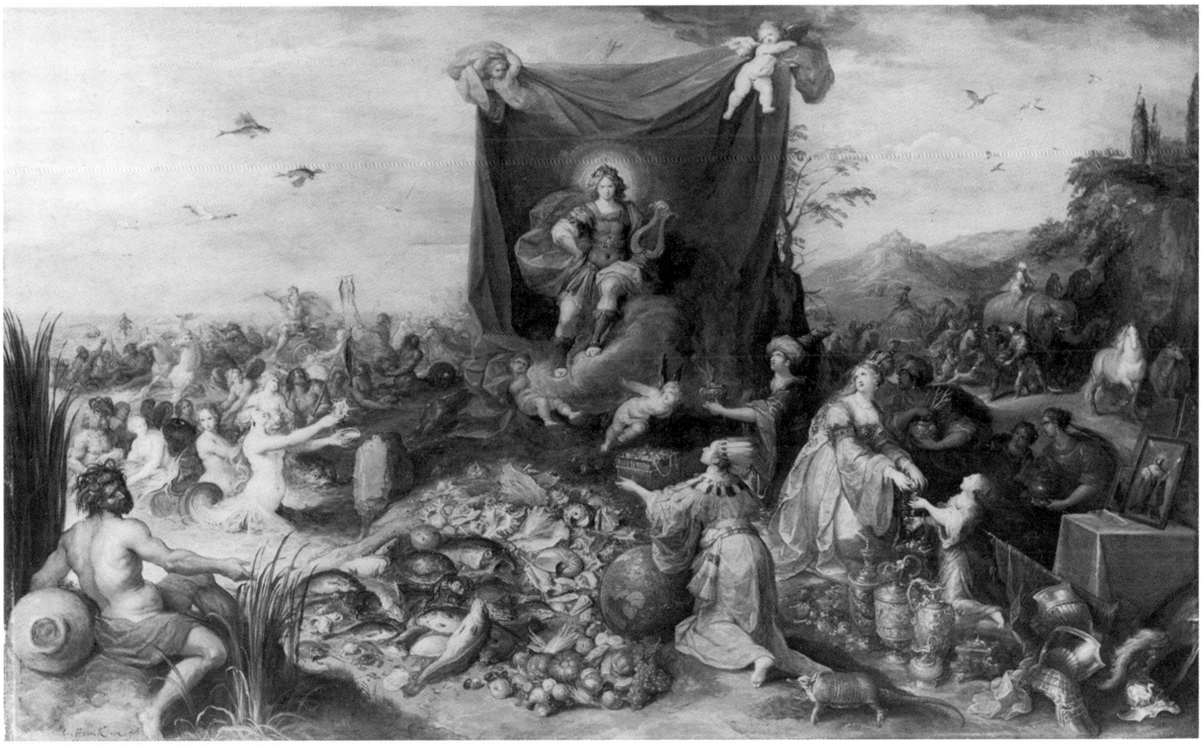

Fig. 29. Frans Francken, *Homage of the Earth and Sea to Apollo*, painting. Oldenburg, Landesmuseum für Kunst und Kulturgeschichte, Gemäldegalerie

within the cup, by a queen-shaped map, with Spain at its head.[102] Francken's two 'imperial' women are perhaps best seen as Imperial Power ('Potestas imperialis'), with sword and orb – very close to an embodiment of the Habsburg Empire – and Imperial Majesty ('Maiestas imperialis'), with the sceptre. Francken (and his adviser, Hannicaert) may well have been influenced here too by the print by Merian (Fig. 27) in which the Continents present themselves, and their gifts, to a figure with imperial crown, double-eagle canopy, sceptre and orb who represents the Holy Roman (i.e. Habsburg) Empire; also relevant, for its distinction between Majesty and Power in a similar context, is the print by Collaert of *c.* 1600 (Fig. 26).[103]

Behind Asia Francken placed a dark-skinned man in a turban who at first sight might seem to be introducing this Continent – or perhaps all three kneeling women.[104] He certainly has something of this role, for he has almost the air of a saint recommending a kneeling donor; but his gesture is, I think, principally that of directing attention to the inscription. This makes it all the more intriguing that he bears a certain resemblance to Mulay Ahmad, the Tunisian ruler who, like his father Mulay Hassan, lived most of his life in the shadow of Charles V.[105] Or rather he recalls Rubens's picture of that ruler, after a lost painting by Jan Cornelisz Vermeyen.[106]

It seems unlikely – especially given the degree of deliberation that must have gone into the iconography of this picture – that Francken did not have a specific idea in mind in deriving his figure from Vermeyen's *Mulay Ahmad* (and he might have known the picture either from the artist's original, then apparently in Antwerp, or from Rubens's version); still, it may be that this specific idea was of a/the ruler of Tunis, rather than of an identifiable individual – and in this context it seems significant that in Rubens's inventory the sitter was referred to simply as 'a King of Tunis'.[107] That Francken should have placed the figure closer to Asia than to Africa might seem remarkable, but this is in part a condition of his marginal role in the picture, as well as the fact that he is, in some sense, a representative of both parts of the world – lighter in skin than the personification of Africa and darker than Asia, yet wearing a turban which is more Asian than African.[108]

Charles V's successful campaign in North Africa in the 1530s, culminating in the Capture

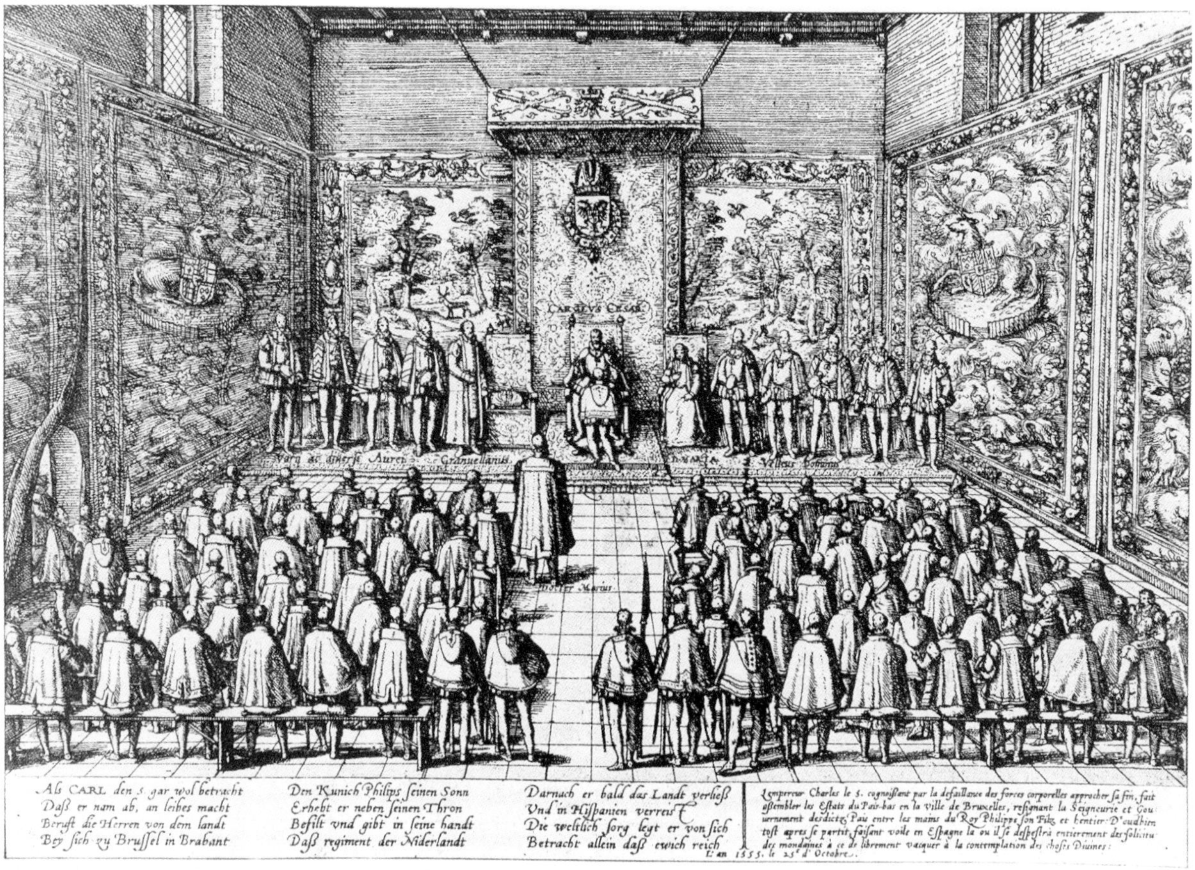

Fig. 30. Frans Hogenberg, *Abdication of Charles V*, etching.

of Tunis, and the reduction/winning over of the Berber kings to a sort of client status, was important not just in itself, but for what it seemed to herald – for its intimate relationship, in the minds of contemporaries, with the greater enterprise against the Turk, the idea of which formed a backdrop to so much sixteenth-century European policy, both in theory (from Erasmus's *Institution of the prince* onwards) and in practice, and which was promoted in the pageants at Antwerp in 1520 and 1549 (Figs. 17, 18).[109] In this context, the fact that a representative loyal 'arab/moor' is given the role of indicating the explanatory inscription is highly significant: a Mediterranean character, he helps to define the essential meaning of both Africa and Asia in this context, for he is appropriately associated with the Emperor's conquest of the old, 'tripartite' world, apparently assured sufficiently to leave Charles free to venture further, *plus ultra*, to the new lands beyond.

In a sense, then, the painting provides a retrospective reworking, in full consciousness of the discovery of the fourth Continent, of the themes of Antwerp pageantry which connected the (three) Parts of the World with Habsburg rule and Charles V, and saw the Emperor's triumph over Moors and Turks as the necessary concomitant, even prelude, to his conquest of the whole globe.[110] Whether the impetus for the inclusion of the Continents in the painting stemmed from Hannicaert, Francken, or a combined resolution of both, is hard to say – though if the *Homage to Apollo* (Fig. 29) indeed came first, the notion should be presumably attributed to the artist.[111] Whatever the case, it seems crucial that the Continents should have been encouraged into Flemish painting by a certain literary, theatrical and humanist influence, and that their entry into this medium should have happened in Antwerp – the very site of their initial invention in literary, theatrical and humanist contexts.

NOTES

I am most grateful to Ann Diels for furnishing me with documentary information from her unpublished thesis on the entry of Archduke Ernest to Antwerp in 1594 and for showing me her notes on the series of drawings by Maarten de Vos in the Plantin-Moretus Museum. I am also grateful to other participants in the conference who offered advice and comments, especially Arnout Balis and Egbert Haverkamp-Begemann. The text published here is modified quite a bit from the account presented at the conference of November 1997, introducing, for example, an account of Francken's paintings of the Continents, and curtailing some material which will be considered more fully in my contribution to a forthcoming volume of *The Image of the Black in Western Art*, sponsored by the Menil Foundation. I have benefited from the help of Jean Michel Massing, who is engaged in the same project. The Editor of the series, Ladislas Bugner, has been more than generous in providing information, ideas and encouragement in the course of many discussions on the subject. To him, above all, my thanks.

1. See generally Jean Seznec, *La survivance des dieux antiques*, ed. Paris, 1980, esp. pp. 247–282; Charles Hope and Elizabeth McGrath, in *The Dictionary of Art*, ed. Jane S. Turner, 34 vols, London, 1996, XV, pp. 84–88, s.v. 'Iconographic programmes'; cf. Ibidem, pp. 82–84, s.v. 'Iconographic handbooks'.

2. On the genre see [cat. exh.] *Alba Amicorum. Vijf eeuwen vriendschap op papier gezet: Het Album Amicorum en het Poëziealbum in de Nederlanden*, ed. K. Thomassen, Maarsen–The Hague, 1990.

3. On the close friendship of Hoefnagel and Ortelius see notably Thea A.G. Wilberg Vignau-Schuurman, *Die emblematischen Elemente im Werke Joris Hoefnagels*, Leiden, 1969, I, pp. 6–8; and for the 'Hermathena' drawing in Antwerp, made by Hoefnagel for Ortelius: Ibidem, 1, p. 195; 2, Fig. 119; Carl Depauw, in Jan Van der Stock ed., [cat. exh.] *Antwerpen, verhaal van een metropool. 16de–17de eeuw*, Antwerp, 1993, p. 298, no. 151. For the *Album* of Ortelius see the facsimile edition *Album Amicorum Abraham Ortelius*, ed. and trans. Jean Puraye, Amsterdam, 1969 (but see also the comments in the article by Müller Hofstede cited below, and Jan van Dorsten and Alistair Hamilton, 'Two puzzling pages in Ortelius' Album Amicorum', in *Time and Tide. Writings offered to A.G.H. Bachrach*, Leiden, 1980, pp. 45–53. The relevant page is fol. 6r-v. Hoefnagel was also a friend of, among others, the historian Emanuel van Meteren, and the merchant-scholar Jan Radermacher. Cf. Frances Yates, *The Valois Tapestries*, London, 1959, pp. 27–28; J.A. van Dorsten, *The Radical Arts. First Decade of an Elizabethan Renaissance*, Leiden–London, 1970, pp. 37–38, 53–54. On the relationship of Bruegel with Ortelius see Justus Müller Hofstede, 'Zur Interpretation von Pieter Bruegels Landschaft. Ästhetischer Landschaftsbegriff und Stoische Weltbetrachtung', in *Pieter Bruegel und seine Welt*, ed. Otto von Simson and Matthias Winner, with Ernst Kreutzer and Hans Mielke, Berlin, 1979, pp. 73–142, esp. 74–80, 127–131 (with much on the epitaph composed by Ortelius in 1574, 5 years after the painter's death, and inscribed on fol. 12v of his *Album Amicorum*).

4. For the contributions of the two humanists to Van Veen's *Album* see J. Van den Gheyn, S.J., *Album Amicorum de Otto Venius*, Brussels, 1911, pp. 46–47, 111–112 (Ortelius), 55, 121–122 (Lipsius). Van Veen's contribution of 1588 to Ortelius's *Album* (for which see previous note) is on fol. 109v. See Mark Morford, *Stoics and Neostoics. Rubens and the Circle of Lipsius*, Princeton, N.J., 1991, p. 188.

5. See esp. *Correspondance de Rubens et documents épistolaires concernant sa vie et ses œuvres*, ed. Charles Ruelens and Max Rooses, 6 vols., Antwerp, 1887–1909; also Morford 1991 (see note 4), pp. 3–13, 41–51, 94–95.

6. See Justus Lipsius, *Epistolarum selectarum centuriae ad Belgas*, 3 vols., Antwerp, 1605, III, pp. 101–103, no. lxxiii; cf. Elizabeth McGrath, *Rubens. Subjects from History*, Corpus Rubenianum Ludwig Burchard, XIII, 1, London, 1997, I, p. 109; Charles Hope and Elizabeth McGrath, 'Artists and Humanists', in *The Cambridge Companion to Renaissance Humanism*, ed. Jill Kraye, Cambridge, 1996, p. 179; Morford 1991 (see note 4), p. 188.

7. [J.]C. Gevartius, *Pompa Introitus honori Serenissimi Principis Ferdinandi... a S. P. Q. Antverp[iensi] decreta et adornata...*, Antwerp, 1641 [1642]) 'Praefatio ad lectorem', fol. **r-v.

8. Gevartius himself leaves us in no doubt that Rubens's part in the imagery of the *Pompa Introitus* was more considerable than his own. This latter was essentially the composition of the inscriptions, though he modestly states that, even if daunted by the importance of the task, he was encouraged to produce his inscriptions by the splendour of the decorations ('Quantum enimipsa operis propositi materies splendore suo me alliciebat, tantum Argumenti Dignitas, velut obiectis Maiestatis suae fascibus, deterrebat.'; Gevartius 1641 (see note 7), fol. **v). Humanists normally put things otherwise, thinking of the texts as the soul to the (mere) body of the imagery. It is worth considering, however, the fact that Gevartius credits Otto van Veen, Rubens's teacher, not only with the painted decoration in 1599 but, parenthetically, with similar work in 1594: 'Ac tum [i.e. for the entry of Albert and Isabella in 1599] Otho Vaenius, pictor celeberrimus et litteratus, icones tabulasque (quod et in praecedenti Ernesti Principis Introitu ab illo praestitum) delinearat.' While it is well known that Van Veen was involved in the entry of 1599 (cf. Irmengard von Roeder-Baumbach with Hans G. Evers, *Versieringen bij Blijde Inkomsten gebruikt in de Zuidelijke Nederlanden gedurende de 16e en 17e Eeuw*, Antwerp–Utrecht, 1943, pp. 114–115), his name is not usually connected with the entry of 1594, nor does it appear in the records of the city archives. And while Bochius mentions him, once, in his account of the 1599 entry (Joannes Bochius, *Historica Narratio profectionis et inaugurationis Serenissimorum Belgii Principum Alberti et Isabellae, Austriae Archiducum...* Antwerp, 1602, p. 201), there is no reference to him at all in Bochius's book about the 1594 entry. Maarten de Vos and Ambrosius Francken are the painters credited with 'diversche inventien' for this in the city's archives. See Antoinette Doutrepont, 'L'entrée triomphale de l'archiduc Ernest d'Autriche à Anvers en 1594', *Bulletin de l'Institut Historique Belge de Rome*, XVIII, 1937, pp. 125–198, esp. 187–190; F.J. Van den Branden, *Geschiedenis der Antwerpsche Schilderschool*, 3 vols., Antwerp, 1883, I, pp. 251–254; the documentary evidence is cited with references in A. Diels, *De Blijde Intrede van aartshertog Ernest van Oostenrijk te Antwerpen in 1594. Een kunstwetenschappelijke benadering*, diss. Vrije Universiteit Brussels, 1994, pp. 123–124; also Carl Van de Velde, 'Portretten van Frans Francken de Oudere', *Jaarboek. Koninklijk Museum voor Schone Kunsten, Antwerpen*, 1962–1963, p. 181. If Gevartius's statement is exaggerated, it is presumably based on some sort of evidence, most probably provided by Rubens. Van Veen then must have worked on one or more of the arches financed by the foreign mer-

chants and not paid for by the city (it was in connection with the Spanish Arch that he was cited in Bochius's book of 1602); the imagery of certain paintings included on these, as recorded in the plates of Bochius's 1595 volume, looks consistent enough with the work of Van Veen: e.g. the Choice of Hercules on the Florentine Arch which resembles the *Allegory for Alessandro Farnese*, engraved by Gisbert van Veen *c.* 1586; see Joannes Bochius, *Descriptio publicae gratulationis, spectaculorum et ludorum, in adventu... Ernesti...*, Antwerp, 1595, pp. 102–103; John Rupert Martin, *The Decorations for the Pompa Introitus Ferdinandi*, Corpus Rubenianum Ludwig Burchard, XVI, Brussels–London–New York, 1972, p. 211, Fig. 108, and, for the print after Van Veen, also Ilja Veldman, in [cat. exh.] Antwerp 1993 (see note 3), pp. 229–270, no. 123.

9. On Montano's talent at drawing see Laevinius Torrentius, *Correspondance*, ed. M. Delcourt and J. Hoyoux, 2 vols., Liège, 1952, II, pp. 3–5. On his designs for the statue of Alva see Jochen Becker, 'Hochmut kommt vor dem Fall. Zum Standbild Albas in der Zitadelle von Antwerpen, 1571–1574', *Simiolus*, V, 1971, pp. 75–115. In general see Sylvaine Hänsel, *Der Spanische Humanist Benito Arias Montano (1527–1598) und die Kunst*, Münster, 1991.

10. See esp. Léon Voet, *The Golden Compasses*, 2 vols., Amsterdam, 1969, I, pp. 362–395.

11. On Ortelius's concern with antiquities and ancient coins, a subject generally neglected, see Godelive Denhaene, 'Un témoignage de l'intérêt des humanistes flamands pour les gravures italiennes: une lettre de Philippe van Winghe à Abraham Ortelius', *Bulletin de l'Institut Historique Belge de Rome*, LII, 1992, pp. 69–137, esp. 69–73. On his religious standpoint see René Boumans, 'The Religious Views of Abraham Ortelius', *Journal of the Warburg and Courtauld Institutes*, XVII, 1954, pp. 374–377; Van Dorsten 1970 (see note 3), passim; Alistair Hamilton, *The Family of Love*, Cambridge, 1981.

12. For Ortelius the word *theatrum* seems to involve the (etymological) sense of something on view as well as the old notion of *Theatrum mundi*, cited, for example, by R.A. Skelton in his introduction to the facsimile edition (Amsterdam, 1964), pp. vii–viii. The *ommegang* pageants at Antwerp in 1564 and 1566 of the 'Theater der Werelt' (*Theatrum Mundi*) are relevant too in more than their titles (for these see below, at notes 57, 46).

13. See notably Werner Waterschoot, 'The Title-page of Ortelius's Theatrum Orbis Terrarum', *Quaerendo*, IX, 1979, pp. 43–68; also further below, at note 69.

14. On which see Frances A. Yates, *The Art of Memory*, ed. Harmondsworth, 1969.

15. On the importance of inscriptions to humanist programmes see e.g. Hope and McGrath 1996 (see note 6), pp. 161–188, esp. 170–171.

16. Sebastiano Erizzo, *Discorso sopra le medaglie antiche*, Venice, 1559; Antonio Agustín, *Dialogos de medallas, inscriciones y otros antiguedades*, Tarragona, 1587, translated into Italian and then Latin (cf. below, note 55); Hubert Goltzius, *C. Iulius Caesar...*, Bruges, 1563; *Fasti magistratuum et triumphorum romanorum*, Bruges, 1566; *Caesar Augustus...*, Bruges 1574, etc. The importance of these works for Rubens and his generation can be judged by the part played by that artist in the republication of the works of Goltzius, for which he also designed titlepages. See J. Richard Judson and Carl Van de Velde, *Book Illustrations and Title-pages*, Corpus Rubenianum Ludwig Burchard, XXI, 2 vols., London and Philadelphia, 1978, I, pp. 334–343; II, figs. 275–281.

17. Vincenzo Cartari, *Imagini de i dei degli antichi*, Venice, 1556, revised and illustrated in many editions from 1571 onwards; Giovanni Pierio Valeriano, *Hieroglyphica*, Basle, 1556, likewise reprinted and translated.

18. Thus the Four Winds on the Portuguese Arch in 1594 were derived from Cartari: Bochius 1595 (see note 8), p. 74; cf. Vincenzo Cartari, *Le Imagini de gli dei de gli antichi*, ed. Venice, 1571, pp. 261–263; also Caterina Volpi, *Le immagini degli dèi di Vincenzo Cartari*, Rome, 1996, pp. 287–8 and pl. xxxix. (This arch also has motifs in roundels taken from the reverses of Roman coins.) Bochius himself tells us that many of the spectators, ignorant of the fact that the figure of Boreas was based on antique authority ('ignari antiquitatis') – he gives us the passage from Pausanias, borrowed from Cartari – were outraged at ('indigne ferebant') the sight of an old man with snaky legs (*anguipes*), carrying off a naked maiden in the bloom of youth. Valeriano was, for instance, behind the symbolism on the arch in the Clothmarket (Bochius 1595 [see note 8], pp. 114–117). He was not only used, but is cited, as 'Pierius', at several points in the account of the 1599 entry for emblematic attributes, e.g. Bochius 1602 (see note 8), pp. 217, 228.

19. Stradanus's famous series of engravings, published by Philips Galle in the late 1580s with the title *Nova reperta*, introduced the (mostly technical) innovations of post-classical Europe with an allegory of the discovery of 'America'; this is plate 1. The titlepage shows a near-naked young man with an armlet (an Indian to represent the New Age?) and carrying the tail-devouring serpent (*ouroboros*) which is the hieroglyph of time (a corresponding old, clothed man of Antiquity disappears with the same attribute), who indicates the first of the new discoveries (only nine are actually included, numbered, on the titlepage; which suggests that the theme was only subsequently expanded to the final total of 19) by pointing to the map of America. On the series see Alice Bonner McGinty, *Stradanus (Jan van der Straet): his role in the visual communication of Renaissance discoveries, technologies and values*, PhD diss., Tufts University, 1974; for the titlepage see esp. p. 14 (in her view the figure indicating the new continent is an 'American Amazon', but the hairstyle seems to me to be that of a young man rather than a woman; in any case the two figures carrying the *ouroboros* ought to be of the same sex, representing Old and New Times or Ages). On the *Nova reperta* see also Alessandra Baroni Vannucci, *Jan van Der Straet detto Giovanni Stradano*, Milan–Rome, 1997, pp. 397–400. For the drawing for *The Discovery of America*, in the Metropolitan Museum, New York, see Ibidem, pp. 282–3, no. 461 (repr.). The five prints published under the title *Americae retectio* constitute a different series, even if they were sometimes appended to the *Nova reperta*.

20. Rubens certainly consulted the books by Bochius on the 1594 and 1599 entries when he was working on the Medici Cycle. See McGrath 1997 (see note 6), 1, p. 65.

21. Cesare Ripa, *Iconologia*, Rome, 1603. See Erna Mandowsky, *Untersuchungen zur Iconologie des Cesare Ripa*, Hamburg, 1934, translated into Italian as *Ricerche sulla Iconologia di Cesare Ripa*, Florence, 1939; Gerlind Werner, *Ripa's 'Iconologia'. Quellen-Methode-Ziele*, Utrecht, 1977.

22. Diels 1994 (see note 8), p. 53; cf. Van den Branden 1883, p. 254, and Doutrepont 1937 (see note 8), pp. 189–190 (these latter, however, provide only part of the quotation).

23. *Prosopographia sive virtutum, animi, corporis, bonorum externorum, vitiorum, et affectuum variorum delineatio, imaginibus accurate expressa a Philippo Gallaeo, et monochromate ab eodem edita. Distichis a Cornelio Kiliano Dufflaeo illustrata.* See Doutrepont 1937 (see note 8), p. 148; also Manfred Sellink, 'Philips Galle als uitgever van prenten aan het einde van de zestiende eeuw', *De zeventiende eeuw*, VIII, 1992, pp. 13–26, esp. 20, dating it *c.* 1590, on stylistic grounds; Ilja M. Veldman, 'Philips Galle: een inventieve prentontwerper', *Oud Holland*, CV, 1991, pp. 262–290, esp. 285 [without suggesting a date]; Eadem, 'Images of Labor and Diligence in sixteenth-century Netherlandish prints: the work ethic rooted in civic morality or Protestantism', *Simiolus*, XXI, 1992, pp. 257–258.

24. As the preface in the copy in Brussels puts it: 'Artes proinde septem liberales, Virtutes cardinales, Peccata capitalia, et plurima huius farinae nunc vulgatissima, variorum industria artificum formata, quibus officinae et tabernae venalibus abunde scatent, omisi'. This preface is, however, not included in the set preserved in Antwerp; see Doutrepont 1937 (see note 8), p. 149, n. 1.

25. See Wilberg Vignau-Schuurman 1969 (see note 3), 1, pp. 5–10, 243–245; Elizabeth McGrath, 'A Netherlandish History by Joachim Wtewael', *Journal of the Warburg and Courtauld Institutes*, XXXVIII, 1975, pp. 195–196; Karel G. Boon, *Netherlandish Drawings of the Fifteenth and Sixteenth Centuries. Catalogue of the Dutch and Flemish Drawings in the Rijksmuseum*, The Hague, 1978, I, p. 132, no. 376; Guido Marnef, in [cat. exh.] Antwerp 1993 (see note 3), pp. 272–273, no. 127 and Carl Depauw, in Ibidem, p. 277, no. 133. *Patientia*'s attribute of the yoke is recorded in Valeriano, *Hieroglyphica*, ed. Basle, 1575, fol. 359.

26. Doutrepont 1937 (see note 8), p. 148: 'En habes, amice Lector, Patientiae, Poenitentiae, Experientiae, Humilitatis, Pietatis, et id genus alias Virtutum, Vitiorum quoque, atque aliorum, suis symbolis pulchre ornatas imagines; pictoribus, sculptoribus, caelatoribus, aurifabris, statuariis, phrygionibus, polymitariis, poetis etiam rhythmicis sive rhetoribus vernaculis, pluribusque aliis apprime necessarias; ut libellum hunc unde effigies quaslibet imitandi copia datur, consulant'.

27. As indeed, etymologically, is the common Latin *personificatio*.

28. That is to say that I can find no single figure which relates directly and exclusively to this source. In an unpublished paper on the drawings in the Plantin-Moretus Museum attributed to Maarten de Vos, Ann Diels has suggested that, even if the entire series of prints eventually published together by Galle was not yet extant in 1594, many of the images might have been available as loose sheets. The prints have been dated *c.* 1590, on stylistic grounds, but they may well have been published as much as a decade later. The dating of 1579 for the inception of the series, mentioned, for example, in Sabine Poeschel, *Studien zur Ikonographie der Erdteile in der Kunst des 16.–18. Jahrhunderts*, Munich, 1985, p. 361, is from a print by Maarten de Vos included as an extra item in the version of the work in Antwerp: see Doutrepont 1937 (see note 8), pp. 148–149. So it can be discounted.

29. See note 23.

30. See note 8.

31. See Doutrepont 1937 (see note 8), pp. 125–195, passim. A few inscriptions include reference to prominent civic officials in Antwerp at the period.

32. Bochius 1595 (see note 8), pp. 110–111; see Doutrepont 1937 (see note 8), pp. 129–30, 135–136, 139, 169–170, Fig. 31. This is inscribed 'voer heere maleneus', evidently Charles Malineus (van Male), who was burgomaster in 1589–1590, and 1594–1595.

33. Doutrepont 1937 (see note 8), p. 174, Fig. 39.

34. See Michael Evans, 'Two Sources for Maimed Justice', *Source*, II, 1, 1982, pp. 12–15.

35. Doutrepont 1937 (see note 8), pp. 152–155, figs 5, 7, 9–10; Poeschel 1985 (see note 28), p. 426, no. 8.

36. Doutrepont 1937 (see note 8), pp. 152–155, figs 6, 8; Poeschel 1985 (see note 28), 75–79, 348–349, no. 37; Ernst Van den Boogaart, in Paul Vandenbroeck ed., [cat. exh.] *America, Bruid van de zon. 500 jaar Latijns-Amerika en de Lage Landen*, Antwerp, 1992, p. 302, no. 75; Friedrich Polleross, in [cat. exh.] *Federschmuck und Kaiserkrone. Das barocke Amerikabild in den habsburgischen Ländern*, Schlosshof im Marchfeld, 1992, p. 233, no. 3.10; C. Schuckman, *Hollstein's Dutch and Flemish Etchings, Engravings and Woodcuts, 1450–1700. Maarten de Vos*, XLIV–XLVI, 1996, ed. D. de Hoop Scheffer, nos. 1396–1399, text, pp. 277–278, pls. 198–199.

37. Both drawings are in Darmstadt, Hessisches Landesmuseum, inv. AE 440 and 441. See G. Bergstrasser, *Niederländische Zeichnungen, 16. Jahrhundert, im Hessischen Landesmuseum Darmstadt*, Darmstadt, 1979, pp. 182–185, nos. 137–138 (repr.). Cf Ernest Van den Boogaart, in [cat. exh.] Antwerp 1992 (see note 36), p. 308, no. 85.

38. The fact that some additional attributes were appended to the figures in the Plantin Museum drawings, with Europe (Figs. 5, 9) acquiring a clock and a mariner's compass which she has to balance on her knee [added from the *Nova reperta*?: for which see note 19], does not to my mind affect the argument.

39. Bochius 1595 (see note 8), pp. 88, 90 (repr.). Doutrepont 1937 (see note 8), p. 138, saw this as the destined setting for the figures on the Antwerp drawings of the Parts of the World (Figs. 5–8), but the little that can be seen in the illustration in the book does not bear this out, and the idea is in any case unconvincing – even though it has been often repeated in the literature.

40. Bochius 1595 (see note 8), pp. 72–75.

41. See the illustration in Lille, Bibliothèque municipale, MS 678, fol. 99. This manuscript appears to date from the eighteenth century, to judge from the style of the handwriting; another, earlier version of the text, with illustrations, is in Paris, Bibliothèque nationale, Cabinet des Estampes, Pd 33. The pageant is mentioned in Bochius 1602 (see note 8), p. 368, with, however, only a brief allusion to the four pictures. A more extensive account is in the manuscript description reproduced in J. Houdoy, *Joyeuse entrée d'Albert et Isabelle. Lille au XVIe siècle*, Lille, 1873, pp. 83–85. This is, according to Houdoy, Lille, Archives municipales, Livre E (Ibidem, 9); but he evidently presents an account corrected with the help of another version of the description: Bibliothèque municipale, MS 295 (Ibidem, 11). This begins: 'Au marchié, au devant de la maison portant pour enseigne *le Lion rouge*, aultre théâtre hault eslevé, composé et rempli de quatre grandes peintures vives en couleur ès quelles estoient représentées les quattre parties du monde: Europe, Asie, Afrique et Amérique, et au milieu, en nice [=niche], un personnaige en face et compartimens fort ressemblant Charles V[e], accoustré d'habits impériaux, au dessus en ung compartiment bien faict selon l'ouvraige... [etc.]' The theatre nearby presented Philip II enthroned between the 'peoples of the two Indies'. See Houdoy 1873, pp. 85–87; Bochius 1602, p. 368.

42. These were held by two soldiers. Between the kneeling Africa and Asia Pax overwhelmed Bellona. See Petrus Aegidius (=Gillis), *Hypotheses sive argumenta spectaculorum quae... Carolo... fides et amor... sunt edituri*, Antwerp, 1520; on this rare pamphlet see Marcus de Schepper, in [cat. exh.] Antwerp 1993 (see note 3), pp. 214–215, no. 64; the text is, however, reproduced in Marquard Freher, *Rerum germanicarum scriptores*, III, Hannover, 1611, pp. 174–177. Cf. Jean Jacquot, 'Panorama des fêtes et cérémonies du règne', in *Les Fêtes de la Renaissance. II. Fêtes et cérémonies au temps de Charles Quint*, Paris, 1960, p. 456.

43. See Cornelius Grapheus (Scribonius), *La tresadmirable... entree du... Prince Philipes... en la tresrenommee florissante ville d'Anvers...*, Antwerp, 1550, sigs. Iiiij–K. [The original text, in Latin is in *Spectacula in susceptione... principis...*, Antwerp, 1550]. The prince was flanked by ancient precedents of youths marked for greatness: Ascanius and Servius Tullius. Cf. Jacquot 1960 (see note 42), p. 465.

44. Grapheus 1550 (see note 43), sigs Kv–Kijv. Presumably these female figures were likewise in a variety of costumes; in

the print (Fig. 18) the representative men and allegorical women are indistinguishable in their turbans. Still the text specifies that the province of Numidia was dark-skinned and that of Ethiopia had a black face.

45. For the imagery of the Continents as subject to Habsburg and other monarchs see notably Polleross, in [cat. exh.] Schlossdorf 1992 (see note 36), esp. pp. 54–84.

46. *Ordinantie inhoudende de nieu Poincten van den Heyligen Besnijdenis Ommeganck, der Stadt van Antwerpen, gheschiet inden Iare 1564*, Antwerp [1564], sig. A2r-v; interestingly the Asian *Keyserinne* is specified as *Turckijen*, the African as *Mooren landt*, which suggests a continuing association with the Mediterranean borders of these 'Continents'; cf. *Ordinantie inhoudende die Oude en Nieuwe Poincten, van onser Vrouwen Ommeganck, der Stadt van Antwerpen, gheschiet inden Iare 1564*, Antwerp [1564], sig. A2r; *Ordinantie inhoudende de niew Poincten vanden Ommeganck halff Oogst, Anno 1566 ghenaempt den Tijt present*, Antwerp [1566], sig. Av. On these *ommegangen* and their mercantile themes see Sheila Williams, 'Les Ommegangs d'Anvers et les cortèges du Lord-Maire à Londres', in *Les Fêtes de la Renaissance. II: Fêtes et cérémonies au temps de Charles Quint*, Paris, 1960, pp. 352–353 (though she wrongly describes it as one of the old tableaux); Ernest Van den Boogaart, 'Keizerin Europa en haar drie zusters...', in [cat. exh.] Antwerp 1992 (see note 36), pp. 122–123.

47. They are indeed presented as such in the frontispiece to the series of prints published by Paul Flindt at Nuremberg in 1611, where they are further related to that theme of universal history, the Four Monarchies from the Book of Daniel (cf. Merian's frontispiece to Sebastian Münster [Fig. 27]): see F.W.H. Hollstein, *et al.*, *German Etchings, Engravings and Woodcuts, ca. 1450–1700*, Amsterdam, 1954–, VIII, pp. 88–91, nos. 100–112. This is entitled: *Quatuor: Monarchiae/ Partes Mundi/ Regiones/ Elementa/ Tempora/ Complexiones*. For the old quaternities of the Middle Ages see Anna C. Esmeijer, *Divina Quaternitas*, Assen–Amsterdam, 1978.

48. See James H. Hyde, 'L'Iconographie des quatre parties du monde dans les tapisseries', *Gazette des Beaux-Arts*, V^e^ série, X, 1924, pp. 253 and 256, note 1. On the Continents in general see notably Erich Köllmann and Karl August Wirth, in *Reallexikon zur deutschen Kunstgeschichte*, V, 1967, cols. 1107–1202, s.v. 'Erdteile'; Poeschel 1985 (see note 28).

49. Witness her role in the *Nova reperta*: see note 19.

50. The 12th-century candlestick in Hildesheim is a curious exception: see Köllmann and Wirth 1967 (see note 48), col. 1133 and Fig. 6.

51. See Köllmann and Wirth 1967 (see note 48), cols. 1127–1132; Poeschel 1985 (see note 28), pp. 15–20; Jean Devisse, *L'Image du Noir dans l'art occidental*, ed. Ladislas Bugner, 2.2, Fribourg, 1979, esp. pp. 216–221; Benjamin Braude, 'The Sons of Noah and the Construction of Ethnic and Geographical Identities in the Medieval and Early Modern Periods', *The William and Mary Quarterly*, 3rd ser., XIV, 1997, pp. 108–20.

52. Herodotus, *Historiae*, IV.45. A distinction between Europe and Asia was reinforced by the hostility between the Greeks and the Persians, as Herodotus also emphasises (Ibidem, I.2ff).

53. For a survey of the iconography of each see *Lexikon Iconographicum Mythologiae Classicae*, Zürich–Munich, 1981–, [hereafter LIMC], s.v. *Africa*, *Asia I*, *Europe II*, *Libye*, with further literature. It might be noted that the term *continens*, meaning 'mainland', does occur in Latin as a feminine noun (or rather as an adjective with the noun *terra* understood with it); but, as far as I know, no classical author talks of the 'tres continentes'.

54. It seems worth noting that Ortelius comments on his map of Africa that the Greeks called it Libya.

55. Witness the efforts of G.Z. Castellini to find an ancient iconography in his commentary on Ripa: Cesare Ripa, *Iconologia*, ed. Padua, 1645, pp. 418–419. Agustín notes that there are no representations of Europe on coins, but that Europa and the bull is a motif on Cretan coins (implying that this might be used as an image of Europe). See Antonio Agostini (Agustín) *Dialoghi... intorno alle medaglie...*, trans. Dionigi Ottaviano Sada, Rome, 1592, pp. 84–86.

56. The Europa whom 'Autocrator' embraced was pronounced to have been 'untouched by Jupiter': see Marcus de Schepper, in [cat. exh.] Antwerp 1993 (see note 3), pp. 214–215, nr. 64

57. The first edition of De Bruyn's book, published at Cologne in 1577 during his exile from Antwerp, was entitled *Omnium poene gentium imagines* and dealt mainly with European costume; the edition published by Plantin at Antwerp in 1581, after his return, was, however, much expanded to include costumes from all the four parts of the world: *Omnium pene Europae, Asiae, Aphricae atque Americae gentium habitus*. On De Bruyn see notably Yates 1959 (see note 3), pp. 13–16, suggesting a connection with the activities of Ortelius. It may be noted that Lucas de Heere's manuscript Costume Book (perhaps compiled from the late 1560s onwards; De Heere died in 1584) was entitled by him 'Theatre de tous les peuples et nations de la terre avec leurs habits, et ornemens divers...'; on this work see Yates 1959 (see note 3), pp. 20–23. On De Bruyn's titlepage see [cat. exh.] *Antwerp's Golden Age*, Smithsonian Institution, 1973–1975, p. 110, no. 79 (1581 Antwerp edition). Europe is, incidentally, shown as Europa on her bull at the side (in the Atlantic) of Ortelius's map of Europe: for an illustration see Dirk Imhof, in [cat. exh.] Antwerp 1993, pp. 306–307, no. 160 from the Dutch edition of 1571.

58. See Jean C. Balty, in *LIMC* (see note 53), II.i: pp. 858–859; ii: pl. 629 (s.v. *Asia II*). For Agustín's illustration and commentary on this see Agostini 1592 (see note 55), p. 97, interpreting the serpent/hook as a sort of cornucopia.

59. See Marcel Le Glay in *LIMC* (see note 53), I.i, pp. 250–255, esp. 254, no. 48; ii, pls 184–190 (s.v. *Africa*). For Agustín's commentary and illustration, used here (Fig. 20), see Agostini 1592 (see note 55), pp. 89–90.

60. The old interpretation of this as the 3 ancient 'continents' is surely wrong, all the more so as it takes the woman in the elephant hat as Asia. The central figure might, however, be Alexandria. See Martin Robertson, in *LIMC* (see note 53), IV.i, p. 92, no. 2 (s.v. *Europa*); Balty, Ibidem, II.i, p. 858, no. 3 (s.v. *Asia I*); Le Glay, Ibidem, I.i, p. 254, no. 51 (s.v. *Africa*); Marie-Odile Jentel, Ibidem, I.i, p. 492, no. 80 (s.v. *Alexandria*); Mary-Ann Zagdoun, Ibidem, VI.i, p. 286, no. 13 (s.v. *Libye*).

61. See E. Babelon, 'Alexandre ou l'Afrique? Etude d'iconographie d'après les médailles et les pierres gravées', *Aréthuse*, I, 1924, pp. 95–107. Jentel in *LIMC* (see note 53), I.i, pp. 488–494. Also Poeschel 1985 (see note 28), p. 13.

62. Pliny, *Historia naturalis*, V.7 (42). Cf. Erwin Panofsky, *The Iconography of Correggio's Camera di San Paolo*, London, 1961, p. 84.

63. Where Valeriano himself got this figure remains for the present mysterious; he seems to refer to an image he has seen in the Pazzi palace (*apud Pactios*) in Florence. See Valeriano 1575 (see note 25), fol. 398(A) [under chapter LIIII: *De malo punico: Poeni*; but this section is indexed under Africa]. He says he has seen in ancient monuments *fercula* adorned with pomegranates, to celebrate those victorious over the Carthaginians: 'Et Africam ipsam muliebri specie apud Pactios Florentiae vidi, in cuius manu altera, laeva quippe, quae decumbentis molliter capiti sustinendo subiecta est, malum Punicum habetur. In

altera flabellum, ad regionis ardores indicandos. Pro pulvillo undae duae, utrunque mare significant, Oceanum & Mediterraneum, quorum circa se ambitum ut ostenderet, anulos etiam duos in extremos digitos induxit.' In this context 'Oceanus' may be the Atlantic, but it could also refer to the encircling Ocean of the ancient *oikumene*. On the different meanings attached to Oceanus see Elizabeth McGrath, 'The Streams of Oceanus. Rubens, Homer and the Boundaries of the Ancient World', in *Ars naturam adiuvans. Festschrift für Matthias Winner*, ed. Victoria von Flemming and Sebastian Schütze, Mainz, 1996, pp. 464–476.

64. It was, however, used for the personification of Africa as one of the Continents on an arch set up for the entry of Charles II to London in 1662: John Ogilby, *The Entertainment of His Most Excellent Majestie Charles II...*, London, 1662, p. 81.

65. *Caesar Augustus sive historiae... ex antiquis numismatibus restitutae liber secundus*, Bruges, 1574.

66. In fact this attribute was later 'authorised' for the 'modern' Continent by its inclusion in Ripa's *Iconologia*, with the personifications of the 'Parti del Mondo'; these first appear in the edition of 1603; for Ripa's direct source see below, note 95.

67. On this titlepage see W. Le Loup, in [cat. exh.] *Hubertus Goltzius en Brugge, 1583–1983*, Bruges, 1983, pp. 136–138, no. 41, referring to Marcel Hoc, in *Bibliotheca Belgica*, III, Brussels, 1964, s.v. *Goltzius*, no. G387.

68. On the statue see Phyllis P. Bober and Ruth Rubinstein, *Renaissance Artists and Antique Sculpture*, London–Oxford, 1986, pp. 102–104, nos. 66–67; Francis Haskell and Nicolas Penny, *Taste and the Antique. The Lure of Classical Sculpture, 1500–1900*, ed. New Haven–London, 1988, pp. 20–22, 272–273, no. 65; also Elizabeth McGrath, 'River-gods, Sources and the Mystery of the Nile. Rubens's "Four Rivers" in Vienna', in *Die Malerei Antwerpens – Gattungen, Meister, Wirkungen (Internationales Kolloquium, Wien 1993)*, ed. E. Mai, K. Schütz, H. Vlieghe, Cologne, 1994, pp. 72–82.

69. See Waterschoot 1979 (see note 13), pp. 43–68, reproducing (pp. 58–68) the explanations provided of the titlepage by Adolphus Merkerus, Pieter Heyns and Gerard Du Vivier; also Van den Boogaart 1992 (see note 46), pp. 120–128 and no. 103; Poeschel 1985 (see note 28), pp. 70–72, 314–315, no. 4, Fig. 12. Merkerus wrote his explanation in honour of his friend, with the help of a drawing from Ortelius and notes used for the texts to the maps of the Parts of the World (Waterschoot 1979 [see note 13], p. 47); the introductory poems subsequently written by Heyns (to the Dutch edition of 1571) and Du Vivier (to the French edition of 1572) were apparently commissioned by Plantin (Ibidem).

70. There appears to be some doubt as to the status Ortelius gave this mostly undiscovered Continent since in the preface (sig. bIIv) he talks of the principal parts of the world as four.

71. Waterschoot 1979 (see note 13), p. 45. Unlike Goltzius, Ortelius himself executed neither the print, nor, most probably, the preparatory drawing for it. Waterschoot suggests that the artist might have been Maarten de Vos, who was in contact with Ortelius at this period: Ibidem, citing two letters. Both on stylistic and iconographic grounds this idea is less than convincing. Might the print not have been made by Hogenberg, who at the end of the preface (sig. Cr) is credited with having engraved 'almost all these plates' ('atque FRANCISCI HOGENBERGI artificiosae manui, cuius unius indefatigabili diligentia fere omnes hae Tabulae caelatae sunt, bene faveto')? J. Denucé, *Oud-Nederlandsche kaartmakers in betrekking met Plantijn*, Antwerp–The Hague, 1912–1913, p. 53, already put this idea forward. The titlepage has, however, also been ascribed to Philips Galle: A.J.J. Delen, *Histoire de la gravure dans les anciens Pays-Bas... Le XVIe siècle. Les graveurs-illustrateurs*, Paris, 1969, p. 157.

72. Waterschoot 1979 (see note 13), pp. 48–56.

73. For the pageants of the 'Theatre of the World' featuring a chariot with the Four Continents in the *ommegangen* of 1564 and 1566, see note 46.

74. In the *ommegang* pageants of 1564 and 1566 (see previous note) all four Parts of the World were described as Empresses, even if there is a notional first (Europe) and last (America).

75. Van den Boogaart, in [cat. exh.] Antwerp 1992 (see note 36), p. 301, no. 74; Edward Hodnett, *Marcus Geeraerts the Elder*, Utrecht, 1971, p. 58 and Fig. 51.

76. For the *Prosopographia* see notes 23, 24.

77. See Waterschoot 1979 (see note 13), p. 51.

78. Van den Boogaart, in [cat. exh.] Antwerp 1992 (see note 36) comments that we might not recognise her as an African without the encouragement of the text.

79. It should be noted that in setting his figures in landscapes De Vos was evidently following the example of Dirck Barendsz's set of prints published by Jan Sadeler in 1581 (Hollstein, *Dutch and Flemish Etchings...*, XXI, p. 164, no. 495; J. Richard Judson, *Dirck Barendsz., 1534–1592*, Amsterdam, 1970, p. 151, no. 104; Poeschel 1985 (see note 28), pp. 81–88, 404–405, no. 89, figs. 49–50; Van den Boogaart, in [cat. exh.] Antwerp 1992, p. 304, no. 79.

80. For example at the corners on the border of Claes Jansz. Visscher's world map of 1639 (C. Schuckman, *Hollstein's Dutch and Flemish Etchings, Engravings and Woodcuts, 1450–1700*, XXXVIII-XXXIX, 1992, ed D. de Hoop Scheffer, no. 209, text, p. 102, pl. 100; on the earlier map of Hondius (1608) they were all gathered in a group in the top border, along with an invented fifth Continent: for an illustration see J. Denucé, *Africa in de XVI^de Eeuw en de Handel van Antwerpen*, Antwerp, 1937, pl. 7. They were also used in the border of a tapestry series in Vienna (Kunsthistorisches Museum) after Raphael's Cartoons from the Geubels workshop in Brussels (*c.* 1595). See E. von Birk, in *Jahrbuch der Kunsthistorischen Sammlungen des allerhöchsten Kaiserhauses*, II, 1884, pp. 208–209, no. CII.

81. For a few examples of their use in decorative ensembles see Köllmann and Wirth 1967 (see note 48), cols 1180–1181.

82. For this print see Polleross, in [cat. exh.] Schlossdorf 1992 (see note 36), pp. 57–58, 258, no. 5.11, Fig. 48. It was published by Philips Galle, with verses below by the Antwerp town secretary, Joannes Bochius. These run: 'Cum Phoebo imperium communi sorte Philippus/ Tertius Austriacae gloriae gentis habet./ Hic sua signifero distinguit tempora circo,/ Servat et aetherias nocte, dieque vices:/ Ille sed in terris est sidus, et orbis ocellus,/ Est Helice populis et Cynosura suis'. A later state of the print with a globe in the circle between Africa and Asia, and the inscription 'Domus Austriacae Maiestas atque Potestas', was published by Jan Galle.

83. For this titlepage, apparently based on an earlier one by Crispin de Passe where the honour is done to Louis XIII, see Polleross, in [cat. exh.] Schlossdorf 1992 (see note 36), pp. 60–61, 266, no. 5.29, Fig. 52; also no. 5.28. Ortelius had exploited an earlier edition of Münster's work in compiling his notes on the Continents; see above, at note 72.

84. Amsterdam, Rijksmuseum, inv. A 112; oil on panel, 134 x 172 cm. Ursula Härting, *Frans Francken der Jüngere (1581–1642). Die Gemälde mit kritischem Œuvrekatalog*, Freren, 1989, p. 343, no. 363, Fig. 344; Poeschel 1985 (see note 28), pp. 359–360, no. 46, Fig. 32; Polleross, in [cat. exh.] Schlossdorf 1992 (see note 36), pp. 59, 67, pl. 60.

85. Expanded, the inscription would read: 'S[ANCTI] R[OMANI] IMPERII SPONTANEA RESIGNATIO A CARLO V. IMP[ERATORE] IN FERD[INANDUM] I FR[ATREM] REGNORUMQ[UE] HAERED[EM] IN PHL[IPPU]M II HISP[ANIAE] REGEM F[I]L[IUM] FACTA BRUX[ELL]AE (?: or BRUXELLAE ANNO?) 1555 EX INVEN[TIONE] D. PETRI. DE HANNICART. F. FRANCK.'

86. See Carl Van de Velde, *Frans Floris (1519/20–1570). Leven en Werken*, 2 vols., Brussels, 1975, I, pp. 102–103, seeing the separation of 'invention' from 'execution' as connected with the organisation of the workshop, as well as ideas about figural compositions; portraits and study heads, if signed, had no more than 'fecit/faciebat'.

87. See esp. Härting 1989 (see note 84), pp. 28–32; her catalogue records the formulae used for any signatures on individual works. See also below, note 90. What exactly he meant by invention has been debated: Härting is puzzled that some pictures claimed as his 'inventions' borrow their compositions from prints by other artists. Francken may well have considered such 'borrowings' legitimate elements in the process of invention; 'invenit' may signify no more than that he was responsible for the choice of how the subject was depicted.

88. See Arnout Balis, 'La destinée d'Anvers. Créatures marines semi-humaines dans l'art des Pays-Bas, du moyen âge à la période baroque', [cat. exh.] *Sirènes m'étaient contées*, Brussels, Galerie CGER, 1993, pp. 109, 115, note 37 and Fig. 12, citing Paul Génard, *P.P. Rubens. Aantekeningen over den grooten meester en zijne bloedverwanten*, Antwerp, 1877, pp. 7, 38, 76, 77, 87, 94. Hannicaert (Hannecaert) is recorded as a councillor in 1643 and again from 1648 until his death in 1655. Generally, the reference to Hannicaert in the inscription has been misunderstood, as, for example, a possible artistic collaborator: Härting 1989 (see note 84), p. 343, under no. 363. He certainly had an interest in art: he was instrumental in publishing the prints by Nicholaas Lauwers after Rubens's Eucharist series made between 1648 and 1652: see Nora De Poorter, *The Eucharist Series*, Corpus Rubenianum Ludwig Burchard, II, 2 vols., Brussels–London–New York, 1978, 1, pp. 214–215, 219–221, with further biographical details. He was Rubens's brother-in-law (see P. Génard, 'Het laatste testament van P.P. Rubens', *Rubens-Bulletijn*, IV, 1896, p. 140), and one of the executors of his will. Seven paintings by Rubens and Van Dyck, bought by Andries Hannicaert and Peter le Cat in the sale of Rubens's works in 1642, appear in the inventory made at his own death, in 1655, including unfinished battle scenes from the Henri IV cycle. Little is known about his activity as a merchant. He is mentioned in 1646–1647 as registered in *De Violieren* (P. Rombouts and T. van Lerius, *De liggeren en andere historische archieven van de Antwerpsche Sint Lucasgilde*, 2 vols., ed. Amsterdam, 1961, II, pp. 183, 185, 228). Particularly interesting in the present context is the Golden Book of the Confraternity of the Holy Sacrament at Antwerp which he produced at his own expense in 1631, since this has on its titlepage an image of the Lamb of God adorned by the Continents. See De Poorter, op. cit., I, p. 214, note 3. For much of the above information on Hannicaert I am indebted to Filip Vermeylen, Nico van Hout and Arnout Balis. Ursula Härting proposed an attribution of this titlepage to Frans Francken the Younger in: *Uit het Gulden Boek van de Kapel van Venerabel in de Kathedraal van Antwerpen*, Antwerp, 1999, pp. 11–13, 15 (repr.)

89. Oldenburg, Landesmuseum für Kunst und Kulturgeschichte, Gemäldegalerie; oil on panel, 64.5 x 104.5 cm. See Härting 1989 (see note 82), pp. 58, 349, no. 377, Fig. 56; Karl-Heinz Kohl ed., [cat. exh.] *Mythen der Neuen Welt*, Berlin, 1982, p. 31, Fig. 25, pp. 329–330, no. 8.13, Fig. 24; Poeschel 1985 (see note 28), pp. 357–358, no. 45; Siska Beele, in [cat. exh.] Antwerp 1992 (see note 36), p. 340, no. 128 [repr. in colour]; Balis 1993 (see note 88), pp. 109–110.

90. It is inscribed *ffranck. in f.A* [=*invenit et fecit Antverpiae*].

91. See Balis 1993 (see note 88), pp. 104–110.

92. Even if it is not quite certain what his use of the term 'invenit' implies: see note 87.

93. See Härting 1989 (see note 82), p. 343, perceiving appropriate distinctions in handling – though given the fact that the *Homage to Apollo* presents a more pleasing equivalence between the offerings of the sea and those of earth, I am less inclined to see a stylistic development. The 1628 titlepage by Merian (Fig. 27) seems to provide a *terminus post quem* for both paintings.

94. There may be a connection here with the idea that America ('India') supplies (to a European, specifically Habsburg ruler) the remaining part of the world, as on the reverse of a medal by Gianpaolo Poggini, of 1561–1562, made for Philip II, and reproduced with a new application to Antwerp (pictured on the obverse) in honour of the governor (1571–1576; 1585–1586) Frederick Perrenot; see Walter Louwet, [cat. exh.] Antwerp 1992 (see note 36), p. 266, no. 26, p. 341, no. 129. On the medal for Philip II and the artist's letter describing it see G. Kubler, 'A medal by G.P. Poggini depicting Peru and predicting Australia', *Mitteilungen des Kunsthistorischen Institutes in Florenz*, XI, 1964, pp. 149–152.

95. See note 83. Siska Beele, in [cat. exh.] Antwerp 1992 (see note 36), p. 340, already drew attention to the relationship to Sebastian Münster, referring, however to the edition of the *Cosmographia* published at Basle in 1544, which did not include images of the Continents. Merian (or De Passe's) own source for the coral was presumably Ripa. See Cesare Ripa, *Iconologia*, Rome, 1603, pp. 335–336. This was likewise the source of Europe's horse. It has not been previously noted that Ripa himself derived his figures, which do not appear in the first edition (1593), from the maps of the four parts of the world of 1597 by Fausto Rughesi (for which see Roberto Almagia, *Monumenta Cartographica Vaticana. II: Carte geografiche a stampa di particolare pregio o rarita dei secoli XVI e XVII*, Vatican City, 1948, pp. 69–73, no. xxix, pls xxi–xxiv).

96. It looks more like a lobster than a crab, but there are precedents for showing Cancer in this form, such as Dürer's famous star map of the Northern Hemisphere.

97. Cancer was, however, in antiquity, and therefore in symbolic terms, the location of the summer solstice.

98. The association is made, in connection with Spanish Habsburg rule, which extends to all four Parts of the World, in the verses by Bochius to the print after Stradanus (Fig. 26): for which see note 82.

99. For accounts of this ceremony see notably William Stirling-Maxwell, *The Chief Victories of the Emperor Charles the Fifth Designed by Martin Heemskerck in MDLV*, London–Edinburgh, 1870, pp. 59–73. See also P. de Sandoval, *Historia de la Vida y Hechos del emperador Carlos V*, 2 vols., ed. Pamplona, 1634, II, pp. 80–114. Francken probably knew Hogenberg's print (Fig. 30), made retrospectively from the descriptions; see Frederik Muller, *De Nederlandsche Geschiedenis in Platen. Beredeneerde Beschrijving van Nederlandsche Historieplaten, Zinneprenten en Historische Kaarten*, 2 vols., Amsterdam, 1863, I, p. 37, no. 408; also p. 44; G. van Rijn with G.W. Kernkamp, *Nederlandsche Historieprenten (1555–1900)*, Amsterdam, 1910, pl. 2. The men behind Philip may represent the officials present at the occasion: royal counsellors as well as Flemish nobles and knights of the Golden Fleece, but only one head (that next to the flag with the arms of the 17 Provinces) looks as if it was based on an old portrait. Given the subsequent course of history, it is unlikely that William of Orange, who was at the Emperor's side (Charles actually leant on him) at the ceremony, is meant to be represented here [in any case he is usually shown with curly hair]; nor can it be Granvelle, since he does

not wear ecclesiastical dress. Mary of Hungary, who was enthroned to one side of Charles V at the abdication ceremony in Brussels (Philip was on the other side), might be expected to have been included by Francken; if so she should be the crowned lady behind the queen near Ferdinand (Eleanor, widow of François I, Charles V's other sister?: both Mary and Eleanor accompanied the Emperor back to Spain). However this may be, it would appear that, for the sake of variety, the artist grouped all the 'real' (historical) women behind the largely male collection of sea-gods, allowing the 'imaginary' (personified) females to appear in front of a group of men.

100. Cf. Poeschel 1985 (see note 28), p. 359, where the identification is simply stated.

101. If not more so, since this woman, who has a dark interior to her crown as distinct from the red of her companion, is looking towards Charles V, in an action which might be interpreted as reflecting the (more humble) poses of the three Continents in the foreground. (In the *Homage to Apollo* only America is kneeling.) But neither of the crowned women in the *Abdication* corresponds in detail to Europe in the *Homage to Apollo*.

102. See Franz Adrian Dreier, in Kohl, in [cat. exh.] Berlin 1982 (see note 89), pp. 111–20; Polleross, in [cat. exh.] Schlossdorf 1992 (see note 36), pp. 56–57, Fig. 47.

103. For this print see note 82.

104. Poeschel 1985 (see note 28), p. 359, says he's pointing to Asia.

105. For the identification of Francken's figure with Mulay Ahmad see Jan-Albert Goris and Julius S. Held, *Rubens in America*, Antwerp, 1947, p. 28, under no. 11.

106. Boston, Museum of Fine Arts; oil on panel, 99.6 x 72.3 cm. See Julius S. Held, 'Rubens's "King of Tunis" and Vermeyen's Portrait of Mulay Ahmad', *Art Quarterly*, III, 1940, pp. 173–181 and Fig. 2, republished in *Rubens and his Circle. Studies by Julius S. Held*, ed. Anne W. Lowenthal, David Rosand and John Walsh, Jr. (Princeton, N.J., 1982), pp. 3–8; Idem, *The Oil Sketches of Peter Paul Rubens. A Critical Catalogue*, 2 vols., Princeton, N.J., 1980, I, p. 600, under no. 433; Hendrik J. Horn, *Jan Cornelisz Vermeyen, Painter of Charles V, and his Conquest of Tunis*, 2 vols., Doornspijk, 1989, I, pp. 15, 19, 73–74; II, pl. A47; Kristin Belkin, in *Flemish Paintings in America*, Flandria extra muros, Hans Vlieghe ed., Antwerp, 1992, pp. 186–189; Marjorie E. Wieseman, in [cat. exh.] *The Age of Rubens*, Peter C. Sutton ed., Boston, 1993, pp. 235–237, no. 9. Rubens may also have known the anonymous sixteenth-century print which identifies the sitter (it has the artist's monogram only).

107. Rubens must have copied Vermeyen's lost portrait of Mulay Hassan as well as that of Mulay Ahmad: they are recorded as 'Deux pourtraits d'un Roy de Thunis, apres Anthoine More/ Two pictures of Kings Tunis, made after Antonio More's' in the inventory taken at his death: see Jeffrey M. Muller, *Rubens: The Artist as Collector*, Princeton, 1989, p. 121, nos. 148–149, pls. 68–69. For the pair of pictures in the collection of Herman de Neyt in 1642 see Jan Denucé, *De Antwerpsche 'Konstkamers'. Inventarissen van de kunstverzamelingen te Antwerpen in de 16e en 17e eeuwen*, Bronnen voor de geschiedenis van de Vlaamsche kunst, II, Antwerp, 1932, p. 101.

108. It would in any case be odd to have a 'straightforward' portrait in this section of the painting (otherwise the portrait-figures are in the background, to either side of Charles V). And had Francken wanted to choose a historical individual to sum up the eventual loyalty secured by Charles V from North African Berbers he would surely have chosen the father of Mulay Ahmad, Mulay Hassan, since this latter had the more direct (and tributary) relationship with Charles V. The figure's turban looks to me more self-consciously (near-)Eastern than African in style: it is different from that shown on Mulay Ahmad in Rubens's painting and in the print: wound a different way and rising in the middle to a (flattened) point: more like those of the Turks in, for example, Pieter Coecke's *Moeurs et fachon de faire de Turcs* of 1553 – for which see Georges Marlier, *La Renaissance flamande. Pierre Coeck d'Alost*, Brussels, 1966, pp. 55–72.

109. See above, at notes 42ff.

110. It seems significant that the scene at Antwerp in 1549 in which Charles and Philip frightened away the infidels (Fig. 18) was crowned by the device of the twin columns with their motto (in this case in the old, Burgundian form *Plus Oultre*). Still, the columnar device and motto was specifically associated with the conquest of Africa by some early sixteenth-century Spanish commentators; see Earl E. Rosenthal, 'The Invention of the Columnar Device of the Emperor Charles V at the Court of Burgundy in Flanders in 1516', *Journal of the Warburg and Courtauld Institutes*, XXXVI, 1973, pp. 221–230. The victory at Tunis and the routing of the Turks was explicitly claimed to herald Habsburg rule over the whole world in an inscription on the Spanish Arch for the 1549 entry: Grapheus 1550 (see note 43), sig. Eiiij.

111. Still, it might be significant that the Continents featured in another work associated with Hannicaert: the titlepage to the book of the Confraternity of the Eucharist in Antwerp Cathedral of 1631 (cf. note 88) even if that book postdates Francken's *Homage to Apollo*.

Bedrooms and Banquets: Mythology in Sixteenth-Century Flemish Painting

Fiona Healy

Possibly the most memorable testimony to the high status accorded to the art of painting in Antwerp is the *Allegory of Sight and Smell* (Fig. 1), presented together with its pendant, the *Allegory of Taste, Touch and Hearing*, to the Archdukes Albert and Isabella by the city of Antwerp in 1618.[1] Executed in the studio of Jan Brueghel the Elder, the *Allegory of Sight and Smell* is, as the sources tell us, the result of the collaboration between the 'twelve most important artists' of the city, each of whom contributed scaled-down reproductions or variations of the genre of painting for which he was most famous.[2] Like a confident self-portrait, the *Allegory* asserts the importance of Antwerp as an artistic centre by illustrating the diversity of its painted output as a collective enterprise while simultaneously upholding the role of the individual participants as contributors to a tradition of innovation which since the sixteenth century shaped the artistic landscape. As the city's most famous painter, Peter Paul Rubens features prominently in the *Allegory*, with no less than seven of his compositions adorning the room. These works reveal a great deal about Rubens's own view of his role as a Flemish painter. Rather surprising is his affirmation of his status as a painter of a 'lesser' genre, namely of hunting scenes, but otherwise he conforms to expectations by asserting his mastery of the established fields of portraiture and history painting. Given, however, that Rubens's public presence in Antwerp prior to 1618 was marked by a number of outstanding religious images, it is indeed surprising that he should have chosen as his contribution to this imaginary gallery history paintings devoted entirely to the activities of the classical gods.[3] This is all the more noteworthy because, with the exception of a *Mars and Venus surprised by Vulcan* by an unidentified artist, he is the only painter to illustrate scenes from ancient mythology. By highlighting this particular part of his artistic personality, Rubens, it would seem, wished to emphasise the importance of mythology as a socially and intellectually valid form of artistic expression. It hardly seems possible that Rubens would have had to justify his commitment to this particular aspect of his art. Yet exactly this appears to have been the case, for as will be shown below, there was no continuous and dominant tradition of depicting pagan subjects in Flemish painting which he could invoke and build upon.

Mythology belongs, of course, to the realm of the history painter, who in Italy reigned supreme in the artistic hierarchy. The situation in the Netherlands was very different, for the sixteenth century saw the emergence of the specialist, the artist who exercised his talent in the fields of landscape, still-life or genre painting. In a manner unthinkable in Italy, those painters specialising in what are frequently called the 'lesser' genres were equated the same high status as history painters; this is particularly evident in works where history and portrait painters collaborated with specialists in landscape or still-life.[4] Scholarly interest has tended to focus on the particularities of these genres as well as on the enormous output of religious art, which, indeed, has more or less become synonymous with sixteenth-century history painting in Antwerp. That the study of mythological painting has been religated to the margins is unfortunate not least because its status as an art form can help shed light on the nature of Flemish society during this period.[5] Given therefore the extremely innovative nature of Flemish sixteenth-century art, is it not curious that at a time when Netherlandish artists journeyed to Italy in search of artistic enlightenment, mythology, as one of the major forces of the ancient and Renaissance worlds, played such a minor role? The acceptance, or in this case non-acceptance of mythology is more than a simple matter of taste, for how else are we to explain the paradoxical situation that the Calvinist North so fervently embraced mythology from the 1570s while the Spanish-ruled South more or less eschewed it. Nor are we

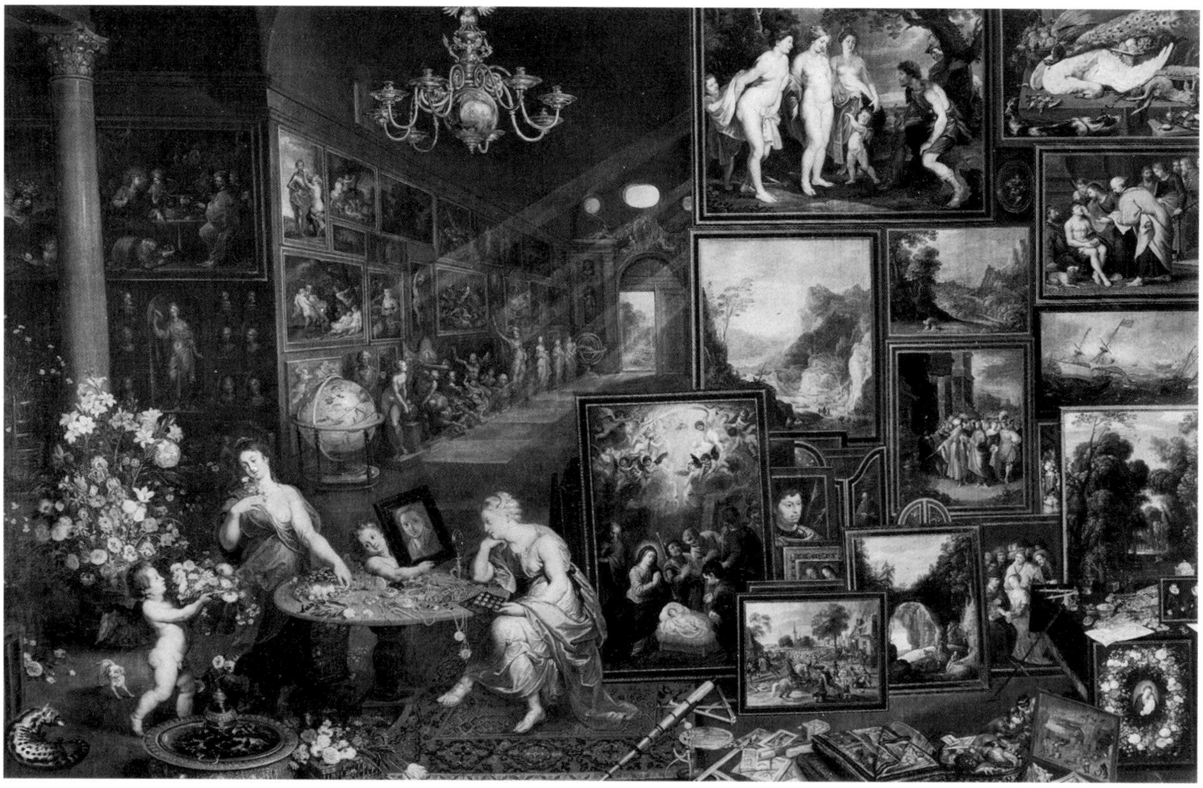

Fig. 1. Jan Brueghel the Elder *et al.*, *The Allegory of Sight and Smell*. Madrid, Museo del Prado

justified in assuming the Netherlandish art-buying public shied away from the depiction of nudity. Indeed, judging by the popularity of paintings emphasising the physical charms of biblical heroines,[6] as well as the choice of scenes for *tableaux vivants* and for the triumphal arches erected for the *Blijde Inkomst* or Joyous Entry of an important personage into a Netherlandish city,[7] the very opposite was the case. Answers to these complex issues can only be attempted after a survey has been undertaken of the comparatively small number of extant mythological paintings, many of which are by lesser-known artists. This study represents a first step in establishing the type of mythological painting produced in Antwerp, following which it should be possible to draw some – very general – conclusions as to the interests of artists and patrons, the choice of subject matter, the manner of representation, and the taste for the sensually pleasing and/or morally edifying. Any discussion of mythology in the Netherlands necessitates looking beyond the period and geographical boundaries set by this Colloquium. For the sake of clarity, neither the role of mythology in the graphic arts, nor in paintings where the landscape is of equal – if not even greater – importance, as in Pieter Bruegel's *Fall of Icarus*, is discussed. Equally, artists of Flemish origin, such as Bartholomeus Spranger, who left to work outside the Netherlands have been omitted.

The apparent low standing of classical mythology among artists and patrons is all the more remarkable given its illustrious and promising introduction to the Netherlands. Jan Gossaert returned from Italy in 1509, bringing with him, to quote Karel van Mander: 'the correct manner of composing and making pictures full of nudes and all kinds of allegories [...], which things were not so common in our country before his time'.[8] But it was not until 1516, when Philip of Burgundy, with whom the artist had visited Rome, commissioned paintings for two of his residences that Gossaert was given the opportunity to put his literary and practical knowledge of ancient art into practice. Surviving testimony of these projects include the artist's *Neptune and Amphitrite*,[9] probably the first-ever rendering of this couple in a large-scale paint-

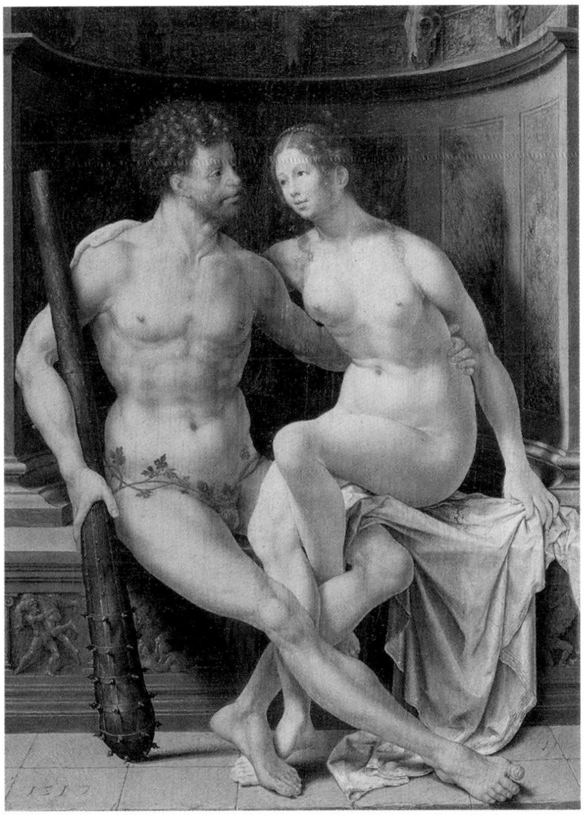

Fig. 2. Jan Gossaert, *Hercules and Deianira*. Birmingham, The Barber Institute

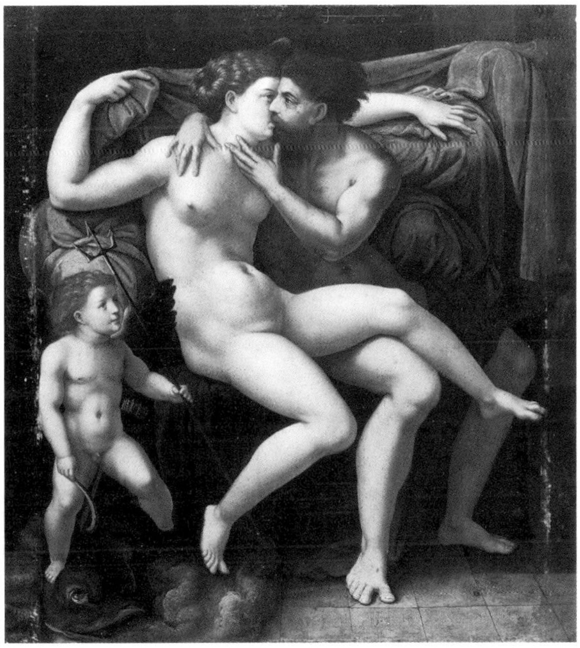

Fig. 3. Master of the Female Half-Lengths, *Neptune and Thetis*. Berlin, Staatliche Museen, Gemäldegalerie

ing, and *Hercules and Deianira* (Fig. 2).[10] In these works Gossaert recalls his experience of Italy, and in particular its ancient art, by placing figures clearly inspired by his study of antique sculpture in a setting which testifies to his detailed investigation of classical architecture. Such depictions must have provoked very mixed reactions in a society still immersed in medieval thinking. At a time when Gothic architecture dominated the skyline of Northern European cities and when didactic-moralising books such as the *Ovide moralisé* were a principal source of information on the ancient deities,[11] Gossaert's 'authentic' pagan gods in their 'authentic' classical setting – although probably accessible only to a select few – must nevertheless have seemed curious, if not altogether mystifying, to those artists and patrons who had not had the opportunity to see for themselves what remained of the glories of ancient Rome. With some hesitation, I venture to suggest that Gossaert's desire to be true to the classical ideal, albeit one seen through Gothic eyes, may, paradoxically, have hindered rather than encouraged the establishment of mythological painting as part of a Netherlandish artist's standard repertoire.

A characteristic feature of Gossaert's mythological paintings, and one which was to continue into the seventeenth century, is the absence of real narrative. Instead of recalling a particular mythological event, we are presented with a 'portrait' of the protagonists, usually a couple. Rather than depicting, for instance, Deianira's dramatic abduction by the centaur Nessus, Gossaert simply seats her next to Hercules. The outwardly simple composition is, however, misleading, for Gossaert's use of the slung-leg motif to refer to the sexual nature of their association and to the jealousy that was to bring about the hero's terrible death,[12] prompts reflection on the complexities of human behaviour as expressed through the male-female relationship.[13] Gossaert's psychologically subtle approach held little appeal for subsequent generations, who instead preferred to focus on the more erotic aspects of sexuality. Instead of devising their own designs, many of these artists copied or emulated inventions by famous Italian masters. During the 1530s, the Master of the Female Half-Lengths executed two paintings showing *Neptune and Thetis* (Fig. 3) and *Venus and Amor* after engravings by Caraglio,[14] while the many renderings of *Leda* by Vincent Sallaert and Cornelis van Cleve

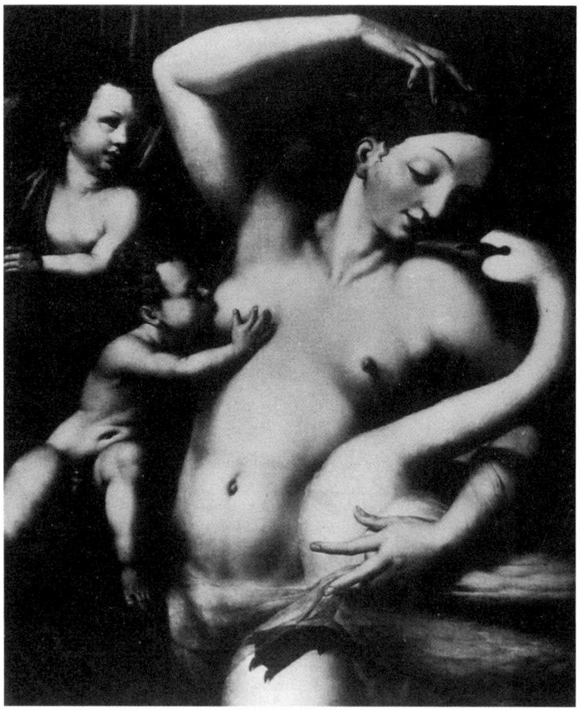

Fig. 4. Cornelis van Cleve, *Leda*. Whereabouts unknown

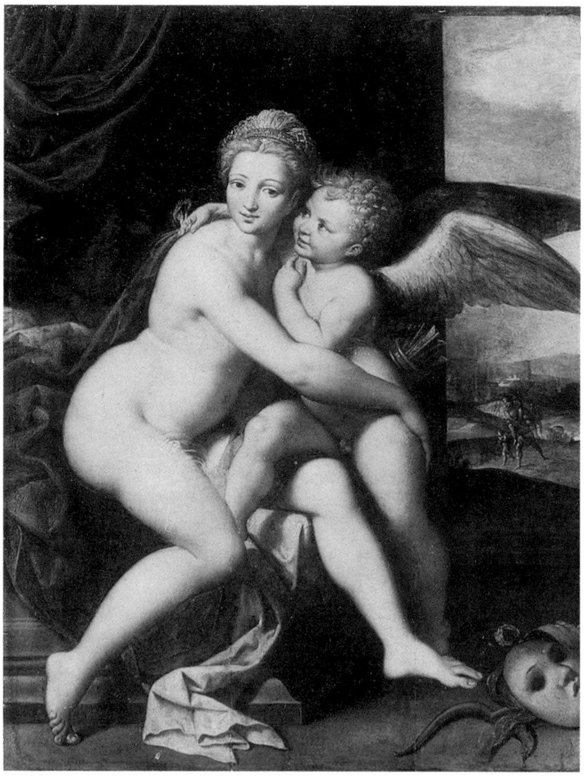

Fig. 5. Jacob de Backer, *Venus and Amor*. Berlin, Staatliche Museen, Gemäldegalerie

(Fig. 4) were surely created with Leonardo's famous compositions in mind.[15] These painters quite obviously catered to a segment of the market eager to possess paintings which depict a lascivious subject executed in the Italian manner. It is difficult to pinpoint the reasons for this reliance on Italian sources. On the one hand, the view may have arisen during the emerging stages of artistic specialisation that mythology was the preserve of the Italian artist. On the other, the choice of subjects of an overtly erotic but essentially non-narrative nature may indicate that such paintings were aimed at a public not particularly well-versed in classical mythology but interested in possessing 'modern' pictures, ones where style and content clearly point to Italy.[16]

While the basic characteristics of this type of non-narrative erotic painting remained valid into the early seventeenth century, a shift in emphasis occurred during the latter half of the sixteenth century. Instead of an indiscriminate illustration of sexual desire, a more critical attitude towards the ancient gods was expressed by superimposing a moralising message onto the erotic scene. Jacob de Backer's painting of *Venus and Amor* (Fig. 5) follows the by now recognisable pattern of placing the nude figures in the foreground. But by adding arrows and a mask, symbols of the power but also the deceitfulness of love, and depicting in the background the flight of Aeneas and his father Anchises from Troy, de Backer introduces an allegorical dimension designed to warn of the dangers overly-familiar association with the realm of Venus and Amor can bring.[17] Moreover, in keeping with artistic developments, more complex compositions were devised which straddle the divide between narrative and non-narrative without, however, completely relinquishing the principle of 'portraying' the gods in a compromising situation. De Backer adopted such an approach in his unusual, if not iconographically singular rendering of Venus handing Paris a tazza containing a skull hidden behind the mask of a beautiful woman (Fig. 6).[18] No textual sources refer to the shepherd ever having entered the goddess's bed, but they do recall Venus's statement that her beauty was matched by that of Helen of Troy, whose bed Paris did share, even though she was married to another. Hence we are invited to identify both women in the figure on the bed, and to read the image as a warning of the dangers of submitting to the temp-

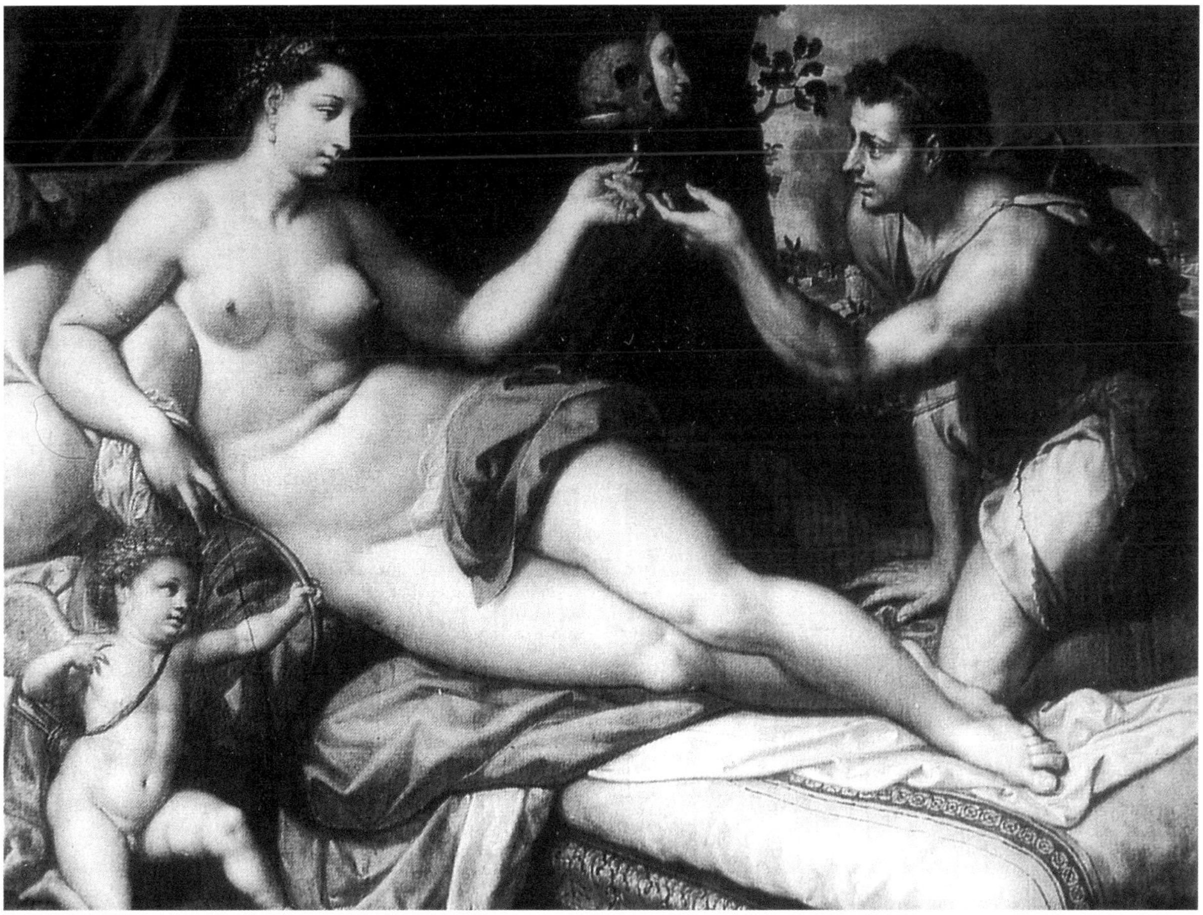

Fig. 6. Jacob de Backer, *Venus and Paris*. Meiningen, Staatliche Museen, Schloß Elisabethenburg

tations of the flesh, and in particular of committing adultery.[19]

A more humorous account of the humiliation experienced through excessive sexual lust is found in the two renderings of *Hercules and Omphale* which Abraham Janssens executed during the first decade of the seventeenth century.[20] Instead of the more usual scene of Omphale degrading the hero by forcing him to don her clothing and spin, Janssens illustrates Ovid's witty account in the *Fasti* (II, 303–358) of Hercules unceremoniously kicking Pan out of Omphale's bed. But whereas Ovid simply recalls the case of mistaken identity by having Pan discover to his detriment that he has attempted to seduce Hercules and not the Lydian queen, Janssens gives the story a novel twist by having Hercules share Omphale's bed – in Ovid they decorously occupy separate beds. The hero's deft defence of the sleeping queen acquires a very different meaning in the artist's second version in Copenhagen (Fig. 7). There Pan not only mistakes Hercules for the object of his desire but has, as Justus Müller Hofstede notes, interrupted the couple's lovemaking. The message of such works is not easy to decipher. Janssens alludes to the power of women to weaken even the strongest of men by depicting Hercules's submission to female domination, yet ironically, he simultaneously portrays the hero as the defender of female virtue; for although their relationship is not sanctioned by marriage, his love of the Lydian queen is noble, whereas Pan simply seeks sexual gratification. So although powerful narratives, these two paintings nevertheless represent the culmination of a century-long preoccupation with sexuality as exercised within the orderly confines of the bedroom. As such they can be classified as illustrating what was apparently considered the favourite occupation of the pagan gods, wherein, of course, lies the moral, should one require one, since their behaviour represented the temptations of the flesh which constantly threatened to undermine Christian values.

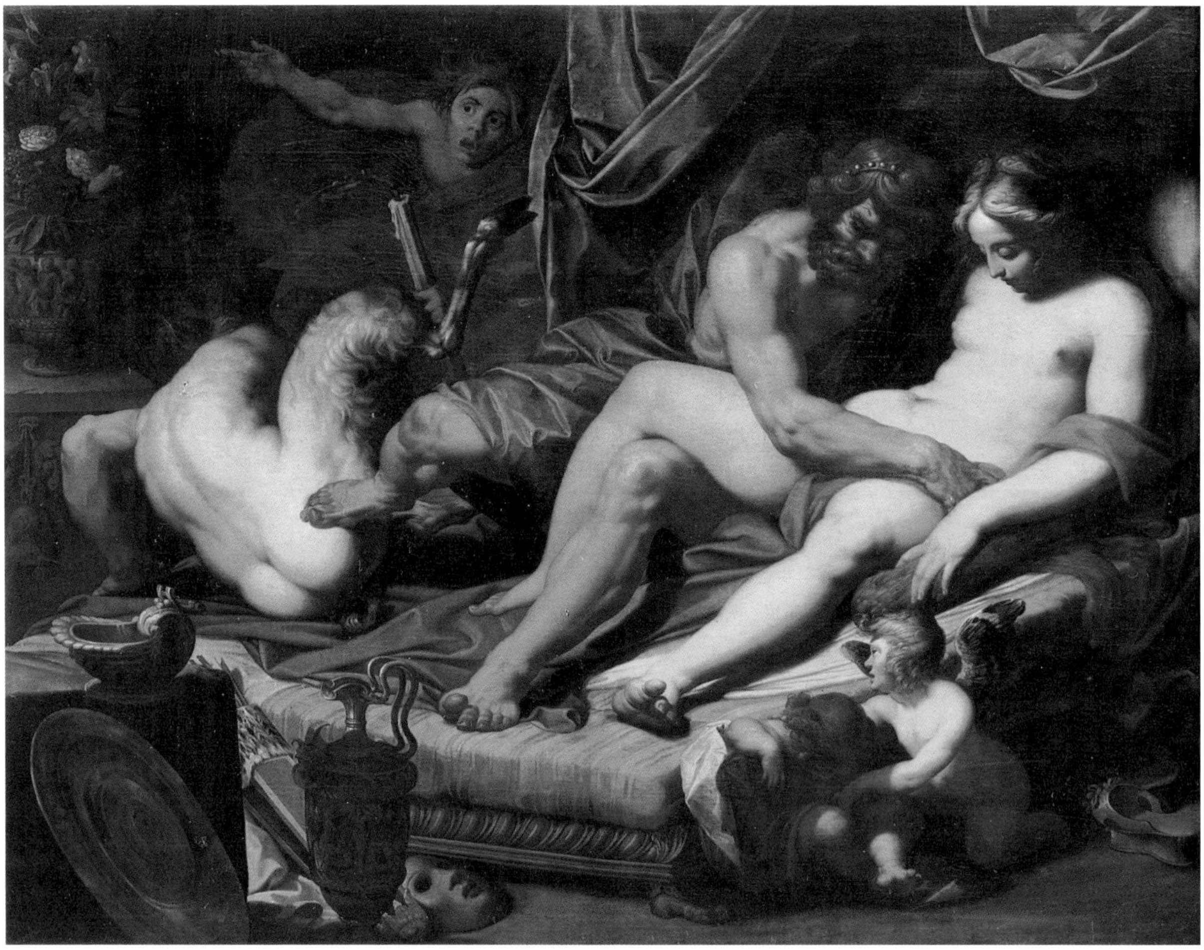

Fig. 7. Abraham Janssens, *Hercules and Omphale*. Copenhagen, Statens Museum for Kunst

The situation regarding painting which can be said to be truly narrative in form and content is less straightforward. The ambivalent attitude towards mythology in general can be best demonstrated by looking at one of the most popular of the ancient myths in the Netherlands and Northern Europe. The fact that the story of Paris and his role in the downfall of Troy was considered to belong to the realm of history rather than mythology only partly explains why, long after the classical version was reinstated in Italian Renaissance art, the Northern European interpretation of the contest for the golden apple as a dream continued to dominate art and literature until well into the sixteenth century.[21] What is probably the first Netherlandish rendering of the classical account of the *Judgement* as opposed to the *Dream* of Paris is attributed, interestingly enough, to the Master of the Female Half-Lengths (Fig. 8), who however counteracts his innovative step by transforming the myth into a moralising allegory on the choices facing man.[22] The decision to resort to the decidedly old-fashioned device of giving each goddess an attribute which alludes to the gift she offers Paris should he award her the apple is all the more astonishing given that the same artist used Italian prints as the source for paintings and was surely acquainted with Marcantonio Raimondi's famous engraving of the *Judgement of Paris* after Raphael. The classical version was thus available in both textual and pictorial form, yet its slow integration into Northern European art suggests a reluctance on the part of the art-buying public to throw old concepts of history overboard and rid the myth of all medieval remnants.

It was only with Frans Floris in the Southern Netherlands and his older contemporary Marten van Heemskerck in the North that a truly narrative rendition of ancient mythology is to be found. Both, for example, painted the Judgement of Paris on a number of occasions,

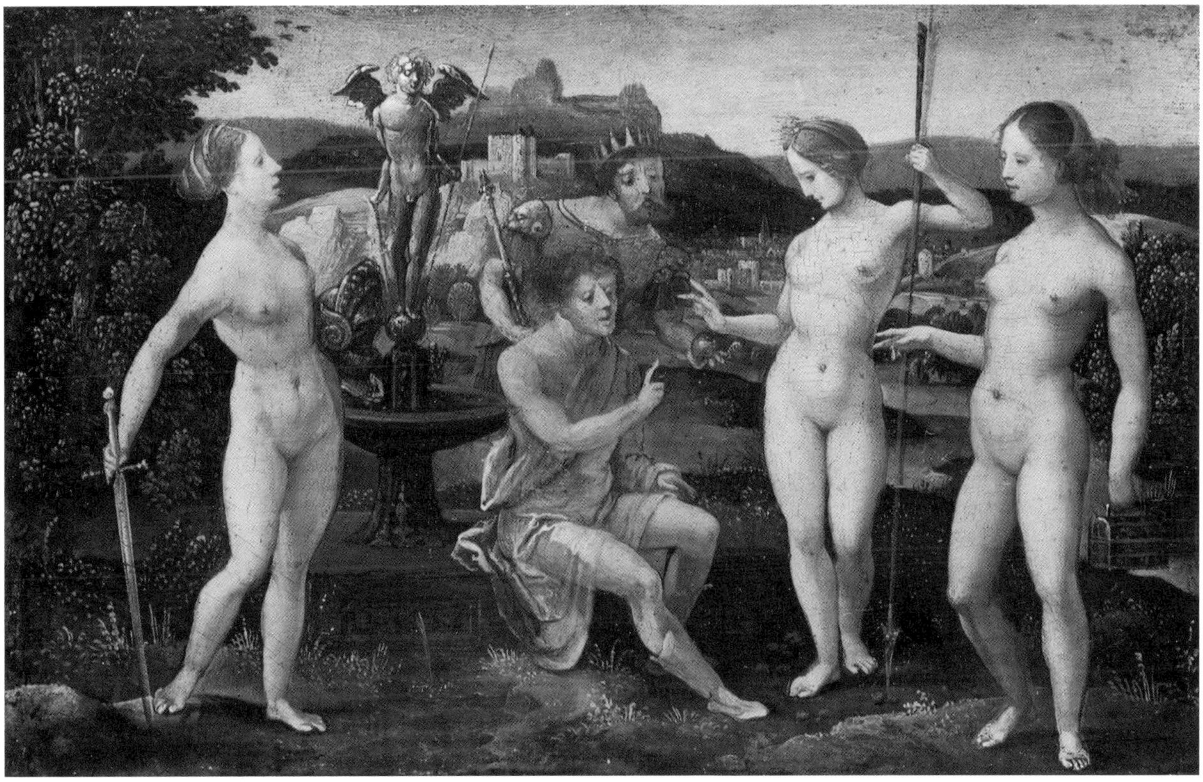

Fig. 8. Master of the Female Half-Lengths, *Judgement of Paris*. The Hague, Mauritshuis

often taking Marcantonio's engraving as their point of departure, as is evident from Floris's *Judgement of Paris* in Kassel (Fig. 9).[23] Typical of their approach is the reduction of the number of figures and the corresponding emphasis on the protagonists Paris and the goddesses. In transforming Raphael's river-god into a stone figure of the type commonly found in Rome at that time, both artists displayed their knowledge of ancient sculpture; they also paid tribute to their own pictorial heritage by modernising the traditional Northern European motif of the fountain beside which Paris fell asleep and dreamt of the goddesses. Floris and Heemskerck would have seen more or less the same ancient works of sculpture whilst in Italy, yet their use of that experience could not be more different. Heemskerck generally sought to capture the atmosphere of the ancient world by placing his figures in a suitably 'authentic' setting,[24] whereas Floris kept the descriptive qualities of place to a minimum. Here is, or so it seems to me, an indication of the different paths the art of history painting was to take in the Netherlands from about the 1580s: Heemskerck's elaborate environments foreshadow the wealth of detail favoured by Dutch Mannerists, while in the Southern Netherlands ambience played a decidedly less-important role.[25] There painters focused on the principal players and the mainstay of artistic inspiration remained the classical style of Raphael and Titian.

The proportionally large number of Flemish renderings of the story of Diana and Actaeon and of Diana and Callisto is surely testimony to the fame of the Venetian artist's adaptation of Ovid's accounts in the *Metamorphoses* (II, 442–496; III, 131–252). How Netherlandish artists would have known these works is not completely clear, for there is no evidence that they ever actually saw Titian's canvases or copies thereof, but would have known Cornelis Cort's engraving of *Diana and Callisto* from *c.* 1566.[26] Moreover, the role played by minor Netherlandish artists in transmitting knowledge of Italian works via drawings and copies has not yet been studied sufficiently.[27] One such artist was Gillis Coignet,[28] whose *Diana and Callisto* (Fig. 10),[29] executed before his emigration to Amsterdam in 1586, combines features from Titian's painting with figures taken

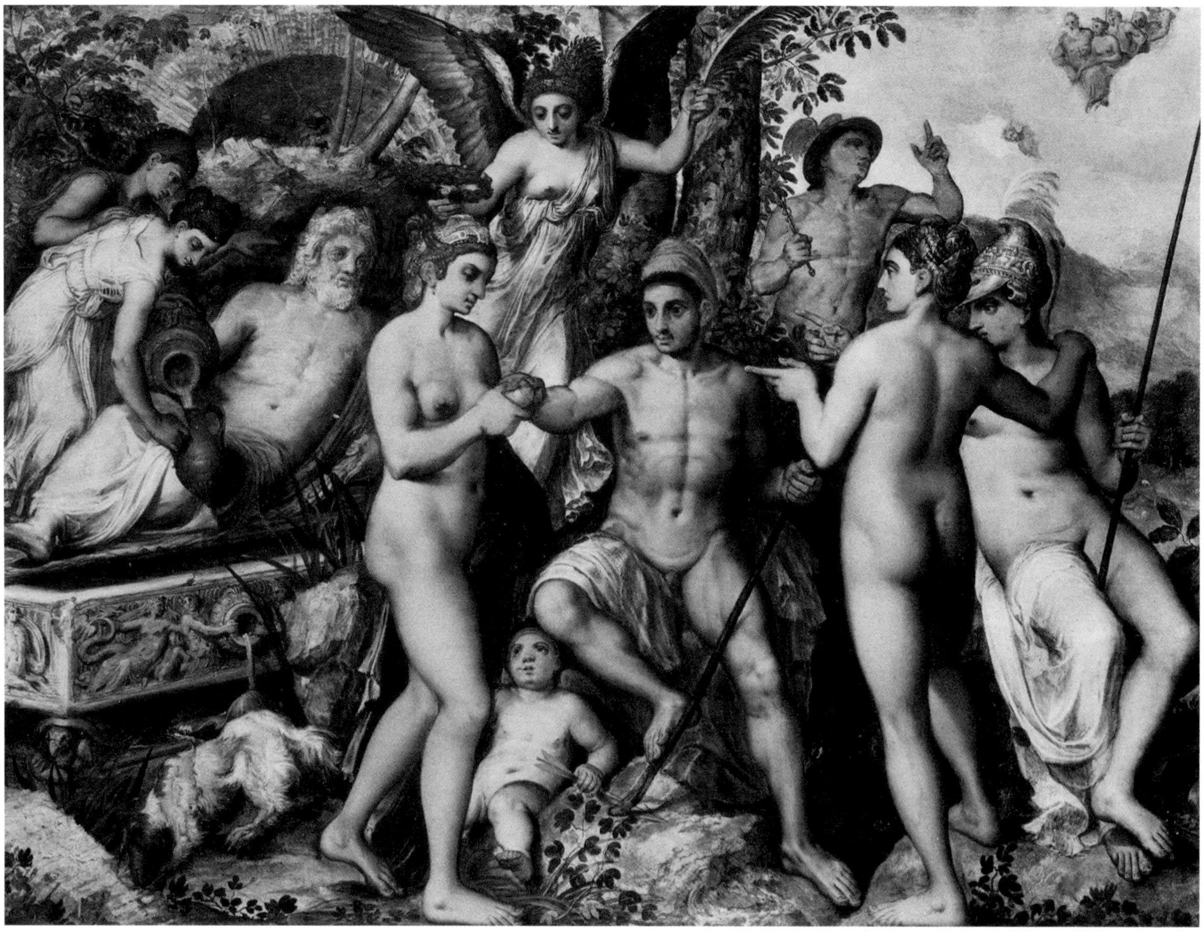

Fig. 9. Frans Floris, *Judgement of Paris*. Kassel, Staatliche Museen, Gemäldegalerie

from Marcantonio's *Judgement of Paris* after Raphael. But instead of showing the virginal and righteous Diana looking down in contempt as she bans Callisto for failing to remain chaste, Cognet paints a physically more brutal account. Bent back by the force of the callous act of revealing her pregnancy, Callisto's twisted body offers a telling contrast to Diana's luxuriant pose, one which would do justice to Venus herself. This juxtaposition, coupled with the goddess's accusing finger pointing to the nymph's exposed intimacy, serves to underline the innocent maiden's suffering at the hands of the Olympian gods: her deception and seduction by Jupiter and subsequent punishment by Diana. The physical and psychological intensity of this work is replaced in Abraham Janssens's interpretation of the myth by the desire to impart the scene with recollections of his study of ancient and contemporary sculpture.[30] Both painters, however, succeed in making Callisto the real subject of their compositions, and so encouraged the viewer to identify with the victim, or at least to reflect on the causes which led to her predicament and on the nature and justification of moralising judgements. This shift away from a single, clearly-recognisable moral message in favour of a more circumspect reading of the activities of the Olympian gods appears to be a characteristic feature of Flemish mythological painting, one which Rubens was to exploit to the full. It deviates considerably from the Italian inclination to see the actions of the ancient gods as being above reproach. It also differs from the readiness of Northern Netherlandish artists and patrons to use mythological subjects as negative *exempla*.[31]

Another painter to look to Titian's mythological works for inspiration was Maarten de Vos. As is attested to by his large œuvre, he was one of the most prolific Flemish masters of the second half of the sixteenth century, yet only two mythological paintings have survived:[32] a *Venus mourning Adonis*[33] and his signed and

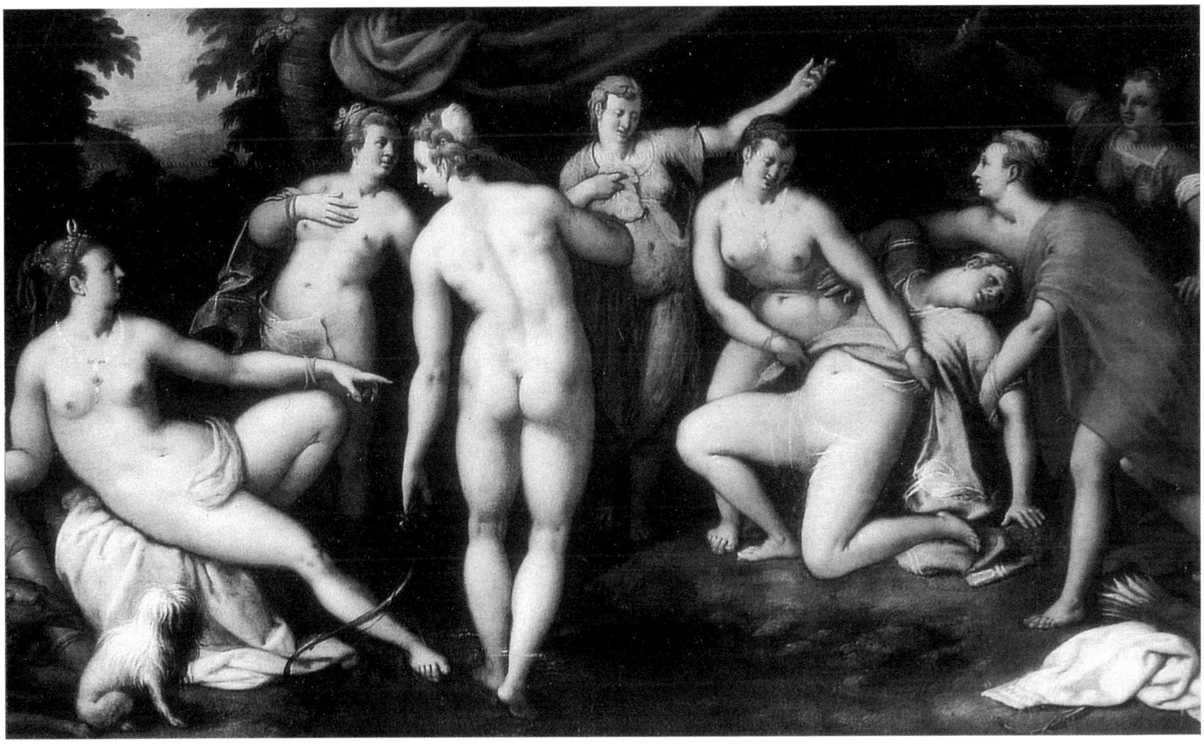

Fig. 10. Gillis Coignet, *Diana and Callisto*. Budapest, Szepmüvészeti Múzeum

dated *Abduction of Europe* (Fig. 11) of 1572.[34] Despite a number of differences, the overall compositional similarity between this latter work and Titian's painting of the same subject in Boston suggests that De Vos must have had access to a copy of some kind.[35] Both focus on Europe struggling to remain on the bull's back as he leaves the shore behind him in the distance. Instead of the atmospheric landscape of Titian, De Vos opts for a more descriptive background. His inclusion of details such as the flower garlands adorning the bull and the temple on the shore have been shown to have come from a number of different classical sources.[36] De Vos put this familiarity with ancient literature to good use in his designs for the 1602 edition of the *Metamorphoses*.[37] Given then that we know De Vos possessed both the necessary erudition and artistic inventiveness, it is surprising that mythology did not feature more prominently in his paintings. One could, of course, speculate that as a Lutheran who only converted to Catholicism after Alessandro Farnese's recapture of Antwerp in 1585, De Vos was more concerned with the didactic function of religious and allegorical art as a moralising and educational tool. Equally, the prudish dress of the goddess in his *Venus mourning Adonis* suggests a reluctance to portray female nudity – an essential ingredient of most mythological images. But neither of these aspects explain the more *risqué* subjects De Vos is said to have painted for foreign patrons, especially royal ones such as Rudolf II and Philip II. Lomazzo describes a picture belonging to Philip as showing Venus with a Satyr, and this painting, or a closely related version, may be recorded in an engraving by Raphael Sadeler of 1583 (Fig. 12).[38] The absence of a narrative context and an explicit moralising message which would justify such an erotic image is surprising in a painting by De Vos, but as a pictorial type it is by no means unique, for it belongs to the Netherlandish tradition of showing the gods within the privacy of their own bedrooms. The portrayal of the goddess engaged with a satyr can, of course, be interpreted as a general warning about the dangers of submitting to carnal desire and this, it may be assumed, was sufficient to squash any qualms Philip II might have had about displaying such titillating pictures in his collection.

Although a more detailed study of sixteenth-century patronage must be undertaken before any conclusions can be drawn, the examples

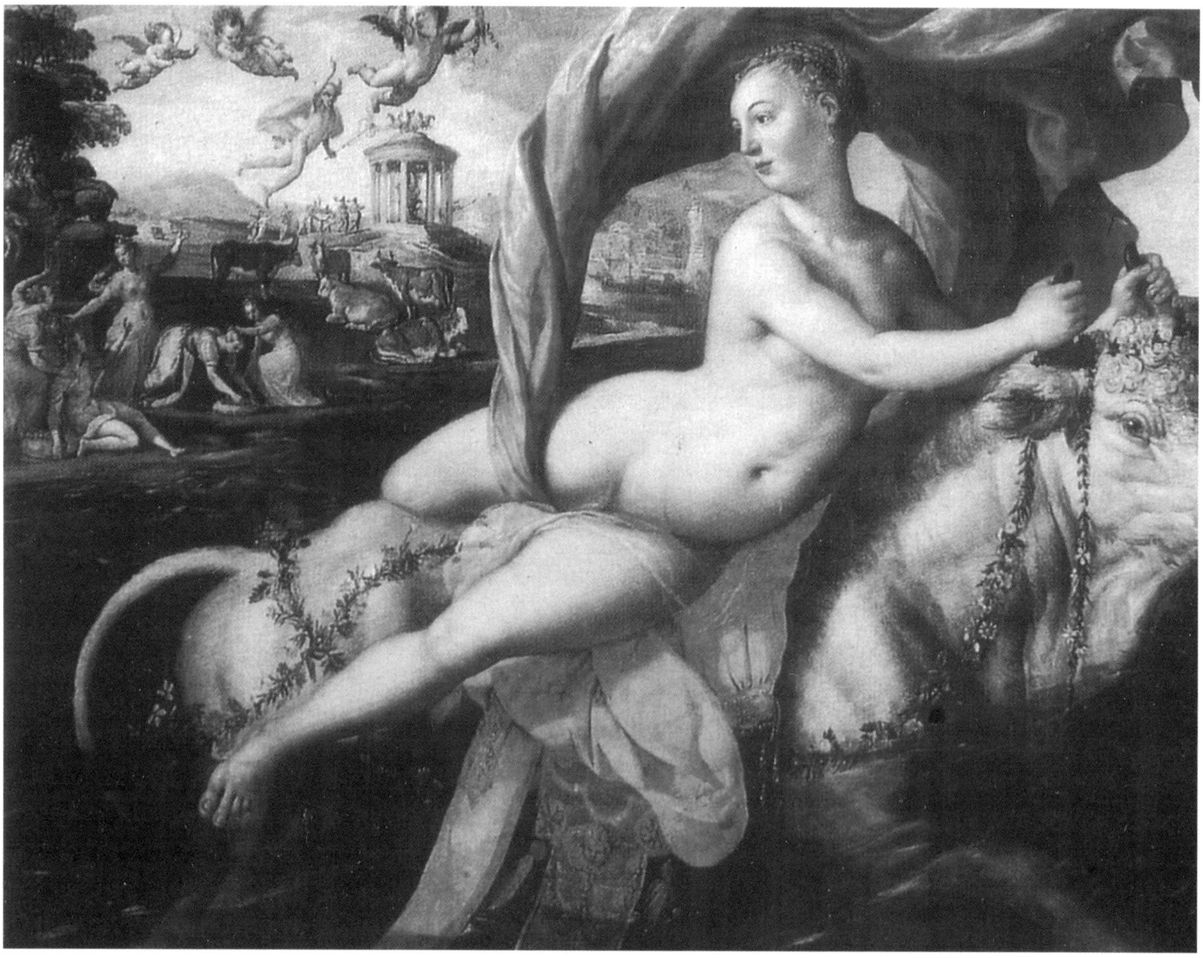

Fig. 11. Maarten de Vos, *The Abduction of Europe*. Bilbao, Museo de Bellas Artes

discussed here do suggest that Flemish artists were capable of adapting both the form and content of their artistic output to suit the very different requirements of foreign and local patrons. The apparent disinterest in sixteenth-century Flanders for paintings depicting mythological themes seems to rest with the patrons rather than the artists. On the one hand Flemish clientele appear to have been reluctant to hang images depicting the deeds of the pagan gods on their walls,[39] while on the other, judging by the frequency with which works such as the *Metamorphoses* were printed, immensely keen to purchase illustrated editions of classical texts.[40] This question is particularly interesting when we consider the situation in the Northern Netherlands from the 1580s, where the wealth of mythological paintings reflects the specific demands of patrons no longer requiring religious works. Many of those who will have purchased such paintings emigrated from Antwerp following its return to Catholicism in 1585. It is noteworthy that the artists producing these works came principally from Utrecht (Abraham Bloemaert and Joachim Wtewael) and Haarlem (Cornelis Cornelisz); of the artistic community who left Flanders, the only prominent member to paint scenes showing the classical gods was Karel van Mander, and these were principally mythological landscapes.[41] The changed religious, social and political climate obviously prompted corresponding changes in the attitude towards art and its subject-matter. With religious paintings no longer very much in demand, mythology was an obvious alternative, but only those tales of the ancient gods were selected which could be used to transport a moralistic message that reflected the religious sensibilities of Northern Netherlandish society.

With the advent of the seventeenth century and the return in 1608 of Rubens to Antwerp,

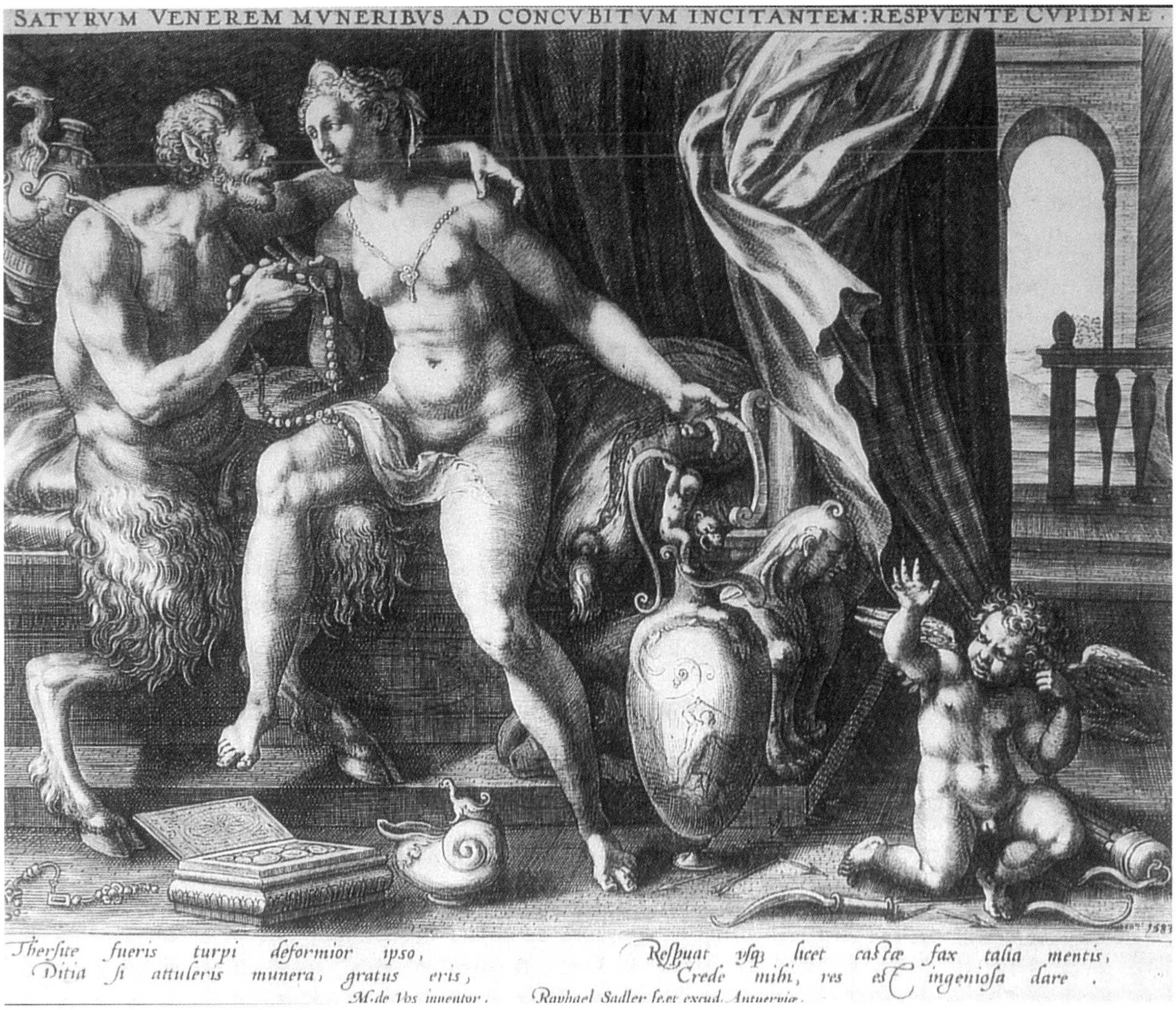

Fig. 12. Raphael Sadeler after Maarten de Vos, *Venus with a Satyr*, engraving

the stage was set for mythological painting to assume a more prominent position in Flemish art. But it was not easy to overcome the reservations which seem to have gone hand in hand with renderings of the ancient gods. The more blatant references to sexuality – and by implication morality – which characterised much of sixteenth-century mythological painting was dropped by Rubens in favour of a more sensitive portrayal of the deeds of the ancient gods as a metaphor for the frailty of human relationships. The sensuality and topicality of these works resulted in numerous commissions, most prominently the project to decorate Philip IV's hunting lodge, the Torre de la Parada, in 1636.[42] Yet even Rubens's international reputation was unable to break the behavioural patterns of Antwerp patrons. Very much the businessman, Rubens responded to the increasing demand for works of all genres by stocking paintings to sell to clients. It is nevertheless fair to assume that most of these 'off-the-peg' mythological paintings were acquired by the many foreign visitors to Antwerp, for as Nora De Poorter has pointed out,[43] neither the Archdukes nor any other Flemish art lovers were moved to commission Rubens to depict a subject from classical mythology.

Frans Floris, the most important painter of mythological subjects in sixteenth-century Flanders, was more fortunate in this respect, for he received the patronage of one of the great art collectors in Antwerp, one for whom mythology was clearly more than the depiction of the erotic. During the late 1550s and early 1560s, Nicolas Jongelinck, best known for his patronage of Pieter Bruegel the Elder,

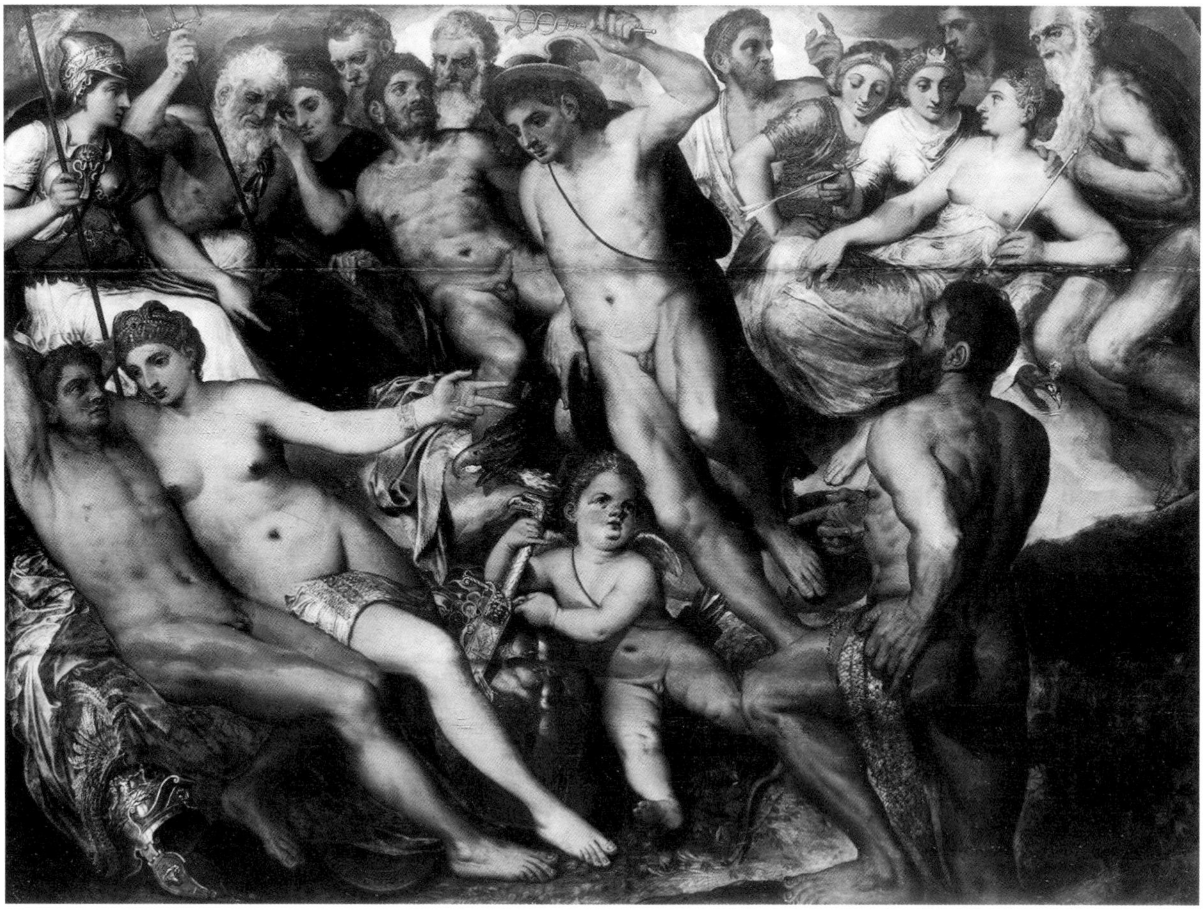

Fig. 13. Frans Floris, *Venus and Mars surprised by Vulcan*. Whereabouts unknown

acquired a number of mythological works from Floris.[44] Among these was a *Judgement of Paris*, which in style and pictorial language differs considerably from the version in Kassel (Fig. 9), executed some twelve years earlier in 1547.[45] Whereas the former isolates Paris and Venus in the background as an allusion to the isolation which the Trojan War will bring, the Kassel painting is far more concerned with Paris's role as judge. Indeed, his position and clearly-visible genitals indicate that Floris sought to make an unmistakable statement about the motivating force of sexuality.

Carnal desire and its consequences was a theme which quite obviously occupied Floris during the 1540s. In his first known depiction of *Venus and Mars surprised by Vulcan* (Fig. 13), probably painted soon after his return to Antwerp in 1547 following a six-year stay in Italy, the explicit rendering of male sexuality is just one of a number of unexpected factors.[46] Both Homer (*Odyssey*, VIII, 266–366) and Ovid (*Metamorphoses*, IV, 171–189) recount the story of how the heavens shook with laughter as Vulcan assembled the Olympian gods to witness his wife Venus caught *in flagrante delicto* with Mars by the finely-woven chains he had forged after Apollo had informed him of their liaison. Floris is indebted to both authors: Ovid mentions the presence of the goddesses, who according to Homer stayed away to spare their embarrassment. Homer alone recounts that Mercury, so prominently placed in Floris's painting, remarked he would willingly put up with such shame for the chance to sleep with Venus. There is no literary precedent for the outdoor setting, although Floris may have had knowledge of Venetian examples, such as Paris Bordone's painting of around 1545.[47] But whereas there Mars tries to protect a blushing Venus from the onslaught of Vulcan while the Olympians watch from afar, Floris's gods have descended to form an impregnable circle around the trapped lovers, who however seem rather unperturbed by such a large audience. The depiction does, of course, fit very nicely

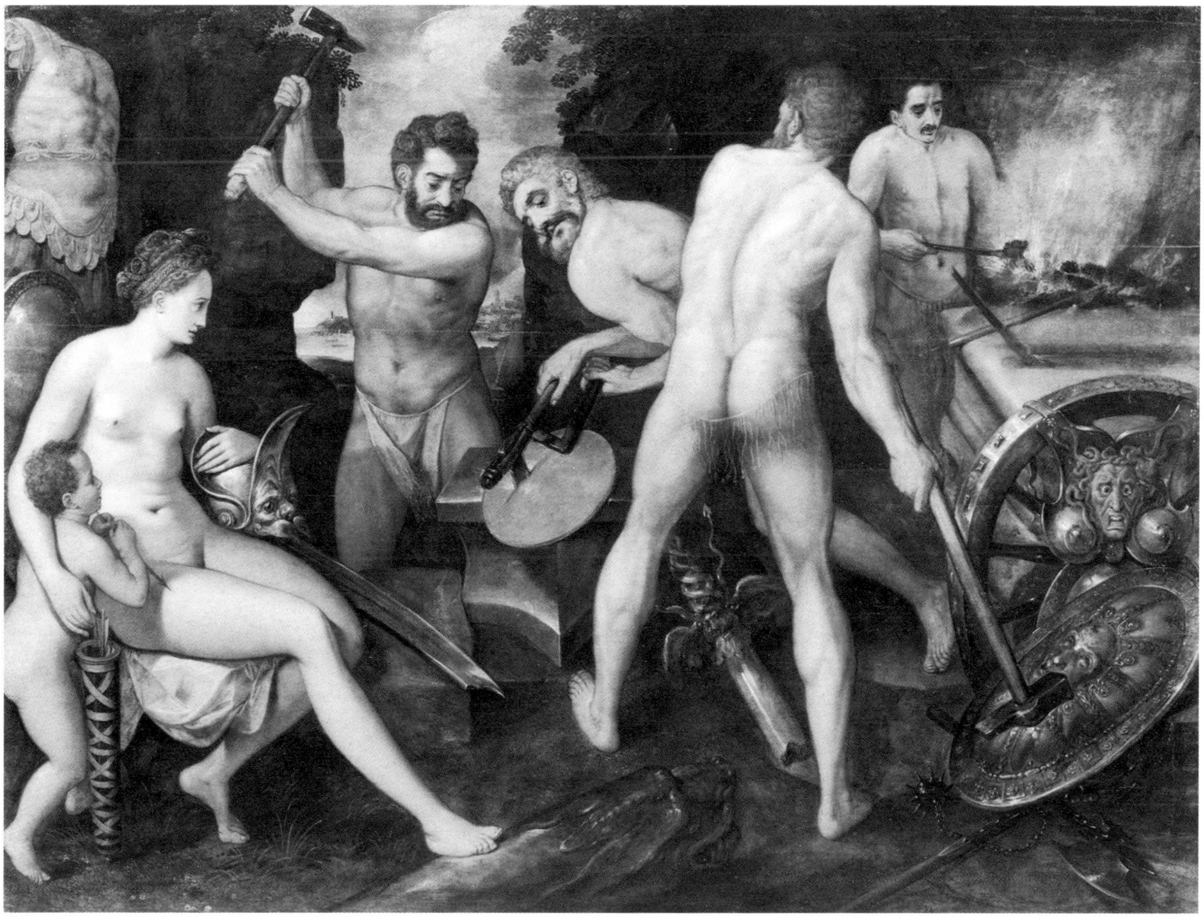

Fig. 14. Frans Floris, *The Forge of Vulcan*. Berlin, Staatliche Museen, Gemäldegalerie

into the series of bedroom trysts which apparently held singular fascination for sixteenth-century Flemish painters and patrons. But the absence of Homeric laughter suggests that Floris intended his painting to be more than simply an illustration of a raunchy story. Venus's gesture clearly identifies Vulcan as a cuckold, the husband of an unfaithful wife. He in turn seems to point towards Mars's clearly visible genitals as the centre of the desire which led him to commit adultery. Equally, the prominent position of the nude figure of Mercury could refer to his eagerness to swop places with Mars; Venus is thus caught between a real and a potential bedfellow while her husband stands accusingly opposite her. The reference to conjugal infidelity continues in the depiction of an equally nude Jupiter, whose many extra-marital affairs were a drain on Juno's resourcefulness as she sought to eliminate her many rivals. The goddess is shown on the right, being comforted by the virgin Diana, who, somewhat paradoxically, seems to be explaining the power of Cupid's arrows. The painting thus warns of the dangers to both sexes of seeking sexual gratification outside the marriage bed, and as if to emphasise the point and show that a happy marriage was not unknown among the Olympians, Floris depicts Amphritrite leaning lovingly on Neptune's shoulder; this may also have been intended as an ironic comment, for according to Homer, Neptune was the only god to urge Vulcan to release Mars. But the liaison between Mars and Venus could also be cast in a positive light, as an allegory of peace and harmony, since the god could not go to war when otherwise engaged with the goddess of love, a union which brought forth a daughter, Harmonia. Only Minerva, prominently placed behind the amorous couple, appears to notice that Cupid has laid aside his bow, as the instrument which awakes love, to draw Mars's sword, the instrument of combat, from its sheath.[48] The allusion is clear. Now that the illicit relationship is over, Mars will have nothing better to do than wage war. The message is twofold,

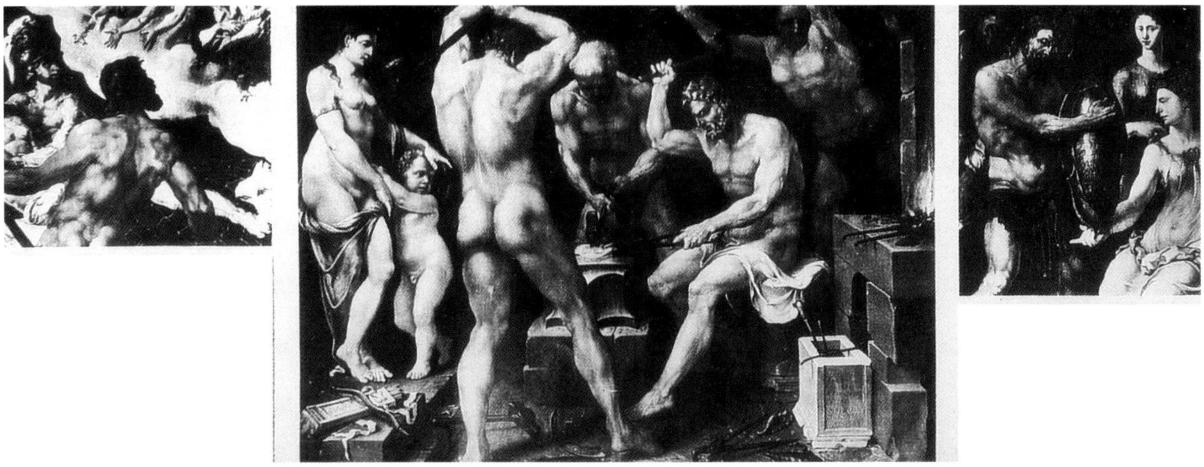

Fig. 15. Marten van Heemskerck, *Vulcan Triptych*. Reconstruction after R. Grosshans

on the one hand a moralising one which seeks to warn of the dangers of unfaithfulness, on the other an allegorical reference to the threat of war.

An unmistakable martial tone dominates Floris's *Forge of Vulcan* in Berlin from the early 1560s (Fig. 14).[49] Amid the fiercesome implements littering the floor of the forge, Venus, accompanied by Cupid, watches the blacksmith and his assistants at work. The composition resembles Heemskerck's *Forge of Vulcan* of 1536.[50] For reasons which will become clear below, this painting deserves closer inspection. Executed on canvas while Heemskerck was still in Italy, in the seventeenth century it formed the central part of a triptych which had as wings the now fragmentary panels of *Venus and Mars Surprised by Vulcan* on the left and *Vulcan Handing the Shield of Achilles to Thetis* on the right (Fig. 15).[51] While it is generally accepted that the *Forge of Vulcan* was not originally conceived as the middle section of a triptych, opinions differ as to whether Heemskerck was responsible for adding the wings.[52] It is true that triptychs with profane subject matter are very rare, but this would have hardly deterred an artist like Heemskerck, whom I suspect would have derived considerable satisfaction from the viewer's surprise upon discovering that the shutters depicting four virtues painted in *grisaille* did not, as one would automatically assume, conceal a sacred subject but instead hid from view a very profane one.[53] Through the addition of the two wings, the purely illustrative character of the central image became part of a complex programme which utilises the story of Vulcan to illustrate that those who have wronged will be punished while the charitable will be rewarded.[54] Although it can only remain a tentative suggestion, it is possible that Floris knew of the triptych and decided to render his own tripartite construction. A candidate for the left section is a panel in Sibiu showing *Venus and Mars Surprised by Vulcan* (Fig. 16), which is dated by Carl Van de Velde to the 1560s, and has an upright format, which is unusual for this subject.[55] Moreover, the measurements of both the Sibiu and Berlin panels allow for such a reconstruction. At present the Sibiu panel is exactly half the width of the Berlin panel (115,5 cm x 231 cm). Another aspect in favour of the Sibiu panel being part of a series is the choice of moment. The story is just unfolding as Mars slips his fingers under the strap holding his cloak in place while Venus lifts her shift to expose her body. Cupid, lying between the couple, fondles his mother's breast while in the background Mercury pulls aside the curtain to reveal the assembly of gods, among them Vulcan who appears to be explaining the function of the chain net in his hands. No rendering of Vulcan and Thetis is known which could serve as the right wing. But then this scene need not necessarily have been part of such a tripartite assembly since Floris might have wished to convey quite a different message; the emphasis could, for example, have been on Cupid, who assumes such a central role in the Sibiu panel and whose wings are possibly being forged in the Berlin painting.[56]

Beyond the scope of this study is the question of whether the story of Vulcan could have

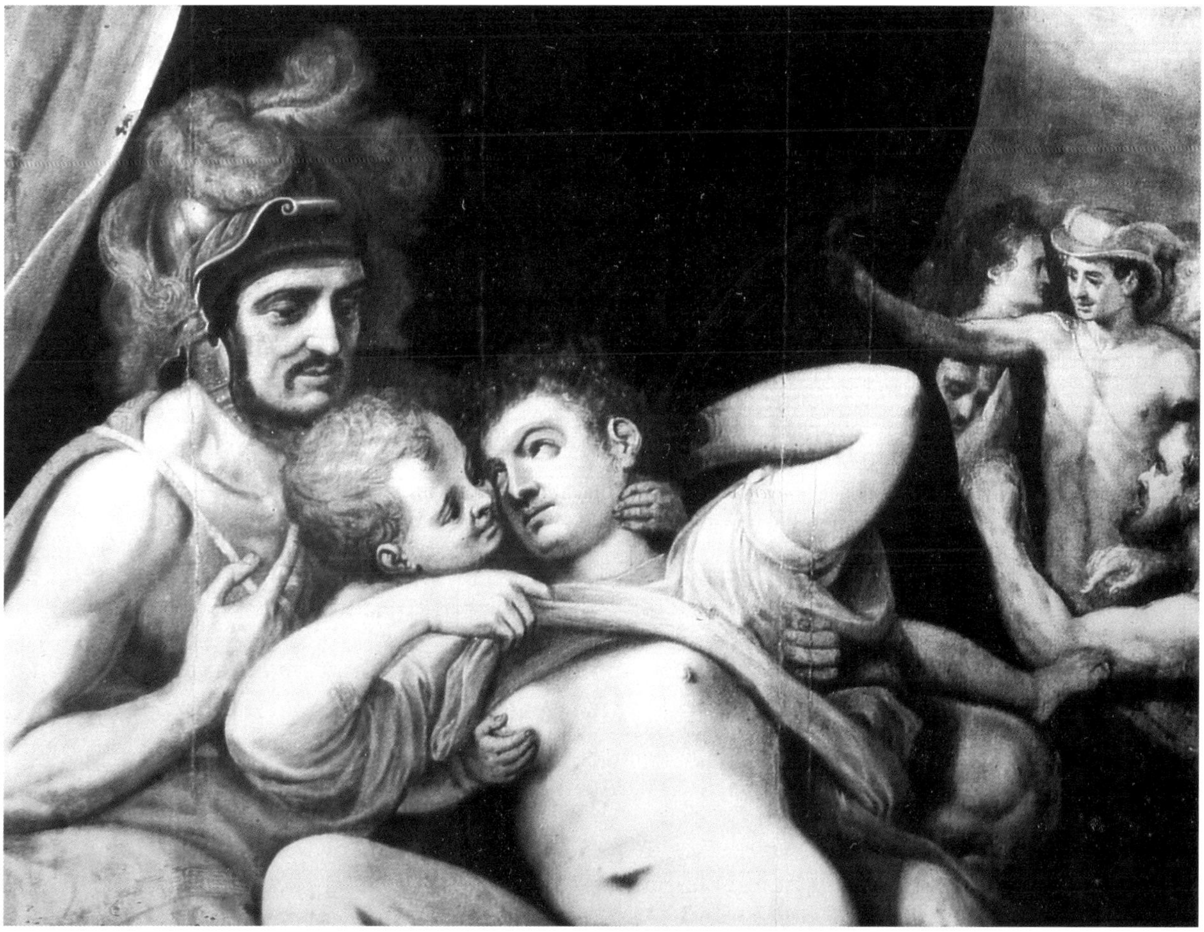

Fig. 16. Frans Floris, *Venus and Mars Surprised by Vulcan*. Sibiu, Museum Brukenthal

had a more topical meaning for sixteenth-century Netherlandish artists. It is noteworthy that interest in a god who although a mere blacksmith nevertheless produced works of outstanding artistic quality was at its highest at a time when painters were seeking to have their art recognised as a Liberal Art.[57] While sixteenth-century artists may have couched their criticism of the prevailing situation beneath the humorous-moralistic blanket of renderings of the blacksmith punishing the adulterous Venus and Mars, seventeenth-century painters showed considerably less enthusiasm for this type of moralistic condemnation, preferring instead to cast Vulcan in a more positive light by focusing on his artistic achievements.[58] At the same time, the love affair between Mars and Venus acquired a new dimension as a political allegory. Rubens in particular was instrumental in devising new iconographical forms of expression to illustrate the consequences of Mars's refusal to succumb to the temptations of Venus, of which the *Horrors of War* in Florence is undoubtedly his emotionally most powerful.[59]

Another firm favourite of Floris's was the Banquet of the Gods. This is a subject more closely associated with the art of Dutch Mannerists such as Cornelis Cornelisz van Haarlem, who around 1593 painted a large *Wedding of Peleus and Thetis* for the Prinsenhof in Haarlem.[60] As an allegory of the Golden Age, the Banquet of the Gods was particularly well suited to such an important location, since it served as an admonition to those in power that such a desirable situation is only possible in times of peace and unity. For this reason, Northern Netherlandish artists were taking nothing for granted when they chose to depict this particular wedding, for it contains a warning about the dangers of complacency. The inclusion of a visual reference to the Judgement of Paris as the starting point for the Trojan war is a continual reminder of how

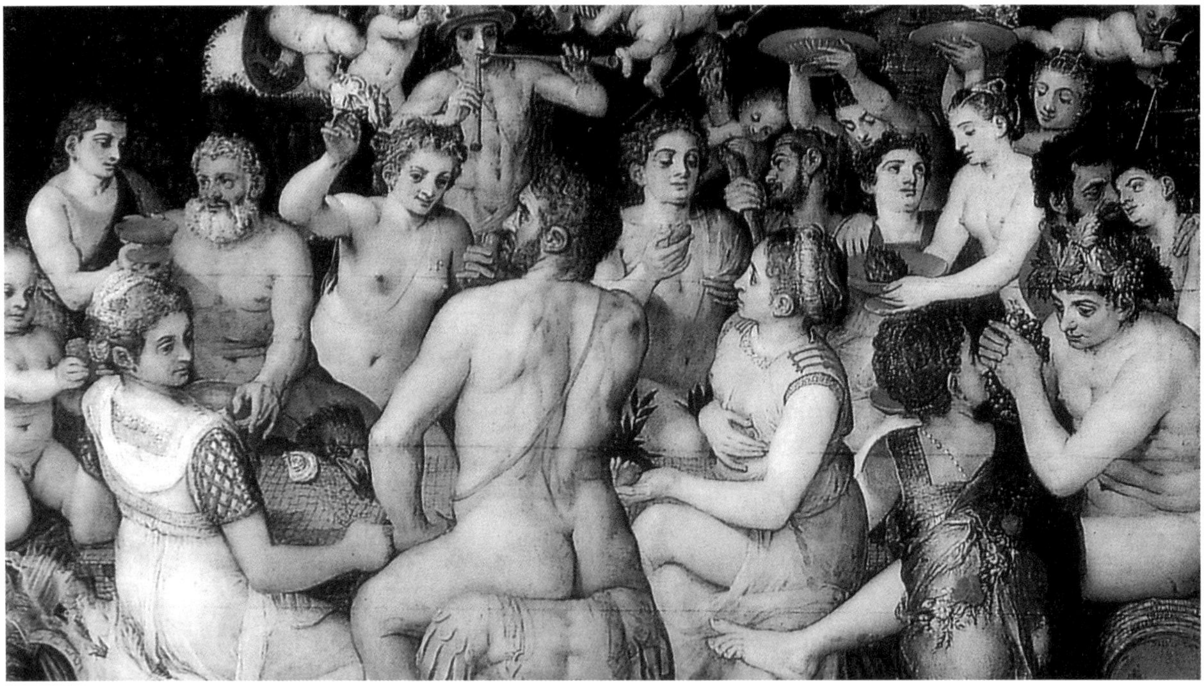

Fig. 17. Frans Floris, *Banquet of the Gods*. Antwerp, Koninklijk Museum voor Schone Kunsten

quickly peace and prosperity can give way to war and depravation; indeed, for Karel van Mander, the Wedding of Peleus and Thetis exemplified the dangers facing the state whose rulers are torn by jealousy and discord.[61]

In the light of this, it would be particularly interesting to know the appearance of the large Banquet of the Gods by Floris which is recorded as having hung in Antwerp's town hall, especially as this may be the first instance of the use of such an iconography in a civic context.[62] Unfortunately it has not survived, but on the basis of two extant versions we can conclude that although Floris probably avoided all reference to a specific celebration, he probably incorporated elements which were quite clearly intended to caution against complacency. Dominating the version of 1550 in Antwerp[63] (Fig. 17) is Mars, who, sitting on his cuirass with his back to the viewer, stares at the small bouquet of red and white flowers – the colours of Antwerp – held aloft by Flora in a manner similar to that in Jan Massys's depiction of 1559 showing the goddess against the backdrop of the city of Antwerp.[64] Is she then in Floris's painting willing Mars to remain at the banquet and so maintain the peace that is essential if Antwerp is to flourish? The desolation wrought by the god of war is evident in the barren earth beneath him, as opposed to the fertile ground of peace on either side, particularly evident in the portrayal to his right of Venus accompanied by Bacchus and Ceres as an illustration of the popular saying that love can only exist where food and wine are plentiful: *Sine Cerere et Baccho friget Venus*.[65] That Floris should have wished to so prominently emphasise the effects of war in a time when Antwerp was enjoying untold economic prosperity should not be taken as a reference to a specific military, political or economic event, but rather as a warning that, just as the Golden Age came to an end, so too must Antwerp and the Netherlands be prepared for possible upheaval. In retrospect, the painting's prophetic message does seem to suggest the presence of an underlying sense of unease in society as a whole, an unease which assumes even greater urgency in the *Banquet of the Gods* in Graz (Fig. 18), which Floris painted towards the end of the 1550s.[66] Saturn has now assumed Mars's central position, leaving the god of war free to engage in a passionate embrace with Venus. The god of time watches his fellow Olympians indulge their amorous desires with what, one feels, is increasing indignation. At the far end of the table, Amor is being feted, while the three parcae or fates to his left take up the theme of the transience of time. Time

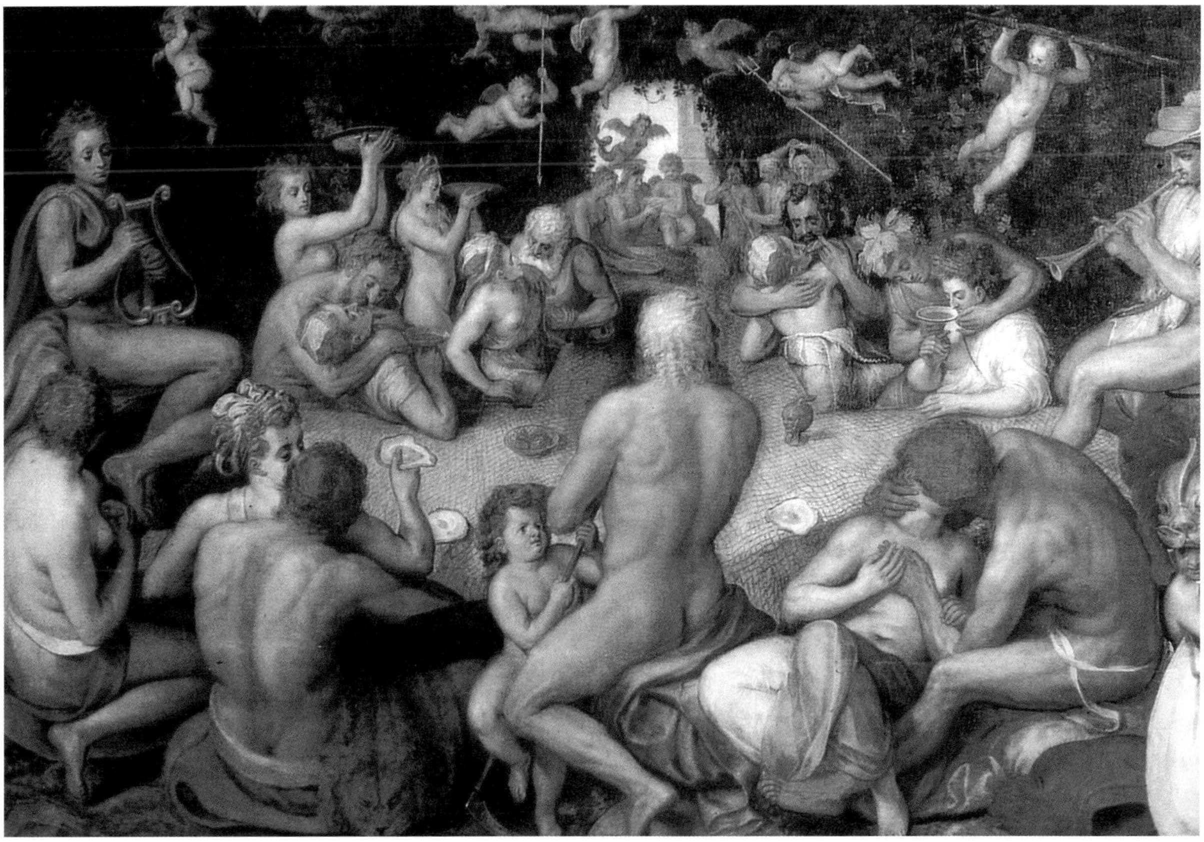

Fig. 18. Frans Floris, *Banquet of the Gods*. Graz, Landesmuseum Joanneum

is indeed here a factor, for in the distance a harpy can be seen approaching, bringing with her doom and destruction. The essence of the picture is surely found in the two playful putti, one of whom vehemently tugs at Saturn's scythe while the other dons Mars's discarded armour. Their seemingly innocent behaviour is surely to be read as symbolising for the sweep of Saturn's implement which will end the Golden Age and the resulting inevitability of war. So for all their apparent revelry, these two paintings mask a very serious and topical subject. According to Ovid (*Metamorphoses*, I, 89–112), the Golden Age, watched over by Saturn, was a period of moral integrity which existed without laws;[67] an age which, as we have seen, signifies an ideal world, but one under constant threat. What is of interest is that Floris has not just portrayed the Golden Age, but rather brings together elements belonging to subsequent Ages; the sheaves of corn are not just the attribute of Ceres but also refer to the Silver Age under Jupiter. It is therefore not surprising to find in a seemingly insignificant detail a reference to the Iron Age as the last and most destructive of the Four Ages. The Olympians are gathered around a table which in both paintings is covered with a particularly suitable tablecloth – a metal net, albeit of gold. As a fishing net it refers to the bounty of the sea, to which the abundant oysters testify. But on a more subtle level it prompts the viewer to recall Vulcan, who is not present, or at least identifiable,[68] and the net he forged to trap Venus and Mars. Here again, two readings are possible: the net alludes to the illicit affair, which in turn points to the collapse of moral standards – clearly the case in the painting in Graz. Equally, it serves as a reminder that Vulcan effectively opened the way for Mars to once again wage war when he brought to an end a love affair which guaranteed peace.[69]

As the most important painter of mythology in sixteenth-century Flanders, Floris knew how to use the ancient myths to address the delicate equilibrium that exists among the gods as a metaphor for the uncertainty of man's existence. Upon his death in 1570, the political situation in the Netherlands had changed for the worst and artistic production came almost to a standstill. Commissions for religious paintings declined dramatically, leaving history painters in a precarious economic situation. Van Mander recalls that Marcus Gheeraerts designed and etched a book of Aesop's Fables in 1566 when 'art was at a stand-still as the result of the new preachings'.[70] This atmosphere was hardly congenial for building on the achievements wrought by Floris in the sector of mythology, but it would be wrong to blame the political situation alone. The majority of history painters appear to have had no great experience in painting mythological subjects and, even more importantly, few patrons were on hand to commission such paintings. So towards the end of the century, while Antwerp sought to come to terms with its dwindling importance and to re-establish its position within the Spanish-controlled Southern Netherlands, the North was in the process of defining its new status; the pioneering atmosphere which dominated all walks of life galvanised artists into adopting new styles and pictorial themes. But the South was also to acquire a new lease of life in the early part of the seventeenth century, when Antwerp once again became a centre of artistic production and the royal courts of England, France and Spain vied with one another in obtaining the services of Rubens and Van Dyck. It comes therefore as no great surprise to find a connection between Frans Floris, as the principal sixteenth-century Flemish painter of mythologies, and Rubens, the Homer of the seventeenth century: both, for example, used mythology to express their concern with human behaviour and political instability. As Floris's, *Awakening of the Muses*,[71] and Rubens's *Peace and War*[72] demonstrate, the choice of subjects may have changed, a shift in emphasis may have occurred, but the themes of war and peace and its effect on the arts are concerns which both artists sought to express in their painting.

NOTES

My thanks to Klaus Junker, Eberhard König and Elizabeth McGrath for their suggestions and criticism. I am especially grateful to Rainald Grosshans for generously supplying photographs.

1. Madrid, Museo del Prado, canvas, 176 x 264 cm. These two paintings are, in my opinion, replicas of the originals presented to the Archdukes and recorded as having hung in Tervuren Castle and destroyed by fire in 1731. See [cat. exh.] *David Teniers, Jan Brueghel y Los Gabinetos de Pinturas*, Madrid, Museo del Prado, 1992, cat. 17; also Fiona Healy, *Peter Paul Rubens and the Judgement of Paris. A Question of Choice*, Turnhout, 1997, pp. 83–88, 83–85, pl. 4.

2. The documents do not unfortunately name the artists, nearly all of whom can however be identified on the basis of their paintings within the painting; cf. [cat. exh.] Madrid 1982 (see note 1). See Healy 1997 (see note 1), p. 188, n. 17, for the documents.

3. The paintings are as follows: on the right-hand wall: the *Judgement of Paris* and a portrait of *Charles the Bold*. On the table on the right part of a double portrait of the *Archdukes*; on the left-hand wall leading to the garden: *The Leopards with Nymphs and Satyrs*, *The Tiger, Lion and Leopard Hunt*, *Mars and Venus* and a *Bacchanal*. On these paintings and their relationship to extant or documented works, see [cat. exh.] Madrid 1982 (see note 1); also Healy 1997 (see note 1), p. 86.

4. This is best illustrated by *The Temptation of St Anthony* in Madrid, Museo del Prado, for which Joachim Patinir executed the landscape and Quentin Massys the figures; the painting is always listed under Patinir despite Massys's apparent 'higher' ranking as a painter of *historia*. For the extensive co-operation between Rubens and Jan Brueghel the Elder and the Younger, see the contribution by Christine van Mulders in this volume.

5. The analysis of the mythological works of individual painters in *catalogues raisonnés* is by the very nature of the task restricted to the literary and visual sources available to the artist rather than a more global investigation of the role of a particular subject in a particular place and time. It is only in recent years that art historians have begun a more detailed investigation of Netherlandish mythological painting, albeit one which concentrates for the most on the Northern Netherlands and on the period from the 1570s onward (see note 25). This restriction is understandable in so far as it covers the most productive time for mythological painting in the sixteenth century. It is, however, misleading, for it suggests that apart from Jan Gossaert, Marten van Heemskerck and Frans Floris, Netherlandish artists did not depict subjects from classical mythology. Moreover, it distracts from pertinent questions, such as why mythology only made isolated appearances in the Netherlands at a time when it was taking Italy by storm. Paul Philippot's *La peinture dans les anciens Pays-Bas. XVe–XVIe siècles*, Paris, 1994, is typical of the degree of attention paid to mythological painting: he illustrates three works – one by Jan Gossaert (*Neptune and Amphitrite*, Berlin) and two by Frans Floris (*Mars and Venus surprised by Vulcan*, Berlin; the *Banquet of the Sea-Gods*, Stockholm). The only author to deal exclusively with mythology is Andrée de Bosque, whose *Mythologie et Maniérisme aux Pays-Bas, 1570–1630. Peinture-Dessins*, Antwerp, 1985, provides an excellent overview of the works of individual artists and the favourite subjects of the period, but fails, for example, to address wider issues, such as why very different degrees of acceptance existed in the Northern and Southern Netherlands. The contribution of Flemish artists to the development of painting in the Northern Netherlands is the subject of a study by Jan Briels, *Vlaamse schilders in de Noordelijke Nederlanden in het begin van de Gouden Eeuw, 1585–1630*, Antwerp, 1987. But neither the different attitudes towards mythological subjects in the two parts of the Netherlands nor the issue of whether Flemish artists exerted any great influence in the area of mytholgical painting in the North is addressed.

6. Among the paintings deserving mention is Jan Sanders van Hemessen's *Judith* (Chicago, The Art Institute) of *c.* 1549/50. Instead of showing the Biblical heroine 'in action', Hemessen shows her so close to the picture plane that only the upper half of her fully-nude body is visible. She holds as identifying attributes Holofernes's head and a sword. Hemessen based his figure on a design for the goddess Juno by Benvenuto Cellini. See Burr Wallen, *Jan van Hemessen. An Antwerp Painter between Reform and Counter-Reform*, Michigan, 1893, pp. 107–108, Fig. 121 and Fig. 122 for Cellini's drawing. See also the many renderings of Susanna, Judith, Bathseba and Lot and his Daughters by Jan Massys in: Leontine Buijnsters-Smets, *Jan Massys. Een Antwerps schilder uit de zestiende eeuw*, Zwolle, 1996.

7. It remains unexplained why female nudity and mythological themes played such an important role in the decoration for Triumphal Entries but were apparently considered unworthy subjects for panel painting. However, it is questionable whether in very early accounts, such as in the *tableau vivant* showing three nude goddesses in a *Dream of Paris*, erected as part of the Triumphal Entry of Joan of Castile into Brussels in 1496 and recorded in a manuscript in Berlin (Kupferstichkabinett, inv. MS 78 D 5), the figures were actually naked or simply 'dressed' so as to appear naked; on this see Healy 1997 (see note 1), pp. 30–32 and Fig. 32 for the *Dream of Paris*. The painted decoration of the arches for the Triumphal Entry of Philip II into Antwerp in 1549 shows extensive use of mythological scenes and nudity, whereby, interestingly, no real difference can be discerned between the arches erected by the city and those by foreign groups resident in Antwerp. However, as we learn from Grapheus's description of the event, the Genoese Arch, for which Frans Floris contributed some of the designs, was adorned with scenes which seem to have been especially explicit; he refers in particular to a picture on the vault showing 'Juno between the Winds, [...] a horrible sight, with enormous members, serving pudency which we here like to have said about all others, completely nude'; see W. Kuyper, *The Triumphant Entry of Renaissance Architecture into the Netherlands: The Joyeuse Entrée of Philip of Spain into Antwerp in 1549, Renaissance and Mannerist Architecture in the Low Countries from 1530 to 1630*, Alphen aan den Rijn, 1994, pp. 49–56, 52.

8. Karel van Mander, *The Lives of the Illustrious Netherlandish and German Painters*, introduction & translation by Hessel Miedema, from the 2nd ed. of the *Schilder-boeck* (1616–1618), Doornspijk, 1994, p. 161. Van Mander's account is remarkably similar to that given by Lodovico Guicciardini in his famous description of the Netherlands: 'Il [Gossaert] quale fu il primo che portò d'Italia in questi paesi, l'arte del depingere Historie, e poesie con figure nude [...]'; cf. Lodovico Guicciardini, *Descrittione di tutti i Paesi Bassi* (Antwerp, 1567), p. 98. For a

discussion of nudity in Gossaert's work, see Larry Silver, 'Jan Gossaert and the Renaissance Nude in the Netherlands', *Nederlands Kunsthistorisch Jaarboek*, XXXVII, 1986, pp. 1–40, esp. pp. 10–19 for the mythologies.

9. Berlin, Staatliche Museen, Gemäldegalerie, panel, 188 x 124 cm. *Gemäldegalerie Berlin. 200 Meisterwerke*, Berlin, 1998, pp. 176–177. The depiction of the mythical couple is most likely to have been conceived as an allegorical tribute to Philip of Burgundy in his rank as admiral and his power over the seas. It was painted for the castle of Suytburg (Souburg, Walcheren Island); see Jozef Duverger, 'Jacopo de' Barbari en Jan Gossaert bij Filips van Burgondië te Souburg (1515)', in *Mélanges Hulin de Loo*, Brussels–Paris, 1931, pp. 142–153.

10. Birmingham, Barber Institute, panel, 36,5 x 26 cm, dated *1517* and inscribed *Hercvles* and *Dyanira*. Although not documented, it is generally thought to have been painted for Philip's residence Wijk-bij-Duurstede, south of Utrecht. See [cat. exh.] *Kunst voor de beeldenstorm. Noordnederlandse kunst 1525–1580*, Amsterdam, Rijksmuseum, 1986, cat. 1.

11. The *Ovide moralisé* gives a Christian interpretation of Ovid's tales and was first written in verse form between 1316–1328. A prose version was compiled in 1467 for René d'Anjou; see *Ovide moralisé, en prose*, ed. C. de Boer, Amsterdam, 1954. For an example of the type of moralising interpretation applied to Ovid's text, see Monika Bierschenk, 'Die Europa-Fabel in der Literatur und in bildlichen Darstellungen des Mittelalters', in [cat. exh.] *Die Verführung der Europa*, Berlin, Kunstgewerbemuseum, 1988, pp. 61–75.

12. Ovid (*Metamorphoses*, IX, 98–272) tells how Nessus, having been fatefully wounded by Hercules, drenched his shirt in his own blood and gave it to Deianira saying it had the power to rekindle the hero's love for her. After Hercules betrayed her for Iole, Deianira sent him the shirt which, however, consumed his body in flames. The prominence given the white garment on which Deianira sits suggests that it is intended as a warning about the nature of deception, since white symbolises purity and innocence.

13. This may also explain the choice of the struggle between Hermaphroditus and Salmacis (Ovid, *Metamorphoses*, IV, 288–388) as the subject for a painting today in Rotterdam (Museum Boijmans Van Beuningen, panel, 32,8 x 21,5 cm), for it addresses the conflict which arises when love is not reciprocated. The depiction of the physical struggle between the couple goes someway towards fulfilling the requirements of narration, yet the painting still retains elements of the static nature of classical sculpture. See [cat. exh.] Amsterdam 1986 (see note 10), cat. 2.

14. Berlin, Staatliche Museen, Gemäldegalerie. *Gemäldegalerie Berlin. Gesamtverzeichnis der Gemälde*, Berlin, 1986, nos. 386, 387; for Caraglio's engravings, which are after designs from the *Loves of the Gods* by Perino del Vaga, see *The Illustrated Bartsch*, XXVIII, p. 88, no. 11 and p. 98, no. 21.

15. Berlin, art dealer B. Lohse, 1938, panel, 85 x 69 cm. Max J. Friedländer, *Early Netherlandish Painting*, Leiden–Brussels, 1972, IX, 1, p. 133, Fig. c 18. Examples by Sallaert include a painting in Cremona (de Bosque 1985 [see note 5], p. 60) and one in the gallery in Schleissheim. The paintings in Cremona and Berlin most closely resemble a composition by Leonardo which is recorded in a copy in the collection of the Earl of Pembroke, Wilton House, Salisbury; see [cat. exh.] *Leonardo da Vinci, artist, scientist, inventor*, London, Hayward Gallery, 1989, p. 38, Fig. 31. The composition gives a more discreet portrayal of the union between Leda and Jupiter than that in the painting which was in Fontainebleu until the seventeenth century and which is recorded in an engraving by Cornelis Bos. Cornelis van Cleve could have seen this painting when he was at the court of François Ier, probably from 1528–1535. He omits almost all landscape background and simply uses the swan as an attribute rather than as an integral part of the story. The *Leda* in Schleissheim shows that Sallaert generally prefers a more opulent landscape background. Common to both artists is the inclusion of two or, more usually, three children, presumably a reference to the offspring of the union: the twins Castor and Pollux and Helen of Troy.

16. Gossaert's *Hermaphroditus and Salmacis* (see note 13) is an interesting case in point. It is thought that Philip of Burgundy presented it to his niece Margaret of Austria (†1530), who was probably familiar with the subject. However, the inventory taken in 1523 of her possessions in Mechlin lists the painting as 'ung beau tableau auquel est painct ung homme et une femme nuz, estant les pieds en l'eaue; [...]'. This suggests the author was unfamiliar with the subject, which may even have been given in the inscription which decorated the original frame.

17. Berlin, Staatliche Museen, Gemäldegalerie, panel, 73 x 52 cm. Another example of the same subject is in Paris (private collection), while a painting in Helsingør (Kronborg Castle) depicts Minerva standing with her back to the viewer and accompanied by a putto. Her Medusa shield and other pieces of armour identify her as the goddess of war while the soldiers and women in the background allude to military conflict. Justus Müller Hofstede, 'Jacques de Backer. Ein Vertreter der florentinisch-römischen Maniera in Antwerpen', *Wallraf-Richartz-Jahrbuch*, XXXV, 1973, pp. 227–260, 245–247, figs. 17–19.

18. Meiningen, Staatliche Museen, Schloß Elisabethenburg, canvas, 145 x 188 cm. Eckhard Leuschner, 'Ein unbekanntes Hauptwerk von Jacob de Backer in Meiningen', *Jaarboek Koninklijk Museum voor Schone Kunsten Antwerpen*, 1994, pp. 51–63, Fig. 1.

19. Leuschner 1994 (see note 18) argues that as the goddess's colouring differs from that of the mask, Helen is present only in the mask. However, given the implied relationship between the couple, a more abstract reading of the situation is called for.

20. (1) London, private collection, canvas, 179 x 210 cm, *c.* 1604–1605; (2) Copenhagen, Statens Museum for Kunst, canvas, 150 x 190 cm. Justus Müller Hofstede, 'Abraham Janssens. Zur Problematik des flämischen Caravaggismus', *Jahrbuch der Berliner Museen*, XIII, 1971, pp. 208–303, 232–233, 247, figs. 9 (London), 19 (Copenhagen). See also [cat. exh.] *Von Bruegel bis Rubens. Das goldene Jahrhundert der flämischen Malerei*, Cologne (Wallraf-Richartz-Museum)–Antwerp (Museum voor Schone Kunsten)–Vienna (Kunsthistorisches Museum) 1992–1993, cat. 38.1 (Copenhagen, colour repro.).

21. See, for example, the painting by Pieter Coecke van Aelst (Paris, Musée du Louvre) showing Paris dressed as a medieval knight rather than as a shepherd. A discussion of the pictorial tradition north and south of the Alps in: Healy 1997 (see note 1), pp. 9–45.

22. The Hague, Mauritshuis, panel, 10 x 15,5 cm, dated *1532*. Healy 1997 (see note 1), p. 36, Fig. 39.

23. Kassel, Staatliche Museen, Gemäldegalerie, panel, 120 x 159,5 cm. Carl Van de Velde, *Frans Floris (1519/20–1570). Leven en Werken*, Brussels, 1975, cat. 6, Fig. 4; [cat. exh.] *Fiamminghi a Roma. 1508–1608*, Brussels (Palais des Beaux-Arts)–Rome (Palazzo delle Esposizioni) 1995, colour repro. p. 25. See Healy 1997 (see note 1), pp. 37–40, for a discussion of paintings of the Judgement of Paris by Heemskerck and Floris.

24. Examples include the *Triumph of Bacchus* (Vienna, Kunsthistorisches Museum, panel, 56,3 x 106,5 cm) of *c.* 1537 and the *Meeting of the Gods* (Rotterdam, Boymans-van Beuningen, panel, 55,7 x 98 cm) of 1556; see Rainald Grosshans, *Maerten van Heemskerck. Die Gemälde*, Berlin, 1980, cat. 24, pl. III, figs. 27, 83, 116.

25. The Dutch Mannerists eschewed the references to the art and architecture of the ancients which so characterise Heemskerck's depictions in favour of a Northern European forest setting, a fact which may go someway towards explaining the predominance of myths which take place outdoors. As has been shown by Eric Jan Sluijter in his excellent study of mythological painting in the Northern Netherlands from 1590–1670, these were: the two scenes of Diana with Actaeon and Callisto, the Judgement of Paris, the Banquet of the Gods, Venus and Adonis, and Vertumnus and Pomona. Eric Jan Sluijter, *De 'Heydensche Fabulen' in de Noordnederlandse Schilderkunst, circa 1590–1670*, The Hague, 1986. For a brief comparison of paintings of the Judgement of Paris by Dutch Mannerists and Flemish artists, see Healy 1997 (see note 1), pp. 40–43.

26. Harold E. Wethey, *The Paintings of Titian*, III, *The Mythological and Historical Paintings*, London, 1975, cat. 9–11 and pl. 216 for the engraving by Cornelis Cort.

27. In 1573 the Antwerp painter Bernaert de Rijckere executed a *Diana and Actaeon* which, although reversed, in the rendering of Actaeon and his dog suggests at the very least indirect knowledge of Titian. But whereas Titian uses a single fleeting moment to 'tell' the story – the surprise of all concerned at the unexpected confrontation – Rijckere relies on the more old-fashioned descriptive tradition of showing Actaeon already sprouting horns as he comes upon the goddess and her nymphs; a feature found in Netherlandish paintings until well into the seventeenth century. On Rijckere's painting (Vienna, Kunsthistorisches Museum, panel, 124 x 168 cm), see Detlev Kreidl, 'Zur Bestimmung des Wiener Diana and Aktäon-Bildes als Werk des Bernaert de Rijckere', *Oud Holland*, XCIII, 1979, pp. 47–51, Fig. 3.

28. Cognet (or Coignet) was born in Antwerp around 1540, spent 8 years in Italy and was back in Antwerp by 1579 at the latest when Cornelis van Haarlem is recorded as working in his studio. Cognet emigrated to Amsterdam in 1586, and then moved to Hamburg, where he died in 1599. His œuvre contains a number of copies and adaptations of Titian's mythological paintings, including a signed and dated *Venus and Cupid* of 1579 in Kassel (Staatliche Museen, Gemäldegalerie, panel, 139 x 96 cm). Also a *Mars and Venus* of 1590 (whereabouts unknown) and a *Danae* (whereabouts unknown), see Briels 1987 (see note 5), figs. 67, 68.

29. Budapest, Szepmüvészeti Múzeum, canvas, 103 x 175 cm. [cat. exh.] Brussels–Rome 1995 (see note 23), pp. 159–161, colour repro.

30. Budapest, Szepmüvészeti Múzeum, panel, 91 x 140 cm, signed: *A. Jansenio. A.o. 1601*. Executed together with Paul Bril while both were in Italy, the figure of Callisto is derived from Michelangelo's *Notte* in the Medici Chapel in Florence, that of the nymph to Diana's right from the ancient statue of the *Spinario*. On the painting, see Müller Hofstede 1971 (see note 20), pp. 227–230, Fig. 5; [cat. exh.] Brussels–Rome 1995 (see note 23), colour repro. p. 39.

31. See in particular Sluijter 1986 (see note 25), who compares the visual evidence with literary texts, in particular Karel van Mander's commentary on the *Metamorphoses*: *Wtleggingh op den Metamorphosis* (1604). The œuvre of Giles Cognet (see note 28) may give an indication of how Netherlandish artists changed their interpretation of mythological subject matter depending on whether they were working in the Catholic South or Protestant North. Although the problem of dating Cognet's paintings is not inconsiderable, he does appear to have adopted a clearly different approach to mythology following his departure from Antwerp in 1586. His *Danae* and *Diana and Callisto* were almost certainly painted earlier, whereas his *Mars and Venus* of 1590 post-dates this event. Based on one of Titian's favourite themes, *Venus with an Organist* or with a *Luteplayer*, Cognet has demonstratively transformed the erotic rendezvous into an encounter between two modestly dressed gods, who as they wine and dine are oblivious to the brutality of war taking place in the background behind them. This painting can surely be seen as a moralising generalisation on the effects of war, but perhaps also as a direct criticism of Spanish rule and the blindness of the King to the suffering of the Netherlandish people. Such an association may have been promulgated because Titian's *Venus and Cupid with an Organist* (Madrid, Museo del Prado) was in the Brussels residence of Antoine Perrenot Granvelle, Archbishop of Mechlin and later Cardinal. On Titian's paintings of this subject, see Wethey 1975 (see note 26) cat. 45–50; on Granvelle as a collector, see Claudia Banz, *Höfisches Mäzenatentum in Brüssel: Kardinal Antoine Perrenot Granvelle und die Erzherzöge Albrecht und Isabella*, manuscript, Ph.D. Thesis, Freie Universität Berlin, 1996.

32. Armin Zweite, *Marten de Vos als Maler. Ein Beitrag zur Geschichte der Antwerpener Malerei in der zweiten Hälfte des 16. Jahrhunderts*, Berlin, 1980. Of the 114 catalogue entries, only two can be said to fall into the category of mythological narratives as opposed to allegories such as *Hercules at the Crossroads* (London, private collection) and *Apollo and the Muses* (Brussels, Musées Royaux des Beaux-Arts), which draw on mythological figures.

33. Blois, Musée Château de Blois, panel, 86 x 120 cm; Zweite 1980 (see note 32), cat. 44, Fig. 54, considers it mostly the work of studio hands and dates it to the middle of the 1570s.

34. Bilbao, Museo de Bellas Artes, panel, 135 x 173 cm, signed and dated: *1572. Fecit Merten de Vos*. Zweite 1980 (see note 32) cat. 46, Fig. 55; also [cat. exh.] Brussels–Rome 1995 (see note 23), p. 30, colour repro. (reversed!).

35. Boston, Isabella Stewart Gardner Museum, canvas, 178 x 205 cm. The picture was shipped to Spain in 1562 and no (known) copies or engravings appear to have been made before Rubens's copy of 1628/1629 (Madrid, Museo del Prado). On these two paintings, see [cat. exh.] *Titian and Rubens. Power, Politics and Style*, Boston, Isabella Stewart Gardner Museum, 1998. For the myth in illustrated editions of Ovid's *Metamorphoses*, see Barbara Mundt, 'Illustrationen zu Ovid', in [cat. exh.] Berlin 1988 (see note 11), pp. 108–114. Typical of depictions prior to Titian is the view from the shore to the sea.

36. B.H.M. Mutsaers, 'Literaire Bronnen voor Maarten de Vos' Ontvoering van Europa', in *Album Discipulorum Prof. Dr. J. G. van Gelder*, Utrecht, 1963, pp. 63–66. Mutsaers has shown that in addition to Ovid, de Vos also knew Lucian, *Dialogi Marini*, XV, for the putti holding torches; Nigidius Figulus (LXXXX), for the temple and rivergod, and Moschos, *Europa*, 33–34, 37–38, 129–130.

37. The seven illustrations were engraved by Crispijn de Passe I. See *Hollsteins's Dutch & Flemish Etchings, Engravings and Woodcuts. 1450–1700*, XLIV, pp. 258–259, nos. 1568–1574.

38. Hollstein (see note 37), p. 164, no. 1292. The engraving may, however, only render a variation of the picture for Philip as the inscription reads *M.d. Vos inventor* and not *pinxit* as is usual if the engraving follows a painting. Crispijn de Passe's engraving after de Vos's *Venus, Bacchus and Ceres* bears the inscription *Martin de Vos pinxit* (Hollstein [see note 37], p. 165, no. 1293), but no corresponding painting is known. Lomazzo (*Idea del Tempio della Pittura*, Milan, 1590, p. 162) describes Philip's painting as follows: 'Venere ignuda, sopra un letto che ride vendendosi comparir auanti un Satiro con molti tesori a donarli per acquistar la gratia di lei. E quiuí e anco un Cupido che piange scorgendo il brutto desiderio di questo et la lascivia grande di quella che per acquistare tesori a ciascun si sottopone.'; see Zweite 1980 (see note 32), pp. 334f.

39. There are, of course, important exceptions, mainly among members of the nobility, such as Charles de Croy, Duke of

Aarschot. The inventory drawn up following his death on April 24, 1613 lists 15 lots by Floris, of which 9 are of mythological subjects. Humanists, in particular those who had spent some time in Italy, also counted among those more open to rendering of the pagan gods. For the house of Hieronymus van Busleyden in Mechlin, Jan Gossaert and Jacopo de Barbari executed frescoes, including a *Banquet of Tantalus* featuring a nude Venus with Cupid; see H. de Vocht, *Jerôme de Busleyden. Founder of the Louvain Collegium Trilingue, his life and writings*, Turnhout, 1950, pp. 50–68, Fig. p. 57.

40. M.D. Henkel, 'Illustrierte Ausgaben von Ovids Metamorphosen im XV., XVI. und XVII. Jahrhundert', *Vorträge der Bibliothek Warburg 1926–1927*, Berlin–Leipzig, 1930, pp. 59–144, esp. p. 61 for the earliest printed edition of the *Metamorphoses* containing illustrations which was published by Colard Mansion in Bruges in 1484. For sixteenth-century illustrated editions of Ovid, see esp. pp. 72–95, which includes a discussion of the profound influence of Bernard Salomon's woodcuts of 1557.

41. On Van Mander and in particular the affinity between landscape and history, see Walter S. Melion, *Shaping the Netherlandish Canon. Karel van Mander's 'Schilder-Boeck'*, Chicago–London, 1991. On Flemish painters in the Northern Netherlands, see Briels 1987 (see note 5).

42. Svetlana Alpers, *The Decoration of the Torre de la Parada*, Corpus Rubenianum Ludwig Burchard, IX, Brussels, 1971.

43. Nora De Poorter, 'Von Olympischen Göttern, Homerischen Helden und einem Antwerpener Apelles', in [cat. exh.] Cologne–Antwerp–Vienna 1992–1993 (see note 20), pp. 121–132, 123.

44. In addition to an *Awakening of the Muses* (see below note 71) and a *Banquet of the Sea-Gods* (see below note 69), Jongelinck also commissioned a series of 10 paintings illustrating the *Labours of Hercules*, of which only the *Hercules and Antaeus* (Brussels, private collection) has survived; all are, however, recorded in engravings by Cornelis Cort; see Van de Velde 1975 (see note 23), cat. 69–78; *Idem*, 'The Labours of Hercules, a lost series of paintings by Frans Floris', *Burlington Magazine*, CVII, 1965, pp. 114–123.

45. Although undocumented, it is generally accepted that this is the painting today in St Petersburg (Hermitage, panel, 134,5 x 188 cm); see Van de Velde 1975 (see note 23), cat. 119, Fig. 57; Healy 1997 (see note 1), Fig. 45.

46. Whereabouts unknown, panel, 150 x 198 cm, signed and dated: *1547 FF.I. V.* See Van de Velde 1975 (see note 23), cat. 2, Fig. 2. The subject was painted by Floris and his studio on a number of occasions. Examples other than those discussed here include: a large *Vulcan's Forge* (lost, canvas, *c.* 300 x 560 cm) executed for the Genoese Triumphal Arch as part of the Triumphal Entry of Philip II into Antwerp in 1549, see Van de Velde 1975, cat. 24; also Kuyper 1994 (see note 7). The 1613 inventory of the possessions of Charles de Croy, Duke of Aarschot, lists two paintings: no. 79 '[...] sur thoille, de vij pied demy de hault et vj de large, [...] représentant Mars, Vénsu et Cupido couchés ensambles, les aultres dieux les regardans [...]', no. 83 '[...] sur bois, d'environ xj pied de longueur et vij pied demy de halteur, [...] contenant la représentation de Mars et Vénus, couché par ensamble, tous les aultres dieux les regardans et prenans au filet [...]'; see Van de Velde 1975 (doc. 108, p. 493), who points out, that no. 79 cannot be identical with the fragment of a painting in Sibiu (see below note 85, Fig. 16) showing a scene similar to that described in the inventory since both support and size differ.

47. Berlin, Staatliche Museen, Gemäldegalerie. G. Canova, *Paris Bordon* (Venice, 1963), pp. 39–43.

48. Showing putti playing with armour is a common motif in renderings of Mars and Venus, one which Jan L. de Jong in his study of Italian examples ('Ovidian Fantasies. Pictorial Variations on the Story of Mars, Venus and Vulcan', *Die Rezeption der Metamorphosen*, eds. H. Walter, H.-J. Horn [Berlin, 1995], pp. 161–171) sees as a way of introducing a lighthearted, comic element. While Netherlandish artists were undoubtedly aware of such a use and indeed applied it on occasions, they also recognised its potential as a carrier of a more serious message.

49. Berlin, Staatliche Museen, Gemäldegalerie, panel, 170 x 231 cm. Van de Velde 1975 (see note 23), cat. 134, Fig. 68.

50. Prague, Národní Galerie, canvas, 166,5 x 207 cm, dated *1536*. The painting was engraved by Cornelis Bos in 1546. See Grosshans 1980 (see note 24), cat. 21, figs. 22 and 147 for the engraving; Ilja M. Veldman, *Maarten van Heemskerck and Dutch humanism in the sixteenth century*, Maarssen, 1977, pp. 21–42, 21–34, figs. 4, 5; [cat. exh.] Brussels–Rome 1995 (see note 23), pp. 218–219, colour repro. p. 219.

51. Vienna, Kunsthistorisches Museum, panel, 96,5 x 99 cm. The first mention of the triptych was made in a letter written before November 13, 1669 by the Antwerp art dealer Gilliam Forchoudt to his sons in Vienna. See Veldman 1977 (see note 50), pp. 34–42, esp. pp. 36–37 for the correspondence, figs. 1–3; Grosshans 1980 (see note 24), cat. 22–23, figs. 24–26; de Bosque 1985 (see note 5), pp. 162–163 for colour repros.

52. Cf. the arguments put forward by Grosshans 1980 (see note 24, p. 121) that Heemskerck himself assembled the triptych and those given by Veldman 1977 (see note 50) against this proposal. Too much importance cannot be given to the fact that the central panel is on canvas whereas the wings are on panel, especially as the central section was painted in Italy.

53. The personifications of *Prudence and Justice* grace the outer left wing, while the outer right probably depicted the virtues *Charity and Temperance*; see Grosshans 1980 (see note 24), p. 122, Fig. 25. Veldman 1977 (see note 50), pp. 38–39, Fig. 3, reproduces all four paintings to scale, presumably to illustrate the difference in the size of the figures. This is not however conclusive evidence that Heemskerck would not have added the wings himself, given that one must allow for stylistic development, while it is not infrequent to find that the figures on the wings of triptychs vary somewhat in scale from those on the central panel. For profane triptychs, see Veldman 1977, p. 38, n. 82. Another tripartite construction which deserves mention here is Hendrick Goltzius's *Mercury, Hercules and Cacus, Minerva* (Haarlem, Frans Halsmuseum), even though it is again unclear if Goltzius was responsible for assembling the three panels; see [cat. exh.] *Dawn of the Golden Age. Northern Netherlandish Art. 1580–1620*, Amsterdam, Rijksmuseum, 1993–1994, cat. 216; [cat. exh.] *Pegasus und die Künste*, Hamburg, Kunsthalle, 1993, p. 87 (colour repros. of side panels).

54. Veldman 1977 (see note 50), pp. 37–42, gives a detailed account of the iconography and interpretation of the three scenes related to Vulcan and their relationship to the Cardinal Virtues on the outer wings.

55. Sibiu, Museum Brukenthal, panel, 93 x 115,5 cm. The fragmentary state of this panel, Floris's second known rendering of this subject, makes it more difficult to interpret. Again a reading of the painting as an allegory of peace is permissible. Yet Floris gives greater prominence to the humorous side of the story by revealing to the viewer that the lovemaking of the couple will soon be dramatically interrupted as Vulcan's chain falls upon them. The picture is discussed by Van de Velde 1975 (see note 23), cat. 133, Fig. 67, who argues convincingly that originally the panel most probably had an upright format. He further notes that the pose of Venus and Cupid is captured in a drawing bearing the name *FFloris* and included in Frans Francken the Younger's *Collector's Cabinet* (Antwerp, Rubenshuis; *ibid.* Fig. 318).

56. The present title of the painting is *Vulcan Forging Arms for Aeneas*. But since the object on the anvil is unidentifiable and Cupid clearly has no wings, it may be that they are in the process of being made by Vulcan.

57. The situation for Netherlandish artists, who were forced to conform to the rules and regulations of a guild system which recognised their art only as a mechanical process and not as a liberal art which relies on a high degree of theoretical and intellectual input, is discussed by Zirka Zaremba Filipczak, *Picturing Art in Antwerp. 1500–1700*, Princeton, 1987. She focuses on subjects which directly address the status of painters, such as St Luke painting the Madonna in the sixteenth century and *Kunstcamer* paintings in the seventeenth. Probably the most forthright artistic expression of the demands of painters is the programme devised by Floris for the decoration of the façade of his house, for which see *ibid.*, pp. 35–39; also Catherine King, 'Artes Liberales and the mural decoration on the house of Frans Floris, Antwerp, *c.* 1565', *Zeitschrift für Kunstgeschichte*, LIX, 1989, pp. 239–256. It has been suggested that Velázquez may have intended such an association in his *Forge of Vulcan* (Madrid, Museo del Prado) because of his knowledge of the *Fabulas* of the mythographer *Juan Pérez de Moya*, see John F. Moffitt, 'Velázquez's "Forge of Vulcan". The Cuckold, the Poets, and the Painter', *Pantheon*, 41 (1983), pp. 322–326.

58. Rubens depicted Vulcan handing Thetis the shield for Achilles as one of the scenes in his *Life of Achilles* tapestry series; see Egbert Haverkamp-Begemann, *The Life of Achilles*, Corpus Rubenianum Ludwig Burchard, X, London, 1975, cat. 4. The artist also depicted the blacksmith alone in his forge in a painting for the Torre de la Parada for Philip IV; see Alpers 1971 (see note 42), cat. 60. Rubens's only *Venus in Vulcan's Forge* (Brussels, Musées Royaux des Beaux-Arts) was originally a depiction of *Sine Cerere et Baccho friget Venus* before the artist cut off the section showing an old woman with glowing coals (now Dresden, Gemäldegalerie Alte Meister) and in her place added the forge; see Konrad Renger, 'Sine Cerere et Baccho friget Venus', *Gentse Bijdragen tot de Kunstgeschiedenis*, XXIV, 1976–1978, pp. 190–203, Fig. 1 for a copy (The Hague, Mauritshuis) after the original painting.

59. Florence, Palazzo Pitti, canvas, 206 x 342 cm. Reinhold Baumstark, 'Ikonographische Studien zu Rubens Kriegs- und Friedensallegorien', *Aachener Kunstblätter*, XLIV, 1974, pp. 125–234, 189–201.

60. Haarlem, Frans Halsmuseum, canvas, 246 x 419 cm; see [cat. exh.] Amsterdam 1993–1994 (see note 53), pp. 19–20, Fig. 8. Of paramount importance for this and other examples was Hendrick Goltzius's engraving (1587) of the *Wedding of Cupid and Psyche* after the drawing by Bartholomeus Spranger which Van Mander brought back to Haarlem; *Ibid*, cat. 1 (Spranger), 2 (Goltzius). For a discussion of both Dutch and Flemish depictions of the Banquet of the Gods, see Eva-Marina Froitzheim-Hegger, *Sie lebten dahin sorglos in behaglicher Ruhe. Studien zum niederländischen und flämischen Göttermahl*, Hildesheim, 1993, esp. pp. 110–114 for Cornelis Cornelisz's painting.

61. Any interpretation depended, of course, on one's individual perspective. Yet the inclusion in many such paintings of the Judgement of Paris, which began at the wedding of Peleus and Thetis when Eris threw the apple among the guests in revenge for not having been invited, clearly alludes to the negative conclusion of the feast and the ensuing Trojan war. Van Mander in particular drew on the precarious nature of the celebrations to warn of the dangers of strife among rulers who place personal gain above common good; see Sluijter 1986 (see note 25), pp. 198–210.

62. A document of October 1, 1571, lists 'een groot stuck schilderye genaempt convivium deorum' by Floris, while another dated December 12, 1571, mentions a Banquet of the Gods in the large state room of the Town Hall, 'het stuck dat opde groote staetcame staet van Mr. Franchoys Floris, het bancket van de goeyen'; see Van de Velde 1975 (see note 23), p. 469, docs. 72, 73.

63. Antwerp, Koninklijk Museum voor Schone Kunsten, panel 150 x 198 cm, signed and dated: *FF. IV. ET. F. 1550.* Van de Velde 1975 (see note 23), cat. 34, Fig. 5; see also [cat. exh.] *Antwerp, story of a metropolis. 16th–17th century*, Antwerp, Hessenhuis, p. 116, Fig. 72.

64. Hamburg, Kunsthalle, panel, 114 x 113 cm, signed and dated: *IOANNIS MASSIIS 1559.* Leontine Buijnsters-Smets 1996 (see note 6), cat. 34. The interpretation of this picture is disputed, one theory being that it is a portrait of a courtesan. However, given the depiction of a statue of Brabo with the arms of Antwerp and the panorama of the city itself, I believe it more probable that here Massys alludes to the prosperity of Antwerp. In addition to the red and white carnations Flora also holds a yellow one; I have been unable to discover if this has a symbolic meaning. In 1561 Massys executed a second version, this time with Genoa in the background (Stockholm, National Museum, panel, 130 x 156 cm); *Ibid.*, cat. 35. Except for a diaphanous veil, Flora is now completely nude, and this has given rise to the question of whether Flora or Venus is depicted. Either way, the more modest rendering of Flora in the painting depicting Antwerp may be an indication that it was intended for a local patron while the uninhibited nudity of her counterpart was perhaps considered to be more in keeping with the expectations of a foreign patron.

65. See Renger 1976–1978 (see note 58).

66. Graz, Landesmuseum Joanneum, panel, 116,5 x 161,5 cm, signed: *FF IV ET FA.*, *c.* 1558–1560. Van de Velde 1975 (see note 23), cat. 116, Fig. 54; also [cat. exh.] Cologne–Antwerp–Vienna 1992–1993 (see note 20), cat. 2.2 (colour repro.).

67. Although difficult to substantiate, one wonder's whether here might not be a subtle reference to Spain's uncompromising rule of the Netherlands and the necessity of the Netherlandish people to adhere to the laws imposed by foreign rulers.

68. Since no particular feast is depicted, Floris may have taken inspiration from numerous pictorial and literary sources, including Apuleius, who in his *Metamorphoses* or *The Golden Ass* (VI, 24) states that Vulcan was responsible for the catering; this could have been taken to mean the god was not actually among the guests at the wedding of Psyche and Cupid.

69. The desire to infuse a seemingly innocent scene with a serious message may also apply to a *Banquet of the Sea-Gods*, which, as Carl Van de Velde has convincingly suggested, was probably painted for Nicholas Jongelinck. In addition to the four couples and the multitude of sea creatures frolicking in the water, Floris shows the forlorn figure of a woman gazing longingly out to sea, and opposite her a male figure whose recumbent pose and oar suggest he might be a river god, even though he does not have, as is usual, a beard. Their prominence suggests they may be the clue to a deeper meaning of the painting, but one that hinges on their identification, and this may prove impossible. On the painting in Stockholm (Nationalmuseum, panel, 126 x 226 cm, signed and dated: *FF IV.ET FA 1561*), see Van de Velde 1975 (see note 23), cat. 137, Fig. 71; also Froitzheim-Hegger 1993 (see note 60), pp. 55–56. For a brief account of Jongelinck's life, see Van de Velde 1975 (see note 23), pp. 114–117; on river-gods, see Elizabeth McGrath, 'River-Gods, Sources and the Mystery of the Nile. Rubens' "Four Rivers" in Vienna', in *Die Malerei Antwerpens – Gattungen, Meister, Wirkungen. Studien zur flämischen Kunst des 16. und 17. Jahrhunderts*, Internationales Kolloquium Wien 1993 (Cologne, 1994), pp. 73–82.

70. See David Freedberg, *Iconoclasm and Painting in the Revolt of the Netherlands 1566–1609*, Ph.D. Thesis, University of Oxford 1972 (New York–London, 1978), p. 192, n. 71. Freedberg (*ibid.*, p. 193, n. 72) also cites an archival entry for 9 January, 1567 which quotes the reasons given by the painter Jacob Gheens when he left Antwerp: 'not because of any debts or ill-deeds, but simply in order to earn a living for himself and his wife, seeing that his aforesaid craft and trade had largely come to a halt'.

71. Ponce, Museo de Arte, canvas, 157 x 238 cm, signed: *FF IV ET FA*. Van de Velde 1975 (see note 23), cat. 120, Fig. 58.

72. London, National Gallery, canvas, 189 x 297 cm. Baumstark 1974 (see note 59), pp. 152–162.

Confraternity and Art in the St Jacob's Church, Antwerp: A Case Study of the Altar of the Brotherhood of St Rochus

Jeffrey M. Muller

In this paper I present the altar of the brotherhood of St Rochus as one example taken from a larger study of art in the St Jacob's Church at Antwerp during the Counter Reformation.[1] St Jacob's is unique among all the churches which proclaimed Antwerp the triumphant cultural and artistic center of resurgent Catholicism in the South Netherlands. It alone survives with art intact and archives complete to document the history of two centuries. St Jacob's was a complex institution with many interacting parts. First and foremost, it was a parish church, invested with twenty-one private chapels flanking the aisles and ringing the ambulatory. From 1656 St Jacob's was home as well to a collegiate chapter of canons, and during the seventeenth and eighteenth centuries a score of brotherhoods affiliated themselves with the church. Works of art provided the focus of devotion and the core of group identity for each corporate body in St Jacob's. Nevertheless, the many paintings and sculptures by Antwerp's finest artists were positioned carefully to respect the communal and unified character of the church's interior, as if a preordained order maintained harmony among the different groups which shared the space. The example I have chosen demonstrates in dramatic fashion that this image of concord sometimes covered over a history of conflict and crisis.

Between 1657 and 1660 the chapel of St Rochus in St Jacob's was decorated with a new altar and altarpiece (see figs. 1–3). A brotherhood dedicated to St Rochus was founded in the same chapel on 12 August 1658.[2] If the thesis I will argue is correct, then it can be said that the magnificent new white marble altar frame and the alabaster image of St Rochus attributed to the sculptor Artus Quellinus the Elder (Fig. 4) and the altarpiece painted by the sculptor's brother, Erasmus Quellinus the Younger (Fig. 5), were at the center of several historical events which resulted in the foundation of the brotherhood and then shaped its distinctive character.[3]

On 14 September 1657 the churchwardens of the St Jacob's Church petitioned the burgomaster of Antwerp.[4] They requested that the burgomaster forbid the masters of the chapel of St Rochus in their church from carrying out plans to decorate the chapel with a new altar which was to be paid for at the expense of the city (gemeijnte) and without due consent of the churchwardens. If the chapel masters built their altar, it would be to the detriment of the church and in contempt of the churchwardens whom the burgomaster had appointed. According to the churchwardens, the chapel masters were only being perverse. They knew very well that leading members of the parish were willing to pay out of their own pocket for a beautiful new marble altar and other costly ornaments in honor of St Rochus and in the interest of the community. And, said the churchwardens reassuringly, this gift would come with no strings attached. St Rochus's chapel would still belong to the community and the chapel masters would continue to exercise their proper function.

Antwerp's burgomaster immediately acted in favor of this request. He ordered the masters of the St Rochus Chapel and the sculptor they hired – Jan van den Cruyce – to cease and desist from building their altar.[5] A few days later, on 28 Sept. 1657, the churchwardens of St Jacob's signed an agreement with the rich donor – Jonker Alexander Balthasar Roelants – accepting his gift of a new altar.[6] Consequently, in place of Jan van den Cruyce it is likely that Artus Quellinus the Elder carved the beautiful altar of white marble, crowned by an image of St Rochus as pilgrim (Fig. 4). The altarpiece, signed and dated to 1660 by Erasmus Quellinus, alludes to a sequence of episodes from the legend of the saint (Fig. 5). Infected

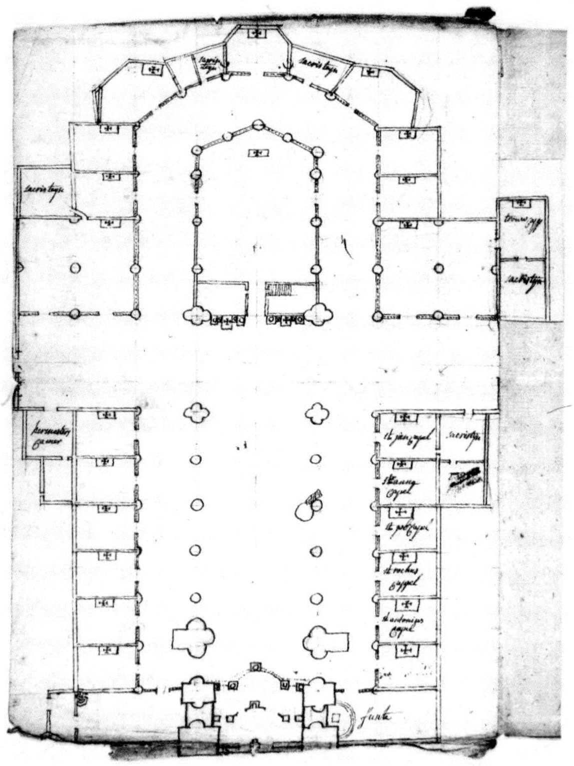

Fig. 1. *Plan of the St Jacob's Church, Antwerp*, eighteenth century. Stadsarchief, Antwerp, K 318. The St Rochus Chapel is clearly marked, the third chapel from the West entrance, flanking the South aisle, on the right in the *Plan*.

with plague, St Rochus hid in the forest where he was fed miraculously by a dog who carried bread to him, and we see the dog with the loaf resting at the saint's feet, one of the holy man's constant attributes. At a later moment an angel announced to St Rochus that god has heard his prayer and cured him of the plague, and in Quellinus's picture we see two angels, one who gives comfort and the second who tends to the afflicted man's sores. Finally, one of the cherubic angels in the clouds above holds a jar of unguent identified by its inscription as 'Treacle of Heaven' [Theriaca Coelestis] and another displays the message sent by god in answer to St Rochus's dying prayer. Written in gold it promises: you will be patron in time of plague [eris in peste patronus].[7]

Despite the reassurances of the churchwardens, actual control of the St Rochus Chapel changed hands between 1657 when the churchwardens requested the burgomaster's intervention and 1660 when Erasmus Quellinus finished his altarpiece. First, in the agreement of 28 Sept. 1657, the churchwardens of St Jacob's granted to Roelants, the donor of the altarpiece, exclusive burial rights in the chapel for himself and his family. Second, they also appointed Roelants as superintendent [hooftman] of the chapel, thus eliminating the chapel masters who had wished to refuse Roelant's gift.[8] Third, in place of the chapel masters a new brotherhood dedicated to St Rochus was erected in the chapel on 12 August 1658, by authority of Ambrosius Capello, bishop of Antwerp.[9] Although the bishop did not explicitly name Roelants as superintendent of the new brotherhood in 1658, Capello later used his authority to confirm in an edict of 19 May 1673, that Roelants was superintendent and patron of both the chapel and brotherhood of St Rochus.[10] Capello set as another condition for founding the brotherhood in 1658, that the bishop always would choose one of the directors of the brotherhood from among the canons of the new collegiate chapter of canons established in St Jacob's only two years earlier in 1656, thus imposing direct episcopal supervision.[11]

My thesis in this paper is that the whole series of events – from burgomaster's intervention, the agreement between Roelants and the churchwardens, elimination of the chapel masters, and foundation of the brotherhood, to completion of the decoration – occurred because during the 1650s the St Rochus Chapel had become a flash-point where several lines of crisis converged and were mediated in the altar decoration and the conflicts that surrounded it.

The clash of interests fought over the new altar in 1657 can best be understood as a symptom of crisis by setting it in contrast with the normal and peaceful development that preceded, during which the St Rochus Chapel fitted easily into the larger history of Counter Reformation institutions, devotions, and art in Antwerp.

After the Catholic conquest of Antwerp in 1585 the St Rochus Chapel was relatively neglected until the mid-seventeenth century. From excerpts made by J. van den Nieuwenhuizen of records in the account books of St Jacob's dealing with expenses for construction and ornament of the church it is possible to conclude that between 1585 and the 1640s most available money was put

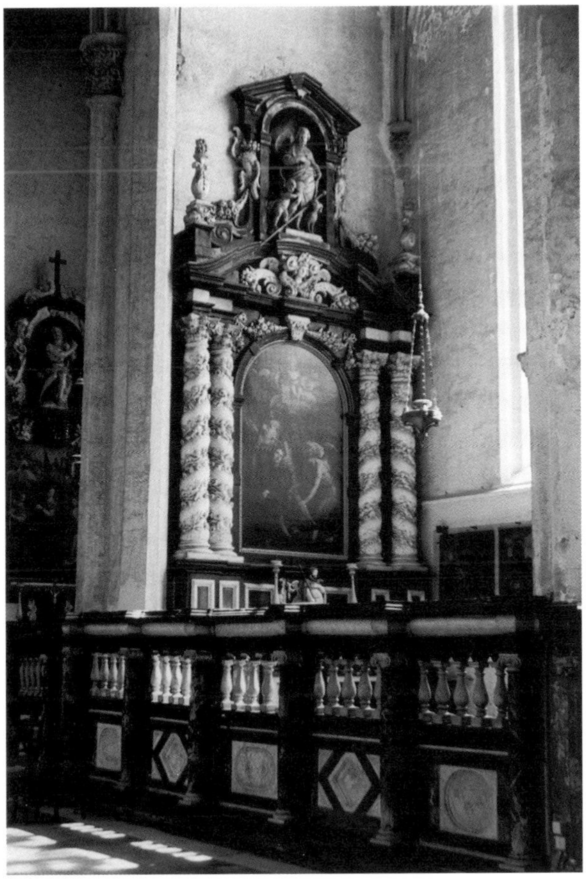

Fig. 2. View of the St Rochus Chapel in St Jacob's Church, Antwerp, from the West looking South East. Marble frame and alabaster image of St Rochus, attributed to Artus Quellinus the Elder, 1658–1660. Altarpiece of St Rochus by Erasmus Quellinus the Younger, 1660

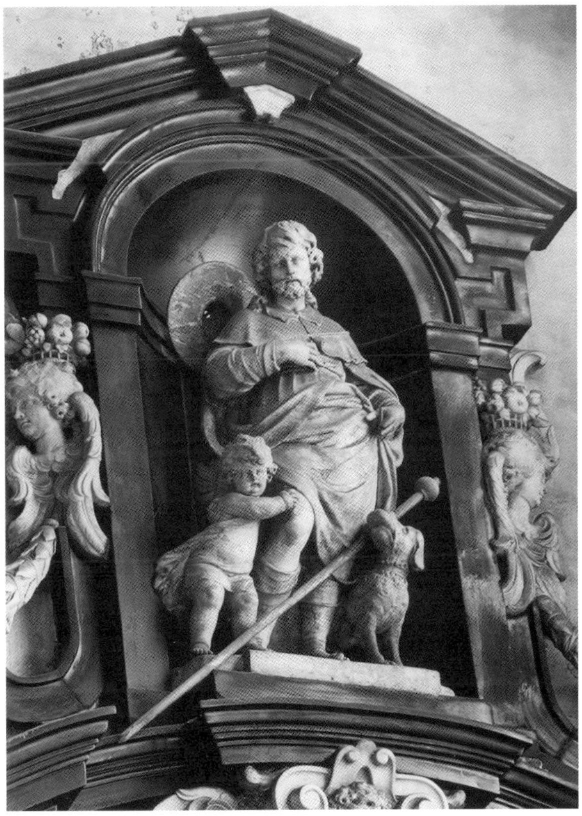

Fig. 3. Attributed to Artus Quellinus the Elder, *St Rochus as Pilgrim*, 1658–1660, alabaster. Antwerp, St Jacob's Church, St Rochus Chapel

towards completion of the choir vault and the nave, decoration of the main altar, construction of the major chapels dedicated to the Eucharist and the Virgin Mary on either side of the main altar, and construction of the ambulatory chapels radiating around the choir (Fig. 1). During this time the St Rochus Chapel was not separately incorporated, and the single expense recorded was payment to a mason in 1607 for repair of the window frames.[12]

Only in July of 1648 did the very active pastor of St Jacob's, Franciscus van den Bossche, renew the account book and appoint chapel masters to revive the St Rochus Chapel as an active institution within his church.[13] Van den Bossche already had put great effort into raising money for completion of the building and attracting new constituents. In 1643 he was instrumental in founding the Archconfraternity of the Holy Trinity in St Jacob's and now in 1648 he turned his attention to fostering devotion to St Rochus.[14] In general Van den Bossche's efforts contributed to the broad shift of emphasis around mid-century away from churches of the regular orders which had led the vanguard of resurgent Catholicism, to the parish churches which the Council of Trent always had designated as the building block of the solid new edifice to be constructed.[15] Van den Bossche chose the new masters of the St Rochus Chapel from a cohesive social group. All whose positions can be identified belonged to the solid middle class of professionals, skilled artisans, and merchants: Aegidius de Witte, dean of the Schoolmasters's Guild; Herman Nesscher, dean of the Bakers's Guild; Jan van den Cruyce, master sculptor in the St Lucas Guild; and, in 1657, Herman Neskens, tailor and silk merchant living in the Paddegracht.[16] Certainly it was no coincidence that in August 1648, the same month he accepted the position of chapel master, the sculptor Jan van den Cruyce signed a contract with his fellow chapel

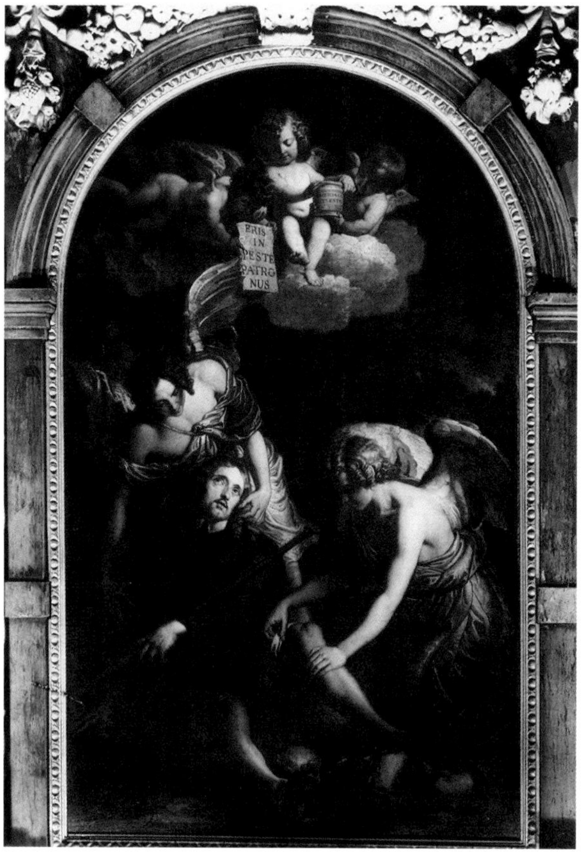

Fig. 4. Erasmus Quellinus the Younger, *St Rochus Cured by Angels*, 1660. Antwerp, St Jacob's Church, St Rochus Chapel

masters and witnessed by Pastor Van den Bossche in which he agreed to make the balustrade or enclosure (tuin) of the chapel for the price of 700 fl. (figs. 2 and 6).[17] Van den Cruyce was to provide all the material – a cornice of blue stone, a frieze of white marble, architrave of blue stone, balusters of white marble, and so on – and to pattern it after the measurements of the balustrade already enclosing the Holy Cross Chapel in St Jacob's. Construction of the enclosure thus exemplified the communal process in which different groups within the church agreed on materials and artist, and cited a precedent within the church, to insure uniformity of measure and style along with subtle and pleasing variety in color. Within the larger Gothic frame of St Jacob's a delicate Ionic order was used to enclose the chapels on a human scale, and the architectural terms used in the contract – cornice, frieze, architrave – indicate a vocabulary derived from the rules of ancient architecture and shared in common by artist, pastor, and patrons – knowledge Cornelis de Bie would try to teach his readers thirteen years later in 1661 in *Het Gulden Cabinet* by means of a catchy verse:[18]

With architrave, cornice, frieze, base, and pedestal
And then add the capital, there you have it all.

After construction of the blue and white enclosure no further work was undertaken in the St Rochus Chapel until 1657 at which time the conflict flared up over plans for a new altar. The proposal of the chapel masters which once again involved Jan van den Cruyce as sculptor, the counter-proposal submitted by the churchwardens, appointment of Jonker Roelants as superintendent and patron of the chapel, the founding of the new brotherhood of St Rochus in 1658, and completion of the altar by Artus and Erasmus Quellinus, all responded first to the immediate crisis of plague.

Marie Juliette Marinus has shown, through a graph of expenditures by the city of Antwerp to care for victims of the plague, that after a calm during the 1640s, the black death raged again in 1652–1653, grew even more virulent during 1655–1656, and claimed a large number of victims in 1658.[19]

Two of the documents concerned with the St Rochus Chapel state explicitly that the new administration, decoration, and brotherhood of the chapel all were motivated by fear of the plague. When, on 28 September 1657, the churchwardens overruled the chapel masters and accepted Roelant's gift of a new altar, they did nevertheless set a number of conditions:[20] 'All services of mass and confession shall continue as previously, because St Rochus is a patron of the plague, where many people have taken their refuge by paying for private masses and lighting candles on ordinary Sundays and feast days as a comfort to the whole community [using the term "gemeijnte" to indicate a city-wide devotion, rather than one based exclusively in the parish], so that the chapel must remain accessible as is true for the other chapels in the nave of St Jacob's, to which end a key to the chapel will be kept in the church for use of the whole community [gemeijnte].' This passage teaches us a great deal about the customs of devotion in the chapel, and explains why a confessional was listed in the inventory of the chapel made by the French Republic on 17 February, 1798.[21] St Rochus was, after all, a confessor saint as well.

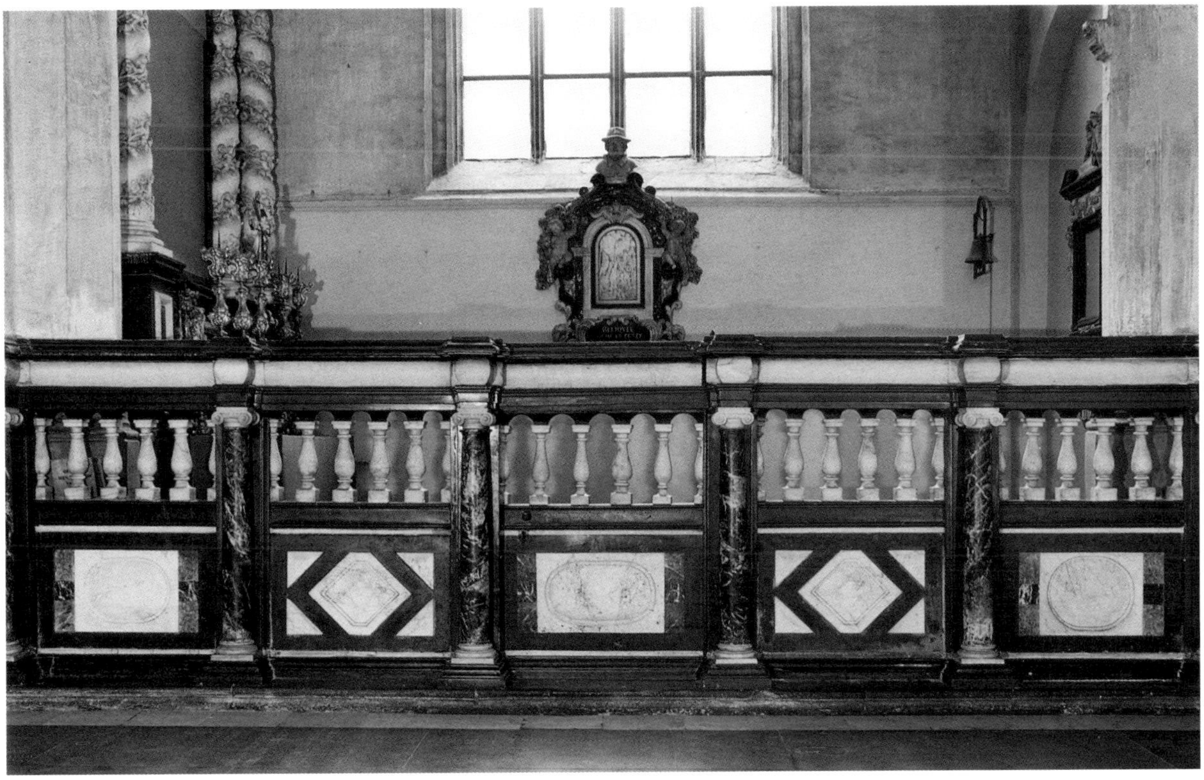

Fig. 5. Jan van den Cruyce, Enclosure Balustrade, 1648, white marble and blue stone. Antwerp, St Jacob's Church, St Rochus Chapel

Ambrosius Capello was even more emphatic in his letter of 12 August 1658 authorizing the establishment of the brotherhood of St Rochus. God in his unfathomable goodness is moved to justified anger by the many sins of humankind and punishes with various scourges even those whom he loves, so that he may convert them and embrace them in his mercy. For this reason Christians in need throughout the ages have taken refuge in god's mercy and the intercession of his saints. St Rochus, because he himself had been infected and helped many others smitten with the black death, was to be invoked as a special patron in time of plague. And since god has seen fit to visit Antwerp and its environs with plague during this and recent years, the bishop has granted the request of several devout Christians who want to found a brotherhood attached to the altar of St Rochus in the St Jacob's Church.[22]

While the crisis of plague is enough in itself to explain the sudden eagerness to decorate the chapel and to found a brotherhood in honor of St Rochus, the outbreak of plague explains neither the conflict fought over the decoration nor the distinctive character of the brotherhood as it took shape in 1658. These new developments were rooted in a second area of crisis which troubled Antwerp during the late 1650s – the decline of the city's economy and the impact of this decline on church finances.[23]

In 1661 the churchwardens of St Jacob's petitioned the old aldermen, superintendents of the citizenry [porterijen], and 'good men' of the guilds – the different members in the Brede Raad ['Broad' Council] of the city government.[24] The churchwardens asked the Brede Raad to restore the annual subvention of 400 fl. which the city of Antwerp had paid to the church for twenty-nine years, between 1624 and 1653. By 1661 St Jacob's was in dire straits. The church was unable to pay the interest on debts incurred during the construction of the choir and ambulatory chapels which had cost more than 100,000 fl. and was dependent on the community for contributions which, because of the hard times, diminished day by day. The shortage of operating funds was so serious that two years earlier in 1659 the church had been forced to suspend all its divine services for the space of nine months, and it is indeed remarkable that St Jacob's kept no

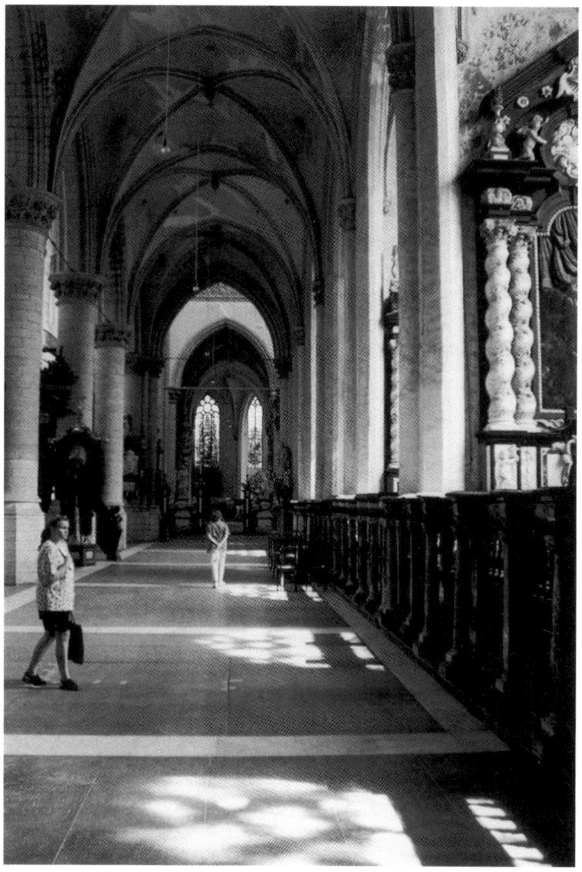

Fig. 6 View of the South Aisle from West to East. Anwerp, St Jacob's Church

accounts for that year.[25] To strengthen their argument for renewed support, the churchwardens insisted that the parish churches had been built at the request of the whole community, and therefore were a public trust as deserving of the city's help as the poor and the hospitals. The implication is clear: that in 1653 the Brede Raad of the city had resolved to divert funds previously reserved for the parish churches to the poor and sick who began to suffer terribly from the plague at exactly that time. As a counter-argument the churchwardens pointed out how the architecture of St Jacob's was a praiseworthy work, serving both to win the admiration of strangers and to ornament the city, thus a tourist attraction of benefit not only to parishioners, but to the whole community of Antwerp as well.[26]

Given the crisis of hard times, it is not surprising that the churchwardens were so eager to accept Jonker Roelants's gift in 1657, exactly at the point when the outbreak of plague created a pressing need to glorify the devotion to St Rochus and when St Jacob's could bring some of its straying flock back again into the fold with the attraction of so potent and magnificent a devotion. Indeed, in the same year, 1657, St Jacob's joined the Minorite Franciscans in a legal action to prevent the Jesuits from building a new church next to the Jesuit College in the Prinsstraat close by St Jacob's, because it was feared that the dynamic Jesuits would use all their arts of persuasion to lure away parishioners and the income they represented.[27] The Jesuits never did build this second church and the following year, in 1658, the new brotherhood of St Rochus founded in St Jacob's was able to offer a regular schedule of indulgences approved by the pope as an important added incentive to visit the chapel.[28]

The twin crises of plague and economic depression explain the intense new devotion to St Rochus, the foundation of the brotherhood, and the decision by the churchwardens to accept Alexander Balthasar Roelants's gift of a the new altar. I think that there is enough consistent evidence to see in this succession of events the workings of still another and third related crisis – the social conflict fought between the aristocratic and patrician classes who controlled most power in the city government and the artisan and working classes whose only official voice in city government was precinct captains (wijkmeesters) and the deans of the privileged guilds who served as members of the Brede Raad.[29] In 1653 it was the Brede Raad which cut off subsidies and plunged St Jacob's into a crisis of debt. The 1657 dispute over the new altar of St Rochus was fought between representatives of these two antagonistic social groups. The chapel masters who were thwarted and forced out of power belonged to the professional and artisan guilds, some of the guilds represented in the Brede Raad. Their victorious enemies were aristocrats and patricians, led by the chief-churchwarden of St Jacob's, Hendrik van Halmale, knight, who served several terms as burgomaster of Antwerp over the decades from 1649 to 1677.[30] Jonker Alexander Balthasar Roelants, donor of the new altar, was a noble landholder and also Royal Postmaster of Antwerp.[31]

What are we to make of the fact that these same two people, Van Halmale and Roelants, were the main targets of the most violent outbreak of civic unrest to occur in seventeenth-

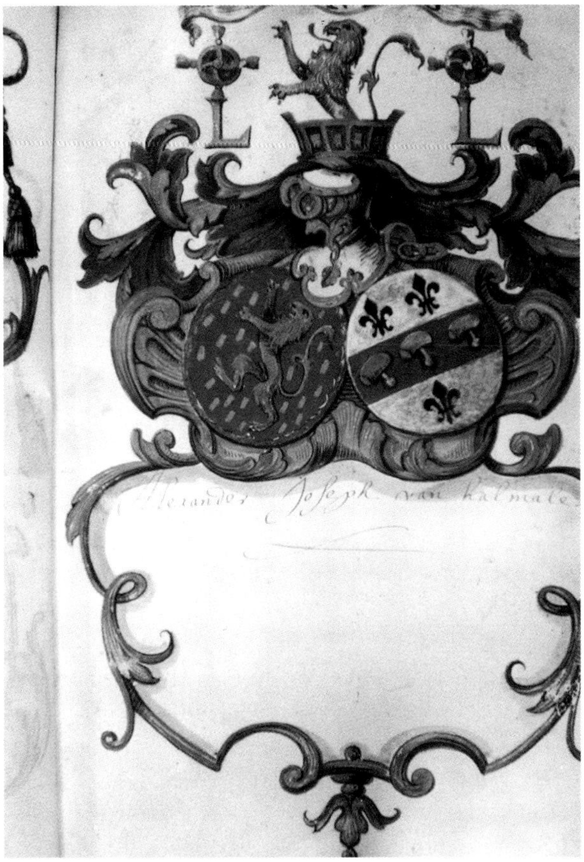

Fig. 7. *Coat of Arms of Alexander Joseph van Halmale in the Members' Book of the St Rochus Brotherhood. c.* 1721, watercolor. Antwerp, Archive St Jacob's Church

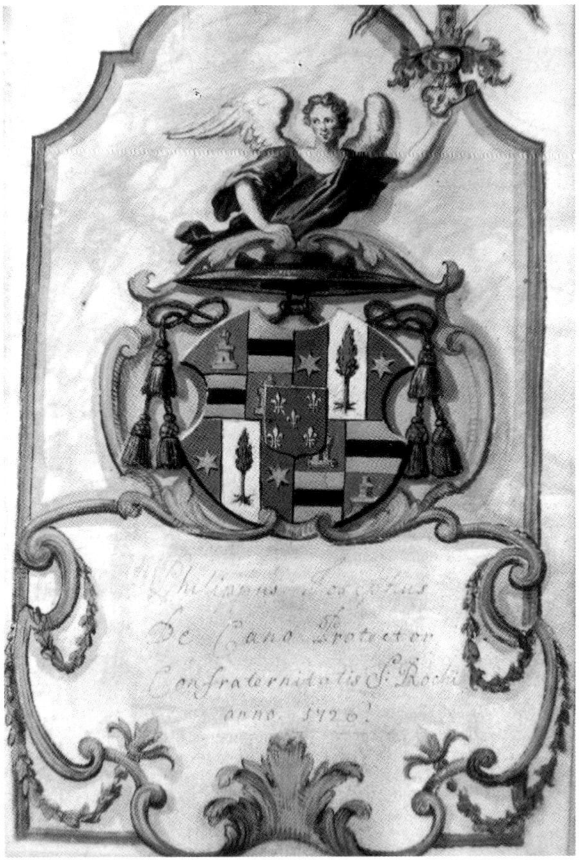

Fig. 8. *Coat of Arms of Philippus Josephus De Cano*, 1726, watercolor. Antwerp, Archive St Jacob's Church

century Antwerp? On 2 September 1658 the Council of Brabant judged that an independent postal service run by the city of Antwerp violated the privileges of the Royal Postmaster – Roelants in Antwerp, the Count of Turm and Tassis for the whole region. Although the city government did submit to this judgment, the fourth member of the Brede Raad – the deans of the guilds – resisted and continued in defiance to operate the independent postal service. On 30 September 1659, rebellious violence was provoked by the public announcement of sentences of banishment against the leaders of the resistance. As sitting burgomaster in 1659, Hendrik van Halmale was the crowd's first target. They ransacked his house and set his coach on fire. In the second wave of violence that broke during the night of 6 October, the rebellious crowd turned its anger against Roelants, the Royal Postmaster, and smashed the windows of his house. In this real test of power between rulers and subordinates, the outcome finally was decided by the external force of the Spanish army which reimposed and strengthened the authority of the Spanish royal government in Brussels.[32]

Van Halmale's position as burgomaster and Roelants's position as Royal Postmaster set up these two men as the obvious symbolic targets for the rebellion and I do not intend to suggest that any direct causal relationship existed between their actions against the chapel masters of St Rochus taken two years earlier in 1657 and the violence directed against them in 1659. I do think, however, that both events represented the same contest for power between clearly defined political and social groups. This view is confirmed further by the distinctive social character of the brotherhood of St Rochus which formed around the chapel in the St Jacob's Church.

While the agreement of 1657 between Roelants and the churchwardens of St Jacob's emphasized the popularity of the devotion to St Rochus and the need to keep the chapel open for all supplicants, and while the rules of

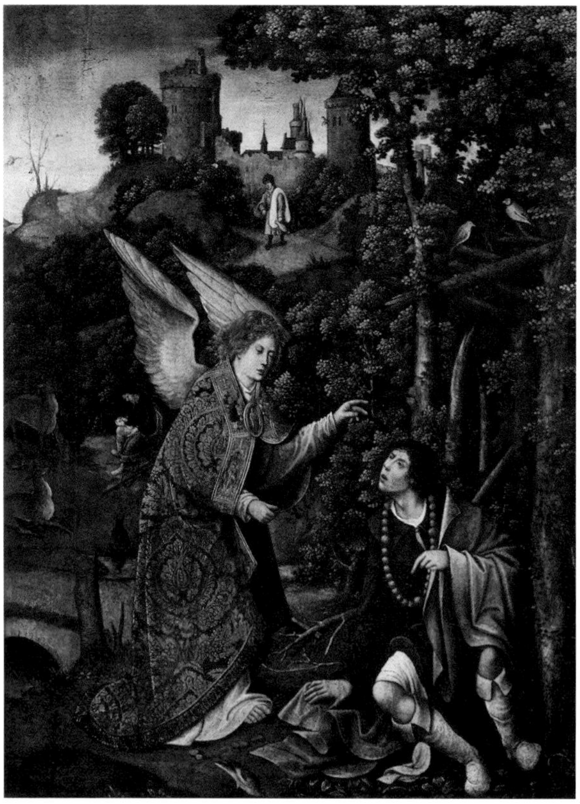

Fig. 9. Anonymous Antwerp painter, *The Angel Tells St Rochus That He Has Been Cured of the Plague*, 1517. Antwerp, St Jacob's Church

the brotherhood founded in 1658 stated that all could join – men and women – simply by inscribing their names, the brotherhood was in fact an exclusive club.[33] Membership remained consistently small – only nineteen in 1721 – and was drawn from precisely the ruling group of aristocrats and patrician magistrates exemplified by Roelants and Van Halmale.[34] The strong identity of the group was both expressed and reinforced in a book illuminated with members' coats of arms: for example those of Alexander Joseph van Halmale, a descendant of Hendrik van Halmale and sitting burgomaster in 1721, and of Philippus Josephus de Cano, canon of St Jacob's who became director of the brotherhood in 1726 – a clear sign of aristocratic and exclusive status different from the illuminated directors' books kept by most other brotherhoods (figs. 7–8).[35] Indeed, the Postmaster of the whole Spanish Netherlands, the Count of Turn and Tassis, inscribed his name in the book when he sought the aid of St Rochus in the chapel during the time of plague.

Alfons Thijs has proposed that the continued devotion shown by guilds towards their patron saints during the seventeenth century was an important component of group identity.[36] Splendid altar decorations and participation in group rituals such as processions were potent symbols of this claim to status through the group. In a similar way, it is easy to imagine that the aristocrats and magistrates who saw their power challenged during the 1650s would have derived a cohesive strength through the exclusive brotherhood of St Rochus with its magnificent marble altar and its membership book of coats of arms. The fine classical style of Artus and Erasmus Quellinus – in contrast to the cruder work of Jan van den Cruyce – could have provided an additional sign of this distinction. By 1658 Artus was famous as the sculptor chosen to decorate Amsterdam's new Town Hall. His brother Erasmus was acknowledged as the greatest successor of Rubens and Van Dyck.

The chapel of St Rochus in St Jacob's also may have served as a symbol of this exclusive group's loyalty to the Spanish king. A letter of 4 May, 1563, from Philip II – King of Castile, Aragon, and other Spanish territories, of Sicily, Naples, and other Mediterranean islands, of the Indian Islands, and also duke of Brabant and other Netherlandish provinces – conferred extraordinary status on the chapel of St Rochus.[37] Philip granted to the masters of the altar, and to the elders of the guild or brotherhood associated in 1563 with the altar of St Rochus, the right to manage their own income separately from the finances of the rest of St Jacob's. Members of the brotherhood and prospective donors, inclined to support the chapel, hesitated because they saw that earlier gifts had been diverted to other purposes by the churchwardens of St Jacob's, and the guild brothers desired only to ornament the altar and the service to God held on it. All the powers that were in 1563 – worldly and spiritual – gave their eternal consent to grant the chapel its independence: the burgomaster, aldermen, and council of Antwerp – the whole city government – and the churchwardens of St Jacob's themselves, who chose not to oppose the request.

Philip's letter conferred extraordinary status on the chapel of St Rochus and it could be partly for this reason that it alone survived unharmed when the Calvinist iconoclasts destroyed all the other eighteen altars in St Jacob's during the evening of 20 August, 1566. Floris Prims asks rhetorically whether the Calvinists held back because they dared not commit sacrilege against St Rochus, the greatest patron among saints in time of plague. But this motivation seems unlikely for a group determined to smash every symbol that might encourage the invocation of saints. Perhaps the aura of direct royal patronage proved decisive and for the same reason convinced Prince William of Orange – as a conciliatory gesture to Catholics and to the king – to hear mass before the altar of St Rochus on Sunday, 13 September 1566.[38]

Along with the consecrated altar of the chapel, the iconoclasts in 1566 spared an elaborate altarpiece which included a narrative cycle of twelve panels depicting the life and miracles of St Rochus, painted and dated by an Antwerp artist to 1517 (figs. 9–10).[39] Six of the panels are also painted on the reverse with grisaille images – one of the Virgin and Child and the others of saints – to decorate the altarpiece when its wings were closed. One of these grisailles has been incorrectly identified until now as St Gudula, patroness of Brussels. Because there is no obvious connection between St Gudula and the St Rochus Chapel, her appearance on the altarpiece introduced some doubt that the series originally was painted for St Jacob's.[40] However, Philip II's letter of 1563 informs us that the altar was dedicated to several saints besides St Rochus, and one of these additional saints was St Genoveva. Her characteristic iconography is almost identical to that of St Gudula. Legend has it that each saint carried a light that the devil maliciously blew out, only to be thwarted by an angel who would rekindle it. In fact the grisaille from the St Rochus Chapel displays the particular attribute which distinguishes St Genoveva from St Gudula. Traditionally St Genoveva is shown holding a candle or wax torch, as she does in the grisaille. St Gudula, by contrast, always holds a lantern. Furthermore, St Genoveva was invoked, like St Rochus, in time of plague. So the match between this grisaille and one of the saints to whom the altar was dedicated increases the probability that the series was painted on commission for the St Rochus Chapel in 1517.[41] The panels probably were removed

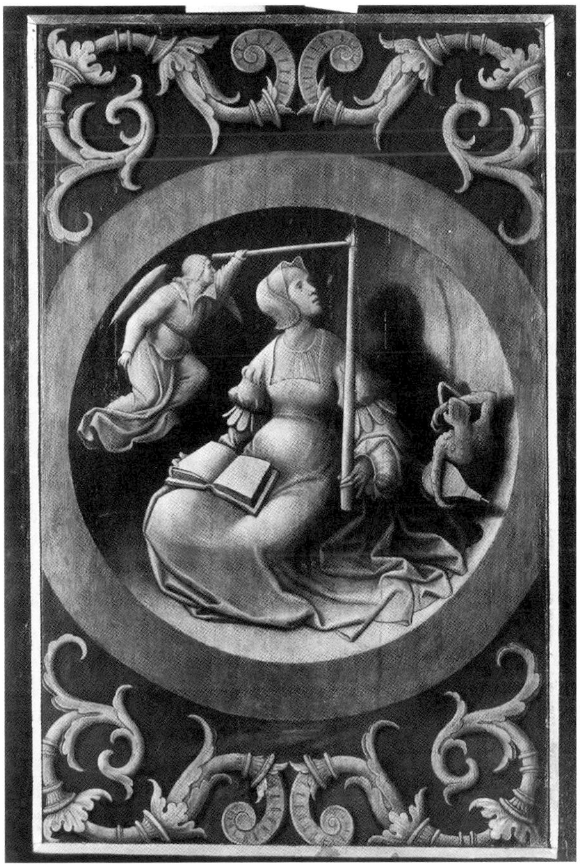

Fig. 10. Anonymous Antwerp painter, *St Genoveva*, 1517. Antwerp, St Jacob's Church

from their original setting during the second, more systematic iconoclasm carried out by the Calvinist magistracy of Antwerp in 1581. While there is no record of them before Jacob de Wit's early eighteenth-century description of art in the churches of Antwerp, all twelve pictures must have been put back in place during the seventeenth century and thus formed an integral part of the decoration of the St Rochus Chapel.[42] At the very least these pictures testified in the seventeenth century to the antiquity of veneration for St Rochus in the chapel, and thus increased the luster and status of the brotherhood, as did the grant from Philip II of 1563 and the claim in the title of the statutes of the brotherhood published in 1658 that the devotion to St Rochus in this chapel was more than one-hundred years old.[43]

I would argue that this display of class identity through art and ritual and the paradox of a popular devotion controlled by the most exclusive group are based above all on the most profound belief. In time of plague and crisis the cult of St Rochus was too important to leave in the hands of the chapel masters who could not give due honor to the saint. A direct equation was made between the power of religion to save the city from divine wrath and the strength of the ruling group of Spanish king, aristocrats, and magistrates to save the city from crisis. Works of art were the active symbols of these beliefs.

I want to point out in conclusion that I am not the first to tell this story. In the third volume of the *Acta sanctorum* for August, published at Antwerp in 1737, Joannes Pinius included an account of the posthumous glory of St Rochus in Antwerp based on many of the same documents from the archive of the chapel and brotherhood of St Rochus in St Jacob's which I have cited in my paper.[44] The crucial difference is that the Bollandists eliminated all traces of conflict. The one document they did not cite is the petition by the churchwardens to block construction of the altar planned by the chapel masters. The Jesuits made selective use of documents to write an untroubled history of glorious devotion in which there were no winners and losers.

NOTES

It is a pleasure to thank Dr. J. Van den Nieuwenhuizen who has been extraordinarily generous and helpful in providing access to the Archives of St Jacob's and in sharing transcriptions he has made from the Archives of documents pertaining to construction and decoration of the church.

1. Théodore van Lerius, *Notice des œuvres d'art de l'église paroissiale et ci-devant insigne collègiale de St Jacques à Anvers, précédé d'une introduction historique et rédigée d'après des documents authentiques*, Borgerhout, 1855, remains the best account of art in St Jacob's. Also see the general and anecdotal introduction by Armand Boni, *Antwerpens Roem St Jacobskerk: Een kultuur-historische schets van Antwerpen en Sint Jacobskerk in de vijftiende, zestiende en zeventiende eeuw*, Antwerp, s.d. [1953]). Anne-Marie Peré, *De St.-Jakobskerk te Antwerpen: Plan en bronnen voor een museologische studie van de kunstschatten*, dissertation KU Leuven, 1971 [copy in Stadsarchief Antwerp, PK3403]), contains valuable bibliographical information. Floris Prims, *De Sint-Rochusschilderijen in de Collegiale Kerk van Sint-Jacob te Antwerpen*, Antwerp, 1933, the only specialized study to-date of the St Rochus Chapel, exclusively treats the twelve narrative panels of the life of St Rochus painted for the chapel in 1517. I discuss these paintings below.

2. *Instellinge ende Onderwijsinghe van Het Broederschap van den H. Rochus Confessoor Inghestelt inde Collegiale Kercke van Sint Jacob binnen Antwerpen 1658. Die over de hondert Iaeren aldaer gheviert is gheweest*, Antwerp, 1658, I, publishes the letter by Ambrosius Capello, Bishop of Antwerp, authorizing the establishment of the brotherhood: 'Aldus ghedaen in onsen Bisschoppelijcken Paleyse binnen Antwerpen den twelfften Augustus Ann 1658.'

3. Van Lerius 1855 (see note 1), p. 62, first proposed the attribution of altar frame and alabaster image to Artus Quellinus the Elder. Juliane Gabriels, *Artus Quellinus de Oude, 'kunstryck belthouwer'*, Antwerp, 1930, pp. 296–297, n. 325, accepted and substantiated both attributions through comparison with documented works by the sculptor. In particular Gabriels drew attention to the similarity between the Solomonic columns of the St Rochus Chapel – decorated with lilies, roses, and angels – and the columns of the Sweet Name of Jesus altar in the St Paul's Church (former Dominican Church) carved by Quellinus's student Peter Verbruggen the Elder in 1656. For the altarpiece by Erasmus Quellinus see Jean-Pierre De Bruyn, *Erasmus II Quelllinus (1607–1678): de schilderijen met catalogue raisonné*, Freren, 1988, pp. 243–244, no. 204.

4. Archive St Jacob's Church, Antwerp, BR 48 (Oud nr. 138/5), (numbers refer to the inventory of Archive St Jacob's Church, Antwerp, by J. Van den Nieuwenhuizen, *Oude broederschappen en kapellen*, and, in parentheses, to the old archival numbers recorded by Van Lerius in the nineteenth century): transcriptions: Theodore van Lerius, *Beschryving der parochiale en voorheen vermaarde Collegiale Kerk van St Jacob te Antwerpen. begonnen in Oct 1846*, Archive St Jacob's Church, Antwerp, Oud nr. 560, Bylage 13; J. Van den Nieuwenhuizen, *Transcriptions from the Archive St Jacob's Church, Antwerp: Chapels and Brotherhoods*, p. 74.

5. Archive St Jacob's Church, Antwerp, BR 48 (Oud nr. 138/5), transcription is my own: 'Opden 14 7bris. 1657. gedaen aen Guilliam Moons Herman Neskens, Cleermaeker, & Zydevercooper opden Paddegracht Cappelmeesters van St Rochus cappelle in St Jacobs kercke, & Jan vanden Cruyce beeltsnyder ten eijnde als in dese bovenstaende. Fiat periculo partis. Actum 11 sept. 1657. Acte vermelt by my H Van Weteringen.'

6. Archive St Jacob's Church, Antwerp, BR 48 (Oud nr. 138/6). Transcriptions: Van Lerius, *Beschryving* (see note 4), Bylage 14; Van den Nieuwenhuizen, *Transcriptions* (see note 4), pp. 74–75

7. For the iconography of St Rochus see Marie-Theres Schmitz-Eichhoff, *St Rochus: Ikonographische und medizin-historische Studien*, Cologne, 1977, p. 288, on Quellinus's picture in particular.

8. Archive St Jacob's Church, Antwerp, BR 48 (Oud nr. 138/6).

9. *Instellinge ende Onderwijsinghe van Het Broederschap van den H. Rochus* (see note 2). Also see the transcriptions of Capello's original letter, the accuracy of which is attested to by Joannes Engelgrave, canon and actuary of the Chapter of St Jacob's, and Apostolic Protonotary, who himself made the transcriptions: Archive St Jacob's Church, Antwerp, BR 48 (Oud nr. 138/7 bis) and BR 48 (Oud nr. 418), Archive St Jacob's Church, Antwerp. This and other transcriptions by Engelgrave from the archive of the St Rochus's Chapel in St Jacob's were published in the account of the posthumous glory of St Rochus at Antwerp given in *Acta sanctorum Augusti ex Latinis & Graecis, aliarumque gentium Monumentis, servatâ primigeniâ veterum Scriptorum phrasi, collecta, digesta, Commentariisque & Observationibus Illustrata a Joanne Bapt. Sollerio, Joanne Pinio, Guilielmo Cupero, Petro Boschio P.M., e Societate Jesu Presbyteris Theologis. Tomus III Quo dies decimus tertius, decimus quartus, decimus quintus, decimus sextus, decimus septimus, decimus octavus, & decimus nonus continentur*, Antwerp, 1737 (repr. ed. Brussels, 1970), pp. 412–413.

10. Archive St Jacob's Church, Antwerp, BR 48 (Oud nr. 138/7 bis), published in *Acta sanctorum Augusti* (see note 9), III, p. 414.

11. Published in *Instellinge ende Onderwijsinghe van Het Broederschap van den H. Rochus* (see note 2), IV; *Acta sanctorum Augusti* (see note 9), III, p. 412. Transcriptions by Engelgrave of the original document: Archive St Jacob's Church, Antwerp, BR 48 (Oud nr. 138/7 bis) and BR 48 (Oud nr. 418), 'Regulen van het broederschap van den H. Rochus Confessor. 1. De directie van dit Broederschap altijdt hebben eenen Canoninck van de selve Collegiale kercke bij ons daer toe te noemen, gelijck wij tegenwoordigh sijn noemende Hr. Franciscus De Wolf Canoninck der selve kercke.'

12. J. Van den Nieuwenhuizen, *Extracten uit de kerkrekeningen van de Sint-Jacobskerk te Antwerpen in verband met de bouw en de stoffering van de kerk*, p. 167.

13. Archive St Jacob's Church, Antwerp, BR 49 (Oud nr. 261), Rekeningboek of the St Rochus Chapel: fol. 1, Franciscus van den Bossche, Pastor of St Jacob's, 'vernieuwt' the book starting July 1648.

14. Archive St Jacob's Church, Antwerp, BR 39 (Oud nr. 140), chronicle of the Archconfraternity of the Holy Trinity in St Jacob's: 'Institutionem huius Archisodalitatis sollicitavit, procuravit, et promovit Franciscus Vanden Bossche Bruxellensis, Pastor Ecclesiae S. Jacobi, tertio anno suae residentiae. Qui & haec Chronica collegit, et descripsit.'

15. For accounts of the rivalry between regular and parish churches in Antwerp see Alfons K.L. Thijs, *Van Geuzenstad tot katholiek bolwerk: Maatschappelijke betekenis van de kerk in contrareformatorisch Antwerpen*, s.l. [Turnhout], 1990, pp. 77–80; Marie Juliette Marinus, *De Contrareformatie te Antwerpen (1585–1676): Kerkelijk leven in een grootstad*, Verhandelingen van de Koninklijke Academie voor Wetenschappen, Letteren en Schone Kunsten van België, Klasse der Letteren, Jaargang 57, 1995, nr. 155 Brussels, 1995, pp. 194–202. The central importance of parish churches is stated explicitly in *Canons and Decrees of the Council of Trent*, ed. and trans. H.J. Schroeder, St Louis–London, 1950, p.204, Twenty-Fourth Session, Chap. XIII.

16. Their names and professions are recorded by the pastor, Franciscus van den Bossche in the *Rekeningboek* of the St Rochus Chapel, which he renewed in 1648: Archive St Jacob's Church, Antwerp, BR 49 (Oud nr. 261), fol. 1–1v: in July 1648, Van den Bossche appointed as chapel masters: 'De eersaemen & gods-dienstige mannen, Meester Aegidius de Witte, Deken vande Scholmeesters binnen Antwerpen. ende Herman Nesscher, Deken vande Backers. etc. die den selven dienst, ter Liefde Godts gewillgslyck hebben aenveerdt ten daghe & iaere als boven.' In August of the same year Van den Bossche and the two sitting chapel masters chose two more chapel masters: Jan van den Cruyce and Franchoijs Peeters; in 1654, Joannes de Medesens. Neskens is recorded as tailor and silk merchant in the order sent by the Antwerp burgomaster on 14 September 1657 to the chapel masters of St Rochus's Chapel, where a second chapel master, Guilliam Moons, also is named (see above, note 5). I have not been able to identify the professions of Franchoys Peeters or Joannes de Medesens.

17. Archive St Jacob's Church, Antwerp, BR 48 (Oud nr. 138/3) 7 August, 1648: transcriptions by Van Lerius (Oud nr. 560, bylage 13, Archive St Jacob's Church, Antwerp); Van den Nieuwenhuizen, *Transcriptions* (see note 4), pp. 73–74. Another old copy, Notarissen, G. le Rousseau 2437, fols. 35–35v, Stadsarchief, Antwerp, is published by J. van Damme, 'Documenten betreffende de Antwerpse beeldhouwers Jan en Jan-Anthoni van den Cruys', *Cornelis Floris Jaarboek*, 1989, pp. 63–64. Jan van Damme kindly drew my attention to this reference. My transcription of the specifications: 'de Cornisse van blauwen steen/ de Fries van witten Marmer/ de Arcketraef van blauwen steen/ de Ballesterkens van witten marmor/ de ronde pilaren van Barbarson steen/ de taeffels mette mollueren oock van blauwen steen/ / de Ingelegde taeffels van witte marmer/ de doorloopende treden oock van blauwe/ de deure met witte marmere Ballusterkens, & de reste gecoloreert/ altemael opde dickte vanden thuijn van het Heijlich Cruijs aultaer Inde voors. kercke.'

18. Cornelis de Bie, *Het Gulden Cabinet vande edel vry schilder const inhoudende den lof vande vermarste schilders, architecten, beldthouwers, ende plaetsnyders, van dese eeuw*, intro. G. Lemmens, Lier, 1661 (repr. ed. Soest, 1971), p. 515: 'In *d'Architraeb'*, *Cornies*, *Phries*, *Baes* en *Peeter-stael*/ En t'*Capiteel* daer by, bestaet'et altemael.'

19. Marinus 1995 (see note 15), p. 28, afb. 2, with analysis on pp. 27–29.

20. BR 48 (Oud Nr. 138/6, see note 6): 'alle diensten van Missen ende Bichten sullen continueren als van voortijden is geweest als wesende Sinte Rochus eenen patroon vande Peste daer vele persoonen haeren toevlucht toenemen van particuliere missen te doen doene ende lichten te ontsteken ende opde gewoonlijcke dagen van Sondagen ende heijlich dagen tot gerieff vande gemeijnte dat de voorschreven Cappelle sal moeten open wesen gelijck als andere Cappellen inden beuck staende waertoe tot dienst vande voorschreven gemeijnte eenen sleutel vande selve Cappelle aende kercke sal blijven.' My understanding of 'gemeijnte' as the community of the whole city rather than the parish, is based on a passage in the appeal for more funds made by the churchwardens of St Jacob's to the the Antwerp city government in 1661 in which the narrow interests of parishioners ('parochianten') are contrasted with the broader concerns of the whole community ('geheele gemijnte'): Stadsarchief, Antwerp, K 318.

21. Rijksarchief Antwerp, Provinciaal Archief, A: 115: 1: fol. 1r: 'Departement des Deux Nêthes/ Canton et Commune d'Anvers/ Inventaire Contenant la description sommaire des effets trouvée dans l'eglise de St Jaque/ Fait conformement a l'art 2. de la loy du 15 fructidor dernier an 5me.' fol. 9r: 'fait clos et arrete par nous commissaires le present etat sincere et veritable Anvers ce 28 Pluviose an 6 [17 February 1798; church reopened 11 February 1798] de la Republique fransaise/ J:B: adnetx/ commissaire/ J:J: Kreijmans/ Commissaire/ J:B: Mortelmans Prêtre/ le 29 Pluviose 6e année [18 February 1798].' fol. 2r: 'Chapelle No 4 de St Rocque': 'un confessional, avec fauteuil.'

22. Archive St Jacob's Church, Antwerp, BR 48 (Oud nr. 138/7bis), 'alsoo de onbegrijpelijcke goetheijdt godt, die in sijne straffe oock bermhertigh is, door de menichvuldighe sonden der menschen tot rech[t]veerdighe gramschap verweckt sijnde, dickwils met verscheijde geesselinge compt te castijden oock de gene, die hij bemint, om die te brengen tot beteringe, ende in genade te ontfangen, ende dat hierom de Christi geloovige van alle tijde in noot sijnde, hunnen toevlucht hebben genomen tot sijne bermhertigheijdt, ende tot de voorspraecke van sijne heijligen, dewelcke hoe wel int' gemeijn bij godt Almachtich uijtter maeten sijn vereert, geacht, en in haere voorspraecke gehoort, soo bevint men nochtans metter daet door de sienelijcke vertroostinge ende baete bij menichvuldige persoonen beproeft, dat godt eenige onder sijne heijligen vrienden in dese ellendige weireldt is aenwijsende voor speciale patroonen ende beschermers tegen diversche soorten van sieckten ende ellenden aen de menschen meest schroomelijck ende schadelijck, als namentlijck is de haestige sieckte, waer tegen onder andere voor eenen besonderen patroon wort geviert ende aengeroepen den H. Rochus Confessor, die hier op der aerden al noch levende heeft gedient met grooten iever, ende geholpen de gene, die met de haestighe sieckte bevangen waeren, ende oock met de selve is besmet geweest, soo dat hij het selve patronaetschap bij godt besonderlijck schijnt verdient te hebben. Allen welcken overmerckende, en daerenboven, dat aen godt heeft gelieft om onse sonden dese stadt, mitsgaders de omliggende plaetsen met de voorseijde haestige sieckte soo in den voorleden, als tegenwoordigen Jaere, ende t'andere tijden swaerlijck te besoecken, gelijck wij alnoch tegenwoordighlijck sijn gevoelende.

Soo ist dat wij op het ootmoedigh versoeck en godtvruchtige begeerte van eenige devote Christi geloovige tot meerder eere godts, vertroostinge der Christene zielen, en afweiringe van dese straffen, hebben goetgevonden mits desen in te stellen ende opterechten een Broederschap in de Collegiale kercke van S. Jacob binnen dese stadt voor allen Christi geloovige soo mans als vrouwen onder den titel ende aenroepinge van den H. Rochus Confessoor in de Capelle, ende aen den autaer t'sijnder eere in de selve kercke gerecht...'

23. The classic analysis of Antwerp's economic crisis during the second half of the seventeenth century is Roland Baetens, *De nazomer van Antwerpens welvaart: De diaspora en het handelshuis De Groote tijdens de eerste helft der 17de eeuw*, Historische Uitgaven Pro Civitate, reeks-in 8(, nr. 45, Brussels, 1976, vol. 1, pp. 49–65. Subsequent publications have confirmed this analysis and placed it in broader contexts: Etienne Scholliers and Chris Vandenbroeke, 'Structuren en conjuncturen in de Zuidelijke Nederlanden 1480–1800', in *Algemene Geschiedenis der Nederlanden*, Haarlem, 1980, V, pp. 252–310.

24. Stadsarchief, Antwerpen, K 318. For the composition of Antwerp's Brede Raad, see Jan van Acker, 'Het stadsbestuur van 1585 tot 1713', in *Antwerpen in de XVIIde eeuw*, Antwerp, 1989, pp. 22–23.

25. Van den Nieuwenhuizen, *Extracten* (see note 12), p. 204. Stadsarchief, Antwerp, K 318: 'misgaeders legaten ende aelmoessen die van de goede luijden moeten worden gecollecteert, & die door de soeberheijt des tijts dagelijcx meer en meer commen te verminderen/ Dat dijenvolgende in cas van geen assitentie alwaet oock soo dat de legaeten & aelmoessen van dach tot dach niet en quamen te verminderen de godts dinsten wederom niet en sullen connen geschieden, gelyck over twee jaeren gebeurt is, als wanneer by gebreck van middelen alle dinsten als mettenen, hoochmissen vesperen, & loven den tyt van negen maenden llanck hebben moeten cesseren.'

26. Stadsarchief, Antwerp, K 318: 'de bouw der voors. kercke is een loffelijck werck dienende tot verwonderinge van alle vremdelinghen tot ciraet deser stadt & dinst niet alleenelijck vande parochianten maer vande geheele gemeijnte der selve./ Daerbeneffens dat de voors. & alle andere parochien kercken soo wel sijn deel ende lidtmaeten deser stadt als den huijsarmen, het gasthuijs ende andere publicque gebouwen, daer van d'een soo veel als d'ander bij gebreck van middelen van wegens desere stadt moeten worden gesecoureert & geholpen./ Te meer de parochiaele kercken wtgenomen de Catedrale wesende tevoorens alleenelijck cappellen (: gelijck by de opene brieven van hunne erectie claerlijck te sien is) niet opt versoeck vande prochianten off van particulieren tot parochien sijn geerigeert maer wel & expresselijck by & opt versoeck vande geheele gemijnte deser stadt.'

27. Stephanus Schoutens, *Geschiedenis van het voormalig Minderbroedersklooster van Antwerpen (1446–1797)*, Antwerp, 1894, pp. 117–121.

28. The list of indulgences and the bull of Alexander VII, dated 28 September 1658, approving the erection of the brotherhood and the indulgences offered at the altar of the chapel, are published in *Instellinge ende Onderwijsinghe* (see note 2).

29. On the composition of the Brede Raad, see Van Acker 1989 (see note 24), p. 22. For the history of social-political conflict in seventeenth-century Antwerp, see Karin Van Honacker, *Lokaal verzet en oproer in de 17de en 18de eeuw: collectieve acties tegen het centraal gezag in Brussel, Antwerpen en Leuven*, Standen en Landen, Wetenschappelijke Bijdragen uitgegeven door de Belgische Afdeling van de Internationale Commissie voor de Geschiedenis van Standen en Landen, XCVIII, Kortrijk–Heule, 1994, pp. 137–162. Marinus 1995 (see note 15), p.74, stresses the representative function of the Brede Raad in opposing subventions for ecclesiastical institutions.

30. Floris Prims, *Geschiedenis van Antwerpen*, repr. ed., Brussels, 1982, vol. 6A, pp. 186–187, for Van Halmale's terms in office. The agreement of 28 September 1657, between the churchwardens of St Jacob's and Alexander Baltasar Roelants, over decoration of the St Rochus Chapel, was made: 'met consent van Heer Hendrick van Halmale Ridder ende opperkerckmeester vande Collegiale kercke van Sint Jacob': Archive St Jacob's Church, Antwerp, BR 48 (Oud nr. 138/6), For the office of chief-churchwarden, see Van Acker 1989 (see note 24), pp. 13–14.

31. 'Jonker Alexander Balthasar Roelants Heere van Heijnthout Comis Postmeester van sijn Conincklijcke Mat': Archive St Jacob's Church, Antwerp, BR 48 (Oud nr. 138/6).

32. Accounts of the so-called 'posterijen' rebellion are given by Prims 1982 (see note 30), vol. 6A, pp. 158–161; Van Honacker 1994 (see note 29), pp. 143–151; and in a contemporary diary, *Dagverhael van den oproer te Antwerpen in 1659*, ed. C. Serrure, Ghent, 1839 [I owe this reference to the kindness of Alfons Thijs], p. XI, on the attack, 30 September 1659, against Van Halmale, his house, and carriage; p.2, on the attack, 6 October 1659, against: 'het huys van mevrau Roelants, op het postcomptoir. Dadelyck beginnen sy de veynsters al uyt te werpen, de Bylen ende hammners waeren verdich om de poorte in te slaen, maer alsoo de clocke soo ras gheluyt was, als de vergaderynghe begont, is ghebeurt dat de borgherye vroegher op de beenen was, als de plunderaers ghedacht hadden, ende namentlyck omtrent het huys van mevrau Roelants, mets dat men wel wiste hoe seer sy in den haet was om dit proces van het postcomptoir.'

33. Archive St Jacob's Church, Antwerp, BR 48 (Oud nr. 138/7bis): 'Regulen van het broederschap van den H. Rochus Confessor': '2. Alle die begeiren in dit Broederschap te comen, sullen bij den voornoemden Directeur, ofte iemanden bij hem te substitueren ingheschreven worden, sonder iet daer vooren te moeten geven, sal nochtans ijder liber sijn te geven t'gene hem belieft.'

34. Archive St Jacob's Church, Antwerp, BR 49 (Oud nr. 261): Rekeningboek van de kapel: fol. 86v: 'Lyste der Namen vande Heeren dewelcke syn in het Broederschap vanden H: Rochus inde vermaerde Collegiale ende Parochiale kercke van St Jacob binnen dese stadt van Antwerpen.'

35. Archive St Jacob's Church, Antwerp, BR 55 (Oud nr. 709). This manuscript is noted in *Acta sanctorum Augusti* (see note 9), above), p. 415: 'Dominos confratres ab erectione confraternitatis semper nobilioris notae huijus urbis viros *fuisse*: cui Comes de la Tour & Tassis primus propria manu adscripsit; ipsius & quàm plurimorum insignibus in libro confraternitatis depictis: inter quae etiam illa Illustrissimorum ac reverendissimorum hujus civitatis quondam antistitum Ambrosii Capello, & Ferdinandi van Beughem emicant. De Praefato Comite de la Tour fertur, quod propter restem tunc temporis grassantem huc fugerit, ut se patrocinio praedicti Sancti, in hac insigni ecclesia à ducentis & ultrà annis celebris, commendaret.' Directors' books kept by most Antwerp brotherhoods commemorated the service of the officers only: see for example, Archive St Jacob's Church, Antwerp, BR 81 (Oud nr. 706): 'Beginsel ende vervolgh der Praefecten van het Loffelijck Broederschap vande Vierthien Daegsche Berechtinge in de Parochiale ende Collegiale Kercke van St Jacob binnen Antwerpen.' A similar collection of members' coats of arms was assembled by the Brotherood of the Sweet Name of Jesus affiliated with the Cathedral of Antwerp, as a sign of that group's exclusive and elite character: see Marie Juliette Marinus, 'De bisschoppen en hun kathedraal', in W. Aerts ed., *De Onze-Lieve-Vrouwekathedraal van Antwerpen*, Antwerp, 1993, pp. 54–55.

36. Alfons K.L. Thijs, 'Religieuze rituelen in het emanciepatieproces van Vlaamse en Brabantse handwerkgezellen (zestiende–negentiende eeuw', in Catharina Lis and Hugo Soly ed., *Werken volgens de regels: Ambachten in Brabant en Vlaanderen 1500–1800*, Brussels, 1994, pp. 231–281.

37. Archive St Jacob's Church, Antwerp, BR 48 (Oud nr. 138/1). This is a copy in an eighteenth-century hand of the original letter which appears to be lost. It is transcribed by Van den Nieuwenhuizen, *Transcriptions* (see note 4), pp. 71–73 and summarized in *Acta sanctorum Augusti* (see note 9), III, p. 412. Marie-Thérèse Claessens, 'De Broederschappen te Antwerpen van de 14de eeuw tot circa 1600', dissertation KU Leuven, 1971 [copy in the library of the Ruusbroecgenootschap, Antwerp], p.34, refers only in passing to this document, without mentioning that it is a letter from Philip II.

38. Prims 1982 (see note 30), vol. 6B, p. 494. Prims 1982, vol. 5, p. 390, determined that nineteen altars stood in St Jacob's by 1524. The account book of the church for 1568 records payment of 7 lb. 4 s. Br. to the suffrigan consecration bishop of Mechelen ('wijbisschop sofhrigaen') for consecration of eighteen altars, which had been consecrated by 7 June 1567, when the mason Machil van Steenwinckel was paid for closing the holes where relics had been placed in the consecrated altars (Van den Nieuwenhuizen, *Extracten* [cited in note 12], pp. 105–106, 'Kladrekening 15 maart – 14 maart 1568;' p. 107, 'Kerkrekening 15 maart – 14 maart 1569'). As Prims figured it, the St Rochus altar, where William of Orange heard mass,

would bring the number of altars back to the full complement of nineteen.

39. These now have been distributed in groups of four to the St Rochus Chapel and to the chapels of St Job and St Anna to the east of the St Rochus Chapel flanking the South aisle of St Jacob's. See Prims 1933 (see note 1), and also Schmitz-Eichhoff 1977 (see note 7), p. 246, who describes the series of pictures in St Jacob's as the most important artistic expression of the early veneration of St Rochus in Western Europe, provides the most judicious discussion of attribution (circle of Bernaert van Orley?), and, pp. 246–260, makes a detailed iconographic analysis.

40. The identification with St Gudula, first made by Van Lerius 1855 (see note 1), p. 66, has been repeated by Prims 1933 (see note 1), p. 26, and Schmitz-Eichhoff 1977 (see note 7), p. 248. Prims 1933, p. 26, noted that the grisailles of 'St Gudula', St Jerome, and St Adriaan have no obvious connection with St Jacob's or with the St Rochus Chapel, and suggested that they could be patron saints of the most important donors, now unknown to us.

41. Archive St Jacob's Church, Antwerp, BR 48 (Oud nr. 138/1), Philip II acknowledges receipt of the petition from: 'Jan de Voocht, Jan van Driesseren, Franchoijs Dijckstraete, ende Adriaen van Stijl als autaermeesteren ende die ouders vander Gulden des autaer van St Rochus, St Genoveve, St Bavo, St Franciscus, ende St Siacre[sic: for Fiacre] gefondeert inde Kercke van St Jacops.' For the iconographies and cults of St Gudula and St Genoveva, see Louis Réau, *Iconographie de l'art Chrétien, vol.3, Iconographie des saints*, 2, G–O, Paris, 1958, p. 618, and pp. 563–568, respectively.

42. Jacobus de Wit, *De Kerken van Antwerpen*, ed. J. de Bosschere, Antwerp–The Hague, 1910, p. 42: 'De Wit, II. – fol. 20v: Eenige klyne stuckjes, verbeeldende de *Historie van St Rochus* (twaalf in getal) door een seer Ouden Meester geschildert.' The pictures also are recorded in the inventory of St Jacob's made by the French on 17 February 1798: Rijksarchief Antwerp, Provinciaal Archief, A: 115: 1, (see note 21), fol. 1v: 'Chapelle No 4 de St Rocque': 'Douze tabelau representant l'histoire du dit Saint.'

43. *Instellinge ende Onderwijsinghe* (see note 2): 'V. Oorspronck ende vermeerderinghe van de aenroepingh', ende Devotie tot den H. Rochus in den tijdt van de haestighe Sieckte.' Remarkable growth of the devotion was above all due to events of 7 June 1414, at the Council of Constance, when the outbreak of plague prompted a procession, carrying the image of St Rochus. The epidemic miraculously ended, encouraging the erection of chapels throughout Germany, France, and other countries: '... alwaer de Beelden, Taeffereelen, ende memorialen der beloften, ghenoech bethoonen, met wat een eere den H. ROCHUS t'alle kanten gheviert wordt.'

44. *Acta sanctorum Augusti* (see note 9), III, pp. 410–415.

Peter Paul Rubens en Jan Brueghel de Oude: de drijfveren van hun samenwerking

Christine Van Mulders

De studie van het creatieve proces in het œuvre van Peter Paul Rubens in samenwerking met Jan Brueghel de Oude[1] kadert binnen de bredere context van de samenwerking tussen zelfstandige schilders in het algemeen. Een analyse van dergelijke samenwerkingsverbanden is dus noodzakelijk, als men het ontstaan en de eigenheid van het teamwork van Rubens en Brueghel wil bestuderen. Bepaalde aspecten van het concept van hun schilderijen in samenwerking, aan de orde in volgend artikel,[2] hebben betrekking op de omstandigheden die het verschijnsel van de samenwerking tussen zelfstandige schilders in het algemeen hebben gestimuleerd en andere houden verband met de precieze feiten die aanleiding hebben gegeven tot het specifiek Rubens-Brueghel-teamwork.

Het corpus van schilderijen van Rubens in samenwerking met Jan Brueghel de Oude omvat een dertigtal werken. Hieronder bevinden zich kransen of guirlandes met meestal religieuze afbeeldingen, interieurs met allegorische voorstellingen en landschappen met historietaferelen. Het zijn oorspronkelijke composities, naar dewelke verscheidene replieken, kopieën en varianten door Jan Brueghel de Jonge, al dan niet in samenwerking met Rubens, of door kunstenaars uit hun ateliers en omgevingen werden geschilderd. De periode waarin de samenwerking tussen Rubens en Jan Brueghel de Oude haar sporen liet, loopt van 1589 tot 1600, de vermoedelijke ontstaansdatum van hun eerste schilderij, tot 1625, het sterftejaar van Brueghel.[3]

Het onderzoek naar het concept van de schilderijen van Rubens in samenwerking met Brueghel concentreert zich grotendeels rond de algemene context waarin dit teamwork ontstond. In verband hiermee stelt zich de vraag naar, enerzijds, de schildersorganisatorische en institutionele en, anderzijds, de culturele en sociaal-economische mechanismen die aanleiding gaven tot de creatie van een kunstwerk in samenwerking en die het concept ervan beïnvloedden.

De eerste, eerder schaarse, vormen van samenwerking tussen zelfstandige schilders zijn reeds te duiden in het eerste kwart van de zestiende eeuw, waar zij ontstonden als een gevolg van de ontwikkeling van verschillende genres en de specialisering binnen de schilderkunst.[4] Zo liet Joachim Patinier, als vaardig landschapschilder – al bestond het landschap nog niet als een zelfstandig genre, toch waren Patinier's religieuze scènes en genretaferelen niet meer dan een voorwendsel om het landschap op zich af te beelden –, zich regelmatig bijstaan door gespecialiseerde figuurschilders, waaronder zijn goede vriend Quinten Metsijs.[5] Soms is het moeilijk uit te maken of het gaat om een daadwerkelijke samenwerking, dan wel om een verregaande onderlinge beïnvloeding. Joos van Cleve, de Meester van de Vrouwelijke Halffiguren, de Meester van de Mansi-Magdalena, Adriaen Isenbrant en Lucas Gassel kunnen hierbij vernoemd worden. De samenwerkingsverbanden bij Jan van Amstel, Jan Sanders van Hemessen, Pieter Coecke van Aelst en anderen dienen verder te worden onderzocht. Rond het midden van de zestiende eeuw betekende het groeiend aantal genres - het narratieve devotietafereel, het landschap, het moraliserend genrestuk, het markt- en keukentoneel, het stilleven, het portret en het historietafereel met religieuze, mythologische en allegorische onderwerpen bestonden naast elkaar - de aanzet tot nog meer doorgedreven specialisering. Deze vormde op haar beurt een voedingsbodem voor productie-eenheden van samenwerkende schilders. Onder de nieuwe kunstenaarsduo's bevonden zich onder meer Cornelis van Dalem-Gillis Mostaert, Jacob Grimmer-Gillis Mostaert, Hans Vredeman de Vries-Gillis Mostaert, Jacob Grimmer-Maarten

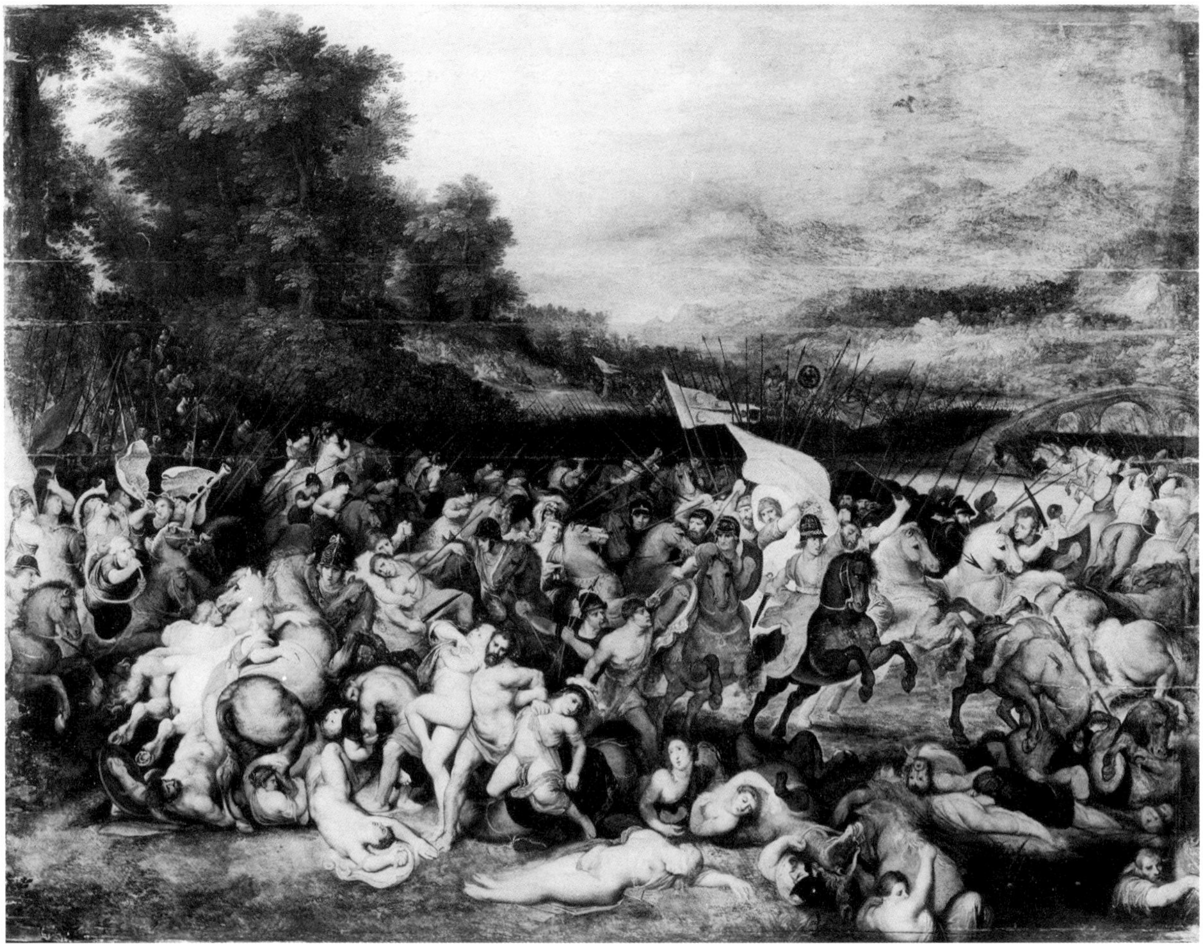

Afb. 1. Peter Paul Rubens en Jan Brueghel de Oude, *Amazonenslag*. Potsdam, Schloß Sanssouci

van Cleve en Cornelis Molenaer-Maarten van Cleve.[6] Schilders zoals Pieter Bruegel en Frans Floris daarentegen kenden het fenomeen van de samenwerking enkel binnen hun atelier.[7] Ook na de beeldenstormcrisis van 1566–1585, overleefde de praktijk van de samenwerkende productie-eenheden. Zowel schilders van autochtone als van classicistische strekkingen bleven hun krachten bundelen. Gillis van Coninxloo werkte samen met Karel van Mander en Gillis Mostaert; Joos de Momper de Jonge met Frans Francken de Jonge, Sebastiaen Vrancx, Hendrick van Balen, Jan Brueghel de Oude en Jan Brueghel de Jonge.[8] Voorts zijn er onder meer de duo's Denijs van Alsloot-Hendrick de Clerck, Abel Grimmer-Hendrick van Balen en David Vinckboons-Hendrick de Clerck.[9]

Tijdens de eerste helft van de zeventiende eeuw, wanneer het herstel van Antwerpen zich verder voltrok en wanneer de stad een beloftevol centrum bleef inzake schildersopdrachten van Kerk, hof, adel en burgerij en bovendien een goed uitgebouwde internationale kunstmarkt kende, verspreidde het fenomeen van de samenwerking zich verder. Productie-eenheden gevormd rond figuren zoals Jan Brueghel de Oude en Peter Paul Rubens hebben hierbij ongetwijfeld een rol gespeeld. Evenals het teamwork van de zestiende eeuw, was hun samenwerking ingegeven door de specialisering, die in de zeventiende eeuw op de spits gedreven werd. Niettegenstaande Brueghel en Rubens zich manifesteerden als allround schilders, waren ook zij zich bewust van hun opperste kwaliteiten: Brueghel als stilleven- en natuurschilder – zijn delicate, haast miniaturistische schildertechniek kwam in deze genres, als nergens anders, tot zijn recht – en Rubens als figuurschilder – met geniale hand wist hij in zijn vluchtige, maar perfect beheerste stijl de lichamen te animeren. Brueghel was gedurende zijn hele loopbaan vertrouwd met teamwork. De vroegste werken van Brueghel

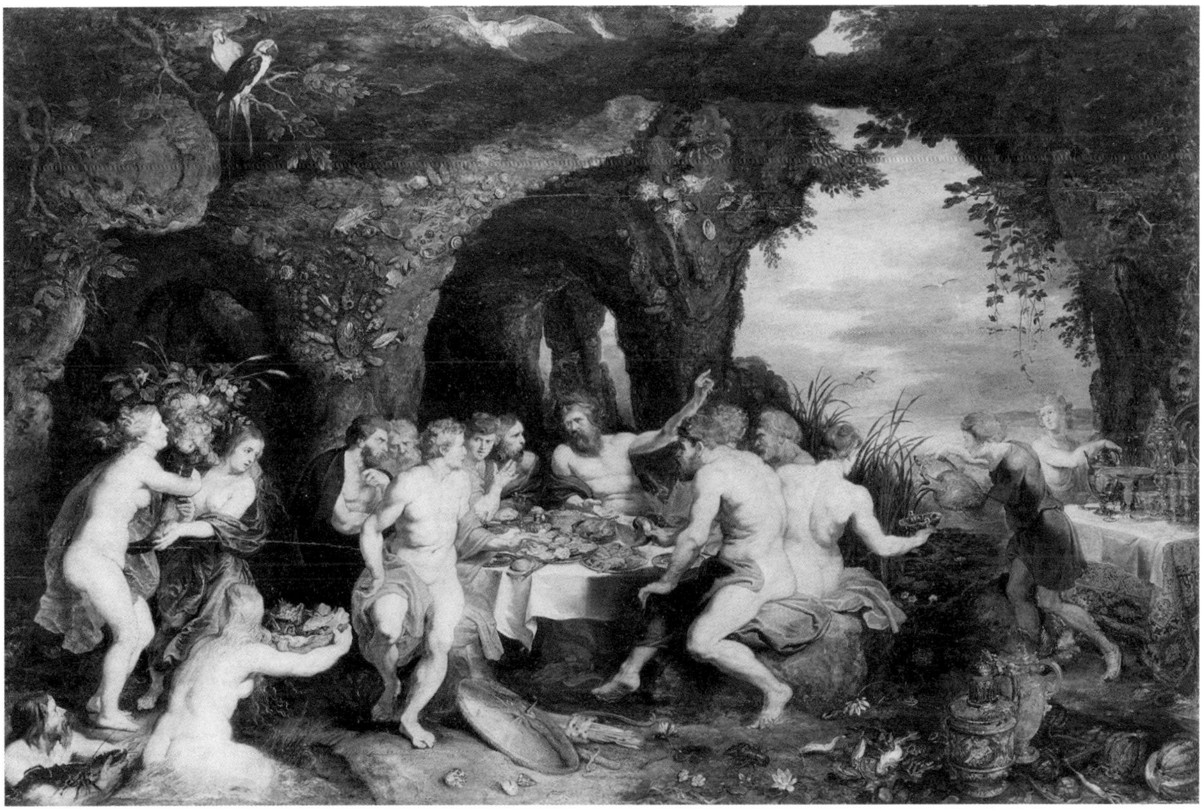

Afb. 2. Peter Paul Rubens en Jan Brueghel de Oude, *Banket van Acheloüs*. New York, The Metropolitan Museum of Art

in samenwerking kwamen tot stand tijdens zijn verblijf van 1589 tot 1596 in Italië, waar hij onder meer werkte voor kardinaal Federico Borromeo.[10] Hij schilderde er samen met Hans Rottenhammer en Jacob de Backer.[11] Ook nadien te Antwerpen, bleef hij schilderijen maken met Rottenhammer.[12] Vermoedelijk kort na zijn terugkeer uit Italië kwam hij in contact met Hendrick van Balen, met wie hij hecht bevriend raakte en voor de rest van zijn leven frequent samenwerkte. De talrijke allegorische taferelen van de zintuigen, de elementen en de seizoenen, waarbij Van Balen de landschappen van Brueghel stoffeerde, getuigen hiervan.[13] Vele van deze schilderijen werden gemaakt in opdracht van of althans voor Borromeo.[14] Ook Tobias Verhaecht, Hendrick van Steenwijck, Sebastiaen Vrancx en Hendrick de Clerck werkten al samen met Brueghel vóór Rubens' terugkeer uit Italië en het begin van diens regelmatige samenwerking met Brueghel.[15] Tijdens de jaren van samenwerking tussen Brueghel en Rubens duurden Brueghel's eerder opgezette teamworks voort en kwamen er zelfs nog nieuwe bij. Zo associeerde Brueghel zich met Joos de Momper de Jonge, waarmee hij het meest samenwerkte, met Frans Francken de Jonge, Peter van Avont, Jan Wildens en Frans Snyders.[16] Ook Rubens was gedurende zijn hele carrière, naast de samenwerking met Brueghel, eveneens werkzaam in andere productie-eenheden; deze met Jan Brueghel de Jonge, Paul Bril, Frans Snyders, Paul de Vos en Jan Wildens waren de voornaamste.[17]

De institutionele context stond de zelfstandige samenwerking niet in de weg. De arbeidsreglementering van het Sint-Lucasgilde bevatte geen specifieke richtlijnen betreffende deze tijdelijke productie-eenheden. Dit is een eerder eigenaardige vaststelling, gezien het feit dat de trend van efficiënte specialisatie en samenwerking in de loop van de zeventiende eeuw uitgroeide tot een kenschetsende modus van artistieke bedrijvigheid. Het streng gildensysteem had echter wel een atmosfeer van collegialiteit gecreëerd. Deze verbondenheid werd in sommige gevallen nog extra ondersteund door de oude traditie van de kunstenaarsfami-

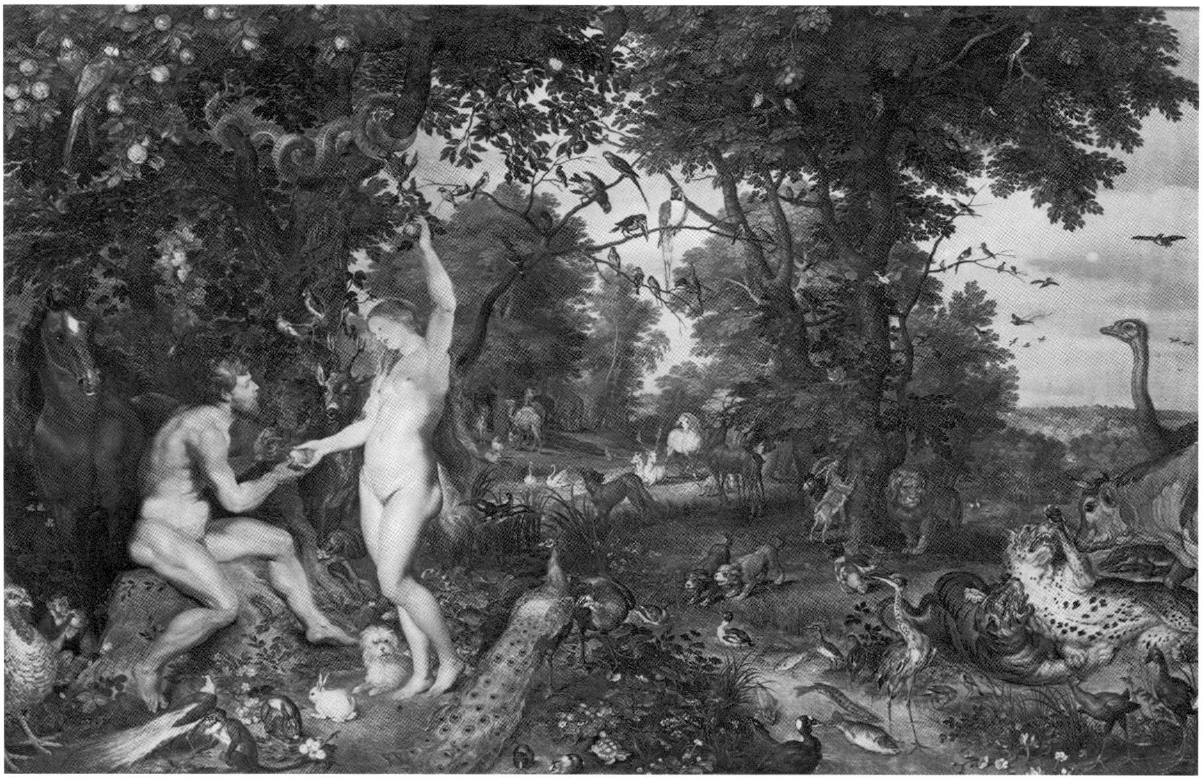

Afb. 3. Peter Paul Rubens en Jan Brueghel de Oude, *Aards Paradijs*. Den Haag, Mauritshuis

lies, die zich regelmatig via het huwelijk met mekaar verbonden. De Brueghel-, De Jode-, Kessel-, en Teniersfamilies zijn hiervan voorbeelden.[18] De impliciete erkenning door het gilde van de zelfstandige samenwerking blijkt, onder meer, uit het groot aantal dekens dat geregeld in dit soort teamwork actief is geweest. Een andere getuigenis van waardering was de schenking door de stad Antwerpen aan de aartshertogen tijdens hun bezoek in 1618 van twee panelen met de *Allegorie van het Gezicht en de Reuk* en de *Allegorie van het Gevoel, het Gehoor en de Smaak*, geschilderd in opdracht door een twaalftal kunstenaars onder leiding van Brueghel.[19] Voorts liet de Antwerpse rederijkerskamer De Violieren in 1618 haar blazoen vervaardigen door een groep van vier schilders: Frans Francken de Jonge, Hendrick van Balen, Sebastiaen Vrancx en Jan Brueghel de Oude.

De culturele en de sociaal-economische context hield verband met de manier waarop schilderijen waarde kregen in de zeventiende-eeuwse Antwerpse cultuur. In het zelfstandig teamwork dient een onderscheid te worden gemaakt tussen verschillende niveaus van samenwerking, die tevens kenmerkend waren voor de sociale status van de kunstenaars. Honig spreekt over 'low- en high-level collaborations'; Van der Stighelen bespreekt 'collaborative circuits'.[20]

Binnen de 'low-level' samenwerkingen opereerden 'tweederangs' schilders uit louter opportunistische overwegingen. Samenwerking was een noodzaak, gezien de eenzijdige vakkundigheid die de specialisering met zich meebracht. Op korte tijd kon bovendien betrekkelijk veel geproduceerd worden. Het auteurschap had quasi geen belang en werd door de handelaar, die dikwijls tussenpersoon en opdrachtgever was van de kunstenaars, geheim gehouden voor de kopers. De handelaars traden in dat geval op als organisator en verdeler.

De samenwerking tussen Brueghel en Rubens behoorde uiteraard tot de 'high-level' categorie. Bepalend voor de stijgende waarde en het groeiend succes van deze schilderijen was eerst en vooral hun grote kwaliteit. Het spreekt voor zich dat de bundeling van de vakkundigheid van twee vooraanstaande schilders als Brueghel en Rubens, opererend in het door hen meest beheerste genre, extra kwaliteit schonk aan hun werken. Waarde en succes van deze werken waren voorts grotendeels te wijten aan de hoge socio-culturele status van de coöpererende schilders, in casu het duo Brueghel-Rubens. De stijgende belangstelling van de zeventiende-eeuwse toeschouwer voor het auteurschap van een schilderij in het algemeen en de daarmee gepaard gaande nieuwe rol en sociale status van de 'connaisseur' populariseerden het beschouwen en trachten onderscheiden van verschillende handen in schilderijen in samenwerking. In tegenstelling tot de renaissancistische gedachte dat het auteurschap in het brein van één kunstenaar lag, los van de eigenlijke uitvoering, die mogelijk door het atelier gebeurde, beoordeelde de nieuwe kunstkenner een in expressie meervoudig auteurschap. Het bezit van schilderijen in samenwerking werd sociaal geprivilegieerd. De waarde van een werk hing af van het al dan niet kunnen toeschrijven van de geschilderde partijen aan bekende specialisten. Naast de canon van belangrijke schilders, ontstond er ook één van de voornaamste samenwerkingsteams; onder de toppers waren de duo's Brueghel-Rubens, Brueghel-De Momper, Brueghel-Van Balen. Omdat de vraag naar schilderijen van deze voorname teams niet altijd kon worden gevolgd en omdat dergelijke werken voor de grootste cliënteel onbetaalbaar waren, kwam een kopieermolen op gang. Weinigen van de eersterangs kunstenaars kloegen dit aan. Integendeel, velen deden er met de hulp van hun atelier zelf aan mee. Zo ontstonden naast het principaal of het oorspronkelijk schilderij, de eigenhandige replieken en varianten en de kopieën.

Het is duidelijk dat met het duo Brueghel-Rubens de samenwerking geen nieuw, evenmin zeldzaam, verschijnsel was. Het was een reeds doorheen de zestiende eeuw ontwikkeld fenomeen, dat zich bij deze kunstenaars evenwel onderscheidde omwille van zijn prestigieus karakter.

Het eerste schilderij van Brueghel en Rubens, namelijk de *Amazonenslag* (Potsdam, Schloß Sanssouci, inv. 10021; afb. 1), dateert van 1598–1600. Hun regelmatige samenwerking startte echter vanaf de terugkeer van Rubens uit Italië op het einde van 1608. Wat hun persoonlijke motieven hierbij betrof, is het bekend

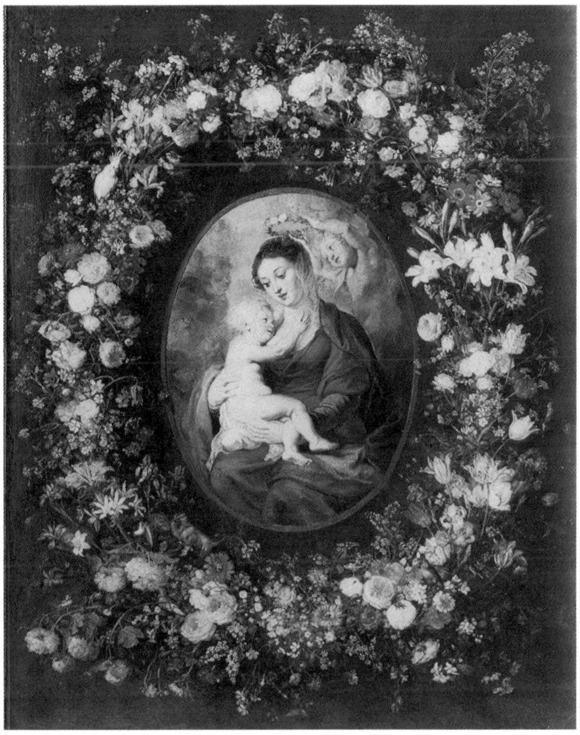

Afb. 4. Peter Paul Rubens en Jan Brueghel de Oude, *Madonna en Kind in krans*. Parijs, Musée du Louvre

dat ze sowieso een wederkerige bewondering voor mekaar koesterden. Van bij het begin van hun carrière genoten ze bekendheid om hun extreme artistieke kwaliteiten. Ze behoorden tot de hoogste klasse van schilders van dat ogenblik te Antwerpen en werden ook zo gerespecteerd door hun tijdgenoten. Dit had tot gevolg dat ze tot eenzelfde artistieke gemeenschap, circuit, behoorden en dat hun sociale contacten en status grotendeels dezelfde waren, net zoals hun opdrachtgevers uit hoofse en diplomatieke kringen. Hun samenvallende of kruisende levenslopen hebben zeker het ideaal kader gecreëerd, waarbinnen een vriendschappelijke relatie en samenwerking kon ontstaan. Hierin lag een stukje van het succes en het exclusieve karakter van hun teamwork, dat zeker niet productiever was dan bijvoorbeeld de samenwerking Brueghel Van Balen of Brueghel-De Momper, vervat.

De artistieke drijfveren lagen vermoedelijk aan de basis van hun initiatief. Zoals reeds eerder gezegd, als allround schilders van de hoogste rang verkozen Brueghel en Rubens, niettegenstaande hun afzonderlijk succes, om toch in team te werken. Door hun krachten te bundelen, konden de verschillende partijen met

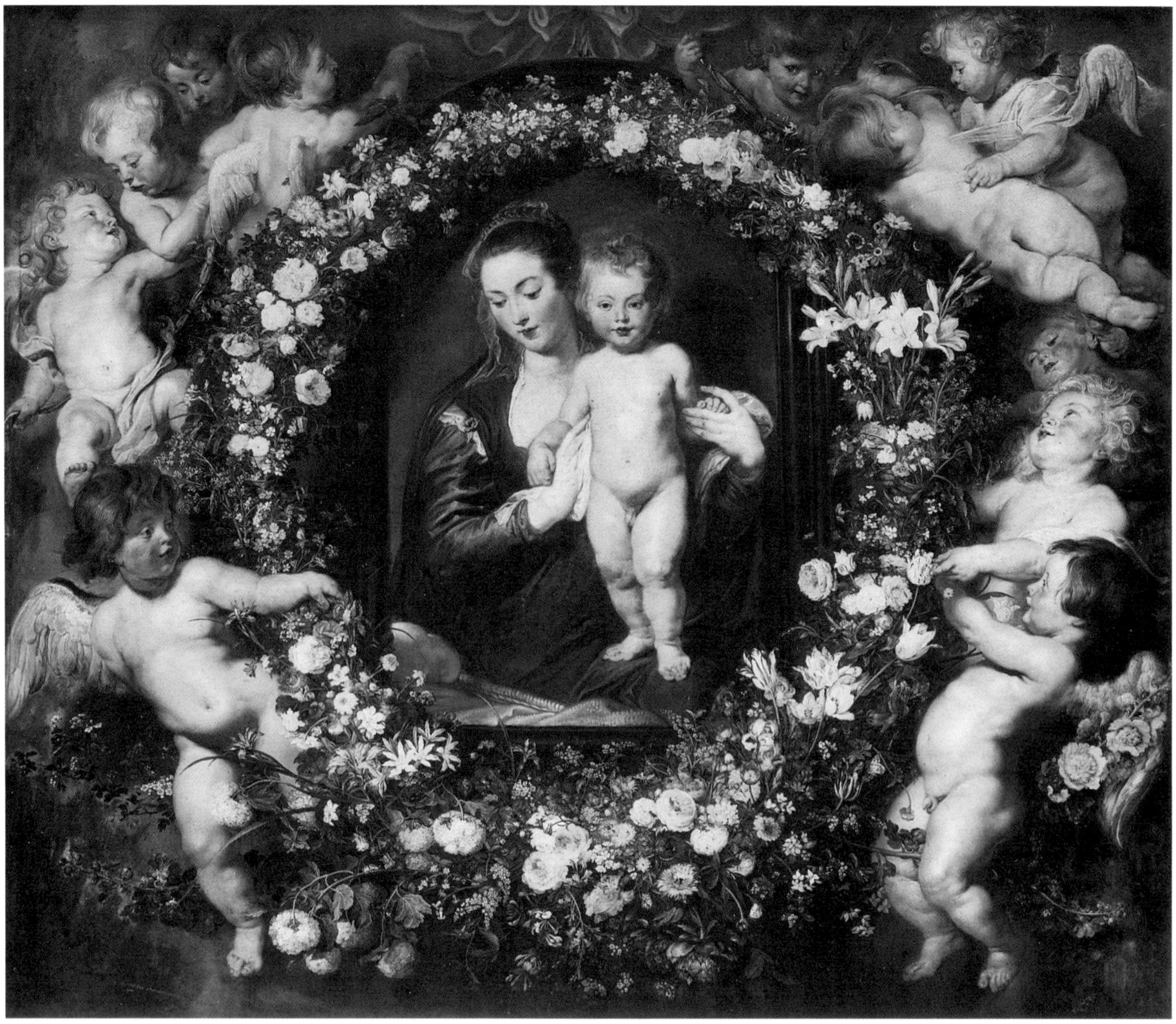

Afb. 5. Peter Paul Rubens en Jan Brueghel de Oude, *Madonna en Kind in krans met engelen*. München, Alte Pinakothek

een uiterste vakkundigheid worden uitgewerkt. Alleen op die manier kon men komen tot de meest perfecte gehelen, in een veelzijdige stijl. Het feit dat ze hun principale schilderijen dikwijls in hun eigen collecties koesterden, zegt iets over hun appreciatie ervan. Hierover getuigen bovendien verschillende brieven van Jan Brueghel de Oude, alsook het dagboek van Jan Brueghel de Jonge.

Wat de consumptie van de schilderijen van Rubens in samenwerking met de Brueghels betreft – Jan Brueghel de Jonge dient hier eveneens in beschouwing genomen te worden, omdat hij na de dood van zijn vader voor continuïteit zorgde in de verspreiding van composities in samenwerking met Rubens –, onderscheidden zich als verbruikers: de schilders zelf, de mecenassen, de vaste cliënteel en de potentiële markt, via de jaarmarkt en de kunsthandel. Het is, onder meer, op basis van de consumptie dat men het samenwerkingstijdperk van Rubens en de Brueghels kan opdelen in grosso modo vier periodes: 1598–1600, 1609–1619, 1620–1625 en 1625–1644. Het duiden van de herkomst van schilderijen is in dit opzicht van groot belang.

Uit de periode van 1598, het tijdstip waarop Rubens als meester werd ingeschreven in de Antwerpse Sint-Lucasgilde, tot 1600, het jaar van zijn vertrek naar Italië, is slechts één schilderij gekend dat met zekerheid aan Brueghel en Rubens kan worden toegeschreven, met name de reeds vermelde *Amazonenslag*[21] (afb. 1). Een repliek[22] van dit werk bevindt zich in een Belgische privé-verzameling. Het Potsdam-schilderij is niet alleen

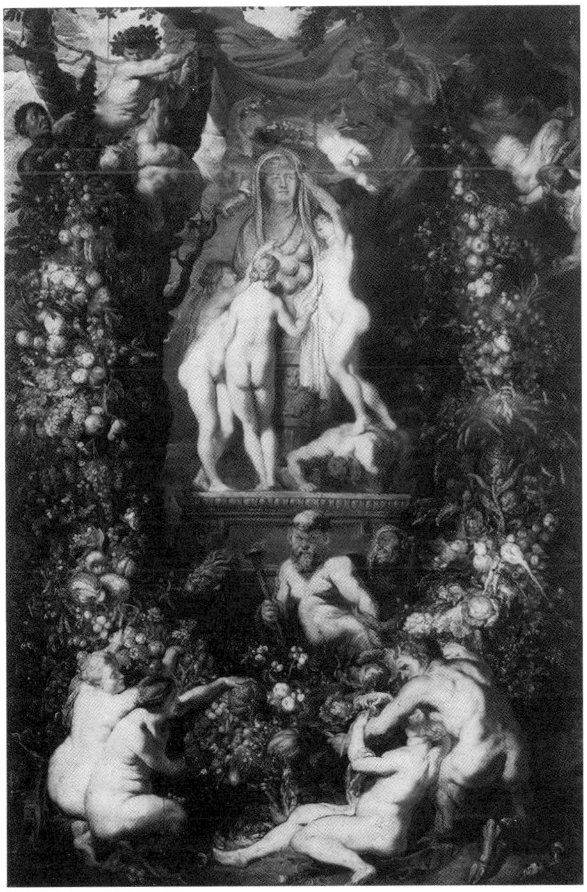

Afb. 6. Peter Paul Rubens en Jan Brueghel de Oude, *Natuur met de Drie Gratiën in guirlande*. Glasgow, Art Gallery

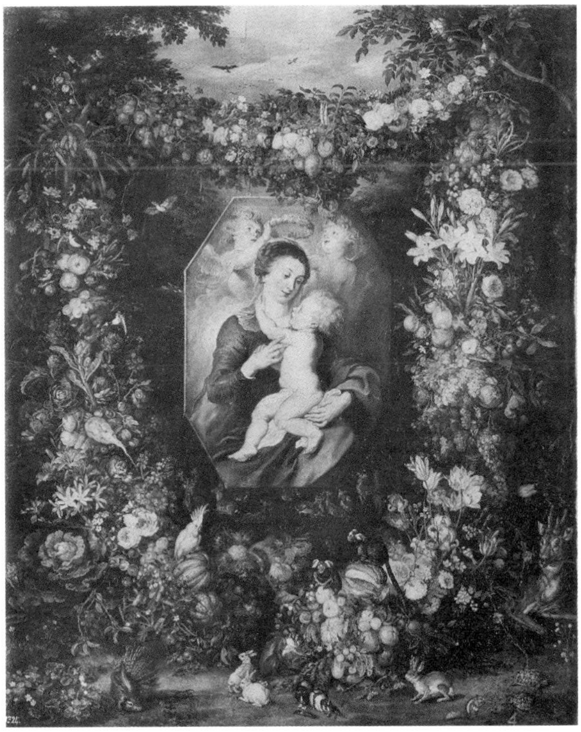

Afb. 7. Peter Paul Rubens en Jan Brueghel de Oude, *Madonna en Kind in guirlande*. Madrid, Museo del Prado

het eerste product van hùn samenwerking, het is tevens de oudste getuigenis van de samenwerking van Rubens in het algemeen en zelfs één van zijn vroegste werken. Het schilderij is vermoedelijk te identificeren met het werk dat vermeld wordt in de 1682 gedateerde inventaris van Diego Duarte de Jonge: 'Van Petro Paulo Rubbens... No. 62 Een stuck op paneel den slagh van de Amasoonen vol werckx van syn vroege manier. Het lantschap ofte verschiet is geheel vanden Fluweelen Bruegel'.[23] Mogelijk kocht Gaspar Duarte de Oude, de vader van Diego, het paneel rechtstreeks van Rubens. In een symposiumbijdrage in 1982 gaf Held[24] reeds een overzicht van de studies en polemieken over de toeschrijving van het Potsdam-schilderij, waarbij het onderzoek van het vroegste œuvre van Rubens en van de betrokkenheid van diens leermeester Van Veen[25] van groot belang was. Uiteindelijk bleek de toeschrijving aan Rubens en Brueghel alge meen aanvaard. De toeschrijving van de Belgische repliek is mijns inziens veel minder overtuigend en dient verder te worden onderzocht.[26] De vermelding in de inventaris van de verzameling van Herman Neyts, opgemaakt op 15–21 oktober 1642, van 'Een stuck van Octavi ende Breugel ende van Rubens eerst geschilderd, met buytenlyst, wesende den berch Parnassus', doet vermoeden dat het tweetal nog meer heeft samengewerkt in deze periode en eveneens in trio met Otto van Veen.[27] Het feit dat Rubens zich, kort na het verlaten van het atelier van zijn leermeester, waagde aan een samenwerking met Brueghel, zegt niet alleen iets over Rubens' prille, hoog artistiek niveau en zijn quasi onmiddellijke plaats binnen het topniveau van schilders op dat ogenblik te Antwerpen; het is tevens een teken aan de wand over de toen reeds heersende vertrouwdheid met het fenomeen van de samenwerking. Vermoedelijk ging het om initiatieven van de betrokken schilders zelf, waarbij deze prestigieuze producten ofwel bewaard bleven in hun eigen verzameling ofwel aangeprezen werden bij belangrijke collectioneurs van het ogenblik, zoals bijvoorbeeld de hoger vermelde Gaspar Duarte de Oude en Herman Neyts.

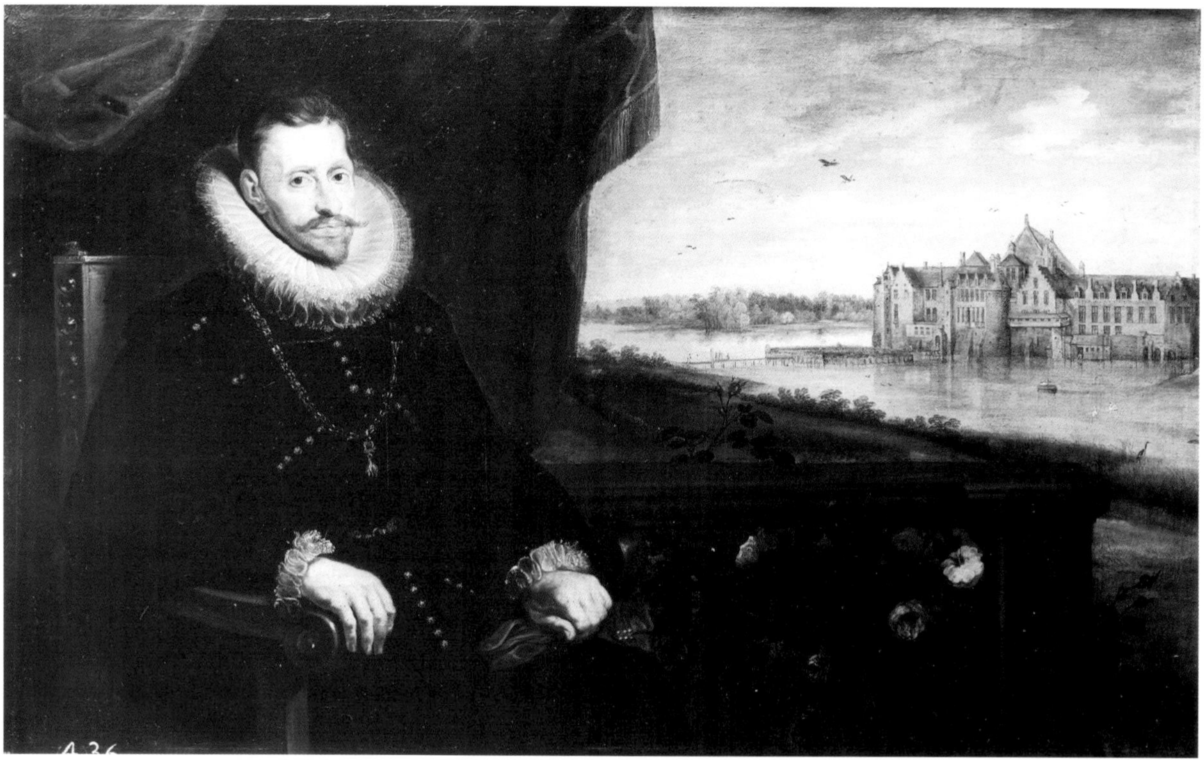

Afb. 8. Peter Paul Rubens en Jan Brueghel de Oude, *Portret van aartshertog Albrecht*. Madrid, Museo del Prado

De belangrijkste tijdspanne inzake de samenwerking Rubens-Brueghel was de periode 1609–1621. Het leek bijna vanzelfsprekend dat hun teamwork na Rubens' terugkeer uit Italië werd hervat, ook al was de samenwerking van Brueghel met voornamelijk Hendrick van Balen intussen erg geactiveerd en begon ook Rubens zich te associëren met andere schilders zoals Paul Bril en Frans Snyders. Wanneer het lot hen bovendien samenbracht aan het aartshertogelijk hof ontstonden ideale omstandigheden die hun samenwerking extra stimuleerden. De aartshertogen Albrecht en Isabella gedroegen zich als ware mecenassen.[28] Brueghel werkte vanaf 1606 geregeld voor hen.[29] Rubens was vanaf 1609 in dienst als hofschilder.[30]

Slechts enkele opdrachten voor Albrecht en Isabella zijn effectief gedocumenteerd. Het vroegste werk dat met de Aartshertogen in verband kan worden gebracht, is het *Banket van Acheloüs*[31] (New York, The Metropolitan Museum of Art, inv. 45.141; afb. 2) van 1614–1615. Het schilderij, of een versie ervan, is afgebeeld in het kabinet op de *Allegorie van de Schilderkunst*[32] (Kasteel van Anet, verzameling C. de Yturbe) van een anonieme Vlaamse meester. Dit kabinet kan, omwille van het kasteel van Mariemont op de achtergrond, geïdentificeerd worden met de verzameling van de Aartshertogen.[33] In het *Banket van Acheloüs* heeft Rubens de compositie vastgelegd en de figuren geschilderd en vervolgens heeft Brueghel het landschap en het decor verder uitgewerkt. Eveneens van 1614–1615 dateert waarschijnlijk het *Aards Paradijs*[34] (Den Haag, Mauritshuis, inv. 253; afb. 3), dat vermoedelijk ooit in het bezit is geweest van de verzamelaar Johann de Bye in Leiden (1666).[35] Ook in dit schilderij was Rubens verantwoordelijk voor de grote lijnen van de compositie, niettegenstaande hij enkel de figuren van Adam en Eva en mogelijk ook het paard effectief uitwerkte; Brueghel leverde vervolgens het landschap en de dieren.[36]

Kort daarna schilderden Rubens en Brueghel enkele *Madonna's in krans*. Een oerversie dateert van 1615–1617 en komt voor op hun *Allegorie van het Gezicht* (Madrid, Museo del Prado, inv. 1394) van 1617, waarop het deel uitmaakt van de verzameling van de Aartshertogen. De grootte van het werk wijst op de mogelijke functie van devotiebeeld voor een kerk of privé-kapel.[37] Vermoedelijk leverden ze, op initiatief van

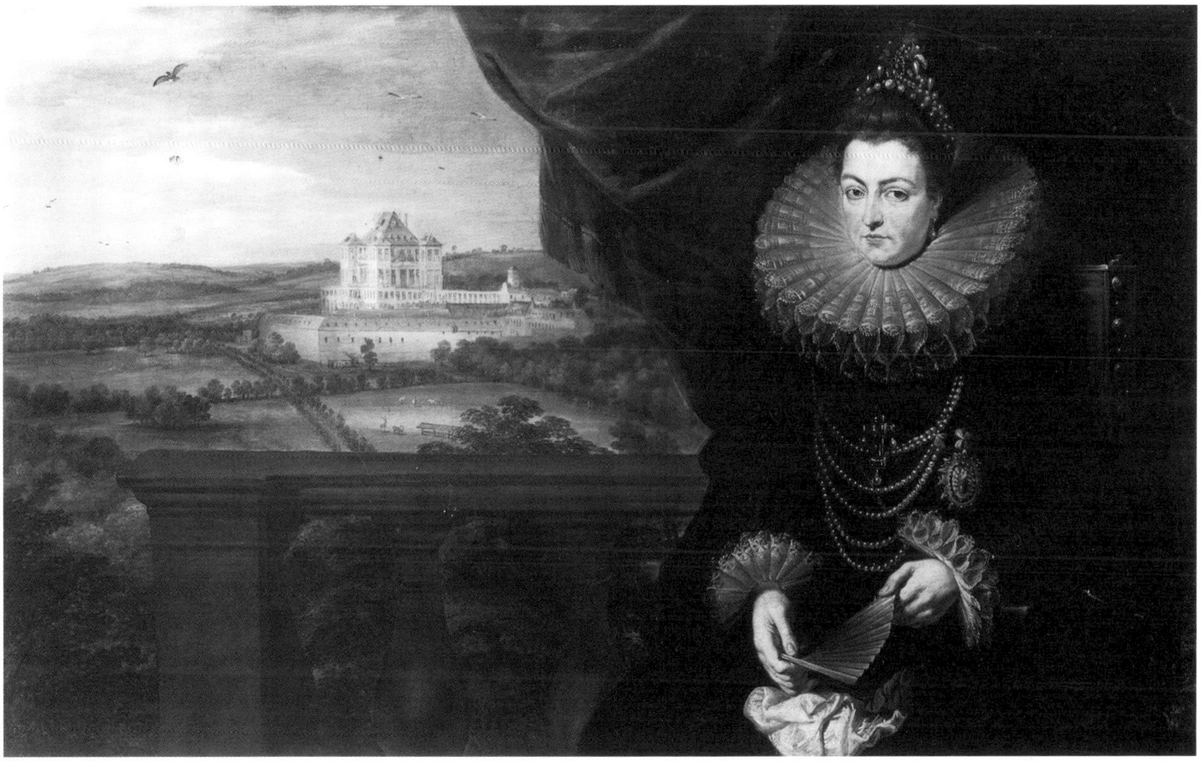

Afb. 9. Peter Paul Rubens en Jan Brueghel de Oude, *Portret van aartshertogin Isabella*. Madrid, Museo del Prado

Brueghel, na 1617–1618 een kleinere variante[38] (Parijs, Musée du Louvre, inv. 1764; afb. 4) voor kardinaal Federico Borromeo. De *Louvre Madonna* was Brueghels eerste werk in samenwerking met Rubens voor de kardinaal.[39] Van dezelfde jaren dateert de *Madonna in krans met engelen*[40] (München, Alte Pinakothek, inv. 331; afb. 5). Het initiatief ging uit van Rubens, die het schilderij mogelijk maakte voor Georges Villiers, hertog van Buckingham, of later aan deze bezorgde.[41] Het feit dat Rubens initiatiefnemer was, komt op verschillende manieren tot uiting. Eerst en vooral is, in vergelijking met de Louvre Madonna, zijn aandeel in de compositie groter; het tafereel van het medaillon loopt uit in de omringende bloemenkrans die door engelen is bevolkt.[42] Het accentueren van de verschillende plans en het onderling verbinden ervan creëert ruimtelijkheid. In de *Louvre Madonna* daarentegen blijft de Rubenspartij nauwkeurig gescheiden van de krans in een vooraf ingekrast ovaal. Het vernieuwend Rubens-concept in het schilderij in München heeft een gelijkaardige evolutie binnen de kransen in het algemeen mede in gang gezet. Bovendien werd, op initiatief van Rubens, de compositie van het werk gewijzigd: het paneel werd vergroot en de schikking van de engelen veranderd.[43] Deze aanpassingen werden doorgevoerd voor Brueghel zijn krans uitwerkte, wat eveneens wijst op het inventorschap van Rubens van de grote lijnen van de compositie. Voorts is de inbreng van Rubens origineel omwille van de keuze van de afgebeelde figuren, Isabella Brant met de kleine Jan II, als Madonna en Kind. Ten slotte onderscheidt het schilderij zich omwille van de buitengewone afmetingen, wat ook hier wijst op een functie als devotiebeeld, bestemd voor een kerk of privé-kapel.[44] In ca. 1619 ontstaat, op initiatief van Rubens, *de Natuur met de Drie Gratiën in guirlande*[45] (Glasgow, Art Gallery, inv. 609; afb. 6). Mogelijk kwam in 1624 het werk, dat tot dan in de Rubensverzameling was gebleven, een tijdje in het bezit van prins Wladislas Sigismund van Polen;[46] in 1625–1627 verkocht Rubens het aan hertog Georges Villiers van Buckingham.[47] Ook in dit schilderij deint het middentafereel uit buiten het vooraf ingekrast ovaal, in en zelfs buiten de bloemenguirlande, die alzo wordt opgenomen in het toneel van het medaillon. Deze betrokkenheid wordt verder ondersteund door de symbolische verwijzingen van de krans naar

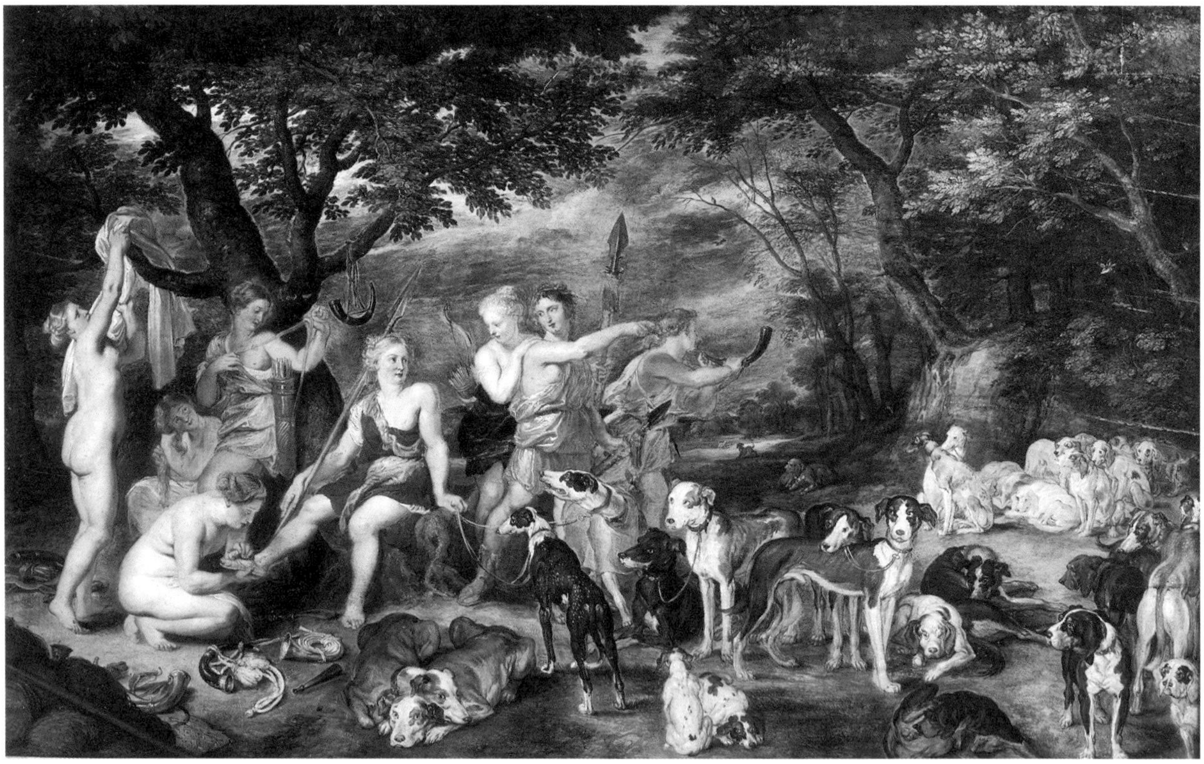

Afb. 10. Peter Paul Rubens en Jan Brueghel de Oude, *Vertrek van Diana naar de jacht*. Parijs, Musée de la Chasse et de la Nature

het centrale tafereel. Een vergelijkbare compositie is deze van het *Offer aan Ceres met vruchtenguirlande* van Brueghel, dit keer in samenwerking met Hendrick van Balen. De oerversie, afgebeeld op de *Allegorie van de Smaak* (Madrid, Museo del Prado, inv. 1397), is meer dan waarschijnlijk te identificeren met de *Ceres*[48] van ca. 1618 in Belgisch privé-bezit. De evolutie van de kransen naar de U-vormige guirlandes zette zich voort, om uiteindelijk te eindigen in het type van de gesloten U-slinger zoals in de *Madonna en Kind in guirlande*[49] (Madrid, Museo del Prado, inv. 1418; afb. 7). Brueghel en Rubens schilderden het, op initiatief van de eerste, voor kardinaal Federico Borromeo en dit kort voor 1621.[50] Borromeo, aanvankelijk niet erg opgetogen over de bijdrage van Rubens en niet geïnteresseerd in het verwerven van het schilderij, kocht het uiteindelijk toch vóór 8 juli 1622; Brueghel ontving 300 scudi en Rubens daarentegen slechts 1 goudstuk.[51] Het Brueghel-stilleven is in dit werk uitzonderlijk breed uitgewerkt.

Omstreeks 1616–1617 schilderde het duo in opdracht van de aartshertogen Albrecht en Isabella hun beider *Portret*[52] (Madrid, Museo del Prado, inv. 1683–1684; afb. 8–9). Brueghels achtergronden bieden een gezicht op enerzijds het hertogelijk kasteel te Tervuren (*Portret van Albrecht*) en het buitenverblijf te Mariemont (*Portret van Isabella*). Zoals Vlieghe[53] stelt, werd bij de uitwerking van de portretten een beroep gedaan op de medewerking van Rubens' atelier. Een hoogtepunt in de samenwerking van Rubens en Brueghel is de vijfdelige allegorische reeks met de *Zintuigen* (Madrid, Museo del Prado, inv. 1394–1398)[54] van 1617–1618. In deze cyclus van een, zowel op artistiek als iconografisch vlak, uitzonderlijk niveau worden de zintuigen uitgebeeld in verschillende hoofse contexten. De serie doet zich voor als een bewuste vormgeving van het aartshertogelijk begrip voor kunst en verzamelen en van de representatieve rol van pracht en praal.[55] De Aartshertogen schonken deze schilderijen aan Wolfgang Wilhelm van Palts-Neuburg, hun belangrijkste bondgenoot binnen de katholieke alliantie. De reeds vermelde pendanten met de *Zintuigen*, in 1618 geschilderd door een twaalftal kunstenaars onder leiding van Brueghel en geschonken door de stad Antwerpen aan Albrecht en Isabella, dienen hier eveneens vernoemd. De werken gingen verloren in de brand van het Coudenberg-

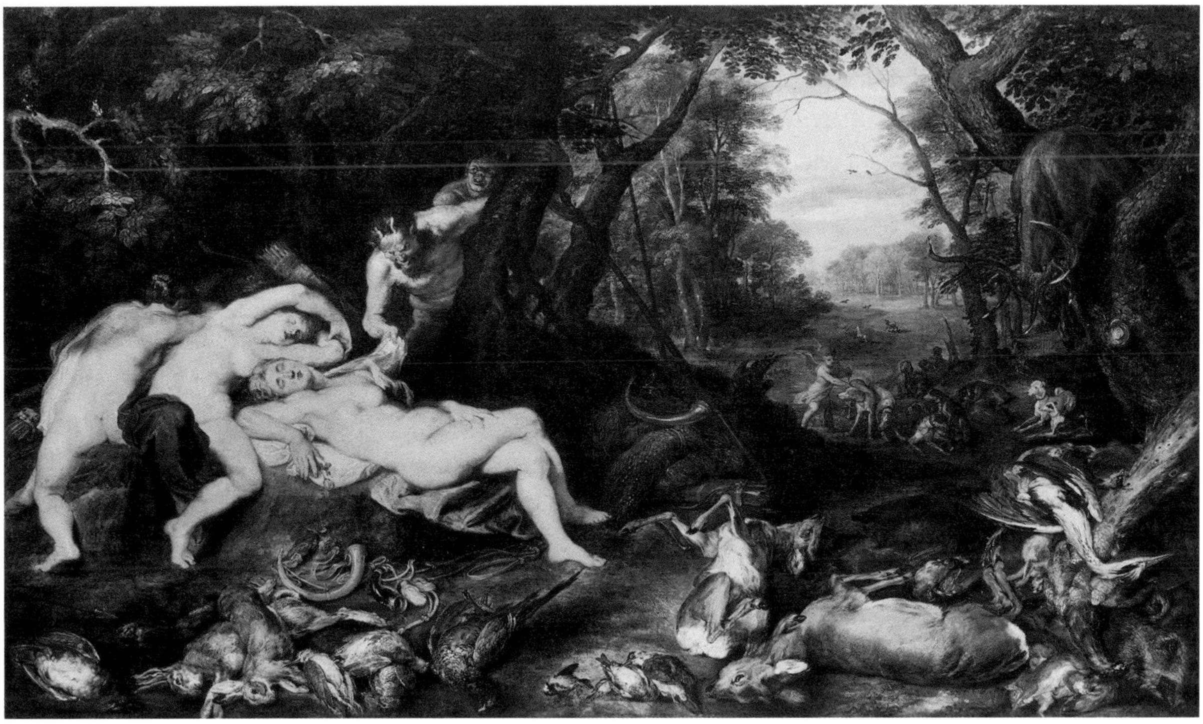

Afb. 11. Peter Paul Rubens en Jan Brueghel de Oude, *Slapende nimfen*. München, Bayerische Staatsgemäldesammlungen

kasteel in 1731, maar bleven bekend via repliekken[56] (Madrid, Museo del Prado, inv. 1403–1404) van Jan Brueghel de Oude in samenwerking met andere kunstenaars.

Het patronage speelde door het stimuleren van de creatie van dergelijke prestigieuze werken een belangrijke rol in de latere popularisatie van het zelfstandig samenwerkingsverband. Pausen, pauselijke nuntii, vorsten, hertogen, diplomaten, edellieden vervulden niet zelden de rol van mecenas.

Ook voor de periode 1621–1625, blijven de gedocumenteerde opdrachten aan Rubens en Brueghel schaars. Toch is het duidelijk dat de vaste cliënteel zich in deze jaren uitbreidde naar een ruimere groep. De verruiming van deze klantenkring was een gevolg van de talrijker wordende relaties van Rubens, via zijn frequentere diplomatieke missies na het overlijden van aartshertog Albrecht. Tijdens deze jaren kregen landschappen met historietaferelen voor het eerst een duidelijk overwicht in de productie van het team. Ze schilderden een *Noli me tangere*, ons bekend via onder meer een repliek[57] (Bremen, Kunsthalle, inv. 73657/3) van 1630–1632 van Rubens en Jan Brueghel de Jonge. In 1620–1621 ontstond een *Visioen van de Heilige Hubertus*, oorspronkelijk in het bezit van Oranje, maar uiteindelijk verloren gegaan in een brand in 1945 in een schilderijendepot van het Kaiser-Friedrich-Museum te Berlijn (inv. 765).[58] De compositie is ons bekend via onder meer een repliek (Madrid, Museo del Prado, inv. 1411) van Jan Brueghel de Oude.[59] Van deze jaren dateert verder een reeks Dianataferelen, met het *Vertrek van Diana naar de jacht*[60] (Parijs, Musée de la Chasse et de la Nature, inv. 6831; afb. 10) – waarvan al dan niet dezelfde versie vermeld is in Rubens' nalatenschap en afgebeeld op een omstreeks 1621 ontstane *Allegorie van de Schilderkunst* (Kasteel van Anet, verzameling C. de Yturbe) van een anonieme Vlaamse meester en op het *Atelier van Apelles* (Den Haag, Mauritshuis, inv. 266) van 1630–1635 van Willem van Haecht, en waarvan in 1645 door handelaar Musson een variante aangeboden werd aan Amalia van Solms, de *Rust van Diana tijdens de Jacht*[61] (München, Bayerische Staatsgemäldesammlungen, inv. 346/3885; afb. 11), *Slapende nimfen*[62] (München, Bayerische Staatsgemäldesammlungen, inv. 344/3884) – mogelijk ooit in het bezit van Oranje in het Lookasteel –, een andere voorstelling van *Slapende nimfen*[63] (Parijs, Musée de la Chasse et de la Nature, inv. 6832) – ooit in het bezit van Frederik de Grote (Potsdam, Schloß Sanssouci) –, een 1620 gedateerde *Terugkeer van Diana*[64] (München, Bayerische Staatsgemäldesammlungen, inv. 842) en ten slotte een *Pan en Syrinx*[65] (Engelse privé-verzameling) – vermeld in de sterfhuis-inventaris van Jan Brueghel de Oude. Twijfelachtiger toeschrijvingen, maar waarbij men overtuigd is dat oerversies van de hand van Brueghel en Rubens hebben bestaan, zijn *Zephyros en Flora* (Dessau, Schloß Mosigkau, inv. 6), *De Emmaüsgangers* (Sint-Petersburg, Hermitage, inv. 525) en de *Drie Gratiën* (Wenen, Akademie der bildenden Künste, inv. 646).[66]

Na het overlijden van Jan Brueghel de Oude is zijn zoon tegemoetgekomen aan een groter wordende cliënteel. Zoals reeds eerder gezegd, kenden deze schilderijen in samenwerking een groeiend succes, niet alleen omwille van de artistieke meerwaarde op zich, maar ook door de toenemende status van de kunstverzamelaar als 'connaisseur' in het onderscheiden van auteurschappen. In het kader van deze modieuze trend is het opmerkelijk hoe de modaliteit van uitvoering van een schilderij, namelijk de samenwerking, een drijfveer werd bij de conceptie ervan. De kunsthandel en jaarmarkten speelden een belangrijke rol bij de popularisatie van de zelfstandige samenwerking. Dit zorgde voor een potentiële cliënteel voor dergelijke schilderijen; men kan in zekere zin spreken van een massaconsumptie-gerichte productie. De grote vraag bracht een kopieercampagne op gang, die zoals bij Jan Brueghel de Jonge dikwijls ondersteund werd door de kunstenaar zelf. Talrijke getuigenissen hiervan komen voor in zijn dagboek. De replieken en kopieën werden aanvankelijk verkocht voor wat ze waren. Dit werkte zolang er een direct contact was tussen de kunstenaar en de handelaar of klanten, maar op de markt verliep het twijfelachtiger. In deze atmosfeer komt de 'low-level' samenwerking sterk op. De tussenkomst van de handelaars Mattijs Musson, Fourmenois, Forchoudt, Goetkint & Van Immerseel zijn hierbij van belang. Inventarissen van kwalitatieve collecties waarin we producten van zelfstandige samenwerking terugvinden, zijn deze van Jan van Meurs, Nicolaas Cornelis Cheeus, Cornelis van der Gheest, Pieter Paul Rubens, Nicolaas Rockox, Arnold Lunden, Peeter Stevens, Peter van Hecke, Dierick Fabri, Gillis de Kimpe, J. Placquet, J. Noydens, H. van Cantelbeeck.

Het verloop van de ontwerp- en de uitvoeringsfases binnen het creatieve proces van schilderijen van Rubens in samenwerking met Brueghel is, zoals eerder gezegd, nu niet aan de orde.[67] Toch moeten we stellen dat de totale kijk op de ontwerp- en de uitvoeringsstadia bijkomende informatie geeft over de conceptfases. Met andere woorden, de inbreng van beide schilders in het ontwerp en de uitvoering zegt ook iets over hun initiatief bij het ontstaan van het concept. Meestal was het de initiatiefnemer die verantwoordelijk was voor de grote lijnen van de compositie, wat niet meteen inhield dat ook hij het grootste gedeelte van de compositie effectief uitwerkte. Het belang van hun aandeel bij de uitwerking was uiteraard afhankelijk van de verhouding tussen het landschaps-stilleven en de figuren binnen de compositie.

Het is duidelijk dat de samenwerking Brueghel-Rubens zeker geen uniek verschijnsel was maar eerder een voorbeeld van een reeds in de zestiende eeuw ontwikkeld fenomeen. Het onderscheidde zich evenwel omwille van zijn prestigieus karakter, een rechtstreeks gevolg van de artistieke en de sociale status van de betrokken grootmeesters Brueghel en Rubens en de uitzonderlijke kwaliteit van hun schilderijen. Als succesvolle schilders waren ze niet verplicht tot samenwerking, maar hun vriendschappelijke relatie manifesteerde zich op de eerste plaats in hun werk.

NOTEN

1. Maakt deel uit van mijn proefschrift in voorbereiding: *Een analyse van het creatieve proces in het œuvre van Peter Paul Rubens in samenwerking met Jan Brueghel de Oude en Jan Brueghel de Jonge.*

2. De stadia van het ontwerp en de uitvoering van hun schilderijen in samenwerking blijven hierna zo goed als onbesproken.

3. Het teamwork van Rubens en Jan Brueghel de Jonge ontwikkelde zich van 1624 – het jaar waarin Brueghel de Jonge terugkeerde uit Italië en het 'atelier' van zijn vader overnam – tot 1644, het sterftejaar van Rubens.

4. Madonna's, narratieve devotietaferelen, moraliserende genretonelen en portretten bestonden toen reeds naast mekaar. Over de evoluties binnen de zestiende-eeuwse Antwerpse schilderkunst zie G.T. Faggin, *La pittura ad Anversa nel Cinquecento*, Firenze, 1968; C.Van de Velde, 'De Schilderkunst', in *Antwerpen in de XVIde Eeuw*, Antwerpen, 1975, pp. 419–445. De florerende handelsmetropool Antwerpen van de zestiende eeuw speelde bij deze ontwikkelingen een stimulerende rol. De grote concentratie van, al dan niet ingeweken, voortreffelijke schilders, de stijgende vraag naar en productie van schilderijen, de groeiende commercialisering – via de handelsstructuren zoals het Onze-Lieve-Vrouwepand tijdens jaarmarkten en de vanaf 1540 permanente schilderijengalerij in de beurs – en serieproductie van deze artefacten waren van groot belang. A. Thijs, 'De Antwerpse luxenijverheid: winstbejag en kunstzin', in [cat. tent.] *Antwerpen. Verhaal van een metropool. 16de-17de eeuw* (Antwerpen, Hessenhuis, 1993), Gent, 1993, pp. 105–113.

5. Bijvoorbeeld *De verzoeking van de Heilige Antonius*, gesigneerd 'OPUS JOACHIM *AT*NIER' (Madrid, Prado, inv. 1615) van Patinier-Metsijs.

6. Bijvoorbeeld *Landschap met kasteel en herberg*, gesigneerd en gedateerd 'IACOB GRI.F.1583 AVG 16/GM' (Wenen, Kunsthistorisches Museum, inv. 5652) van Grimmer-Mostaert; *De parabel van de Barmhartige Samaritaan* (Berlijn, Staatliche Museen, inv. 706) van Molenaer-Van Cleve.

7. In het atelier naar Italiaans model, rond het midden van de zestiende eeuw in de Nederlanden geïntroduceerd door Frans Floris, was de meester op de eerste plaats verantwoordelijk voor de inventie van een schilderij en werd de uitvoering ervan dikwijls overgelaten aan meerdere gespecialiseerde medewerkers. De atelierwerking is niet te vergelijken met de samenwerking van zelfstandige schilders en is hier niet aan de orde. Mogelijk heeft de vertrouwdheid met de 'ondergeschikte' samenwerking van gespecialiseerde helpers binnen het atelier de 'zelfstandige' samenwerking mede gestimuleerd.

8. Bijvoorbeeld *Landschap met het oordeel van Midas* (Dresden, Staatliche Kunstsammlungen, inv. 857) van Van Coninxloo-Van Mander; *Bezoek van Minerva aan de muzen*, gesigneerd 'BALE MOMP..BRVEGH..' (Antwerpen, Koninklijk Museum voor Schone Kunsten, inv. 957) van De Momper-Van Balen-Brueghel.

9. Bijvoorbeeld *Woudlandschap met Kephalos en Prokris*, gesigneerd en gedateerd 'D:ab Alsloot S:A: Pict:1608//H. de Clerck' (Wenen, Kunsthistorisches Museum, inv. 1077) van Van Alsloot-De Clerck; *Antwerpen met de Schelde en de Heilige Drievuldigheid*, gesigneerd en gedateerd 'ABEL GRIMMER FECIT 1600' (Antwerpen, Koninklijk Museum voor Schone Kunsten, inv. 817) van Grimmer-Van Balen.

10. Vanaf zijn verblijf te Milaan in 1595–1596, had de schilder zich onder de hoede geplaatst van deze mecenas. Tot aan de dood van Borromeo bleef Brueghel met hem in nauw contact en leverde voor hem talrijke werken.

11. Bijvoorbeeld *Circe en Odysseus*, gesigneerd en gedateerd *Brueghel 1595* (Toronto, Art Gallery of Ontario) van Brueghel-Rottenhammer; *Landschap met Diana en Aktaion*, ca. 1591 (Stockholm, Nationalmuseum, inv. NM 367) van Brueghel-De Backer. De vermelding 'een Badt van Diana van de Bacquer ende Breugel' in een rekening van de Antwerpse kunsthandel Forchoudt van 4 augustus 1702, No. 4, no. 2.1 kan met dit laatstgenoemde werk in verband worden gebracht. J. Denucé, *Kunstuitvoer in de 17e Eeuw te Antwerpen. De Firma Forchoudt*, Bronnen voor de Geschiedenis van de Vlaamsche Kunst, I, Antwerpen, 1931, pp. 258–259.

12. Bijvoorbeeld *Engelenkoor*, 1605–1606 (Milaan, Ambrosiana, inv. 70). Een onbetwijfelbare bron over de samenwerking Brueghel en Rottenhammer in het *Engelenkoor* is de stichtersbrief van Borromeo van 1618; de kardinaal schreef over het werk in zijn verzameling 'il paradiso l'ha fatto Rotenhamer, i fiori ce li aggiunse Brueghel'. G. Crivelli, *Giovanni Brueghel, pittor fiammingo. Sue lettere e quadretti esistenti presso l'Ambrosiana*, Milaan, 1868, p. 22; S. Bedoni, *Jan Brueghel in Italia e il Collezionismo del Seicento*, Firenze–Milaan, 1983, pp. 44–45, 83; P.M. Jones, *Federico Borromeo and the Ambrosiana: Art Patronage and Reform in Seventeenth-Century Milan*, Cambridge, 1993, p. 352, IA i100.

13. Bijvoorbeeld *Allegorie van de elementen*, gesigneerd en gedateerd 'BRVEGHEL 1604' (Wenen, Kunsthistorisches Museum, inv. 815). Verder werden sommige figurencomposities van Van Balen door Brueghel voorzien van een landschap. Bijvoorbeeld *Het huwelijksfeest van Peleus en Thetis*, gesigneerd en gedateerd 'H v Bael 1608' (Dresden, Gemäldegalerie, inv. 920). Hun bloemenkransen vertonen dan weer een meer gescheiden samenwerking. Bijvoorbeeld de zogeheten *Milanese Madonna*, 1608 (Milaan, Ambrosiana, inv. 71).

14. De eerste opdracht van een allegorisch tafereel van Borromeo aan Brueghel, een *Allegorie van de elementen*, 1605 (Milaan, Ambrosiana, inv. 74, 6–16), is gemaakt in samenwerking met Hendrick van Balen. Een brief van Brueghel aan de kardinaal van 8 augustus 1605 is met dit werk in verband te brengen (Crivelli 1868 [zie noot 12], pp. 50–51). In de briefwisseling van Brueghel aan Borromeo of zijn secretaris Ercole Bianchi zijn er naast de expliciete opdrachten vooral sporen van spontane aanbiedingen.

15. Bijvoorbeeld *De toren van Babel*, 1602–1610 (Antwerpen, Koninklijk Museum voor Schone Kunsten, inv. 947) van Brueghel-Verhaecht; *Binnengezicht van de kathedraal van Antwerpen*, gesigneerd en gedateerd 'STEENWIJCKI 1583' (Budapest, Szépmüvészeti Múzeum, inv. 579) van Brueghel-Van Steenwijck; *Overval in het bos*, ca. 1605 (Warschau, Muzeum Narodowe w Warszawie, inv. 622) van Brueghel-Vrancx; *Diana en Aktaion*, 1606–1609 (Praag, Národní Galerie, inv. DO-4130) van Brueghel-De Clerck. *De Amazonenslag* (Potsdam, Schloß Sanssouci, Bildergalerie, inv. 10021) van Rubens-Brueghel is daarentegen het enige werk van Rubens in samenwerking dat ontstond vóór zijn terugkeer uit Italië op het einde van 1608. Verder kan de samenwerking met zijn leermeester Otto van Veen bezwaarlijk voor een zelfstandige samenwerking genomen worden.

16. Bijvoorbeeld *Heuvellandschap met reizigers*, 1610–1615 (Vaduz, Sammlungen des Fürsten von Liechtenstein, inv. G748) van Brueghel-De Momper; *'Konstkabinet' met de aartshertogen Albrecht en Isabella*, ca. 1620 (Baltimore, The Walters Art Gallery, inv. 31.2010) van Brueghel-Francken; *Vruchtenguirlande met Heilige Familie*, ca. 1623 (München, Alte Pinakothek, inv. 149) van Brueghel-Van Avont.

17. Bijvoorbeeld *Madonna en Kind met vergeet-mij-nietjes* (Brussel, Koninklijke Musea voor Schone Kunsten van België, inv. 2850) van Rubens-Brueghel de Jonge; *Landschap met Psyche en Jupiter* (Madrid, Prado, inv. 1849) van Rubens-Bril; *Putti met guirlande* (Madrid, Prado, inv. 1420) van Rubens-Snyders; *Krijgsgodin kroont Mars* (München, Bayerische Staatsgemäldesammlungen, inv. 4813) van Rubens (atelier)-De Vos; *Philopoemen wordt herkend door zijn gastheer en -vrouw* (Madrid, Prado, inv. 1851) van Rubens-Wildens.

18. Voor een genealogische tafel van de Brueghels zie K. Ertz, *Jan Brueghel der Ältere (1568–1625). Die Gemälde; mit kritischem œuvrekatalog*, Keulen, 1979, p. 13.

19. Opmerkelijk in het stadsbesluit omtrent de aankoop van beide schilderijen in 1618 is de precisering dat 'tweelff diversche van de principaelste meesters deser stadt' hadden meegewerkt. M. De Maeyer, *Albrecht en Isabella en de schilderkunst. Bijdrage tot de geschiedenis van de XVIIe-eeuwse schilderkunst in de Zuidelijke Nederlanden*, Verhandelingen van de Koninklijke Vlaamse Academie voor Wetenschappen, Letteren en Schone Kunsten van België. Klasse der Schone Kunsten, 9, Brussel, 1955, p. 342, doc. 139. Deze schilderijen van de hand van onder meer Peter Paul Rubens, Hendrick van Balen, Frans Snyders, Frans Francken de Jonge, Jan Wildens, Joos de Momper, Sebastiaen Vrancx, Andries van Ertveld, Peter van Avont, Alexander Keirincx en Jan Brueghel de Oude gingen verloren in de brand van het Coudenbergkasteel in 1731. Replieken van Jan Brueghel de Oude in samenwerking met andere kunstenaars zijn voorhanden (Madrid, Prado, inv. 1403, 1404).

20. E.A. Honig, 'The beholder as work of art: A study in the location of value in seventeenth-century Flemish painting', *Nederlands Kunsthistorisch Jaarboek*, 1995, pp. 253–297; E.A. Honig, 'Value in Display and the Aesthetic of Judgment', in *Painting and the Market in Early Modern Antwerp*, New Haven–Londen, 1998, pp. 170–212; K. Van der Stighelen, 'Produktiviteit en samenwerking in het Antwerps kunstenaarsmilieu, 1620–1640', *Gemeentekrediet*, XLIV, 1990/2, 172, pp. 5–15.

21. G. Eckardt, *Die Gemälde in der Bildergalerie von Sanssouci*, Potsdam Schloß Sanssouci, 1980, p. 80, nr. 74; E. Mai en H. Vlieghe eds., [cat. tent.] *Von Bruegel bis Rubens. Das goldene Jahrhundert der flämischen Malerei* (Keulen, Wallraf-Richartz-Museum, 1992; [Antwerpen, Koninklijk Museum voor Schone Kunsten, 1992–1993]; Wenen, Kunsthistorisches Museum, Wenen, 1993), Keulen, 1992, pp. 343–344, nr. 44.1.

22. D. Bodart ed., [cat. tent.] *Petro Paolo Rubens (1577–1640)* (Padua, Palazzo della Regione; Rome, Palazzo della Esposizioni; Milaan, Società per le Belle Arti ed Esposizione Permanente, 1990), Milaan, 1990, p. 36, nr. 1; [cat. tent.] *Pieter Breughel de Jonge (1564–1637/8) - Jan Brueghel de Oude (1568–1625). Een Vlaamse schildersfamilie rond 1600* ([Essen, Villa Hügel, 1997; Wenen, Kunsthistorisches Museum, 1997–1998], Antwerpen, Koninklijk Museum voor Schone Kunsten, 1998), Lingen–Antwerpen, 1998, pp. 217–220, nr. 70.

23. G. Dogaer, 'De inventaris der schilderijen van Diego Duarte', *Jaarboek van het Koninklijk Museum voor Schone Kunsten*, Antwerpen, 1971, pp. 195–221.

24. J.S. Held, 'Thoughts on Rubens' Beginnings', in H. Wilson ed., *The John and Mable Ringling Museum of Art. Papers Presented at the International Rubens Symposium April 14–16, 1982*, Sarasota, 1983, pp. 21–25; J.S. Held, 'Gedanken über die Anfänge von Rubens. Die Amazonomachia in Potsdam', in *Rubens-Studien*, Leipzig, 1987, pp. 9–22.

25. J. Müller Hofstede, 'Zum Werke des Otto van Veen, 1590–1600', *Bulletin des Musées Royaux des Beaux-Arts de Belgique*, VI, 1957, pp. 127–174; J. Müller Hofstede, 'Zur Antwerpener Frühzeit von Peter Paul Rubens', *Münchner Jahrbuch der bildenden Kunst*, III, 13, 1962, pp. 179–216; F. Baudouin, 'Een jeugdwerk van Rubens, *Adam en Eva*, en de relatie Van Veen en Rubens', *Antwerpen*, XIV, 1968, pp. 45–61; J. Müller Hofstede, 'Rubens in Italien', in [cat. tent.] *Peter Paul Rubens 1577–1640* (Keulen, Kunsthalle, 1977), Keulen, 1977, p. 181, onder nr. 24.

26. De stijlanalyse wordt sowieso bemoeilijkt door de schaarste aan Rubens-schilderijen uit deze vroege periode. De slechtere toestand van het Belgische werk hindert bovendien de vergelijkende studie met het Potsdam-schilderij. Niettegenstaande beide panelen reeds aan technisch onderzoek werden onderworpen, bleven expliciete conclusies inzake de toeschrijving van het Belgische schilderij naar mijn mening uit. Een studie van de, voor Rubens althans, intrigerende ondertekening in dit werk dient te worden ondernomen.

27. J. Denucé, *De Antwerpsche 'Konstkamers'. Inventarissen van kunstverzamelingen te Antwerpen in de 16e en 17e eeuwen*, Bronnen voor de geschiedenis van de Vlaamsche Kunst, II), Antwerpen, 1932, p. 100, onder nr. 362.

28. De Maeyer 1955 (zie noot 19); [cat. tent.] *Albrecht & Isabella, 1598–1621* (Brussel, Koninklijke Musea voor Kunst en Geschiedenis, 1998), Turnhout, 1998.

29. Een mogelijke benoeming als hofschilder is in geen enkele bron gedocumenteerd. Passages uit Brueghels brieven getuigen over bepaalde dagdagelijkse aspecten van zijn verblijf aan het hof met onder meer de langdurige observatie van dieren in de menagerie van Albrecht en Isabella (Crivelli 1868 [zie noot 12], p. 272.

30. M. De Maeyer, 'Rubens' terugkeer uit Italië naar Antwerpen', *Gentse Bijdragen tot de Geschiedenis en Oudheidkunde*, XI, 1945–1948, pp. 147–165; H. Vlieghe, 'Rubens back in Antwerp. Reflections on the Change of his Style and the Taste Pattern of his Public', in *Actes du XVIIe Congrès International d'Histoire de l'Art (1989)*, Straatsburg, 1993, pp. 49–54; C. Brown, 'Rubens and the Archdukes', in [cat. tent.] Brussel 1998 [zie noot 28], pp. 121–128. Ook al zijn er geen expliciete aanwijzingen van een Rubens-Brueghel-samenwerking tijdens hun vroege jaren in dienst van Albrecht en Isabella, toch vermoedt men dat ze aan bepaalde opdrachten samen hebben gewerkt. In 1609–1610 verbleef Brueghel enkele maanden aan het hof, wat eerder uitzonderlijk was, voor een opdracht van een elftal werken (De Maeyer 1955 [zie noot 9], p. 147).

31. J.S. Held, 'Acheloüs' Banquet', *The Art Quarterly*, IV, 2, 1941, pp. 122–133; Ertz 1979 (zie noot 18), pp. 415, 613, nr. 335; W.A. Liedtke, *Flemish Paintings in the Metropolitan Museum of Art*, New York, 1984, pp. 194–198. Een repliek van Rubens en Jan Brueghel de Jonge vormt een pendant van een *Vertumnus en Pomona* (Sorrento, Museo Correale di Terranova) van Rubens-Brueghel de Jonge.

32. De Maeyer 1955 (zie noot 9), pp. 49–49, 118–119, pl. VI.

33. Er dient echter rekening gehouden te worden met de mogelijkheid dat de schilder ook werken afgebeeld kan hebben die niet tot de verzameling behoord hebben. S. Speth-Holterhoff, *Les peintres flamands de cabinets d'amateurs au XVIIe siècle*, Brussel–Parijs, 1957, p. 88.

34. Gesigneerd 'PETRI PAVLI RVBENS FIGR / IBRUEGHEL FEC'. Ertz 1979 (zie noot 18), pp. 236, 245–246, 248, 391, 608, nr. 308; C. Van de Velde, 'Het Aards Paradijs in de beeldende kunsten', in [cat. tent.] *Het Aards Paradijs* (Antwerpen,

Zoo, 1982), Antwerpen, 1982, pp. 17–35; B. Broos, *De Meesterwerken in het Mauritshuis*, Den Haag, 1987, pp. 323–329; B. Broos, *Liefde, List en Lijden - Historiestukken in het Mauritshuis*, Den Haag, 1993, nr. 8; *Mauritshuis. The Royal Cabinet of Paintings. Illustrated General Catalogue*, Amsterdam–Den Haag, 1993, p. 129, nr. 253; D. Beaujean, 'Jan Brueghel d.Ä, Peter Paul Rubens und Bernard Salomon: Zur Entstehunsgeschichte des "Paradiesbildes" im Haager Mauritshuis', *Zeitschrift für Kunstgeschichte*, IL, 1, 1996, pp. 123–127.

35. In 1718 vermeldde Houbraken: 'Dog het alleruitmuntenste in Konst dat ik van hem (=Joan Bruegel, bygenaamt den Fluweelen) gezien heb, is het zoo genaamde Paradys, by den Heer Le Court van der Voort, tot Leiden, waar in zig een menigte van allerhande Dieren op 't allerkonstigst, in een niet min konstig geschildert Landschap doen zien: en de Adam en Eva op 't alleruitvoerigst door Rubbens geschildert. Dit stuk is gekomen uit het beruchte Kabinet van den Heer de Bie, den Mecenas van G. Dou.' (A. Houbraken, *De groote Schouburgh der Nederlantsche Konstschilders en Schilderessen*, I, Amsterdam, 1718, p. 87).

36. Brueghel schilderde verscheidene dierenmotieven naar bestaande Rubensontwerpen. Broos belicht in detail de uitvoerige beïnvloeding van Rubens op de ontwerpen van Brueghel in dit schilderij; desalniettemin schrijft hij het ontwerp van de gehele compositie toe aan Brueghel. Broos 1993 (zie noot 34), nr. 8.

37. D. Freedberg, 'The Origins and Rise of the Flemish Madonnas in Flower Garlands. Decoration and devotion', *Münchner Jahrbuch der bildenden Kunst*, III, 32, 1981, pp. 115–150.

38. De Maeyer 1955 (zie noot 9), pp. 156–157; Ertz 1979 (zie noot 18), pp. 304–306, 309, 313, 316, 323, 324, 611, nr. 325; A. Brejon de Lavergnée, A. Foucart en M. Reynaud, *Catalogue sommaire illustré des peintures du Musée du Louvre. I. Ecole flamande et hollandaise*, Parijs, 1979, p. 115; K. Ertz, 'Jan Brueghel de Oude', in [cat. tent.] *Bruegel. Een dynastie van schilders* (Brussel, Paleis voor Schone Kunsten, 1980), Gent, 1980, p. 203, nr. 141.

39. Borromeo heeft enigszins bijgedragen tot het populariseren van het type van madonna in krans. Talrijke schilderijen van Brueghel in samenwerking met Van Balen zijn dit werk voorafgegaan.

40. E. Kieser, 'Rubens' Madonna im Blumenkranz', *Münchner Jahrbuch*, III, 1, 1950, pp. 215–225; Ertz 1979 (zie noot 18), pp. 271, 313, 611, nr. 326; *Bavarian State Picture Collection. Alte Pinakothek Munich. Explanatory notes on the works exhibited*, München, 1986, pp. 448–449, nr. 331; K. Renger e.a., *Flämische Barockmalerei. Meisterwerke der Alte Pinakothek München*, München, 1996, pp. 92–95.

41. In 1625 trad de hertog van Buckingham via Gerbier in contact met Rubens, en dit in verband met de aankoop van een collectie antieke beelden en medailles, evenals enkele schilderijen. De inventaris van George Villiers van 1635 vermeldt een *Madonna in krans*; de identificatie met de madonna uit München is echter nog niet bewezen.

42. De inbreng van engelen sluit aan bij Rubens' *Maria della Vallicella* van 1608 (Grenoble, Musée des Beaux-Arts).

43. Renger heeft deze problematiek uitvoerig belicht. V. Poll–Frommel, K. Renger en J. Schmidt, 'Untersuchungen an Rubens Bildern: Die Anstückungen der Holztafeln', *Bayerische Staatsgemäldesammlungen: Jahresbericht*, 1993, pp. 24–35; K. Renger, 'Anstückungen bei Rubens', in E. Mai, K. Schütz en H. Vlieghe, ed., *Die Malerei Antwerpens - Gattungen, Meister, Wirkungen. Studien zur flämischen Kunst des 16. Und 17. Jahrhunderts. Internationales Kolloquium Wien 1993*, Keulen 1994, pp. 156–167.

44. Het devote karakter wordt extra benadrukt door het intiem en menselijk karakter van het madonnatafereel, met Jezus die hier naar voor treedt. Dit werk contrasteert met vele andere Madonna's in krans waar de decoratieve functie van de krans soms overweegt. In het schilderij van München verwijst de krans, door de symbolische betekenis van sommige van zijn componenten, bovendien naar de inhoud van het medaillon. Freedberg 1981 (zie noot 37), p. 132.

45. *Glasgow Art Gallery and Museum. I. Dutch and Flemish Netherlandish and German Paintings*, 1961, pp. 117–120, nr. 609; Ertz 1979 (zie noot 18), pp. 316, 325, 616, nr. 394; Freedberg 1981 (zie noot 37), p. 132.

46. J. Müller Hofstede, 'Rubens und Jan Brueghel: Diana und ihre Nymphen', *Jahrbuch der Berliner Museen*, X, 1968, p. 225, noot 52.

47. Vermelding in inventaris van hertog Georges Villiers van Buckingham van 1648. B. Fairfax, *A Catalogue of the Curious Collection of Pictures of George Villiers, Duke of Buckingham*, Londen, 1758, p. 16, nr. 11. Naast dit schilderij bezat Georges Villiers ook de enige andere natuurlijke allegorie van Rubens in samenwerking met Frans Snyders, namelijk een *Ceres* (Sint-Petersburg, Hermitage, inv. 504).

48. Ertz 1979 (zie noot 18), pp. 316, 614, nr. 341; C. Van Mulders, in A. Balis en P. Coessens, ed., [cat. tent.] *Kunst in de Bank. Een keuze van Rubens tot Magritte* (Brussel, Paleis voor Schone Kunsten, 1997–1998), Antwerpen, 1997, pp. 104–108, nr. 49; [cat. tent.] (Essen–Wenen)–Antwerpen (1997)–1998 (zie noot 22), pp. 268–271, nr. 87. Een, mogelijk maar weinig waarschijnlijk eigenhandige, variante (Den Haag, Mauritshuis, inv. 233) is ontstaan na dit zogeheten oertype; onder verschillende veranderde motieven in de Mauritshuis-versie gaan de oorspronkelijke schuil. De verschillende kwaliteit en schildertechniek van de krans in dit schilderij doen op zijn minst een inbreng van het atelier van Jan Brueghel de Jonge vermoeden. Ertz 1979 (zie noot 18), p. 614, nr. 340; [cat. tent.] (Essen–Wenen)–Antwerpen (1997)–1998 (zie noot 22), pp. 266–268, nr. 86.

49. M. Díaz Padrón, *Museo del Prado. Catalogo de Pinturas. I. Escuela Flamenca Siglo XVII*, I, Madrid, 1975, pp. 313–314, nr. 1418; Ertz 1979 (zie noot 18), pp. 304–306, 311, 320, 620, nr. 368; A. Balis, M. Díaz Padrón, C. Van de Velde en H. Vlieghe, *De Vlaamse schilderkunst in het Prado*, Flandria Extra Muros, Antwerpen, 1989, p. 131, nr. 38; M. Díaz Padrón, *El siglo de Rubens en el Museo del Prado. Catalogo razonado de pintura flamenca del siglo XVII*, Barcelona, 1995, pp. 290–291, nr. 1418.

50. In een brief van 5 september 1621 aan de secretaris van Borromeo, Ercole Bianchi, meldde Brueghel dat hij buiten het door Borromeo bestelde schilderij, *Allegorie van de Lucht* (Rome, Galleria Doria Pamphilj, inv. 328), een guirlande had meegestuurd naar Italië. Crivelli 1868 (zie noot 12), pp. 271–274.

51. Deze kwestie is uitvoerig gedocumenteerd door Brueghels briefwisseling met de kardinaal van 1621–1622. Crivelli (zie noot 12), 1868, pp. 274, 283, 287, 296, 298.

52. De Maeyer 1955 (zie noot 9), pp. 101–109; Díaz Padrón 1975 (zie noot 49), pp. 314–317, nrs. 1683–1684; Ertz 1979 (zie noot 18), pp. 338, 608–609, nrs. 309–310; H. Vlieghe, *Rubens Portraits of Identified Sitters in Antwerp*, Corpus Rubenianum Ludwig Burchard, XIX, 2, Londen–New York, 1987, pp. 43–45, nrs. 66–67; Díaz Padrón 1995 (zie noot 49), pp. 1076–1083, nrs. 1683–1684; [cat. tent.] Brussel 1998 (zie noot 28), pp. 149, nrs. 202–203.

53. Vlieghe 1987 (zie noot 52), p. 43.

54. *Het Gezicht*, *De Geur* en *De Smaak* zijn gesigneerd en gedateerd, respectievelijk, 'BRVEGHEL F. 1617', 'BRVEGHEL' en 'BRVEGHEL fe. 1618'. In *De Smaak* is een participatie van Frans Snyders niet uitgesloten. De Maeyer 1955 (zie noot 9), pp. 42–43, 112, 114, 118; Speth-Holterhoff 1957 (zie noot 33), pp. 29, 52 ev.; Díaz Padrón 1975 (zie noot 49), pp. 40–46,

nrs. 1394–1398; Ertz 1979 (zie noot 18), pp. 328–356, 611–612, nrs. 327–331; [cat. tent.] *Brussel 1980* (zie noot 38), p. 204, nr. 142; J. Müller Hofstede, '"Non Saturatur Oculus Visu" - Zur "Allegorie des Gesichts von Peter Paul Rubens und Jan Brueghel d. Ä"', in H. Vekeman en J. Müller Hofstede, ed., *Wort und Bild in der niederländischen Kunst und Literatur des 16. und 17. Jh.*, Erfstadt, 1984, pp. 243–286; Balis, Díaz Padrón, Van de Velde, Vlieghe 1989 (zie noot 49), pp. 280–287, nrs. 294–298; Díaz Padrón 1995 (zie noot 49), pp. 264–287, nrs. 1394–1398.

55. B. Welzel, 'Armoury and Archducal Image: The Sense of Touch from the Five Senses of Jan Brueghel and Peter Paul Rubens', in [cat. tent.] Brussel 1998 (zie noot 28), pp. 99–106. Over de 'konstkamer' zie Speth-Holterhoff 1957 (zie noot 33); Z.Z. Filipczak, *Picturing art in Antwerp 1550–1700*, Princeton, 1987, pp. 47–72; E. Mai, 'Pictura in der "Constkamer" - Antwerpens Malerei im Spiegel von Bild und Theorie', in [cat. tent.] Keulen–(Antwerpen)–Wenen 1992–1993 (zie noot 21), pp. 39–54; K. Schütz, 'Das Galeriebild als Spiegel des Antwerpener Sammlertums', in [cat. tent.] Keulen–(Antwerpen)–Wenen 1992–1993 (zie noot 21), pp. 161–170; U. Härting, 'Doctrina et Pïetas. Über frühe Galeriebilder', *Jaarboek Koninklijk Museum van Antwerpen*, 1993, pp. 95–133; J. Müller Hofstede, 'Zur Theorie und Gestalt des Antwerpener Kabinettbildes um 1600', in Mai, Schutz en Vlieghe 1994 (zie noot 43), pp. 39–43.

56. Over de eigenhandigheid en de inbreng van de andere schilders in deze replieken bestaat onenigheid. Frans Snyders werkte waarschijnlijk mee aan de *Allegorie van het Gevoel, het Gehoor en de Smaak*. Vermoedelijk schilderden ze deze replieken in opdracht van de Aartshertogen kort nadat de originelen aan deze laatste waren geschonken. De Maeyer 1955 (zie noot 9), pp. 43 e.v., 47–49, 112, 118 ev., 152–154, 156, 171, 342 (doc. 139); Speth-Holterhoff 1957 (zie noot 33), pp. 58–59; Díaz Padrón 1975 (zie noot 49), pp. 61–64, nrs. 1403–1404; Ertz 1979 (zie noot 18), pp. 158–159, 305, 336, 356–362, 400, 459, 612–613, nrs. 332–333; [cat. tent.] Brussel 1980 (zie noot 38), p. 205, nr. 143; Müller Hofstede 1984 (zie noot 54), p. 275; Díaz Padrón 1995 (zie noot 49), pp. 236–244, nrs. 1403–1404; [cat. tent.] *Pieter Breughel der Jüngere–Jan Brueghel der Ältere. Flämische Malerei um 1600. Tradition und Fortschritt* (Essen, Villa Hügel, 1997; Wenen, Kunsthistorisches Museum, 1997–1998; [Antwerpen, Koninklijk Museum voor Schone Kunsten, 1998]), Lingen, 1997, pp. 310–314, nr. 95a.

57. K. Ertz, *Jan Brueghel d.J. Die Gemälde, mit kritischem Œuvrekatalog*, Flämische Maler im Umkreis der grossen Meister, I, Freren, 1984, p. 68, nr. 155.

58. Inventaris van het Stadhouderlijk Kwartier, Den Haag, 16–31 augustus 1632: 'Op de Galderije van mevrouw de princess: een stuck van Rubbens ende 't landtschap door Bruegel gedaen, hangende boven de deur van het cabinet'. *Oud-Holland*, 1930, p. 213, nr. 84. *Staatliche Museen zu Berlin. Beschreibendes Verzeichnis der Gemälde im Kaiser-Friedrich-Museum und Deutschen Museum*, Berlijn, 1933, p. 10, nr. 765. Müller Hofstede 1968 (zie noot 46), p. 226; Ertz 1979 (zie noot 18), pp. 393, 480, 619, nr. 365.

59. Was ooit in het bezit van de Leganés; in de inventaris van diens verzameling van 30 maart 1642 wordt het toegeschreven aan Brueghel en Rubens: 'Otra pintura de ssan huberto de mano di Rubens el País cierbo perros y caballos de mano de Bruxel' (Archivo de Protocolos, 6210, fols. 1163v–1186v, passim, no. 38). Ertz 1979 (zie noot 18), p. 619, nr. 366; M. Crawford Volk, 'New Light on a Seventeenth Century Collector: the Marquis of Leganés', *The Art Bulletin*, LXII, 1980, pp. 262, 267; Díaz Padrón 1995 (zie noot 49), pp. 288–290, nr. 1411. Een andere versie, vernoemd in de inventaris van de Brusselse Sinte-Goedelekerk van 1639, was vermoedelijk oorspronkelijk in aartshertogelijk bezit.

60. Gesigneerd 'P.P.R.' Müller Hofstede 1968 (zie noot 46), pp. 200–207; Ertz 1979 (zie noot 18), pp. 391–394, 406, 617, nr. 354.

61. Müller Hofstede 1968 (zie noot 46), pp. 207–215; Ertz 1979 (zie noot 18), p. 401.

62. Mogelijk met medewerking van F. Snyders. Houbraken 1718 (zie noot 35), I, pp. 85–87; Hoet, 1752, I, p. 150. Müller Hofstede 1968 (zie noot 46), pp. 221–222; Ertz 1979 (zie noot 18), pp. 402, 618–619, nr. 358.

63. Met medewerking van Frans Snyders. Müller Hofstede 1968 (zie noot 46), pp. 218–219; Ertz 1979 (zie noot 18), pp. 394, 395, 398, 400, 406, 617, nr. 355.

64. Met medewerking van Frans Snyders; gesigneerd en gedateerd 'BRVEGEL 1620'. Müller Hofstede 1968 (zie noot 46), p. 218; Ertz 1979 (zie noot 18), pp. 394, 400, 406, 617–618, nr. 356.

65. Ertz 1979 (zie noot 18), pp. 417, 420, nr. 384a.

66. Müller Hofstede 1968 (zie noot 46), p. 226.

67. Het is vooral de technische studie, met het blote oog, infraroodfotografie, infraroodreflectografie, X-radiografie en verfmonsteranalyse, die hierin duidelijkheid kan scheppen.

II. Design

Working it out: Design Tools and Procedures in Sixteenth- and Seventeenth-Century Flemish Art

Arnout Balis

The European Context

An artist can conceive any given work in his mind, see it, as it were, with his mind's eye, but bringing this initial conception to an adequate form can involve some considerable trouble. Bridges may be needed, constructed to connect inner vision to artistic production, the ethereal to the material. Here it is a matter of overcoming the inherent limitations which typify the human mind as a performing system; and at particular periods, within certain historical traditions, a whole variety of such design aids have been arrived at. Taken together they consitute a sort of visual technology: a set of tools for the mind. It is the job of these tools to ensure the eventual realisation of what was initially conceived in rather vague, or at least immaterial terms. The artist's design aids form the subject of the second part of this publication devoted to the creative process in its broadest sense. It is only when these bridgeheads have been installed, when this scaffolding with all its various platforms has been erected, that the definitive execution can be carried out and the work brought to a proper completion.[1]

To be sure, some exceptionally gifted artists, endowed with a highly developed visual imagination, can do without such intermediary steps. It is said of the Greek painter Theophanes, active in Moscow around 1400, that he never consulted models as his more timid colleagues did, but immediately delineated his compositions on the wall.[2] Still, it could be maintained that in some artistic contexts the tasks set to painters were not very complex, and that in such cases reliance on simple mnemotechnics could, given a particularly ready visual talent, yield the expected results. But even within pictorial traditions such as those of Byzantium or the Western Middle Ages, where much stress was laid on the repetition of authoritative models and formulae, some external memory aid was often found handy: the 'exempla', copied down in model books, proved a great help in the labour of composition.[3] These might include samples of entire figures, figure groups, or significant parts such as heads, or again details of costume or of natural phenomena.

It has been pointed out that for this early period very few compositional drawings have come down to us, and very few sketches. Does this point to a gap in the record or does the situation simply reflect something fundamental about art as it was practiced at the period? The relatively simple logical process employed in the assembly of a new composition may be a factor in this debate, as may be the circumstance that drawings were often made immediately onto the panel (as is now detectable by infrared techniques) or onto the wall (the 'sinopie', under the final layer of plaster). But it remains a fact that here too we seldom encounter very rough sketches, all shapes having already more or less found their final formulation. On the other hand it may be that less definitive studies have simply not come down to us because they were executed on perishable or re-usable supports; and it has recently been demonstrated how widespread was the use of study tools such as erasable tablets even as late as the sixteenth and seventeenth centuries.[4] Whereas one may then be inclined to accept that until the early fifteenth century many fewer preparatory steps were inserted into the process of creation than our knowledge of later traditions would invite us to suppose, more informal drawing procedures may have existed than the now extant corpus of drawings suggests.

In at least one province of art compositional drawings were made – and survive – from the thirteenth century onwards, namely that of architecture.[5] Here the task in hand was of course very complex and entailed not only the elaboration of a very (and towards the end of the Gothic period ever more) intricate type of pattern. But concerns for stability and the coordination of an heterogeneous team of workers most have highlighted the need for the existence of some visual entity on which decisions could be based and procedures determined in advance. For such designs too the more tentative stages escape us (even if some preliminary rough incisions are sometimes visible), and we are presented with well finished renderings of a complex whole. But individual parts and details were also worked out in drawing: mostly on 'tracing floors' or on wall surfaces and in actual size. In this province of design, then, we find a visual system that reflects operational procedures as they were habitually carried out in practice and that has a hierarchical structure – a system which then ensured the successful organization of labour. Later practices involving the systematic organisation of different stages of design – especially relevant for complex tasks, or where a whole range of competencies was required, and needed to be coordinated (in fields such as glass painting and tapestry weaving) – may well have taken their inspiration from architectural precedents.

It is striking that around 1400 there was an increasing demand for forms that were more natural, more closely imitative of the real world.[6] Nature studies were made, especially of animals – domestic as well as exotic – and the repertory of characteristic figure types was expanded and diversified. Sometimes it looks as if these new collections of motifs were jealously restricted to individual studios. The Renaissance saw another category enter the artistic vocabulary: forms derived from the Antique. Many model books now specialised in this new material.[7] Both trends, one finding its resource in nature, the other in the Antique, were to continue through the sixteenth and seventeenth centuries, in Italy and elsewhere in Europe, even if at times or in specific regions the balance between the two might vary considerably.

With the Renaissance the situation also changed in another, perhaps more decisive respect. New and more complex requirements were introduced for the structure, the syntax of a composition, and theoretical writings anchored these conceptions firmly to an artistic ideology.[8] A coherent dramatic scene had to be constructed, which entailed new requirements for the composition as a whole as well as for the way figures and figure groups functioned therein. Figures were expected to assume more complex roles, and if they were to deal properly with these requirements and represent convincing dramatic 'actors' artists needed a better understanding of the organic structure of the human body – thus, by implication an appreciation of anatomy. To achieve a coherent whole, poses of figures had to be individually worked out for any given composition. This entailed some playing around with alternatives. Simply assembling bits and pieces copied from elsewhere was no longer adequate as a way of proceeding.

Designing a composition now seemed to require more preparation than ever before: old methods of storing visual material were no doubt perpetuated, but new procedures had to be thought out to deal with the new and more complex requirements of invention. More and more recourse was had to drawing, and new types of drawing were created, such as the tentative sketch, the 'open' figure drawing (with the definitive contours as yet unspecified), and the study from the live model in a specific pose.[9] Different sorts of drawing served different functions in the creative process, and they could be ordered into a complex system of design procedures. But other media could also be functionally integrated into the logic: sketches in oil, for example, or 'bozzetti' in wax or clay. Ways had to be devised to transfer the results of one stage to the next. Thus the 'modello' functioned as a temporary, summing-up stage, while the full-scale cartoon provided the final formulation, ensuring the easy transfer of the composition to its eventual support.

It would appear that much of the new 'design technology' summarily sketched in the previous paragraphs was evolved in fifteenth- and early sixteenty-century Italy, with its culmination in the work of Leonardo, Michelangelo and above all Raphael.[10] Still, some artists such as Titian seem to have relied less on drawings as intermediate stages in the elaboration of a composition, making the definitive support itself the arena for creative activity, sketching and redefining forms in layers of paint, in a manner which implied a more dynamic approach to underpainting and 'dead colouring' than was traditional.[11]

Early Netherlandish Art

Let us turn from this overview of Italian design procedures to the Netherlands, and specifically to Flanders. For the 'Early Netherlandish' school (fifteenth and early sixteenth centuries) relatively few drawings on paper or parchment are preserved (maybe some six hundred altogether), and most of these are copies after finished paintings (whether the entire compositions or details) rather than preparatory to them; sketches do not feature among them.[12]

It is true that to this corpus of drawings we may add the underdrawings on the final support (mostly panel) which can now often be discerned by infrared photographs or 'reflectograms', but these too rarely reveal a tentative first approach such as it seems reasonable to suppose must have preceded the sometimes complex, and not simply 'additive', compositions typical of the best products of this school.[13] Whether this circumstance is an indication that the creative process for these painters should be located more firmly than it usually is in the imagination, or whether it should be taken to testify to a lacuna in the surviving material, is, I'd say, very difficult to decide.

Still, it should not be forgotten that tentative first outlines may have been applied in charcoal on the panel's white chalk ground, to be wiped off once a satisfactory compositional pattern had been achieved.[14] Very instructive too, as a possible parallel in the procedure of working out compositions, are the preliminary marginal drawings found in manuscripts: some of these are simply programmatic instructions in (rudimentary) visual form, stemming from a scholar or 'learned adviser' and quite often accompanied by written instructions, but others (e.g. those of the Boucicaut Master) are clearly the artist's own short-hand sketches of first ideas.[15] These latter may allow us an insight into a lost category of drawing also used by panel painters.

In any case, it seems certain that for many of the elements from nature (for the most part plants, but also portrait heads) which we find painted in elaborate detail, and which sometimes feature in almost identical form in more than one painting, there must have existed preliminary studies on a 'mobile' support – and one that is at the same time easy to file away, such as paper.[16]

In the context of the Flemish school of the sixteenth and seventeenth centuries,[17] it is clear that some of the Northern traditions of design methods and tools would have been perpetuated in local studios, especially in the earlier period. Also, since the Flemish school developed some particular specialities, such as landscape painting (and prints), it seems likely that for this category of work certain typical and regional design procedures were evolved.

But a highly important feature of Flemish (and more broadly Netherlandish) art of this period certainly is that in the course of the sixteenth century the Italianate history piece was embraced with enthusiasm as the most significant genre. Not only were Italian forms adopted (as in the case of Gossaert), it is evident that Italian design procedures were likewise taken over.

At what rate and to what degree of consistency is for the present not quite clear. Nor is it clear by which channels this transfer of 'technology' came about. Some Flemish artists of course travelled to Italy and could have picked up knowledge of Italian procedures on the spot. On the other hand Italian products reached the Netherlands. And if it is rather unlikely that the more 'intimate' studio material ever became accessible to Northerners in this way at an early date, there are certainly cases of material that was very revealing about certain studio practices being imported to Flanders. An obvious example are the Italian designs for tapestries woven in workshops in Brussels. Raphael's cartoons of the *Acts of the Apostles* (executed in full colour) arrived in 1517, but for subsequent tapestry series 'modelli' were sent, and Tommaso Vincidor came to Brussels to supervise the later stages of the execution – and in so doing no doubt offered a direct insight into the preparatory procedures elaborated in the Raphael workshop.[18]

Around this time military engineers arrived in the Netherlands from Italy: their design strategies may have influenced the existing practices of Northern architects.[19]

So much for design traditions in habitual use in Italy as well as in the Netherlands in the period just preceding that chosen as the focus for this publication. In what follows I propose to identify a few design features which were more or less standard in Flemish art of the sixteenth and seventeenth centuries. I shall first look at compositional drawings, and then at more detailed studies.

The Compositional Drawing in the sixteenth and seventeenth centuries

It is of course artificial to make a sharp subdivision, as I shall do in the remainder of my text, between stages in the design process which offer a representation of the composition as a whole, and stages which concentrate on isolated elements. In any chronological sequence both types may alternate in a kind of platform construction, in such a way that the installation of one is a prerequisite for the fabrication of the next – which in turn makes an extension or partial extension possible. In the process earlier stages may have to be strengthened to provide for stability, and 'ready made' elements as well as features devised 'ad hoc' may prove functionally useful.

For any major project it was in the Middle Ages perhaps most often the architect (usually also, as we noted, a good draughtsman) who directed and coordinated the contributions of the various skilled artisans (sculptors, painters, glass painters etc.) – sometimes maybe without going further than giving general instructions, but at other times producing visual directions in the form of drawings. On some architectural drawings quite detailed sketches for sculpture appear, though it is not always clear whether they are by the same hand as the design for the masonry.[20] More and more, however, painters seem to have taken on the role of overall designers.

In sixteenth-century Flanders we know of quite a group of such 'peintres-inventeurs' who usually remained active as painters within their own ateliers while devising compositions for colleagues in other fields.[21] Certainly the emphasis on 'inventio' in the new artistic programme for painters, as it had been formulated by Alberti and others in Italy, had its effect on Northern painters – on their status and ambitions.

Thus an artist such as Bernard van Orley, although also active as a painter in his own right, can almost be called a professional 'inventor':[22] he made cartoons for stained glass (Brussels cathedral), but was especially prolific as a designer of tapestries. We are poorly informed about the details of his practice: what have been preserved are his fully worked out 'modelli' (in the technical literature on tapestry usually called 'petits patrons') sometimes in more than one version – a circumstance which suggests that one set was part of the legal, rather than the artistic process, functioning as the contract drawing or 'vidimus'. It is, however, clear from the 'mature' formulation of many elements in them that these 'modelli' incorporate and subsume previous design activities of which no trace remains – by Van Orley himself and by others. More tentative compositional sketches must have existed as well as detailed figure drawings (although perhaps not necessarily from the live model; sometimes a small statuette viewed from various angles might have served the purpose), and in some cases detailed nature studies (landscapes and individual plants, as well as animals) for which Van Orley could call in a specialist (most possibly the now almost forgotten Tons, who also collaborated with other masters).[23] It was from these 'modelli' that the full-scale cartoons had to be composed, and this was not done slavishly or mechanically: the processes of elaborating and refining the composition often continued. None of Van Orley's cartoons survive, but judging from the detailed stylistic conformity of the end product (the tapestries) to his personal idiom, it would seem that the master himself (as well as the nature specialist, where appropriate) at least participated in the production of the cartoons.[24] For less important tapestry series apparently a more routine process was adopted, and most of the work was left to narrowly specialised 'cartoonists'.

However little we know for certain about the specifics of Van Orley's design procedure, and all the preparation that went into it, it seems that he took his lead from the practices evolved in the studio of Raphael. Given that we still have no evidence that he ever made a trip to Italy, his familiarity with these practices would have come from the material that reached the Brussels workshops from Raphael's studio. An acquaintance with particular design tools such as cartoons and 'modelli' may have offered him insights – possibly supplemented by advice from Italian artists such as Vincidor.

Apart from Van Orley, quite a few Netherlandish artists proved to be very prolific designers for tapestries: Pieter Coecke started up in Antwerp as a rival to the Brussels design school (and in his case we have both 'modello'-like drawings and full-size cartoons),[25] and we are of course lucky with the case of Jan Vermeyen, who designed the tapestry series of *The Battle of Tunis*: here, finally, is a very well-documented series, with some of the original cartoons still preserved (and on permanent view in Vienna).[26]

Once established, the tradition of painters assuming the role of tapestry designers persisted undiminished through the seventeenth century. Newly designed cartoons continued to be highly valued especially in Brussels, where the weavers catered for an international clientele of sophisticated art lovers who would not have been content with yet another edition of a familiar set. As a result the best painters of Brussels and of Antwerp were constantly under pressure to supply new inventions. Rubens and Jordaens here figure prominently,[27] but the list of those seventeenth-century Flemish painters who worked for the tapestry industry, either occasionally or regularly, is an impressive one, and includes names such as the 'figure painters' Abraham van Diepenbeeck, Justus van Egmont, Willem van Herp, Jan van den Hoecke, Erasmus Quellin, Cornelis Schut, Thomas Willeboirts Bosschaert, David Teniers, as well as landscape or still life specialists or animal painters such as Denijs van Alsloot, Lodewijk de Vadder, Lucas van Uden, Pieter Boel and Adriaan van Utrecht. Quite often they supplied not only the small 'modelli' but also the full-scale cartoons (on paper or – surprisingly? – on canvas).[28] Some of these 'modelli' and cartoons are still preserved, but here again most of the other stages in the elaboration of these complex projects are less well documented.

Design for tapestry forms an evident case where there is a clearcut distinction between invention on the one hand and execution in the final medium on the other. In other branches of the arts this sort of rigid separation can also apply at times, even if it need not always do so. Stained glass windows, for example, were regularly designed by an overall painter-inventor,[29] who usually also supplied the full-size cartoons; the execution was then left to specialised glass painters. But some of

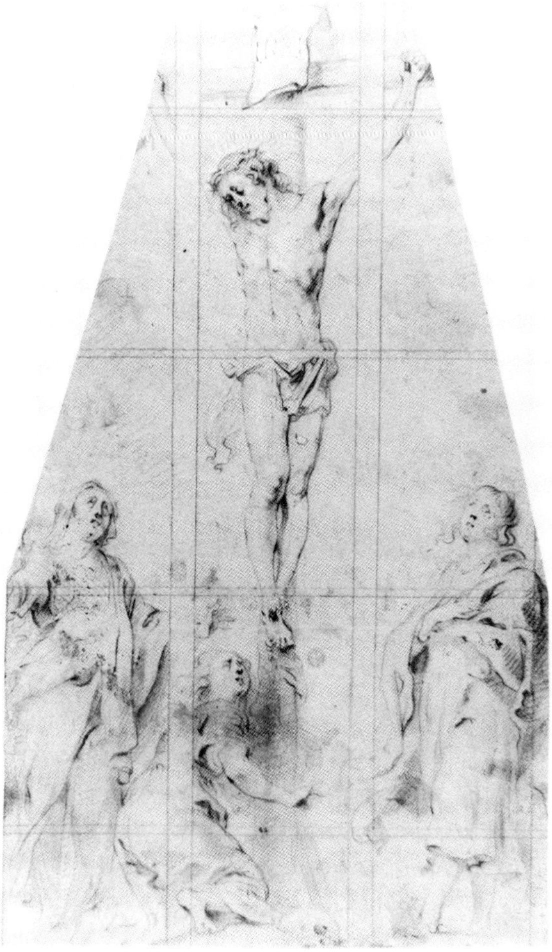

Fig. 1. Abraham van Diepenbeeck, *Christ at the Cross*, drawing. Antwerp, private collection

the designers for stained glass, such as Dierick Vellert in the sixteenth and Abraham van Diepenbeeck in the seventeenth century, themselves executed the glass panels (or roundels).[30] The case of Jean de Labarre is particularly interesting: this glass painter, who came from 's-Hertogenbosch but was active in Antwerp, himself drew the cartoons for a window which he then went on to execute and install in a chapel in the Brussels collegiate church (now cathedral) of St Michael and St Gudule in 1654. In the years to follow he executed three further windows for the same chapel, but for these the full-scale cartoons had been supplied by Theodoor van Thulden, better known as a painter and maybe for this reason preferred by the patrons.[31] Full-size cartoons for glass were most often made on paper, but occasionally they are on canvas.[32] Already at the 'modello' stage the designer had to take account of the structural and decorative elements of the window itself, such as tracery (and often he also indicated the horizontal saddle bars). An artist such as Van Diepenbeeck could in his small-scale designs adopt various techniques, such as the monochrome chalk drawing (Fig. 1), and the monochrome or coloured oil sketch – although the latter is exceptional in works designed for this purpose, and was apparently influenced by Rubens's design methods.[33]

Most of the designers and cartoon painters mentioned above were of course also, and some of them mainly, painters in the normal sense of the term (and other painters never had anything to do with 'inter media' designing, sticking strictly to their trade). When painters are designing their own pictures there is obviously no need for sharp distinctions between invention and execution: the process of creation can be viewed as an organic and continuous one, from invention through elaboration and crystallisation of visual ideas to final realisation of a 'product'. In fact, and especially in the large workshops of painters that had come to be formed (alongside the still frequent one-man shops), a degree of division of labour was experimented with, which in certain ways was not so dissimilar from the situation regarding designs for other media: tasks had to be apportioned and delegated, each individual executant being at least temporarily left on his own, while overall coherence was assured, on the one hand, by a high degree of pre-determination of specific elements (detailed studies could serve this purpose, as we shall see) and, on the other hand, by the provision of precise instructions for the assemblage of the parts into a whole. A detailed composition sketch (whether drawn or painted) might suffice for this; if this sketch was formulated with sufficient clarity, it could presumably just be scaled up and the detailed studies dispensed with. (The same logic of course also applies to the cartoons discussed above, in cases where the execution was left to the atelier). In the studio practice of Flemish seventeenth-century painters we have documentation for many such intermediate stages, evidently intended to serve a specific function; relatively little concrete evidence of this kind seems to have come to us from the sixteenth century, but it is clear that many of these procedures were already firmly established. A word of warning, though: the existence of a graduated sequence of intermediary steps does not 'per se' point to a sort of factory-like organisation of work; the possibility remains that the artist, when faced with a relatively complicated project, chose the security of progressing step by step. Still, a painter gifted with the ebullient creativity of a Rubens, when he made himself responsible for all stages of a work, would normally relinquish or abbreviate the 'standard procedure'. But a degree of standard procedure there certainly was, evolved throughout the sixteenth and seventeenth centuries, mainly under Italian influence (even if in some areas local traditions seem to have persisted – as the case of the sixteenth-century carved altarpieces would indicate).

One highly significant sixteenth-century example of a large-scale painter's studio was that of Frans Floris (who according to Van Mander must have employed, all in all, some 120 pupils or assistants).[34] Unfortunately, little is known in detail about its working procedures. Floris must have had a ready hand at inventing, and a number of his compositional drawings are preserved – few of them, however, in the nature of initial sketches. No studies from the live model are known; but head studies in oils exist (apparently imaginary, as most of his figure types seem to be) and their application in his studio practice can easily be charted (as will be indicated). Students/assistants must of course have played a large part in the execution of some of his paintings, but it is not clear how he organised this multifarious band. In any case, the Italian practice of working with full-scale cartoons seems not to have been adopted by this or any other 'typical' Flemish workshop, whether of the sixteenth or the seventeenth century, that concentrated on painting as an end-product.[35]

Rubens of course epitomises, for the seventeenth century, the image of the painter in charge of a densely populated workshop.[36] And we are in his case well informed about working procedures thoughout the entire sequence of stages of compositional elaboration. Even tentative, preliminary composition sketches are well represented (although in terms of his surviving work certainly not in proportion to their original number). Here truly is an artist who exploited to the full the suggestive quality of the 'pentimento sketch' or 'brainstorming drawing' as initiated by Leonardo. From this base he went on calmly to define and redefine his compositions, giving the actors in the drama he intended to evoke individuality and emotional presence. Much of this preparatory work apparently flowed facily from the incredible visual store of his imagination, but at a certain point he sometimes needed the impetus of direct observation from reality, and had models take up and 'flesh out' his preconceived poses and attitudes (see below). His system of making compositional studies evolved in the course of time: in his early years he favoured paper and pen, supplemented by wash, for a sort of provisional effect of the final formulation; later he came to prefer the oil sketch on panel (a design tool he had already occasionally explored earlier), which could be left inchoate or worked up to an extreme level of definition which nevertheless has nothing of the 'over-determination' of pedantry (see Logan's contribution for further comments on Rubens's more or less systematic approach).[37]

For Rubens's Flemish contemporaries fewer tentative or frankly exploratory sketches are preserved. And the logistics of their step-by-step procedure in the elaboration of a composition cannot always as yet be defined clearly. As a rule Van Dyck seems to have preferred ink (pen and brush with an important component of wash) on paper in his search for adequate formulations – a search which certainly in his early years was a laborious one, with attempt following experimental attempt, not necessarily in a clearly comprehensible continuous sequence;[38] but Van Dyck sometimes also took advantage of the fluidity of the oil sketch.[39] Jordaens stubbornly kept to paper, working with ink as well as body-colour.[40] Other Flemish artists seem to have alternated: the oil sketch was certainly much in favour, following Rubens's example. For Gaspar de Crayer there is evidence of a heavy reliance on paper (pen and ink, but also body-colour); but he often produced very competent oil sketches on panel too.[41] Cornelis Schut likewise repeatedly sketched in oils, but some of his 'modelli' are in ink on paper (Fig. 2).[42] The implications of all this for a more or less coherent design routine are still uncertain. Unfortunately, there is no convenient corpus of Flemish drawings or oil sketches[43] apart from those relating to Rubens, Van Dyck and Jordaens (although some more recent monographs on the 'secondary' masters offer useful starting points).

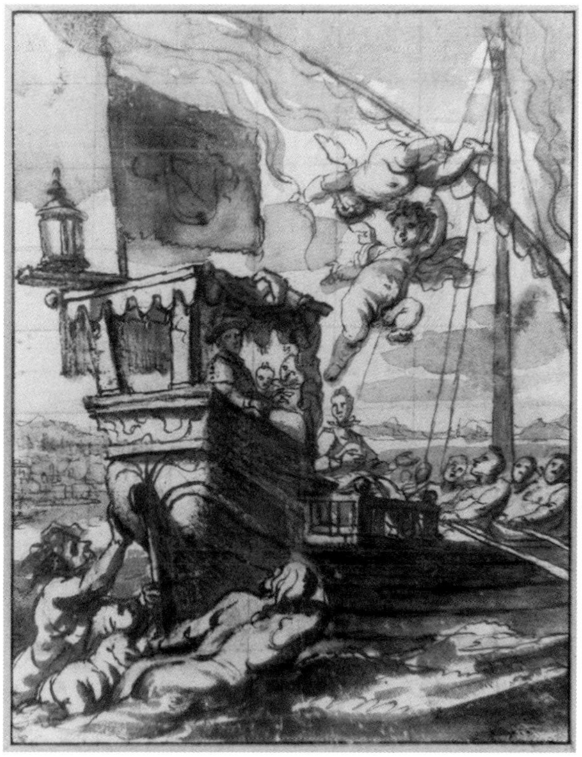

Fig. 2. Cornelis Schut, *The Voyage of the Cardinal-Infante Ferdinand by Sea to Genoa*, drawing. Antwerp, private collection

Finally, there are designs for sculpture. Sometimes in the past sculptors had relied on designs provided by others as a basis for their work – indeed labour – of adding and removing substances of an emphatically material nature, in order to realise a 'form', which generally (and certainly in the period we are considering) had to be of a stereometric complexity such that simple 'thought exercises' or imagination alone might not be able to realise and materialise. Sometimes a painter-designer's two-dimensional impressions might give a helpful hint.[44] On occasion the painter even supplied a series of views. But the sixteenth- and seventeenth century sculptor obviously was not totally dependent on this kind of instruction, and often was his own designer. He himself often resorted to drawing in two dimensions as a first exploratory medium to test out vague visual ideas. But a more natural preparatory tool seems to have been the small three-dimensional sketch (in clay or wax) known as a 'bozzetto'.[45] Quite a few of these (mostly in

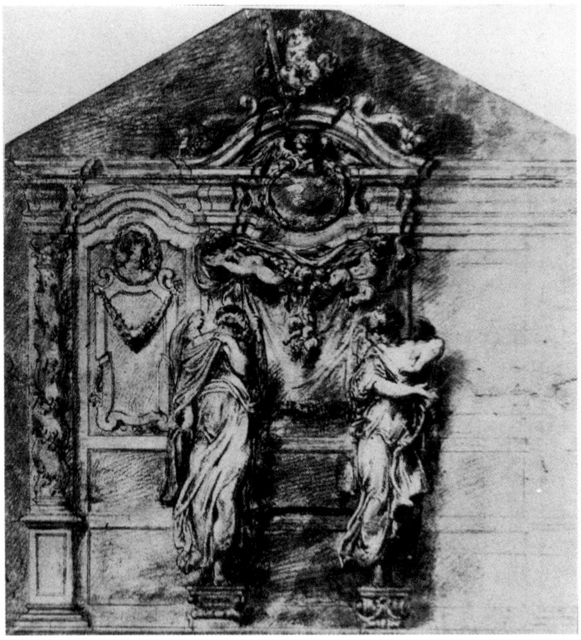

Fig. 3. Artus Quellinus the Younger, *Design for a Confessional*, drawing. Copenhagen, Printroom

'terracotta') have happily been preserved for Flemish seventeenth-century sculpture.[46]

Still, some sculptor's drawings were worked out in great detail, and could serve for contracts, as was, for example, the case for a wonderfully subtle sheet showing a confessional signed on the back by Artus Quellinus the younger, as well as by the patron of the work, the parish priest of Beringen (Fig. 3).[47] This serves as a reminder that many compositional drawings which have been preserved were expressly made with just such an intent.

Such, then, is a sample of artists, of all sorts of background and formation (though mostly painters), who possessed some level of skill, talent and expertise as designers of compositions (or sometimes just freestanding figures) in different media. It may be clear that many Flemish artists of the sixteenth and seventeenth centuries – some of them not particularly well known or even mentioned in general surveys – were really very competent designers or 'inventors' of compositions. The basis of this competence was perhaps in part, simply, talent (the essence of which still awaits an explanation from psychologists), in part it may have been the result of training (and here we have a straightforwardly art-historical question). How were these artists trained in the art of invention; or how did they train themselves?

Theoretical literature offered some kind of support, or encouragement. Alberti's treatise (*De pictura*, 1436) posed the challenge, but at the same time suggested some helpful practical guidance as to how to implement it. Van Mander (1604) devoted a whole chapter (Ch.5) of his *Den grondt der edel vry schilder-const* to invention ('Van der Ordinanty ende inventy der Historien'), which certainly must have helped to make a rather abstract requirement into something more practically realisable.[48] But for all that, the business of art as a serious category of human endeavour needed more than this kind of very general advice to a youthful public (the essence of Van Mander's approach).

Rubens was of course not the first Flemish artist to treat this problem of invention as a central one, but he was certainly among the most original. At a certain point (early) in his career he provided himself with a notebook in which he systematically combined literary citations (above all from the ancient poets) with visual 'quotations' (mostly from his immediate artistic predecessors, such as Raphael).[49] This process seems to reflect a particular sort of intellectual training as well as a manner of thinking which conceived of an easy transition between visual imagery and the world of words.

Other painters in seventeenth-century Flanders seem to have shared this conviction, and have succeeded in marrying the visual to the intellectual. Boeckhorst, Van Diepenbeeck, Willeboirts, Van Thulden, Boeyermans, Frans Francken II – all of these were effective designers of intricate compositions, sometimes with a densely abstract content.[50] How exactly they had trained themselves to reach proficiency in this demanding field we do not, however, know.

Studies of individual elements as components of design strategy

Various distinctions can be made in the way individual elements are generated and utilised in the process of creation. Some elements predate the project in hand having been kept in stock, as visual capital; they may originally have been freely invented or copied, either after nature or after a prototype – so fulfilling the

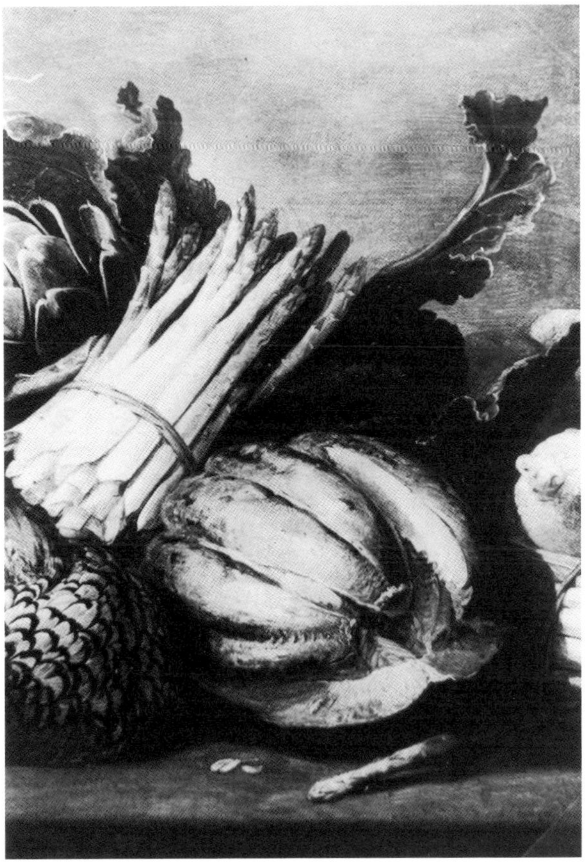

Fig. 4. Frans Snyders, *Game, Fruit and Vegetables* (detail). Laren, Singer Museum, Collection Van Dongen

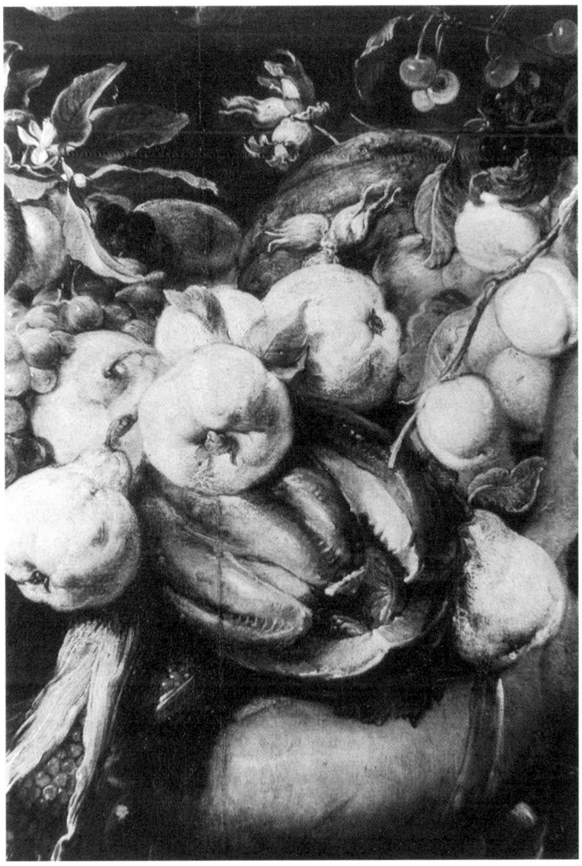

Fig. 5. Frans Snyders, *Fruit Garland* (detail). Brussels, City Museum

same function as the 'pattern drawings' in late-medieval model books. Other elements are made specifically for the project, as one of the stages in the elaboration (even if, once realised, they join the workshop's store of motifs, to serve some later purpose). Reuse of pre-existing motifs remains a familiar strategy in working out new compositions in the sixteenth and seventeenth century. It may be that this practice was sometimes treated with caution, what with the new demand for originality which accompanied the arrival of the Renaissance.[51] But at times the borrowings are so clearly emphasised that it looks as if the artist wanted to insert a deliberate quotation from the work of a revered predecessor. Reuse of material, be it borrowed or self-generated, may accordingly be differently motivated.

This sort of practice should be distinguished from studies made as a form of training, to gain fluency in the depiction of complicated figures or figure groups: many drawings by Lambert Lombard in the *Arenberg Album*, which presents freely invented variations on selected figures, are of this type.[52]

Given that nature played such a prominent role in much of Flemish art from the fifteenth century onwards, it must have been the case that numerous studies were made of flora and fauna, to be used once or repeatedly. Relatively few such studies have, however, come down to us[53] (an exception being those albums of nature studies which constituted a collector's item in themselves, only occasionally and incidentally used as a resource in painting production).[54] As was noted above, from the early sixteenth century it was often a dedicated 'nature' painter who contributed his particular skill to a history painting, and by the end of the century the flower piece, still life, landscape and animal piece were coming into their own as specialities. Painters working in these developing genres likewise exploited a repertoire of nature studies – both new and old.

In Frans Snyders's will of 1655 it is stipulated that he leaves all his painted studies on paper

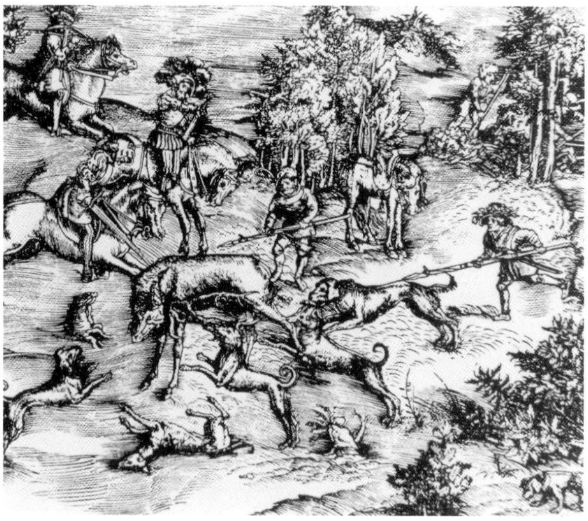

Fig. 6. Lucas Cranach, *Stag Hunt* (detail), woodcut

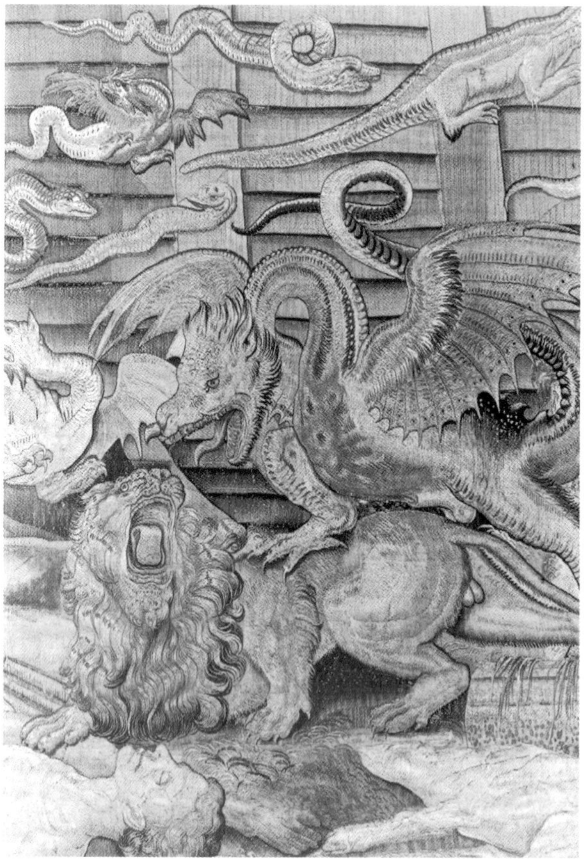

Fig. 7. After Michiel Coxcie, *The Animals leaving the Ark* (detail), tapestry by Jan van Tieghem. Cracow, Wawel Castle

of 'Italian fruit' to his nephew Hendrik de Rasiers.[55] These studies seem not to survive. But the use of one of them at least can be proved: there is an overripe melon burst open, which we encounter time and again in his compositions (Figs. 4–5).[56] The motif certainly derived from his collection of exotic fruit studies.

The problem of presenting a convincing depiction of a live animal in movement was of another order of complexity. In late-Gothic model books such motifs were a standard feature, and they were intensively (re)used. Other channels of transmission were loose drawing sheets, as well as prints, which had of course a broader diffusion. Thus we find a Cranach motif of a fighting stag (Fig. 6) in a Brussels tapestry from around 1520,[57] and an impressive group of a lion fighting a dragon in a tapestry (*The Animals leaving the Ark*) designed by Michiel Coxcie (Fig. 7) appears to be literally transcribed from a Leonardesque prototype.[58] Thus animals could migrate from one studio to another, sometimes over large distances in time and space. But again, few of the drawings or other studies are preserved, which, as it were, formed the passport in this migration process. A fortunate exception, also from the Coxcie workshop, is a sheet with studies of a lioness and a lynx-like beast (Fig. 8): the two animals turn up in different works by Coxcie: the lioness in another Coxcie tapestry, the lynx in his painting of the *Expulsion of Adam and Eve from Paradise* (Vienna; Fig. 9). This drawing later came into the hands of Rubens, who partly reworked it, and who may have had it in mind when he painted the tigress in his *Four Rivers* (Vienna) in a crouching position.[59]

Rubens was of course an animal painter 'hors pairs', and whenever possible he studied live animals; they were 'cavati dal naturale' as he proudly announced to one of his correspondents. He had an eye for the determining characteristics of a species as well as typical poses and their potential for both motion and expressiveness.[60] His animals (from lions and leopards to dogs and horses) were immediately copied and can count among the most popular animal motifs ever painted. Even Jan Brueghel, who was himself a very competent animal painter, as is evident from his sketches after life, borrowed from Rubens's animal material in several paintings:[61] it is obvious that this was not a furtive use of somebody else's model collection, but rather a deliberate citation, a visual tribute.

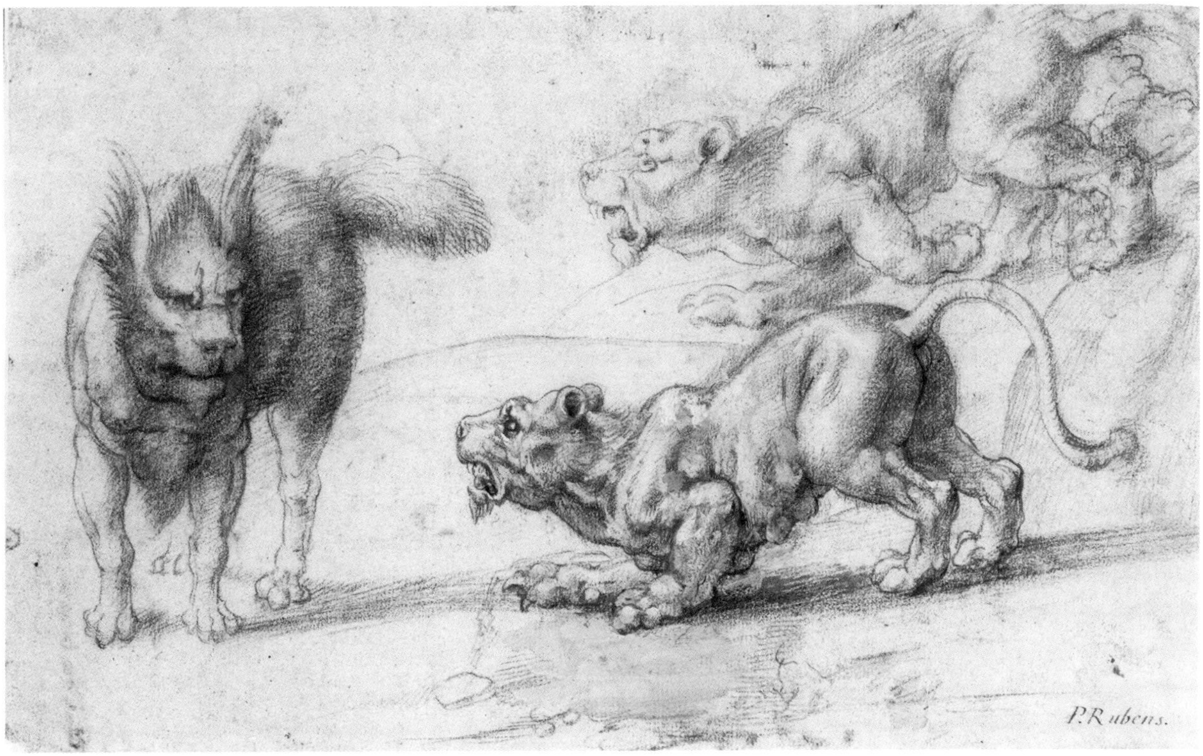

Fig. 8. Anonymous draughtsman, retouched by Rubens, *A Lynx (?) and a Lioness*, drawing. Whereabouts unknown

Last, but hardly least (given that we are ascending the scale of nature): studies after the human figure, the most important ingredient in the highest pictorial genre: history painting. And an even more complex problem than the previous categories of artistic subject, since not only did specific human (and sometimes individual) characteristics have to be observed, but also rhythm and movement, and attitudes expressive of intentions as well as emotions – and this in a functional relationship with the theme of the composition and with interactions of figures within it. For some artists (indeed for some whole periods of history) it was enough to represent a rather general or generic cast of types, which the trained practitioner could effortlessly recreate in a form of artistic cloning, but for any remotely sophisticated artist of the sixteenth and seventeenth century a degree of complexity and at least a suggestion of individuality was a basic requirement. Insight into the organic structure of the body had to be manifested and the sense of a real encounter with a human being had to be conjured up.

Much of this the artist had to master and assimilate in a period of training, before any specific project was taken up – although for the true artist such training was really never over. There were a number of methods of approach (usually these were used combined, more or less facily, although certain individuals or certain schools might choose to concentrate on one rather than the other).

Study after the Antique was one important means of arriving at an adequate understanding of the human figure as it was now conceived (in terms of pose, type, anatomy, expression). Some artists (such as Frans Floris) made only very superficial sketches after ancient prototypes,[62] others (such as Rubens or Van Lint) entered into an intricate exploration of the sculptures in their full detail and their three-dimensional materiality[63] (Rubens even adding the dynamic element of an unexpected viewpoint).

The time-honoured procedure of copying after the master, or an admired recent artist, was evidently still much in use as a way to acquire formal skills (at one time it was virtually the only method of teaching). Rubens's copies after his northern as well as southern predecessors are well known; but again he supplemented this rigorously literal form of copying with anoth-

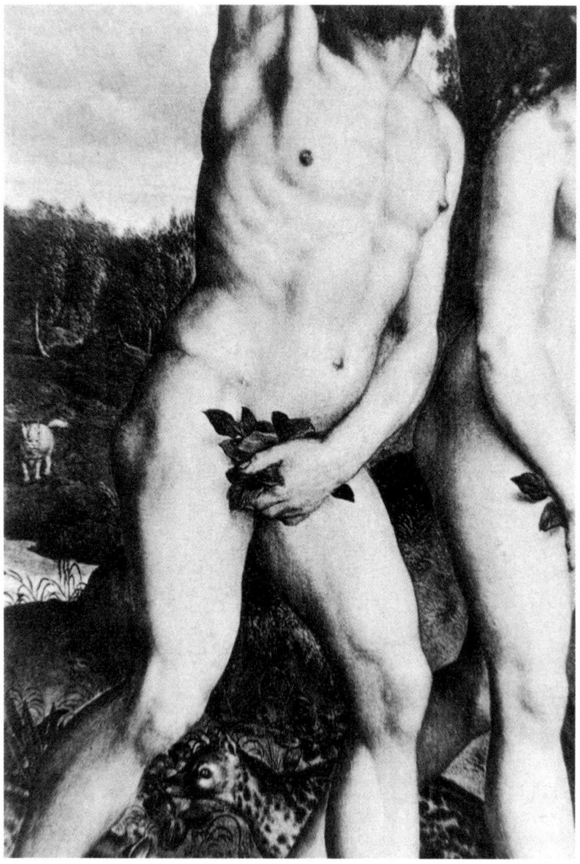

Fig. 9. Michiel Coxcie, *The Expulsion of Adam and Eve from Paradise* (detail). Vienna, Kunsthistorisches Museum

er procedure of self-training, which consisted of freely reformulating elements 'borrowed' from elsewhere, recombining selected fragments (see J. Wood in this publication) or enhancing specific effects.[64]

Studies of the posed model (often nude or quasi-nude) was of course another way to gain insight into the organic structure of the human body. For sixteenth-century Flemish art surprisingly few such studies from the model are known;[65] they are much more familiar for the seventeenth century (although actually rather rare if we discount the study sheets by Rubens, Jordaens and Van Dyck).[66] Sometimes such model studies feature as 'exempla' in the published drawing books.[67]

There is also the matter of the detailed, quasi-scientific study of human anatomy. Dissection of corpses does not seem to have been much practiced (if at all) by Flemish artists working in the Netherlands, but they must have shared with their Italian colleagues the conviction that some knowledge of the disposition and function of the muscles is a prerequisite, and that this knowledge should even determine and inform the interpretation of features observed in live models as well as in exemplars from ancient and modern art. Again for the sixteenth century there is but meagre evidence, but it is hard to imagine how Frans Floris could have had depicted the convincing nudes in his *Fall of the Rebel Angels* (Antwerp), without an awareness of subcutaneous features of anatomy. It seems probable that he used medical publications, or an écorché model – that is a sculpted figure in which the muscular structure of the human body was displayed in all its detail.[68] Such a procedure can now be documented for Rubens: several sheets of his anatomy book are preserved, and we there see how accurately and intensively the young artist studied (and again often from unexpected viewpoints) several such écorché models.[69] Some of these were, after Rubens's death, reproduced in print in Pontius's *Livre à dessiner* and so became more widely available; but it is clear that certain of Rubens's anatomy studies had also been copied before, in drawings, in the studio.

These observations about the study of the human figure have more to do with the general *training* of the young artist than the *design* procedures he adopted when engaged on actual projects. Still, as I have indicated, this sort of categorisation is somewhat artificial: in Rubens's case, for example, it has been shown that at times, even in his later works, he might transcribe an écorché study he had earlier made with no more specific purpose than for practice.

But let us return to the central subject of this paper – the deliberately *design*-oriented graphic (or pictorial) tools which Flemish artists used and developed – concentrating now on the isolated components rather than (as in the last section, pp. 132–136) on the composition as a whole. In this context it should be reiterated that this two-part subdivision (composition/elements) entails no notion of a sequentional logic: some of the fragmentary studies to be considered here would have been sandwiched, as it were, between more compositionally oriented stages such as we have studied above (and some, such as reused items, obviously antedate them in 'real' time; a point which will be taken up later). And the sort of simple 'stratigraphy' that might here seem to be implied does not of course do justice to the important role some of these inter-

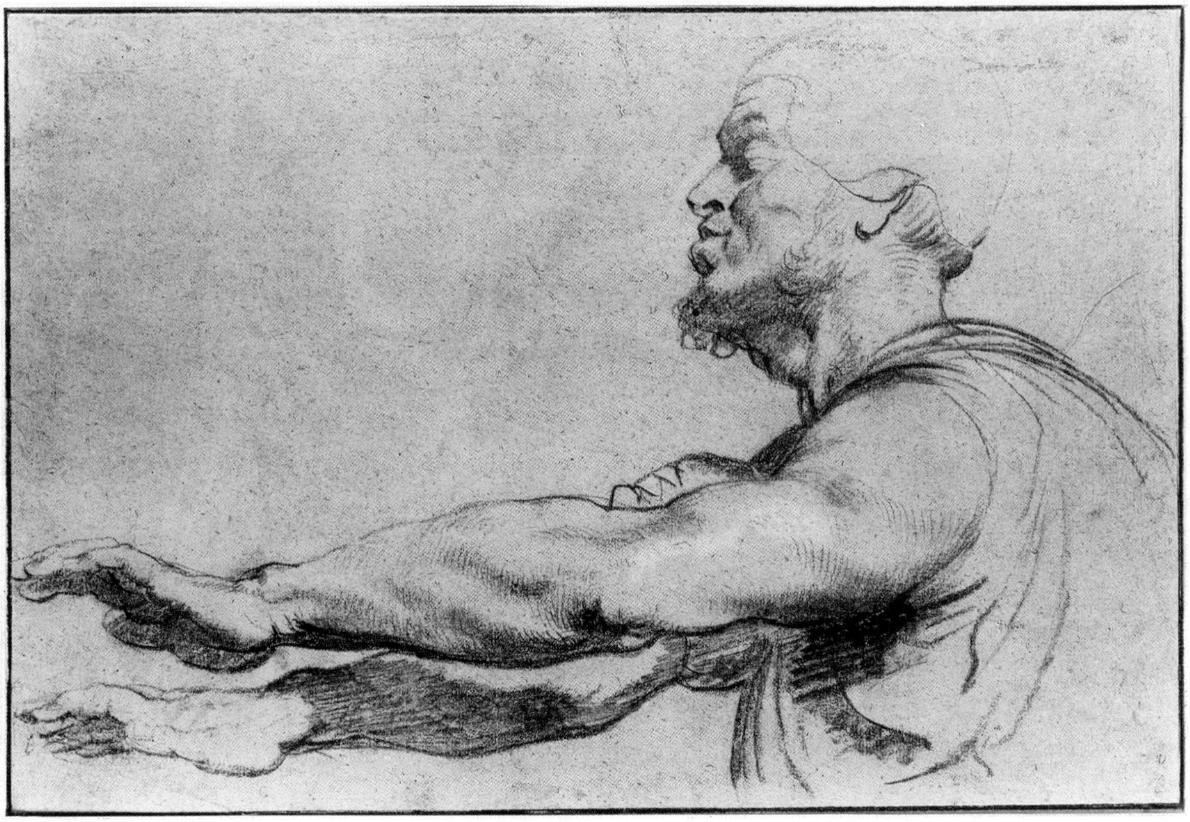

Fig. 10. Peter Paul Rubens, *Study of a Blind Man stretching his Arms forward*, drawing. Vienna, Albertina

mediate stages actually played, in moving the whole machinery up into another gear.

Again the distinction should be articulated between graphic and pictorial tools which *antedate* a given project (*a*), but were designed or generated with a view to their potential later usefulness (the store of visual capital); and those (*b*) which were made 'ad hoc', to meet the need for a particular sort of visual information at a specific point in a project.

To begin with the second group (*b*): the 'additional' studies required to bring the individual elements of the composition to life and to a definitive and convincing form. This normally implies studies from life, from the model posing in a predetermined attitude in the studio. Few such studies remain for the sixteenth century. But they are abundantly preserved for Rubens, and in most cases they can neatly be located at a particular circumstantial nexus: they 'implement' a situation (a pose) which has been previously indicated in the 'modello' stage apparently by a complete reliance on visual imagination. The studio model was simply required to approximate to the pose indicated; was drawn in some detail, in such a way that even the fall of light was carefully noted; and this image (the imaginary form now made concrete) was almost literally transfered to the painting (although this particular procedural formulation is more typical of some stages in Rubens's career than others). Hardly any of Rubens's known model studies do not relate to a specific project; and rather few of these were later reused (contrary to what one might have expected of this supposedly opportunistic, time saving painter). And some of these reuses (as when he adapts the muscular arms of a 'blind man' for the figure of a woman in a later painting; Figs. 10–11) may prove rather surprising.[70]

A similar procedure may have at times been used by other artists such as Van Dyck and Jordaens; but in dealing with studies from the model it is essential to attempt to establish in each instance whether or not they were indeed made for a specific project, and at which point in the elaboration of the composition they were inserted (for example, before or after the 'modello' stage was reached). But not all detailed figure studies need be after the live model: inten-

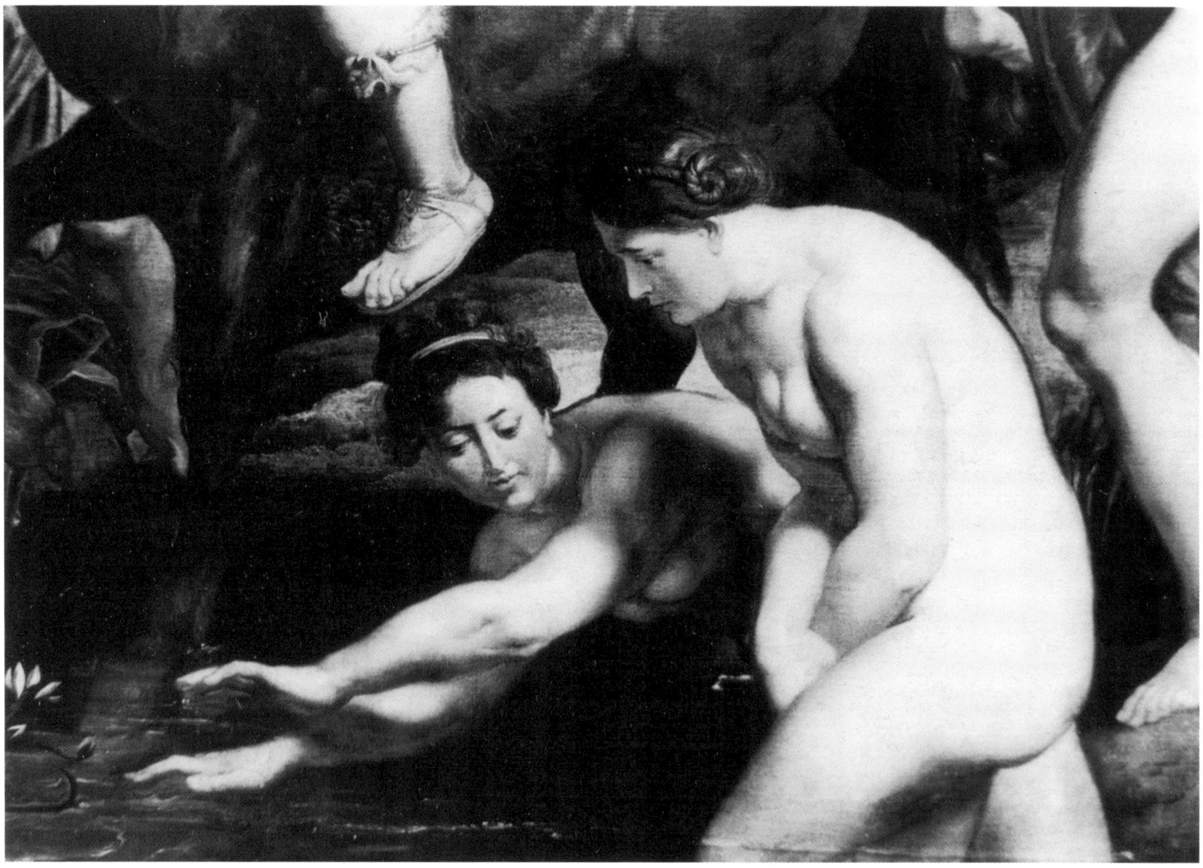

Fig. 11. Peter Paul Rubens and Studio, *The Flight of Cloelia* (detail). Formerly Berlin, Kaiser-Friedrich-Museum

sive training had prepared artists to work out elaborate formulations of individual features without reference back to real life.

Rubens, in the course of a design sequence, sometimes also had recourse to studies of particular features (rather than overall views) of his characters, these also made 'ad hoc'. Hands as well as heads were especially so devised, adapted to a specific situation; a live model might be consulted for such details, but at times the artist took as his guide antique heads or busts which figured in his collection.[71]

But Rubens also took full advantage of another preparatory procedure, in this instance generic (*a*, above) rather than specific – one which had been introduced to the Netherlands by Frans Floris. This was the pre-existing, almost fully finished (and painted) study head.[72] Such a resource was of course immensely useful when part of the execution was to be left to assistants.

Floris's head studies had been worked out in colour (in oil on panel), and so were Rubens's (oils, sometimes on paper that was later laid down on panel). In this context the Rubensian attribution refers primarily to the artist's role as studio director, since we are informed that at least some of these head studies were supplied for him by Van Dyck (although a certain number are clearly by Rubens himself). And we find them used time and again in the workshop's production, although (again) more in certain periods of his career than in others.

Rubens's exploitation of this store of head studies might be far from mechanical. In a few instances (for example Figs. 12–13)[73] his compositions (apparently executed largely or entirely by studio assistants, among them certainly Van Dyck) seem not just to make use of the available heads, but to be altogether conceived on the basis of them: to such effect that nothing in the result betrays any sense of an additive, jigsaw-like assembly procedure, since the composition as a whole 'functions' with perfect dramatically coherence. We might easily suppose that each of these heads had been specifically painted for its role in the compo-

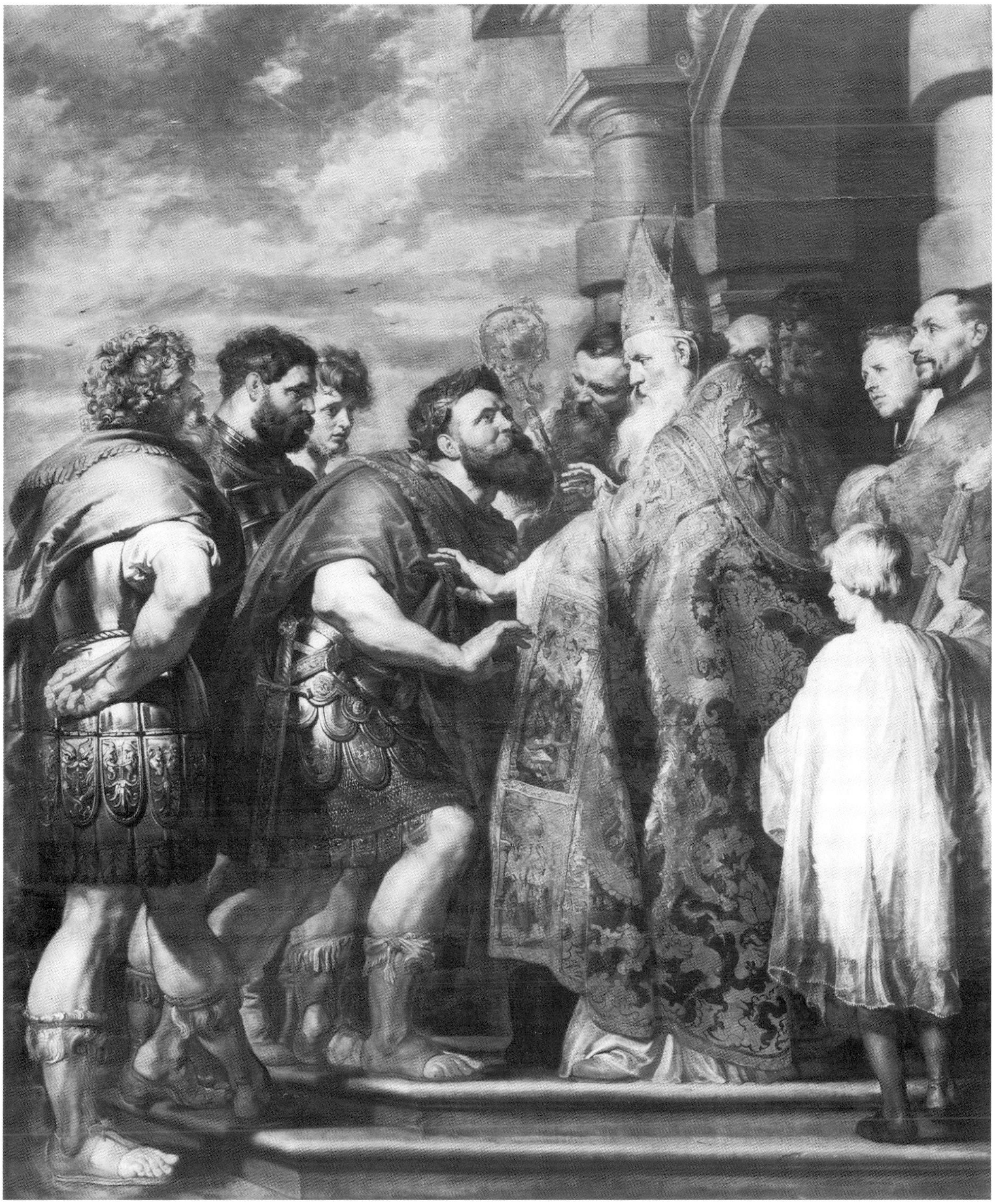

Fig. 12. Peter Paul Rubens and Anthony van Dyck, *St Ambrose and Theodosius*. Vienna, Kunsthistorisches Museum

sition. Apparently, however, it was the other way around. This highlights one feature of the head studies: we hardly ever find in them an emotional charge that is specific: most are portrayed in what might be termed an 'average' mood (testifying to 'ethos' rather than 'pathos'). But when brought together in a particular sort of narrative context, they seem to assume 'personae', restrained but nevertheless adequately expressive. For situations of more dramatic intensity, Rubens seems to have relied on 'ad hoc' study drawings.

Head studies were ubiquitous in Flemish seventeenth-century art. Like other patterns,

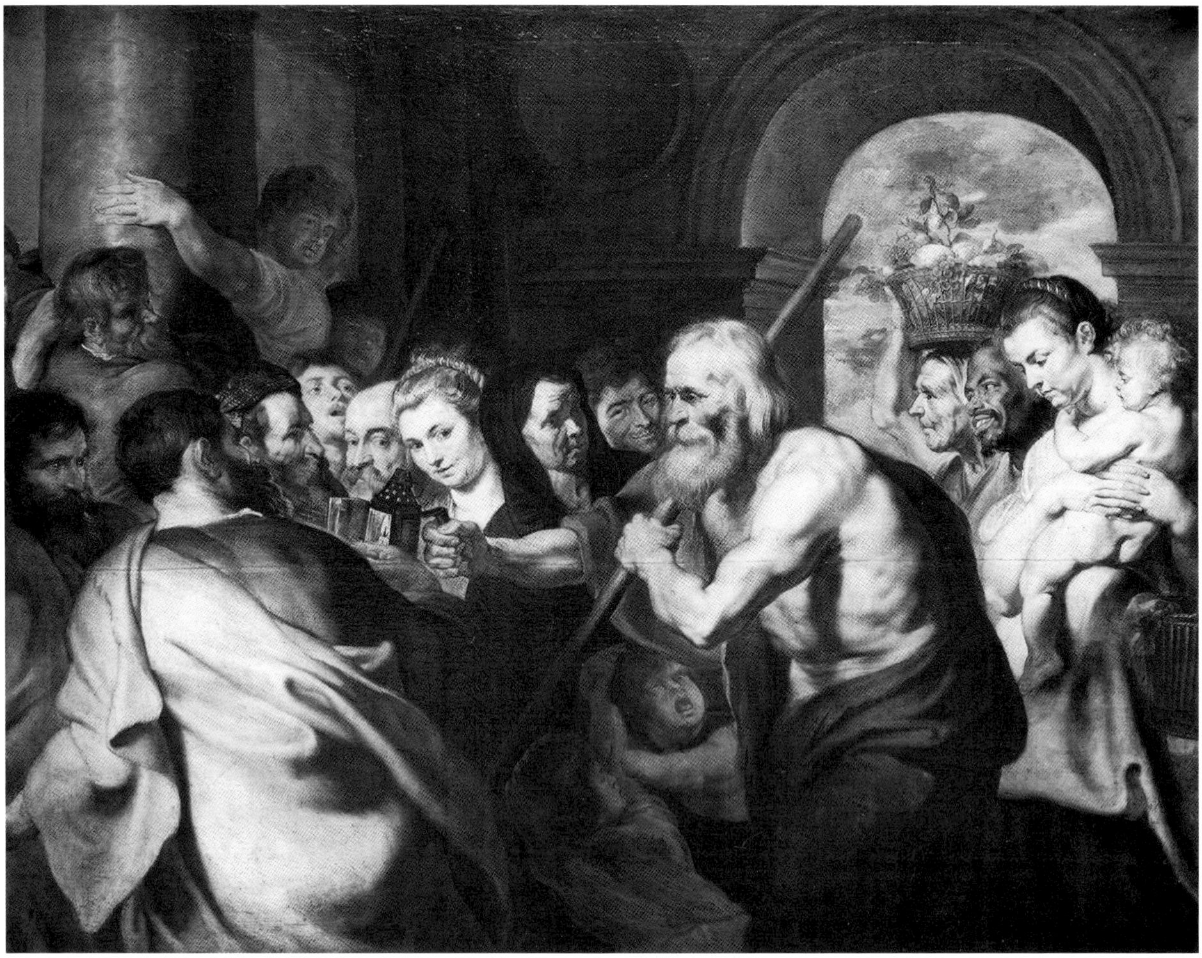

Fig. 13. Studio of Peter Paul Rubens, *Diogenes seeking a True Man*. Paris, Musée du Louvre

these were copied, inherited, and reused in other artistic studios. A case in point is the very popular head of a curly-haired boy (Fig. 14),[74] apparently painted as a head study by Willeboirts Bosschaert and used by him in his own art, but taken up and exactly reproduced by such diverse artists as Jan van den Hoecke and David Ryckaert (the last a curious case of transference to the realm of genre painting). What strikes one is that in both cases we can speak of a literal repetition, with no attempt on the part of the borrower to make a personal reformulation. Maybe this practice should not be seen merely as a labour-saving device; rather it could be an opportunistic manœuvre to integrate into a composition as many attractive features as possible; in other words, it is not the ease with which it could be reproduced which explains the popularity of this paricular head study, but its catchy appeal.

In conclusion

Before a painting was actually executed on its definitive support (and this in itself was also a complicated matter, involving phases of sketching or underdrawing and several layers of 'dead colouring' – see Nico Van Hout in this publication), quite a lot of preparatory or intermediary material might have been generated, varied in its focus and technique, and with paper as the most popular (but not the only) support.

Some of this material was made in advance and kept in stock, other items were prepared in connection with specific works. Certain of these latter might have been immediately discarded after performing their function, but much was probably stored away with an eye to its possible usefulness in the future.

As a body, the material was treasured and sometimes, it seems, jealously guarded from the eyes of strangers, since the sum of information it embodied was vital to the workshop as an economic unit and to its distinctive character – what might be called its individualised profile – in the market. Sometimes, however, an artist's collected store was deliberately destroyed, for one reason or another (Michelangelo supposedly did not want the laborious creative process behind his work to be revealed, while Pieter Bruegel had ideological reasons for wanting many of his drawings to be obliterated). Normally, however, rich collections of design material were passed on to the next generation as – being real (visual) capital – an important part of the artistic estate.[75]

Since most of these 'fonds d'atelier' are now lost, or depleted and dispersed, and moreover not usually studied for what they were (i.e. functional, rather than more generally aesthetic items), many of the specifics of the design procedures they might document are as yet poorly understood – as was not infrequently evident in the above survey. How varied was this sort of preparatory visual material, and how was it stored away for later retrieval?

Only exceptionally have such artistic estates been preserved, even in part.[76] In the case of Rubens we are fortunate to have Panneels's copies after part of his master's 'cantoor' (although this source has not yet been exploited to its full potential).[77] Sometimes artists' probate inventories provide a measure of enlightenment about the richness of such holdings (see Katlijne Van der Stighelen later in this publication): lay-models, pieces of sculpture that served as study models, sketchbooks and portfolios with study drawings, albums with drawings and engravings pasted in (and the inventory of the estate of Erasmus Quellin is especially informative in this respect).[78] But individual drawings are usually not described in such notarial documents.

If a few sketchbooks are still preserved more or less intact or can be tentatively reconstructed,[79] the functional purpose of individually preserved drawings can now sometimes only be guessed at, and a more sophisticated typology is needed in order to classify them. Some very finished drawings might be 'ricordi' (that is, records made 'ex post facto', in order to preserve visual information for possible later use) rather than real compositional drawings, 'modelli', or contract drawings.[80] Sometimes the existence of intermediate material can be reconstructed (as we saw above) on the basis of the repetition of a motif in different paintings; but in such cases attention must be paid to the extent of the closeness in detail, as well as the relative size (where the correspondence between motifs extends to the actual size, this may indicate the use of a partial cartoon).[81]

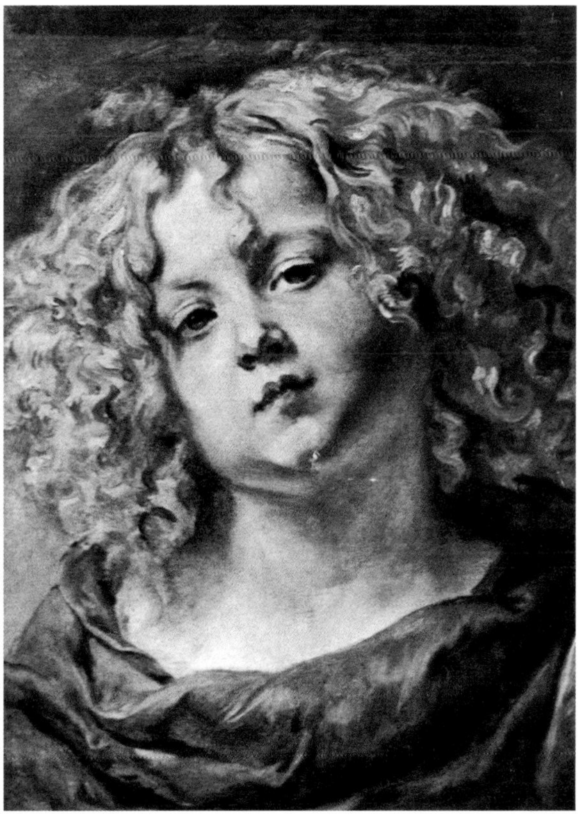

Fig. 14. Thomas Willeboirts Bosschaert, *Head of a Boy*. Whereabouts unknown

And, last but not least, one would like to know how the artists ordered their material:[82] was it classified according to subject-matter or just added to the growing stack in the course of time? It may be clear from these remarks and from the various threads I have left dangling that much work remains to be done in this vital field of study.

NOTES

I would like to thank Elizabeth McGrath for her help with the English and for stimulating suggestions.

1. Seminal for the approach here attempted have been two important articles by J. von Schlosser, 'Zur Kenntnis der künstlerischen Überlieferung im späten Mittelalter', *Jahrbuch der kunsthistorischen Sammlungen des Allerhöchsten Kaiserhauses*, XXIII, 1902, pp. 279–338; 'Aus der Bildnerwerkstatt der Renaissance', Ibidem, XXXI, 1913–1914, esp. pp. 100–135 (the use of sculptural models). And of course Joseph Meder's great book on drawing (*Die Handzeichnung: ihre Technik und Entwicklung*, Vienna, 1919).

2. See the reference in Scheller (see note 3), pp. 23, 389.

3. The last word on medieval model books (and medieval drawing traditions) is now R.W. Scheller's masterly *Exemplum: Model-Book Drawings and the Practice of Artistic Transmission in the Middle Ages (ca. 900–ca. 1470)*, Amsterdam, 1995 (encompassing the entire previous literature, and including an exceedingly rich bibliography).

4. E. van de Wetering, 'Lost Drawings and the Use of Erasable Drawing Boards and "Tafeletten"', in his *Rembrandt. The Painter at Work*, Amsterdam, 1997, pp. 47–72.

5. An excellent overview is G. Binding *et al.*, *Baubetrieb im Mittelalter*, Darmstadt, 1993, pp. 171–234 (covering subjects such as drawings on parchment and paper as well as tracings on chalk floors and walls, model books and templates). For the Netherlands in particular see: R. Meischke, 'Het architectonische ontwerp in de Nederlanden gedurende de late middeleeuwen en de zestiende eeuw', in his *De gotische bouwtraditie. Studies over opdrachtgevers en bouwmeesters in de Nederlanden*, Amersfoort, 1988, pp. 127–207; R. Tijs, 'De architect en de ontwerptekening tijdens de 16de en de 17de eeuw', in *Architectuurtekeningen uit de historische steden van België*, s.l., 1985, pp. 10–21. Instructive is also E.S. Ferguson, *Engineering and the Mind's Eye*, Cambridge, Mass.–London, 1994.

6. O. Pächt, 'Early Nature Studies and the Calendar Landscape', *Journal of the Warburg and Courtauld Institutes*, XIII, 1950, pp. 13–47; O. Pächt, '"Simon Mormion myt deer handt"', *Revue de l'art*, XLVI, 1979, pp. 7–15; F. Koreny, *Albrecht Dürer and the Animal and Plant Studies of the Renaissance*, Boston, 1988; W. Prinz and A. Beyer, ed., *Die Kunst und das Studium der Natur vom 14. zum 16. Jahrhundert*, Weinheim, 1987.

7. P.P. Bober and R. Rubinstein, *Renaissance Artists & Antique Sculpture. A Handbook of Sources*, London–Oxford, 1986 (with a list of individual artists and 'sketchbooks', pp. 451–470).

8. M. Baxandall, *Giotto and the Orators. Humanist Observers of Painting in Italy and the Discovery of Pictorial Composition 1350–1450*, Oxford, 1971; see now, for a different interpretation of Alberti's ideas on composition, a forthcoming article by C. Hope.

9. R. Oertel, 'Wandmalerei und Zeichnung in Italien. Die Anfänge der Entwurfszeichnung und ihre monumentalen Vorstufen', *Mitteilungen des Kunsthistorischen Institutes in Florenz*, V, 1940, pp. 217–313; E.H. Gombrich, 'Leonardo's Method for Working out Compositions (1952)', in his *Norm and Form. Studies in the Art of the Renaissance (I)*, 3rd ed., Oxford–New York, 1978, pp. 58–63; E.H. Gombrich, 'Watching Artists at Work: Commitment and Improvisation in the History of Drawing', in his *Topics of Our Time. Twentieth-Century Issues in Learning and in Art*, London, 1991, pp. 92–130; P. van den Akker, *Sporen van vaardigheid. De ontwerpmethode voor de figuurhouding in de Italiaanse tekenkunst van de renaissance*, Abcoude, 1991; M. Shelley, (art.) 'Drawing', in *The Dicitonary of Art*, ed. J. Turner, London–New York, 1996, IX, pp. 212–233 (esp. pp. 213–215: 'Function and purpose').

10. F. Ames-Lewis, *Drawing in Early Renaissance Italy*, New Haven–London, 1981; P. Joannides, *The Drawing of Raphael, with a Complete Catalogue*, Oxford, 1983; F. Ames-Lewis, *The Draftsman Raphael*, New Haven–London, 1986.

11. Van Mander also refers to the practice of painting out of one's head directly on the surface, and correcting in dead colouring ('herdootverwen'), without bothering about preliminary drawings, but this is only given to the 'Augusten' among artists (Karel van Mander, *Den grondt der edel vry schilderconst*, ed. H. Miedema, Utrecht, 1973, chapt. 12.6–7, I, pp. 252–255).

12. A succinct and rather unhelpful treatment is M. Comblen-Sonkes, 'De tekening', in R. Van Schoute and B. de Patoul, ed., *De Vlaamse primitieven*, Leuven, 1994 (French language original: *Les primitifs flamands et leur temps*, Brussels, 1994), pp. 117–123, with useful bibliography on p. 631. But see also the same author's more detailed study: *Dessins du XVe siècle: Groupe Van der Weyden*, Les primitifs flamands, III, 5, Brussels, 1969.

13. An exemplary study of the relationship between drawing and underdrawing (as revealed by the technique of infrared reflectography) is M.W. Ainsworth, 'Northern Renaissance Drawings and Underdrawings: A Proposed Method of Study', *Master Drawings*, XXVII, 1989, pp. 5–38. Underdrawings in early Netherlandish art have been exhaustingly studied over the last decades (by such leading authorities as J.R.J van Asperen de Boer and M. Faries). The proceedings of regularly held colloquia *Le dessin sous-jacent* in Louvain-la-Neuve and Leuven, and organised by R. Van Schoute, H. Verougstraete and M. Smeyers, always contain a wealth of new information.

14. '...to draw in your ancona or panel with those willow coals... But the charcoal wants to be tied to a little cane or stick, so that it comes some distance from the figures; for it is a great help to you in composing. And keep the feather handy; so that, if you are not satisfied with any stroke, you may erase it with the barbs of the feather, and draw it over again... [W]hen the figure is satisfactory, take the feather and rub it over the drawing very lightly, until the drawing is practically effaced...[;] reinforce your whole drawing, with a small pointed minever brush [and ink]. Then take a little bunch of feathers, and sweep the whole drawing free of charcoal' (Cennino d'Andrea Cennini, *The Craftsman's Handbook. The Italian 'Il libro dell' arte'*, transl. D.V. Thompson, New York, 1960, p. 75.

15. J.J.G. Alexander, *Medieval Illuminators and their Methods of Work*, New Haven–London, 1992, pp. 56–71, and Appendix 2, pp. 184–186.

16. A very suggestive study is F. Koreny, 'Coloured Flower Study by Martin Schongauer and the Development of the Depiction of Nature from van der Weyden to Dürer', *The Burlington Magazine*, CXXXIII, 1991, pp. 588–597.

17. On sixteenth-century drawing as a functional unit in the total creative process, see W.W. Robinson and M. Wolff,

'The Function of Drawings in the Netherlands in the Sixteenth Century', in [cat. exh.] *The Age of Bruegel: Netherlandish Drawings in the Sixteenth Century* (Washington, National Gallery; New York, Pierpont Morgan Library, 1986–1987), Cambridge, 1986, pp. 25–40. For the seventeenth century see A.M. Logan, [cat. exh.] *Flemish Drawings in the Age of Rubens. Selected Works from American Collections*, Wellesley, Mass., Wellesley College, 1993; U. Westfehling, 'Zeichenkunst in Antwerpen 1600–1650', in [cat. exh.] *Von Bruegel bis Rubens. Das goldene Jahrhundert der flämischen Malerei* (Cologne–[Antwerp]–Vienna), Cologne, 1993, pp. 235–248.

18. J. Shearman, *Raphael's Cartoons in the Collection of Her Majesty the Queen and the Tapestries for the Sistine Chapel*, London, 1972. On the physical make-up of these cartoons see most recently S. Fermor, *The Raphael Tapestry Cartoons: Narrative - Decoration - Design*, London, 1996; S. Fermor and A. Derbyshire, 'The Raphael Tapestry Cartoons re-examined', *The Burlington Magazine*, CXL, 1998, pp. 236–250. N. Dacos, 'Tommaso Vincidor. Un élève de Raphael aux Pays-Bas', in *Relations artistiques entre les Pays-bas et l'Italie à la Renaissance: Etudes dédiées à Suzanne Sulzberger*, Brussels–Rome, 1980, pp. 61–99; N. Dacos, 'Cartons et dessins raphaélesques à Bruxelles: l'action de Rome aux Pays-Bas', in *Fiamminghi a Roma 1508–1608* (*Bolletino d'arte*, C, 1997: *Supplemento*), pp. 1–22.

19. C.M.J.M. van den Heuvel, *'Papiere Bolwercken'. De introductie van Italiaanse stede- en vestingbouw in de Nederlanden (1540–1609) en het gebruik van tekeningen*, Alphen aan de Rijn, 1991.

20. See e.g. the drawing on parchment (height 400 cm), *c.* 1360–1365, for part of the tower of Strasbourg cathedral, containing detailed drawings in colour for figural sculpture, presumably by another hand ([cat. exh.] *Die Parler und der Schöne Stil 1350–1400*, Cologne, Kunsthalle, 1978, I, p. 280, with illustrations pp. 279, 280, 281 and colour plate 9). On designs for late-Gothic sculpture in general: H. Huth, *Künstler und Werstätte der Spätgotik*, 1923, pp. 36–53 and n. 75, 94 (with illustrations).

21. For an important early sixteenth-century example see E. Dhanens, 'Jan van Roome alias van Brussel, schilder', *Gentse bijdragen tot de kunstgeschiedenis*, XI, 1945–1948, pp. 41–146.

22. See, e.g., M.W. Ainsworth, *Bernart van Orley as a Designer of Tapestry*, Ph.D. Diss, Yale University, 1982 (distributed by University Microfilm International, Ann Arbor, Mich.), esp. chapt. 3: 'The Creative Act: the Drawings', pp. 63–98.

23. A. Balis, K. De Jonge, G. Delmarcel and A. Lefébure, *Les tapisseries des Chasses de Maximilien*, Paris, 1993, pp. 54–79 for the designs and cartoons, and pp. 72–74 for Jan (II?) Tons.

24. Large cartoons of course were not entirely the work of the head of the studio (in this case: Van Orley): he must have ordinarily relied on assistants (see, e.g., Balis, De Jonge, Delmarcel en Lefébure 1993 (see note 23), pp. 74–78 for the hypothetical identification of one of these collaborators). See, for a more reductionist statement (separating designer from cartoon-painter): T. Campbell, 'New Light on a Set of *History of Julius Caesar* Tapestries in Henry VIII's Collection', *Decorative Arts*, V, 2, 1998, esp. pp. 29–32. The relative share of the 'designer' and the 'cartoonist(s)' has been debated in the past and will continue to be in the future.

Three systems (at least) were operational: (1) the designer with his atelier being in charge of the cartoon (working from the small-scale *modello* towards the full-scale cartoon); (2) the designer as only a first purveyor of the general composition ('le petit patron' or *modello*), with the specialised cartoon painter continuing from there on (with no extra pictorial information to guide him?); (3) the reassemblage by a cartoon specialist of elements (fragments of cartoons) which were at hand (but of course, painters could themselves also have recourse to this sort of recuperation: see the contribution by N. De Poorter to the present publication).

25. G. Marlier, *La Renaissance flamande. Pierre Coeck d'Alost*, Brussels, 1966, pp. 311–342. Recently Coecke's cartoon of *The Beheading of St Paul* (Brussels, City Museum) has been restored.

26. H.J. Horn, *Jan Cornelisz Vermeyen Painter of Charles V and his Conquest of Tunis*, Doornspijk, 1989, I, pp. 109–298; II, pp. 343–411, figs. B1–102. A few further sixteenth century Flemish tapestry cartoons are preserved. Among other painters who were active in this field should also be mentioned Jan van Roome, Lambert Lombard, Michiel Coxcie, Lucas de Heere, Peter de Kempeneer. Surprisingly, however, many designs for Flemish sixteenth-century tapestries remain without a convincing attribution. For a recent proposal see N. Dacos, 'Léonard Thiry des Belges, peintre excellent: de Bruxelles à Fontainebleau en passant par Rome', *Gazette des Beaux-Arts*, May–June 1996, pp. 199–212; N. Dacos, 'Léonard Thiry des Belges, peintre excellent: de Fontainebleau à Bruxelles', *Gazette des Beaux-Arts*, July–August 1996, pp. 29–34.

27. N. De Poorter, *The Eucharist Series*, Corpus Rubenianum Ludwig Burchard, II, Brussels, 1978, 2 vols.; K. Nelson, *Jacob Jordaens: Design for Tapestry*, Pictura Nova, V, Turnhout, 1998.

28. On Van Diepenbeeck's cartoons on paper in St Petersburg, see A. Balis, 'Abraham van Diepenbeeck and Pieter Boel as Designers of Tapestries: the Holstein Hunts', in E. Mai, K. Schütz and H. Vlieghe, ed., *Die Malerei Antwerpens - Gattungen, Meister, Wirkungen. Studien zur flämische Kunst des 16. und 17. Jahrhunderts. Internationales Kolloquium, Wien 1993*, Cologne, 1994, pp. 168–177; on the tapestry cartoons on canvas by Jan van den Hoecke et al. in Vienna see G. Heinz, 'Studien über Jan van den Hoecke und die Malerei der Niederländer in Wien', *Jahrbuch der Kunsthistorischen Sammlungen in Wien*, LXIII, 1967, pp. 130–143. The Rubens workshop generally supplied canvas cartoons; Jordaens worked on paper.

29. A very early instance of a design for a glass window (if rather hypothetical): H. Wentzel, 'Un projet de vitrail au XIVe siècle', *Revue de l'art*, X, 1970, pp. 7–14; for a fourteenth-century wooden glazier's table on which the pattern of the leading is traced: J. Vila-Grau, 'La table de peintre-verrier de Gérone', *Revue de l'art*, LXXII, 1986, pp. 32–34.

30. E. Konowitz, 'The Glass Designer Dierick Vellert', in V. Chieffo Raguin et al., [cat. exh.] *Northern Renaissance Stained Glass: Continuity and Transformation*, Worcester, Mass, I. and B.G. Cantor Art Gallery, 1987, pp. 22–28. A very rich mine of material about Netherlandish sixteenth-century designers and executors of glass roundels is T.B. Husband et al., [cat. exh.] *The Luminous Image. Painted Glass Roundels in the Lowlands, 1480–1560*, New York, The Metropolitan Museum of Art, 1995. Other important designers (though not executors) of glass windows include Van Orley and Coxcie (Y. Vanden Bemden, 'Michel Coxcie, créateur de vitraux', *Handelingen van de Koninklijke Kring voor Oudheidkunde, Letteren en Kunst van Mechelen*, XCV, 2, 1992 [=1993], pp. 141–159). For fragments of glass panels actually painted by Diepenbeeck see D.W. Steadman, *Abraham van Diepenbeeck, Seventeenth-Century Flemish Painter*, Ann Arbor, Mich., 1982, figs. 14–15 (with on pp. 51–53 a list of his designs for glass). Other stained glass panels attributed to Van Diepenbeeck and, interestingly, to Rubens (by whom no glass designs are known) are mentioned in the sale catalogue of the collection of F.A.E. Bruynincx (Antwerp, C. de Vil, 10–20 October 1791, eight lots, nos. 233–236 as by Rubens and 237–240 as by Van Diepenbeeck: 'Tous ces verres sont à-peu-près de même grandeur, & ont servi de fenêtres à la sodalité des ci-devant Jésuites à Anvers; ils sont plus ou moins endommagés mais rare & peut-être unique exemple de trouver de Rubens d'ouvrages sur verre'; see P. Delsaert and D. Vanysacker, 'The Library of Franciscus Bruynincx, Official Principal, Learned Canon and Bibliophile from Antwerp [1719–1791]', *Revue d'histoire ecclésiastique*, XCII, 1997, p. 774).

31. Y. Vanden Bemden, C. Fontaine-Hodiamont and A. Balis, *Cartons du XVIIe siècle: La cathédrale Saint-Michel, Bruxelles*,

Corpus vitrearum, Belgique: Etudes, I, Brussels, 1994. For the rich collection of cartoons preserved in Gouda see H. van Harten-Boers and Z. van Ruyven-Zeman, *The Stained-Glass Windows in the Sint Janskerk at Gouda. The Glazing of the Clerestory of the Choir and of the Former Monastic Church of the Regulars*, Corpus Vitrearum, Amsterdam, 1998.

32. Van Mander mentions that Jacob Jansz. van de Gheyn (*c.* 1532–1582) at the end of his life used to paint his glass cartoons in oils on canvas (Karel van Mander, *Het Schilder-Boeck*, Haarlem, 1604, fol. 294).

33. See Steadman 1982 (see note 30), fig. 1 (ink on paper); figs. 7–11 (oils on panel, grisaille); fig. 13 (oils on panel, full colour); (fig. 12, ink on paper, is a rare example of an initial, tentative design, for the same composition). The present drawing (Fig. 1), here attributed to Van Diepenbeeck, is in black and red chalk, 361 x 203/95 mm; sale Brussels (Simonson), 13 February 1993, lot 117 (as Jordaens). The figure style can be compared with Steadman, figs. 33 and 47.

34. C. Van de Velde, *Frans Floris (1519/20–1570): leven en werken*, Verhandelingen van de Koninklijke Academie voor Wetenschappen, Letteren en Schone Kunsten van België, Klasse der Schone Kunsten, XXXVII, no. 30, Brussels, 1975, I, pp. 99–119 (atelier), and pp. 84–98, 335–381 (drawings), pp. 69–74 (head studies).

35. In early Netherlandish (or more generally: Northern) painting, cartoons (pricked or incised) were mostly used for repetitions and copies (and sometimes portraits); Van Mander in his *Grondt* refers to the use of cartoons, on the one hand by the earlier Netherlandish painters, on the other by the modern Italians, and he recommends it as an aid (when kept hanging next to one's painting) to work out the distibution of light and shade; but apparently very few artists took over this practice (Van Mander [see note 11], chapt. 12.9–17, I, pp. 254–257). In his life of Pieter Aertsen he mentions that painter's use of detailed full-sized cartoons; this question has been much debated: J.R.J. van Asperen de Boer, M. Faries, J.P. Filedt Kok, 'Painting Technique and Workshop Practice in Northern Netherlandish Art of the Sixteenth Century', in [cat. exh.] *Kunst voor de beeldenstorm* (Amsterdam, Rijksmuseum, 1986), The Hague, 1986, pp. 110–111; J.M.C. Boreel and F.W.H. van Zon-Christoffels, 'Enkele aspecten van de schilderspraktijk in het atelier van Pieter Aertsen natuurwetenschappelijk nader bekeken', *Nederlands kunsthistorisch jaarboek*, XL, 1989 [=1990], pp. 167–196; Y. Bruijnen, 'Fruits and Vegetables: New Information on the Workshop Practice of Pieter Aertsen', *Oud Holland*, CVIII, 1994, pp. 120–126. For cartoons in general see R. Bacou, [cat. exh.] *Cartons d'artistes du XVe au XIXe siècle*, Paris, Musée du Louvre, 1974.

36. A. Balis, '"Fatto da un mio discepolo": Rubens's Studio Practices Reviewed', in T. Nakamura, *Rubens and his Workshop. The Flight of Lot and his Family from Sodom*, Tokyo, 1994, pp. 97–127.

37. See also G. Aust, 'Entwurf und Ausführung bei Rubens', *Wallraf-Richartz-Jahrbuch*, XX, 1958, pp. 163–212; J. Müller Hofstede, 'Aspekte der Entwurfszeichung bei Rubens', in *Stil und Überlieferung in der Kunst des Abendlandes. Akten des 21. Internationalen Kongresses für Kunstgeschichte in Bonn 1964*, Berlin, 1967, III, pp. 114–125; J.S. Held, *Rubens: Selected Drawings*, 2nd ed., Oxford, 1986, pp. 16–41 ('types and techniques of Rubens' drawings'); J.S. Held, *The Oil Sketches of Peter Paul Rubens: a Critical Catalogue*, Princeton, NJ, 1980, 2 vols.

38. H. Vey, *Die Zeichnungen Anton van Dycks*, Brussels, 1962, 2 vols.; C. Brown, [cat. exh.] *The Drawings of Anthony van Dyck*, New York, The Pierpont Morgan Library, 1991.

39. H. Vey, 'Anton van Dycks Ölskizzen', *Bulletin des Musées Royaux des Beaux-Arts (Brussels)*, V, 1956, pp. 167–208; J.S. Held, 'Van Dyck's Oil Sketches', in [cat. exh.] *Anthony van Dyck*, Washington, National Gallery of Art, 1991, pp. 327–366.

40. R.A. d'Hulst, *Jordaens Drawings*, Brussels, 1974, 4 vols. Only a few oil sketches (on canvas) by Jordaens are known.

41. H. Vlieghe, *Gaspar de Crayer. Sa vie et ses œuvres*, Brussels, 1972, 2 vols; H. Vlieghe, 'Drawings by Gaspar de Crayer from the Ghent Album', *Master Drawings*, XXI, 1988, pp. 119–132.

42. G. Wilmers, *Cornelis Schut (1597–1655): Flemish Painter of the High Baroque*, Pictura Nova, I, Turnhout, 1996, esp. pp. 40–41. The drawing here reproduced (Fig. 2) surfaced only recently: *The Voyage of the Cardinal-Infante Ferdinand by Sea to Genoa*, pen and brown ink and brown wash over black chalk, squared in black chalk, 208 x 159 mm.; sale Amsterdam (Christie's), 11 November 1996, lot 37 (as Van Diepenbeeck); now in a private collection in Antwerp. The corresponding painting (Wilmers, cat. A20, repr. p. 355), is in the Oudheidkundig Museum van de Bijloke, Ghent; an engraving after this composition figures in G. Becanus, *Serenissimi Principis Ferdinandi... Introitus in Flandriae Metropolim Gandavum*, Antwerp, 1636, pl. 7 (see C. Van de Velde and H. Vlieghe, *Stadsversieringen te Gent in 1635 voor de Blijde Intrede van de Kardinaal-Infant*, Ghent, 1969, fig. 24). The present drawing deviates in various points from the painting as well as the engraving (most notably in not including the portrait of the Marquis of Leganés next to Ferdinand) and can accordingly be recognised as a preliminary compositional drawing, rather than as the drawing after the painting made in preparation for the engraving (the same applies to another drawing connected with another composition for this project; see Wilmers, cat. A21a, repr. p. 356 and commented on in n. 69 p. 27).

43. Some studies on oil sketches in general (the literature is, of course, enormous) are: L.B. Freeman Bauer, *On the Origin of the Oil Sketch: Form and Function in '500 Preparatory Technique*, Ph.D. Diss, New York, 1975; R.K. Klessmann and W.A.L. Beeren, [cat. exh.] *Malerei aus erster Hand: Ölskizze von Tintoretto bis Goya*, Brunswick, Herzog Anton Ulrich-Museum; Rotterdam, Museum Boijmans van Beuningen, 1984; followed by a symposium, *Beiträge zur Geschichte der Ölskizze, vom 16. bis zum 18. Jahrhunderts*, Brunswick, 1984 (with a.o. contributions on Venius, Rubens and Cornelis de Vos); O. Ferrari, *Bozzetti italiani dal Manierismo al Barocco*, Naples, 1990.

44. See C. Bambach Cappel, (art.) 'Modello: drawn', in *The Dictionary of Art*, ed. J. Turner, London–New York, 1996, XXI, pp. 762–767. Rubens's role as a designer for sculpture is well known (F. Baudouin will treat this aspect of his activity in a part XXII of the *Corpus Rubenianum Ludwig Burchard*). Such designs could be drawings (Held 1986 [see note 37], nos. 50, 125–127, 133) or oil sketches (Held 1980 [as in note 37], nos. 419, 420). See: R. Oldenbourg, 'Die Plastik im Umkreis von Rubens', in his *Peter Paul Rubens*, ed. by W. von Bode, Munich–Basle, 1922, pp. 194–211; F. Baudouin, 'Rubens en de Antwerpse jezuïetenkerk', in his *Pietro Paolo Rubens*, Antwerp, 1977, pp. 143–155 (and see also pp. 168–171); J.S. Held, 'Rubens' Designs for Sepulchral Monuments', in his *Rubens and his Circle*, ed. by A.W. Lowenthal et al., Princeton, NJ, 1982, pp. 80–93. For the recent identification of a stucco relief in the church of Our Lady at Neuburg for which Rubens's drawing has been preserved, see E. McGrath, [Review of K. Renger, *Peter Paul Rubens, Altäre für Bayern*, 1990], *The Burlington Magazine*, October 1991, p. 717, figs. 60 and 61.

45. There are interesting comments on preparatory stages (drawings as well as three-dimensional models) in the realisation of sculpture throughout the ages in R. Wittkower, *Sculpture: Processes and Principles*, Harmondsworth, 1991 (1st edn 1977): *passim*; I. Lavin, 'Bozzetti and Modelli. Notes on Sculptural Procedures from the Early Renaissance through Bernini', in *Stil und Überlieferung in der Kunst des Abendlandes. Akten des 21. Internationalen Kongresses für Kunstgeschichte in Bonn 1964*, Berlin, 1967, III, pp. 114–125; J. Montagu, *Roman*

Baroque Sculpture: The Industry of Art, New Haven–London, 1989 (esp. pp. 99–125: 'The sculptor as Designer'); C. Avery, (art.) 'Modello: sculpted', in *The Dictionary of Art*, ed. J. Turner, London–New York, 1996, XXI, pp. 767–771. See also note 20 above for the early northern tradition. For Baroque sculpture in general: P. Volk, *Entwurf und Ausführung in der europäischen Barockplastik*, Munich, 1986; K. Kalinowski ed., *Studien zur Werkstattpraxis der Barockskulptur im 17. und 18. Jahrhundert*, Poznan, 1992.

46. Recently the King Baudouin Foundation has acquired a very important collection (Van Herck) of Flemish sculptors' *bozzetti* as well as drawings; see F. Baudouin, 'Van concept tot beeldhouwwerk: ontwerptekeningen', in [cat. exh.] *Tekeningen uit de 17e en 18e eeuw*, Antwerp, Koninklijk Museum voor Schone Kunsten, 2000 pp. 23-46; idem, 'Van concept tot beeldhouwwerk: terracotta's, in [cat. exh.] *Terracotta's*, Antwerp, Museum Plantin-Moretus, 2000.

47. Copenhagen, Printroom; inscription on the verso: 'Volgens dit concept ben accordert met Sr. Artus Quilinus ende soude moeten hebben twe hondert ende viertich gulden brabants gelt. Ita testor A. Wuestenraedt pastuer jn Beringhen'. - 'Ende ick belouf volgens het selven modelle het selven vromelyck uyt te vueren. By my Artus Quellin. Actum Antwerpen den tweden Junius 1665' (S. Zajadacz-Hastenrath, *Das Beichtgestühl der Antwerpener St Pauluskirche und der Barockbeichtstuhl in den Südlichen Niederlanden*, Brussels, 1970, pp. 218–219, no. 164, fig. 274). In the estate, dated 15 april 1671, of the artist's widow a debt of 60 florins of 'the pastoor van Beiringen' is noted as still outstanding (E. Duverger, *Antwerpse kunstinventarissen uit de zeventiende eeuw*, IX, Brussels, 1997, p. 297).

48. Van Mander (see note 11), I, pp. 126–157; II, pp. 459–492.

49. M. Jaffé, *Van Dyck's Antwerp Sketchbook*, London, 1966, 2 vols.; J. Müller Hofstede, in [cat. exh.] *Peter Paul Rubens. Katalog I: Rubens in Italien...*, Cologne, Kunsthalle, 1977, pp. 55 ff. and under cat. 25A; J. Bolten, *Dutch and Flemish Drawing Books 1600–1750: Method and Practice*, Landau, 1985, pp. 107–116; H. Braham, [cat. exh.] *Rubens: Paintings. Drawings. Prints, in the Princes Gate Collection*, London, Courtauld Institute Galleries, 1989, pp. 50–53, cat. 58–59; the present author is preparing a critical edition of this material (to appear in the *Corpus Rubenianum Ludwig Burchard*).

50. Many of these Flemish history painters are treated in M.L. Hairs, *Dans le sillage de Rubens: les peintres d'histoire anversois au XVIIe siècle*, Liège, 1977. For a helpful survey and bibliography see now H. Vlieghe, *Flemish Art and Architecture 1585–1700*, New Haven–London, 1998.

51. Van Mander advises the young painter to copy as many motifs as possible from the masters, to steal like a thief (but he implies that this is no more than part of the training process): 'Steelt armen, beenen, lijven, handen, voeten. T'is hier niet verboden; die willen moeten wel spelen Rapiamus personnage. Wel ghecoockte rapen [turnips: a wordplay on the Latin "rapere"] is goe pottage' (Van Mander [see note 11], chapt. 1.46, I, p. 87; Miedema's instructive commentary in II, pp. 388–389, referring also to another piece of advice, given by Philips Angel in his *Lof der schilder-const* of 1642, namely to insert deliberate quotes from the works of great artists in order to bring them honour). Plagiarism that went too far was frowned upon, as Van Diepenbeeck experienced: E. Duverger, 'Abraham van Diepenbeeck en Gonzales Coques aan het werk voor de stadhouder Frederik Hendrik, prins van Oranje', *Jaarboek Koninklijk Museum voor Schone Kunsten Antwerpen*, 1972, pp. 181–237; J. Wood, 'Padre Resta's Flemish Drawings. Van Diepenbeeck, Van Thulden, Rubens and the School of Fontainebleau', *Master Drawings*, LXXVIII, 1990, p. 22 (but see also Jeremy Wood's contribution to the present publication).

52. G. Denhaene, *Lambert Lombard. Renaissance et humanisme à Liège*, Antwerp, 1990, pp. 141–165, 281–311.

53. See note 16 above.

54. M.-C. Maselis, A. Balis and R.H. Marijnissen, *The Albums of Anselmus de Boodt (1550–1632). Natural History Painting at the Court of Rudolph II in Prague*, Rotthalmünster: Heribert Tenscher, 1999; L. Hendrix, 'Natural History Illustration at the Court of Rudolf II', in E. Fucikova et al., ed., *Rudolf II and Prague*, Prague–London–Milan, 1997, pp. 157–171; M. Pinault, *Le peintre et l'histoire naturelle*, Paris, 1990.

55. 'Item aen Heyndrick de Rasiers... alle mijne beschilderde papieren met Italiaensche Vruchten' (E. Duverger, *Antwerpse kunstinventarissen uit de zeventiende eeuw*, VII, Brussels, 1993, p. 188; 21 December 1655).

56. This melon appears in the following paintings by Snyders (the reference is to H. Robels, *Frans Snyders, Stilleben- und Tiermaler 1579–1657*, Munich, 1989): *Fruit Market*, St Petersburg, Hermitage (Robels, cat. 26); *Still Life with Game and two Dogs*, V.D. Spark, New York, 1957–1963 (Robels, cat. 71); *Game, Fruit and Vegetables*, dated 1613, Laren, Singer Museum, Van Dongen Collectie (Fig. 4; Robels, cat. 113); *Garland of Fruit and Vegetables*, Philadelphia, Museum (Robels, cat. 170); *Garland of Fruit and Vegetables*, Althorp House (Robels, cat. 171); *Garland of Fruit and Vegetables*, Antwerp, Rubenshuis (Robels, cat. 173I); *Fruit Garland*, Brussels, City Museum (Fig. 5; Robels, cat. 175); (with Rubens) *Pythagoras advocating Vegetarianism*, London, H.M. the Queen (Robels, cat. 277).

57. Cranach's woodcut of a *Stag Hunt* (with a largely different composition) dates from *c.* 1506 (F.X.H. Hollstein [et al.], *German Engravings, Etchings and Woodcuts 1400–1700*, VI, Amsterdam, 1959, p. 92, no. 115. The *Stag Hunt* tapestry is one of a series of four, one of which contains the (Brussels weaver's) signature of Jan van Antwerpen; see [cat. exh.] *Chefs-d'œuvre de la tapisserie du XIVe au XVIe siècle*, Paris, Grand Palais, 1973–1974, no. 66, p. 158, repr. (as in a private collection). Not only the stag but the hounds too are carefully copied (and duly appear in reverse).

58. For Leonardo's prototype see Zoan Andrea's engraving (*The Illustrated Bartsch*, XXV, New York, 1980, p. 163) and a drawing (considered a copy after Leonardo) discussed by W. Suida, *Leonardo und sein Kreis*, Munich, 1929, p. 105, fig. 117. The tapestry is part of a Genesis series designed by Michiel Coxcie and preserved in Cracow (J. Szablowski et al., *Les tapisseries flamandes du Wawel*, Antwerp, 1972, ill. p. 147); see for this connection already my 'Facetten van de Vlaamse dierenschilderkunst van de 15de tot de 17de eeuw', in [cat. exh.] *Het Aards Paradijs. Dierenvoorstellingen in de Nederlanden van de 16de en de 17de eeuw*, Antwerp, Zoo, 1982, p. 41.

59. Formerly in the George L. Hersey collection. Published by A.M. Logan as a North Italian drawing (which it might of course be, if Coxcie acquired it in Italy), reworked by Rubens ('Some Early Drawings by Rubens', *Gentse bijdragen tot de kunstgeschiedenis*, XXIV, 1976–1978 (*Internationaal Rubenscolloquium Anwerpen, 1977*), p. 110, fig. 3; and see my 'Facetten', as in the previous note, p. 52 n. 21); it has since appeared on the art marked as a drawing entirely by Rubens's hand (*Old Master Drawings*, P. & D. Colnaghi, London, 25 June–13 July 1985, no. 26: catalogue entry by Michael Jaffé).

60. A. Balis, *Rubens: Hunting Scenes*, Corpus Rubenianum Ludwig Burchard, XVIII, 2, London, 1986, pp. 70–87 ('Rubens as an Animal Painter'). For his drawings of lions see R.A. d'Hulst and M. Vandenven, *Rubens: The Old Testament*, Corpus Rubenianum Ludwig Burchard, III, London, 1989, under no. 57, figs. 139, 142–151; six of his lion motifs were etched by Wenzel Hollar in 1646 (Ibidem, fig. 138), and altogether ten were brought together by an anonymous draughtsman (Van Thulden?) on one sheet, in the manner of a model-

book (Ibidem, p. 188, copy 20; E. Mitsch, *Die Rubenszeichnungen der Albertina*, Vienna, 1977, pp. 216–217, no. 112, repr.).

61. K. Ertz, *Jan Brueghel der Ältere (1568–1625). Die Gemälde mit kritischem Œuvrekatalog*, Cologne, 1979, cat. 273 (*The Animals entering the Ark*; now in the Getty Museum); cat. 308 (*Adam and Eve in the Earthly Paradise*, figures by Rubens).

62. Van de Velde 1975 (see note 34), pp. 335–361, cat. T.1–25 (the *Basle sketchbook*). See also, for a sketchbook, possibly from the Southern Netherlands, but derived in part from Heemskerck's Italian sketchbook: M.M.L Netto-Bol, *The so-called Maarten de Vos Sketchbook of Drawings after the Antique*, Kunsthistorische studiën van het Nederlands Instituut in Rome, IV, The Hague, 1976; for Heemskerck's celebrated sketchbooks, see C. Hülsen and H. Egger, *Die römische Skizzenbücher von Marten van Heemskerck...*, 2 vols., Berlin, 1913–1916.

63. M. van der Meulen, *Rubens: Copies after the Antique*, Corpus Rubenianum Ludwig Burchard, XXIII, London, 1994–1995, 3 vols.; for Van Lint's drawings after the Antique: [cat. exh.] *Flemish Drawings of the 17th Century [Frits Lugt collection]*, London, Victoria and Albert Museum; Paris, Institut Néerlandais; Berne, Kunstmuseum; Brussels, Bibliothèque royale Albert Ier, 1972, nos. 48–49. Apart from these, relatively few Flemish artists of the seventeenth century seem to have made detailed drawings of antique sculpture; for the Dutch one should of course refer to that superlative draughtsman, Hendrick Goltzius: E.K.J. Reznicek, *Die Zeichnungen von Hendrick Goltzius*, Utrecht, 1961, II, pls. 142–186.

64. These subjects will be treated by K. Belkin and J. Wood in forthcoming volumes of the *Corpus Rubenianum Ludwig Burchard* (part XXV: *Copies and Adaptations from Renaissance and Later Artists*); both authors have already published widely in this field. See also M. Jaffé, *Rubens and Italy*, Oxford, 1977; J.M. Muller, 'Rubens's Theory and Practice of the Imitation of Art', *The Art Bulletin*, LXIV, 1982, pp. 229–247.

65. A few model studies by Lambert van Noort are extant: Müller Hofstede 1967 (see note 37), pl. 19.1–2; Z. van Ruyven-Zeman, *Lambert van Noort Inventor*, Brussels, 1995, cat. T34.a–b.

66. Under the title *Studi di figura nelle botteghe italiane e neerlandesi* a symposium devoted to the study from the model has been held in the Istituto Olandese di Storia dell'Arte in Florence on 7–8 June 1996 (with a contribution by the present author on Rubens's studies); the papers have, however, not been published.

67. J. Bolten, *Dutch and Flemish Drawing Books 1600–1750: Method and Practice*, Landau, 1985, *passim*.

68. For a few suggestions about Van Heemskerck's anatomical knowledge, see I.M. Veldman, *Maarten van Heemskerck and Dutch Humanism in the Sixteenth Century*, Amsterdam, 1977, pp. 111–121: 'St Luke's Medical Books'.

69. For Rubens's anatomies: J.M. Muller, 'Rubens' Anatomy Book', in [cat. exh.] *Rubens Cantoor: Een verzameling tekeningen ontstaan in Rubens' atelier* (Antwerp, Rubenshuis, 1993), Ghent–Antwerp, 1993, pp. 78–107; U. Heinen, *Rubens zwischen Predigt und Kunst. Der Hochaltar für die Walburgerkirche in Antwerpen*, Weimar, 1996, pp. 136–142, figs. 17–21 (Ulrich Heinen has pointed out to me that relevant Rubens material is also comprised in the following, which I have not had a chance to see: L. Price Amerson Jr, *The Problem of the écorché: A Catalogue Raisonné of Models and Statuettes from the Sixteenth Century and Later Periods*, Ph.D. Diss, Pennsylvania State University, 1975).

70. The drawing from the model (Vienna, Albertina) is H. Vlieghe, *Saints*, Corpus Rubenianum Ludwig Burchard, VIII, II, Brussels, 1973, no. 104d, fig. 13; this drawing was made in preparation of the altarpiece *The Miracles of St Francis Xavier* (now Vienna); the same drawing was later reused for one of the (female) companions of Cloelia in *The Flight of Cloelia* (formerly Berlin, Kaiser-Friedrich-Museum; see E. McGrath, *Rubens: Subjects from History*, Corpus Rubenianum Ludwig Burchard, XIII, London, 1997, I, cat. 47; II, fig. 170). The literalness of the reuse is striking.

71. Vlieghe 1973 (see note 70), II, no. 115b, fig. 43; see also further comments in Van der Meulen 1994–1995 (see note 63), I, p. 78; III, Fig. 225.

72. For Floris's study heads see note 34 above. A selection of Rubens's head studies have been discussed in Held 1980 (see note 37), I, pp. 597–614, nos. 432–450 (with reference to the earlier literature, among which important contributions by J. Müller Hofstede and M. Jaffé). See now also M. Eidelberg, 'An Album of Drawings from Rubens' Studio', *Master Drawings*, XXXV, 1997, pp. 234–266.

73. For this painting of *St Ambrose and Theodosius* and the related head studies see McGrath 1997 (see note 70), under no. 55; her no. 12, *Diogenes seeking a True Man*, offers a similar case where a host of available head studies seem to have suggested the major lines of the composition, rather than the other way around.

74. Various authors have commented on this head study, only gradually realising that an intricate issue of creation versus borrowing was at stake; at first this 'head' was recognised as occuring in the œuvre of David Ryckaert III and accordingly attibuted to that master (R.A. d'Hulst, 'Over een schilderij en een schets van David III Ryckaert', *Gentse bijdragen tot de kunstgeschiedenis en oudheidkunde*, XIX, 1961–1966, pp. 95–101); but it was soon noticed that the head had previously been used by Willeboirts Bosschaert, who remains the most plausible author of the original head study (see Z.Z. Filipczak, in *Gentse bijdragen tot de kunstgeschiedenis en oudheidkunde*, XXII, 1969–1972, pp. 199-210). The reuse of this attractive head by Jan van den Hoecke had in the meantime also been noted (R.A. d'Hulst, 'Nog over een olieverfstudie van een knaap in de Kunsthalle te Hamburg', *Gentse bijdragen tot de kunstgeschiedenis en oudheidkunde*, XXII, 1969–1972, pp. 211–218). It is attributed to Ryckaert, however, in B. Van Haute, *David III Ryckaert, a Seventeenth-Century Flemish Painter of Peasant Scenes*, Pictura Nova, VI, Turnhout, 1999, p. 131, cat. A117, fig. 117. In a way the question still stands: what was the real original (and by whom), and how did it become, as it were, public property. Stylistically it is now clear that neither Van den Hoecke nor David Ryckaert was the originator of this so popular, cloying Head. The implied emphatic emotion and the evident charm which this study exudes point indeed to Willeboirts rather than to any other artist. The only remaining question is now: which of two extant versions of the study head of the same curly-haired boy is by him (Willeboirts)? Judging from the material to hand (photos or published reproductions), I think that the real original is not the picture till now reproduced in the literature as the original (Kunsthalle, Hamburg), but rather a painting (Fig. 14) that was with Leonard Koetser (London) in 1963 (Autumn exhibitions, no. 29, as Van Dyck).

75. In Rubens's will it was, e.g., stipulated that '... the drawings which he had collected and made he ordered to be held and preserved for the benefit of any of his sons who would want to follow him in the art of painting...' (Held 1986 [see note 37], p. 16; see P. Génard, 'Het laatste testament van P.P. Rubens', *Rubens-Bulletijn / Bulletin-Rubens*, IV, 1895, p. 139.

76. See, e.g., the Metsu family estate, preserved in Amsterdam (Rijksprentencabinet).

77. J. Garff and E. de la Fuente Pedersen, *Rubens Cantoor. The Drawing of Willem Panneels, a Critical Catalogue*, Copenhagen, 1988, 2 vols.; [cat. exh.] Antwerp 1993 (see note 69).

78. J.P. De Bruyn, *Erasmus II Quellinus (1607–1678): de schilderijen met catalogue raisonné*, Freren, 1988, pp. 298–328, doc. 17 (previously published by Denucé).

79. For sixteenth-century sketchbooks see already note 62 above. For some sketchbooks from the seventeenth century: K.L. Belkin, *The Costume Book*, Corpus Rubenianum Ludwig Burchard, XXIV, Brussels, 1980; Jaffé 1966 (see note 49): authorship still debated; G. Adriani, *Anton Van Dyck, Italienisches Skizzenbuch*, Vienna, 1960; H. Vlieghe, 'De leerpraktijk van een jonge schilder: het notitieboekje van Pieter van Lint in het Institut Néerlandais te Parijs', *Jaarboek Koninklijk Museum voor Schone Kunsten Antwerpen*, 1979, pp. 249–279; for Rubens's lost theoretical notebook, see note 49; for his anatomy book see note 69.

80. It may be wondered, e.g., whether some of the detailed drawings by Frans Snyders, which happen to show a very close approximation to the paintings, even in secondary detail, might not be such 'ricordi', rather than 'modelli'; for some 'ricordi' drawings by de Crayer see Vlieghe 1988 (see note 41).

81. See Bruijnen 1994 (see note 35).

82. See, e.g., K.L. Belkin, 'The Classification of Rubens's Drawings Collection', *Wallraf-Richartz-Jahrbuch*, LV, 1994, pp. 105–114.

Rubens as Thief: His Use of Past Art and Some Adaptations from Primaticcio

Jeremy Wood

The notes that Sir Joshua Reynolds made during his visit to Antwerp in 1781 not only reveal an attentive study of Rubens's works, but also an interest in Rubens's use of past art, and his comments provide an excuse for the title of this essay: 'Rubens as thief'. Reynolds believed he could identify a source that Rubens had adapted in one of his major altarpieces, the *Descent from the Cross* in Antwerp Cathedral (Fig. 1), and this led him to remark that 'what was stollen by Rubens, the possessor knew not how to value; and certainly no person knew so well as Rubens how to use'.[1] Nevertheless, an early manuscript draft of this text, now in the Institut Néerlandais, Paris,[2] contains a number of revisions which reveal Reynolds's perplexity that such a great artist could adapt the ideas of others with so little shame. Another version of the same passage goes so far as to defend Rubens from being 'barren of invention', arguing that 'to adopt and improve a happy composition invented by an artist who probably could only invent... can be no disgrace to Rubens'.[3]

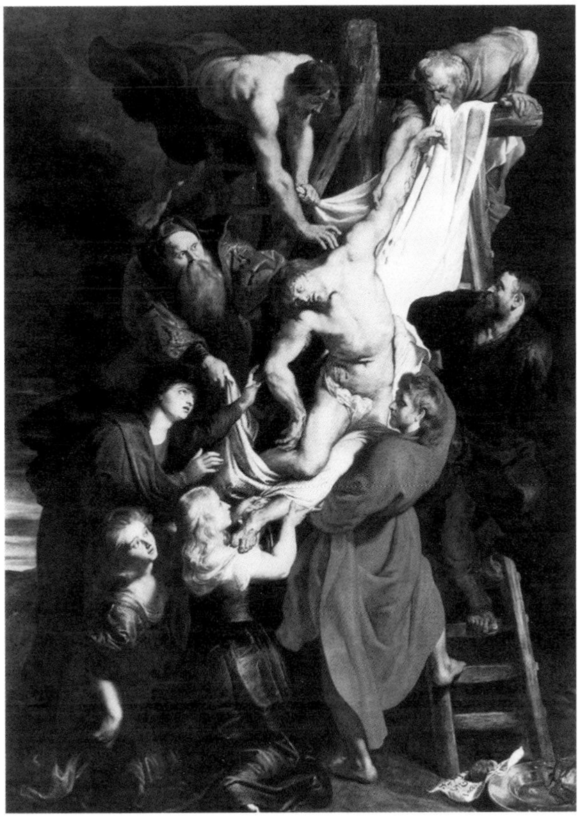

Fig. 1. Peter Paul Rubens, *The Descent from the Cross*. Antwerp, Cathedral

In fact, Jean François Marie Michel had already identified a model for the *Descent from the Cross* in an engraving by Hieronymus Wierix after Bernardo Passeri (Fig. 2) from a collection of devotional images, the *Evangelicae historiae imagines* of Hieronymus Natalis, published in 1593.[4] Michel made this identification in his life of Rubens published in 1771,[5] and since Reynolds is known to have consulted this book during his travels in Flanders it was probably his source. What Michel has to say is of interest because Rubens's borrowings were seldom identified in the early literature, although his work was sometimes compared to that of his sixteenth-century predecessors, and, more rarely, his contemporaries (such as Caravaggio). Michel's observation – itself an early example of the modern taste for identifying sources – is convincing at least as regards those men who lower Christ's body from the cross (as Michel himself noted).[6] It was – until recently – overlooked by modern historians,[7] who turned more predictably to the work of Daniele da Volterra,[8] Francesco Salviati, Federico Barocci and Lodovico Cigoli for Italian models that Rubens might have used.[9] It has also been claimed that the body of Christ was adapted from the *Laocoon*.[10] But Michel and Reynolds, who were writing only a little more than a century after Rubens's death, may have had a better understanding of the artist's use of past art. As will be implied later in this essay (in relation to Rubens's adaptations from the work of Primaticcio), modern art historical prejudices are not always helpful when trying to understand Rubens's debt to the past.

From the late eighteenth century onwards Rubens's work has come to be discussed as a

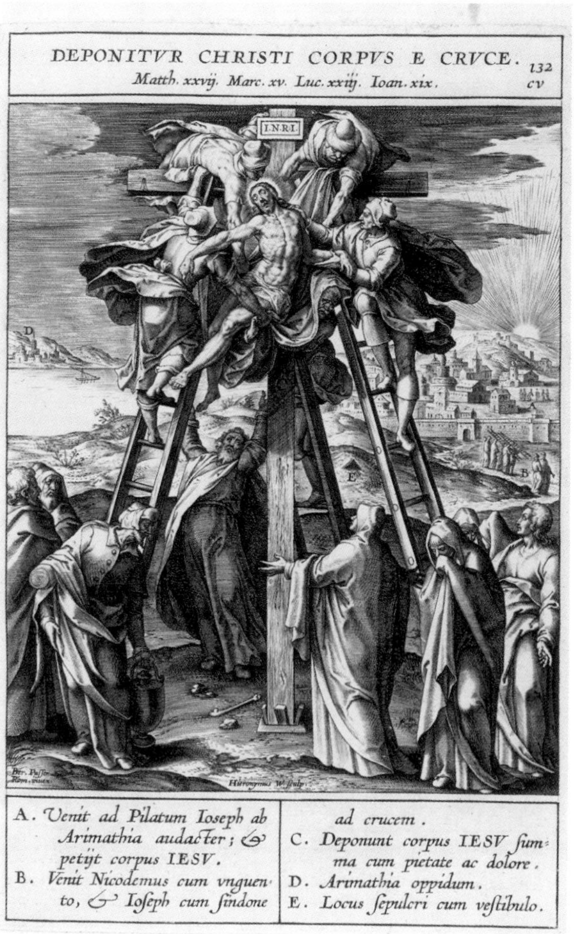

Fig. 2. Hieronymus Wierix (after Bernardo Passeri), *The Descent from the Cross*, engraving

synthesis of Venetian colour and Roman design,[11] based on a study of the work of Titian, Michelangelo and Raphael as seen through the eyes of a non-Italian. However, in the seventeenth century much less emphasis was placed on Roman sources. Roger de Piles, in his account of the paintings by Rubens in the collection of the Duc de Richelieu (published in 1681) compared his work to that of Raphael, Titian, Correggio, Veronese and the Carracci,[12] although this was less an analysis of how Rubens had formed his style and more a definition of his position in the pantheon of late-renaissance art. Unlike modern historians, many of Rubens's early critics and biographers actually placed him in the Venetian School. According to Bellori (writing in 1672), Rubens was essentially a colourist who, while in Venice, based his work on that of Titian, Veronese, and Tintoretto, and followed them in the treatment of light and shade (a statement which was stolen by Félibien who inserted it into his Seventh *Entretien* of 1679).[13] This idea runs throughout the writings of de Piles,[14] who, on one occasion, wrote that Rubens absorbed everything he could from this triumvirate of Venetian artists 'to enhance his style'.[15] Elsewhere de Piles characterised Tintoretto's work as having *force* and Veronese's as having *magnificence*, which helps flesh out what he meant when he called Rubens's work Venetian.[16] Few other Italian artists are ever mentioned by Rubens's biographers, although on several occasions de Piles noted his debt to Giulio Romano,[17] and also claimed that he began by following Caravaggio's manner but found it too laborious.[18]

For these critics Rubens was not only an honourary Venetian, his work was explicitly said not to resemble the antique or Raphael. Bellori admitted that Rubens admired the art of antiquity, but wrote that though he imitated models such as the *Apollo Belvedere*, *Medici Venus*, and the *Gladiators*, they remained unrecognisable because his style was so dissimilar (another idea that Félibien translated and slipped into his *Entretien*).[19] It is therefore paradoxical that Rubens should have made numerous drawings after antique sculptures but few after Venetian paintings.[20] This is no less true of the numerous drawn copies that Rubens bought and retouched, which provide relatively few examples from Venetian art,[21] although this certainly does not apply to Rubens's well-known painted copies many of which reproduce works by Titian.[22] A large proportion of the sheets that Rubens retouched are copies after finished compositions (rather than preparatory studies) by Central Italian artists such as Raphael, Giulio Romano, and Polidoro. This bias cannot be explained solely because the Venetians did not like making drawings, since Rubens could have obtained drawn copies after Venetian paintings had he so desired. It may well be that he valued Venetian art for qualities of handling and colour that could only be conveyed in painted copies and not in drawn ones.

According to Félibien, Rubens transported Lombard (by which he meant both Emilian and Venetian) colour into Flanders.[23] This was the background to Reynolds's more emphatic claim in his *Discourses* that 'the Flemish School, of which Rubens is the head, was formed upon that of the Venetian'. For Reynolds, 'the

Venetian style cannot improve the great style', and Rubens 'was more gross than they [the Venetians], and carried all their mistaken methods to a far greater excess'.[24]

It is not the purpose of this essay to argue whether or not Rubens should be classed as a Venetian painter, but rather to reconsider one aspect of his use of past art, his debt to the work of Francesco Primaticcio, which does not fit easily into either the older or more modern views of his artistic concerns. Because Primaticcio was born in Bologna he is classed as belonging to the Emilian School, but his style was formed at Mantua, and Vasari implies that Giulio Romano, a pupil of Raphael, was his first master. The most productive part of Primaticcio's career was spent at Fontainebleau and it was in France that he had his greatest influence. As a result Primaticcio's work has been divided uncomfortably between the competing national claims of Italian and French art, and may therefore seem difficult to categorise.

The most familiar example of Rubens's interest in Primaticcio's work is a sheet in the Museum Boijmans van Beuningen, Rotterdam, which contains some adaptations by Rubens of stucco caryatids by Primaticcio which were made on the verso of a sixteenth-century Fontainebleau School drawing that he must have owned.[25] Rubens also painted a substantial copy in oil on panel, now in the Neuerburg Collection, Cologne, after Primaticcio's *Apollo in his Chariot surrounded by the Hours*,[26] which is closely based on one of the ceilings from the Galerie d'Ulysse,[27] but, unlike all of Rubens's other painted copies, it resembles an oil sketch in technique.[28] Both these copies present problems as to when and where they were made. It has been assumed that Rubens visited Fontainebleau in 1600 (which seems far from certain).[29] More plausibly he went there during his trips to Paris in 1622, 1623 and 1625.[30] The Rotterdam drawing, which is on one side of an earlier sheet, need not have been made *in situ* if Rubens was reworking – and virtually obliterating – a pre-existing chalk drawing,[31] while the *Apollo and his Chariot* is so large that it seems unlikely to have been made in front of the original (although this is not impossible) and it has been claimed that Rubens used a drawing by Primaticcio as model.[32] Rubens's retouched copies after Italian art have been dated to the eight years when he stayed in Italy,[33] and described as part of his apprenticeship in Italian art, but in my opinion Rubens kept them throughout his life, and their reworking was carried out over a long period and as a result of mature reflection. It follows that the drawing in Rotterdam and the painted copy of *Apollo in his Chariot* do not have to be attached to any particular date or period, either during his years in Italy or his visits to Fontainebleau itself, although this is not to undermine the importance for Rubens of seeing the frescoes themselves.

Much the same arguments apply to several free adaptations in coloured wash which Rubens made from compositions by Primaticcio;[34] these are divided between several collections, and one which is in the Rijksprentenkabinet, Amsterdam, will be discussed in some detail below. All of these drawings contain adaptations from Primaticcio's work in France (largely – but not exclusively taken from the Galerie d'Ulysse at Fontainebleau), but in some cases with changed subject matter so that any connection between the group as a whole and Homer's narrative is lost. This group of works can be securely dated to the 1630s towards the end of Rubens's career. There is evidence that Rubens not only possessed some of Primaticcio's own *modelli* (or early copies of them),[35] which he could have obtained at almost any time, but that he had access to an extensive series of more recent copies after Primaticcio's frescoes, made by two of his pupils and followers in the 1630s. Since the coloured adaptations are demonstrably based on those copies they must be later than 1625, the date assigned to them until recently.[36]

While it is widely recognised that Rubens used the art of the past in a voracious way, and that he often placed visual sources in new contexts of his own devising, less attention has been given to these aspects of his working practice for those artists who imitated his example or had access to his workshop. Primaticcio's frescoes at Fontainebleau appear to have been of great interest to some of the artists in Rubens's circle. (The subject matter of the Galerie d'Ulysse itself may have attracted attention, and, in the mid-1630s, Jacob Jordaens was working on a cycle of tapestries depicting the story of Ulysses).[37] There is evidence to suggest that Rubens encouraged this interest in Primaticcio's designs, and, as will be suggested

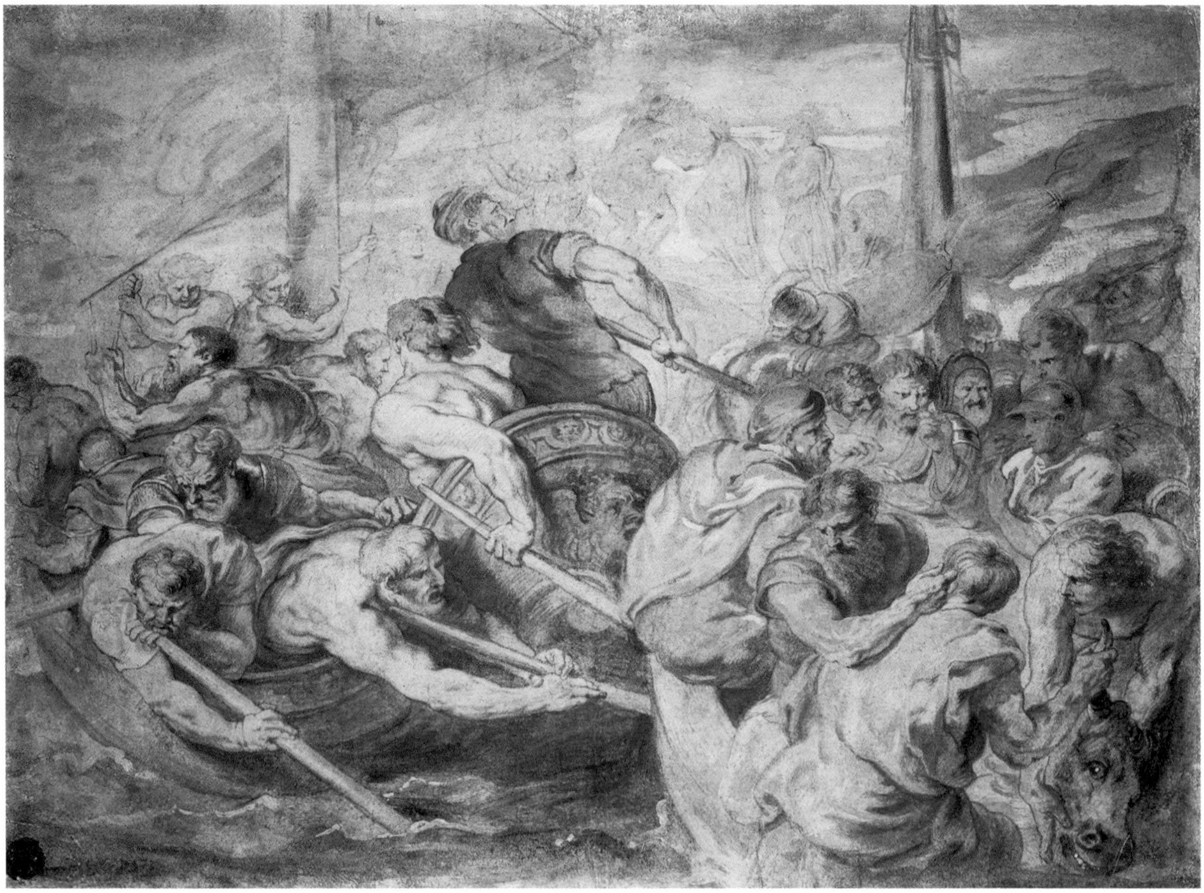

Fig. 3. Peter Paul Rubens (after Francesco Primaticcio), *Ulysses and his Companions on Circe's Island*. Amsterdam, Rijksprentenkabinet

below, at least one of his imitators learned from him how to steal from past art.

Art historians may feel uncomfortable when a particular visual debt does not fit into preconceptions of Rubens's development or style. Indeed, his interest in Primaticcio's work as late as the 1620s and 1630s has been found 'surprising'.[38] Although Primaticcio's contribution at Fontainebleau had been given less attention than Rosso's during the sixteenth century (at least as registered by printmakers),[39] this was reversed in the seventeenth century when the Galerie d'Ulysse, in particular, became a source that was widely imitated. Poussin, for example, commented warmly on the Galerie as an admirable model for artists,[40] and a *Bacchus and Ariadne* by the Le Nain brothers at the Musée des Beaux-Arts, Orléans, reuses a group taken from one of the frescoes in the Galerie d'Ulysse which was also adapted by Rubens and some of his followers on several occasions (as will be shown later in this discussion).[41] All of this suggests that Rubens's interest was typical of his age.

Two works traditionally attributed to Rubens share the same motif borrowed from Primaticcio. The better-known, which will be considered first, is an elaborate drawing in bodycolour and wash, now in the Rijksprentenkabinet, Amsterdam (Fig. 3),[42] which has been little discussed since the exhibition of drawings by Rubens in Antwerp in 1956.[43] It belongs to a series of works, mentioned briefly above, which are all of similar technique and size. The attribution to Rubens of this group of coloured drawings has been widely – but not unanimously – accepted.[44] In my opinion the technique employed is compatible with the extensive use of wash found throughout the drawings that Rubens retouched, but this particular drawing (like all the others in the group) is entirely by one hand.[45]

The Rijksprentenkabinet drawing adapts details from three separate compositions from

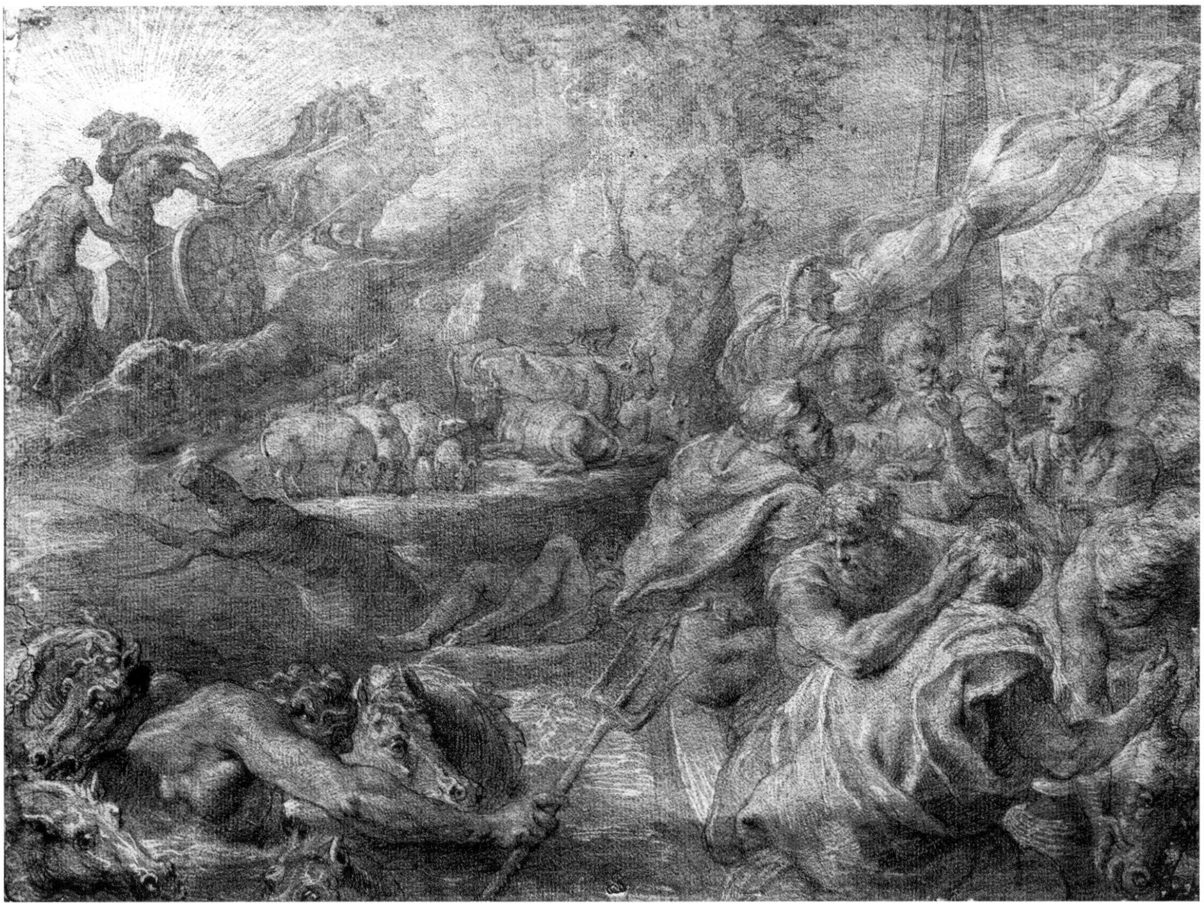

Fig. 4. Francesco Primaticcio (retouched by Rubens), *The Companions of Ulysses stealing the Cattle of the Sun*. Vienna, Albertina

the Galerie d'Ulysse.[46] These lost frescoes are recorded in Primaticcio's own *modelli*, a series of etchings by Theodoor van Thulden dated 1633,[47] and a large group of detailed chalk copies now mostly in the Albertina, Vienna. These have also sometimes been attributed to Van Thulden and wrongly said to have been made by him in preparation for his etchings. I have argued elsewhere that they are by Abraham van Diepenbeeck, who is also known to have visited Paris in the 1630s,[48] and they will be discussed as his work here.[49] There is not only a difference between the visual style of the drawn copies in the Albertina and Van Thulden's etchings, but there are significant variations of detail between them, so that the drawings are unlikely to have been used as models for the etchings, and it follows that there is no logical reason why the copies in the Albertina need to have been made by Van Thulden.[50] More importantly in this context, there is sufficient evidence to establish that the entire group of drawn and etched copies by Flemish artists after frescoes from the School of Fontainebleau were brought from Paris to Antwerp in the mid-1630s and were known to Rubens.[51]

The way in which the Rijksprentenkabinet drawing creates a new composition out of three separate fragments by Primaticcio is an extreme and blatant example of artistic theft. This raises several questions: how far is the drawing a copy after Primaticcio or a new work by Rubens, and, in particular, what was its original function? In addition, it is puzzling that not all the works in this group of colour adaptations from Primaticcio's work seem to be by Rubens himself.[52] It might follow that some are copies after lost works by Rubens (which would explain the variation in quality), or, alternatively, it may be that a nucleus of copies by Rubens himself was later enlarged by one of his imitators. The original reason why these drawings were made is problematic, to say the

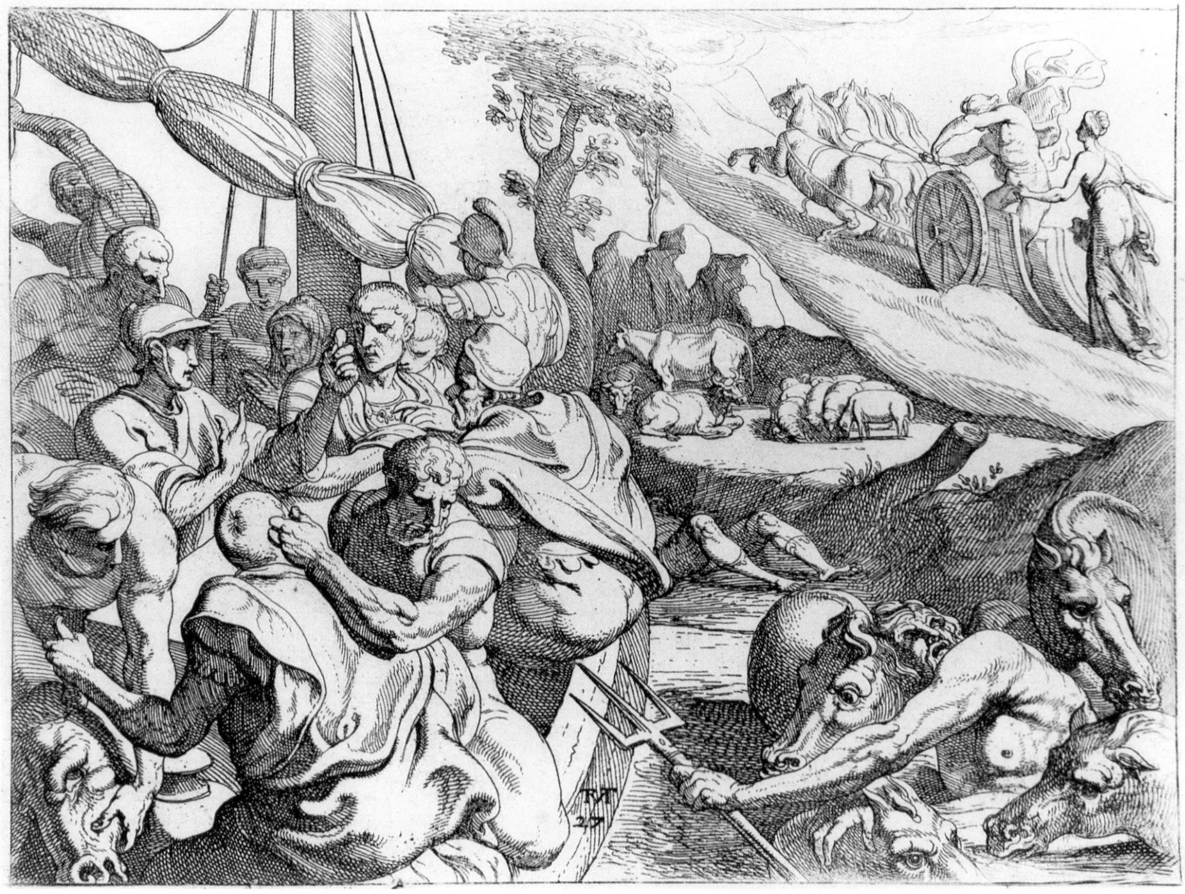

Fig. 5. Theodoor van Thulden (after Francesco Primaticcio), *The Companions of Ulysses stealing the Cattle of the Sun*, etching

least, and it has been suggested that they were designs for a set of tapestries ordered by the Count of Monterrey but shipwrecked en route to Spain.[53] However, it would seem most unlikely that Rubens would make such blatant use of another artist's work in a large and costly commission of this kind, and some of the new subjects introduced would make a set of tapestries incoherent. These problems are resolved if the series was made by Rubens for instruction, using adaptations from past art as examples for his pupils, and demonstrating how to create new compositions out of old ones. This would also explain why some of the weaker drawings were added in emulation of Rubens's example.

The boat on the right in Rubens's drawing (Fig. 3) adapts a detail from one of the Galerie d'Ulysse frescoes, *The Companions of Ulysses stealing the Cattle of the Sun*.[54] Although Rubens certainly saw the fresco itself during one of his visits to Paris, it was also known to him from a *modello* in red chalk heightened with white by Primaticcio, now in the Albertina, Vienna (Fig. 4), that Rubens himself owned and retouched.[55] In the *modello* (and the lost fresco) Ulysses lies asleep on the island of Thrinacie while his companions are depicted with one of the cows that they have sacrilegiously stolen from the Sun. (Although it seems, in the fresco, that the helmeted man in the boat is Eurylochus, who incites the starving men to kill and eat Apollo's cattle, in Rubens's adaptation this may no longer be the case once the group is removed from its context). Rubens omits all those details found in Primaticcio's *Companions of Ulysses* which explain its narrative: Neptune in the left foreground who has raised a storm which forced Ulysses on to the island; Ulysses himself asleep on the shore (only his legs are visible); the Cattle of the Sun seen grazing further inland; and, at the upper left in the heavens, Lampetie calling on her father the Sun God to punish the slaughter of his herds.

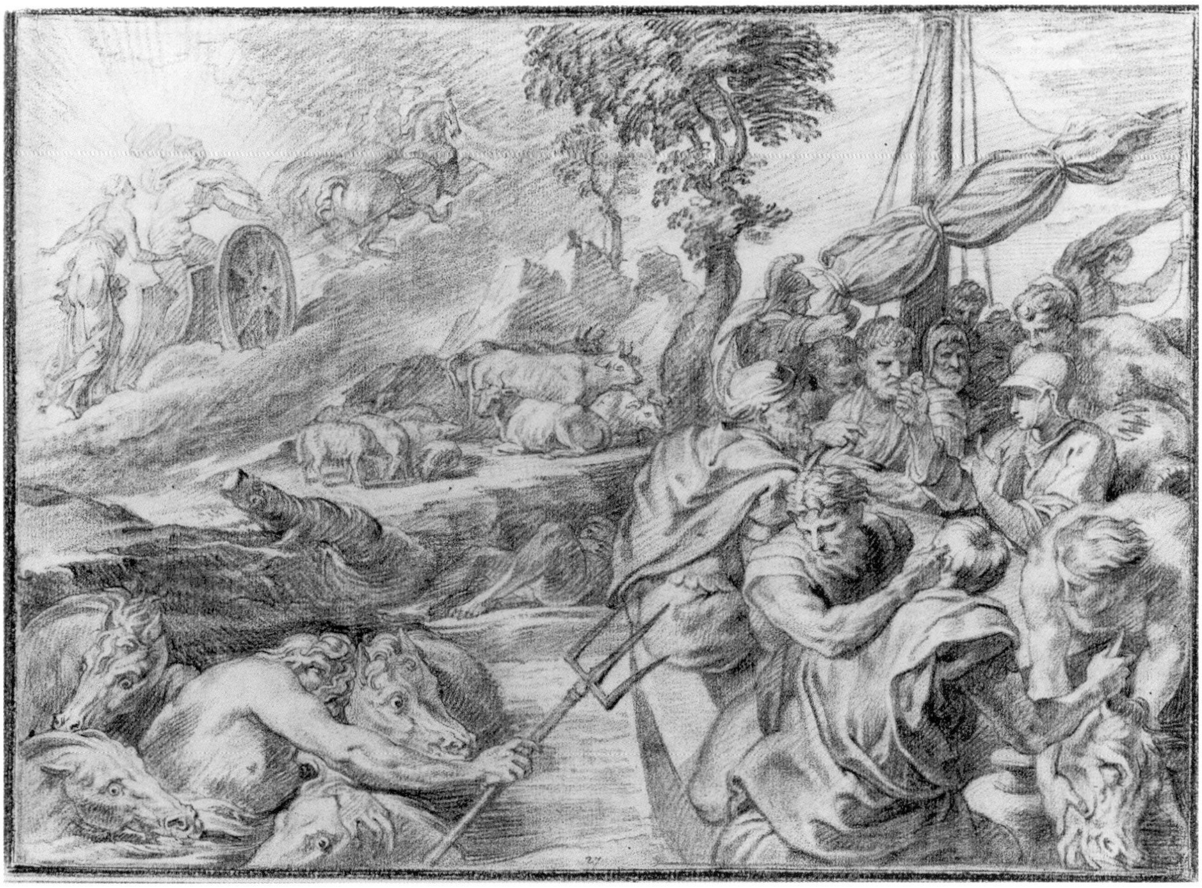

Fig. 6. Abraham van Diepenbeeck (after Francesco Primaticcio), *The Companions of Ulysses stealing the Cattle of the Sun*. Vienna, Albertina

The Primaticcio *modello* that Rubens owned (Fig. 4) cannot have been his only source for this borrowing, since the head of a man next to the mast looks upwards in the *modello* but downwards in the Rijksprentenkabinet drawing (Fig. 3),[56] as in other early copies. More conclusively, the pot being emptied by a man at the far right in Rubens's version is hard to read in the *modello* but looks like a face, and is very clumsily drawn in Van Thulden's etching (Fig. 5). Rubens clearly derived the upended pot from the precise chalk copy in the Albertina by Van Diepenbeeck (Fig. 6).[57] There are good reasons, therefore, to believe that although Rubens had knowledge of several copies after these frescoes, he used the most accurate available, even if it was recent in date and lacked the authority of Primaticcio's own working drawing.

In the background of the Rijksprentenkabinet drawing (Fig. 3) an embracing man and woman are visible. This is a less conspicuous borrowing from another of Primaticcio's frescoes in the Galerie d'Ulysse, *The Burning of Elphenor's Body and Ulysses's return to Circe*, an episode which takes place after Ulysses's visit to the Underworld,[58] and which is most clearly recorded in a copy in the Albertina by Van Diepenbeeck (Fig. 7).[59] Here Ulysses, having burned the body of his former companion Elphenor, is met by the enchantress who leads a train of servants bringing food and wine (Book XII, 7–20). The borrowed scene is a subsidiary detail taken from the left-hand background of Primaticcio's composition and Rubens omits the much more prominent funeral pyre, shown in the foreground surrounded by Ulysses's companions. Although in terms of Primaticcio's design this seems a very specific meeting between Ulysses and Circe, this particular episode may not be what is inferred in the Rijksprentenkabinet drawing.

The last of these borrowings is the most important one for this discussion. The entire

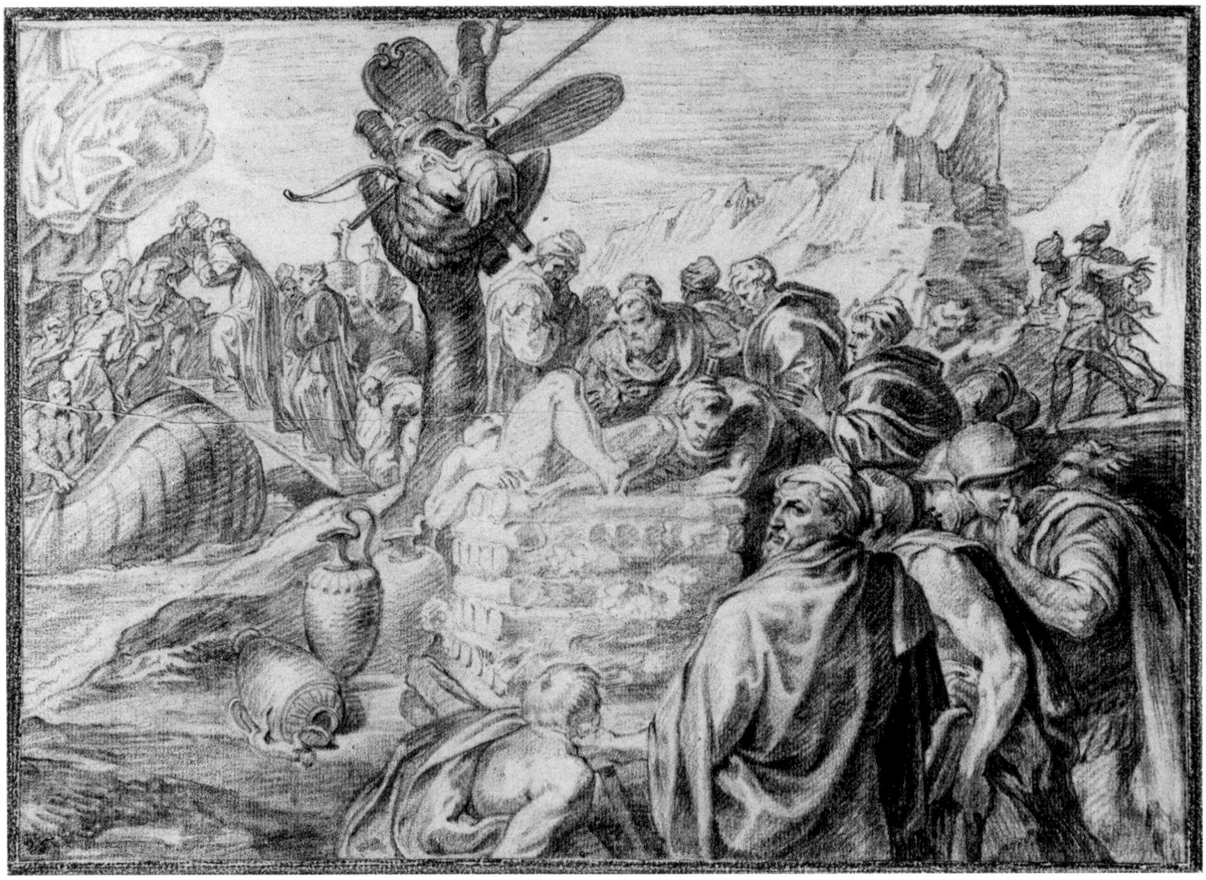

Fig. 7. Abraham van Diepenbeeck (after Francesco Primaticcio), *The Burning of Elphenor's Body and Ulysses's Return to Circe*. Vienna, Albertina

boat with oarsmen placed on the left in the Rijksprentenkabinet drawing (Fig. 3) is taken from yet another of Primaticcio's compositions for the Galerie d'Ulysse, *Ulysses and his Companions arriving on the Shores of the Underworld*. In this episode Ulysses and his men have reached the River of Ocean (Book XI, 18–22) intending to summon the Theban seer, Tiresias, from the dead.[60] A reliable and detailed copy of the original is provided by Van Diepenbeeck's drawing in the Albertina (Fig. 8),[61] and a more summary one is found in Van Thulden's etching (Fig. 9). Although the figures in the boat are generalised in appearance, the bearded man with outstretched arms was almost certainly intended by Primaticcio to represent Ulysses, who is identified by the armour that he wears throughout the cycle, and who looks towards the figure of Ocean (Rubens modifies both his arms in the Rijksprentenkabinet drawing so that he becomes more actively occupied). The part of Primaticcio's composition that Rubens omits shows Ulysses's companions disembarking,[62] and Rubens also leaves out the figure of Ocean (at lower left), from whose penis the sea flows.[63]

As has already been shown, there is some evidence which copy or copies after Primaticcio were used by Rubens. For example, the youth clutching the mast of the boat in the Rijksprentenkabinet drawing (Fig. 3) is shown very differently in Van Thulden's etching of *Ulysses and his Companions* (Fig. 9), but Rubens's adaptation depicts him with his head tilted and his right hand clenched exactly as in Van Diepenbeeck's copy in the Albertina (Fig. 8) where he is grasping a rope. The other surviving copies of Primaticcio's composition suggest that in the original this hand was more elegant and ineffectual. In addition, all of Rubens's borrowings are in the same direction as Van Diepenbeeck's chalk copies, and, if he had used Van Thulden's etchings (which anyhow have significant differences of detail), he would have had to reverse them deliberately. All of this further strengthens the assumption

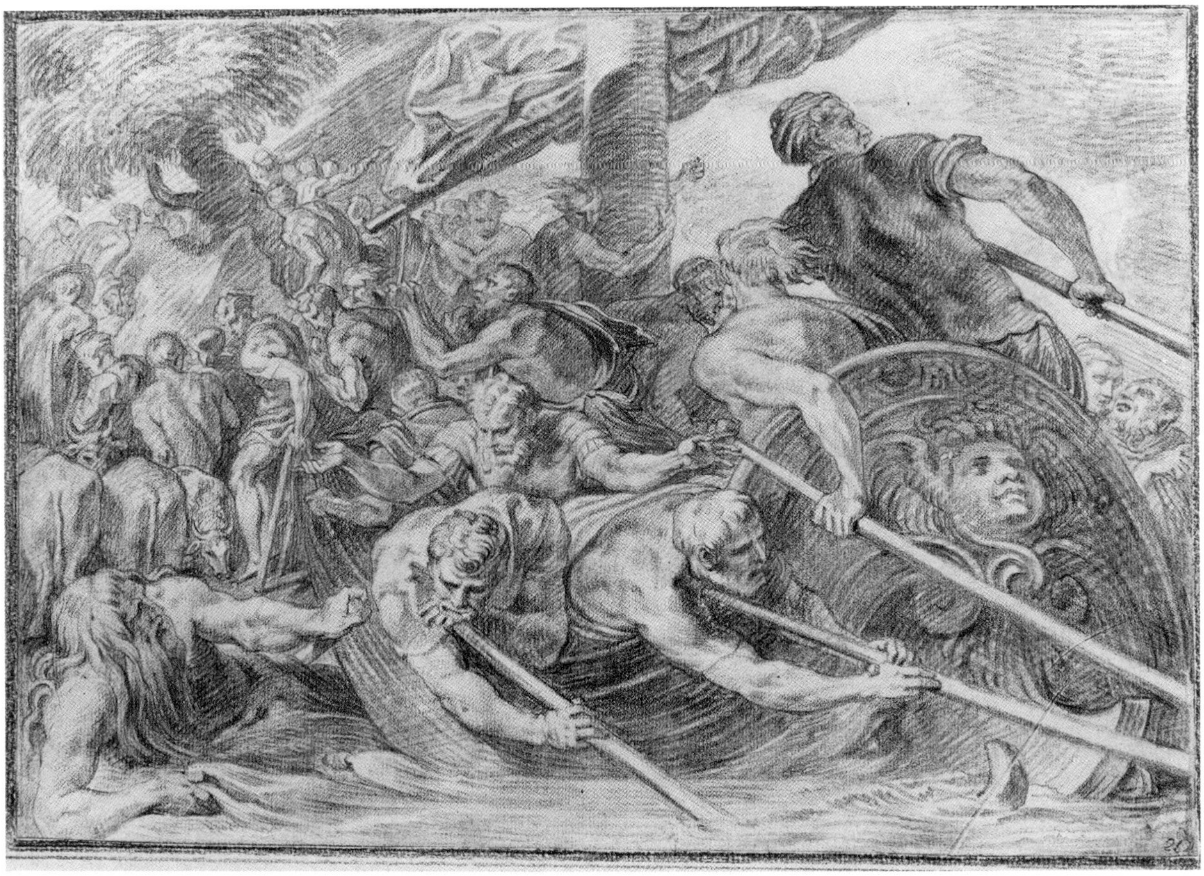

Fig. 8. Abraham van Diepenbeeck (after Francesco Primaticcio), *Ulysses and his Companions arriving on the Shores of the Underworld*. Vienna, Albertina

that the Rijksprentenkabinet sheet was made from the drawn copies brought back to Antwerp by Van Diepenbeeck in the mid-1630s.

It has to be admitted, though, that this particular group of figures in a boat had already been adapted by Rubens a decade earlier. This visual debt is evident in an oil sketch of around 1625–1626 in the collection of Richard E. Feigen, New York. Made for the Eucharist cycle but then discarded, it is currently called an *Allegory* or *Triumph of Hope* (Fig. 10),[64] and contains both a generically Primaticcian boat and the youth clutching the mast taken from *Ulysses and his Companions arriving on the Shores of the Underworld*, although here transformed by Rubens into a winged angel. From this it seems that the stimulus of visiting Fontainebleau at various times between 1622 and 1625 while working on the Medici Cycle had an immediate impact on his work. Rubens became particularly interested in the oddly unseaworthy boats depicted throughout the Galerie d'Ulysse (as will also emerge when looking at one of the canvases from the Medici Cycle later in this discussion); this led to some confusion in his mind as to whether the oarsmen should face towards the bow or the stern of a ship.[65] Rubens's interest in Primaticcio's frescoes was clearly intensified by his visits to Paris in the mid-1620s; this had an immediate impact on his work and can be traced later in his career.

Rubens's assemblage in the Rijksprentenkabinet drawing (Fig. 3) of these details from various frescoes in the Galerie d'Ulysse poses a problem as to what subject he created out of them. Is it an entirely new one, or do vestiges of the original narrative remain in the new composition? Indeed, is one episode depicted or – as in some of Primaticcio's own compositions in the cycle – are several different episodes taking place simultaneously? It seems unlikely that Rubens would have adopted such a mid-sixteenth century approach to narrative as that, indeed, his revision of Primaticcio's work may have been done to 'correct' the syn-

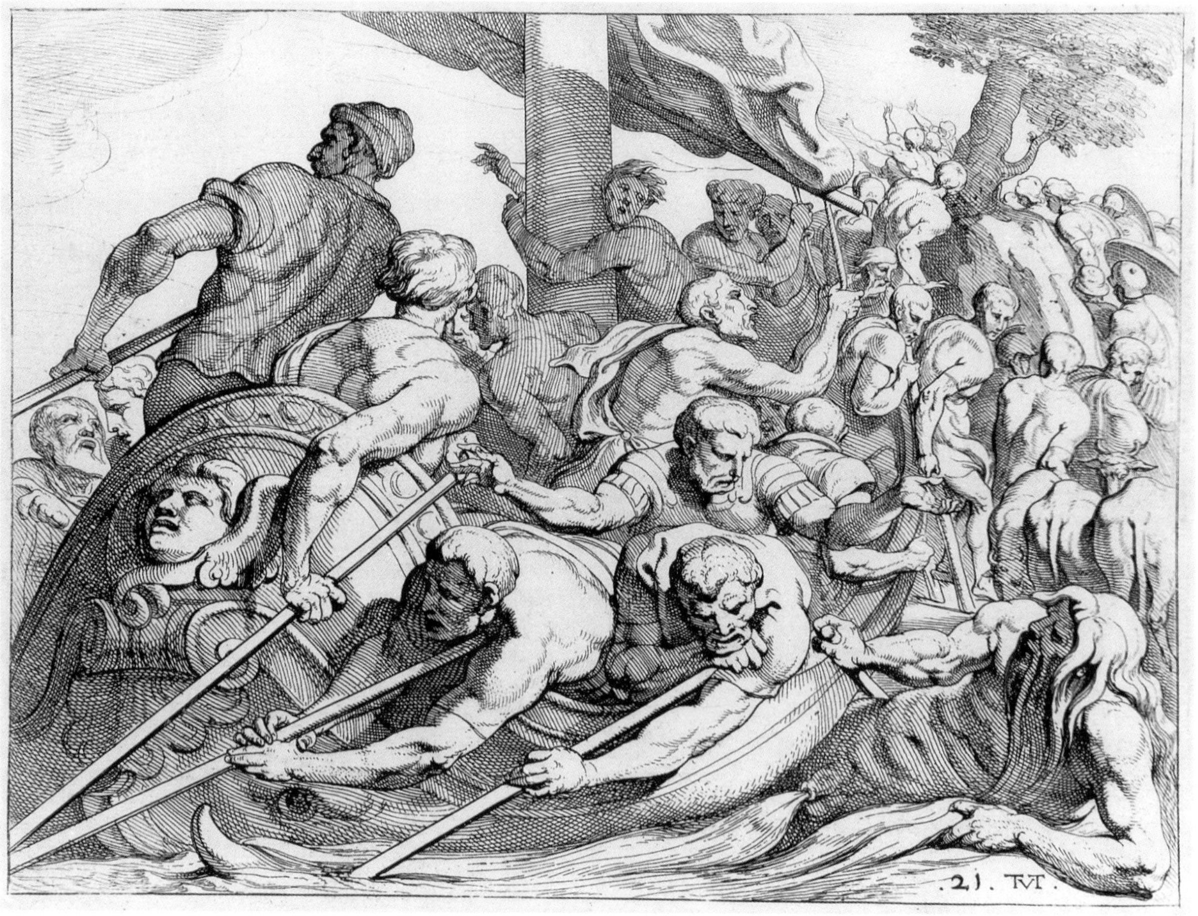

Fig. 9. Theodoor van Thulden (after Francesco Primaticcio), *Ulysses and his Companions arriving on the Shores of the Underworld*, etching

chronistic story-telling. But, if Rubens's drawing represents one unified incident it can no longer show Ulysses being welcomed back from the underworld by Circe because this would conflict with the apparent departure of his men in the right foreground. This departure is confirmed by the way Rubens omitted the small figure (completely out of scale from those in the foreground), who climbs down a ladder at the side of the boat and makes it clear, in the fresco, that Ulysses's men are landing (figs. 8, 9).[66] It would be tempting to assume that Rubens simply turned the scene from a reunion into a farewell, when, at dawn, Ulysses left Circe who summoned up a favourable wind to assist his departure from the island. However, before arriving on Circe's island, Ulysses's fleet had been pelted with rocks by the Laestrygonians and only one boat survived. The presence of two boats in the Rijksprentenkabinet drawing means that the subject cannot be either Ulysses's reunion with Circe nor his departure from her island. It seems unthinkable that Rubens would have worked without a subject in mind but here the exact episode remains a mystery.

The second of the two works, already mentioned, that reuses the boat from Primaticcio's *Ulysses and his Companions arriving on the Shores of the Underworld,* is a little-known composition of *Arion saved by the Dolphins*, a story taken from Herodotus (I, 23–24), Lucian (*Dialogi Marini*, VIII), and Ovid's *Fasti* (II, 83–118). It is known through six different versions, none of which is easily accessible and the group as a whole has never been studied in a systematic way. One of these versions, whereabouts currently unknown (Fig. 11), has been attributed to Rubens and dated around 1625 to 1628,[67] although to my mind the composition was probably designed at least ten years later (possibly more) and not by Rubens himself. Another version, formerly in the collection of Adolphe Schloss, Paris, has recently been attrib-

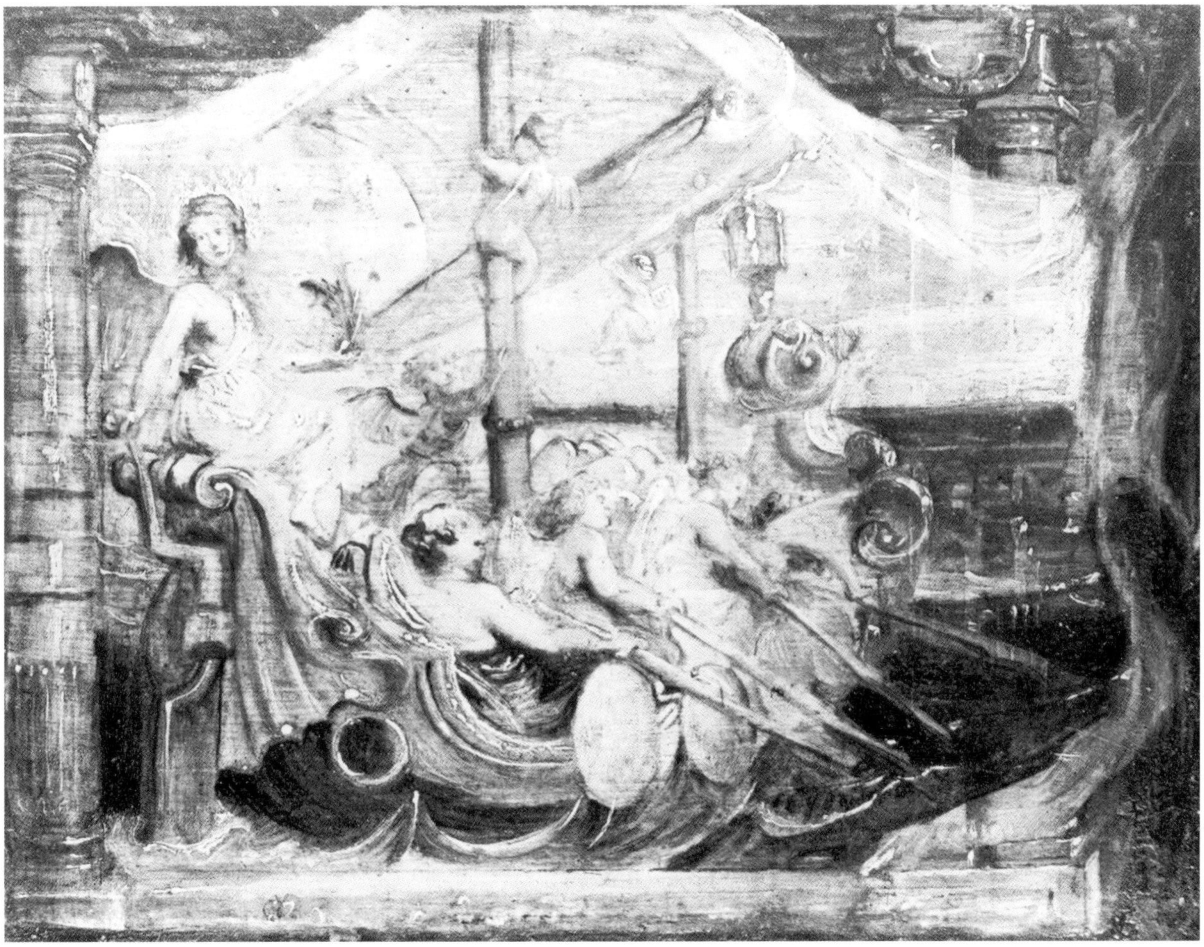

Fig. 10. Peter Paul Rubens, *Allegory of Hope*. New York, Richard L. Feigen

uted to Abraham van Diepenbeeck,[68] apparently only on the basis of an old photograph,[69] but though this attribution has not been argued with any cogency it is worth taking seriously. Yet another version, the only one in the group on canvas, was recorded in Berlin in 1925 as signed with the monogram 'TvT',[70] and is presumably by Theodoor van Thulden. The fact that the composition was repeated several times,[71] could point to a lost prototype by Rubens himself, although there are iconographic and stylistic reasons why this is unlikely.

The composition of *Arion saved by Dolphins* departs from previous treatments of the subject, such as Jan Muller's engraving after Cornelis van Haarlem,[72] by showing the sailors witnessing Arion's escape. Arion was a poet, famous for his skill on the lyre, who was threatened with robbery and murder by the crew of a boat on which he was sailing to Corinth. To pacify the sailors, Arion put on his best singing robes and, having sung his last song, threw himself overboard only to be carried to the shore by a dolphin who had been delighted by the sound of his music. It is hard to think that Rubens would have shown the sailors witnessing Arion's escape because it is crucial to the story that they believed Arion to have drowned, since this is what they claimed when they were caught and punished for their duplicity.[73]

The *Arion saved by Dolphins* contains a quotation – which has not been identified before – of a very similar high-prowed boat to the one found in the fresco at Fontainebleau of *Ulysses and his Companions arriving on the Shores of the Underworld* (figs. 8–9), already discussed. Several of the oarsmen are derived from this source and, consequently, are close to the adaptation of them found in the Rijksprentenkabinet drawing (Fig. 3). How far can this borrowing be linked to the drawn and etched copies after Primaticcio's work that were made by Van

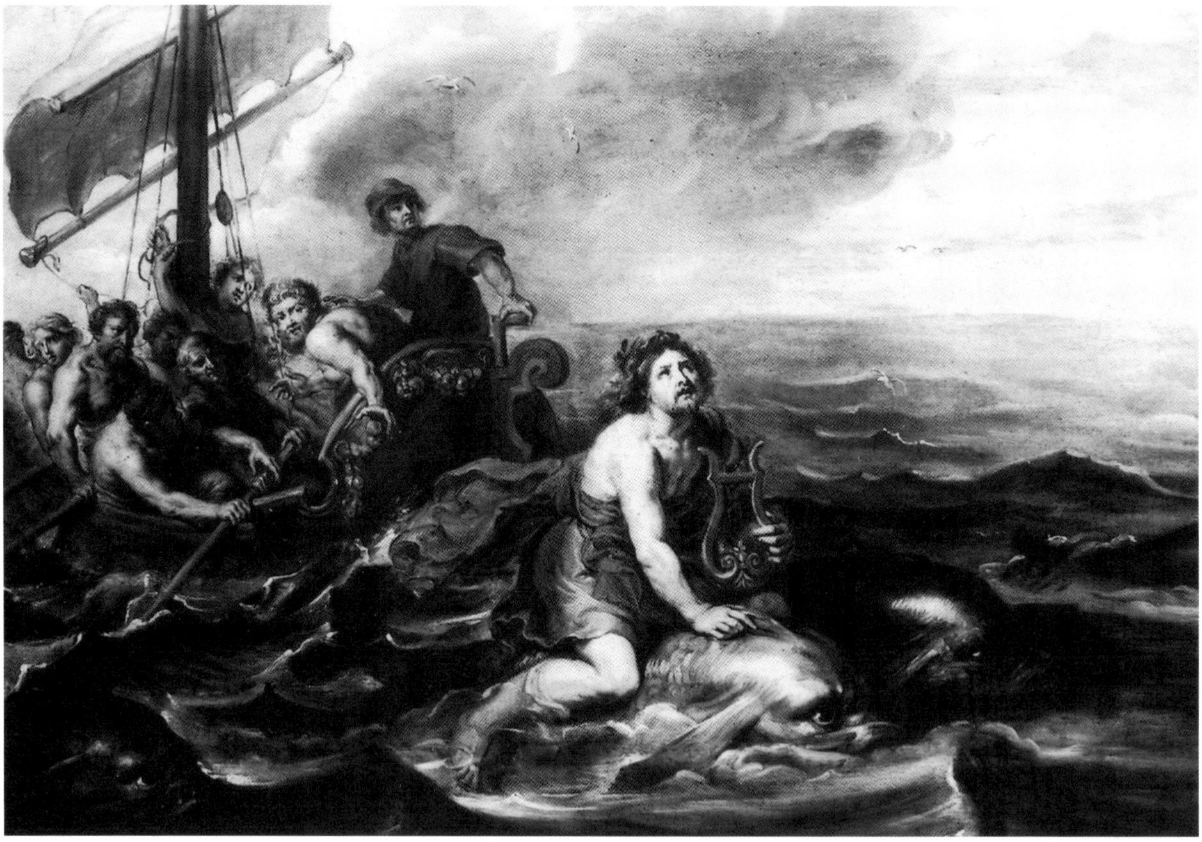

Fig. 11. Anonymous Flemish Seventeenth-Century Artist, *Arion saved by Dolphins*. Formerly Allan MacKay, Petersfield. Present location unknown

Thulden and Van Diepenbeeck? Does the presence of this adaptation from Primaticcio make the attribution of the *Arion saved by Dolphins* to Rubens more or less likely? If the *Arion* was not designed by Rubens, is it possible to identify the artist responsible?

Primaticcio's conception of a small, high-prowed vessel in which the figures are densely packed has been retained in the *Arion saved by Dolphins* (figs. 11–12), but a rudder is added to the boat. The man who stands at the prow in Primaticcio's composition (figs. 8–9) with his back turned to the spectator is turned around and is given the rudder to hold rather than an oar.[74] The oarsman seated next to the steersman is made to look over his shoulder towards the escaping poet, and he is not given anything to hold in his hands. But, even though most of the figures in the *Arion* no longer resemble the model very closely, there is one particularly precise echo of Primaticcio's design: the young man who clings to the mast and pulls on a rope. Oddly this figure recalls the corresponding detail in Van Thulden's etching (Fig. 9), which reverses the direction of the original fresco and the other copies and adaptations. While this suggests that the etching may have been known to the artist who designed the *Arion* (and it is worth recalling that one of the versions is signed with Van Thulden's monogram), the fact that the remainder of the adaptation is in the same direction as Primaticcio's original, the Albertina copy (Fig. 8), and the Rijksprentenkabinet drawing (Fig. 3), suggests that some or all of these were also used as models. Interestingly, the youth clutching the mast and holding onto a rope reappears in one of Van Diepenbeeck's illustrations to Michel de Marolles's *Tableaux du Temple des Muses* of 1655,[75] which depicts *Jason* disembarking from a typically Primaticcian boat (Fig. 13). In short, it seems that while the *Arion* is closely connected to the Flemish copies and adaptations made from the frescoes in the Galerie d'Ulysse, there is nothing very specific to connect the *Arion* with the Rijksprentenkabinet drawing, and there are closer points of contact with copies by both Van Thulden and Van Diepenbeeck.

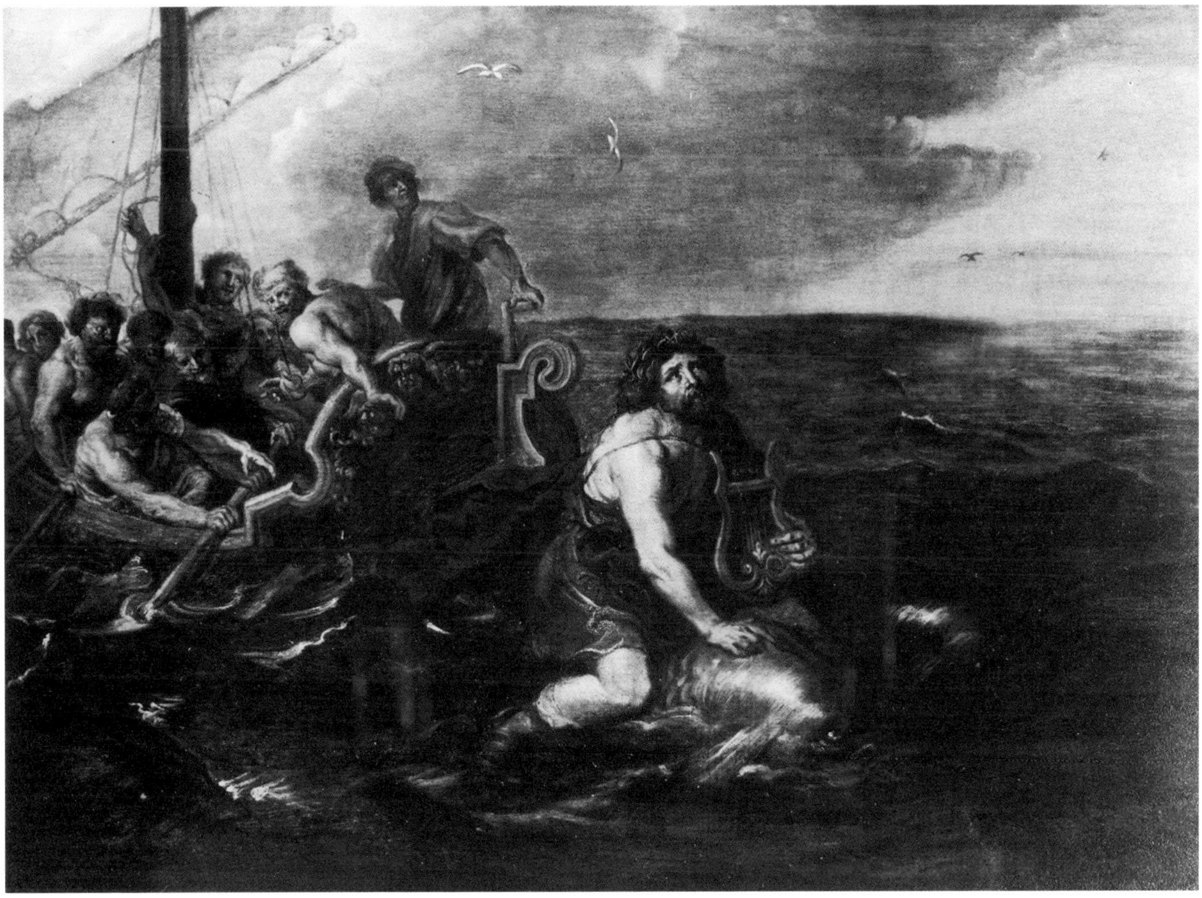

Fig. 12. Anonymous Flemish Seventeenth-Century Artist, *Arion saved by Dolphins*. Present location unknown (formerly Antoon van Welie, The Hague)

What other reasons can be used to argue for an attribution to Van Diepenbeeck? As already noted, one of the paintings of *Arion saved by Dolphins* has recently been attributed to him. The main reason given was that 'the figure of Arion is very close to the same figure in Van Diepenbeeck's drawing of *Arion and the Dolphin*, engraved for [the] *Tableaux du Temple des Muses*'.[76] (The dating of this project may seem relevant but it is complex: even though the book was not published until 1655, it is clear that Van Diepenbeeck's illustrations were commissioned much earlier by Jacques Favereau, and within a few years of the latter's death in 1638).[77] However, there is little connection between the painting of *Arion* and Van Diepenbeeck's illustration of the same subject in the *Temple des Muses* (Fig. 14). The engraving shows Arion inappropriately naked when he should be dressed in his singing robes, as he is, correctly, in the painting.[78] But though there is a fundamental difference between these two depictions of the same subject, it has been shown above that there is a plausible link between the youth hugging the mast of the boat in the various painted compositions and the similar figure in another of Van Diepenbeeck's engravings from the *Temple des Muses*: *Jason* (Fig. 13). In both the painting and the engraving the treatment of the head is very alike, seen frontally and with compactly shaped hair, at variance with the various copies of Primaticcio's original design where the youth's hair streams in the wind. These examples point in different directions: in one case suggesting that Van Diepenbeeck had no connection with the design of the *Arion*, but in the other suggesting that there might be a link between it and the engraving of *Jason*. There is also evidence that one of the versions of the *Arion* was signed by Van Thulden, and it seems unlikely – although not entirely impossible – that Van Diepenbeeck would paint a copy of a picture that was signed (and may therefore also have been designed) by this artist.

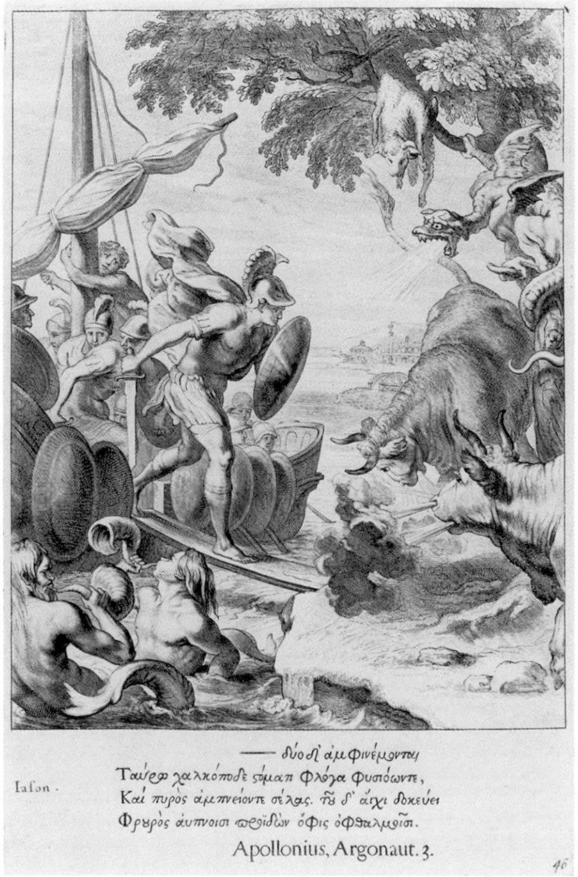

Fig. 13. Abraham van Diepenbeeck, *Jason* from Michel de Marolles: *Tableaux du Temple des Muses* (Paris, 1655), engraving. London, The British Library

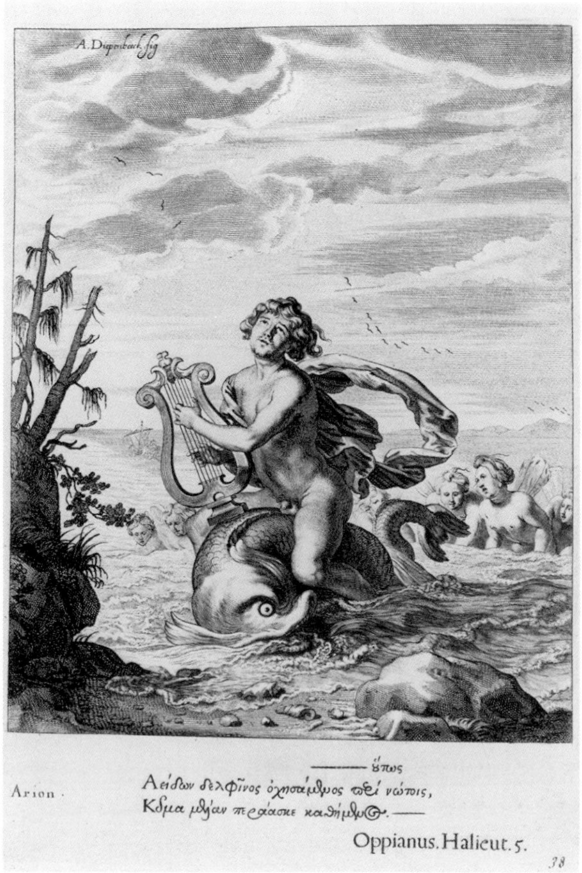

Fig. 14. Abraham van Diepenbeeck, *Arion* from Michel de Marolles: *Tableaux du Temple des Muses* (Paris, 1655), engraving. London, The British Library

It must be admitted, however, that it was Van Diepenbeeck, not Van Thulden, who was well-known to his contemporaries as a skilful plagiarist,[79] and who specialised in imitating Primaticcio's designs for the Galerie d'Ulysse, as can be seen from the illustrations that he provided for several books: not only the *Temple des Muses* of 1655, but also the editions of the *Iliad* and *Odyssey* published by John Ogilby in 1660 and 1665 respectively.[80] Some years ago it was pointed out how the sirens in the foreground of a fresco from the Galerie d'Ulysse were used by Van Diepenbeeck in one of the engravings for the *Temple des Muses*, and that the boat on the left of the same composition from the Galerie was used, in reverse, in one of his later illustrations to the *Odyssey*.[81] This fresco by Primaticcio was cannibalized in a direct and blatant manner, very similar to the clumsy use of ideas from another of the Galerie d'Ulysse frescoes in the *Arion saved by Dolphins* (figs. 11–12), but these examples are unlike the more complex and considered adaptations from similar sources in Rubens's drawing in the Rijksprentenkabinet (Fig. 3). Although the reasons for associating the *Arion* with Van Diepenbeeck and Van Thulden have been argued above, it is difficult to attribute any of the surviving versions to either artist with confidence, not least because the scattered or unknown location of these pictures makes close stylistic analysis impossible.

The key to understanding how a detail from one of Primaticcio's lost frescoes at Fontainebleau became transformed by a follower of Rubens into *Arion saved by Dolphins*, is to be found in another and perhaps unexpected source, Rubens's *Majority of Louis XIII* (Fig. 15) from the Medici cycle. This contains an obviously Primaticcian boat with a high prow and its sides hung with shields.[82] The women propelling the boat provide obvious echoes of Primaticcio's oarsmen as found in the fresco of *Ulysses and his Companions arriv-*

ing on the Shores of the Underworld (figs. 8–9), though Rubens thinks about how differently men and women hold the oars. The figure of Force or perhaps Fortitude (identified by the lion with a column on her emblematic shield) in the *Majority of Louis XIII*,[83] recalls the man who leans forward from the ship, chin almost resting on the end of his oar in Primaticcio's composition. Piety (identified by the altar encircled with a snake on her shield),[84] is a female version of the heroically muscled oarsman near the prow of the boat in the fresco. Rubens must have been conscious that the great cycle he was painting for the French queen followed in the footsteps of Primaticcio's work at Fontainebleau, and such reminiscences show his sensitivity to both context and pictorial tradition. The idea for *Arion saved by Dolphins* must have originated directly from the *Majority of Louis XIII*, since it is based on a combination of elements that are not in Primaticcio's fresco. The *Arion* freely adapts the boat, inverts the sail, turns Louis XIII at the rudder into a common sailor, and – most tellingly of all – transforms the dolphin who alludes to the dauphin into the dolphin who saves Arion. In short, the artist who designed the *Arion* knew both the Galerie d'Ulysse and the Medici Cycle, and also knew that Rubens had himself echoed Primaticcio's work in that cycle. The complex links between these works point to an artist who had been to Paris, and this would fit both Van Diepenbeeck and Van Thulden. Not least, this points to Rubens's genius in creating a school for artistic thieves.

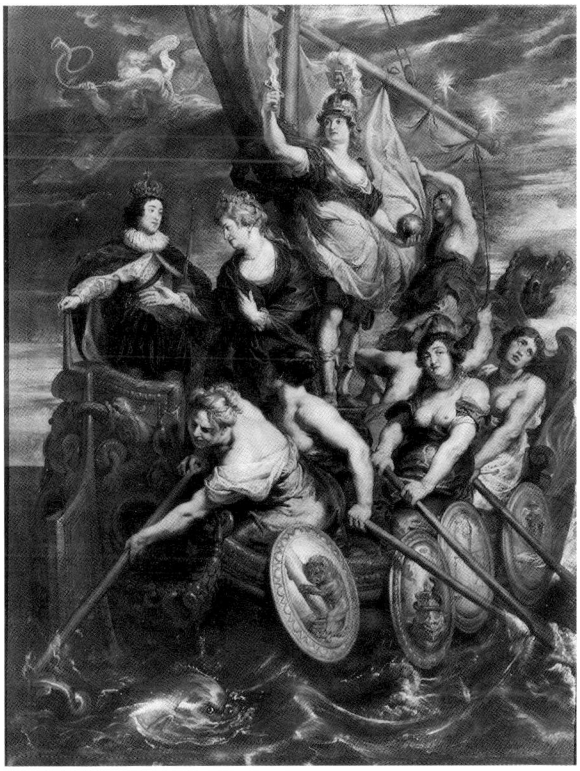

Fig. 15. Peter Paul Rubens, *The Majority of Louis XIII*. Paris, Musée du Louvre

NOTES

My warm thanks to Arnout Balis, Gregory Martin, and Harry Mount, for much help and advice. Elizabeth McGrath generously allowed me to read her unpublished draft discussion of the *Arion saved by Dolphins*. Clare Tilbury read a version of this text and her comments did much to clarify the argument.

1. Sir Joshua Reynolds, *A Journey to Flanders and Holland*, ed. Harry Mount, Cambridge, 1996, pp. 32–33.

2. My thanks to Hans Buijs for providing a photograph of this document.

3. The passage continues: 'at least there is this apology that he stole what no person but himself knew how to use'; Reynolds 1996 (see note 1), p. 33 note a.

4. Marie Mauquoy-Hendrickx, *Les estampes des Wierix conservées au Cabinet des Estampes de la Bibliothèque Royale Albert Ier: Catalogue raisonné*, 3 vols., Brussels, 1978–1983, III, 1, no. 2100.

5. Jean François Marie Michel, *Histoire de la vie de P.P. Rubens, Chevalier, et Seigneur de Steen, illustrée d'anecdotes, qui n'ont jamais paru au public...*, Brussels, 1771, p. 54, who gives the measurements of the engraving and quotes the inscription very precisely.

6. Michel 1771 (see note 5), p. 54: 'Par cette preuve [Wierix's engraving] on peut constater, que Rubens s'est servilement servi de cette estampe pour la grande grouppe, excepté fort peu changement dans les aires des têtes, mais principalement dans la position de la Madelene, qui est entiérement tournée & changée, la figure du Christ, les corps & attitudes de ceux qui le descendent de la croix sont tous conformes à ladite estampe, dont un exemplaire est soigneusement gardé, par un curieux à Anvers'.

7. As observed by Harry Mount in Reynolds 1996 (see note 1), p. 157, note 141.

8. For Rubens's interest in Daniele da Volterra's version of this subject see his inscription on a drawing of the *Descent from the Cross* in the Hermitage, St Petersburg; Julius S. Held, *Rubens: Selected Drawings*, 2 vols., London, 1959, pp. 93–94, no. 3; and *idem*, *Rubens: Selected Drawings*, Oxford, 1986, p. 71, no. 15.

9. See the summary provided by Thomas L. Glen, *Rubens and the Counter Reformation: Studies in his Religious Paintings between 1609 and 1620*, New York–London, 1977, p. 65.

10. Ludwig Burchard and Roger-A. d'Hulst, *Rubens Drawings*, 2 vols., Brussels, 1963, I, p. 32; and John Rupert Martin, *Rubens: The Antwerp Altarpieces. The Raising of the Cross. The Descent from the Cross*, London, 1969, pp. 48–49.

11. For example, see Michel 1771 (see note 5), p. 35: 'Venise fut son idole pour le Coloris, & Rome pour la Correction du dessin'.

12. Roger de Piles, *Dissertation sur les ouvrages des plus fameux peintres, dediée à Monseigneur le Duc de Richelieu*, Paris, 1681, pp. 18, 40–46.

13. Giovanni Pietro Bellori, *Le vite de' pittori, scultori et architetti moderni*, Rome, 1672, p. 247: 'Circa il colore, hebbe il Rubens una stupenda libertà; egli studiò in Venetia, e mirò sempre à Titiano, Paolo Veronese, e Tintoretto con le osservationi del chiaroscuro, e delle masse delle tinte. Colorì dal naturale, e fù vehemente nella mistioni, radiando il lume con la contrarietà de'corpi ombrosi, siché fù mirabile nelle oppositioni dell'ombre, e de'lumi'. Cf. André Félibien, *Entretiens sur les vies et sur les ouvrages des plus excellens peintres anciens et modernes; avec la vie des architectes*, 6 vols., Trevoux, 1725, III, p. 429: 'A l'égard du Coloris qui est son principal talent, il travailla avec une liberté de pinceau tout-à-fait surprenante. Il se servit toujours heureusement de l'étude qu'il avoit faire à Venise après le Titien, Paul Veronese, & le Tintoret, s'attachant à leurs maximes dans la conduire & la distribution des jours, des ombres, & des reflets de lumieres'. For the importance of Titian and Veronese, in particular, see Bellori 1672, p. 222; Félibien 1725, III, p. 407; and Roger de Piles, *Abrégé de la vie des peintres, avec des reflexions sur leurs ouvrages, et un traité du peintre parfait, de la connoissance des dessins, et de l'utilité des estampes*, Paris, 1699, p. 394 (mentioning Titian alone).

14. For de Piles's biography of Rubens see Bernard Teyssèdre, *Roger de Piles et les débats sur le coloris au siècle de Louis XIV*, Paris, 1957, pp. 228–232; for his place in French criticism see Thomas Puttfarken, *Roger de Piles' Theory of Art*, New Haven–London, 1985.

15. Roger de Piles, 'La vie de Rubens', in De Piles 1681 (see note 12), p. 8: 'Et en effet, il tira des Ouvrages du Titien, de Paul Veronése, & du Tintoret, tout le profit qu'on en peut tirer, dont il embellit sa manière.'

16. De Piles 1699 (see note 13), p. 276.

17. Roger de Piles, 'La Vie de Rubens', in De Piles 1681 (see note 12), p. 6, and De Piles 1699 (see note 13), p. 395.

18. De Piles 1699 (see note 13), pp. 400–401; see Bernard Teyssèdre, *L'histoire de l'art vue de Grand Siècle: Recherches sur l'Abrégé de la Vie des Peintres, par Roger de Piles (1699), et ses sources*, Paris, 1964, pp. 134–135, who links this to Sandrart's comment that Rubens's productivity damaged his reputation.

19. Bellori 1672 (see note 13), p. 248: 'E benché egli stimasse sommamente Rafaelle e l'antico, non però imitò mai l'uno, o l'altro in parte alcuna; e se havesse voluto seguitare i lineamenti delle statue di Apolline, di Venere, ò del Gladiatore, li alterava tanto con la sua maniera, che non lasciava di esse forma, ò vestigio per riconoscerle'. Cf. Félibien 1725 (see note 13), III, p. 430: 'Et quoiqu'il estimât beaucoup les Antiques & les Ouvrages de Raphaël, on ne s'apperçoit pas qu'il ait tâché d'imiter ni les unes, ni les autres. Au contraire, on peut dire qu'il s'en éloignoit si fort, que s'il eût copié les statuës d'Apollon, de Venus, ou les Gladiateurs, on ne les auroit pas reconnus, tant sa maniere de dessiner étoit differente de ce goûte-là'.

20. For a notable exception see Held 1986 (see note 8), pp. 137–138, no. 175.

21. For one particularly elaborate exception, a drawing after Veronese's *Christ in the House of Simon* in the British Museum, London (inv. 18959151053), which Rubens retouched and inscribed with the artist's name, see Jeremy Wood, 'Rubens's Collection of Drawings: His Attributions and Inscriptions', *Wallraf-Richartz-Jahrbuch*, LV, 1994, p. 340. For an attribution of this work to Erasmus Quellinus rather than Rubens see Hans Vlieghe, 'Erasmus Quellinus der Jüngere und Italien' in E. Mai, K. Schütz, H. Vlieghe, ed., *Die Malerei Antwerpens – Gattungen, Meister, Wirkungen: Studien zur flämischen Kunst des 16. und 17. Jahrhunderts, Internationales Kolloquium Wien 1993*, Cologne, 1994, p. 219.

22. See Julius S. Held, 'Rubens and Titian', in *Titian: His World and his Legacy*, ed. David Rosand, New York, 1982,

pp. 283–339; and Jeffrey M. Muller, *Rubens: The Artist as Collector*, Princeton, 1989, pp. 103–109, 111.

23. Félibien 1725 (see note 13), III, p. 430.

24. Sir Joshua Reynolds, *Discourses on Art*, ed. Robert R. Wark, New Haven–London, 1975, p. 68.

25. See Held 1959 (see note 8), I, pp. 161–162, no. 166.

26. See J.Q. van Regteren Altena, 'Rubens en de Galerie d'Ulysse', *Bulletin van het Rijksmuseum*, I, 1953, pp. 11–12; and Michael Jaffé, *Rubens: Catalogo completo*, Milan, 1989, p. 286, no. 796. It is oddly described as 'a small sketch in oils' by Michael Jaffé, *Rubens and Italy*, Oxford, 1977, p. 45.

27. For Primaticcio's lost original, see Sylvie Béguin, Jean Guillaume and Alain Roy, *La galerie d'Ulysse à Fontainebleau*, Paris, 1985, pp. 173–176.

28. Because not preparatory (although 'sketchy' in treatment) this work was excluded from the standard discussion of Rubens's oil sketches: Julius S. Held, *The Oil Sketches of Peter Paul Rubens: A Critical Catalogue*, 2 vols., Princeton, 1980, I, p. 3, note 2.

29. Jaffé 1977 (see note 26), p. 19.

30. For convenient summaries of Rubens's visits to Paris see Held 1980 (see note 28), I, pp. 89–90, and Held 1986 (see note 8), p. 130, under no. 155.

31. Egbert Haverkamp Begemann, 'Rubens' "Three Caryatids"', in *Boymans bijdragen: Opstellen van medewerkers en oud-medewerkers van het Museum Boymans-van Beuningen voor J.C. Ebbinge Wubben*, ed. J.R. ter Molen and A.W.F.M. Meij, Rotterdam, 1978, p. 48, argued that Rubens drew over an earlier copy (rather than that he simply made a new drawing on one side of this sheet) and suggested that as a consequence Rubens's intervention need not have been made at Fontainebleau. This led him to date Rubens's reworking early in his career between 1600 and 1608; this was repeated in Anne-Marie Logan and Egbert Haverkamp Begemann, 'Dessins de Rubens', *Revue de l'Art*, 42, 1978, p. 94. It is difficult to be certain whether there was an earlier drawing on this side of the sheet but, logically, this assumption could also be used to argue that Rubens intervened at a later date. In a letter to me (dated 14 December 1998) A.W.F.M Meij has described his thorough technical examination of this sheet, including the lifting of two pasted-on sections, and concluded that Rubens did not retouch an earlier drawing.

32. Held 1986 (see note 8), p. 142.

33. For comments on dating the retouched drawings see Anne-Marie Logan, 'Review of Julius S. Held, *Rubens: Selected Drawings*', *Master Drawings*, XXV, 1, 1987, p. 65.

34. For these see Jeremy Wood, 'Padre Resta's Flemish Drawings: Van Diepenbeeck, Van Thulden, Rubens, and the School of Fontainebleau', *Master Drawings*, XXVIII, 1, 1990, pp. 23–32, 49 (notes 87–89), 50 (note 102).

35. Among these is a drawing of the *Daughters of Minyas* in the Hessisches Landesmuseum, Darmstadt (inv. AE 1419), which Rubens retouched and inscribed with Primaticcio's name; see Wood 1994 (see note 21), pp. 337–340.

36. Van Regteren Altena 1953 (see note 26), p. 10 (citing Rooses).

37. See Roger-A. d'Hulst, [cat. exh.] *Jacob Jordaens (1593–1678)*, II: *Drawings and Prints*, Antwerp, Koninklijk Museum voor Schone Kunsten, 1993, pp. 40–45, nos. B21–23 (with further references).

38. Held 1959 (see note 8), I, pp. 161–162, under no. 166; Jaffé 1977 (see note 26), p. 45; Haverkamp Begemann 1978 (see note 31), p. 48, and Logan 1987 (see note 33), p. 74.

39. William McAllister Johnson, 'Pictures from the School of Fontainebleau in Seventeenth-Century Guise', *Art Quarterly*, XXVIII, 4, 1965, p. 293.

40. Poussin said of the Galerie d'Ulysse 'qu'il ne connoissoit rien de plus propre à former un peintre et à échauffer son génie'; P. de Chennevières and A. de Montaiglon, eds., 'Abecedario de P.J. Mariette et autres notes inédites de cet amateur sur les arts et les artistes', *Archives de l'art français*, 6 vols., 1851–1860, IV, p. 212.

41. For the use of a Primaticcio composition in the Le Nain, see [Jacques Thuillier], [cat. exh.] *Les frères Le Nain*, Paris, Grand Palais, 1978, pp. 94–96, no. 1.

42. Inv. 1948: 419; brush with bodycolour, wash and heightening in oils, 420 x 569 mm. See Van Regteren Altena 1953 (see note 26), pp. 12–13.

43. Ludwig Burchard and Roger-A. d'Hulst, [cat. exh.] *Tekeningen van P.P. Rubens*, Antwerp, Rubenshuis, 1956, pp. 94–95, no. 111.

44. See Burchard-d'Hulst 1963 (see note 10), pp. 250–253, under no. 163; Jaffé 1977 (see note 26), p. 45, and Held 1986 (see note 8), pp. 130, 138, 140 (both Burchard-d'Hulst and Held dated these works slightly too early at 'about 1630'). Against this should be set the doubts of Logan 1987 (see note 33), p. 75. In addition, the entire group were questioned by Kristi Nelson, *Jacob Jordaens as a Designer of Tapestries*, Ph.D., The University of North Carolina, Chapel Hill, 1979, p. 63 note 24.

45. I argued in Wood 1990 (see note 34), p. 25, that some of these drawings may have been prepared by assistants and then reworked by Rubens, but, in re-examining these sheets, I have come to the conclusion that in each case they are the work of one hand and show no signs of retouching.

46. As established by Van Regteren Altena 1953 (see note 26), p. 12.

47. For an edition dated 1633 see Béguin, Guillaume and Roy 1985 (see note 27), p. 78 and note 39 (without citing the location of the copies consulted). I have used British Library 745.b.6: *Errores Ulyssis, adumbrati a S. Martino* [=Niccolo dell Abbate], *ut in Regia Fontis-bellaquae spectantur. A Nicolao depicti; et in aes incisi a Theodoro Van-Thulden. Una cum argumento, & interpretatione morali cujuslibet fabulae apud Melchiorem Tavernier, Sculptorem Regium, in Insula Palatina morantem, in angulo Plateae de Harlay, ad insigne Rosae rubrae*, Paris, 1634.

48. For Van Diepenbeeck's work in Paris see Hans Vlieghe, '"De Peintures très exquises": Abraham van Diepenbeecks Schilderwerk te Parijs', *Wallraf-Richartz-Jahrbuch*, LV, 1994, pp. 269–286.

49. See Wood 1990 (see note 34), pp. 3–53. My attribution was emphatically rejected by Alain Roy who defended his previous opinion in [cat. exh.] *Theodoor van Thulden: Een Zuidnederlandse barokshilder*, 's-Hertogenbosch (Noordbrabants Museum), Strasbourg (Musées de la Ville de Strasbourg), Zwolle, 1991, pp. 116, 124. For my response see Jeremy Wood, ''s-Hertogenbosch and Strasbourg: Theodoor van Thulden', *Burlington Magazine*, CXXXIV, 1992, pp. 327–330.

50. In addition, another series of drawings of these frescoes survives which is close in style to Van Thulden's etchings, but in reverse direction as would be expected in preparatory studies. See Wood 1990 (see note 34), pp. 22–23, and Anne-Marie Logan, [cat. exh.] *Flemish Drawings in the Age of Rubens: Selected Works from American Collections*, Wellesley, Davis Museum and Cultural Center, Wellesley College, 1993, p. 49 note 34.

51. Wood 1990 (see note 34), pp. 30–31.

52. In my opinion the two weakest sheets are *The Seven Sages at the Temple of the Delphic Apollo* in the Prado, Madrid

(inv. T.994), and *Aeneas questioning his Father, Anchises, in the Underworld* (?), present whereabouts unknown (see Wood 1990 [cited in note 34], pp. 23–30).

53. See Van Regteren Altena 1953 (see note 26), p. 13; for the reference by François Mols to this cycle see Nora De Poorter, *The Eucharist Series*, Corpus Rubenianum Ludwig Burchard, London–Philadelphia, 1978, II, 2, pp. 461–462.

54. For the lost original see Béguin, Guillaume and Roy 1985 (see note 27), pp. 258–259.

55. Inv. 1981; red chalk with white heightening, 243 x 320 mm. See Michael Jaffé, 'Rubens as a Collector of Drawings: Part One', *Master Drawings*, II, 4, 1964, p. 392 (as Primaticcio retouched by Rubens); Jaffé later changed his mind over the attribution (Jaffé 1977 [cited in note 26], p. 45 and pl. 117, as 'Theodoor van Thulden, after Primaticcio [retouched by Rubens]'). See also [Erwin Mitsch], [cat. exh.] *Die Rubenszeichnungen der Albertina: Zum 400. Geburtstag*, Vienna, Graphische Sammlung Albertina, 1977, p. 154, no. 66. In addition, Diane DeGrazia, [cat. exh.] *Correggio and his Legacy: Sixteenth-Century Emilian Drawings*, Washington, National Gallery of Art, 1984, pp. 238–240, no. 77, provided full references to the earlier literature but overlooked all discussion of Rubens's intervention.

56. Van Regteren Altena 1953 (see note 26), p. 13, puzzled over this discrepancy. He noted the differences between Rubens's adaptation, Primaticcio's *modello* and Van Thulden's etching, without realising that Van Diepenbeeck's copy (which he did not cite) resolves this question.

57. Inv. 8951; black chalk, 230 x 317 mm.

58. For the lost original see Béguin, Guillaume and Roy 1985 (see note 27), pp. 252–253.

59. Inv. 8949; black chalk, 208 x 290 mm. No *modello* by Primaticcio survives for this composition.

60. For the lost original see Béguin, Guillaume and Roy 1985 (see note 27), pp. 244–245. This interpretation of the scene is confirmed by the inscription on Van Thulden's etching after Primaticcio's original.

61. Inv. 8945; black chalk, 218 x 310 mm.

62. The cattle seen on the river banks may have been included by Primaticcio mistakenly, unless they are intended as victuals, because Ulysses took a 'young ram and a black ewe' to offer in sacrifice; the cattle may be based on Homer's reference to the heifers that Ulysses slaughtered on his return home.

63. This is reproduced unambiguously in Van Thulden's etching of the fresco. The conceit is also found in Giulio Romano's work.

64. See De Poorter 1978 (see note 53), I, pp. 401–408; and Held 1980 (see note 28), I, pp. 165–166, but neither author comments on the influence of Primaticcio in this composition.

65. For this confusion (but with no discussion of Primaticcio's influence), see Held 1980 (see note 28), I, pp. 165–166; and Charles Scribner, III, *The Triumph of the Eucharist: Tapestries designed by Rubens*, Ann Arbor, 1982, p. 109. In the *Allegory of Hope* the rowing angels are facing the wrong way, but in the Rijksprentenkabinet drawing (Fig. 3) the oarsmen should be interpreted as fending off the second boat, which is perilously close, rather than rowing.

66. A remaining discrepancy is the large bull's head held by two men in the right-hand foreground which, in the original context, must be one of the Cattle of the Sun. Here it could simply be understood as part of the provisions that are being put on board in preparation for the voyage.

67. Jaffé 1989 (see note 26), pp. 297–298, no. 868 ('originale'). Formerly in the collections of Thomas Harris, London (1930), and Allan Mackay, Petersfield, the panel was sold at Christie's, London, 2 May 1958, lot 40.

68. David W. Steadman, *Abraham van Diepenbeeck: Seventeenth-Century Flemish Painter*, Ann Arbor, 1982, p. 88, no. 11. The dimensions given by Steadman (56 x 89 cm) fit none of the recorded versions, but '89' is presumably a slip for 79. This would agree with the work formerly owned by Adolphe Schloss and the other references provided by Steadman.

69. Adolf Rosenberg, *P.P. Rubens. Des Meisters Gemälde*, Klassiker der Kunst, V, Stuttgart–Leipzig, 1905, p. 55. My thanks to Gregory Martin for the information that this version is currently in the possession of Jean-Max Tassel, Paris.

70. 59 x 67 cm. Formerly collection of Dr Fritz Rothmann, Berlin, 1925.

71. For example one formerly in the collection of Antoon van Welie, The Hague (Fig. 12); panel, 56 x 79 cm; sale Mak van Waay, Amsterdam, 7 April 1936, lot 67.

72. See Hans Mielke, [cat. exh.] *Manierismus in Holland um 1600: Kupferstiche, Holzschnitte und Zeichnungen aus dem Berliner Kupferstichkabinett*, Berlin, Staatliche Museen, 1979, pp. 29–30, no. 12.

73. My thanks to Elizabeth McGrath for this observation.

74. In the original this oar was simply cut by the edge of the frame, but, in the Rijksprentenkabinet drawing (Fig. 3), it is at the centre of the composition, and appears awkward and unfunctional.

75. Michel de Marolles, *Tableaux du Temple des Muses; tirez du cabinet de feu Mr Favereau Conseiller du Roy en sa Cour des Aydes; & gravez en Tailles-douces par les meilleurs Maistres de son temps, pour représenter les Vertus & les Vices, sur les plus illustres Fables de l'Antiquité avec les descriptions, remarques & annotations*, Paris, 1655. I have consulted British Library 82.l.14.

76. Steadman 1992 (see note 68), p. 88. He presumably means 'design' rather than 'drawing' since no surviving study for this illustration is included in his list of drawings by Van Diepenbeeck (pp. 59–67).

77. Elizabeth McGrath, 'The Black Andromeda', *Journal of the Warburg and Courtauld Institutes*, LV, 1992, p. 13.

78. In terms of treatment of subject matter, Van Diepenbeeck's engraving is far closer to Jan Muller's earlier print after Cornelis van Haarlem, mentioned above. Assuming Van Diepenbeeck's involvement with both compositions, the difference between the painted *Arion* and the illustration in the *Temple des Muses* could be used to argue that the former is later in date than the latter and improves upon it by showing Arion clothed; this would help move the dating of all the painted versions of this subject to the period shortly after Rubens's death.

79. See Wood 1990 (see note 34), p. 22 (with further references).

80. *Homer his Illiads translated, adorn'd with sculpture and illustrated with annotations*, London, 1660; *Homer his Odysseys translated, adorn'd with sculpture and illustrated with annotations*, London, 1665.

81. McAllister Johnson 1965 (see note 39), pp. 293–295.

82. Even if, as has been widely agreed, the symbolic meaning of the boat derives from a medal by Guillaume Dupré showing the ship of the French state.

83. See Ronald Forsyth Millen and Robert Erich Wolf, *Heroic Deeds and Mystic Figures: A New Reading of Rubens' 'Life of Maria de' Medici'*, Princeton, 1989, p. 170.

84. Or perhaps *salus augusti*, the health of the emperor, as suggested by Millen and Wolf 1989 (see note 83), pp. 170–171.

Rubens's Paintings for the Banqueting House: A Talk Partially Recaptured

To the memory of Roger d'Hulst

Gregory Martin

A thief in Barcelona Airport is the last person to have seen the notes for my talk on the ceiling paintings of the Banqueting House. The talk, here partially summarised, straddled two of the topics with which the Symposium was concerned by touching briefly on the preparatory work and by then dwelling on the execution of the paintings and their treatment before installation.

The preparatory work must have been far more extensive than what is extant.[1] It seems inconceivable that no drawings were made,[2] although no trace of any exists or is recorded. At the very least Rubens when he was in London may well have made a drawing – similar to that of Robin the Dwarf[3] – to record the physiognomy and uniform of the Sergeant-at-Arms, who appears in the *Union of the Crowns*. Rubens would have made records, too, of the physiognomy of King James I, his Parliamentary Robes and the Regalia, which also feature prominently in the three main paintings. These drawings may have been made after the completion of the initial preparatory work which culminated in the Glynde sketch (Fig. 1), re-christened in my forthcoming Corpus volume as the multiple *Bozzetto*.[4] Grisaille sketches, like those which it comprises, may have been executed for the two compositions – the *Union of the Crowns* and the *Wise Rule of King James I* – not there considered. Four works – two in the deposit of the Hermitage,[5] one on the German art market in 1993[6] and another known only by a reproduction in the commemorative volume for the 1930 Antwerp exhibition[7] – are probably records of lost *modelli*.

The preparatory work subsequent to the multiple *Bozzetto* should be divided into three types: compositional and figural *modelli* and a combination of the two, which last prepared chiefly for the corner ovals. The four presumed copies are likely to record the first type. That last recorded on the German art market provides the clearest evidence that one of Rubens's concerns in the compositional *modelli* was to establish a degree of foreshortening for the compositions as a whole and for the figures within them that would be visually convincing and acceptable when viewed as approached from 16.5 metres below. Rubens later referred to the time consuming trouble, which could not be avoided in making foreshortenings, when justifying his fee for the projected ceiling paintings for the Queen's House at Greenwich.[8] The degree of tilt in the composition of the *Wise Rule*, as determined in the presumed copy of this lost *modello*, was to be abandoned as he arrived at the most visually satisfactory solution. A similar process was followed in his development of all the other compositions, even to a degree with the Processions.

Of the figural *modelli*, the majority made in preparation for the *Apotheosis* is lost, a fate which has befallen all those for the two *Processions*. The latter were early recorded in an artful combination of autonomous sketches to form an incoherent aerial progress, which is known in several versions.[9] The figural *modelli* were presumably executed to assist in the transfer of the designs on a very large scale onto the canvases and in the execution of the paintings, which latter might seem to presuppose Rubens's anticipated reliance on assistants. The view that he had help in the execution of the paintings goes back at least to Kneller, who had been in Antwerp probably in the 1660's.[10] It is hardly surprising that Rubens did turn to assistants because of the great size of the areas to be filled; the *Apotheosis* is larger than Veronese's *Triumph of Venice* in the Doge's Palace. The *amoretto* flying inwards in the centre right of the aerial progress provides a clue as to who one of the assistants may have been.

The *amoretto* reappears as an angel in a *Nativity*, which has been on display at the National Gallery with its old and traditional

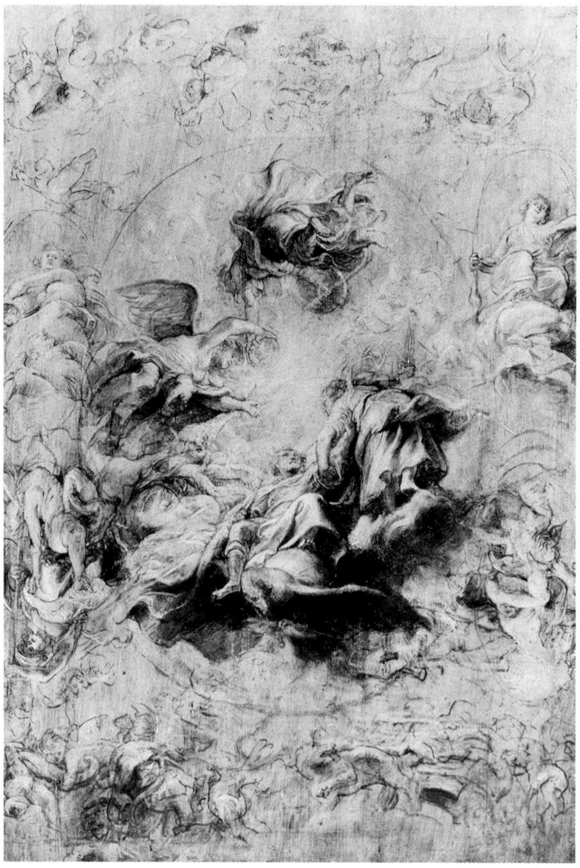

Fig. 1. Peter Paul Rubens, *The Apotheosis of James I and other studies*, oil sketch. Private collection, on loan to the National Gallery, London, from 1981

attribution to Rubens; Jaffé, while dating the work too early, believed it to be by the master and an assistant.[11] Recently Arnout Balis has attributed the painting as a whole to Jan van den Hoecke.[12] The precise status of the *Nativity* is not our concern for a comparison between Minerva in the *Union* or Minerva in *Minerva triumphant over Ignorance* in the Banqueting House ceiling with Van den Hoecke's *Cardinal Infant Ferdinand* or *Liberality of the King* – whether partially retouched by Rubens or assisted by a studio hand – for the Arch of Ferdinand in the *Pompa Introitus Ferdinandi* and thus executed not long after the completion of the Banqueting House commission,[13] shows that he is the most likely candidate to have been Rubens's chief assistant.

His presence in Rubens's studio while preparatory work was in progress for the commission is suggested by the oil sketch at Boston of *Mercury and Argus* (?), which has been thought to have been executed by Rubens as a figural *modello* in preparation for the *Wise Rule* and *Union*, in which the two protagonists appear.[14] The handling is very similar to that in the sketches for *Moses's Song of Praise and Miriam's Dance* at Karlsruhe and *David with the Head of Goliath* at Fort Worth, which Hans Vlieghe has recently attributed to Jan van den Hoecke.[15]

The Boston sketch is one of three hitherto generally accepted *modelli* for the ceiling paintings whose attribution to Rubens is to be questioned. The other two are the *Hercules overcoming Discord(?)* also at Boston[16] and the *Apotheosis* in the Hermitage.[17] The attribution of the *Hercules* was questioned in sale catalogues in the early part of the twentieth century,[18] while the *Apotheosis* has been doubted by Sir Oliver Millar.[19]

The *amoretto* in the aerial progress appears in a much altered and subsidiary role in the *Procession* for which he was designed. His fate provides evidence that the painting had to be reduced before installation; that this happened to the other eight paintings has not been generally appreciated, although such was suggested towards the end of the nineteenth century,[20] while the *Minerva triumphant over Ignorance* was recognised as having been cut about the time of its exhibition in 1950 in the Orangery of Kensington Palace.[21]

The paintings had to be reduced because of confusions over measurements; the operation presumably took place in the Banqueting House and may well have resulted in some drastic improvisation to at least two of the compositions. The *amoretto* in the *Procession* was originally to have held the end of the festoon; after the painting was cut down the festoon was extended so that its end could be held by the genius hovering above the chariot (who also appears in the *Nativity*). His original task had been to hold the reins attached to the yoke, which would join together the bear and lion. The oval *Apollo triumphant over Avarice* probably also had a substantial alteration: the money bag had to be transferred from Avarice's right hand – lost in the reduction – to a newly introduced left hand.

Yet in spite of studio assistance, mutilation of the supports and subsequently on at least two occasions, drastic interventions to mitigate damage caused by the canvases sagging from their stretchers,[22] the power and intensity of the paintings cannot be denied. This is evidence of the extent to which Rubens worked on them himself, as we would have expected of him when executing such a prestigious, royal commission.

NOTES

1. This is contrary to the view of Julius S. Held, in *The Oil Sketches of Peter Paul Rubens. A Critical Catalogue*, Princeton, 1980, I, p. 189. Held's discussion of the extant oil sketches is by far the most comprehensive.

2. Although Julius Held did not seem to think so, see *ibid.*

3. Robin the Dwarf stands beside the Countess of Arundel in the Munich group portrait, see Michael Jaffé, *Rubens: Catalogo Completo*, Milan, 1981, no. 652; for the drawing, see Ludwig Burchard and Roger-A d'Hulst, *Rubens Drawings*, I, Brussels, 1963, no. 127, II, pl. 127.

4. See Gregory Martin, *The Whitehall Ceiling*, Corpus Rubenianum Ludwig Burchard, XV (forthcoming), no. 1.

5. Nos. 2576 and 2579; see Martin forthcoming (see note 4), under nos. 5H and 3H.

6. With Galerie Traude Sauer, Schweinfurt; see Martin forthcoming (see note 4), under no. 3B.

7. See *Trésor de l'Art Flamand... Mémorial de l'Exposition d'Art Flamand à Anvers, 1930*, Paris, I, 1932, no. 244; see Martin forthcoming (see note 4), under no. 5E.

8. As rather obscurely reported by Scaglia, see Max Rooses and Charles Ruelens, *Correspondance de Rubens et documents épistolaires concernant sa vie et ses œuvres, publiés, traduits, annotés par Ch. Ruelens* (I), *par Max Rooses et feu Ch. Ruelens* (II-IV), Antwerp, VI, 1909, p. 287.

9. That recently acquired by the Museo Soumayo, Col. Tizapán San Angel, Mexico, is probably the best; see Martin forthcoming (see note 4), nos. 10D and 11D Copies (?) 1.

10. See *Vertue Note Books*, Volume V, *The Walpole Society*, vol. XXVI, 1937–1938, 1938, pp. 25–26. For the date of Kneller's sojourn in Antwerp, see J. Douglas Stewart, *Sir Godfrey Kneller and the English Baroque Portrait*, Oxford, 1983, pp. 2–3 and note 11, p. 3.

11. See Jaffé (see note 3), no. 660.

12. Arnout Balis, '"Fatto da un mio discepolo". Rubens's Studio Practice Reviewed', in *Rubens and his Workshop. The Flight of Lot and his Family from Sodom*, ed. T. Nakamura, The National Museum of Western Art, Tokyo, 1994, p. 115 and note 193, p. 126.

13. See John Rupert Martin, *The Decorations of the Pompa Introitus Ferdinandi*, Corpus Rubenianum Ludwig Burchard, XVI, London–New York, 1972, nos. 39 and 42, figs. 70 and 75.

14. See Held 1980 (see note 1), I, no. 139, II, pl. 145; see Martin forthcoming (see note 4), under nos. 3J and 5G.

15. See Hans Vlieghe, 'Nicht Jan Boeckhorst, sondern Jan van den Hoecke', *Westfalen*, LXVIII, 1990, pp. 167–172 and figs. 13 and 14; for more accessible reproductions, see Held 1980 (see note 1), II, pls. 489 and 490.

16. See Held 1980 (see note 1), I, no. 141, II, pl. 147; see Martin forthcoming (see note 4), under nos. 6E.

17. See Held 1980 (see note 1), I, no. 135, II, pl. 139; see Martin forthcoming (see note 4), under nos. 4E.

18. In the Fontaine-Flament of Lille sale, Galerie Georges Petit, Paris, 10 June 1904, lot 67, and in the Marczèll de Nemès sale, Dubourg, Paris, 19 March 1919, lot 19.

19. See Oliver Millar, [cat. exh.] *The Age of Charles I, Painting in England 1620–1649*, Londen, The Tate Gallery, 1972, under no. 39.

20. See R.A.M. Stevenson, *Peter Paul Rubens*, London–New York, 1898, p. 83.

21. See Ludwig Burchard, [cat. exh.] *A Loan Exhibition of Works by Peter Paul Rubens, Kt.*, London, Wildenstein, 1950, under no. 24. (This exhibition took place shortly before the Orangery exhibition.) See also Michael Jaffé, 'Painting and History I', *History Today*, January 1951, p. 71. See also Martin forthcoming (see note 4), Introduction, Delivery and Installation

22. See Martin forthcoming (see note 4), Introduction, The canvases from *c.* 1700–*c.* 1830.

Consistency and Change in Rubens's Drawings

Anne-Marie Logan

In order to discuss 'consistency and change' in Rubens's drawings one needs to be aware of the fact that for the most part they served a specific function, namely to prepare a finished work of art, be it a painting, sculpture, or a print. Anyone studying Rubens's drawings, therefore, needs to have a thorough knowledge of his entire œuvre. In the first survey of Rubens as a draftsman, published just about 40 years ago, Julius Held[1] clearly showed how essential it was to always be aware of this, since a drawing's function may dictate a strikingly different technique and manner of execution. This separation in accordance with a drawing's purpose is clearly evident in the plate volume of Held's 1959 edition of his *Selected Drawings*, where the illustrations are grouped by function, namely for compositions, studies from the model, portraits, landscapes, and designs for sculptures, engravings and woodcuts, to allow for a clearer idea of the wide ranging scope of Rubens as a draftsman.

As a rule, Rubens made preliminary drawings on paper which may either follow or precede color sketches in oil on panel. He drew predominantly on single, at times exceptionally large sheets rather than in sketchbooks. The Rubens drawings that have been preserved are for the most part compositional studies, drawn predominantly with pen and brown ink, frequently over slight outlines in black chalk and, – especially during Rubens's early years – enhanced with brush and brown wash. In addition, there exist numerous studies of individual figures, animals, or landscape motifs, most often drawn in black chalk, heightened with white, at times with additional touches of red chalk for faces and hands, or strengthened with pen and brown ink. The most memorable chalk studies, especially those drawn from the model, date from the second decade when Rubens's studio was in full swing, and again from the early 1630s. These detailed preliminary drawings were useful not only to Rubens himself but also to his assistants. The quick first thoughts or *crabbelinge* were basically only meaningful to Rubens himself and hence could be discarded more easily; for this reason they are less numerous. Although we can never be certain about the number of preliminary studies the artist drew for a given work, we nevertheless are able to establish a fairly consistent working procedure that changes relatively little over the course of time.

One noticeable shift away from the preliminary compositional drawings in pen and wash or – less often in chalk – in favor of colored sketches in oil on panel happens at the beginning of the 1620s and lasts – with a few exceptions in the early 1630s – until Rubens's last commissions shortly before his death in 1640. This change may be partly explained by the growing number of large commissions and the involvement of well trained assistants in the Rubens studio. Moreover, Rubens's increased skill in composing paintings and cycles must have lessened the need for these detailed studies.

The following brief overview discusses some of these aspects in more detail.

One example has been preserved where the preliminary drawing and the oil sketch have merged into one and the same, namely in Rubens's late drawing of *c.* 1635–1637, representing *Hercules and Minerva Fighting Mars* in the Louvre, Paris (Fig. 1),[2] drawn with the brush and colored gouache over black chalk, very much in the manner of an oil sketch. Rubens sketched the same composition also in oil on panel, today in the Koninklijk Museum voor Schone Kunsten, Antwerp (Fig. 2).[3] Julius Held reasoned that the gouache, which is more detailed and more colorful, must have followed the oil sketch, which is more monochrome. This procedure was most unusual for Rubens because the compositional drawing traditionally came first, the oil sketch followed as we will see later on. The reason for this exception remains unknown. Both studies relate to

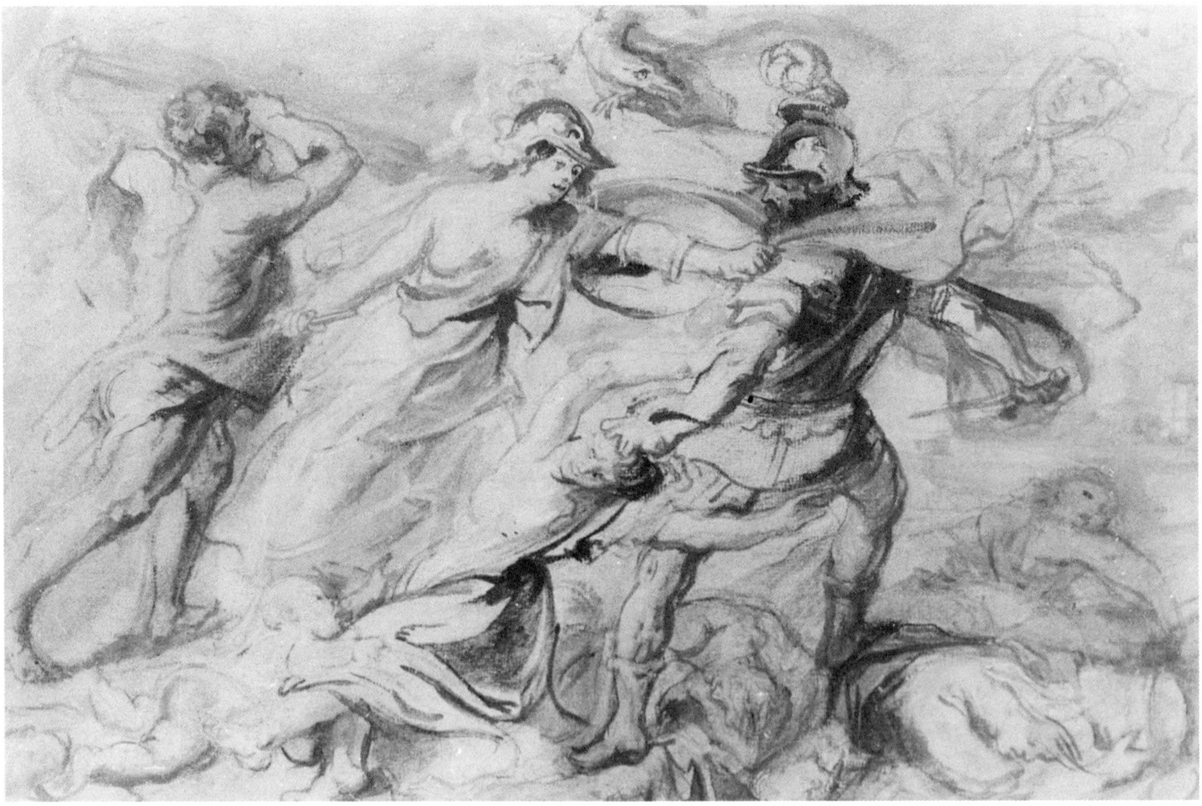

Fig. 1. Peter Paul Rubens, *Hercules and Minerva Fighting Mars*. Paris, Musée du Louvre, Département des Arts Graphiques

Rubens's large *Allegory on the Horrors of War* in the Palazzo Pitti, Florence, of the mid-1630s.[4]

Of the two main groups of drawings that have been preserved, Rubens was more consistent with regard to the studies in chalk, which therefore appear to pose fewer problems regarding their attribution. Often they tie in closely with a sketch in oil, which they follow as the last step in preparation for the final work, or with the final painting itself. Many of these chalk studies count among Rubens's most sensitive and beautiful works. Foremost in the group is the highly finished, exceptionally large portrait of his second wife, Helena Fourment (1614–1673), wearing a 'heuke' and holding a small prayer book, today in the Princes Gate Collection at the Courtauld Institute Galleries, London (Fig. 3),[5] which he drew shortly after their marriage in 1630. The drawing rightly counts among Rubens's masterpieces. The uniqueness of this portrait may be explained by the fact that it represents 'family' and thus has a more private side to its origin. The drawing has been associated with the full-length portrait of Helena Fourment in the Louvre, Paris[6] – which was originally planned as a half-length figure – and may have been an early inspiration for it. In the painting, Helena is rendered less frontally and seen emerging from a doorway.

With few exceptions Rubens used such chalk drawings as direct preparatory studies for specific figures in paintings, such as the head of a *Young Boy with a Coral Necklace* of about 1619, in the Albertina, Vienna (Fig. 4),[7] another one of Rubens's widely admired and often reproduced studies. The child is believed to represent his son Nicolas, born in March of 1618. Rubens used the drawing for the head of the Christ Child in his painting of the *Virgin and the Penitent Sinners* in Kassel,[8] which is dated accordingly to *c.* 1619–1620.

The sequence of these chalk studies for individual figures becomes more specific when Rubens also painted a preparatory sketch in oil on panel. In that case the preliminary studies in chalk follow *after* the colored oil sketch, as a last detailed drawing for a specific figure in the final painting, an observation that goes back to Haberditzl.[9] An especially beautiful example is the black chalk study of a *Man Falling from a Horse* in the British Museum, London

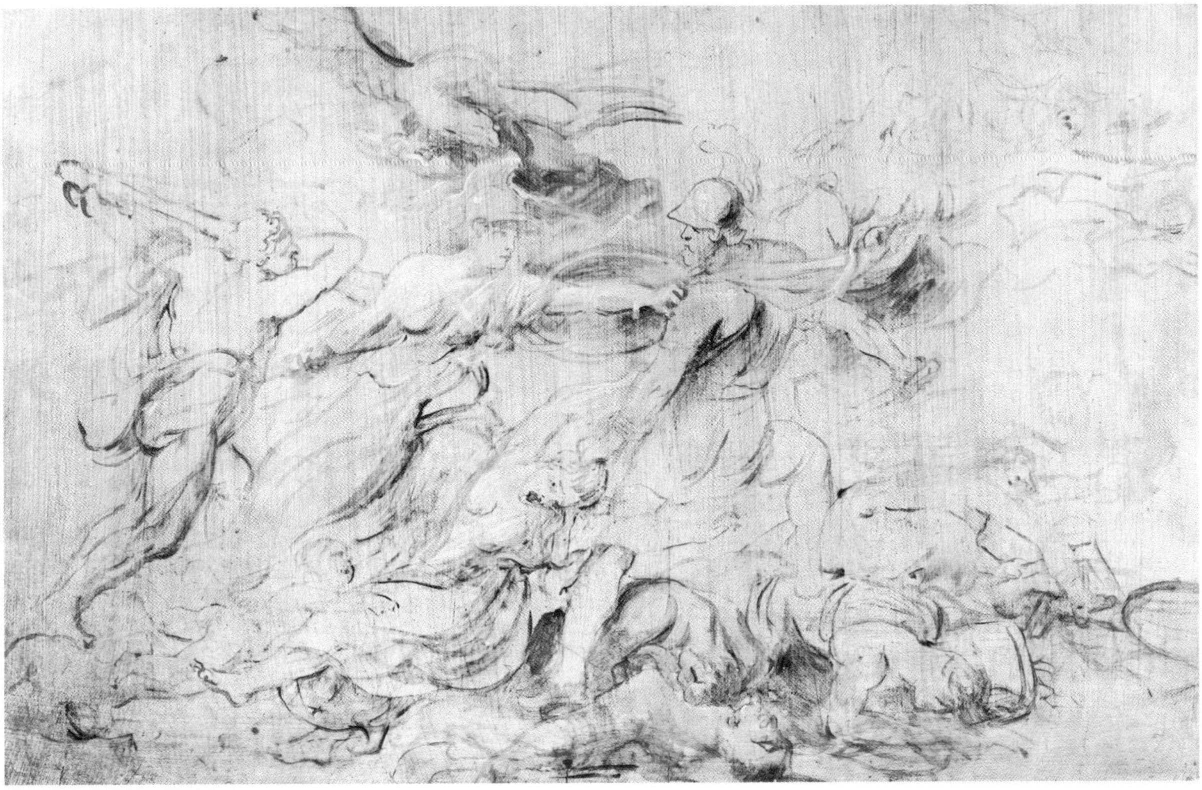

Fig. 2. Peter Paul Rubens, *Hercules and Minerva Fighting Mars*. Antwerp, Koninklijk Museum voor Schone Kunsten

(Fig. 5),[10] which was drawn from the model. The close-up follows the oil sketch that was recently acquired by the Alte Pinakothek in Munich (Fig. 6),[11] which Rubens painted in preparation for the Munich *Lion Hunt* of about 1621. Originally the sheet was larger, since the detailed study of the man's left hand, now added at the top left on a separate piece of paper, must have followed below, but was cut at a later date. In the chalk drawing Rubens rendered a close-up of the man's face, distorted by fright and terror caused by the lion's attack, an expression taken over without any change in the final painting of the *Lion Hunt*.

The sequence and function of these detailed chalk drawings remains quite consistent throughout Rubens's drawn œuvre. Due to the fact that in the course of time, Rubens reused certain figures in his paintings, discrepancies occasionally occur regarding the dating of such studies. A case in point is the black chalk drawing of a so-called *Mercury Descending* in the Victoria and Albert Museum, London (Fig. 7).[12] Julius Held associated it with the *Education of Maria de' Medici*, one of the paintings in the Medici cycle now in the Louvre, Paris, although the figure of Mercury descending toward the young Maria appears in reverse. Accordingly he dated the drawing to about 1622.[13]

J.G. van Gelder,[14] on the other hand, re-dated the study on the basis of the paper's watermark to about 1613–1614, and associated it with the angel figure in the same sense, descending toward the *Four Evangelists* in Rubens's painting in Potsdam of about 1614 (Fig. 8).[15] Here, the figure follows the chalk drawing rather closely except for the fact that Rubens added wings, and in so doing transformed the angel's left leg into a wing. Van Gelder's argument, supported by the paper's watermark, that Rubens was more likely to draw such a chalk study around 1613 than during the time of the Medici cycle seems convincing; the only surviving studies in chalk for that cycle are Rubens's portraits of Maria de' Medici and Henry IV.

Preliminary drawings in black and red chalk for specific figures become rare in the 1620s until they resurface again in the 1630s with new vigor and splendor. Foremost among them are the exceptionally large and beautiful figure studies Rubens drew in preparation for the

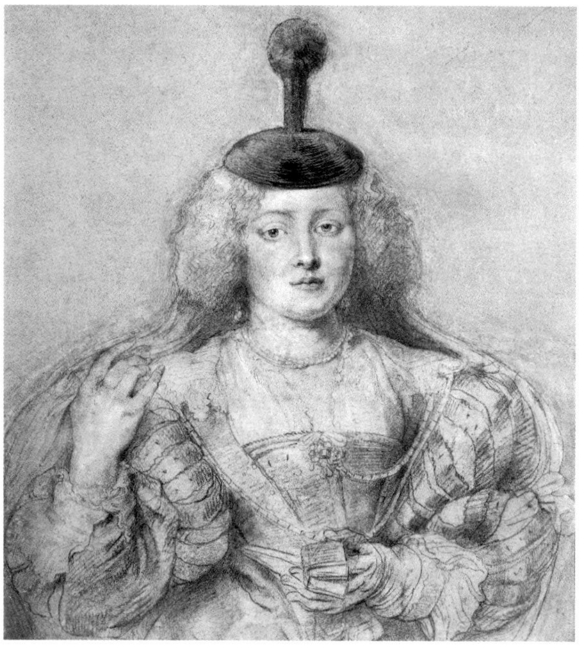

Fig. 3. Peter Paul Rubens, *Helena Fourment*. London, Courtauld Institute Galleries, Princes Gate Collection

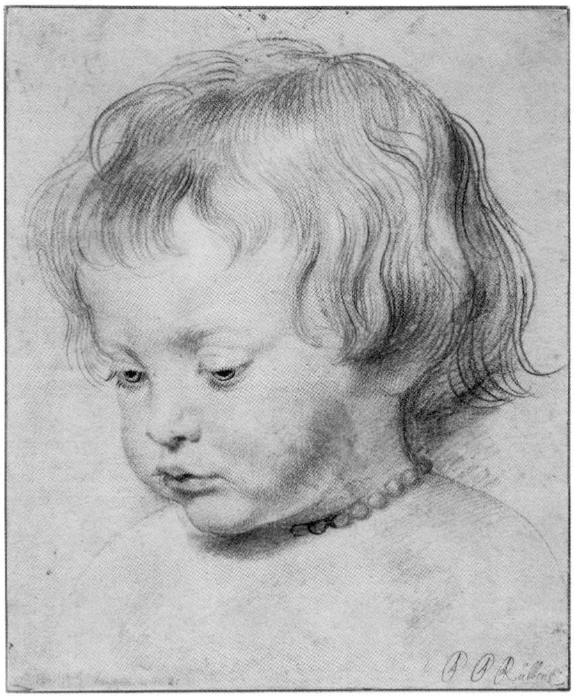

Fig. 4. Peter Paul Rubens, *Head of a Young Boy With a Coral Necklace*. Vienna, Albertina

Garden of Love painting in Madrid, such as the *Young Man Walking* in Amsterdam (Fig. 9).[16]

Rubens was also consistent in yet another respect in his preliminary drawings in chalk, namely in their respective sizes. On average, he used sheets that were more or less of the same format, filling up the entire surface with the individual study. Relatively small-sized drawings, especially of heads, therefore, immediately fall out of the norm and thus attract closer scrutiny.

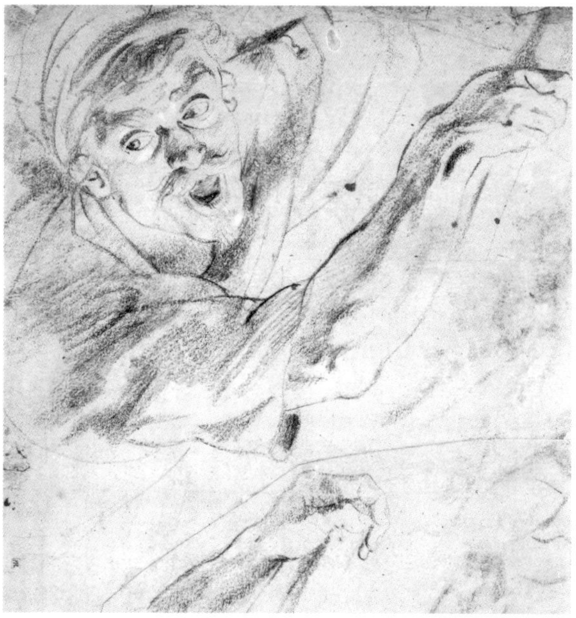

Fig. 5 Peter Paul Rubens, *Man Falling from a Horse*. London, British Museum

Recently, Martin Eidelberg[17] has shown convincingly that head studies such as the one of *Juno*, in the British Museum, London (Fig. 10)[18] may be traced back to an album containing ninety-four such sheets, once in the collection of Roger de Piles where they were attributed to Rubens himself. Today, they are widely dispersed and identified as copies based on Rubens or Rubens school paintings. The small drawing with the *Head of Juno* clearly belongs to this group and thus was correctly eliminated from Rubens's authentic works.

A second group of drawings to be mentioned briefly concern Rubens's more elaborate compositional studies for finished works of art rather than for individual figures, drawn with a fine to medium-fine pen and brown ink. At times, Rubens also used the brush for additional details, and often introduced a light brown wash to unify the composition and indicate the distribution of light and shade. These drawings seem to pose more problems when we investigate their respective consistency within Rubens's œuvre.

In his early pen sketch of *St George Killing the Dragon*, in the Louvre, Paris (Fig. 11),[19] for

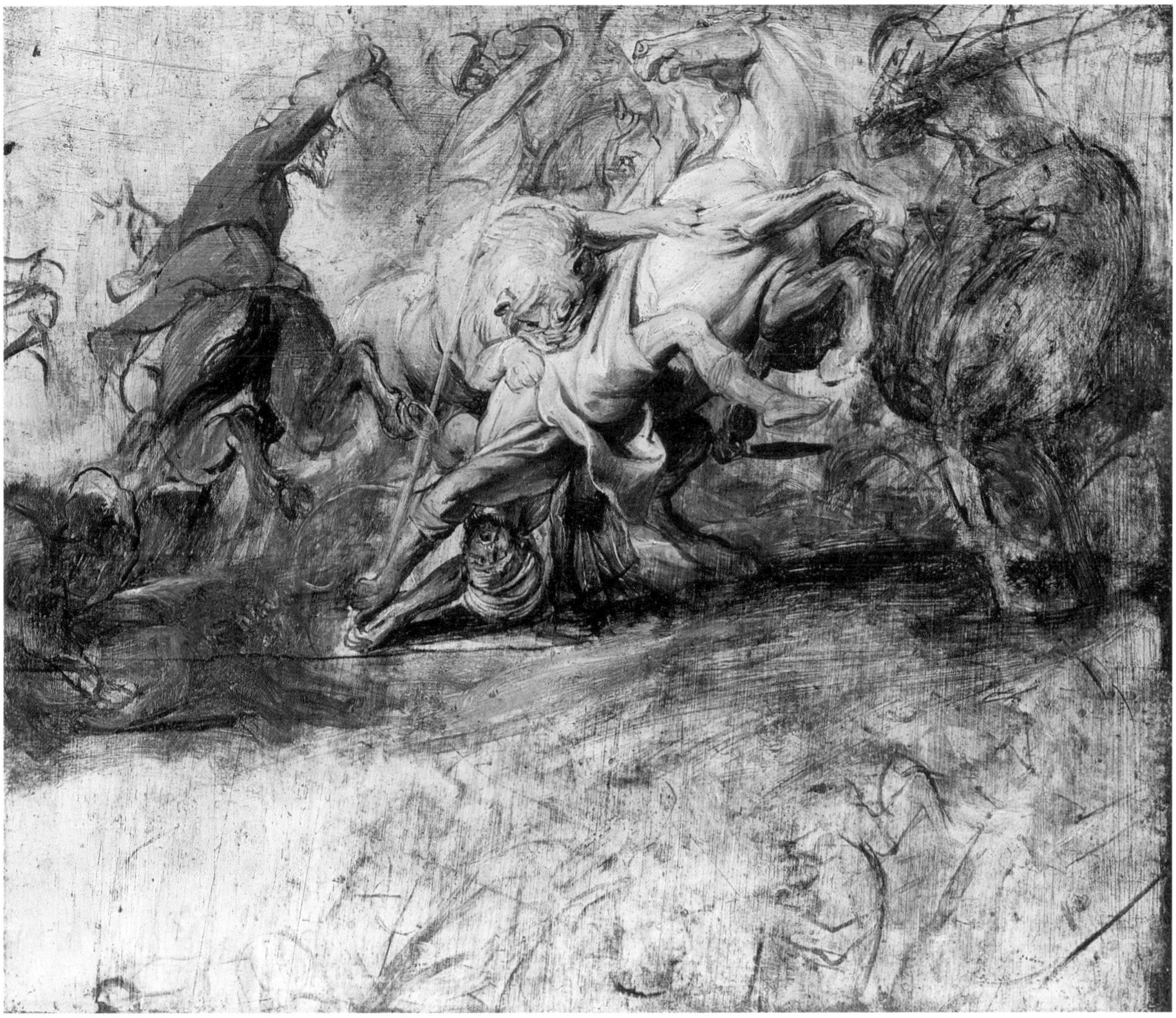

Fig. 6. Peter Paul Rubens, *The Lion Hunt*, oil sketch. Munich, Alte Pinakothek

the painting of the same subject in the Prado, Madrid (Fig. 12),[20] Rubens used fine, fluid strokes for the saint and his rearing horse, but changed the execution to angular, blunt strokes for the succumbing dragon trying to defend itself against the attacker. A horrified, fleeing figure at the far left who will be transformed in the painting into an immobile, docile princess is indicated with a few abbreviated strokes that delineate the barest minimum. This is a rather typical first draft for Rubens, where the lines end abruptly, the figures are given in outline only and the general impression is of great speed in execution, combined with an angularity in pose and gestures. Although Rubens will introduce major changes in the painting, especially in the dragon in the foreground, which he will paint in much greater foreshortening with a dramatically opened mouth, we notice almost no pentimenti, except in the monster's twisting body.

There can hardly be a more striking contrast between this drawing of *St George*, for a painting of about 1606, and Rubens's *Man on Horseback*, the portrait drawing (Fig. 13)[21] associated with his signed painting of the *Duke of Lerma* in the Prado, Madrid (Fig. 14), dated 1603.[22] A comparison with the *St George* drawing also makes blatantly clear just how inconsistent and flexible Rubens's manner of execution could be: one full of movement, the other utterly controlled to the point that a connoisseur like Lugt supposed that it might have been intended as a design for a print.[23]

The discrepancy in style and execution observed in these two drawings may possibly reflect the fact that in his studies for works commissioned by private collectors Rubens

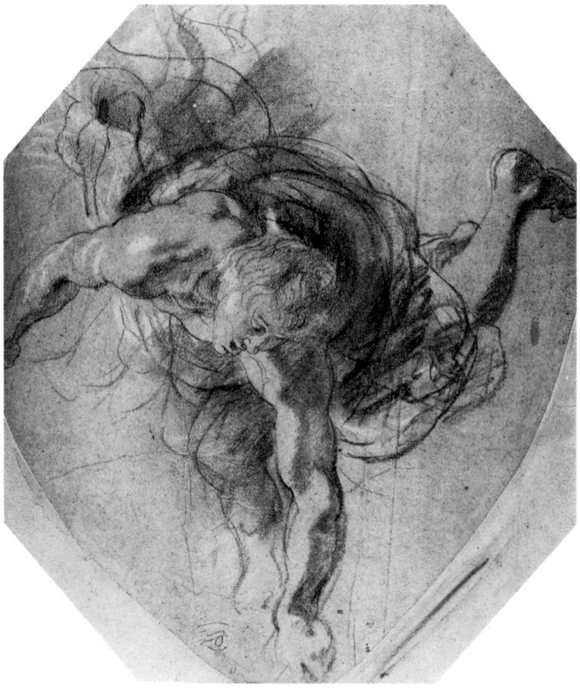

Fig. 7. Peter Paul Rubens, *Mercury Descending*. London, Victoria & Albert Museum

chose to be more exuberant and free spirited. His more restrained, formal side of drawing may have come to the fore when working on official, more public commissions as in this portrait study for the Duke of Lerma. At that time Lerma was more powerful than King Philip III and the driving force in art patronage in Spain, as Susan Schroth established. In her opinion, Rubens's equestrian portrait should be placed in context with Lerma's memorial that outlined the heroic deeds of his ancestors, the Sandoval, serving the Spanish crown, alluded to in the charging warriors on horseback seen in the background.[24]

As is well known, the long lost drawing which only now is being re-introduced into the Rubens scholarship, is closely followed in the painted portrait, except for the portrayed, who does not represent the Duke of Lerma; furthermore, the order of Santiago the Duke is wearing in Rubens's painting, is missing.[25] The relationship of the drawing in Munich to Rubens's painting is complicated further by a second, closely related drawing in the Louvre, Paris (Fig. 15),[26] considered to be another study, also by Rubens, for the same Lerma portrait in the Prado. Since both depict only a stand-in, the function of the two drawings is not easily established and different interpretations have evolved. To some, both drawings are studies by Rubens for the painting, to others, both follow it, and may possibly even have been made in preparation of an engraving, as mentioned earlier.[27]

The *Man on Horseback* in Munich is of exceptional size and very finished. Three areas show what appear to be pentimenti that were obliterated; most noticeable is the one at the lower right, where the tip of the rider's shoe appears to have protruded slightly behind the horse's left foreleg, only to be erased through scratching out. This would speak against the drawing following the painting. Another erasure took place where the Paris drawing and the painting show the hilt of a sword, which would indicate that the sheet in Paris is linked more closely with the painting, while the sheet in Munich reveals an earlier stage in the preparation with modifications.

The large size of the Munich drawing and its meticulous attention to detail in the execution would suggest that it had a special purpose, most likely to be shown to the Duke of Lerma who commissioned the work. The drawing's provenance from Spain would support this notion.[28] In a direct comparison, the version in the Louvre is only about half the size of the sheet in Munich (673 x 410 mm. versus 298 x 216 mm.), lacks the additional strip at the top (88 mm.), and the head of the portrayed is drawn on a separate piece of paper that was pasted in, although there is nothing beneath it, as a close examination has shown. The Paris version bears the Jabach collector's mark and belongs to the drawings that were put into new mounts (*remontés*) once they entered the Royal collection but the work has not been identified in the Jabach inventory.[29]

Of the two studies, the one now in Munich corresponds well with the draftsmanship of the young Rubens, for example in a comparison with his preliminary compositional drawing for the Chiesa Nuova altarpiece, the *Image of the Virgin Adored by Angels* (see below, Fig.17), or the *Head of an Unknown Man*, both in the Albertina, Vienna (Fig. 16).[30] The latter is dated to Rubens's first years in Italy. Although drawn with black and red chalk rather than pen and brown ink, albeit with a very pointed piece of black chalk, there appears a similarity in the attention to detail in the finely drawn hair and

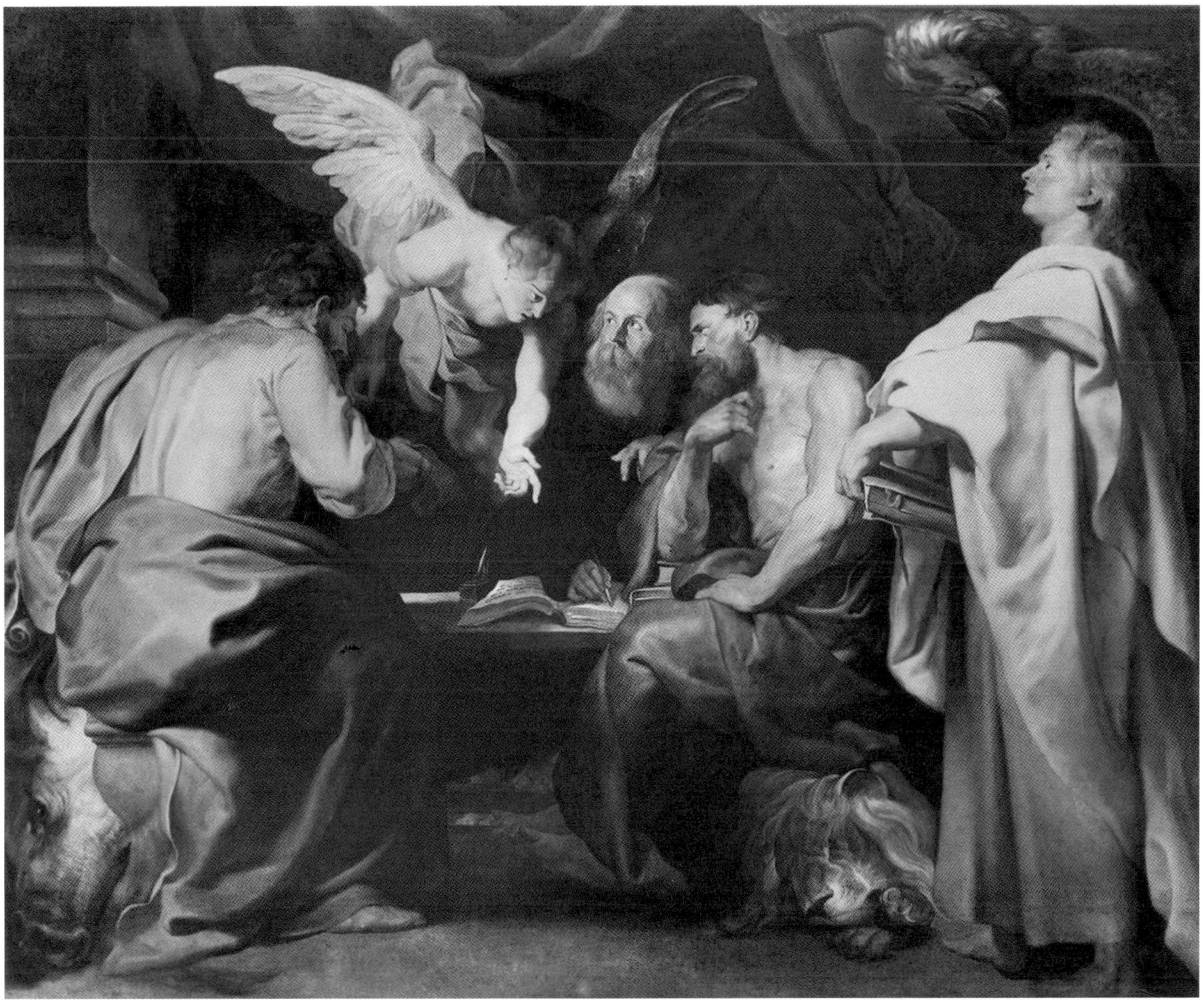

Fig. 8. Peter Paul Rubens, *The Four Evangelists*. Potsdam, Sanssouci, Bildergalerie

beard, not unlike the use of the fine pen in the Munich portrait.

Now that a direct comparison of the drawing in Paris (Fig. 15), associated with the Duke of Lerma painting, with the large portrait study in Munich has become possible, the traditional attribution of the Paris drawing to Rubens becomes more doubtful. The latter shows rather coarsely applied pen strokes and a somewhat pedantic way of cross hatching, especially in the horse, which is not customary in Rubens's early drawings and is indeed reminiscent of designs for prints.

Most vexing, furthermore, is the question why Rubens would have needed two such similar studies for his Lerma portrait? Except for an obvious difference in size, the compositions are nearly identical. In conclusion it seems more likely that of the two versions, Rubens's *Man on Horseback* in Munich served as the preliminary drawing for the portrait of Duke of Lerma in the Prado, Madrid, while the sheet in Paris appears to be more derivative since it includes no meaningful pentimenti; it may even be by another artist who accompanied Rubens in Spain and recorded the painting.

The restrained side of Rubens is also evident in the initial compositional drawing in the Albertina of the *Image of the Virgin adored by Angels,* (Fig. 17),[31] which he then followed up with an oil sketch, now in the Akademie der Bildenden Künste, Vienna.[32] Both are preparatory works for Rubens's revised, second altar painting on the High Altar in the Chiesa Nuova (Sta. Maria in Vallicella) in Rome, finished in 1608.[33] Again, we notice a highly controlled execution with fluid penlines that are continuous and securely placed with hardly any pentimenti. Washes add subtle tonal effects and introduce modeling and depth. Despite the

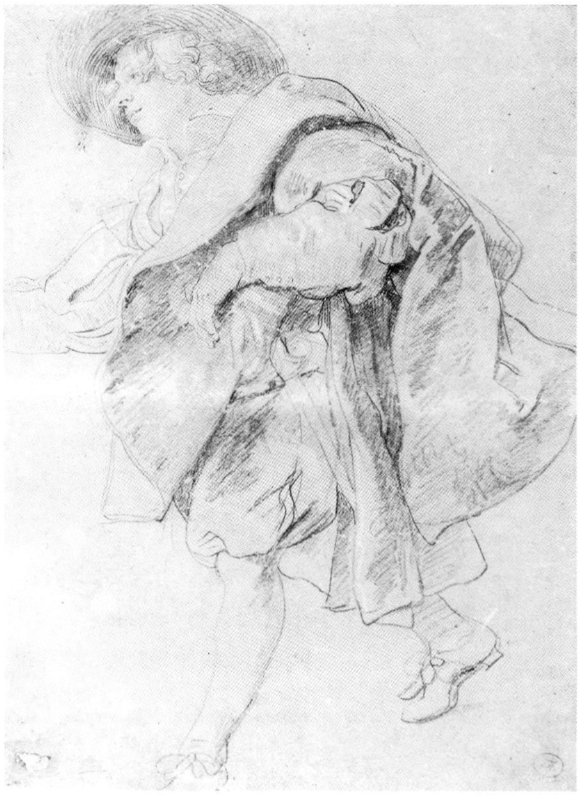

Fig. 9. Peter Paul Rubens, *Young Man Walking*. Amsterdam, Gemeentemuseum, Fodor Collection

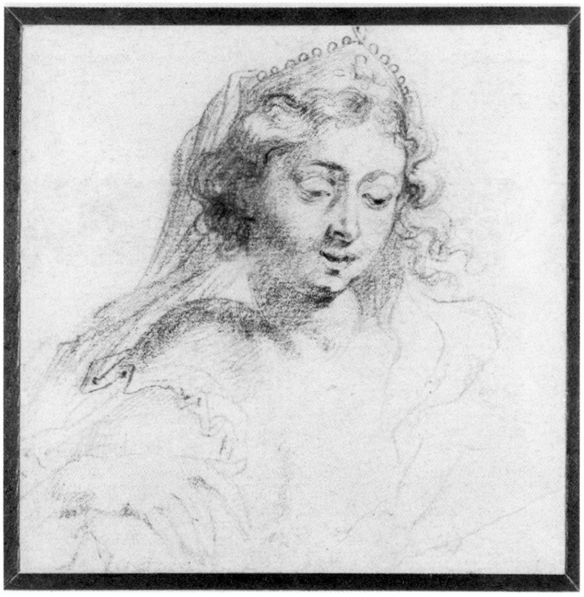

Fig. 10. Peter Paul Rubens (copy after), *Head of Juno*. London, British Museum

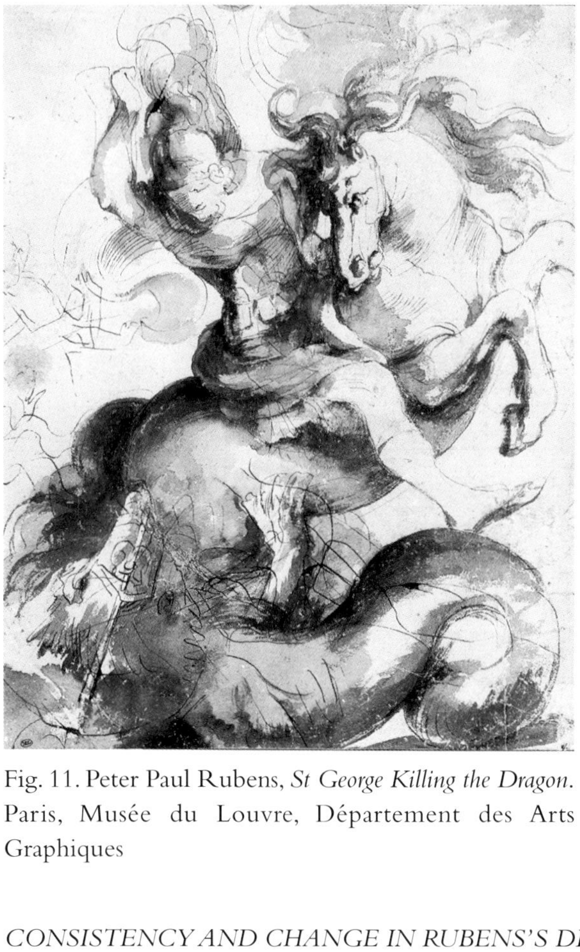

Fig. 11. Peter Paul Rubens, *St George Killing the Dragon*. Paris, Musée du Louvre, Département des Arts Graphiques

multitude of figures, Rubens securely positioned the composition right from the start in the center of the page and needed hardly any corrections to fix his idea of the altarpiece-to-be. It is difficult to imagine that no other quick thoughts preceded the drawing, so precisely is every individual placed. The most noticeable change in the subsequent oil sketch is the elimination of the angel at the right, the increased size of the adoring angels kneeling below, as well as a consolidation of the putti around the image of the Virgin and Child which is now placed in an oval frame. The final altarpiece, painted on slate, shows still a few additional changes. No other compositional drawings have survived, however, just a close-up study in black and red chalk of the framed image of the *Virgin and Child, Supported by Angels*, in the Pushkin Museum, Moscow.[34]

Moving on to the first half of the following decade, to *Silenus, Aegle and Other Figures* in the Royal Collection at Windsor Castle (Fig. 18),[35] dated to about 1612–1614, we encounter for the first time another trait of Rubens's compositional drawings that will continue until the end. In this case clarity gives way to an open-ended composition full of pentimenti and overlapping figures. In addition we find the repetition of figures such as the twisting, reclining naiad Aegle, rendered no less than three times, which Svetlana Alpers described as a 'serial

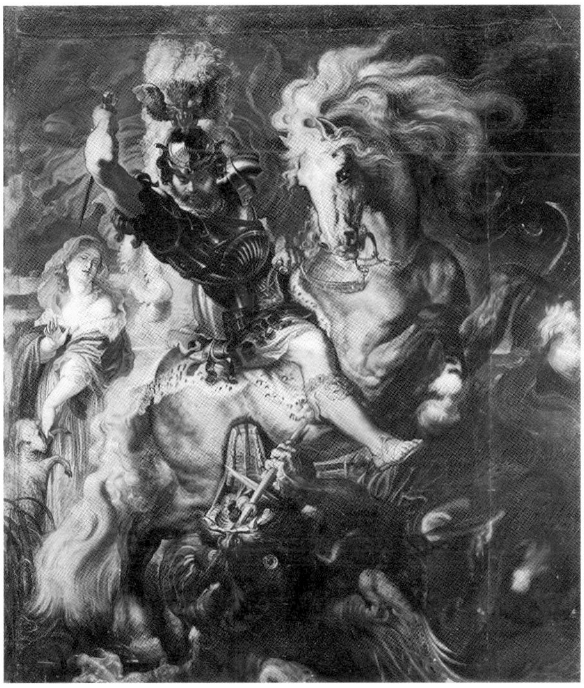

Fig. 12. Peter Paul Rubens, *St George Killing the Dragon*. Madrid, Museo del Prado

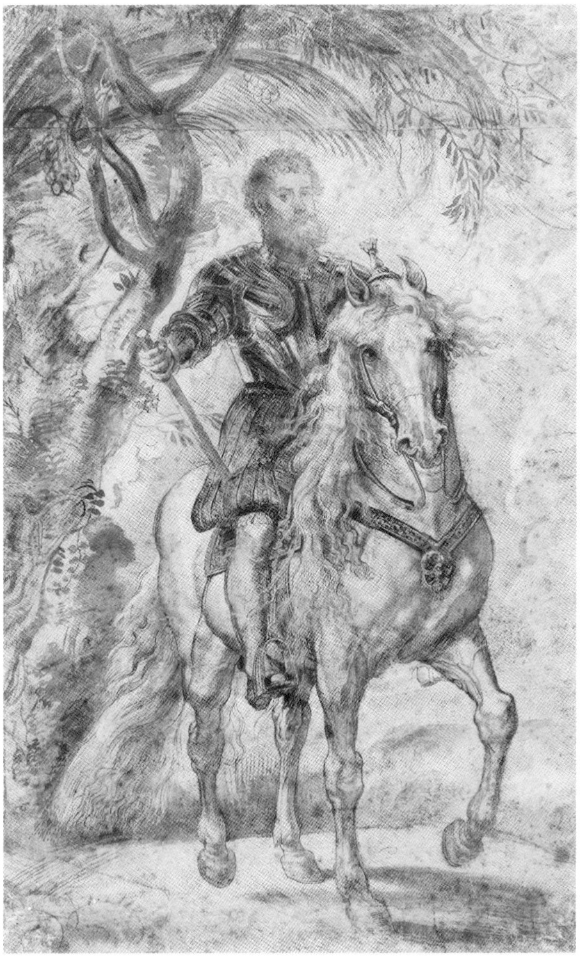

Fig. 13. Peter Paul Rubens, *Study for The Duke of Lerma*. Munich, Staatliche Graphische Sammlung

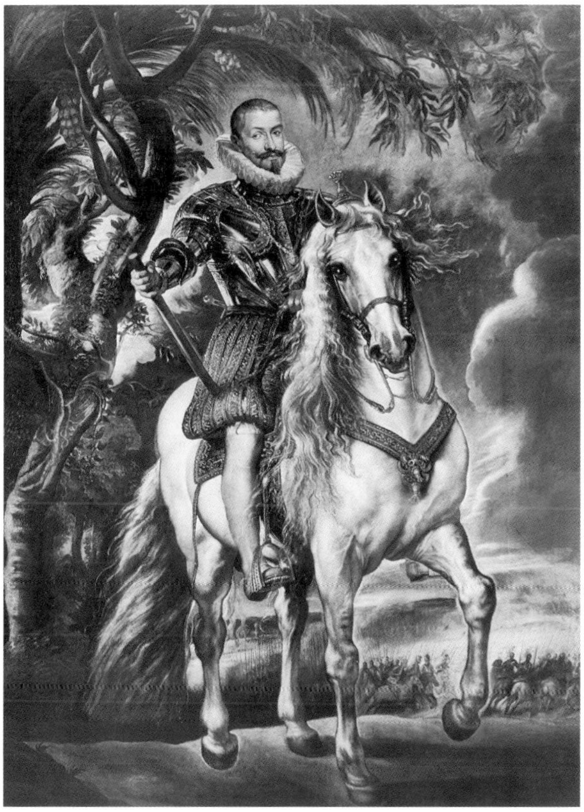

Fig. 14. Peter Paul Rubens, *The Duke of Lerma*. Madrid, Museo del Prado

invention unfolding and repeating across and up the sheet'.[36] Since Rubens rather consistently draws counterclock-wise I wonder whether in fact he did not work in the opposite direction, beginning at top right with a slight outline drawing of the reclining Aegle figure and adding the words – that Elizabeth McGrath[37] deciphered as 'vitula gaud[ium]', – or 'vitula' means joy, which she associated with Virgil's sixth *Eclogue*. In the context of this drawing the inscription may well represent Rubens's shorthand indication for the drunken Silenus, who will be made to sing, in accordance with Virgil. Rubens continued and repeated his study in the center section of the sheet, where he firmed up Aegle's pose and figure, and associated her with a barely recognizable slumped figure, an obvious early indication of the drunken Silenus, who is fully developed and finalized in the group at the lower left. Here Rubens repeated Aegle's position,

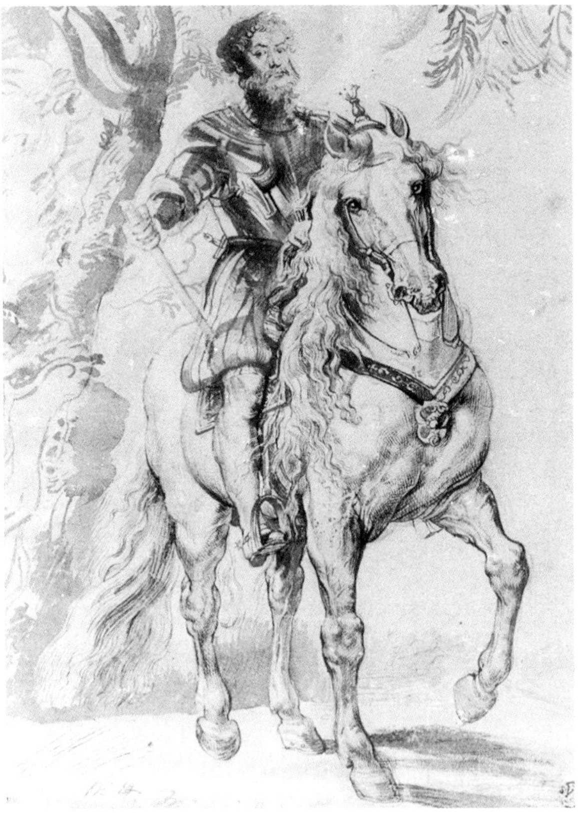

Fig. 15. Peter Paul Rubens (?), *Study for The Duke of Lerma*. Paris, Musée du Louvre, Département des Arts Graphiques

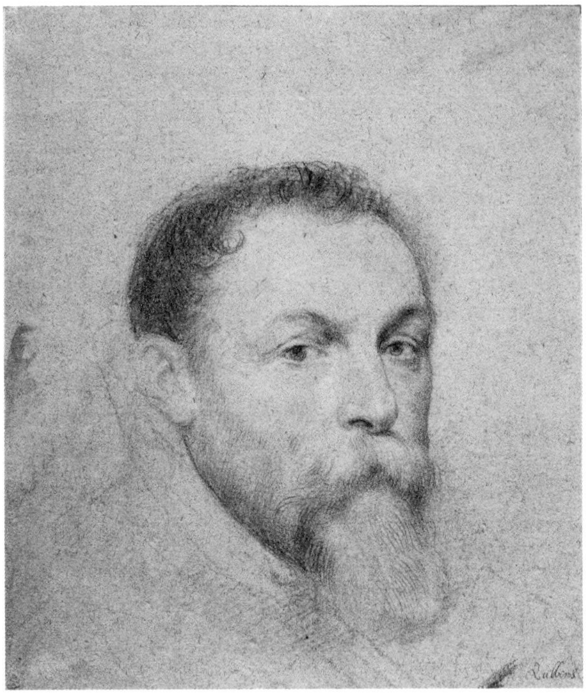

Fig. 16. Peter Paul Rubens, *Head of an Unknown Man*. Vienna, Albertina

but now her action is clarified, for she is staining Silenus's face and brow with crimson mulberries, thus awakening him, whereupon he begins his extended song. It is to this group alone that Rubens added a transparent, light brown wash to unify it and introduce modeling at the same time.

Two especially fine compositional drawings of about 1616–1617, for a painting of the same subject that was lost in a fire in 1836 have been preserved with the theme of the *Continence of Scipio*, where Scipio Africanus releases a captive Spanish bride to her rightful groom and returns the ransom her family had offered as a dowry. The version in Berlin (Fig. 19),[38] which focuses on the bride, is slightly earlier than the example in Bayonne (Fig. 20),[39] where Rubens reversed the composition and added some brisk parallel hatching to indicate slightly more modeling. In this latter study the groom instead of the bride now is placed in the center. The precision and economy of Rubens's line and the clarity with which he formulated the event with few hesitations or corrections is an impressive testimony to his ability to visually formulate an entire composition and bringing it to paper as is. The few minor changes, more noticeable in the sheet in Berlin (Fig. 19), are found – as so often in Rubens – in the hands and legs, where he would experiment with alternate positions.

The reversal of the scene appears to have posed no problems either. His hand and eye coordination must have been truly outstanding, to place the entire composition with such sweeping pen strokes effortlessly on the page without a preliminary underdrawing in chalk. The ink spots on both drawings resulted from Rubens's pen resting just a trace too long on the absorbent paper.

While these two sheets with the Continence of Scipio theme are quite consistent within Rubens's accepted draftsmanship, the drawing in Berlin with the *Reconciliation of Esau and Jacob* at the top and the *Fortitude of Mucius Scaevola* below (Fig. 21)[40] includes some elements which appear to deviate from his traditional working procedure.

Both scenes relate to paintings King Philip IV of Spain had commissioned from Rubens in 1625 through his aunt, Archduchess Isabella. They were shipped to Madrid in 1628, at the time Rubens travelled there himself, where they were placed in the *salón nuevo* of the Alcázar.

The scene of the *Reconciliation* relates to a Rubens sketch in oil on panel in the National Gallery of Scotland, Edinburgh (Fig. 22),[41] and his large painting based on it, now in the Bayerische Staatsgemäldesammlungen,[42] since Charles II of Spain presented the picture in 1694 to his brother-in-law, Johann Wilhelm of Neuburg, the founder of the Düsseldorf Gallery. Rubens's oil sketch and the painting, which follows it with minor changes, are of an upright format and dated to about 1625–1627. In contrast, the two scenes in the Berlin drawing, dated often to *c.* 1616–1618, are arranged in a horizontal format. The *Fortitude of Scaevola* below today is known only from a painting in Budapest, considered to be a studio replica, while the original supposedly was destroyed in the Alcázar fire of 1734. There is general agreement that the two studies in pen must be by the same hand, and date from the same time, but cannot be later than 1628. Opinions are divided, however, about the function of this drawing in Berlin. In 1956, Burchard and d'Hulst interpreted the scenes as so-called *ricordi* by Rubens and placed them *c.* 1616–1618, a position repeated in the Corpus volume of the Old Testament scenes, published in 1989.[43] Held[44] kept the date of *c.* 1617–1619 but strongly argued in favor of a 'first thought', since

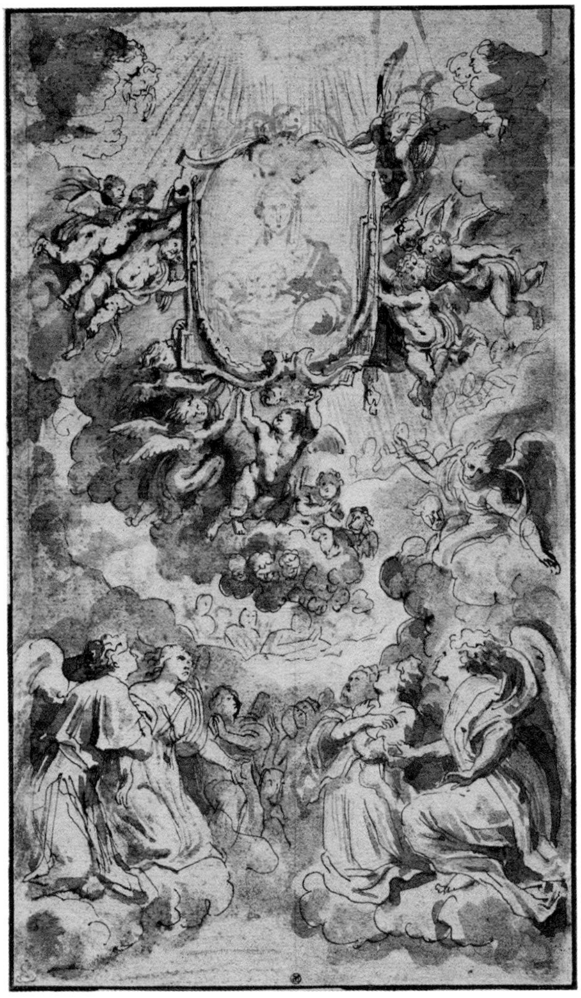

Fig. 17. Peter Paul Rubens, *The Image of the Virgin Adored by Angels*. Vienna, Albertina

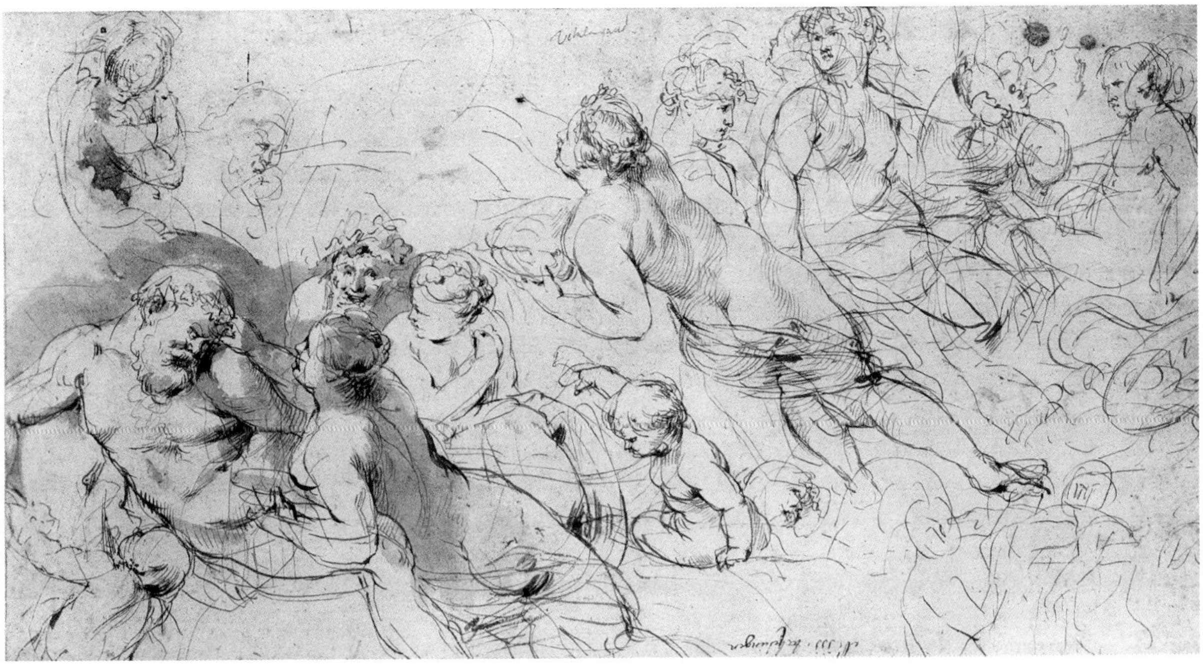

Fig. 18. Peter Paul Rubens, *Silenus and Aegle*. Windsor Castle, Royal Collection (copyright Her Majesty The Queen)

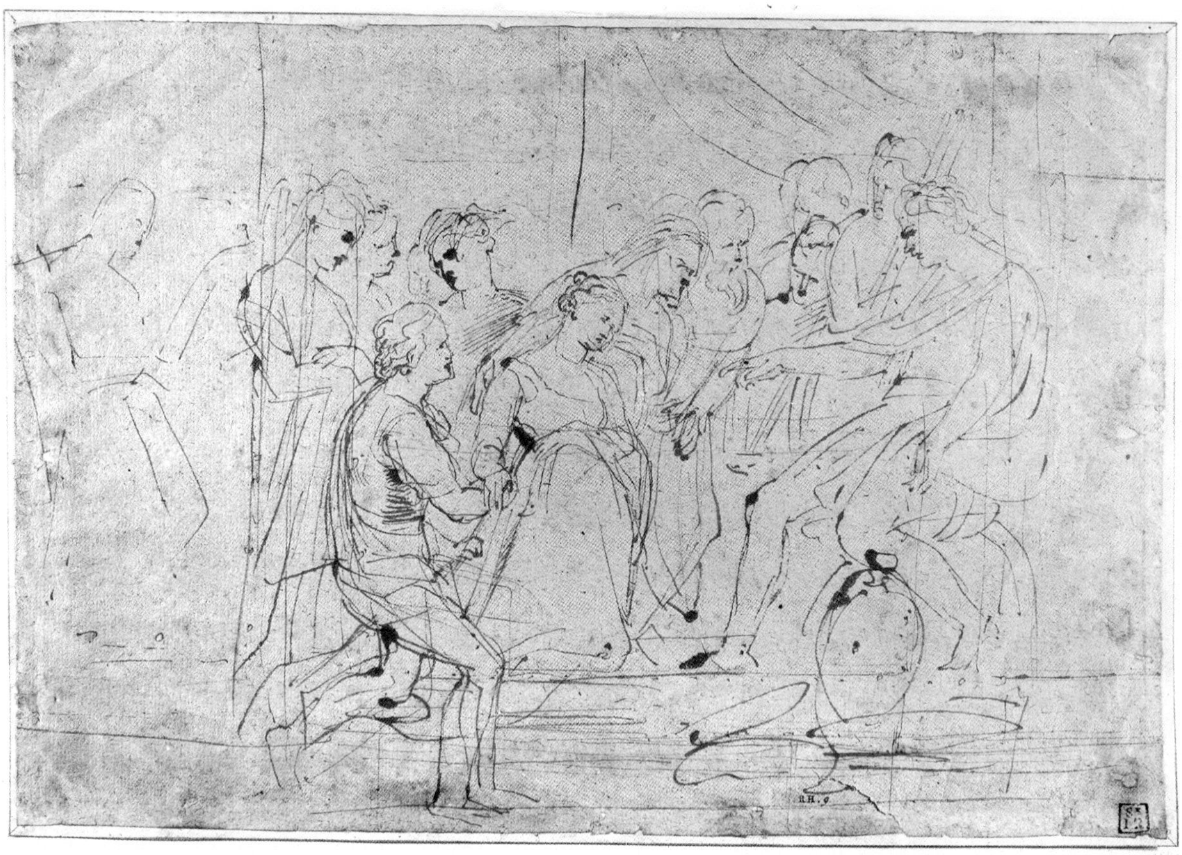

Fig. 19. Peter Paul Rubens, *The Continence of Scipio*. Berlin, Staatliche Museen, Kupferstichkabinett

he considered it highly unlikely that Rubens would have copied his own oil sketches. Therefore he assigned the Berlin sheet to Rubens himself, although he noted an inconsistency in the fact that there were two compositional studies on one sheet and that in the Scaevola scene Rubens omitted the dead scribe in the foreground which was an essential figure in the story. To rationalize this 'awkwardness' as Held described it, he reasoned that the drawing had occupied Rubens toward the end of the second decade, and that he then incorporated essential elements seven to eight years later, or between 1624–1626 in his oil sketch in Edinburgh, where the composition is more spatially developed. Most recently, Elizabeth McGrath[45] has supported this attribution to Rubens, and argued for a date of *c.* 1622–1623, that is before the artist knew the required measurements for the Reconciliation picture. This would place the sheet right at the time of the Medici cycle. She interpreted the drawings as proposals for the paintings' hanging in the *salón nuevo* in the Alcázar.

We should remember, however, that compositional drawings by Rubens are extremely rare in the second decade. There are but three small pen sketches known for the Medici cycle, for example, which would be close in time to the date of the Berlin drawing, as suggested in the latest corpus volume. A comparison with Rubens's drawing of about 1622 representing *Louis XIII Coming of Age*, in the Louvre (Fig. 23),[46] which is a quick first thought that will lead to a very different composition in the oil sketch in Munich before Rubens finalizes it in the painting for the Medici cycle, also in the Louvre. When the sheet in Berlin therefore includes not just two, but actually three such compositional drawings on one sheet – the third one is the *Meleager and Atalante* scene on the verso – we witness here a most inconsistent, unusual and unprecedented working procedure for Rubens.

The hastily drawn lower part, and in particular the flourishes in the rendering of Porsenna's armor, characterized by the late Hans Mielke[47] as 'schnörkelige Ziellosigkeit

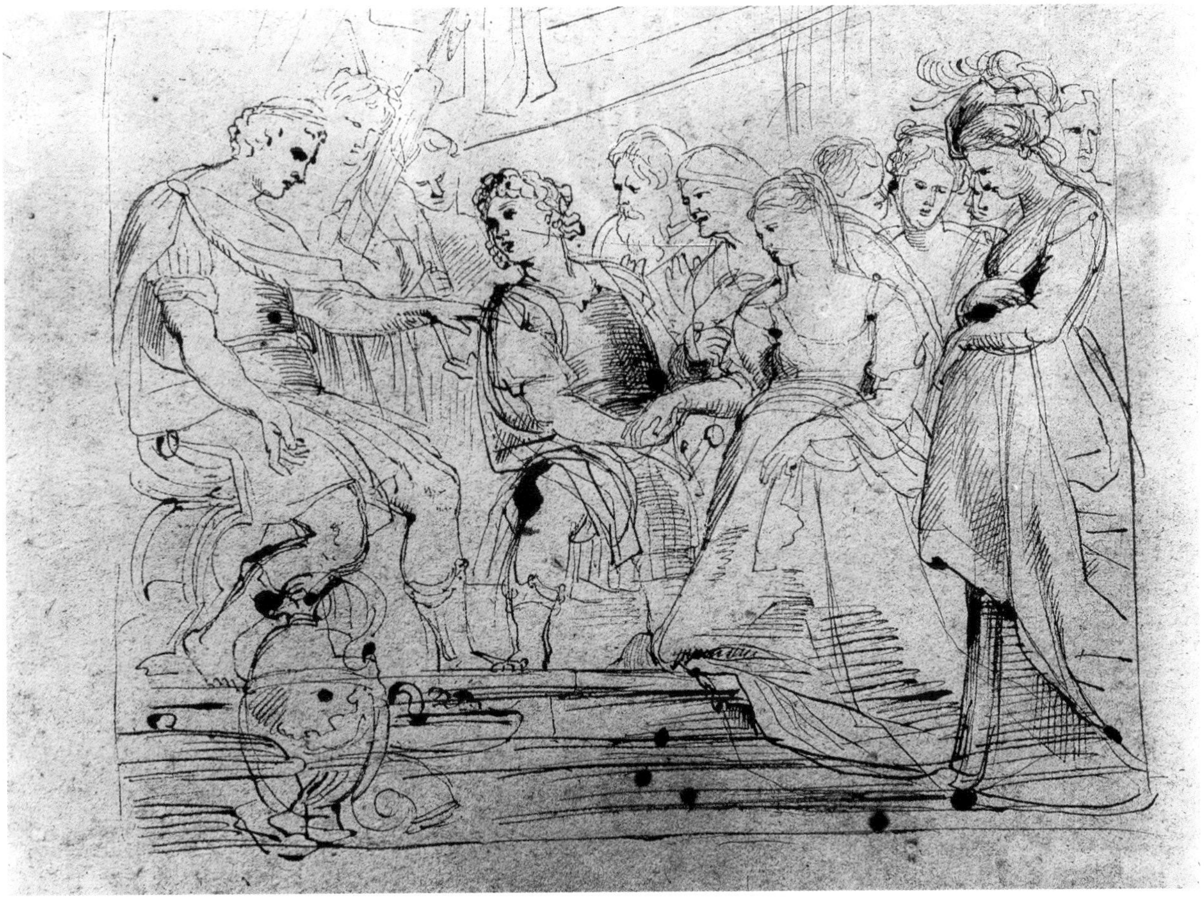

Fig. 20. Peter Paul Rubens, *The Continence of Scipio*. Bayonne, Musée Bonnat

des Federverlaufs', are difficult to reconcile with Rubens's fluid, sinuous lines as we saw in the Continence of Scipio scenes. When Rubens was in a hurry, as is exemplified in the just mentioned drawing for the Medici cycle (Fig. 23), he tended to be more abstract, linear and reduced the figures to angular outlines without flourishes. In the Louvre sheet, as seen earlier in the *Silenus and Aegle* drawing, Rubens abbreviated figural sketches by indicating the type of personage through hastily written identifications such as *prudentia*, *forza* and so on. What I am suggesting therefore is that the drawing most likely is not by Rubens, despite the fact that its attribution goes back to the seventeenth century and Matthäus Merian. Instead another artist all together comes to mind, namely Abraham van Diepenbeeck, who would have drawn these quick copies after Rubens's compositions around 1627, the year he designed the title page for Rosweyde's *Vitae patrum* in accordance to Rubens's instructions.

Van Diepenbeeck's drawing representing *Four Saints Distributing Alms* (Fig. 24)[48] in the Ecole nationale supérieure des Beaux-Arts, Paris, long considered to be by Rubens himself until Julius Held associated it with Van Diepenbeeck's oil sketch in Philadelphia, seems a most appropriate point of reference. In the Paris drawing we recognize strong reminiscences of Rubens, such as the blind man, approaching from the right who was adapted from Rubens's figure in his altar of the *Miracle of Saint Francis Xavier,* today in Vienna.[49] There exists a close similarity in the handling of the pen-lines, especially in the *Reconciliation* scene, with Van Diepenbeeck's drawing of the *Four Saints Distributing Alms*. In both examples the lines are not smooth but broken, and there is a certain scratchiness to the outlines, in addition to a density in the hatching that would be unusual for Rubens. Furthermore, the animals in the Berlin sheet are so ineptly drawn – in particular the cattle in the center, which are difficult to reconcile with the same artist, namely Rubens, who drew

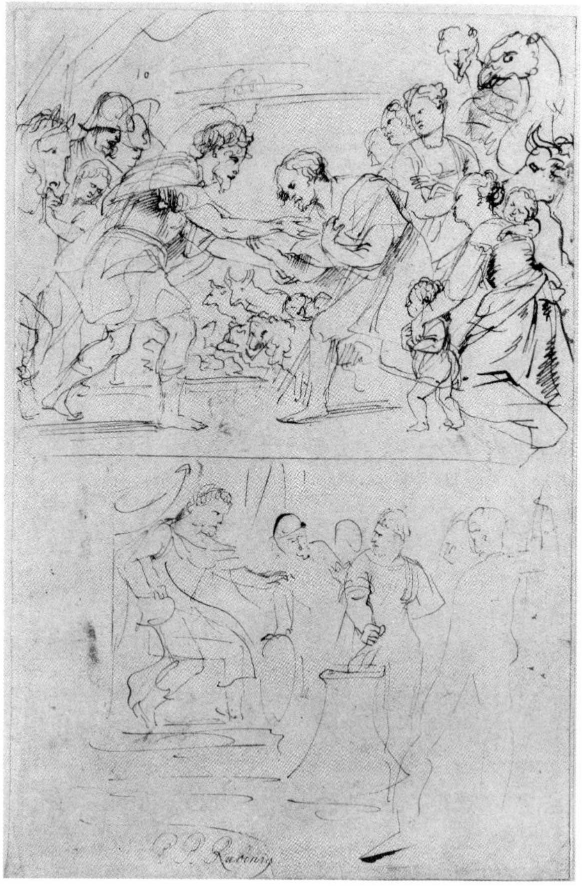

Fig. 21. Peter Paul Rubens (?), *The Reconciliation of Esau and Jacob / The Fortitude of Mucius Scaevola*. Berlin, Staatliche Museen, Kupferstichkabinett

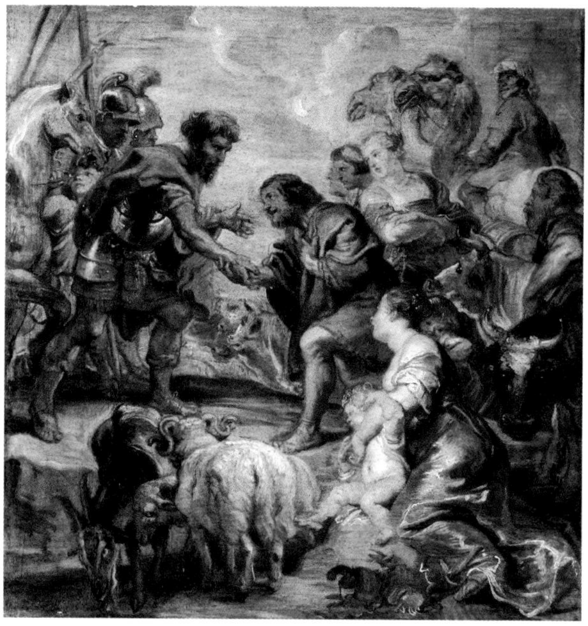

Fig. 22. Peter Paul Rubens, *The Reconciliation of Esau and Jacob*, oil sketch. Edinburgh, National Gallery of Scotland

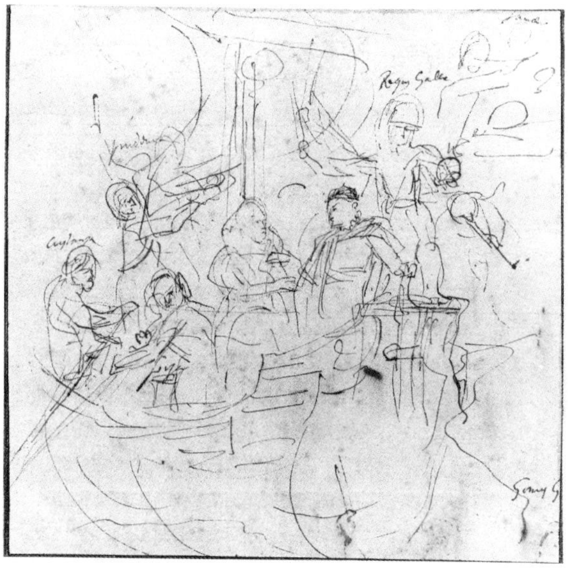

Fig. 23. Peter Paul Rubens, *Louis XIII Comes of Age*. Paris, Musée du Louvre, Département des Arts Graphiques

during those very same years, 1618–1620, at least one of the extraordinary pen studies of cows, known in two almost identical versions in Chatsworth and the British Museum.[50]

The few compositional studies of the 1630s that have been preserved show Rubens drawing with a much thicker, but still free flowing pen on coarse, heavily absorbent paper. Furthermore, the trend to break up the composition into individual figural groups, remarked upon earlier in the *Silenus and Aegle* drawing of the middle of the second decade, culminates in the early 1630s in the *Studies of Peasants Dancing* (Fig. 25), a very large, double-sided sheet in the British Museum,[51] which Rubens filled with figure studies drawn in connection with the painting of the *Flemish Kermesse* in the Louvre,[52] dated to the early 1630s. The recto is covered with seventeen studies of peasant couples dancing. Rubens began with black chalk, but reworked those figures that seemed to matter to him more with pen and brown ink, often introducing some changes. Some of the dancers' movements are repeated up to three times, almost as if Rubens was carried along with their rhythmic motions. Despite the drawing's size and the sheer number of figures, not to mention the complexity of placing so many twisting and swirling figures on the sheet without losing legibility, we easily move along with Rubens and follow the couples' dancing

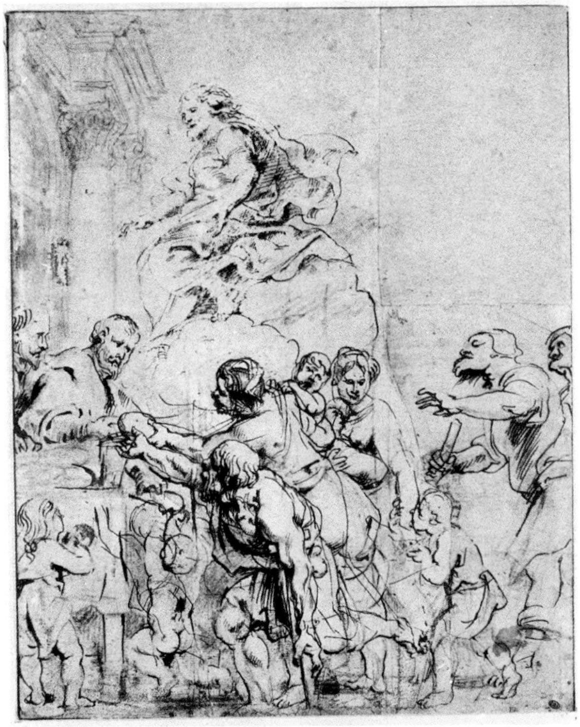

Fig. 24. Abraham van Diepenbeeck, *Four Saints Distributing Alms*. Paris, Ecole Nationale Supérieure des Beaux-Arts

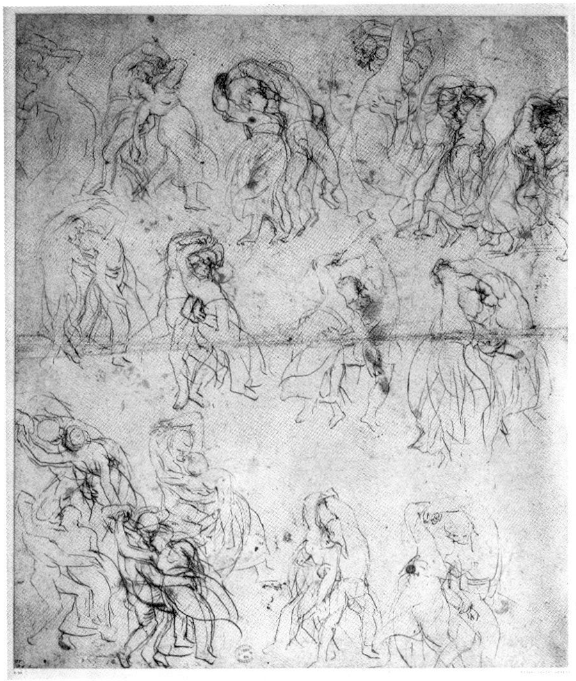

Fig. 25. Peter Paul Rubens, *Peasants Dancing*. London, British Museum

from many different angles. In this case it is difficult to venture a sequence in which Rubens progressed.

Although Rubens studied the individual groups seemingly at random and without assigning them a final place, he did incorporate a number of them in the painting, at times even reversing their sequence. Left are the barest outlines, pentimenti are more common, gone is the brushwork, gone are the modeling and details. Where once we saw carefully prepared compositions we now witness a free form, open-ended approach to composing which seems to reflect the great pleasure Rubens must have experienced when drawing these images toward the end of his life.

NOTES

1. Julius S. Held, *Rubens, Selected Drawings*, London, 1959; revised edition Mount Kisco, NY, 1986.

2. Held 1959 (see note 1), cat. 66, pl. 74 and color plate facing p. 64 [*c.* 1635–1637]; Held 1986 (see note 1), cat. 229, color plate 8 [*c.* 1635–1637].

3. Julius S. Held, *The Oil Sketches of Peter Paul Rubens*, Princeton, N.J., 2 vols., 1980, cat. 244, pl. 254 [*c.* 1634–1635].

4. Michael Jaffé, *Rubens: catalogo completo* (trans. Germano Mulazzani), Milan, 1989, cat. 1353 [*c.* 1637–1638].

5. Held 1959 (see note 1), cat. 114, pl. 125 [*c.* 1630–1632]; Held 1986 (see note 1), cat. 200, pl. 191 [*c.* 1630–1632]; [cat. exh.] *The Princes Gate Collection*, London, Courtauld Institute Galleries, 1981, cat. 147, repr. in color; Hans Vlieghe, *Rubens Portraits of Identified Sitters painted in Antwerp*, Corpus Rubenianum Ludwig Burchard, XIX, 2, London–New York, 1987, cat. 100a, Fig. 105 [for the Louvre portrait].

6. Vlieghe 1987 (see note 5), cat. 100, figs. 103–104 [*c.* 1639]; Jaffé 1989 (see note 4), cat. 1400 [*c.* 1639].

7. Held 1959 (see note 1), cat. 98, pl. 100 and color plate facing p. 16 [*c.* 1619]; Held 1986 (see note 1), cat. 144, pl. 156 [*c.* 1619].

8. Jaffé 1989 (see note 4), cat. 541 [*c.* 1619–1620]; Bernhard Schnackenburg, *Staatliche Museen Kassel. Gemäldegalerie Alte Meister, Gesamtkatalog*, 2 vols., Mainz, 1996, I, pp. 262–263, cat. GK 119; II, pl. 40 [*c.* 1619].

9. F.M. Haberditzl, 'Über einige Handzeichnungen von Rubens in der Albertina', *Die graphischen Künste*, XXXV, 1912, pp. 2–7.

10. Held 1959 (see note 1), cat. 97, pl. 111 [*c.* 1618–1620]; Held 1986 (see note 1), cat. 142, pl. 140 [*c.* 1618–1620].

11. Konrad Renger, [cat. exh.] *Die Pranke des Löwen*, Munich, Neue Pinakothek, 1997–1998, cat. 1a, Fig. 1.

12. Held 1959 (see note 1), cat. 102, pl. 112 [*c.* 1622]; Held 1986 (see note 1), cat. 157, pl. 153 [*c.* 1622].

13. Held 1980 (see note 3), under cat. 58.

14. J.G. van Gelder, 'Rubens Marginalia I', *The Burlington Magazine*, CXX, 1978, p. 457.

15. Hans Vlieghe, *Saints I*, Corpus Rubenianum Ludwig Burchard, London, 1972, cat. 54, pl. 96 [*c.* 1614]; Jaffé 1989 (see note 4), cat. 259 [*c.* 1614].

16. Held 1959 (see note 1), cat. 119, pl. 134 [*c.* 1632–1635]; Held 1986 (see note 1), cat. 209, pl. 202 [*c.* 1632].

17. Martin Eidelberg, 'An Album of Drawings from Rubens' Studio', *Master Drawings*, XXXV, 3, 1997, pp. 235–236, 246, Fig. 27 [as Rubens workshop].

18. John Rowlands, [cat. exh.] *Rubens: Drawings and Sketches*, London, British Museum, 1977, cat. 151 [as Rubens].

19. Ludwig Burchard and R.A. d'Hulst, *Rubens Drawings*, 2 vols., Brussels, 1963, cat. 31, pl. 31 [*c.* 1606; not in Held 1959 (see note 1)]; Arlette Sérullaz, [cat. exh.] *Rubens, ses maîtres, ses élèves*, Paris, Musée du Louvre, 1977, cat. 5, repr.

20. Matías Díaz Padrón, *El Siglo de Rubens en el Museo del Prado*, 3 vols., Madrid, 1996, pp. 878–881, cat. 1644, repr. in color.

21. Inv. 1983:84 Z. Pen and brown ink, brush and brown wash, over black chalk, heightened with white, 673 x 410 mm; strip of paper, added at top, 88 mm. high. See Thea Vignau-Wilberg, 'Rubens' Study in Munich for "The Duke of Lerma" on Horseback', *Master Drawings*, XXXVI, 3, 1998, pp. 275–287, repr. in color; Díaz Padrón 1996 (see note 20), pp. 1066–1067, repr. in color.

22. Díaz Padrón 1996 (see note 20), pp. 1064–1067, cat. 3137, repr. in color. Other recent studies where Rubens's portrait of Lerma is discussed are Xanthe Brooke, *The Patronage and Art Collection of the Duke of Lerma* (M.Phil. thesis), London, Courtauld Institute, 1983, which laid the ground work for Susan Schroth's investigation (as she acknowledged in her introduction), *The Private Picture Collection of the Duke of Lerma* (Ph.D. diss. New York University), Ann Arbor, MI, 1990, pp. 11, 24, 27, 49, 99–102, 111, Fig. 8. Further discussions are found in Simon A. Vosters, *Rubens y España*, Madrid, 1990, pp. 41–45, no. 1.3.; and W. Alexander Vergara, *The Presence of Rubens in Spain*, 2 vols. (Ph.D. diss. New York University), Ann Arbor, MI, 1994, pp. 3, 7 and cat. A74, Fig. 25, A75–A76; Alexander Vergara, *Rubens and His Spanish Patrons*, Cambridge, 1999, pp. 11–17.

23. Frits Lugt, *Musée du Louvre. Inventaire général des Ecoles du Nord. Ecole Flamande*, II, Paris, 1949, no. 1018, pl. XIX.

24. Schroth 1990 (see note 22), p. 10–11. Xanthe Brooke (e-mail of 22 June 1998) assumed that the cavalry 'charge' in the background alluded to Lerma's nomination to the honorary post of Captain General of the Cavalry at the time Rubens painted his portrait.

25. Sarah Schroth has an idea who the rider is and will publish it in the near future (verbal communication, 27 July 1998). Xanthe Brooke (e-mail of 22 June 1998) kindly informed me that the Duke of Lerma had been granted the encomienda of Merida of the Order of Santiago in 1580, based on Augusto de Burgos, *Blason de España*, 1858, III, p. 623 and Salazar de Mendoza, 'Chronico de la Casa de Sandoval. 1600 elogio XXI' (manuscript preserved in a private collection, Madrid). She pointed out, however that the order of Santiago was also missing from Pompeo Leoni's tomb sculpture of Lerma, cast in gilt bronze in 1608. The order's absence in either drawing probably is to be explained by the fact that the portrayed is not the Duke of Lerma himself.

26. Lugt 1949 (see note 23), no. 1018; Held 1959 (see note 1), cat. 71, pl. 83; Sérullaz 1978 (see note 19), cat. 1; Held 1986 (see note 1), cat. 26, pl. 38 [1603]; Díaz Padrón 1996 (see note 20), pp. 1066–1067, repr. in color.

27. Besides Lugt (see note 23) also Manuel Lorente, 'Sobre algunos retratos de Rubens en España', *Miscellanea Prof. Dr. D. Roggen*, Antwerp, 1957, pp. 184, 191. Sarah Schroth kindly informed me (verbally) that she found no mention in the Lerma archives of another work by Rubens pertaining to this commission; see also Sarah Schroth, *Los inventarios del Duque de Lerma*, I, *Las Pinturas*, Toledo, 2000 (forthcoming).

28. John Smith, *A Catalogue Raisonné of the Works of the Most Eminent Dutch, Flemish and French Painters*, II, London, 1830, p. 134, cat. 465.

29. See *Musée du Louvre. Cabinet des Dessins. Répertoire systématique des Fonds, Collections 1, Dessins de la Collection Everard Jabach acquis en 1671 pour la collection royale*, Paris, 1978, Liste A.

30. Erwin Mitsch, [cat. exh.] *Die Rubenszeichnungen der Albertina*, Vienna, Albertina, 1977, cat. 3, ill. in color [*c.* 1602].

31. Held 1959 (see note 1), cat. 17, pl. 19 [1608]; Mitsch 1977 (see note 30), cat. 5, ill. in color; Held 1986 (see note 1), cat. 42, pl. 43 [1608].

32. Held 1980 (see note 3), cat. 397, pl. 387 and color plate 1 [1608]; Jaffé 1989 (see note 4), cat. 76 [1608].

33. Jaffé 1989 (see note 4), cat. 82A [1608].

34. Michael Jaffé, 'Peter Paul Rubens and the Oratorian Fathers', *Proporzioni*, IV, 1959, Appendix, Fig. 51.

35. Held 1959 (see note 1), cat. 29, pl. 30 [*c.* 1611–1613]; Held 1986 (see note 1), cat. 81–82, pls. 77–78 [*c.* 1612–1614]; Christopher White and Charlotte Crawley, *The Dutch and Flemish Drawings of the Fifteenth to the Early Nineteenth Centuries in the Collection of Her Majesty the Queen at Windsor Castle*, Cambridge, 1994, cat. 435, repr. [*c.* 1611–1613 or *c.* 1612–1614].

36. Svetlana Alpers, *The Making of Rubens*, New Haven–London, 1995, pp. 141–146, pl. 112, repr. in color.

37. Elizabeth McGrath, in Alpers 1995 (see note 36), p. 142.

38. Held 1959 (see note 1), cat. 38, pl. 40 [*c.* 1615–1617]; Hans Mielke and Matthias Winner, [cat. exh.] *Peter Paul Rubens. Kritischer Katalog der Zeichnungen. Originale - Umkreis - Kopien*, Berlin, Kupferstichkabinett, 1977, cat. 24, repr. [*c.* 1615–1617]; Held 1986 (see note 1), cat. 123, pl. 123 [*c.* 1617–1618].

39. Held 1959 (see note 1), cat. 39, pl. 41 [*c.* 1615–1617]; Held 1986 (see note 1), cat. 124, pl. 124 [*c.* 1617–1618].

40. Burchard and d'Hulst 1963 (see note 19), cat. 80, pl. 80 [ricordo of lost Rubens sketch; *c.* 1616–1618]; Held 1980 (see note 4), under cat. 286 [*c.* 1617–1619] and 310; R.-A. d'Hulst and M. Vandenven, *Rubens. The Old Testament*, Corpus Rubenianum Ludwig Burchard, III, London–New York, 1989, cat. 15, Fig. 41 [*c.* 1616–1618]; Vergara 1994 (see note 22), pp. 38–43, and cat. A53, A97, Fig. 31 and Vergara 1999 (see note 22), pp. 45–53, 183 ans 210–211, note 104. See also Gary Schwartz, 'Love in the Kunstkamer. Additions to the Work of Guillam van Haecht (1593–1637)', *Tableau*, XVIII, 6, 1996, pp. 48–51, repr. in color; the Berlin drawing is reproduced as 'Pieter Paul Rubens?'. Schwartz (letter of 11 December 1997) now favors an attribution of the drawing to Guillam van Haecht (Willem van Haecht II), especially if compared to Van Haecht's etchings.

41. Held 1980 (see note 4), cat. 310, pl. 312 [*c.* 1624–1626]; d'Hulst and Vandenven 1989 (see note 40), cat. 16a, Fig. 43 [*c.* 1625–1628]; Jaffé 1989 (see note 4), cat. 862 [*c.* 1625–1626].

42. d'Hulst and Vandenven 1989 (see note 40), cat. 16, Fig. 42 [*c.* 1625–1628]; Jaffé 1989, cat. 863 [*c.* 1626–1628].

43. See note 40 above.

44. Held 1980 (see note 4), under cat. 310, p. 428.

45. Elizabeth McGrath, *Rubens, Subjects from History*, Corpus Rubenianum Ludwig Burchard, XIII, 2 vols., London, 1997, cat. 46a, Fig. 162 [*c.* 1622–1623]. Gary Schwartz (see note 40 above) favors an attribution of the drawing to Guillam van Haecht (Willem van Haecht II).

46. Held 1959 (see note 1), cat. 50 verso, pl. 53 [*c.* 1622]; Held 1986 (see note 1), cat. 159, pl.157 [ca.1622].

47. Mielke and Winner 1977 (see note 38), cat. 27, p. 76.

48. Held 1959 (see note 1), p. 8, note 1 and figs. 8 [drawing] and 9 [oil sketch in Philadelphia]; David W. Steadman, *Abraham van Diepenbeeck*, Ann Arbor, MI, 1982, pp. 10–11 [still accepts it as by Rubens; publishes a more hastily drawn study in Rennes (his Fig. 13) as Diepenbeeck's preliminary study for the oil sketch which in turn was preparatory to a stained glass window in the entrance way to the Church of the Beggars, Antwerp, preserved in fragments only; his figs. 14–15]; Emmanuelle Brugerolles, *Les dessins de la collection Armand-Valton*, Paris (Ecole Nationale Supérieure des Beaux-Arts), 1984, cat. 169, repr.

49. Hans Vlieghe, *Saints II*, Corpus Rubenianum Ludwig Burchard, VIII, London–New York, 1973, cat. 104. A working proof of Marinus van der Goes after Rubens's altarpiece, which Rubens extended on both sides by 8–10 mm, was recently acquired by the Albertina, Vienna. In black chalk Rubens also added legs and feet to the cripples in the foreground at the left, altered the gravedigger's knee and face, and introduced retouches with gray and black wash and white bodycolor (see C.G. Boerner, *Schongauer bis Whistler. Die schönsten Neuerwerbungen. Graphik aus fünf Jahrhunderten, Neue Lagerliste Nr. 104*, 1995, no. 27, repr. in color). These changes were all incorporated in the engraving of *c.* 1633–1635 (see Vlieghe 1973, Fig. 16, under cat. 104h).

50. Held 1959 (see note 1), p. 12, Fig. 21.

51. Held 1959 (see note 1), cat. 57, pls. 70–71; 67–69 [*c.* 1629–1632]; Held 1986 (see note 1), cat. 193–194, pls. 184–185 and frontispiece [*c.* 1630–1632]; Alpers 1995 (see note 36), figs. 28–29, repr. in color.

52. Jaffé 1989 (see note 4), cat. 1213 [*c.* 1635–1638].

III. Execution

The Execution of Flemish Paintings between 1550 and 1700: A Survey of the Main Stages

Hans Vlieghe

The execution of a painting may be said to relate to the final result of the process of creation. It starts at the moment the artist enters his workshop to make his preparations. It ends when the final result is displayed and accepted. It is my aim to go into the various stages of this process in the light of an anthology of relevant documentary evidence from the later sixteenth and from the seventeenth centuries.

Time of Execution

The expected duration of commissioned paintings is normally described in detailed contracts. For various reasons it was often necessary to extend the deadline. Usually payment was made in three instalments. Thus an instalment might be paid in advance at the signing of the contract, a second instalment might be expected when the work was half completed, while the remaining instalment was due after the work had been delivered.

The free market and growing demand encouraged painters to find technical means and devices to enable them to increase their output. We know from Montias's investigations how this affected specific stylistic changes in seventeenth-century Dutch art, such as a more sketchlike treatment and a more economic use of colours.[1] Montias's remarks can also be applied to the Southern Netherlands. Especially seventeenth-century Antwerp witnessed a boom in workshops and workshop clusters producing pictures 'en masse' for cheaper national and international markets. A specific aspect

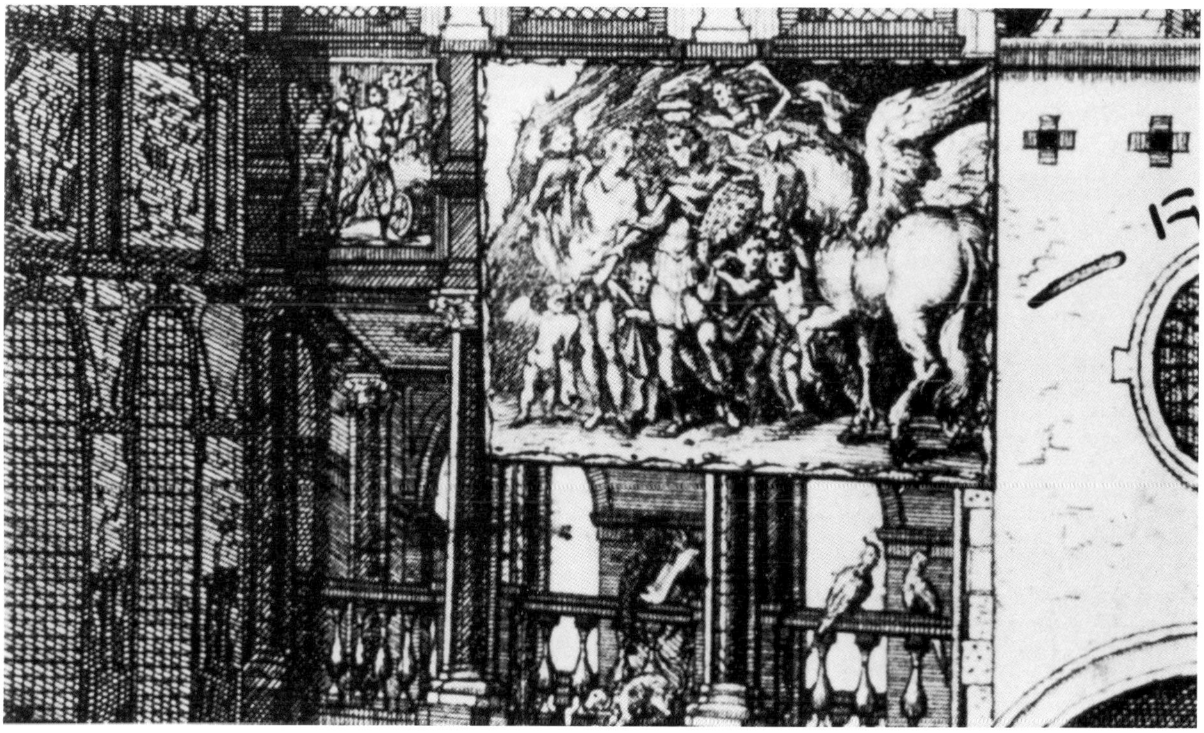

Fig. 1. Jacobus Harrewyn, *View of the Garden Façade of Rubens's House*, detail, engraving

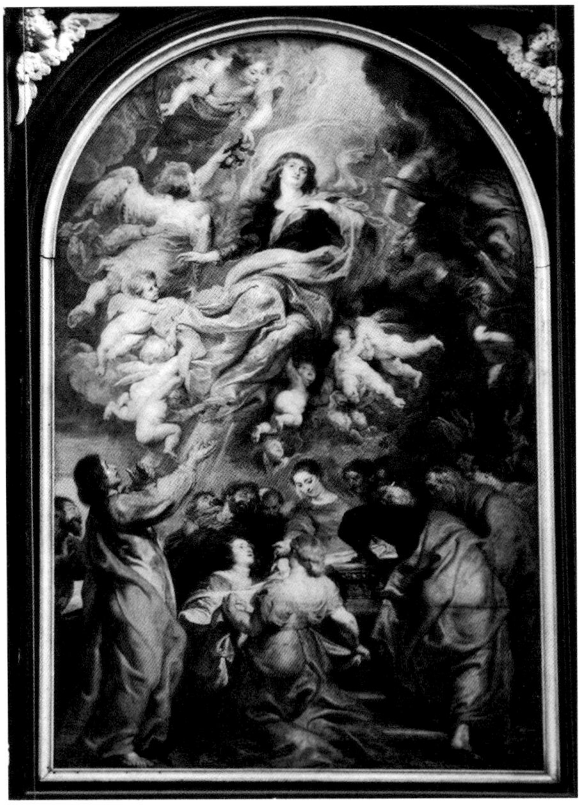

Fig. 2. Peter Paul Rubens, *The Assumption of the Holy Virgin*. Antwerp, Cathedral

of this 'pre-industrial' system was the emergence of labour-sharing devices such as the production of paintings jointly executed by specialists in various aspects of painting.[2]

Rather accurate comments on the state of execution are quite common in seventeenth-century descriptions and listings of pictures. Thus it is striking to find such distinctions as those between paintings that were 'onvolmaeckt', 'beghost', or 'voltooid'. But there are also more precise descriptions, especially on the initial state of execution, clearly defined by terms such as 'doodtverwe' or 'gheprimueerden doeck'. Normally a painter did not complete one painting before starting the next, but was working on several paintings at the same time, dividing his efforts as economically as possible over a number of paintings in varying states of execution. This working method is recorded clearly in the notebook of the young Pieter van Lint and provides a very rare and detailed account of the workshop practice of an Antwerp painter active in the mid and late twenties of the seventeenth century.[3]

After its completion a painting had to dry for a certain length of time. Here Rubens's correspondence is very informative. In May 1618 he writes that his pictures for Sir Dudley Carleton '... are not yet thoroughly dry, and still need to remain on the stretchers for some days before they can be rolled without risk'. And he adds: 'In this fine weather they will be put out in the sun'.[4] It has been convincingly suggested that the 'trompe l'oeil' painting of a Perseus freeing Andromeda which once appeared on the garden façade of Rubens's workshop (Fig. 1), was intended to create the illusion of a painting hung in the sun for drying.[5]

The place of execution

The normal place for the execution of an easel painting was the workshop of an artist. In regard to the contents of a workshop information can be found in probate inventories or other documents about goods found in artists' houses at the time of their death.[6] Among the usual descriptions of furniture and home decoration, we often find detailed information on e.g. the material of the support used by the painter, on utensils for grinding and mixing pigments, on plaster casts based on ancient sculpture, on prints after famous Italian compositions, on books about the theory of art, books containing technical information, and works on ancient mythology, Roman history, numismatics, etc. In rare instances this documentary evidence can be completed by means of visual evidence from drawings by young assistants of the contents of their masters' studios. The most interesting example is, of course, the famous Copenhagen set of drawings made in Rubens's 'Cantoor' by his pupil Willem Panneels.[7]

The growth of an artist's production can be deduced from the size and/or enlargement of his house and/or workshop. We are well informed about the construction and rebuilding of the houses of such painters as Frans Floris, P.P. Rubens, Jacob Jordaens and David Teniers the Younger.[8] The dates of construction of these houses are known to us and coincide with the time of the establishment of their owners' reputations as artists. At the same time the size and specific decoration of these houses also expressed the self-consciousness of such leading artists. The growing activity of these painters demanded adequate space. A specific case is that of Cornelis Schut, who in search of

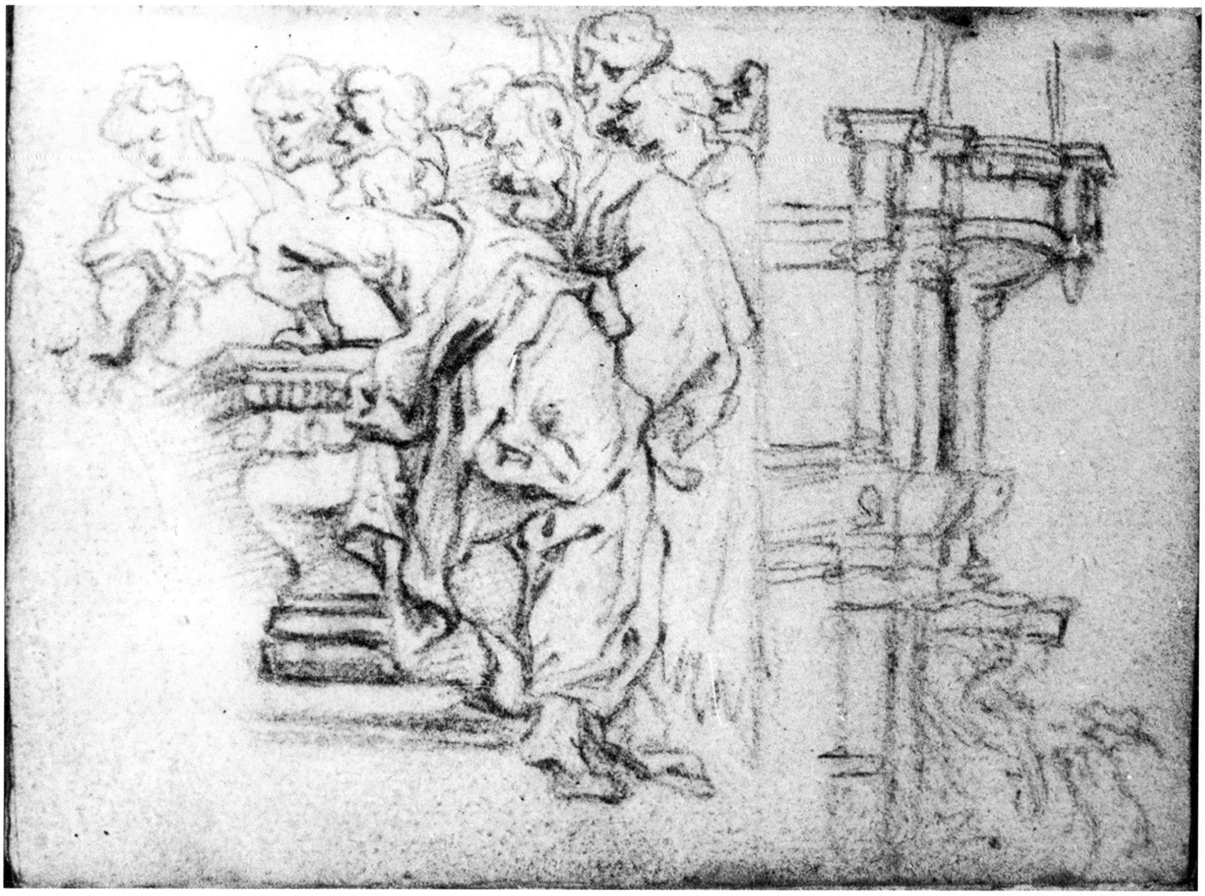

Fig. 3. Pieter van Lint, Page from a Notebook, with Details from Rubens's *Assumption of the Holy Virgin*, drawing. Paris, Institut Néerlandais, Fondation Custodia

space even left Antwerp in 1652, in order to purchase the 'Huis met den toren' in Borgerhout. We also know that Schut had ordered a carpenter to construct him there a workshop measuring *c.* 10 by *c.* 6 m.[9]

In some cases it became necessary to complete a painting at its destination. Thus we are informed how Rubens in 1626 finished his *Assumption* for the high altar of Antwerp cathedral 'in situ', especially after the extension of the panel to the right with a strip measuring *c.* 20 cm., for which extra wooden panels had to be added (Fig. 2).[10] A drawing by Pieter van Lint in his notebook, which I already mentioned, gives us an idea of what Rubens's altarpiece looked like, just before its necessary extension (Fig. 3).[11] Obvious practical reasons also urged Jan Cossiers in 1655 to finish his enormous *Passion* scenes on the spot, i.e. placed between ogival bays at the end of the choir of the Beguinage church in Malines (Fig. 4). However, the Malines painters guild prevented Cossiers from carrying out his plan, a protectionist reaction which obliged him to take his canvases back to Antwerp in order to retouch them there.[12] This incident provoked a violent reaction from Cossiers's Antwerp fellow-artists, who stated that in their town it was usual for Antwerp as well as for non-Antwerp painters to retouch altarpieces after their instalment in the appropriate church and to add and correct whatever seemed necessary to them. The terms of this document make it clear that completion on the spot at their destination was certainly not an uncommon practice at least for altarpieces.[13]

Material aspects

For commissioned works especially, preference for specific materials was strongly determined by local tradition. Thus the fact that in Flanders old-fashioned triptychs remained in demand until the thirties of the seventeenth century (and in certain cases even beyond that date)

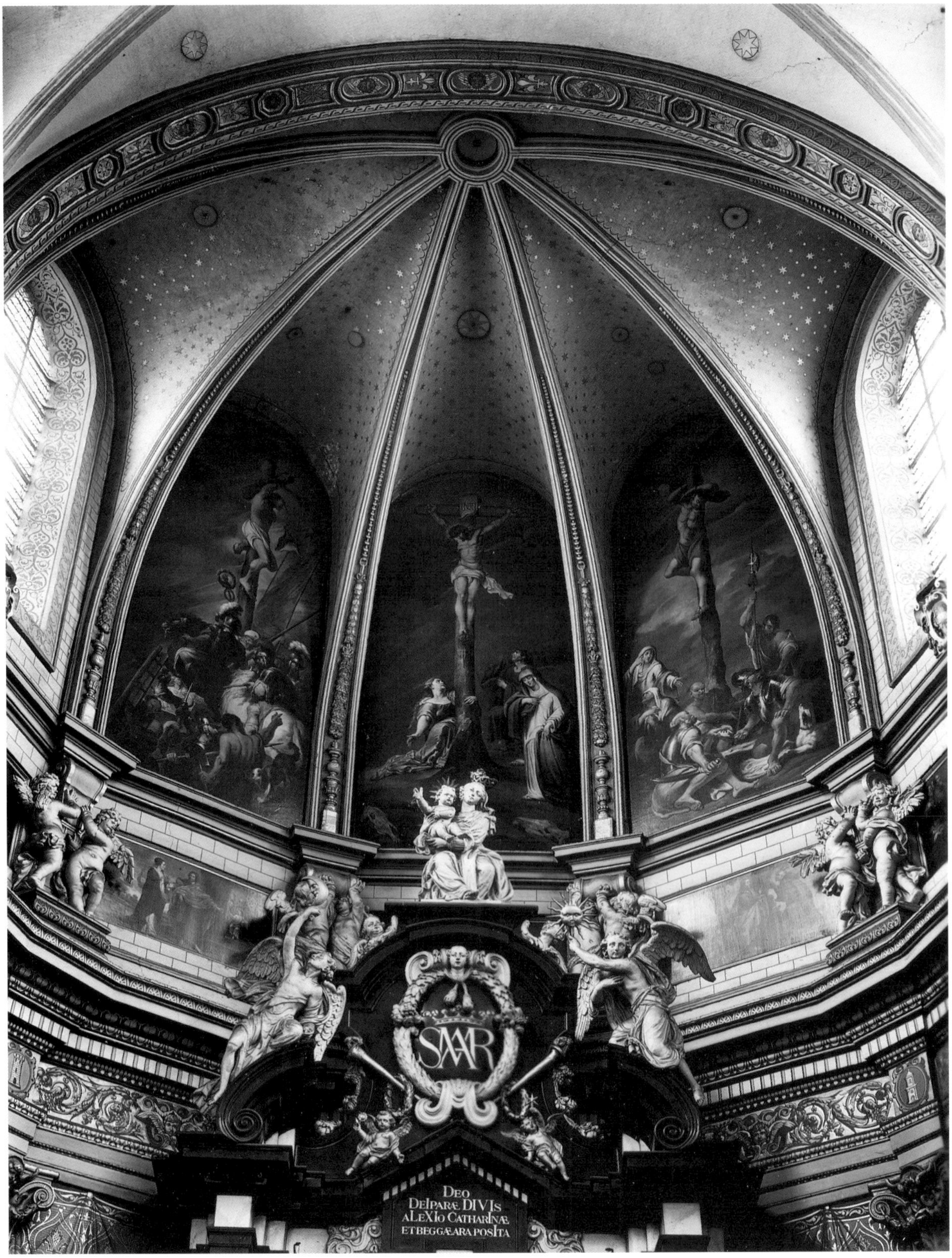

Fig. 4. Jan Cossiers, *The Passion of Christ*. Malines, Beguinage Church

may partially explain the long-lasting use of oak supports.[14] But also apart from their connection with traditional devotional imagery, oak panels, often branded with the guild marks of the renowned Antwerp panel makers as an established form of quality control, long remained in use as the customary support material.[15] However, from the forties onward, and certainly by the middle of the seventeenth century canvas had become the more usual choice.

It was the free market rather than commissioned works that stimulated the use of less weighty and cheaper supports than wood. It is unnecessary to refer here to the importance of the fifteenth-century 'Tüchlein'.[16] And we are also familiar with the importance of the 'waterschilders' from Malines, who specialized in landscape paintings on canvas, intended for the cheaper end of the market.[17] In the seventeenth century, besides canvas, metal, especially copper plate, also became used as a support for cabinet-sized paintings intended for exportation. Increasingly metal plate seems to have been preferred for trade in often rather cheap devotional imagery intended for Spain and its South American colonies. It is not easy to discover specific reasons for this particular preference. These may have been esthetic, as metal plate could guarantee an even smoother surface than a primed wooden panel. On the other hand, this particular kind of support may also have been considered appropriate for the export trade, as it was less vulnerable than either wood or canvas; in particular, it may have proved very stable when submitted to climatic changes.[18] Supports must have been purchased both in a prepared as well as in unprepared condition. Inventories of goods and the correspondence and account books of the seventeenth-century art trade in Antwerp refer to both kinds.[19]

Linked to serial production is the standardizing of formats. For Flemish sixteenth- and seventeenth-century art there is extensive documentation. Again, inventories and records from the art trade are a mine of information. It has also become clear how differences and variations in sizes and types refer to prices (e.g.: 'stuyversmate'), provide measurements (e.g.: 'enckelen doeck' or 'dobbelen doeck'), or refer to a specific function (e.g.: 'troniepaneel', i.e. the size of a 'tronie').[20]

The mere fact that certain standard measurements of supports were sometimes described by referring to their cost price makes it clear that there must certainly have been a proportional relationship between size and price. The lists of goods sold by Antwerp merchants such as Musson or the Forchondt firm demonstrate this very clearly.[21] Detailed lists of paintings pawned by their makers are also very instructive. Thus we are well informed about the value of the works of David Teniers the Elder.[22] But this more or less fixed connection between format and price was not merely the rule for commercialized art production. It also seems to have been usual for large-sized commissioned paintings, such as altarpieces. From the extensive but scattered information it becomes clear that for a large altarpiece measuring between 3 and 4 metres a price of *c.* 500 to 600 guilders had to be paid.[23]

Apparently only the most famous artists were able to impose their artistic 'surplus value' by demanding much higher prices. This was obviously the case with Rubens, who soon after his definitive establishment in Antwerp was renowned there as an expensive artist, reputed to be 'diere'.[24] Van Dyck may also be mentioned in this context, although only at the very end of his life. Shortly before his death in 1641, he was trying to settle in Antwerp again, and on that occasion he was asked to execute a painting for the altar of the guild of the Young Crossbowmen for no less than 2200 guilders.[25] But already in the sixteenth century originality of style, i.e. a certain artistic virtuosity, as a qualitative aspect, must have played a major role in determining prices. This may be conjectured from the fact that the income of a painter like Frans Floris was seven times that of a stonemason. Floris's excellence may have been due not least by his renowned originality of invention. His contemporary Guicciardini praised him for this reason[26], and in a very explicit way Floris emphasized this originality by proudly signing his works: 'Franciscus Floris Invenit et Fecit'.[24]

Aspects of Authenticity

That authenticity as a criterion for valuing and pricing paintings had long played an important role is clear from the obvious terminological difference made between 'principaelen' and 'copijen'.[28] In the case of Rubens we have several important indications of how much importance was attached to the fact that he himself had integrally executed a given painting.with his own hand. We only have to think here of the stipulations in the contract for the Medici series, in which it is specified that all of the paintings should be 'de sa propre main'.[29] And, of course, there is the well known and very enlightening correspondence dating from 1618 between Rubens and Sir Dudley Carleton.[30] Not only does Rubens's valuation of his own pictures offered to his British correspondent make evident the direct correlation between the authenticity of a painting and its high price, but it also offers an interesting insight into the various degrees of that authenticity. Rubens clearly distinguishes between those pictures entirely by himself and those executed, albeit under his supervision, by his assistants. And that these were not average trainees is made clear in the same documents, where mention is made of no less an artist than the young Anthony van Dyck.[31] Probably the most enlightening detail in Rubens's correspondence with Dudley Carleton is his notion about a specific category of paintings, begun by his assistants but finally entirely retouched by himself. Hence, he goes on, these too should be regarded and sold as originals 'da mia mano'.[32] As to those paintings finally touched up by himself, but largely executed by his most skilful assistants, we have evidence of several names, including those of Van Dyck, Jordaens, Boeckhorst and others.[33] This system must have been common practice in seventeenth-century Antwerp. In seventeenth-century probate inventories the specification that a painting was retouched or a retouched copy often appears quite apart from any connection with Rubens. Nevertheless, this 'elastic' interpretation of the concept of 'authenticity' may not have been generally accepted, and certainly was not in the case of artists with a rather modest profile. Thus Carel van Mander mentions that there were complaints about the painter Gillis Coignet who sold copies made by his pupils, after retouching them to some extent.[34]

A very illuminating example of how much value was attached to authenticity is the lawsuit of 1660–1662, which attempted to put an end to a discussion raised by the doubts advanced by Canon Hillewerve of Antwerp in regard to a set of paintings representing apostles which he purchased as Van Dyck's work. In order to arrive at a decision on the quality and genuineness of these works some of the most reputed painters in Antwerp were invited to testify both as experts and as contemporaries of Van Dyck.[35]

Such concerns about authenticity are, of course, directly linked to the type of workshop organization which, as from at least the middle of the sixteenth century, had become common practice in Antwerp, i.e. the close collaboration with the master of a staff of well-trained assistants, who were expected to copy partially or entirely the master's originals, in order to meet the demands of a constantly growing art trade. Indeed, among other examples the Van Dyck case of 1660–1662 may prove that the discussion on authenticity focused on whether or not the disputed paintings were to be considered originals or copies. A rather early example of how reputed artists made good use of the skills of their best-trained assistants in order to have their compositions multiplied is provided by the testimony of Frans Francken the Elder in 1576. In the document in question Francken declares that when he was still working as an assistant to Frans Floris, he had been ordered by the latter to make a copy of his *Caïn and Abel*. Francken also declares that he saw Floris executing the original.[36] We are familiar enough with the fact that Rubens had copies made almost continuously under his supervision.[37] But we also have information about copies of the works of many other artists. Thus, for instance, we know of copies of his own originals which De Crayer kept in his house in Brussels, with a view to having them sold on the free market.[38] An interesting case is that of the painter Marten Pepijn, who in 1626 protested against a painting being sold publicly in Antwerp as an original of his, despite the fact that it was a copy made by one of his pupils:[39] this is a very instructive testimony about how jealously the master himself wished to ensure that the originality of his own work should be respected.

In principle, making copies of the work of an established master was not tolerated without the latter's strict control. We know that painters very jealously tried to protect their inventions. We are familiar with Rubens's admonition to his assistant Lucas Faydherbe to take care 'that everything is well locked up, and that no originals remain upstairs in the studio, or any sketches', for the duration of his absence.[40] Recently another interesting document was published on Cornelis Schut, who

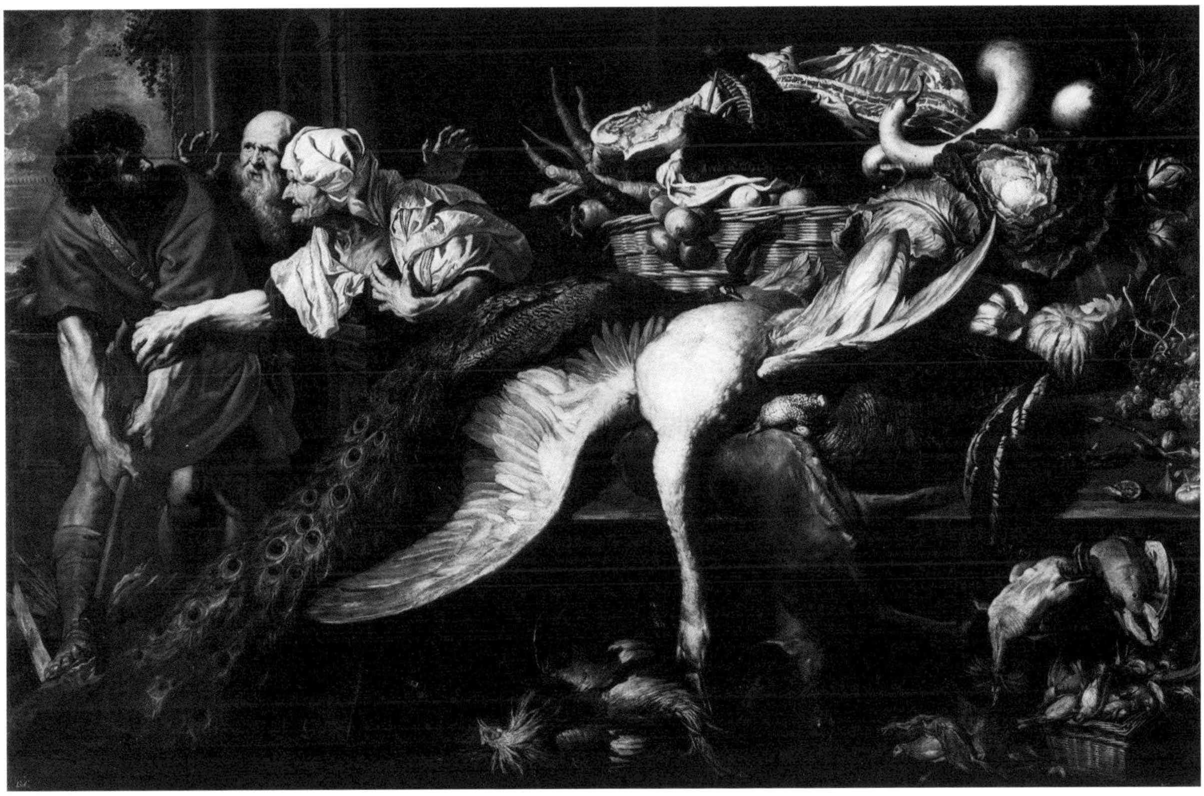

Fig. 5. Peter Paul Rubens and Frans Snyders, *Philopoemen*. Madrid, Museo del Prado

was very upset when his pupil Hans Popels took advantage of his master's absence in 1637, in order to take with him one of the latter's sketches and copy it secretly in his father's house in the form of a full-size painting.[41]

But the skills of those artists who in their youth were trained by reputed masters were also called on long after they had left their master's workshop and in their turn had established themselves as renowned masters. Thus Rubens sought the assistance of the more important Antwerp history painters, when in the late thirties he was ordered to execute his large painting cycles for the Pompa Introitus Ferdinandi and the Torre de la Parada.[42] Hence also painters who at the start of their careers had become familiar with a specific master's style were invited to finish or to retouch certain works left unfinished upon the master's death. Thus Jordaens finished certain paintings by Rubens[43] and work initially ordered from Gaspar de Crayer and Cornelis de Vos was posthumously executed by painters who had been trained by them.[44] An extremely interesting case arises from the will of the landscape painter Abraham Govaerts, dated 1629. Among other items, this document lists a number of unfinished works still in the house of the deceased artist at the time of his death. At the wish of Willem Govaerts, the brother of the deceased painter and the executor of his will, they were completed by no less than eleven painters who all had been familiar with Abraham Govaerts's specific studio practice.[45]

The collaboration described above between a renowned master and his pupils and/or assistants who worked according to his directives can best be described as the vertical workshop organization. Another form of artistic collaboration can be labelled "horizontal", i.e. the precise sharing of tasks among specialists. As we know, this highly specialized form of workshop activity goes back to the beginning of the emergence of the Antwerp pictorial tradition: already in the early decades of the sixteenth century the history painter Quinten Matsys worked together with the landscapist Joachim Patinir. From then on this form of task sharing remained characteristic for Antwerp painting. Probably in the same way also Frans Floris appealed to the skills of Hendrik van Cleef, for the execution of background vistas.[46] The clas-

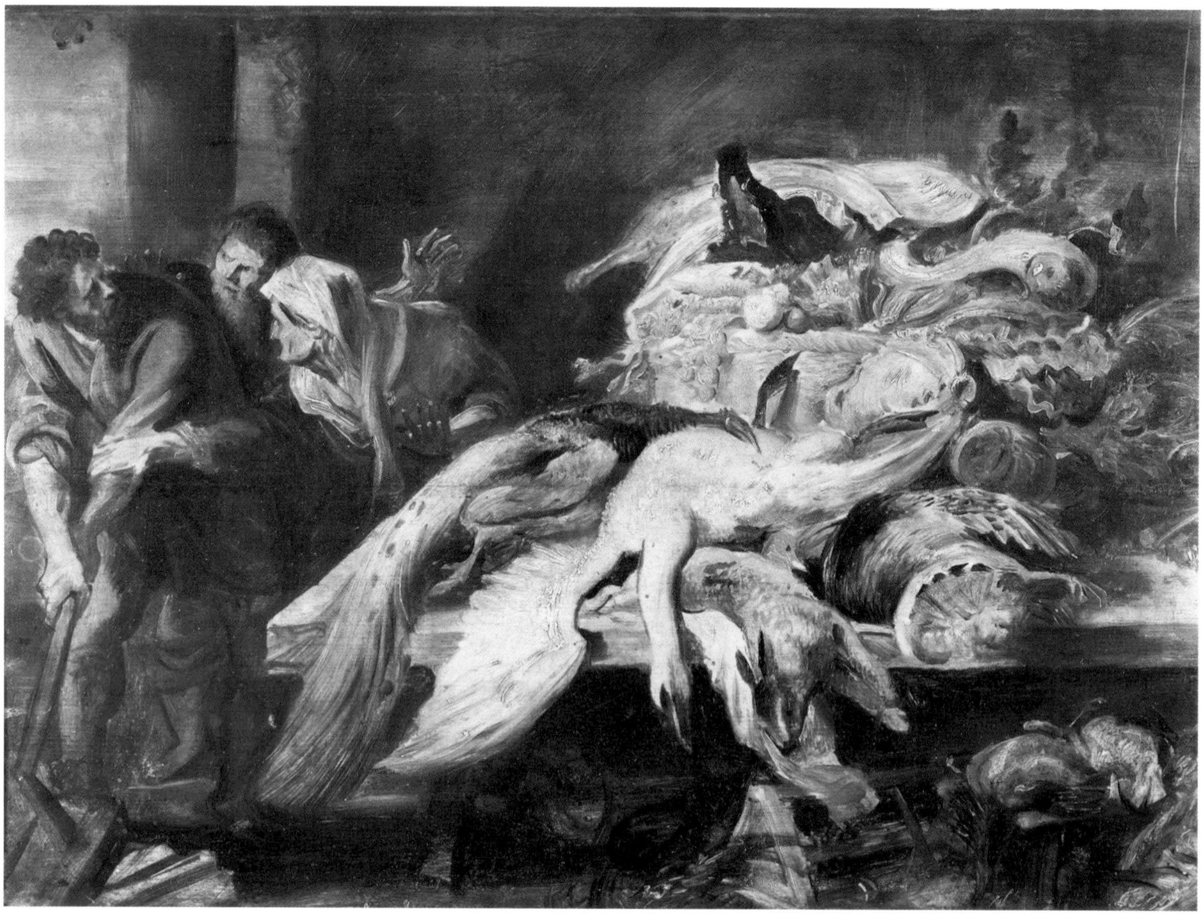

Fig. 6. Peter Paul Rubens, *Philopoemen*, oil sketch. Paris, Musée du Louvre

sical case is that of the history painter who wanted his compositions enlivened with still-life details or to have them opened up onto landscape vistas. Here again Rubens's practice offers the most striking examples. I need hardly refer here to his fruitful partnership – as Michael Jaffé once very aptly called it [47] – with Frans Snijders, Paul de Vos, Jan Wildens or Jan Brueghel. Although this specific form of workshop collaboration was based on what we may best describe as a form of 'equal partnership', in some very specific cases it is obvious how Rubens also took a hand in directing the execution of specific still-life details. A well-known case is that of the *Philopoemen* of *c.* 1610, which is now in the Prado (Fig. 5). The monumental kitchen still-life is a brilliant example of Frans Snijders's art. However, Rubens's modello, in the Louvre (Fig. 6), corresponds very closely to it, and this makes it very clear how in every respect Snijders had to follow Rubens's guidelines.[48] Indeed, the striking monumentality of this still-life was conceived by Rubens himself. We are also informed how other important artists likewise shared labour: in fact the greater part of established history painters in seventeenth-century Antwerp had specialized landscape or still-life painters 'hired' in to execute some of the details which did not form part of the 'historia'. We can even recognize specific clusters. The best-known case is that of Cornelis de Vos who worked in close connection with members of his own family, more especially with his brother Paul de Vos, and his brothers-in-law Frans Snijders and Jan Wildens (Fig. 7).[49] We also know that Theodoor Rombouts occasionally worked with Adriaen van Utrecht,[50] and that Abraham van Diepenbeeck and Pieter Thijs had their own specific contacts with Pieter Boel and Jan Fyt.[51]

We may wonder how these collaborative efforts came about. We can only guess how history painters and still-life and/or landscape specialists made their mutual arrangements. The most likely supposition seems to be that in the cases of paintings of a monumental size show-

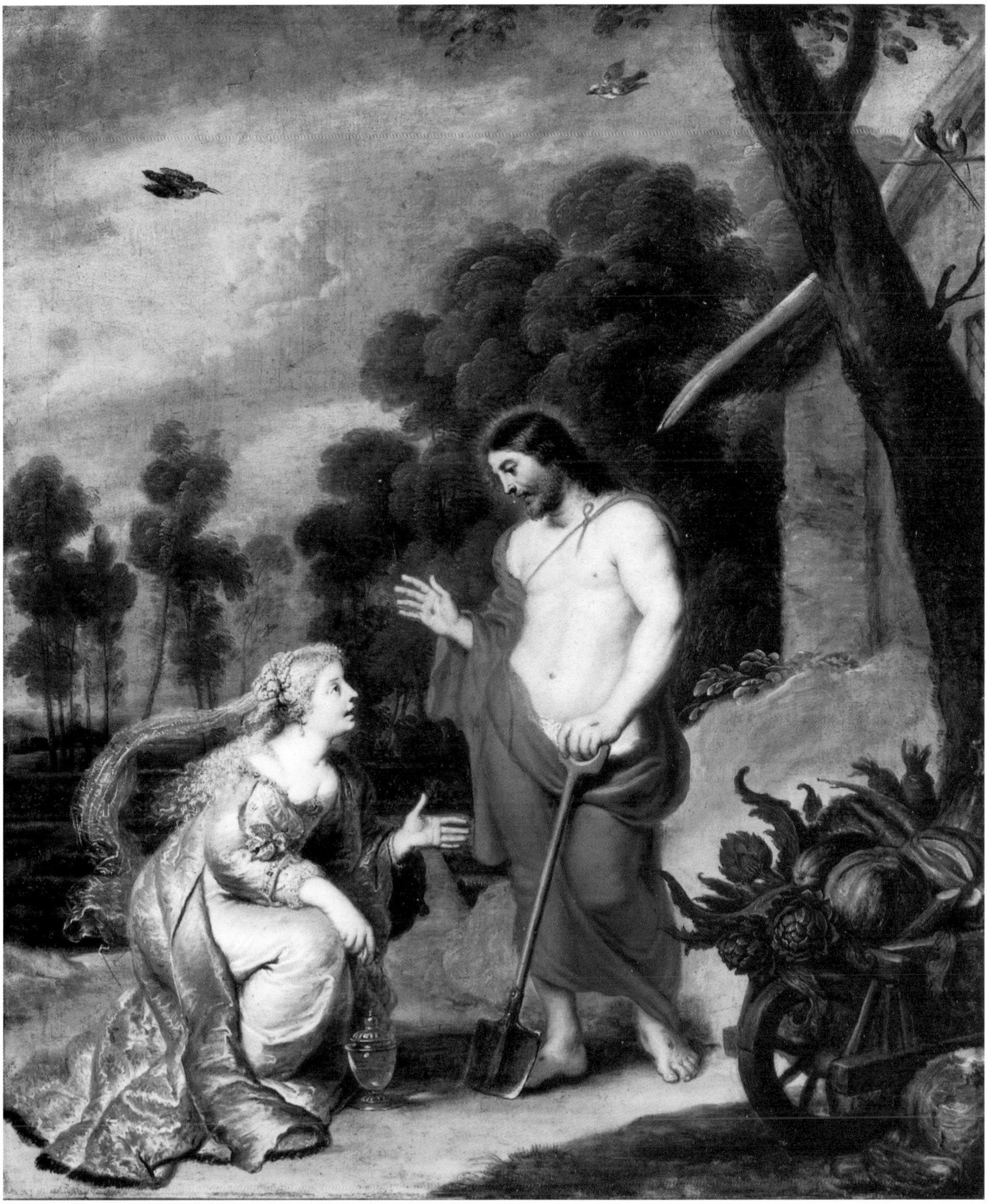

Fig. 7. Cornelis de Vos and Jan Wildens, *Noli Me Tangere*. Whereabouts unknown

ing life-size figures all the work was carried out in the workshop of the artist whose contribution was the more important one. Thus we may think of Frans Snijders inviting Cornelis de Vos to add one or two figures in order to enliven his monumental still-lifes, but that on the other hand De Vos himself would ask Jan Wildens to come over to his own house, in order to fill in a few landscape details in the background to his biblical or mythological scenes.[52] However, paintings executed as a joint effort were much more the rule in the area of smaller-scale, so-called cabinet-size work. It has been made clear in detailed monographs recently published on such artists as the two Jan Brueghels, Joos de Momper, and Frans Francken the Younger, how regularly these artists worked together with a large number of other specialists.[53] Smaller scale compositions may be supposed to have been more easily brought from one workshop to another. A clue to this practice may be found in the circumstance that a considerable number of landscape specialists engaged in relatively cheap serial work, so-called 'dozijnwerk', which was ordered by the leading art trade firms, such as those of Chrysostoom van Immerseel, Matthijs Musson or the Forchondt family, just to mention the more important ones. It has been shown how these dealers acted as genuine entrepreneurs, not only supplying the support material for 'their' artists but even ensuring that paintings were moved from the house of the landscape specialist to that of the figure or still-life painter, in order for them to be properly completed.[54] But also outside the circle of the 'bread and butter' artists it must have been a rather common practice that unfinished canvases or panels of a rather moderate size were thus transported from one workshop to another.[55] It is further interesting to know that certain still-life specialists, renowned for their flower wreaths intended to frame some devotional or other subjects, in a number of cases kept this particular kind of still-life work in stock, irrespective of the kind of subject that would be painted in later. We know examples of such empty wreaths by Daniel Seghers, and mention of them is found in contemporary documents also.[56]

Delivery

As we know, a very large number of Antwerp paintings were made for the free market. This means that they were either made at the request of some dealer-middleman, or were kept by the painter himself in his own house, where they were stocked until a favourable opportunity to sell them arose. This is really what Rubens did, as we can see when we analyze his very instructive correspondence with Sir Dudley Carleton from the year 1618.[57] But this kind of speculative attitude towards the final profit to be made from one's own artistic output must have been common practice. There are numerous examples known of painters, who kept certain works at home, waiting for an opportunity to sell them on the Antwerp Vrijdagmarkt or on the Paris market of St Germain.[58] Sometimes a painting remained in the house of the artist for years, sometimes even for the rest of his life, as we may deduce from the inventories of goods drawn up after their death. This may also explain why some compositions were enlarged or retouched in order to make them more 'up to date', according as new tastes arose or their destination changed. The 'Anstückungen' on Rubens's and Jordaens's compositions are well-known, and this procedure will also become clear from Nora De Poorter's and Konrad Renger's investigations.[59]

But let us return to those paintings executed on command. After a painting was finished, it had to be accepted by its commissioner. This usually took place in the painter's workshop or on the spot, where he had completed his work. We know some details about the specific circumstances under which this visitation took place. Thus in the case of De Crayer's *St Guido*, painted for the church devoted to that saint in what is now the Brussels district of Anderlecht, it was stipulated in 1633–1634 that the visitation had to take place under daylight circumstances, 'opt ghesicht vanden dach'.[60] Special visitations, however, also took place where disputes arose between painter and commissioner, especially in regard to the exact price of the final product. These visitations could take the form of true peer reviews. Thus in 1588 a number of outstanding Antwerp artists, including Marten de Vos, Ambrosius Francken, Gillis Mostaert and Bernard de Rijckere, were invited by the municipality of Ghent to give a binding advice on the price to be paid for Raphael Coxcie's *Last Judgement*, which was considered too high by the commissioners.[61]

In order to arrive at a clear judgement, commissioners sometimes made use of a contest. Normally – as in the case of Rubens and Van Veen in the contest for the high altar of Antwerp cathedral in 1611[62] – the decision was based on the modelli. Hence it seems rather odd that in one well-known case two painters were asked to present a final product to their judges, 'in casu' the deans of St Luke's guild. This occurred in 1643 in the case of Thomas Willeboirts Bosschaert and Cornelis Schut who both competitively executed a *Martyrdom*

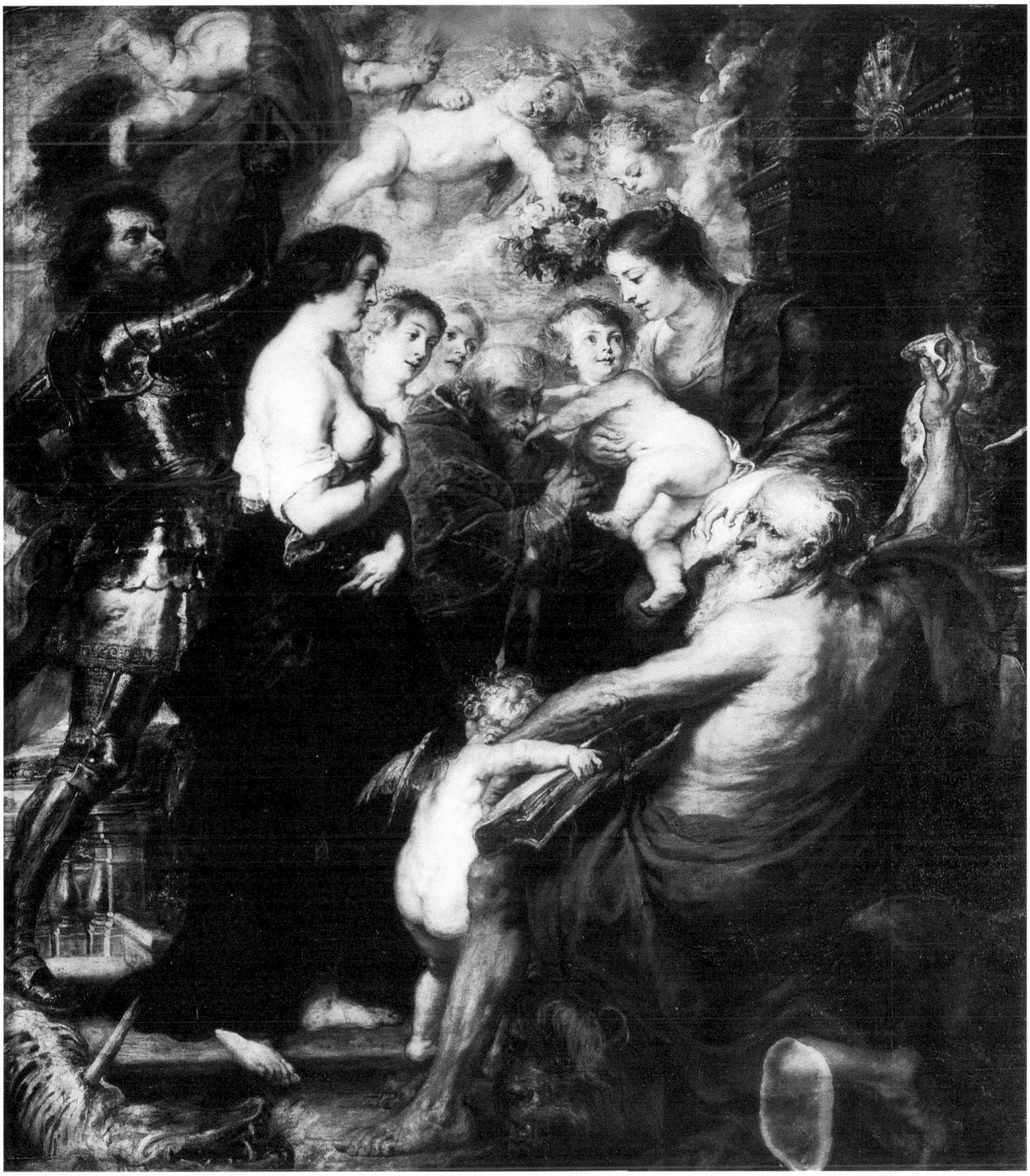

Fig. 8. Peter Paul Rubens, *Madonna and Saints*. Antwerp, St Jacob's Church

of St George for the altar of the chapel of the guild of the Young Crossbowmen in Antwerp cathedral. A degree of over-concern about obtaining final good result may have played a role here, for, as we know, this was not just an average commission. Indeed, a few years earlier the deans of the guild had tried to attract Van Dyck for the execution of this altarpiece for an exorbitant amount of money.[63]

The final effect could prove disappointing for both the artist and the commissioner. We are all familiar with the disappointment about Rubens's first altarpiece for Sta. Maria in Vallicella in Rome, which had to be replaced by a new composition on slate, because of the disturbing light reflections.[64] But there is also the fact that artists sometimes kept in their houses or workshops large-scale altarpieces which cannot at all be considered as having been executed in anticipation of some opportune moment for putting them on the market. In all likelihood such was the case with Rubens's *Madonna and Saints*, a painting which, to judge from its very specific iconography, must have been ordered for the decoration of some altar (Fig. 8). Nevertheless it remained in Rubens's house until the painter himself considered it suitable for the decoration of his tomb chapel, to which the various saints represented do not, however, relate at all.[65] It seems likely, therefore, that this painting had been commissioned and had been rejected by its commissioner.

We also have some information about the way, in which the final products of the artistic process were packed and wrapped before being brought to their destination.

Panels and copper plates were packed in special packing-cases. There is quite some information about them in accounts and correspondence relating to the Antwerp art trade.[66] Canvases were rolled up and put on their stretchers upon arrival: we are e.g. well informed about the usual procedure from the evidence concerning the delivery in 1631 to the Onze-Lieve-Vrouwekerk in Courtray of Anthony van Dyck's *Erection of the Cross* (Fig. 9).[67]

It is quite understandable that especially for transportation to distant foreign countries special attention was devoted to the most adequate packing system, in order to protect the shipment in the best possible way. Thus we know that Rubens's *Adoration of the Shepherds* and *Pentecost*, destined for the side-altars of the Jesuit church in Neuburg, were wrapped in special cloths impregnated with wax.[68] It was no easy task to dispatch a finished painting to a remote destination in Germany or Spain. It might take months to find suitable and reliable carriers, as is clear from the correspondence regarding one of Rubens's pictures for the city of Neuburg. Thus for the transport of his *Fall of the Rebel Angels*, destined for the Sankt-Peterskirche of the Bavarian town, several agents had to be found in various towns, and the definitive route to be taken largely depended on the political and military situation of the moment.[69]

Transportation of paintings was either by waggon or by boat: there is plenty of archival information about both these means of transport. It may be interesting to dwell here on the somewhat enigmatic case of a special chariot which Cornelis Schut in 1648 boasted he had invented, 'wesende eene nieuwe inventie, te vorens noyt gesien noch gepractiseert'. In the same document Schut further states that this chariot is to the benefit of the arts, 'streckende de consten te favoriseren'.[70] This makes me wonder whether he had not been constructing a personal means of transport for the delivery of his altarpieces and other monumental history paintings, the production of which reached its culmination point around the year when the invention took place.... We have also to consider here that – as we saw – Schut had meanwhile established himself in his 'Huys metten Toren' outside the city walls of Antwerp, a situation which will certainly have prompted him to reorganize in some way or other his regular contacts with commissioners, colleagues and various tradesmen residing in the centre of the town. His new chariot may have proven a very helpful tool for this purpose also.

In the case of large-scale compositions unloading, unpacking and setting may have been a rather complex operation. Thus we are well informed of how painters and/or commissioners could make use of specific types of workers. These people were usually known as 'knechten'. In specific cases we know from the relevant documents that these 'knechten' were the artist's own employees.[71] They also included artists-to-be. This is made clear by the classical case of Rubens's Medici series, where we see Justus van Egmont being sent to Paris by his master in 1625, in order to supervise the delivery of the entire set of paintings.[72] Another less well known example is that of Cornelis Schut, who was helped for this purpose by the above mentioned Hans Popels.[73]

After the painting had been set up, it was sometimes appropriate to make final corrections rendered necessary either by the transportation of the work or by the specific site where it was to be hung, e.g. when the measurements of the altarframe did not always correspond exactly to the dimensions of the work. A good example of such an accommodation is the strip of *c.* 20 cm. which Rubens had to add to his *Assumption of the Virgin*, after it was hung in the choir of Antwerp cathedral (Figs. 2, 3), when it turned out that the dimensions of the altar frame were somewhat wider than those

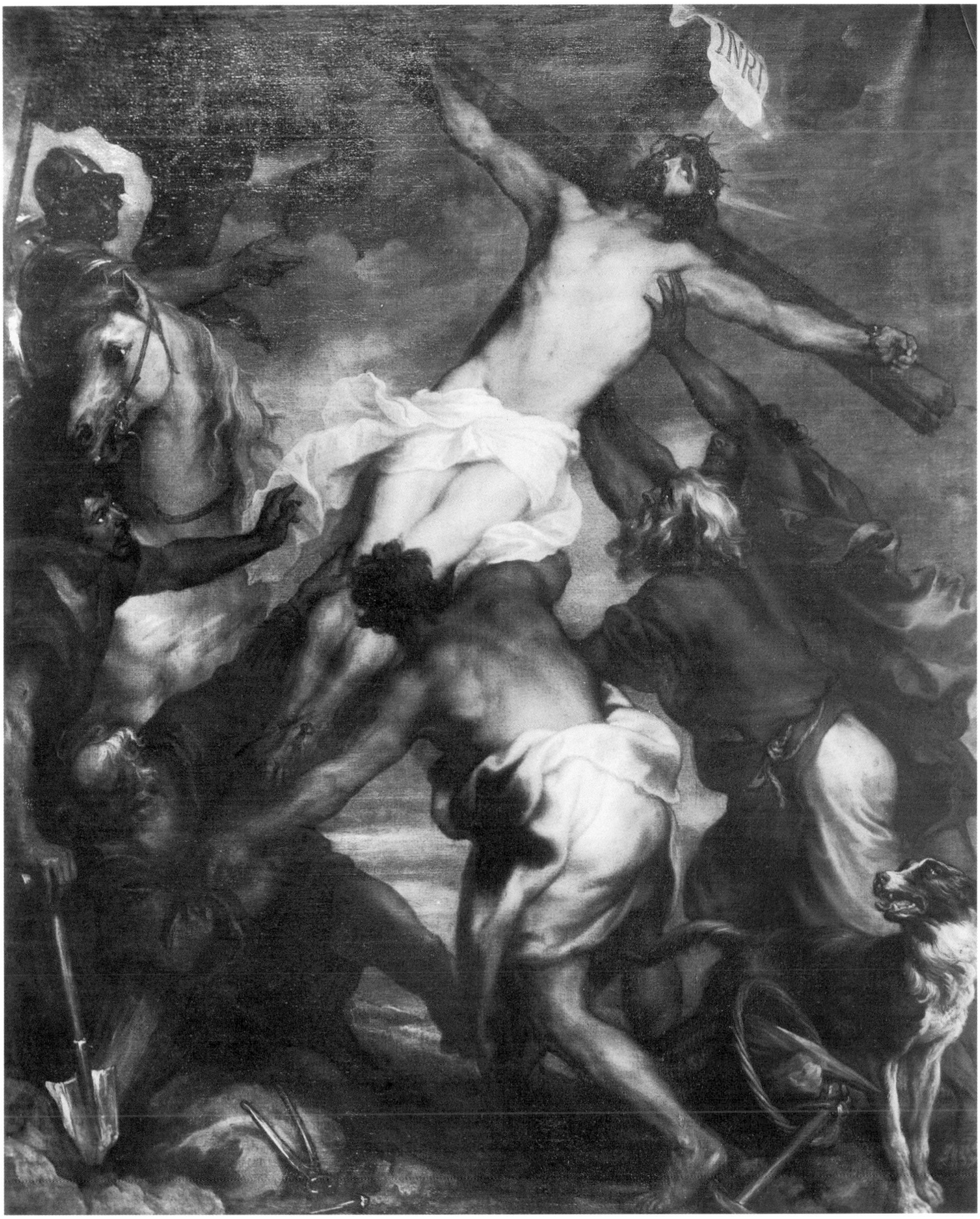

Fig. 9. Anthony van Dyck, *Erection of the Cross*. Courtray, Onze-Lieve-Vrouwekerk

of the painting itself.[74] Of course, this kind of adjustment became problematic in cases where the painting had to be sent off to a remote country. Such cases called for more creative solutions, as is exemplified by two of Rubens's paintings for the Jesuit church at Neuburg which, upon arrival, turned out to be too small for their frames: here Rubens suggested filling in the empty space with a kind of wooden inner frame.[75] Whether such adjustments had implications on the final amount paid to the artist must have depended on the terms of the contract. We know that when Lucas Franchoys in 1669 had to paint some additions to his St Anthony altarpiece for the Sint-Janskerk in Malines, he was rewarded with an extra 13 guilders.[76]

All is well that ends well. After a commissioned painting had received its final fiat and had been installed into its proper place, some festive rounding off may have appeared appropriate. There is information in church account books of drinking and also of some eating. Often the painter's wife was offered a gift which could take the form of a pair of gloves or a hat.[77] But the painter could also receive a bonus. We know how Rubens received a golden chain as a sign of the king's satisfaction, after the installation of the Whitehall Ceilings.[78] But extras could be more modest. Thus we are informed about the delivery of Van Dyck's *Erection of the Cross* in the Onze-Lieve-Vrouwekerk in Courtray. Here in addition to the payment of 100 Pounds or 600 guilders due to him, the painter received a dozen 'Kortrijkse wafeltjes', but these may just have been a consolation prize for the fact that he did not succeed in obtaining the amount of 800 guilders which he had demanded initially.[79]

NOTES

I am greatly indebted to Dr. John Dudley (Leuven), for his very careful revision of the English style of this text.

1. J. H. Montias, 'The Influence of Economic Factors on Style', *De Zeventiende Eeuw*, VI, 1990, 1, pp. 49–57.

2. See e.g. K. Van der Stighelen, 'Produktiviteit en samenwerking in het Antwerpse kunstenaarsmilieu, 1620–1640', *Driemaandelijks Tijdschrift Gemeentekrediet*, XLIV, 1990, pp. 5–15; H. Vlieghe, 'Maatwerk en confectie. Over de functie van historieschilderkunst in de Vlaamse stad van de 17de eeuw', in J. Van der Stock ed., [cat. exh.] *Stad in Vlaanderen. Cultuur en maatschappij 1477–1787*, (Brussels–Schallaburg), Brussels, 1991, p. 264.

3. Relevant passages in this notebook were published in H. Vlieghe, 'Zwischen Van Veen and Rubens. Artus Wolffort (1581–1641), ein vergessener Antwerpener Maler', *Wallraf-Richartz-Jahrbuch*, XXXIX, 1977, p. 136; for the importance of Van Lint's notebook, see H. Vlieghe, 'De leerpraktijk van een jonge schilder: het notitieboekje van Pieter van Lint in het Institut Néerlandais te Parijs', *Jaarboek Koninklijk Museum voor Schone Kunsten Antwerpen*, 1979, pp. 249–279.

4. '... e ben vero che non sono ancora ben secchi ansi hanno di bisogno di star cosi nelli loro telari ancora alcuni giorni inansi che si potranno inrollare senza pericolo...'; as a marginal note Rubens adds: 'Con questo bel tempo, si mette... nel sole...' (M. Rooses & C. Ruelens, *Codex Diplomaticus Rubenianus. Correspondance de Rubens, et documents épistolaires concernant sa vie et ses œuvres*, II, Antwerp, 1898, p. 162); the English translation is that of R. Saunders Magurn, *The Letters of Peter Paul Rubens*, Cambridge, Mass., 1955, pp. 63–64.

5. See J. M. Muller, 'The Perseus and Andromeda on Rubens's house', *Simiolus*, XII, 1981–1982, pp. 131–146.

6. See especially the relevant documentary evidence published by J. Denucé (*De Antwerpsche 'Konstkamers'. Inventarissen van kunstverzamelingen te Antwerpen in de 16e en 17e eeuwen*, Bronnen voor de geschiedenis van de Vlaamsche kunst, II, Antwerp, 1932) and E. Duverger (*Antwerpse Kunstinventarissen uit de zeventiende eeuw*, Fontes Historiae Artium Neerlandicae. Bronnen voor de kunstgeschiedenis van de Nederlanden, I–, Brussels, 1984– [in progress]).

7. See [cat. exh.] *Rubens Cantoor. Een verzameling tekeningen ontstaan in Rubens' atelier* (Antwerp, Rubenshuis, 1993), Antwerp–Ghent, 1993.

8. See the relevant information in C. Van de Velde, 'The Painted Decoration of Floris's House', in G. Cavalli-Björkman ed., *Netherlandish Mannerism. Papers Given at a Symposium at Nationalmuseum Stockholm*, September 21–22, 1984, Stockholm, 1985, pp. 127–134, R. J. Tijs, *P.P. Rubens en J. Jordaens. Barok in eigen huis, een cultuurhistorische studie over groei, verval en restauratie van twee 17de-eeuwse kunstenaarswoningen te Antwerpen*, Antwerp, 1983, and G. des Marez, 'La maison de David Teniers II et l'hôtel Ravenstein', *Annales de la Société royale d'archéologie de Bruxelles*, XXVI, 1912, pp. 5–55. For a more general survey of artists' houses and their importance, including Rubens's house, see also E. Hüttinger ed., *Künstlerhaüser von der Renaissance bis zur Gegenwart*, Zürich, 1985.

9. See G. Wilmers, *Cornelis Schut (1597–1655): A Flemish Painter of the High Baroque*, Turnhout, 1996, p. 233.

10. The details of this necessary enlargement are described in the relevant *Acta Capituli* in the Antwerp Cathedral Archives: 'Placuit ad relationem edituorum ut tabula depingenda in summo altari ob defectum latitudinis ad implendum dilatetur, adglutinatur aliis tabulis, idque quam primum ne differatur occasio pingendi' (see D. Freedberg, *The Life of Christ after the Passion*, Corpus Rubenianum Ludwig Burchard, VII, London–New York, 1984, pp. 176–177).

11. See Vlieghe 1977 (see note 3), pp. 264 (Fig. 44), 266.

12. See F.J. Van den Branden, *Geschiedenis der Antwerpsche schilderschool*, Antwerp, 1883, pp. 895–897; see also M.-L. Hairs, *Dans le sillage de Rubens: les peintres d'histoire anversois au XVIIe siècle*, Liège, 1977, p. 32.

13. '... dat alhier binnen Antwerpen het gebruyck is ende gepermiteert wordt, aen alle onvrije schilders, van wat natie dat sij sijn, die alhier in de kercken commen stellen eenighe aultaerstucken ofte andere schilderijen, bij hun buyten dese stadt geschildert, dienende tot ciraet van de kercken, dat den voorschreven meester, sijn stuck gestelt hebbende, alsdan vermach, naer sijn gelieven, tselve veranderen, vuyt te doen schilderen ende herschilderen, tot dat hij daer over contentement heeft, vuyt dien, als 't voorschreven stuck gestelt staet, dat men alsdan can sien wat datter aen is gebrekende, ende 't selve alsdan wordt herschildert, verandert ende verbetert, volgens de gesteltenisse van de plaetse, gelijck alle constlievende geesten behoorden te laten doen, nyettegenstaende d'ordonnantie, dat geene onvrije meesters er vermogen te schilderen.' (Published by Van den Branden 1883 [see note 12], p. 896).

14. The survival of this tradition well into the seventeenth century is clearly explained by F. Baudouin, 'Altars and Altarpieces before 1620', in J.R. Martin ed., *Rubens before 1620*, Princeton, 1972, pp. 73 ff.

15. On quality control of oak panels in Antwerp, see J. Van Damme, 'De Antwerpse tafereelmakers en hun merken. Identificatie en betekenis', *Jaarboek Koninklijk Museum voor Schone Kunsten Antwerpen*, 1990, pp. 193–236.

16. See D. Wolfthal, *The Beginnings of Netherlandish Canvas Painting*, Cambridge, 1989.

17. On these cf. the standard article by E. Van Autenboer, 'Nota's over de Mechelse waterverfschilders', *Mechelse Bijdragen*, XI, 1949, pp. 33–43.

18. See in this respect e.g. K. Nicolaus, *DuMont's Handbuch der Gemäldekunde. Material-Technik-Pflege*, Cologne, 1979, pp. 53–57.

19. Apart from the above-mentioned publication of the Antwerp probate inventories by Denucé and Duverger (see above, note 6), see also J. Denucé, *Kunstuitvoer in de 17e eeuw te Antwerpen. De firma Forchoudt*, Bronnen voor de geschiedenis van de Vlaamsche kunst, I, Antwerp–The Hague, 1931, *passim*; J. Denucé, *Brieven en documenten betreffend Jan Breugel I en II*, Bronnen voor de geschiedenis van de Vlaamsche kunst, III, Antwerp–The Hague, 1934, *passim*; J. Denucé, *Na Peter Pauwel Rubens. Documenten uit den kunsthandel te Antwerpen in de XVIIe eeuw van Matthijs Musson*, Bronnen voor de geschiedenis van de Vlaamsche kunst, V, Antwerp, 1949, *passim*.

20. See for this particular terminology L. De Pauw-De Veen, *De begrippen 'schilder', 'schilderij' en 'schilderen' in de zeventiende*

eeuw, Verhandelingen van de Koninklijke Vlaamse Academie voor Wetenschappen, Letteren en Schone Kunsten van België. Klasse der Schone Kunsten, XXII, Brussels, 1969, pp. 127–128; on this aspect in the context of Dutch painting, cf. especially J. Bruyn, 'Een onderzoek naar 17de-eeuwse schilderijformaten, voornamelijk in Noord-Nederland', *Oud Holland*, XCIII, 1979, pp. 96–115.

21. See the relevant literature mentioned above, in note 19, *passim*.

22. See E. Duverger and H. Vlieghe, *David Teniers der Ältere. Ein vergessener flämischer Nachfolger Adam Elsheimers*, Utrecht, 1971, pp. 22 ff.

23. See Vlieghe 1991 (see note 2), p. 260; H. Vlieghe, 'Thoughts on Van Dyck's Early Fame and Influence in Flanders', in S. Barnes, and A.K. Wheelock, Jr, ed., *Van Dyck 350*, Studies in the History of Art, XLVI, Washington, 1994, pp. 199–200.

24. See A. Monballieu, 'P.P. Rubens en het "Nachtmael" voor St Winoksbergen (1611), een niet uitgevoerd schilderij van de meester', *Jaarboek Koninklijk Museum voor Schone Kunsten Antwerpen*, 1965, p. 195.

25. See F. Baudouin, 'Van Dyck's Last Religious Commission: an Altarpiece for Antwerp Cathedral', *Journal of the Warburg and Courtauld Institutes*, LVII, 1994, pp. 175–190.

26. '... pittore tanto eccellente nella sua propria professione d'inventione & di disegno...' (L. Guicciardini, *Descrittione di Tutti i Paesi Bassi, altrimenti detti Germania Inferiori*, Antwerp, 1567, p. 99; see also C. Van de Velde, *Frans Floris (1519/20–1570). Leven en Werken*, Verhandelingen van de Koninklijke Academie voor Wetenschappen, Letteren en Schone Kunsten van België, XXX, Brussels, 1975, pp. 3–4).

27. See in this context Van de Velde 1975 (see note 26), pp. 102–103.

28. See De Pauw-De Veen 1969 (see note 20), pp. 107–109.

29. See J. Thuillier & J. Foucart, *Rubens. La Galerie Médicis au Palais du Luxembourg*, Milan, 1969, p. 98.

30. See Rooses and Ruelens 1898 (see note 5), pp. 130–183; see also the English translation in Magurn 1955 (see note 5), pp. 59–68.

31. Rubens calls him the 'meglior mio discepolo'; see Rooses and Ruelens 1898 (see note 5), p. 137; see also the English translation in Magurn 1955 (see note 5), p. 61.

32. See Rooses and Ruelens 1898 (see note 5), p. 137; see also the English translation in Magurn 1955 (see note 5), pp. 60–61.

33. See in this respect H. Vlieghe, 'Antwerpener Historienmaler und Rubens' Atelier', in E. Mai and H. Vlieghe, ed., [cat. exh.] *Von Bruegel bis Rubens. Das goldene Jahrhundert der flämischen Malerei* (Cologne, Wallraf-Richartz-Museum; Vienna, Kunsthistorisches Museum 1992–1993), Cologne, 1993, pp. 133–141; H. Vlieghe, 'Rubens' Atelier and History Painting in Flanders: A Review of the Evidence', in [cat. exh.] P. Sutton ed., *The Age of Rubens* (Boston, Museum of Fine Arts; Toledo, Toledo Museum of Arts, 1993–1994), Boston–Ghent, 1993, pp. 158–170.

34. 'Van hem werdt doch met meerder reden gheclaeght dat hy zyn Jonghers Copien vercocht voor zijn werck wanneer hij daer so wat aen gedaen hadde' (C. van Mander, *Het schilder-boeck*, Haarlem, 1604, fol. 262r).

35. See L. Galesloot, 'Un procès pour une vente de tableaux attribués à Van Dyck', *Annales de l'Académie d'Archéologie de Belgique*, XXIV, 1868, pp. 561–606.

36. See Van de Velde 1975 (see note 26), pp. 472–473.

37. Plenty of these were still in Rubens's workshop at the time of his death; in the inventory of his goods, which was drawn up on that occasion, they are described as one item: 'Une quantité des Copies, faictes d'après les originaux du feu Monsr. Rubens' (Denucé 1932 (see note 6), p. 70; H. Vlieghe, *De schilder Rubens*, Utrecht–Antwerp, 1977, pp. 42–43, 169).

38. This becomes clear from a letter which De Crayer wrote to the dealer Matthijs Musson in 1645 in which he mentions 'veel diversche coppyen... van kerckstucken als ander pleysante dingen'; see Denucé 1949 (see note 19) p. 36; H. Vlieghe, *Gaspar de Crayer. Sa vie et ses œuvres*, Brussels, 1972, p. 313.

39. 'Marten Pepijn, schilder... gehoort ende gesien heeft dat Peeter van Haelen oudecleercooper... een stucxken schildery de ommestaenders was aendienende dattet gemaect was als principael doir de voorseyde deponent (i.e. Pepijn) daer aff hy deponent den zelven Van Haelen was reprehenderende overmits hy deponent bevont dattet geen principael van hem en was maer wel een copyken by zynen knecht gemaect'; unpublished document in the Stadsarchief, Antwerp (*Notarissen*, 3380). This evidence was included in the licentiate thesis *Maarten Pepyn (1575–1642/3). Leven en werk van een Antwerps schilder uit de tijd van Rubens*, written for the University of Leuven by my student Beatrijs Wolters van der Weij in 1995.

40. 'Siet toch wel toe, als ghij vertrecken sult, dat alles wel opgesloten sij ende datter geene originaelen in blijven staen boven op het schilderhuys oft enige schetsen...'; Rooses and Ruelens 1898 (see note 5), VI, p. 223; the English translation from Magurn 1955 (see note 5), p. 411.

41. See the publication in extenso of this interesting document, in Duverger 1984– (see note 6), IV, p. 79; Wilmers 1996 (see note 10), p. 227.

42. See J. R. Martin, *The Decorations of the Pompa Introitus Ferdinandi*, Corpus Rubenianum Ludwig Burchard, XVI, Brussels–London–New York, 1972, and S. Alpers, *The Decoration of the Torre de la Parada*, Corpus Rubenianum Ludwig Burchard, IX, Brussels–London–New York, 1971.

43. See J. R. Martin, 'Rubens's Last Mythological Paintings for Philip IV', *Gentse Bijdragen tot de Kunstgeschiedenis*, XXIV, 1976–1978 (*Internationaal Rubenscolloquium Anwerpen, 1977*), pp. 113–118.

44. See H. Vlieghe, 'Gaspar de Crayer: addenda et corrigenda', *Gentse Bijdragen tot de Kunstgeschiedenis*, XV, 1979–1980, pp. 187–188; K. Van der Stighelen & H. Vlieghe, 'Cornelis de Vos (1584/5–1651) als historie- en genreschilder', *Academiae Analecta. Mededelingen van de Koninklijke Academie voor Wetenschappen, Letteren en Schone Kunsten van België. Klasse der Schone Kunsten*, LIV, 1994, p. 48.

45. See Duverger 1984– (see note 6), III, pp. 164–165.

46. As stated explicitly by Carel van Mander, in his *Schilderboeck*, Haarlem, 1604, fol. 230v; see also Van de Velde 1975 (see note 26), pp. 104–105.

47. M. Jaffé, 'Rubens and Snyders, a Fruitful Partnership', *Apollo*, XCIII, 1971, pp. 184–196.

48. See the insights into this composition by Arnout Balis, in A. Balis, M. Diaz Padron, C. Van de Velde, H. Vlieghe, ed., *Vlaamse kunst in het Prado*, Flandria Extra Muros, Antwerp, 1989, pp. 217–218.

49. See in this respect Van der Stighelen 1990 (see note 2), pp. 5–11; K. Van der Stighelen, 'Zum Problem der Zusammenarbeit: nicht Jan Boeckhorst sondern Cornelis de Vos', in [cat. exh.] *Jan Boeckhorst. Maler der Rubenszeit* (Antwerp, Rubenshuis; Münster, Westfälisches Landesmuseum für Kunst, 1990), Freren, 1990, pp. 87–89.

50. See e.g. K. Zoege von Manteuffel, in U. Thieme & F. Becker, *Allgemeines Lexikon der Bildenden Künstler von der Antike bis zur Gegenwart*, XXXIV, Leipzig, 1940, p. 12; M. Gregori, 'Adriaen van Utrecht e la natura morta italiana', *Paragone*, IX, 1959, pp. 50–54.

51. See A. Balis, 'Pieter Thys, Marten Pepyn und der dritte "Pseudo-Boeckhorst"', in [cat. exh.] Antwerp–Münster 1990 (see note 49), pp. 98–100; A. Balis, 'Abraham van Diepenbeeck and Pieter Boel as Designers of Tapestries: the Hollstein Hunts', in E. Mai, K. Schutz, H. Vlieghe, ed., *Die Malerei Antwerpens-Gattungen, Meister, Wirkungen. Studien zur flämischen Kunst des 16. und 17. Jahrhunderts. Internationales Colloquium Wien 1993*, Cologne, 1994, pp. 169–177.

52. See Van der Stighelen 1990 (see note 49).

53. See. e.g. K. Ertz, *Jan Brueghel d. Ä. Die Gemälde mit kritischem Œuvrekatalog*, Cologne, 1979; K. Ertz., *Jan Brueghel d. J. Die Gemälde mit kritischem Œuvrekatalog*, Freren, 1984; K. Ertz, *Josse de Momper der Jüngere. Die Gemälde mit kritischem Œuvrekatalog*, Freren, 1986; U. Härting, *Frans Francken der Jüngere (1581–1642). Die Gemälde mit kritischem Œuvrekatalog*, Freren, 1989.

54. See Van der Stighelen 1990 (see note 2), pp. 12–14; K. Van der Stighelen, 'De (atelier-)bedrijvigheid van Andries Snellinck (1587–1653) en Co', *Jaarboek Koninklijk Museum voor Schone Kunsten Antwerpen*, 1989, p. 319.

55. Thus in 1663 Theodoor van Thulden sent two unfinished canvases, representing a *Holy Virgin* and a *Vanitas*, to his colleague, the still-life painter Adriaen van Utrecht. Thereby he asked the latter to paint some fruit and flower details. See Duverger 1984– (see note 6), VIII, pp. 346–347.

56. See the record of 'een cartelle daer niet in was geschildert' in the list of paintings Seghers drew up at the end of his life (published in W. Couvreur, 'Daniël Seghers' inventaris van door hem geschilderde bloemstukken', *Gentse Bijdragen tot de Kunstgeschiedenis en de Oudheidkunde*, XX, 1967, p. 124).

57. See above, note 30.

58. See the case of Cornelis de Vos, as illustrated by K. Van der Stighelen, 'Van "marchant" tot "vermaert conterfeyter": het levensverhaal van Cornelis de Vos", *Jaarboek Koninklijk Museum voor Schone Kunsten Antwerpen*, 1991, pp. 106–107, 141.

59. See e.g. J.S. Held, 'Nachträglich veränderte Kompositionen bei Jacob Jordaens', *Revue belge d'archéologie et d'histoire de l'art*, III, 1933, pp. 214–233; K. Renger, 'Anstückungen bei Rubens', in Mai, Schutz and Vlieghe 1994 (see note 51), pp. 156–167; K. Renger, 'Rubens-Stücke. Die Anstückungen von Münchner "Silen" und "Schäferszene"', *Wallraf-Richartz-Jahrbuch*, LV, 1994 (*Studien zur niederländischen Kunst des 16. und 17. Jahrhunderts. Festschrift für Prof. Dr. Justus Müller Hofstede*), pp. 171–184; see also K. Renger and N. De Poorter, further in this volume, on pp. 213-232, 261-265.

60. See H. Vlieghe, 'Ongepubliceerde documenten over het werk van Gaspar de Crayer', *Gentse Bijdragen tot de Kunstgeschiedenis en de Oudheidkunde*, XX, 1967–1968, pp. 182, 187; Vlieghe 1972 (see note 38), p. 306.

61. See E. De Busscher, *Recherches sur les peintres et sculpteurs à Gand aux XVIe, XVIIe et XVIIIe siècles*, Ghent, 1866, pp. 220–221; A. Zweite, *Marten de Vos als Maler*, Berlin, 1980, p. 374.

62. See H. Vlieghe, 'Rubens and Van Veen in Contest. A Marginal Note', in *Ars Auro Prior. Studia Joanni Bialostocki Sexagenario Dicata*, Warsaw, 1981, pp. 477–482.

63. See the relevant evidence in Wilmers 1996 (see note 9), p. 229; see further also Baudouin 1994 (see note 25), pp. 187–188.

64. See e.g. H. Vlieghe, *Saints*, Corpus Rubenianum Ludwig Burchard, VIII, II, Brussels–London–New York, 1973, pp. 49–50.

65. See U. Söding, *Das Grabbild des Peter Paul Rubens in der Jakobskirche zu Antwerpen*, Hildesheim–Zürich–New York, 1986, esp. pp. 87 ff.

66. See especially the very informative details found in the correspondence of the Antwerp dealers Musson and Forchondt (see above, note 19).

67. See especially the most recent and detailed study of this particular altarpiece, by R. De Man: 'Het schilderij "De Kruisoprichting" door Anton van Dyck in Onze-Lieve-Vrouw te Kortrijk', *Handelingen van de Koninklijke Geschied- en Oudheidkundige Kring te Kortrijk*, XLVII, 1980, pp. 53–154, more particularly p. 55.

68. See K. Renger, [cat. exh.] *Peter Paul Rubens: Altäre für Bayern* (Munich, Alte Pinakothek), 1990–1991, pp. 57, 92.

69. Ibidem, pp. 60–61.

70. See Wilmers 1996 (see note 10), p. 232.

71. See e.g. the details about the delivery in Hulst in 1628 of Cornelis de Vos's monumental view of that city (Van der Stighelen 1991 [see note 58], p. 145).

72. See Thuillier and Foucart 1969 (see note 29), p. 126.

73. See Wilmers 1996 (see note 9), p 223.

74. See Freedberg 1984 (see note 10), pp. 176–177.

75. See K. Renger, [cat. exh.] Munich 1990–1991 (see note 68), pp. 57–58, 95.

76. See H. Colsoul, 'Lucas Franchoys de Jonge. Œuvrecatalogus', *Handelingen van de Koninklijke Kring voor Oudheidkunde, Letteren en Kunst van Mechelen*, XCII, 1988, p. 268.

77. The latter was the case with De Crayer's wife in 1622 (Vlieghe 1972 (see note 38), p. 302, doc. 19).

78. See e.g. H.G. Evers, *Rubens und sein Werk. Neue Forschungen*, Brussels, 1943, p. 88.

79. See e.g. De Man 1980 (see note 67), p. 55.

Seriewerk en recyclage: doorgedreven efficiëntie in het geroutineerde atelier van Jacob Jordaens

Nora De Poorter

Met de dood van Rubens, op 30 mei 1640, verdween niet enkel een van de belangrijkste artistieke persoonlijkheden in Europa. Ook kwam er plots een einde aan een goed draaiend bedrijf: Rubens' atelier in Antwerpen dat een grote internationale faam genoot en omvangrijke opdrachten had uitgevoerd. Naast dit atelier was in de Zuidelijke Nederlanden het belangrijkste dat van Jacob Jordaens, die in meer dan één opzicht in de voetsporen van Rubens was getreden. Hij legde zich toe op de grootfigurige historieschilderkunst en kon werk leveren van groot of zeer groot formaat. In de jaren dertig had Jordaens trouwens meegewerkt aan opdrachten van Rubens' atelier: naar olieverfschetsen van Rubens had hij een aantal doeken geschilderd voor de *Pompa Introitus Ferdinandi* en voor de reeks voor de Torre de la Parada.

Antoon van Dyck, die reeds acht jaar in Engeland verbleef, heeft in 1640 wellicht gehoopt Rubens' rol als succesrijk historieschilder te kunnen overnemen. Hier is echter niets van terechtgekomen: Van Dycks carrière werd abrupt afgebroken door zijn vroege dood op 42-jarige leeftijd op 9 december 1641.

Jordaens werd aldus onbetwistbaar de belangrijkste schilder in de Zuidelijke Nederlanden. Hij zal zijn beide collega's nog 37 jaar lang overleven en kijkt met veel optimisme vooruit op de toekomst. Op dit moment, van 1639 tot ca. 1641, is hij bezig met het uitbreiden van zijn atelier door het aankopen van een aangrenzend pand, en met verbouwingswerken aan zijn huis en dit vanzelfsprekend met het doel de omvang van de productie te kunnen opdrijven.[1] Zijn optimisme was gerechtvaardigd. Zijn bedrijf draaide uitstekend en Jordaens werd de meest welvarende schilder in de Scheldestad. Omstreeks 1660 behoort hij zelfs tot de rijkste vierhonderd inwoners van de stad.[2]

Jordaens' faam reikte ver buiten Antwerpen. Wat de buitenlandse opdrachten betreft, zijn te vermelden de reeksen van de *Geschiedenis van Amor en Psyche*, die hij vervaardigde voor het Engelse hof en voor Christina van Zweden. De belangrijkste opdrachten van buiten de Zuidelijke Nederlanden waren echter zonder twijfel deze uit de Noordelijke Provinciën. Het meest opmerkelijke is zijn medewerking aan de Oranje-zaal, de centrale koepelzaal in het Huis ten Bosch bij Den Haag, vervaardigd door meerdere kunstenaars in opdracht van Amalia van Solms. Jordaens maakte voor deze monumentale decoratie twee schilderijen, waaronder het grote centrale tafereel met als onderwerp de *Triomf van Frederik Hendrik*, voltooid in 1652 (afb. 1). Het schilderij van 7,5 m hoog en 7,5 m breed, wellicht het grootste dat hij ooit vervaardigde, is in situ bewaard gebleven. In de jaren zestig verleende Jordaens bovendien zijn medewerking aan het nieuwe Stadhuis van Amsterdam. Voor de boogvelden van de galerijen omheen de 'Burgerzaal' schilderde hij vier doeken van 5,5 m breed, die eveneens nog ter plaatse zijn.

De archivalische bronnen leren ons nagenoeg niets over Jordaens' werkwijze, zijn medewerkers, of de organisatie van zijn zeer productieve atelier. Zoals voldoende bekend, vernemen wij wel een en ander over het tot stand komen van het grote schilderij voor Amalia van Solms uit de briefwisseling die Jordaens hierover voerde met Constantijn Huygens. In een brief van 8 november 1651 verklaart hij aan de secretaris van de vorstin hoe het komt dat *De triomf van Frederik Hendrik* niet zo snel kan vlotten als hij zou wensen. Hieruit blijkt dat de omvang van het enorme doek voor problemen zorgde. Hij is van een trapladder gevallen en werd daarbij ernstig gekwetst aan de schenen. Hij zegt dat hij gevallen is 'door eenen trap die omsloech', en de hele maand oktober aan de gevolgen ervan heeft geleden 'met overgroote pyne'. Verder wijst hij erop dat het werken aan het zeer groot formaat moeilijker is dan hij had

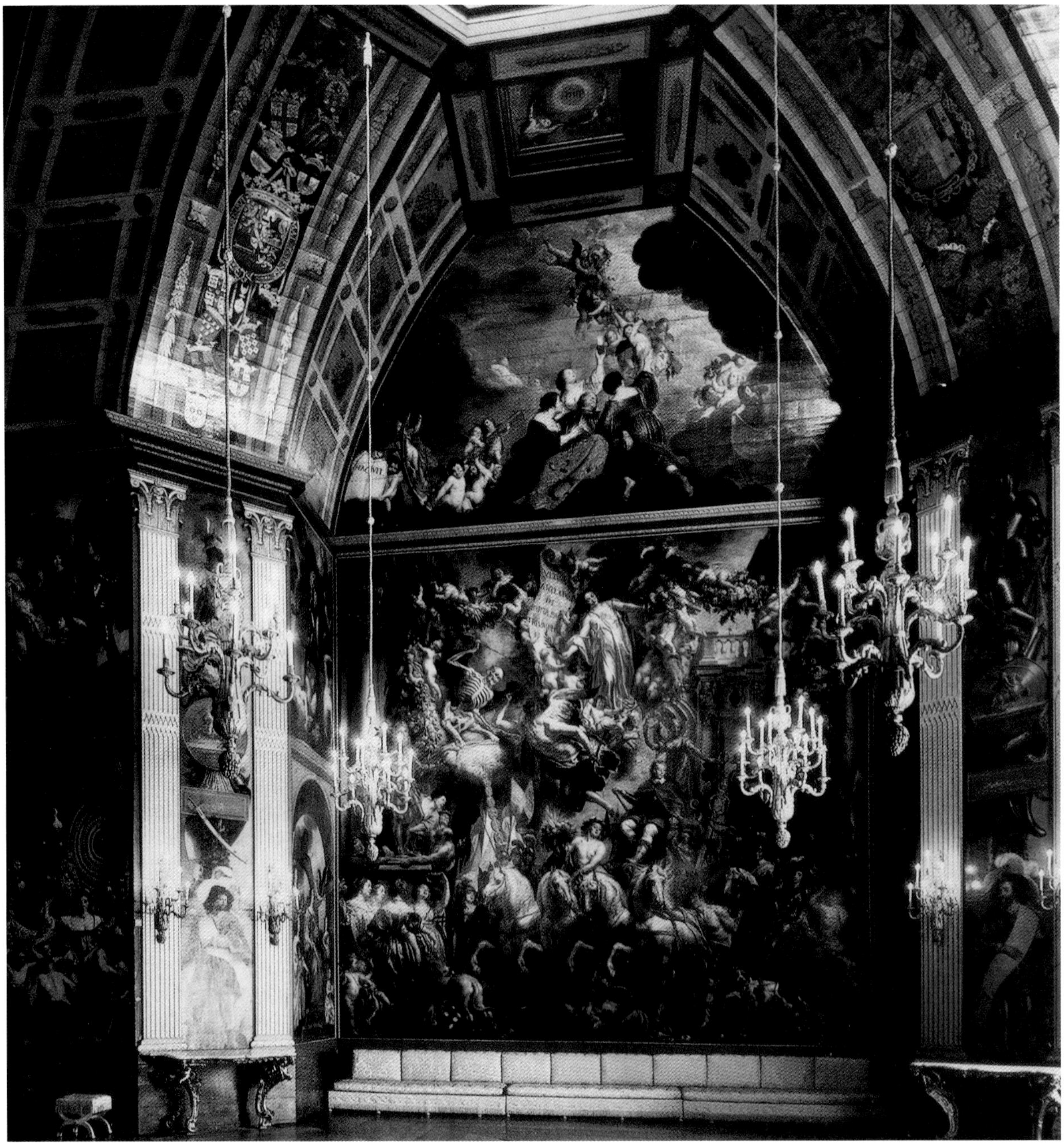

Afb. 1. Jacob Jordaens, *De Triomf van Frederik Hendrik*. Den Haag, Huis ten Bosch

gedacht omdat hij het doek in zijn atelier nooit in zijn geheel kon overzien: '...het aldermoeyelckxste [is], dat ick t niet en can geheel in myn huys wtspannen, soodat ick t meer met het concept int hooft dan met het gesicht heb moeten wtvoeren...'.[3] Hij werkte dus met het doek opgerold of opgeplooid.

Een veel bescheidener opdracht, archivalisch gedocumenteerd en daterend uit de jaren zestig, wanneer Jordaens een uitzonderlijk productief atelier leidt, leert ons ook iets over zijn werkwijze, en het loont de moeite deze daarom van naderbij te bekijken. Opdrachtgever is de stad Hulst, gelegen 27 km ten westen van Antwerpen en behorend tot de Noordelijke Provinciën. In 1663 wenst de Magistraat van het Hulsterambacht een schilderij te bestellen voor de schouw van de Vierschaar, dus de kamer waar recht werd gesproken. Over deze aankoop is een kort verslag neergeschreven in juni–juli 1663 in het resolutieboek van het Hulsterambacht, bewaard in het Rijksarchief

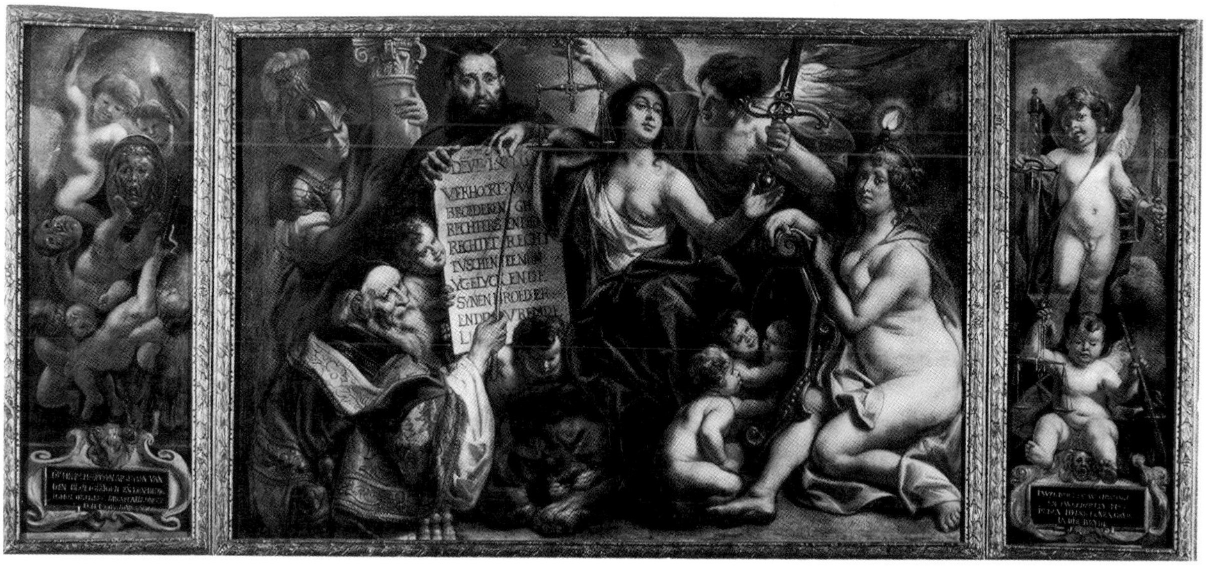

Afb. 2. Jacob Jordaens, *Justitia*. Hulst, Stadhuis

te Middelburg (zie bijlage II). Het bestaan van dit archiefstuk is reeds lang bekend, maar de tekst zelf werd niet gepubliceerd, zodat een interessant gegeven onopgemerkt bleef.

Het college van Hulst had overwogen 'een fray stuck schilderye te laten maecken, en voorden schoorsteen inde groote camer en vierschaer op te hangen... representerende de justitie'. Na enig rondvragen bij 'persoonen van de cunst' had men zich hiervoor gewend tot Jordaens ('den here Jacques Jordaens tot Andwerpen'). Nadat de magistraat beslist had tot de belangrijke aankoop, begaf een delegatie van de Stad Hulst zich naar Antwerpen om de zaak bij de schilder te gaan bespreken. Vooraf was overeengekomen welke som besteed zou worden, namelijk 'ontrent hondert ducatons', dit is 315 gulden.

De 70-jarige Jordaens blijkt een goed onderhandelaar. Hij is in principe akkoord om de opdracht te aanvaarden en hij heeft reeds een aantal schetsen ('verscheyden schetsen') gemaakt met het gewenste onderwerp; waarschijnlijk zijn dit tekeningen. Over de prijs wil Jordaens zich niet uitspreken, maar het is duidelijk dat hij de som die het college wenste te besteden, te laag vindt. Hij komt dan echter met een wat vreemd voorstel dat een licht werpt op de rationeel uitgebouwde werkwijze in zijn atelier. Hij zal niet één, maar drie of vier schilderijen vervaardigen met hetzelfde onderwerp ('dry a vier verscheiden stucken by naer van een subject'); als hij hiermee klaar is, zal hij de vertegenwoordigers van het college van Hulst verwittigen en dan kunnen zij er één uit kiezen; het staat hen daarbij vrij het te nemen of te laten. Ze hoeven zich dus niet te engageren tot de aankoop. Hij zal zich *dan* pas – dus na de voltooiing – over de prijs uitspreken. Het gaat dus *niet*, en dit dient benadrukt, om het maken van een aantal schetsen, maar wel van een aantal voltooide schilderijen met varianten van eenzelfde thema (een *Justitia*), en vermoedelijk ook met precies dezelfde afmetingen, overeenkomend met de schouw in Hulst.

Dit voorstel wordt aanvaard. Wanneer de drie of vier schilderijen voltooid zijn, spreekt Jordaens zich eindelijk uit over de prijs: hij vraagt 800 gulden, dus aanzienlijk meer dan de 315 gulden die het Hulsterse College wilde besteden. Er volgt dan nog wat correspondentie heen en weer, tot uiteindelijk een overeenkomst wordt getroffen. Het allerlaatste bod van Hulst is 500 gulden, een bedrag dat vertegenwoordigers van de stad in de vorm van 200 rijksdaalders in een zak aan Jordaens gaan aanbieden op 29 juni 1663. Er wordt beslist '... daer voor te bieden tweehondert ryxdaelders in specien, en in cas daer mede geen genoughen werd genomen, datmen dito jordaens sonder verder bedancken syn stuck sal laten houden, en daer op hem aengeschreven dat op vrydach den 29 deser twee gedeputeerden sullen aldaer syn, om het wterst en laetste gebodt hem in een sacke contant mede te brengen.'

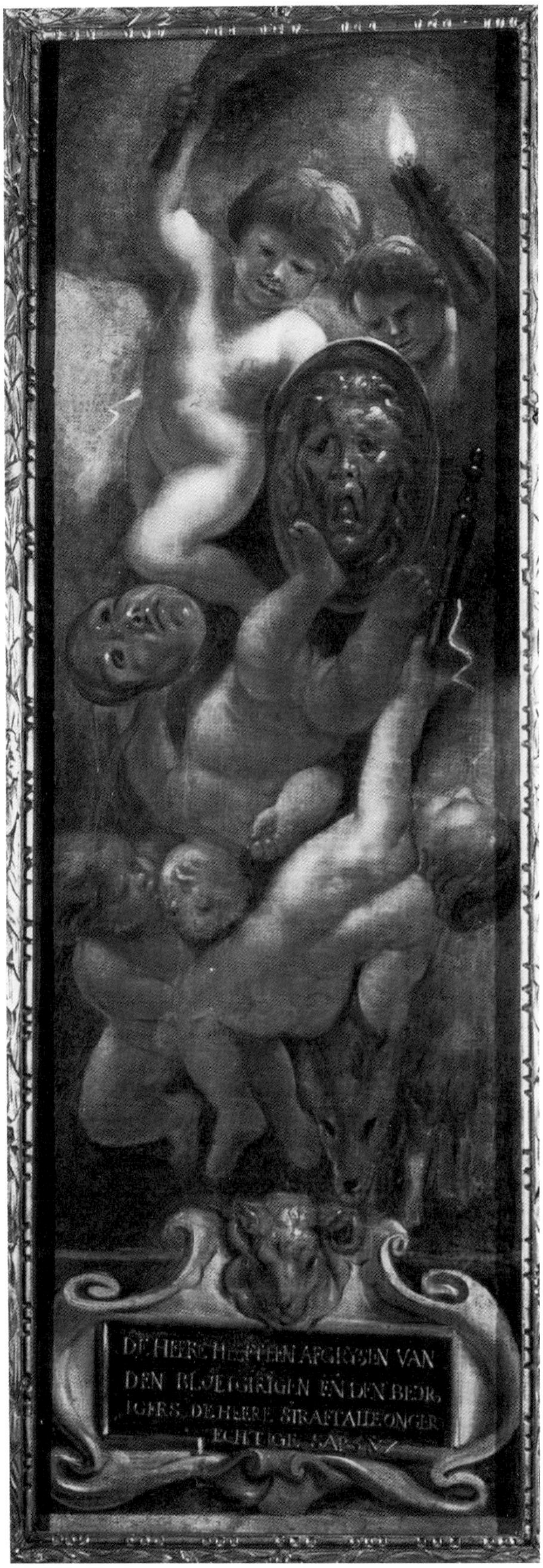

Afb. 3. Jacob Jordaens, *'De Heere heeft een afgrysen...'*. Hulst, Stadhuis

Jordaens gaat in op dit 'wterst en laetste gebodt'; in het resolutieboek wordt het akkoord met de schilder op 2 juli 1663 genoteerd. Door Hulst werd dus één van de afgewerkte schilderijen gekocht voor 500 gulden, een bedrag dat zowat het midden houdt tussen de geboden 315 en de gevraagde 800 gulden.

De *Justitia* die Jordaens vervaardigde voor Hulst wordt er nog steeds bewaard, zij het niet meer in het 's Landshuis, waar de Vierschaar zetelde, maar wel in het Stadhuis (afb. 2).[4] Deze *Justitia* is onderaan rechts gesigneerd en gedateerd 1663, een datum die overeenstemt met de notitie in het resolutieboek. Het schilderij, dat bestemd was voor de schouw van de Vierschaar, kwam overeen met de volledige breedte van de schouwmantel, en bovendien waren er nog twee smalle doeken die tegen de zijkanten werden geplaatst.[5] Van deze zijstukken is in het geciteerde archiefdocument geen sprake. Nu worden de drie doeken in de trouwzaal van het Stadhuis tentoongesteld als een triptiek.

Het hoofdtafereel toont, centraal afgebeeld, een personificatie van de Gerechtigheid, geblinddoekt met een doorschijnende sluier over de ogen. De gebruikelijke attributen, de weegschaal en het zwaard, worden aangereikt door een engel, waardoor hun goddelijke oorsprong wordt benadrukt. Justitia is gezeten op een liggende leeuw, en is vergezeld van de oudtestamentische figuren Mozes en Aaron, en van de personificaties Constantia (de Standvastigheid) en Veritas (de Waarheid). De twee smalle zijtaferelen (afb. 3, 4) geven afbeeldingen die het centrale thema expliciteren; putti met attributen illustreren bijbelse teksten die de rechters waarschuwen om op een rechtvaardige manier hun oordeel te vellen.[6]

Iconografisch gezien kan dit hoofdtafereel als traditioneel worden bestempeld. Het college van Hulst wenste een voor de hand liggende afbeelding voor de kamer van de Vierschaar, namelijk een personificatie van Justitia. Jordaens heeft voor deze compositie wellicht gekeken naar veel oudere schilderijen met gelijkaardige voorstellingen; er zijn in elk geval verwante elementen terug te vinden in het werk van Maarten de Vos.[7]

Het verslag in het Hulsterse resolutieboek leert ons dat Jordaens een succesvolle strategie aanwendde om een schilderij te verkopen voor een merkelijk hogere prijs dan oorspronkelijk de bedoeling was. Maar toch heeft zijn werkwijze in verband met de meerdere *Justitia*-taferelen wellicht niet het resultaat opgeleverd dat hij had gehoopt. Men kan aannemen dat Jordaens drie of vier schilderijen met hetzelfde onderwerp maakte omdat dit een tijdbesparende manier van werken was: hij hoefde zich slechts eenmaal in het onderwerp te verdiepen en enkele varianten te ontwerpen. Het uitschilderen op groot formaat kon dan in één moeite door gebeuren, eventueel met de hulp van medewerkers. Bovendien hoopte hij wellicht dat andere gelijkaardige bestellingen zouden volgen, en dat er dus voor zijn *Justitia*'s interesse zou zijn vanwege andere vierscharen of rechtbanken. Dit laatste bleek echter een misrekening. Door het aandachtig bekijken van andere versies met dit onderwerp, zijn wij er immers achter gekomen dat Jordaens in elk geval voor twee van zijn *Justitia*'s van 1663 geen koper heeft kunnen vinden.

Een ervan is waarschijnlijk tot aan Jordaens' dood in zijn atelier gebleven. Er was namelijk een versie onder de schilderijen afkomstig uit zijn nalatenschap, die geveild werden in Den Haag in 1734: 'No. 73. Een dito [groot stuck] Vierschaar of Moses en Aaron, h. 5 v. 7 en een half, b. 8 v.' (verkocht voor 30 gulden).[8] Zeer waarschijnlijk is deze *Vierschaar* te identificeren met een stuk dat veel later nog steeds in dezelfde stad te vinden was. Het hing tot 1908 in de Gevangenis van Den Haag, werd dan eigendom van het Rijksmuseum te Amsterdam, maar in bruikleen gegeven aan het Gerechtshof in Den Haag in 1937. In dat gebouw ging het verloren door het oorlogsgeweld in 1945 (afb. 5).[9]

Niet alleen het onderwerp en de afmetingen bevestigen de identificatie met een van de drie of vier versies die Jordaens maakte naar aanleiding van de Hulsterse bestelling, maar ook de datum: het doek droeg Jordaens' signatuur en de datum 1663. Het toont een variant met een Justitia die enigszins anders is afgebeeld; Constantia ontbreekt, en een groter deel van de compositie wordt ingenomen door Mozes' tafelen (hier twee in de plaats van een). Aaron is van plaats veranderd, en de figuur van Veritas is op de rug gezien. Op de linkertafel is precies dezelfde tekst geschreven als in het schilderij van Hulst.

Ook een derde *Justitia* konden wij terug vinden. De schilder zelf gaf er een wat onver-

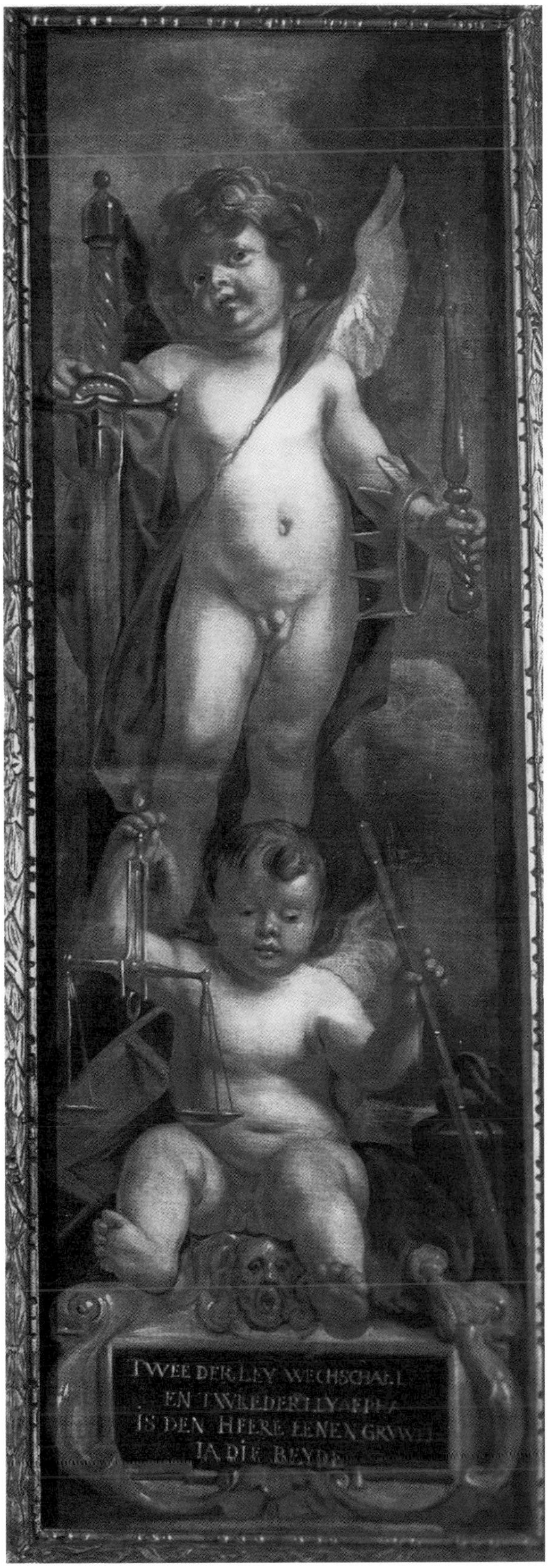

Afb. 4. Jacob Jordaens, *'Tweederley wechschael...'*. Hulst, Stadhuis

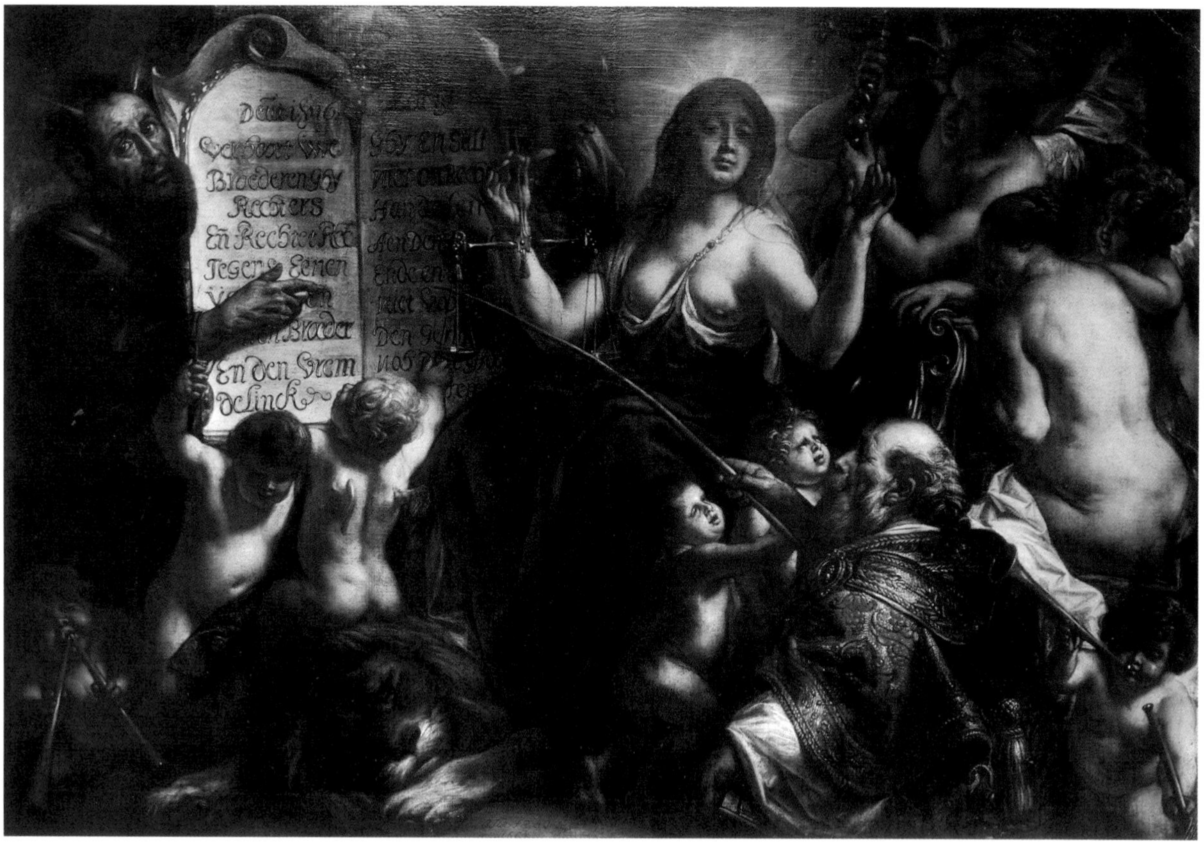

Afb. 5. Jacob Jordaens, *Justitia*. Voorheen Amsterdam, Rijksmuseum (in bruikleen aan Gerechtshof, Den Haag; daar vernield)

wachte bestemming aan. Begon het Jordaens twee jaar na zijn overeenkomst met Hulst duidelijk te worden dat hij de andere Gerechtigheid-doeken moeilijk aan de man zou kunnen brengen? In elk geval wachtte hij in 1665 voor één doek niet langer op een koper: hij gaf het ten geschenke, samen met twee andere schilderijen, aan de nieuw opgerichte kunstacademie in Antwerpen, om er de zaal boven de oude beurs mee te versieren. Deze zaal, de zogenaamde 'schilderskamer', werd ook gebruikt voor toneelopvoeringen door de Rederijkers 'De Violieren' en 'De Olijftak'.[10]

Deze derde *Justitia*, nu bewaard in het Koninklijk Museum voor Schone Kunsten te Antwerpen (afb. 6), werd door Jordaens aangepast aan de vermelde bestemming.[11] Indien het doek de datum 1663 droeg, heeft hij deze weggehaald of overschilderd. Bovendien werd het werk aanzienlijk vergroot: links en rechts werd een smalle strook toegevoegd, onderaan een brede strook en bovenaan nog eens twee stroken. Voor dit geschenk deed Jordaens weinig moeite om de compositie tot een aanvaardbaar groter formaat om te vormen; zowel bovenaan als onderaan is op de vergrotingen slechts een vage wolkachtige achtergrond aangebracht; enkel het gewaad van Aaron werd naar onderen toe uitgebreid; om de lege partij bovenaan enigszins op te vullen, zijn het grote zwaard en de engelenvleugels recht naar omhoog afgebeeld. Bij vergelijking met de andere *Justitia*'s lijkt het overigens waarschijnlijk dat Jordaens het zwaard en de weegschaal van hand heeft verwisseld, om zodoende het geheven zwaard centraal in de compositie (maar in de iconografisch onjuiste rechterhand) te kunnen afbeelden.

Zowel Constantia als Veritas ontbreken in deze variant. Links van Justitia is een engeltje met een brandende fakkel afgebeeld, waarschijnlijk verwijzend naar het licht van de waarheid; van de twee putti draagt er één een maatstok, en de andere misschien een weegsteen; zoals in een van de Hulsterse zijtaferelen verwijzen zij naar het gebod om niet met twee maten en gewichten te oordelen. Mozes' tafelen geven exact dezelfde teksten als in het schilderij van het Rijksmuseum. De oorspron-

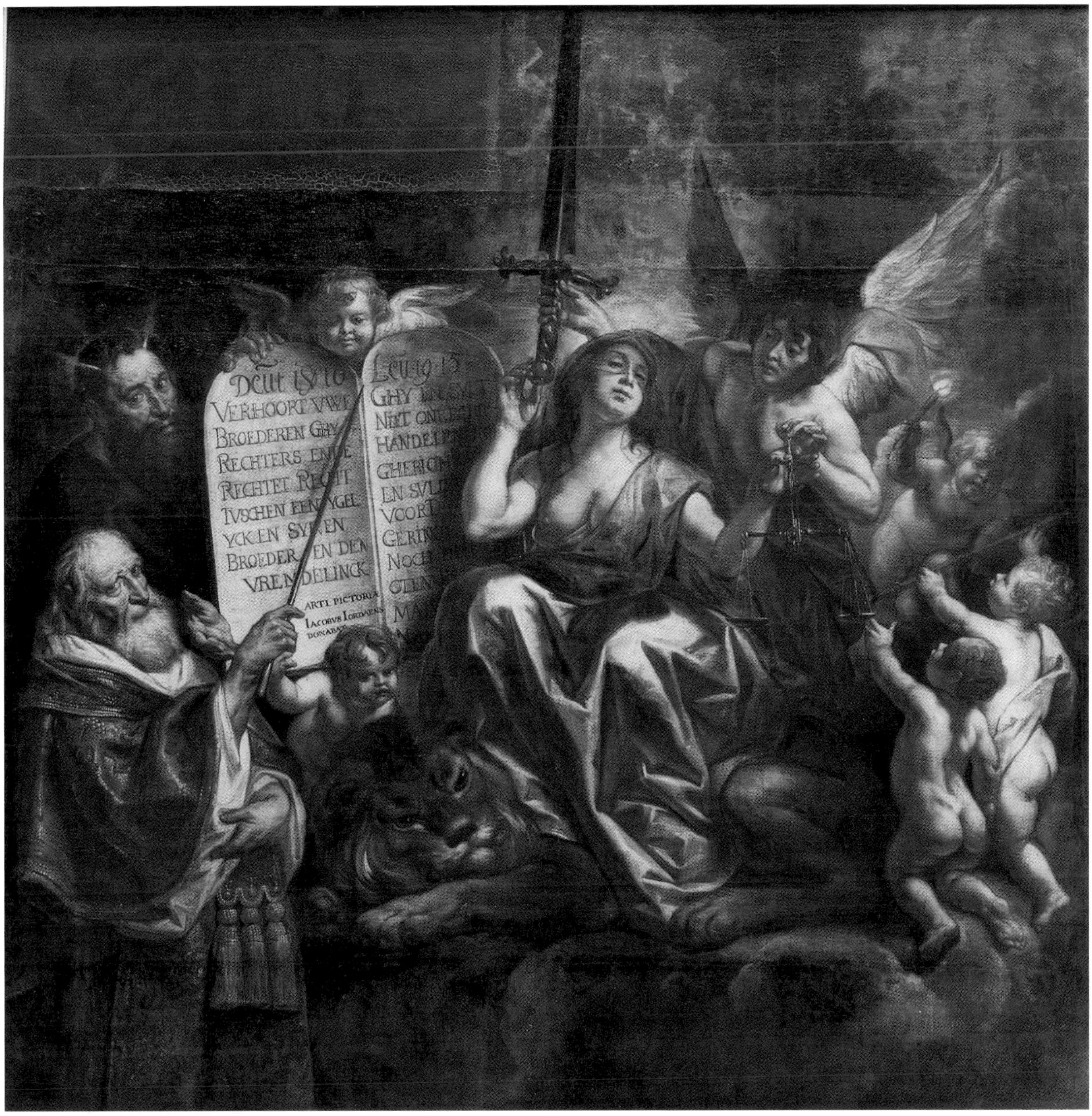

Afb. 6. Jacob Jordaens, *Justitia*. Antwerpen, Koninklijk Museum voor Schone Kunsten

kelijke tekst in ronde letters, die tevoorschijn komt bij infraroodonderzoek (afb. 7), werd overschreven met kleinere kapitalen, zodat er onderaan plaats vrijkomt voor een bijkomend opschrift. Speciaal voor de schilderskamer heeft Jordaens immers onder de bijbelse tekst nog een opdracht toegevoegd: 'ARTI PICTORIAE IACOBUS JORDAENS DONABAT'.

De twee andere doeken die Jordaens in 1665 samen met de uitgebreide *Justitia* schonk aan de kamer van de schilders en de rederijkers, hebben onderwerpen die beter aansloten bij hun bestemming. Het ene doek is een wat onduidelijke allegorie, onder meer betiteld als *De Allegorie van de Dichtkunst*.[12] Het toont een gelauwerde dichter die zich laaft aan een beker die hem door een muze (?) wordt aangereikt, in aanwezigheid van onder meer Apollo, Mercurius en Pictura. Het tweede verbeeldt het gevleugelde paard *Pegasus*, springend van de Helicon, waarbij het met zijn hoeven de bron slaat, die de letterlijke inspiratiebron werd voor de muzen en de kunstenaars (afb. 8).[13]

Wij hebben er het raden naar welke verklaring Jordaens gaf aan de rederijkers en de schilders voor het weinig toepasselijke onderwerp

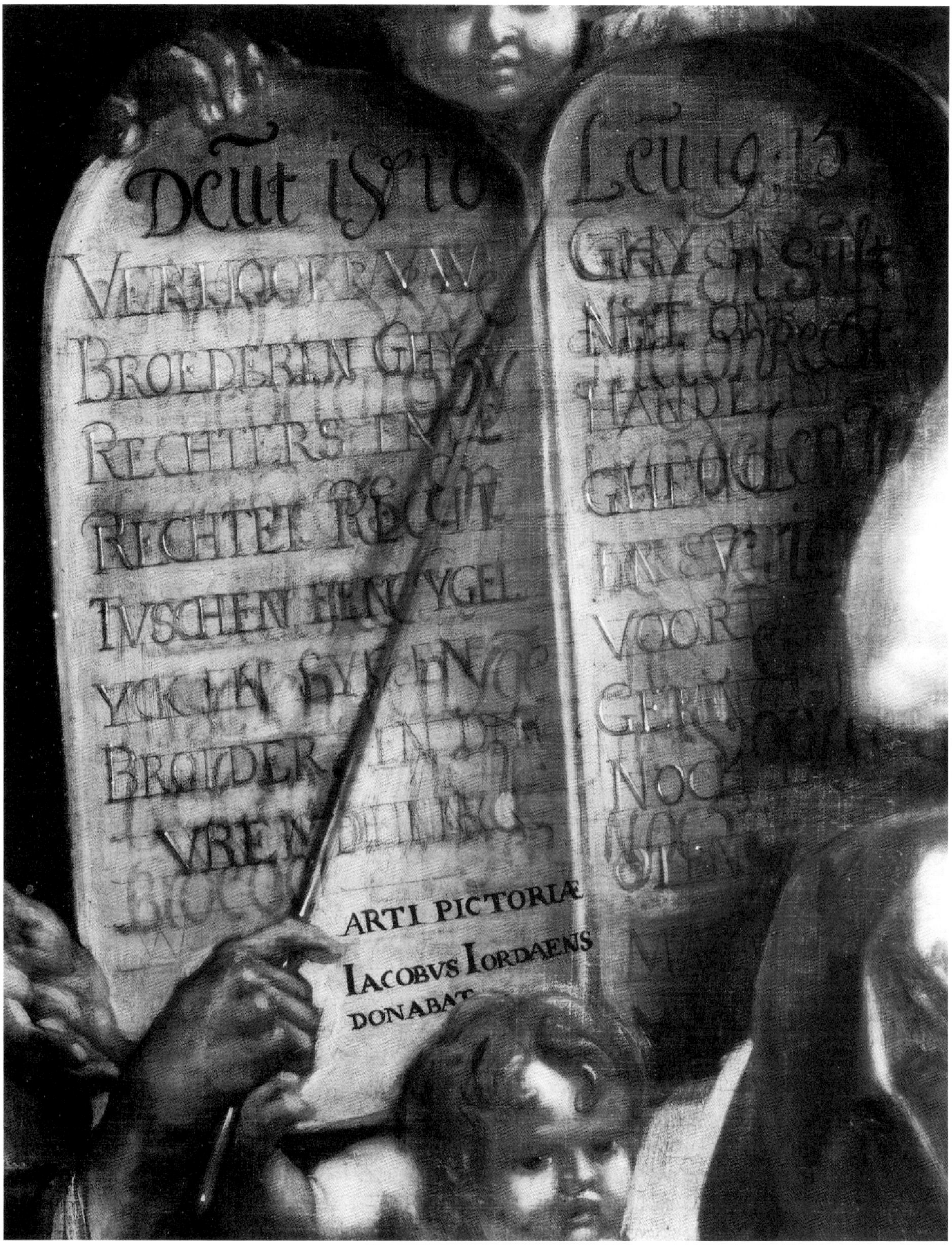

Afb. 7. Infraroodfoto van het opschrift op de tafels (detail van afb. 6)

van zijn geschenk, namelijk een *Justitia*. De kunsthistorici, die er ten onrechte van uitgingen dat hij het vreemde werk speciaal voor de kamer schilderde, deden geen poging om een verklaring te vinden voor het thema. In de literatuur kreeg het de titel *De menselijke wet gegrondvest op de goddelijke* en er wordt geopperd, zonder enige grond, dat het kan worden

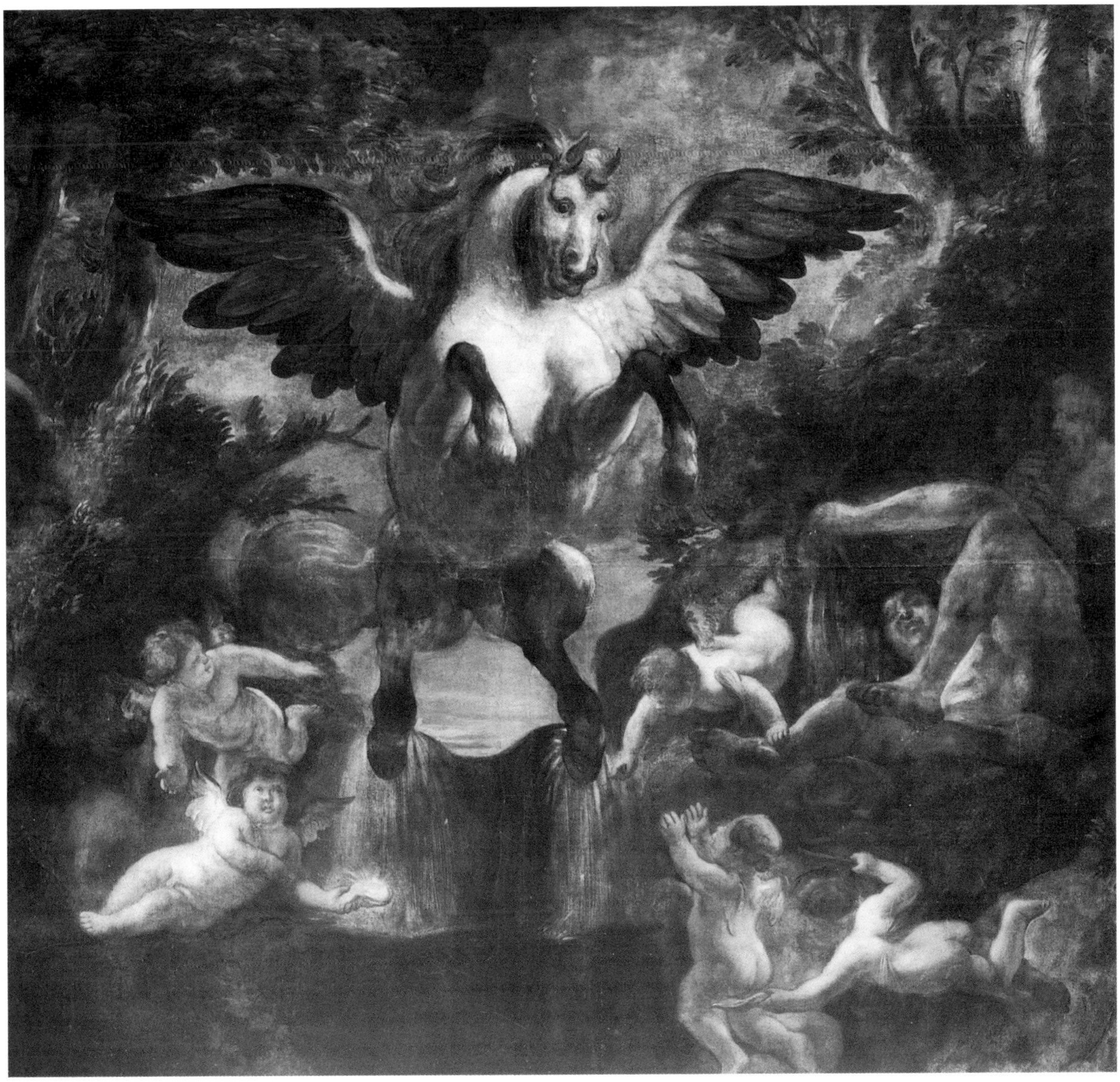

Afb. 8. Jacob Jordaens, *Pegasus*. Antwerpen, Koninklijk Museum voor Schone Kunsten

gezien als een 'kritiek van Jordaens op de politieke en kerkelijke toestand in zijn tijd'.

Dat het ging om een opgelapt 'afdankertje' van de schilder, was misschien wel voor Jordaens' tijdgenoten duidelijk. De Academie vereerde hem met een lovend gedicht en met een zilveren schotel, maar dit was waarschijnlijk vooral een obligate beleefde bedanking voor de man die dertig jaar voordien nog met Rubens zelf nauw had samengewerkt.

Het resolutieboek van het Hulsterambacht vermeldt dat Jordaens aan de opdracht begonnen was met het 'maecken van verscheidene schetsen'. Waarschijnlijk waren dit tekeningen op papier, die in grote trekken overeenkwamen met de naderhand uitgevoerde *Justitia*-schilderijen. Geen van deze tekeningen is bewaard, althans niet in origineel. Een kopie die overeenkomt met het schilderij in Hulst, bevindt zich in de Hermitage.[14] Daarnaast zijn er twee kopieën bekend van detailstudies die met de Antwerpse variant te maken hebben: een studie voor een putto met een liggende leeuw[15] en een tekening van de Aaron-figuur zoals die oorspronkelijk in het Antwerpse doek voorkwam, dat wil zeggen ten halve lijve en vanzelfsprekend nog niet vergroot onderaan (afb. 9).[16]

Jordaens' werken uit de jaren zestig kunnen voor het overgrote deel geen vergelijking door-

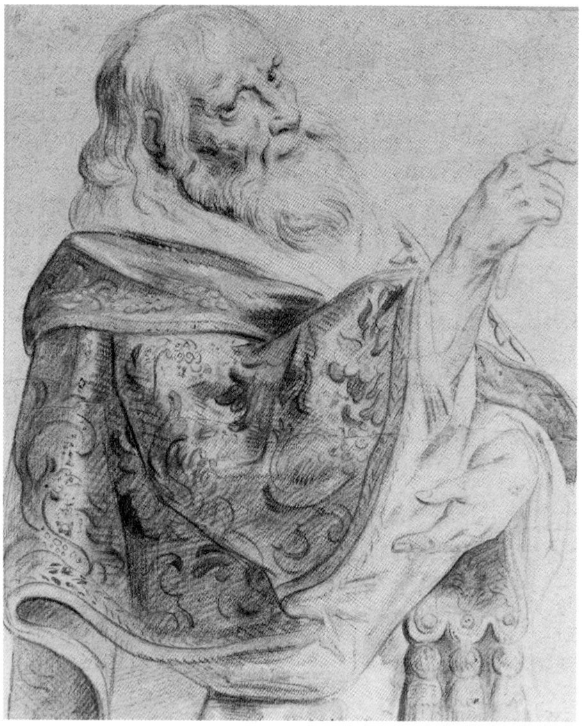

Afb. 9. Kopie naar Jacob Jordaens, *Aaron*, tekening. Londen, Courtauld Art Galleries

staan met zijn productie uit de jaren twintig en dertig, toen hij een zeer eigen stijl ontwikkelde, maar zich toch bleef laven aan de onuitputtelijke en inspirerende bron die het werk van Rubens hem verschafte. Het kleurenpalet verliest zijn glans. Vele doeken zijn als het ware composities in bruin, ruw geborsteld, waarschijnlijk in grote mate door het atelier; zij vertonen qua kleurgebruik een evolutie die men nauwelijks voor mogelijk zou houden bij het bekijken van de meesterwerken uit de vroegere decennia. Het componeren wordt vaak herleid tot een routinematig hernemen en combineren van steeds dezelfde figuren, die soms karikaturale trekken krijgen. Veel van deze wijzigingen hebben vanzelfsprekend te maken met het opdrijven van de productie en een veel grotere participatie van het atelier.

Jordaens' overeenkomst met het College van Hulst geeft inzicht in enkele aspecten van de doorgedreven rationalisering die zijn hoge productie mogelijk maakte. Vooreerst is er sprake van wat wij zouden kunnen omschrijven als 'seriewerk': een aantal doeken wordt gelijktijdig opgezet en uitgeschilderd. In het geval van de Hulsterse opdracht gaat het om varianten die aan de klant de nodige keuze geven. Naderhand kunnen deze doeken nog aan de noden van de opdrachtgever worden aangepast door een wijziging van het formaat (meestal een vergroting van het doek) of eventueel ook door een wijziging van bepaalde details in de compositie.

Er zijn geen andere documenten bekend die melding maken van dit 'seriewerk'-systeem, maar de studie van Jordaens' œuvre laat toe vast te stellen dat de *Justitia* geen uitzonderlijk geval was. Integendeel, het lijkt wel of dit systeem reeds tientallen jaren een essentieel onderdeel was van Jordaens' atelierpraktijk.

Men kan er inderdaad van uitgaan dat hij meer dan eens een reeks werken met dezelfde, of nagenoeg dezelfde compositie, gelijktijdig opzette. Dit was waarschijnlijk het geval bij de veelvuldige quasi gelijke versies van thema's zoals *De Aanbidding van de herders*, *De Vlucht naar Egypte*, *De Bewening van Christus*, *De sater en de boer* of *Mercurius en Argus*. Bij *De Vlucht naar Egypte*, waarvan een zestal versies bekend zijn, is er in de schilderijen zelf een bevestiging te vinden van het gelijktijdig uitvoeren. Eenzelfde belangrijk 'pentimento' komt immers voor in meerdere versies, onder meer die in Belgisch privé-bezit[17], en die in het Poesjkin-Museum te Moskou (afb. 10).[18] De rechtervleugel van de engel, die oorspronkelijk naar rechts gedraaid was, werd naderhand door Jordaens in beide doeken op dezelfde manier gewijzigd, namelijk met de vleugelpunt omhooggericht.

Dit systeem van het werken in serie kan wellicht ook een verklaring bieden voor het voorkomen van meerdere reeksen van de *Geschiedenis van Amor en Psyche*. Naast de reeks die Jordaens vervaardigde voor het Engelse hof, maakte hij nog minstens twee reeksen met plafondstukken, waarvan er een in zijn huis was aangebracht en een tweede in het huis van zijn kleinzoon in Den Haag.[19]

Zowel bij de Antwerpse *Justitia* als bij de Moskouse *Vlucht naar Egypte* werd het doek aan meerdere zijden vergroot. Het was ongetwijfeld zo dat Jordaens in zijn atelier een voorraad schilderijen had staan die dienden als in serie uitgevoerd basismateriaal dat hij kon aanpassen door vergrotingen of overschilderingen. Indien het hem zinde, kon hij onverkochte stukken ook ingrijpend veranderen, eventueel jaren nadat hij met het doek was begonnen.

Het tweede systeem, naast en in samenhang met het 'seriewerk', is dus het vergroten van

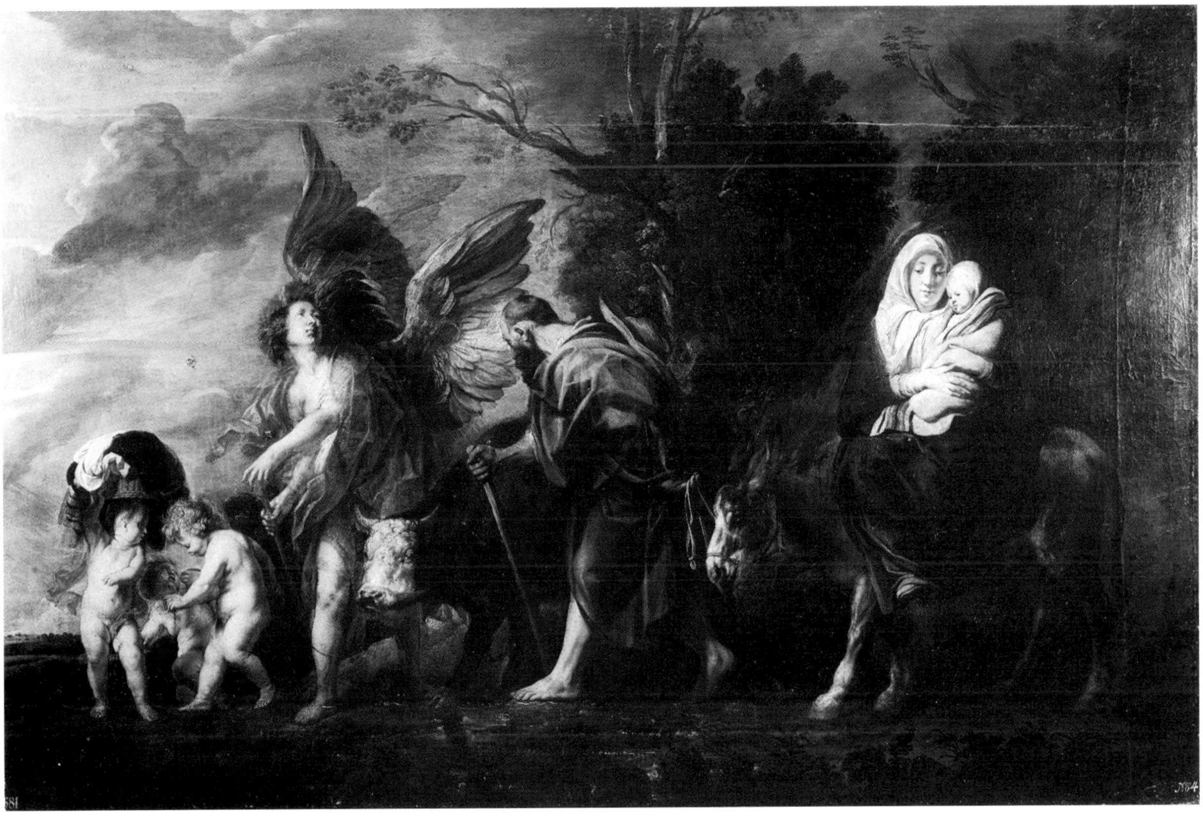

Afb. 10. Jacob Jordaens, *De Vlucht naar Egypte*. Moskou, Poesjkin-Museum

doeken of het op een andere wijze aanpassen aan een bepaalde bestemming. In een aantal gevallen kan uit de schilderwijze worden afgeleid dat er niet enkele jaren, maar wel tien of meer jaren liggen tussen het opzetten van het schilderij en het eindresultaat zoals wij het nu kennen.

Een eenvoudig voorbeeld is de *Meleager en Atalante* bewaard in het Prado.[20] Uit de datering van de schilderwijze is af te leiden dat het werk in twee fasen ontstond. De rechterhelft was een zelfstandig schilderij uit de jaren twintig, dat echter omstreeks 1640 werd verdubbeld tot een breedteformaat met toegevoegde figuren.

Een extremer voorbeeld is een groot genrestuk, een *'Zo de Ouden Zongen'* bewaard in de Alte Pinakothek te München. Het is geschilderd op een complex samengesteld doek dat in meerdere stadia tot stand kwam, zoals gedeeltelijk te zien is met het blote oog, maar ook wordt bevestigd door röntgenonderzoek. Onze afbeelding, overgenomen van een onderzoek door Konrad Renger (afb. 11), toont door aflijningen het ingewikkelde aanvullingsschema. Het werk draagt de datum 1646, maar het werd ongetwijfeld tien jaar vroeger begonnen als een compositie met een zevental familieleden ten halve lijve aan tafel, naar afkadering overeenkomend met de bekende *'Zo de Ouden Zongen'* in het Antwerps Museum. Een aantal figuren werd bovendien volledig overschilderd door personages met een geheel andere fysionomie.[21]

Het vergroten en aanpassen van composities is een essentieel onderdeel van Jordaens' werkwijze, en dit zowel voor tekeningen op papier als voor doeken. Ongetwijfeld hangt zijn vaardigheid op dit gebied samen met zijn activiteit als ontwerper van tapijtkartons. Bij het maken van tapijten was het immers gebruikelijk om het formaat, indien nodig, aan te passen aan de bestelling, en een goed gecomponeerd karton moest deze mogelijke wijzigingen enigszins kunnen opvangen. Het is inderdaad opmerkelijk dat Jordaens in veel van zijn composities als het ware de mogelijkheid inbouwde om het tafereel zonder veel problemen op aanvaardbare wijze te kunnen uitbreiden. Vaak is de vlakvulling zo opgevat dat een uitbreiding tamelijk gemakkelijk is te verwezenlijken, dat wil zeggen op zo'n manier dat de vergrote compositie toch harmonieus en decoratief blijft.

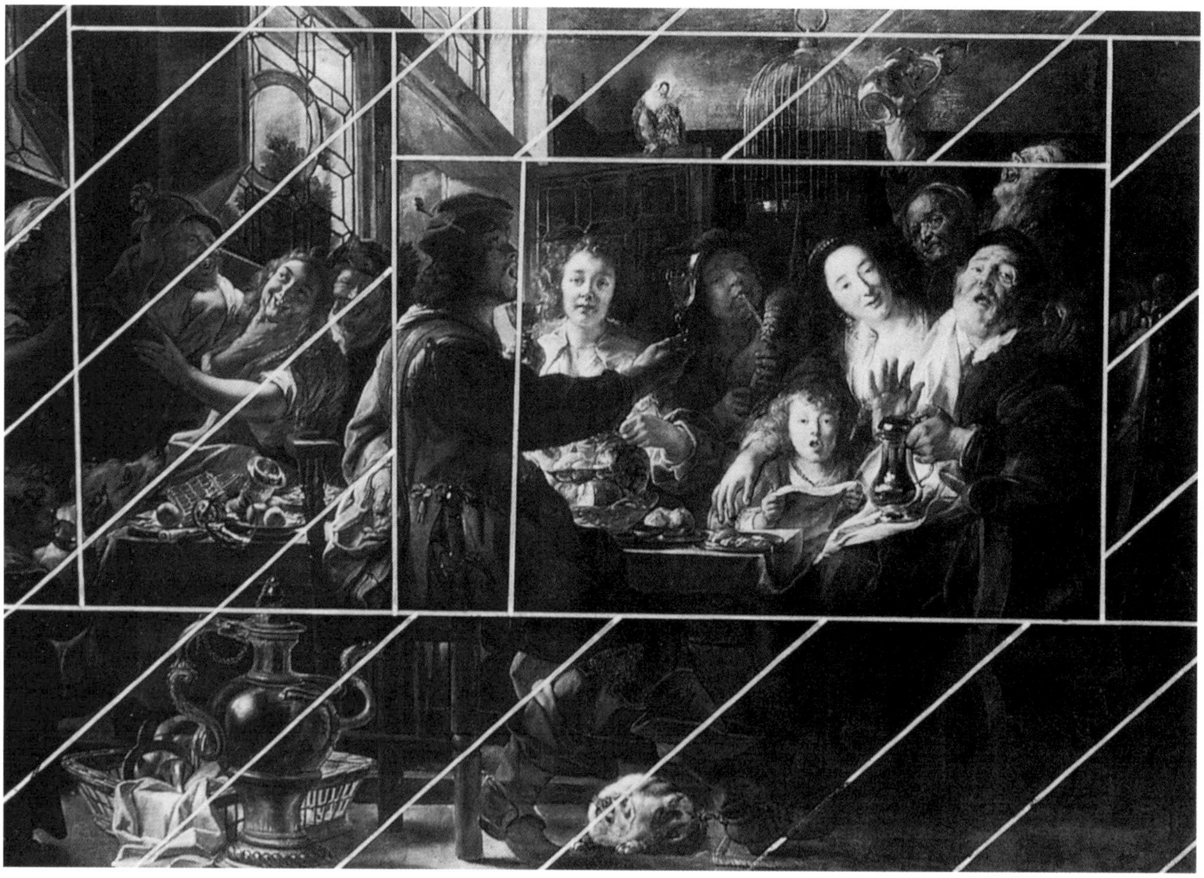

Afb. 11. Jacob Jordaens, *'Zo de Ouden Zongen'* (met aflijning van de aanvullingen, naar Konrad Renger). München, Alte Pinakothek

Kenmerkend voor Jordaens' kunst is onder meer dat hij vaak het volledige beeldvlak vult, vooral met personages. Een van zijn procédés bestaat erin om systematisch een aantal van deze figuren door de beeldrand te oversnijden. Zij zijn bijvoorbeeld ten halve lijve uitgebeeld en kunnen naar wenselijkheid worden aangevuld als figuren ten voeten uit; bovendien kunnen er weer andere figuren worden toegevoegd, al dan niet weer oversneden en voor uitbreiding vatbaar.

Het duidelijkst nawijsbaar is deze werkwijze in een aantal van Jordaens' tekeningen, waarbij de compositie in verschillende stadia werd uitgebreid op aaneengeplakte of overplakte stukken papier. Een ontwerp voor *De kruik gaat zolang te water tot ze breekt* toont het gebeuren eerst afgelijnd tot de knieën; dan aanmerkelijk uitgebreid, ten voeten uit, en met een decoratieve omraming.[22] Een goede illustratie van Jordaens' vergrotingstechniek biedt eveneens een *Aanbidding van de herders* (afb. 12). Een centraal tafereel met enkele hoofdpersonages kan als het ware eindeloos verder uitgebreid worden met meer 'omstanders', figuranten die niet essentieel zijn, maar gaan behoren tot een voorraad types, en uiteindelijk verworden tot stereotypen: de jonge vrouw met kinderen, de tandenloze oude vrouw, de vrolijke zeer zwaarlijvige man, enz.[23]

De klant kan dus kiezen wat hem het meest bevalt: de eenvoudige overzichtelijke compositie, die met enkele hoofdfiguren de essentie van het uitgebeelde tafereel toont, of de meer gediversifieerde, die allerlei personages ten tonele voert en meer inspeelt op de decoratieve en onderhoudende functie van een schilderij. Hoe later in Jordaens' œuvre, hoe routinematiger dit systeem van aanvullen wordt. De opbouw van composities met een overvloed aan personages wordt trouwens een van de kenmerken van zijn late werken, vanaf 1650.

Een derde werkwijze, die nog verder gaat dan vergroten en aanpassen, zou men wat oneerbiedig 'recyclage' kunnen noemen. De allegorie van Justitia, hét onderwerp voor een rechtsprekende schepenbank, werd door Jordaens omgebouwd tot een moeilijk in zijn context te plaatsen tafereel voor de Antwerpse 'schilderskamer'. Een tweede vorm van recyclage bestaat uit het polyvalent gebruiken van gelijkaardige delen van een compositie in een iconografisch geheel verschillende context. Deze werkwijze was vanzelfsprekend ook gebruikelijk in de ateliers van Rubens en andere historieschilders, maar in minder ver doorgedreven vorm. Kenmerkend voor Jordaens' werk vanaf de jaren zestig is immers de neiging om voor bepaalde opdrachten deze tijdbesparende werkwijze systematisch toe te passen.

Een goed voorbeeld biedt *De hulde van Haroen alRasjid aan Karel de Grote*, een modello voor een tafereel uit de tapijtenreeks van *De Geschiedenis van Karel de Grote*, te situeren in de jaren zestig (afb. 13).[24] Deze compositie gaat in grote lijnen terug op een oudere tekening van Jordaens (afb. 14).[25] Dit blad toont

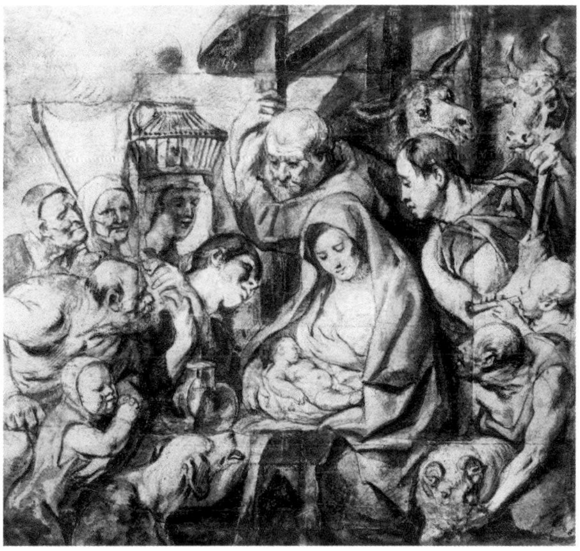

Afb. 12. Jacob Jordaens, *Aanbidding van de herders*, tekening. Londen, British Museum

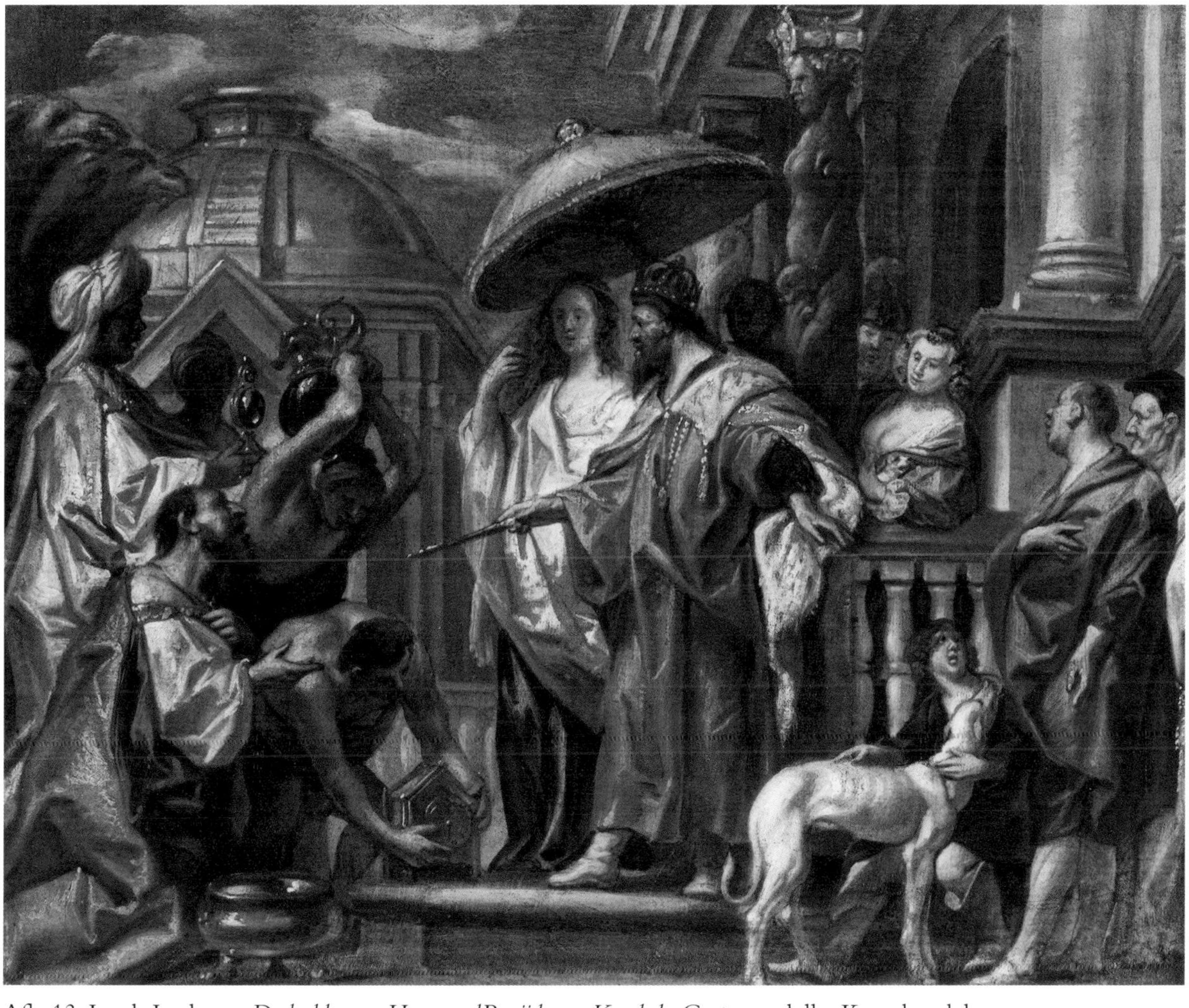

Afb. 13. Jacob Jordaens, *De hulde van Haroen alRasjid aan Karel de Grote*, modello. Kunsthandel

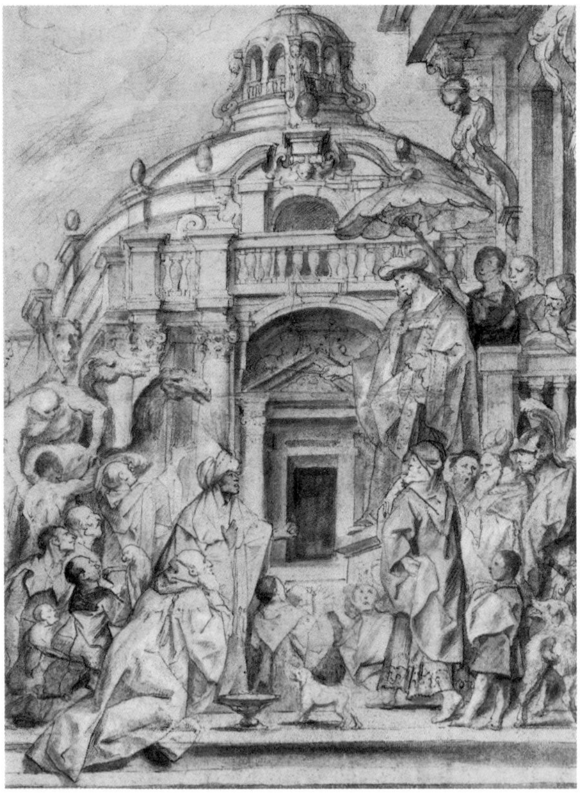

Afb. 14. Jacob Jordaens, *Tafereel uit het leven van Koning Salomon (?)*, tekening. Privé-verzameling

inderdaad een zeer gelijkaardige compositie, maar toch gaat het ons inziens in de tekening niet om de afbeelding van *De hulde van Haroen alRasjid* zoals steeds wordt opgegeven. De baardeloze vorst met een grote tulband, en in wiens gevolg men een hogepriester aantreft, kan immers onmogelijk Karel de Grote zijn, maar is veeleer een oudtestamentische koning. Wellicht gaat het om een tafereel uit het leven van koning Salomon, waarbij het indrukwekkende gebouw op de achtergrond de Tempel van Jeruzalem verbeeldt. De overname van de compositie uit een andere context, verklaart het vreemde exotische motief van de grote parasol die in het 'modello' boven het hoofd van de Frankische vorsten wordt gehouden.

Nog opvallender is deze 'recyclerende' werkwijze bij de tapijtkartons. Men krijgt zelfs de indruk dat Jordaens, misschien in opdracht van de wevers, ontwerpen maakte die toelieten de bestaande oude kartons zelf, of fragmenten ervan, om te vormen tot 'nieuwe' reeksen met een ander onderwerp. De dure investering kon op die wijze – na enkele aanpassingen – nogmaals worden gebruikt voor een nieuwe reeks. Van deze werkwijze zijn meerdere voorbeelden te vinden. Figuren en composities uit de

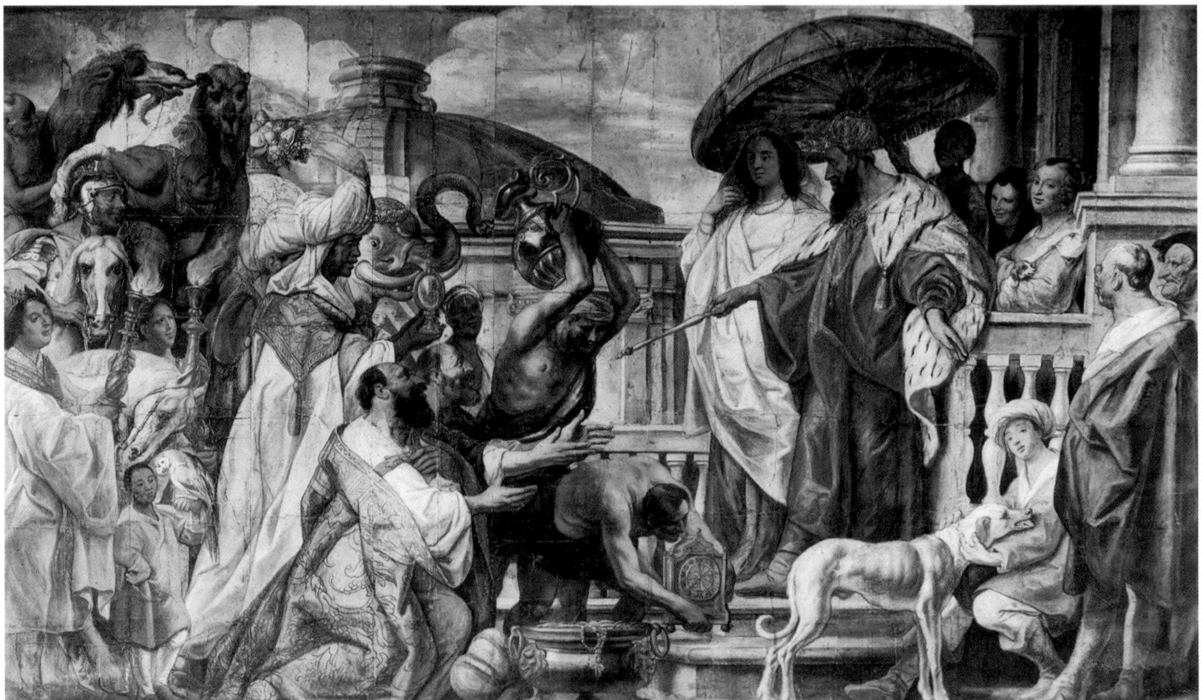

Afb. 15. Jacob Jordaens, *De hulde van Haroen alRasjid aan Karel de Grote*, karton. Parijs, Musée du Louvre (in bruikleen aan Musée des Beaux-Arts, Arras)

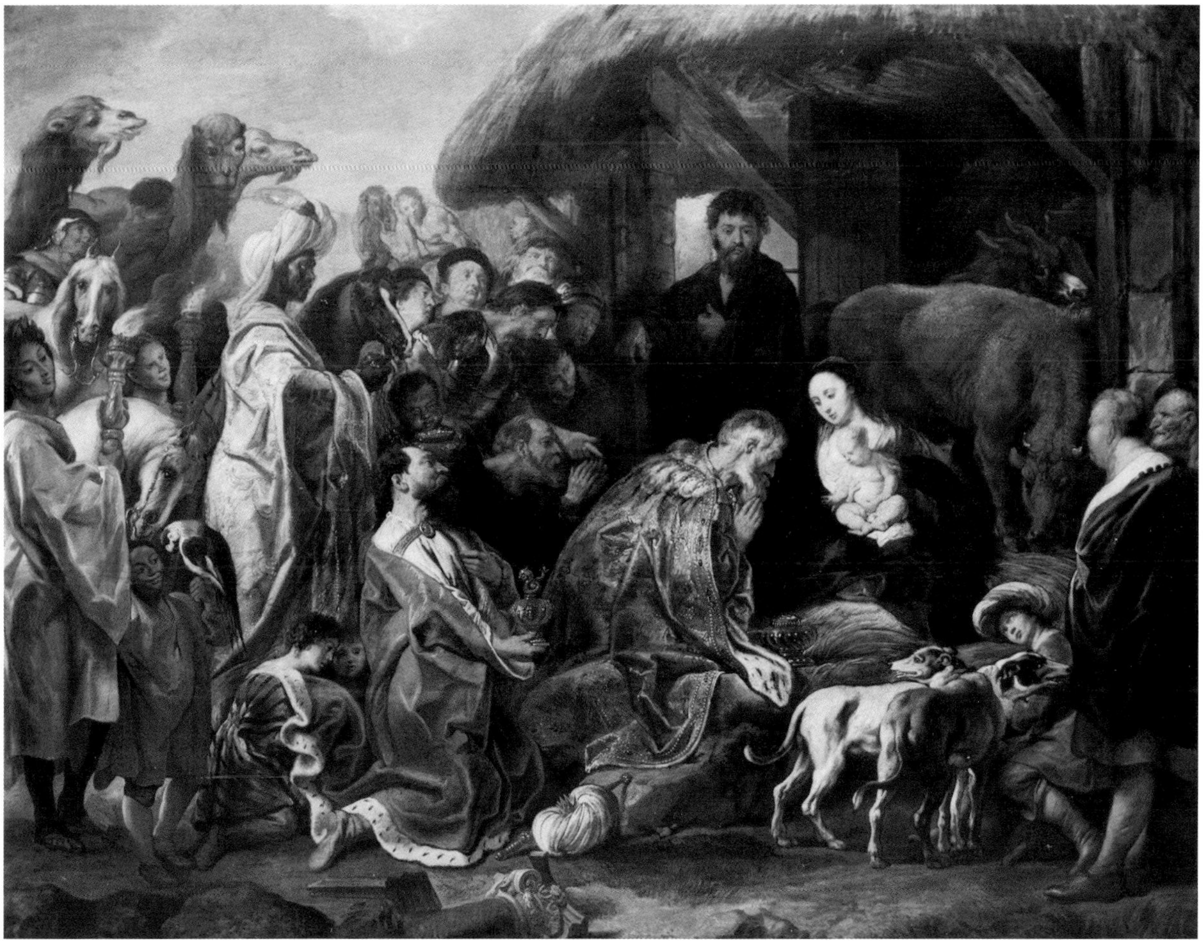

Afb. 16. Jacob Jordaens, *Aanbidding van de koningen*. Cherbourg, Musée Thomas Henry

Beroemde vrouwen werden omgevormd tot aanvullingen op de *Spreekwoorden*.[26] Bepaalde compositieschema's konden dienen voor het uitbeelden van de heldendaden van meer dan één beroemde vorst. Uit de opschriften in de cartouches bovenaan het tapijt blijkt dat identiek dezelfde taferelen (of delen ervan) gebruikt zijn zowel voor de *Geschiedenis van Karel de Grote* als voor de *Geschiedenis van Alexander de Grote*.[27] De figuur van Karel onderscheidt zich enkel door zijn volle zwarte baard van de jonge baardeloze Alexander. Een fragment van een karton met een tafereel uit het leven van de oudtestamentische Gideon werd gebruikt voor het tapijt met *Karel de Grote in gebed*.[28]

Of voor het tafereel *De hulde van Haroen alRasjid aan Karel de Grote* ook een ouder tapijtkarton is gebruikt, is niet vast te stellen. Opvallend is wel dat de hele linkerhelft van het karton (afb. 15)[29] met de afbeelding van het Perzische gezantschap bijzonder rommelig en onhandig is samengesteld. Twee figuren van het 'modello', de geknielde man en de man met de tulband, zijn letterlijk verdubbeld. In belangrijke mate zijn de motieven die erin verwerkt zijn – de kamelen, de jongens met de kandelaars, het knaapje met de papegaai, de donkere man in profiel met de tulband – terug te vinden in afbeeldingen van *De aanbidding der koningen*. Opmerkelijk is inderdaad de overeenkomst van het merendeel van de personages, ook die op de voorgrond rechts, uit de *Hulde van Haroen alRasjid*, met die in Jordaens' *Aanbidding der koningen* bewaard in het Musée Thomas Henry te Cherbourg (afb. 16).[30] Alle figuren zijn ook tientallen malen elders terug te vinden in andere combinaties. Elementen van de oosterse figurengroep zijn bijvoorbeeld eveneens herkenbaar in de 1669 gedateerde *Aanbidding der koningen* in de kathedraal van Sevilla, een schilderij dat met zijn pendant van dezelfde datum, *De Besnijdenis van Christus*, gerekend moet worden tot de laatste werken die wij van Jordaens kennen.[31]

Uit de gedocumenteerde opdracht voor Hulst en uit de geciteerde voorbeelden moge blijken dat het correct dateren van composities van Jordaens niet steeds een eenvoudige opgave is. Men kan er bovendien van uit gaan dat Jordaens niet als enige in Antwerpen de beschreven rationele werkprocédés heeft toegepast.

De kunsthistoricus, die zo graag werken dateert en alles in het œuvre van een kunstenaar op een rijtje zet, heeft ons inziens te weinig rekening gehouden met deze gebruiken in de goed draaiende en zeer productieve Antwerpse ateliers. Als te vanzelfsprekend ging men ervan uit dat eenvoudigweg het ene schilderij na het andere werd begonnen en afgewerkt. Talloos zijn in de literatuur de voorbeelden waarbij gepoogd wordt, zij het voor tekeningen, schetsen of afgewerkte schilderijen met eenzelfde thema of eenzelfde compositie, een 'logische' volgorde van ontstaan vast te leggen, en dit op grond van de kleine wijzigingen ('verbeteringen') in de compositie of op grond van een datering van de schilderwijze. In het licht van het voorgaande moge voldoende blijken dat het vastleggen van een dergelijke volgorde niet kan stroken met de realiteit, en dat de waarde van dit soort hypotheses sterk dient te worden gerelativeerd.

Bijlage I - De Justitia-taferelen van 1663

Bijbelse teksten op Mozes' tafelen:
Deuteronomium 1:16 - '[Uw rechters heb ik toen voorgehouden:] Gij moet beide partijen horen en rechtvaardig vonnis vellen, zowel bij rechtszaken met volksgenoten als met vreemdelingen'
Leviticus 19:15 - 'Wees niet partijdig bij het rechtspreken: begunstig de arme niet en zie de rijke niet naar de ogen. Spreek rechtvaardig recht over uw volksgenoten.'

1. De *Justitia* van Hulst (bestaande uit drie doeken)
Hulst, Stadhuis

1a. Hoofdtafereel: *Justitia* (afb. 2)
Doek, 153 x 222,5 cm; gesigneerd en gedateerd onderaan rechts: 'J. Jord. fe. A°1663'
Literatuur: P. Buschmann, *Jacob Jordaens*, Brussel, 1905, pp. 45–46; M. Rooses, *Jordaens' leven en werken*, Amsterdam–Antwerpen, 1906, pp. 209–210; R.-A. d'Hulst, *Jacob Jordaens*, Antwerpen, 1982, pp. 35–36, 262; [cat. tent.] *Jacob Jordaens (1593–1678)*, Antwerpen, Koninklijk Museum voor Schone Kunsten, 1993, p. 18; M.A. Moelands en J.Th. de Smidt (ed.), [cat. tent.] *Weegschaal & zwaard, De verbeelding van recht en gerechtigheid in Nederland*, Den Haag, Haags Historisch Museum, 1999, nr. 38, kleurafb.

Tekst op Mozes' tafel, gedeeltelijk verborgen onder de mantel van Justitia en de hand van Aaron (Deuteronomium 1:16, zie hoger):
DEVT.1.V.16 / VERHOORT VW[E] / BROEDEREN GH[Y] / RECHTERS ENDE / RECHTET RECHT / TVSCHEN EENEN / YGELYCK ENDE / SYNEN BROEDER / ENDEN VREMDE / LIN[CK].

In het midden zit de Justitia (de Gerechtigheid), 'geblinddoekt' met een doorschijnende sluier over de ogen. Haar gebruikelijke attributen, de weegschaal en het zwaard, worden aangereikt door een engel, waardoor hun goddelijke oorsprong wordt benadrukt. Justitia zit op een leeuw, wellicht een verwijzing naar de kracht van het gerecht, hoewel misschien ook kan gedacht worden aan een verwijzing naar de leeuwentroon waarop Salomon – de wijze rechter bij uitstek – zetelde. Rechts van haar is Mozes te zien met de tafelen van de Wet (hier één brede 'tafel' met opschrift), refererend aan de tien geboden waarop de christelijke rechtspraak is gebaseerd. Het opschrift is echter niet de tekst van de tien geboden, maar wel een andere bijbelse passage, die ook een gebod van Jahwe verwoordt, nl. een aanmaning voor de rechters om rechtvaardig te oordelen. De figuur in priesterlijke gewaden op de voorgrond kan worden geïdentificeerd als Aaron; hij wijst naar de bijbelse tekst met een twijg. Dit is de staf of de twijg die in de hand gehouden werd door de rechtsprekende, en hét traditionele symbool is van de rechtspraak. Naast deze bijbelse figuren zijn er twee personificaties die de gerechtigheid bijstaan: Constantia (de Standvastigheid) een geharnaste vrouw met helm en kolom en Veritas (de Waarheid), een naakte jonge vrouw met een brandende olielamp op het voorhoofd.

1b. Linker zijstuk: *'De heere heeft een afgrysen...'* (afb. 3)
Doek, 153 x 50 cm

Tekst in de cartouche onderaan:
DE HEERE HEEFT EEN AFGRYSEN VAN / DEN BLOETGIRIGEN EN~ DEN BEDR / IGERS DE HEERE STRAFT ALLE ONGER / ECHTIGE. SAP.5 V..7

Psalm 5:7 - Gij vernietigt wie leugentaal spreekt, de Heer gruwt van wie moorden en bedriegen.

Twee putti, waarvan één met een brandende fakkel en één met een geselroede en een medusaschild, verdrijven drie andere putti, die de bloeddorstigen ('bloedgierigen') en de bedriegers verbeelden. Een van hen, met het masker van het bedrog in de hand, stort naar beneden. Een tweede steekt een scepter omhoog en houdt onder de rechterarm een dierenvel dat niet met zekerheid is te identificeren: het zou kunnen gaan om een geitenvel of een vossenvel (die beide door Ripa worden opgegeven als attributen van bedrog of listigheid).

1c. Rechter zijstuk: *'Tweederley wechschael...'* (afb. 4)
Doek, 153 x 50 cm

Tekst in de cartouche onderaan:
TWEEDERLEY WECHSCHAEL / EN TWEEDERLEY AEPHA IS DEN HEERE EENEN GRVWEL / IA DIE BEYDE

Na enig zoeken konden wij deze tekst (zonder referentie) terugvinden: Spreuken 20:10 - Tweeërlei gewichten, tweeërlei maten: zowel het een als het ander is een gruwel voor Jahwe.

Twee engeltjes met attributen van de gerechtigheid verbeelden deze spreuk. Een van hen, zittend op de voorgrond, houdt een weegschaal en een maatstok (een ellemaat), terwijl achter hem nog andere meetinstrumenten liggen. Deze illustreren letterlijk de geciteerde bijbelse woorden en geven Jordaens' interpretatie van een 'aepha' (een inhoudsmaat, hier afgebeeld als een korenmaat), en een weegsteen.

2. De *Justitia* van Den Haag en Amsterdam (afb. 5)
Voorheen Rijksmuseum, Amsterdam, inv. A 2367 (bruikleen gegeven aan het Gerechtshof in Den Haag, 1937; in maart 1945 door oorlogsgeweld verwoest).
Doek, 176 x 242 cm; gesigneerd en gedateerd: 'J Jōr fēc et inv̄ 1663'
Literatuur: *Alle schilderijen van het Rijksmuseum, Volledig geïllustreerde catalogus*, Amsterdam, 1976, p. 309, no. A 2367.

Afgezien van Constantia, die ontbreekt, toont deze variant dezelfde figuren, echter in een andere houding. Er wordt meer plaats ingenomen door de twee tafelen in de plaats van één.

Tekst op de linkertafel (Deuteronomium 1:16, zie hoger): Deut.i v. 16 Verhoort Uwe Broederen Ghy Rechters en Rechtet Recht Tegens Eenen IJ[gelyken] En [Synen] Broeder En Den Vremdelinck

Tekst op de rechtertafel (Leviticus 19: 15, zie hoger) Lev 19 [v.15] Ghy en Sult Niet Onrecht Handelen Aen Den [Gerichte] Ende En Sult Niet Voor [trekken] Den Geringen Nog Den Groot[en] [Ee]ren

3. De Antwerpse *Justitia* (afb. 6)
Antwerpen, Koninklijk Museum voor Schone Kunsten, inv. 220
Doek, 244 x 236 cm; geen signatuur of datum te onderscheiden

Literatuur: F.J. Van den Branden, *Geschiedenis der Antwerpsche Schilderschool*, Antwerpen, 1883, pp. 839, 840; P. Buschmann, *Jacob Jordaens*, Brussel, 1905, pp. 45–46, 130; M. Rooses, *Jordaens' leven en werken*, Amsterdam–Antwerpen, 1906, pp. 210–213; R.-A. d'Hulst, 'Jacob Jordaens en de Schilderskamer van de Antwerpse Academie', *Jaarboek Koninklijk Museum voor Schone Kunsten Antwerpen*, 1967, pp. 131–150; M. Vandenven, [cat. tent.] *Jordaens in Belgisch bezit*, Antwerpen, Koninklijk Museum voor Schone Kunsten, 1978, nr. 42; *Koninklijk Museum voor Schone Kunsten, Antwerpen, Catalogus Schilderkunst, Oude Meesters*, Antwerpen, 1988, p. 206, als *De gerechtigheid*, of *De menselijke wet gegrondvest op de goddelijke*; W. Pleister en W. Schild, *Recht und Gerechtigkeit im Spiegel der europäischen Kunst*, Keulen, 1988, p. 93, kleurafb. als frontispice; M.A. Moelands en J.Th. de Smidt (ed.), [cat. tent.] *Weegschaal & zwaard, De verbeelding van recht en gerechtigheid in Nederland*, Den Haag, Haags Historisch Museum, 1999, nr. 39, kleurafb.

In deze variant, die werd omgevormd tot een groter schilderij, ontbreken zowel Constantia als Veritas. Links van Justitia is een engeltje met een brandende fakkel afgebeeld, waarschijnlijk verwijzend naar het licht van de waarheid; van de twee putti draagt er één een maatstok, en de andere misschien een weegsteen (dit is moeilijk te onderscheiden); in elk geval is hun betekenis verwant aan deze op het Hulsterse zijstuk waarin verwezen wordt naar het gebod om niet met twee maten te oordelen.

Opschrift: uit infraroodonderzoek (afb. 7) blijkt dat de oorspronkelijke tekst in ronde letters (zoals in het Amsterdamse doek) werd overschreven met kleinere kapitalen.

Op de linkertafel (Deuteronomium 1:16, zie hoger):
Deut.1.V.16 / VERHOORT VWE / BROEDEREN GHY / RECHTERS ENDE / RECHTET RECHT / TVSCHEN EEN YGEL / YCK EN SYNEN / BROEDER EN DEN / VREMDELINCK

Onderaan in kleinere letters:
ARTI PICTORIAE / IACOBUS JORDAENS / DONABAT

De tekst op de rechtertafel (Leviticus 19:15, zie hoger) is in grote mate verborgen door de arm en de knie van Justitia, en is gedeeltelijk te reconstrueren:
Lev.19:15 / GHY EN SULT / NIET ONRECHT / HANDELEN [AEN DEN] / GHERICHTE / EN SVLT NI[ET] / VOORTRE[CKEN DEN] / GERINGEN / NOCH DEN GRO / OTEN E[EREN] / MAE [...] / NAE [...]

Bijlage II - Verslag van de aankoop van Jordaens' schilderij door het Hulsterambacht

Den 22 Junij 1663

[in de marge] *[...] het stuck schilderye voor de [...] in de [...] caemer*
Naerdien in het collegie by [ver]scheiden occasien gesproocken was van een fray stuck schilderye te laten maecken, en voorden schoorsteen inde groote camer en vierschaer op te hangen, crachtich representer[ende] de justitie, en daer aen te besteden ontrent hondert ducatons, en daertoe [ver]scheiden persoonen

van[de] cunst, van d'een en d'ander waren voortgebracht is eyndelyck gesproocken met den here Jaques Jordaens tot Andwerpen, den welcke naer het maecken van [ver]scheyden schetsen, [...]elle aengenomen heeft en sich over den prijs niet geerne willen [ver]cleiren, maer gepresenteert indien het stuck gemaect synde, het collegie niet en behaeghde dat hij dat houden soude, en daer op dry a vier [ver]scheiden stucken by naer van een subject gedaen en den magistraet daervan geadverteert hebbende, om haer [...]e te nemen, is by eenige leden tot Andwerpen geweest synde gerapporteert dat [...]elle Jordaens elck stuck hielt op acht hondert guldens, en daer elck eenighe brieven gins en weder gewisselt en insonderlyck wegens dit collegie gesecht synde, –gesecht synde,– dat men van geen hooger prys gedacht hadde als van 100 ducatons en dat mits de voors. hooger eysen en indien die niet notabel gemindert wierd men genootsaekt soude syn te anpplickeren de voors. conditie by hem gepresenteert en lestlyck [...] geresolveert daer voor te bieden tweehondert ryxdaelders in specien, en in cas daer mede geen genoughen werd genomen, datmen dito jordaens sonder verder bedencken syn stuck sal laten houden, en daer op hem aengeschreven dat op vrydach den 29 deser twee gedeputeerden sullen aldae [...] om het wterst en laetste gebodt hem in een sacke contant mede te brengen.

Den 2 Julij 1663

De voors. gedeputeerden hebben gerapporteert dat het accord van[den] schilder hier voors. met de voors 200 Rijxdaelders is d[...] gegeven.

Resolutieboek van de magistraat van het Hulsterambacht, 22 juni 1663 en 2 juli 1663 (Middelburg, Rijksarchief in Zeeland, Archief Hulsterambacht, inv. 25a, folio 211r); vermeld door M. Rooses, *Jordaens' leven en werken*, Amsterdam-Antwerpen, 1906, p. 210.

NOTEN

1. R.J. Tijs, *P.P. Rubens en J. Jordaens, Barok in eigen huis. Een architectuurhistorische studie over groei, verval en restauratie van twee 17de-eeuwse kunstenaarswoningen te Antwerpen*, Antwerpen, 1984, pp. 272, 275–279, 291.

2. Bij een haardstedetelling, in 1659 georganiseerd door het stadsbestuur, wordt de huurwaarde van Jordaens' huis geschat op 450 gulden. Dit is veruit het hoogste bedrag opgetekend voor een schilder (F. Van Cauwenberghe-Janssens, 'De sociale toestand van de Antwerpse schilders in de 17de eeuw', *Jaarboek Koninklijk Museum voor Schone Kunsten Antwerpen*, 1970, pp. 233–240).

3. J.H.W. Unger, 'Brieven van eenige schilders aan Constantin Huygens', *Oud Holland*, IX, 1891, pp. 195–196; M. Rooses, *Jordaens' leven en werken*, Amsterdam–Antwerpen, 1906, pp. 162, 256–257.

4. Voor technische gegevens en een transcriptie van de opschriften, zie: Bijlage I, 1a.

5. Zie Bijlage I, 1b–1c; Max Rooses heeft de drie doeken nog gezien op hun oorspronkelijke plaats, tegen de schouw van de grote zaal, weleer de Vierschaar in het zogenaamde 's Landshuis: 'Deze schilderingen bekleeden de drie zijden van den schoorsteen... De stukken staan nog op hunne oorspronkelijke plaats en zijn in hun oorspronkelijken toestand, maar vervuild en verdoofd...' (Rooses 1906 [zie noot 3], pp. 209–210). Dit huis bestaat nog – er zijn nu overheidsdiensten in gevestigd –, en de schouw is eveneens nog aanwezig. Volgens (mondelinge) informatie ter plaatse zou de *Justitia* in 1949 naar het Stadhuis zijn overgebracht.

6. Over het recht en de rechtspraak in de kunst, zie: R. Jacob, *Images de la justice, Essai sur l'iconographie judiciaire du Moyen Age à l'âge classique*, Parijs, 1994; W. Pleister en W. Schild, *Recht und Gerechtigkeit im Spiegel der europäischen Kunst*, Keulen, 1988. Voor een studie over gerechtigheidstaferelen, waar taferelen met personificaties van Justitia echter *niet* worden bijgerekend, maar wel *Het Laatste Oordeel* en de *Exempla iustitiae*, zie: J. De Ridder, *Gerechtigheidstaferelen voor schepenhuizen in de Zuidelijke Nederlanden in de 14de, 15de en 16de eeuw* Verhandelingen Koninklijke Academie, Klasse der Schone Kunsten, XLV, Brussel, 1989. Na de redactie van deze studie verscheen: M.A. Moelands en J.Th. de Smidt ed., [cat. tent.] *Weegschaal & zwaard, De verbeelding van recht en gerechtigheid in Nederland*, Den Haag, Haags Historisch Museum, 1999.

7. Men vergelijke Jordaens' figuur van Mozes met rechterstwijg en de tafelen van de wet met de centrale figuur in Maarten de Vos' zogenaamd Panhuyzen-paneel, gedateerd 1575, nu in het Mauritshuis in Den Haag (A. Zweite, *Marten de Vos als Maler*, Berlijn, 1980, nr. 59). Dichter bij het schilderij van Hulst staat de *Gerechtigheid* die Maarten de Vos in 1594 schilderde voor de Eed van de Brabantse Munters in Antwerpen, nu in het Rockoxhuis in Antwerpen; dit toont ook een combinatie van een Justitia-personificatie met oudtestamentische figuren en tekstmateriaal (Ibidem, nr. 83).

8. In 1733 overleed in Den Haag Hillegonda Maria van Heemskerk, de weduwe van Jordaens' kleinzoon. In haar nalatenschap bevonden zich meer dan 100 schilderijen, waaronder 52 op naam van Jordaens (A. Bredius, 'Jacob Jordaens, beeldhouwer', *Onze Kunst*, XXVI, 1914, pp. 107–110). De meeste van deze schilderijen werden geveild in Den Haag op 22 maart 1734 (G. Hoet, *Catalogus of Naamlyst van Schilderyen* ..., Den Haag, 1752, I, pp. 400–406; Rooses 1906 (zie noot 3), pp. 259–262, Doc. B).

9. Zie Bijlage I, 2.

10. Uitvoerig over Jordaens' bijdrage aan de decoratie van deze kamer, zie: R.-A. d'Hulst, 'Jacob Jordaens en de Schilderskamer van de Antwerpse Academie', *Jaarboek Koninklijk Museum voor Schone Kunsten Antwerpen*, 1967, pp. 131–150.

11. Zie Bijlage I, 3.

12. Koninklijk Museum voor Schone Kunsten, Antwerpen, inv. 219; doek, 190 x 492 cm; *Koninklijk Museum voor Schone Kunsten, Antwerpen, Catalogus Schilderkunst, Oude Meesters*, Antwerpen, 1988, p. 205, nr. 219 (met drie betitelingen: *Nijverheid en handel die de bloei van de kunst bevorderen*, *De allegorie van de dichtkunst* of *De inspiratie van de dichter*); zie ook onze noot 10, en M. Vandenven, [cat. tent.] *Jordaens in Belgisch bezit*, Antwerpen, Koninklijk Museum voor Schone Kunsten, Antwerpen 1978, nr. 41.

13. Koninklijk Museum voor Schone Kunsten, Antwerpen, inv. 218; doek, 265 x 267 cm; Catalogus 1988 (zie noot 12), p. 205, nr. 218; zie ook onze noot 10, en Vandenven 1978 (zie noot 12), nr. 40.

14. R.-A. d'Hulst, *Jordaens Drawings*, Monographs of the 'Nationaal Centrum voor de Plastische Kunsten van de XVIde en XVIIde eeuw', V), Brussel–Londen–New York 1974, nr. C112.

15. d'Hulst 1974 (zie noot 14), nr. C116.

16. d'Hulst 1974 (zie noot 14), nr. C115.

17. Doek, 103 x 191 cm; gesigneerd en gedateerd, onderaan rechts 'J Jor.fe / 1641'; M. Vandenven, in [cat. tent.] *Jacob Jordaens (1593–1678)*, Antwerpen, Koninklijk Museum voor Schone Kunsten, 1993, nr. A65. Voor referenties over vier andere versies, zie: Ibidem, nr. A65, n. 7–10.

18. Inv. 1717; doek, 135 x 201 cm; gesigneerd en gedateerd 'I.Ior fec 1640'; X. Egorova, 'Changements autographes dans les peintures de Jordaens conservées au Musée Pouchkine de Moscou (d'après les examens radiographiques)', *Jaarboek Koninklijk Museum voor Schone Kunsten Antwerpen*, 1993, pp. 165–185.

19. N. De Poorter, in [cat. tent.] Antwerpen 1993 (zie noot 17), pp. 259–262, onder nrs. A84–A86.

20. R.-A. d'Hulst, in [cat. tent.] Antwerpen 1993 (zie noot 17), nr. A29.

21. K. Renger, '"Wie die Alten sungen, ...". Kompositionsänderungen im Werk von Jacob Jordaens', *Kunst und Antiquitäten*, 1989, 4, pp. 52–58. Deze aanvullingen zijn vergelijkbaar met de samenstelling van *De koning drinkt* te Kassel, waarvoor een tekening bekend is van het centrale, oudste gedeelte (R.-A. d'Hulst, 'Nieuwe gegevens omtrent enkele tekeningen van Jakob Jordaens', *Gentse Bijdragen tot de Kunstgeschiedenis en de Oudheidkunde*, XVII, 1957–1958, pp. 138–139, 143, afb. 3–4).

22. d'Hulst 1974 (zie noot 14), nr. A190; K. Nelson, *Jacob Jordaens, Design for Tapestry*, Brussel, 1998, nr. 28a.

23. Reeds opgemerkt door Julius Held, die een afbeelding met afkadering van het centrale deel geeft (J. Held, 'Nachträglich veränderte Kompositionen bei Jacob Jordaens', *Revue belge d'Archéologie et d'Histoire de l'Art*, III, 1933, pp. 214–223.

24. N. De Poorter in [cat. tent.] Antwerpen 1993 (zie noot 17), nr. A93; Nelson 1998 (zie noot 22), nr. 51a.

25. d'Hulst 1974 (zie noot 14), nr. A403.

26. Zie onder meer: Nelson 1998 (zie noot 22), nrs. 55–59, pl. 122–123, 128–129.

27. Men vergelijke onder meer de wandtapijten afgebeeld bij Nelson 1998 (zie noot 22), pl. 102–103, 108–109, 113–114; tevens zijn fragmenten van kartons bewaard die voor beide geschiedenissen werden gebruikt (Nelson 1998 [zie noot 22], pl. 100–101, 104–106).

28. Een groot deel van het *Gideon*-karton, waarop de krijgers van Gideon zijn afgebeeld, werd weggelaten in het tafereel met Karel de Grote (Nelson 1998 [zie noot 22], pl. 116–119).

29. d'Hulst 1974 (zie noot 14), nr. A418; Nelson 1998 (zie noot 22), nr. 51b, pl. 112.

30. Doek, 134 x 167 cm; M. Hours, 'A propos de quelques radiographies récentes', *Bulletin du Laboratoire du Musée du Louvre*, 1968, p. 54, afb. 1–2.

31. [Cat. tent.] *Pedro Pablo Rubens. Exposición Homenaje*, Madrid, Palacio de Velázquez, 1977–1978, nr. 51; Diego Angulo Iñiguez et al., *La Catedral de Sevilla*, Sevilla, 1991, p. 460, afb. 439.

Van zelfbeeld tot ezel: kunstenaarsalaam op zestiende- en zeventiende-eeuwse zelfportretten

Katlijne Van der Stighelen

Van spiegel tot zelfbeeld

In 1993 verscheen Joseph Leo Koerners imposante studie *The Moment of Self-Portraiture in German Renaissance Art*.[1] *The Painter's Eye: Hans Holbein's Self-Portraits and the problem of the artistic representation* is de titel van de lezing die Jürgen Müller op 22 november 1997 in The National Gallery of Art in Washington op het Holbein-Symposium heeft gehouden. De kunstenaar en zijn artistieke zelfbeeld blijken in een tijd van 'egoscopie' als de onze een 'hot topic' te zijn.

H.J. Raupp heeft aan deze problematiek al meer dan een decennium geleden zijn *Untersuchungen zu Künstlerbildnis und Künstlerdarstellung in den Niederlanden* gewijd.[2] Zijn conclusie was duidelijk. Het Nederlandse picturale zelfbeeld baant geen onmiddellijke weg naar de eigenheid van de kunstenaar maar biedt een allegorisch en/of emblematisch geïnspireerde boodschap die sociaal-maatschappelijke en artistieke aspiraties versluiert of verraadt. Het geschilderde zelfportret is 'programmatisch' en de typologische ontwikkeling wordt bepaald door 'aemulatio' en decorumvoorschriften. De kunstenaar legt zijn ziel niet bloot maar identificeert zich met het meer algemeen concept van de (liefst geleerde) schilder, de 'pictor doctus'. In zijn besluit oppert Raupp: 'Zum Einen ist die Frage nach dem "Realitätsgehalt" neu zu stellen [...]. In jedem Falle aber ist es notwendig, die Frage nach dem dokumentarischen Wert der Künstlerdarstellungen erneut aufzuwerfen'. Belangrijk is tevens zijn stelling: 'die Frage nach dem Realitätsgehalt schliesst die Frage nach dem "persönlichen" individuellen Aussagegehalt der einzelnen Bildnisse ein'.[3] Dit laatste verantwoordt hij door te stellen dat 'die psychologische Deutung bei Bildnissen dieser Zeit methodisch nicht zu rechtfertigen ist'; een mening die ook reeds aan bod kwam in zijn bijdrage voor de tentoonstelling over kunstenaarsportretten in Braunschweig (1980).[4]

Het opzet van deze bijdrage is tweevoudig. Primo: een voorzichtige kanttekening maken bij Raupps 'psychologisch voorbehoud' en secundo: de documentaire waarde van het geschilderde kunstenaarsalaam toetsen aan wat wordt meegedeeld in zeventiende-eeuwse boedelinventarissen van kunstenaars. Wat zeggen de inventarissen en wat toont de kunstenaar als zijn/haar attribuut?

Van zelfbeeld tot ziel(enroerselen)

In 1965 schreef J.A. Emmens in de inleiding van de tentoonstellingscatalogus *De schilder in zijn wereld. Van Jan van Eyck tot Van Gogh en Ensor*: 'Kunstenaarsportret en ateliervoorstelling [...] kunnen beide worden beschouwd als de uitdrukking van het zelfbewustzijn van de kunstenaar, zoals zich dit in de laatste vijf eeuwen heeft ontwikkeld'.[5]

De vraag naar het realiteitsgehalte van de voorstelling houdt dus verband met de vraag naar de persoonlijke boodschap die de kunstenaar met behulp van zijn zelfbeeld doorgeeft. Anders gezegd: waarheid en fictie moeten in het portret van elkaar worden onderscheiden om te kunnen achterhalen waar de kunstenaar naar toe wil. H.J. Raupp is eerder sceptisch in dit opzicht. We kunnen wel voorgestelde realia identificeren maar een psychologische 'Deutung' of analyse van toenmalige gemoedsgesteldheden lijkt hem onmogelijk omdat 'auch die seelische, charakterliche und emotionale Verfassung der Künstlerpersönlichkeit bis hin zu ihrer libido entsprechende Regeln unterworfen wurde'.[6] In voetnoot merkt de auteur, verwijzend naar Emmens' recensie van Wittkowers *Born under Saturn* op dat het zelfportret als genre best zou worden bekeken in samenhang met de biografische lite-

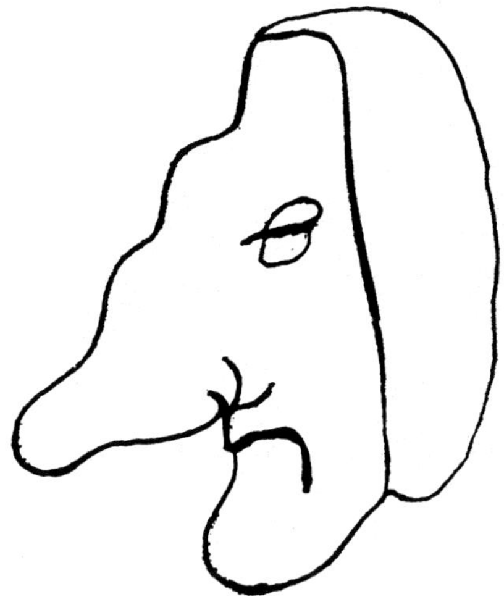

Afb. 1. Erasmus, *Zelfportret*, uit P. Spigt, Het ontstaan van de autobiografie in Nederland, Amsterdam, 1985, p. 75

ratuur, waaruit zou kunnen blijken dat kunstenaars mogelijk hun concrete levenswijze afstemden op 'literaire topoi'. Hier wordt aldus de vraag gesteld of men een gelijkaardig 'conformisme' ontmoet in de kunstenaarsiconografie en in het literaire genre van de biografie.[7]

Deze vraag vormt een boeiend uitgangspunt om metabletisch even na te gaan of beide genres ontstonden in een zelfde context. Allereerst moet worden getoetst wanneer beide 'zelfbeschrijvende' genres actueel werden en wat er met en rond het 'individu' gebeurde op het ogenblik waarop in de Nederlanden de eerste zelfportretten verschijnen. Decennia geleden (1952) schreef Friedländer dat men zou kunnen verwachten dat de geschiedenis van de portretkunst evenwijdig loopt met de geschiedenis van de biografie en de geschiedenis van het zelfportret met deze van de autobiografie.[8] Hij beroept zich op Burckhardt die al eerder had vastgesteld dat de jonge Renaissance een tijd was waarin zowel biografie als autobiografie als een min of meer specifiek genre waren verschenen.[9] Psychologen spreken over 'beginnende of verhevigde subjectivering' en aanzien Petrarca's klim naar de top van de Mont Ventoux als een exponent van een reeks nieuwe ervaringen.[10] Volgens de overlevering – en dit is niet zonder belang – is het ook Petrarca die rond 1335–1340 bij Simone Martini in Avignon een portret bestelt van Laura.[11]

In de Nederlanden kan men een vergelijkbare 'intensivering van het subject' pas vaststellen bij het begin van de zestiende eeuw. In 1538 publiceert Juan Luis Vives *De anima et vita libri tres*. In het boek stelt hij dat al te veel naar de Oudheid wordt gekeken wanneer men de ziel wil doorgronden. Volgens hem moet men niet zozeer onderzoeken wat de ziel is, maar achterhalen hoe zij werkt.[12] Twee jaar later verschijnt Melanchtons *Commentarius de Anima*, een soort fysica waarbij vooral de zintuigen onderzocht worden. Belangrijk is dat het zien zich volgens hem afspeelt in het oog, – niet in de wereld – en dus mag worden bevestigd als een zaak van het subject.[13] Deze opvatting heeft mogelijk het gebruik van de bril als 'Symbol der Selbsterkenntnis'[14] mede beïnvloed. Simon Bening beeldt zich af op een blad van 1558, bewaard in het Victoria & Albert Museum,[15] met een bril in de hand zoals iets eerder de intellectualistisch ingestelde Lambert Lombard (Luik, Musée de l'Art Wallon) het ook al deed (1549–1550).[16] De mens bekijkt zichzelf vanop een afstand en precies de afstand is nieuw. De in 1536 overleden Erasmus schrijft in 1524 een 'levensbericht' in een brief aan Conrad Goclenius. Het is een mengsel van 'modern-aandoende ijdelheid en de grote schroom daar iets van te laten merken'; een eeuwige strijd tussen ikzucht en zelfironie.[17] In zijn autobiografie schrijft hij over zichzelf in de derde persoon, wat nogmaals illustreert dat men het 'ik' als subject tracht te objectiveren: 'Ja, in zijn eijghen aanzicht hadde hij gheen behaghen en men heeft hem door gheen bidden en smeecken nauwelijks zoo verre konnen bringhen dat hij hemzelven zoude laten uijtschilderen'.[18] Portretten zijn er nochtans toch en daar draagt hij steeds de baret die de weinig fraaie vorm van zijn schedel moest verbergen. Interessant is te zien dat hij ooit ook eens een zelfportret krabbelde: meedogenloos intiem en dus enkel voor strikt privé-terrein bedoeld (afb. 1).[19] Erasmus, door Stefan Zweig de eerste 'bewuste Europeaan' genoemd,[20] beschikte over een ruime zelfs 'modern aandoende' dosis zelfbesef en deed dan ook op tweeërlei wijze aan zelfbeschrijving. U kan opmerken dat de geschilderde portretten meer decorum bezitten dan het getekende zelfportret en dan heeft u volkomen gelijk. Belangrijk is echter dat de psychologische boodschap van beide types vergelijkbaar is voor wie over voldoende informatie beschikt. Het decorum is alom aanwezig maar fungeert enkel als verpakking van een diepere inhoud. Men selecteert vormen van decorum die men van toepassing acht op de eigen persoonlijkheid.

Bovendien kan er even worden op gewezen dat sinds het begin van de zestiende eeuw, wel licht in 1503, voor het eerst een vlakke spiegel wordt gemaakt.[21] Dit materieel 'novum' liet de mens letterlijk anders naar zichzelf kijken. Men kwam 'natuurgetrouwer' en geleidelijk aan ook 'groter' in beeld. Spigt spreekt over de uitvinding van het 'verrukkelijkste en afgrijselijkste voorwerp uit onze huishoudelijke beschaving...'[22] Dat het spiegelen zijn consequenties heeft, leerde al de antieke mythe van Narcissus, een god die leed aan zijn zelfbeeld.[23]

De afstand tussen het vroegere en het huidige omgaan met zichzelf lijkt me dan ook veel kleiner dan algemeen wordt aangenomen. Het zelfportret als genre op zich ontsluit zich echter niet voldoende om de volledige draagkracht ervan in te schatten. Niet de traditie van het portret biedt sleutels aan voor de grondige interpretatie, wel een interdisciplinair onderzoek naar het eigentijdse mensbeeld. Er kan bovendien op gewezen worden dat het woord 'Psychologia' voor het eerst in 1590 werd gebruikt als titel van een boek van de Marburgse hoogleraar Rudolphus Goclenius: *Psychologia, hoc est de hominis perfectione, animo, et in primis ortu hujus*.[24] Het gaat nog altijd over de 'ziel' maar nu dan wel over de menselijke ziel (de hominis). Vanaf 1580 was ook Montaigne bezig met zijn *Essais*, waarin hij onomwonden schrijft: 'Ainsi, lecteur, ie suis moy mesme la matière de mon livre'.[25] Er zit canon in zelfportretten maar ze ontstaan niet krachtens de canon alleen.

Van ziel(enroerselen) tot genre 'sui generis'

Wanneer we het hebben over het beeld van de 'kunstenaar die zichzelf achter de ezel ziet zitten', dan dient het zelfportret van Catharina van Hemessen als het oudst bekende Zuid-Nederlandse exemplaar te worden voorgesteld (afb. 2). Het portret is voluit gesigneerd 'Ego Caterina de Hemessen me pinxi 1548. Etatis suae 20'.[26] Raupp aanzag het vroege zelfportret als een uiting van 'aemulatio' ten opzichte van de legendarische schilderes Marcia, wat door Günter Schweikhart in zijn boeiende bijdrage over Boccaccio's *De claris mulieribus und die Selbstdarstellungen von Malerinnen im 16. Jahrhundert* wordt bijgetreden.[27] Boccaccio ontleende zijn gegevens aan Plinius die een aparte paragraaf wijdde aan 'Pinxere et mulieres', of schilderende vrouwen, waarbij natuurlijk ook Marcia, die bij hem nog Iaia van Cyzicus heette, wordt opgevoerd. 'Iaia Cyzicena, perpetua virgo, M. Varronis iuventa Romae et penicillo pinxit et cestro in ebore imagines mulierum maxime et Neapoli anum in grandi tabula, suam quoque imaginem ad speculum. nec ullius velocior in pictura manus fuit, artis vero tantum, ut multum manipretiis antecederet celeberrimos eadem aetate imaginum pictores Sopolim et Dionysium, quorum tabulae pinacothecas inplent'.[28] (De eeuwige maagd Iaia schilderde met een penseel en bewerkte ivoor met een cestrum en ze portretteerde vooral vrouwen. Om een voorbeeld te geven: zo maakte ze een groot schilderij op hout van een oude vrouw en portretteerde ze zichzelf met behulp van een spiegel. Niemand had een vaardiger hand dan zij waardoor ze zelfs hogere prijzen kon vragen dan bekende schilders als Sopolis en Dionysius van wiens hand in elke galerij wel iets hangt.)

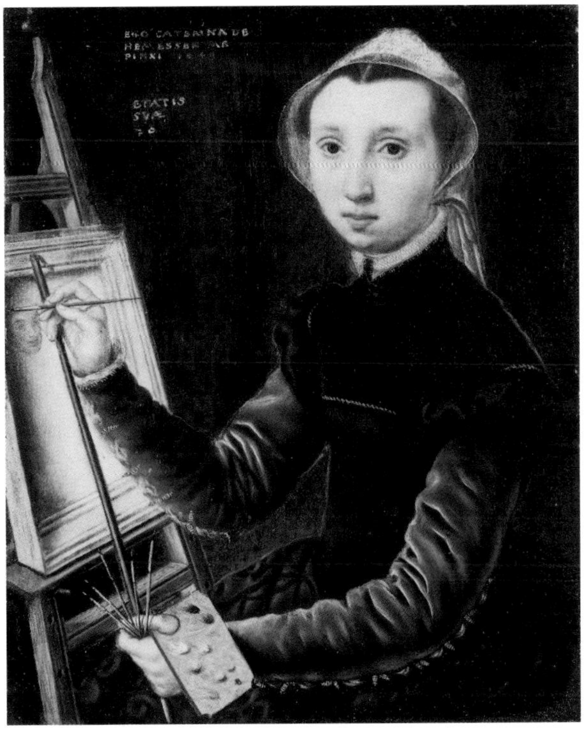

Afb. 2. Catharina van Hemessen, *Zelfportret achter de ezel*, 1548. Bazel, Öffentliche Kunstsammlung

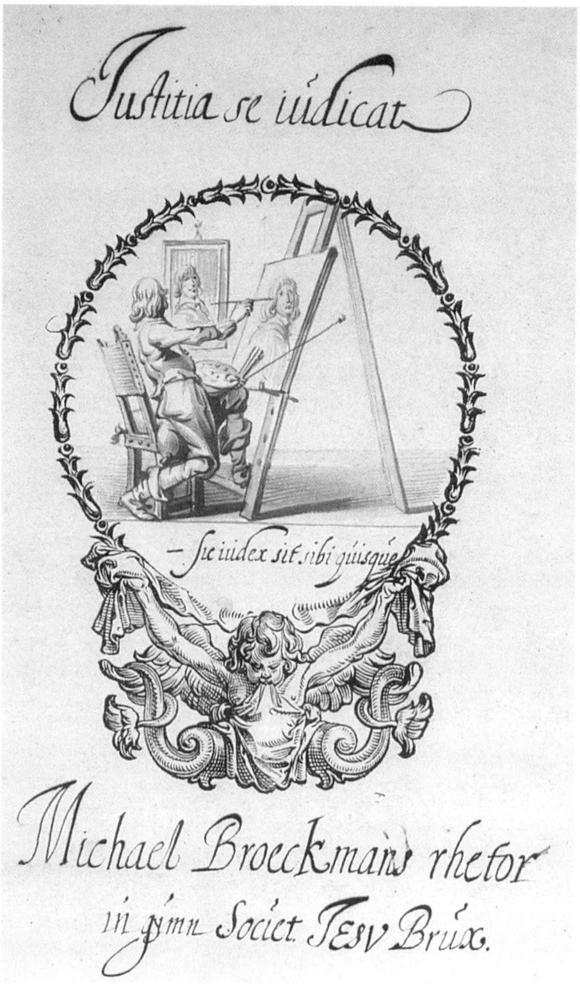

Afb. 3. Anoniem, *Een schilder in zijn atelier*, Handschrift van de Brusselse jezuïeten. Brussel, Koninklijke Bibliotheek, inv. 20.303, fol. 48v

Wat is nu de relatie met Catharina van Hemessen? Was zij vertrouwd met de voorstelling van Marcia of Iaia van Cyzicus vanuit de miniatuurtraditie of kende zij ook de teksten?[29] Het gaat ver om te veronderstellen dat zij Latijn kende maar zij had in ieder geval iemand in haar onmiddellijke omgeving die haar kon adviseren zoals blijkt uit de 'sprekende' signatuur 'ego me pinxi'. Bij vergelijking tussen tekst en portret komt tot uiting dat ze accenten legt op aspecten die ook bij Iaia aanwezig zijn 'penicillo pinxit [...], suam quoque imaginem ad speculum'. Met behulp van het penseel geeft ze haar eigen gelaat weer. Haar schildersezel is eigentijds: het gaat om een mooi geprofileerde eikenhouten driepootezel met op verschillende hoogte instelbaar draagvlak. De spiegel is overbodig omdat, zoals Günter Schweikhart reeds opmerkte,[30] de compositie op het paneeltje in spiegelbeeld Catharina's portret toont. Als schilderes suggereert ze dus tegelijk beeld en spiegelbeeld, wat zij in haar spiegel ziet, valt samen met de voorstelling op het paneel. Haar kunst en/of kunde maakt de spiegel als attribuut overbodig. Voor zover mij bekend, komt hij ook op latere zelfportretten zo goed als niet meer voor. Een enkele uitzondering is te vinden in een aan Sallaert toe te schrijven monochrome gouache in de emblematabundel die hij in 1644 illustreerde voor de Brusselse jezuïeten. Een zichzelf schilderende artiest (afb. 3) poseert onder het motto 'Iustitia se iudicat' en het onderschrift luidt: 'Sic iudex sit sibi quisque'[31] wat zoveel betekent als 'laat ieder zijn eigen rechter zijn'. De zelfafbeelding wordt hier dus duidelijk overdrachtelijk geïnterpreteerd hoewel de zelfbetrokkenheid als gegeven belangwekkend blijft.

Volgens Plinius en Boccaccio was Iaia een hooggewaardeerde artieste en dus rijk. 'Werkkledij' heeft ze in miniatuurvoorstellingen niet of slechts zelden aangetrokken. Ook Catharina poseert in een fluwelen ensemble met modische splitmouwen. Schweikhart ziet in de 'würdevolle Haltung und Kleidung' een referentie aan het feit 'dass sich die Malerin nicht bei einer niedrigen handwerklichen Tätigkeit vorstellt, sondern das Selbstporträt dazu nutzt, den höheren Anspruch der Malerei zur Geltung zu bringen'.[32] Naar mijn bescheiden mening was het de jonge vrouw niet om een theoretische opwaardering van het 'ambacht' te doen maar veeleer om een opwaardering van zichzelf. Zij schildert geen allegorie van dé Pictura maar maakt een portret van zichzelf, zoals ze dagelijks verschijnt, dus in fraaie, 'burgerlijke' uitdossing. De activiteit waarmee ze zichzelf kan legaliseren ('ego me pinxi...') stelt ze aanwezig door attributen, die als pars pro toto functioneren. Het voorbeeld van Marcia dient eerder ter verantwoording dan tot aemulatio. Het opzet blijft bescheiden en ze heeft indringend de compositie van de middeleeuwse miniaturen gewijzigd. Ze treedt naar voor in het beeldvlak en viseert de potentiële kijker. Zo introduceert ze vooral zichzelf of koestert ze tegelijk de ambitie zich in te schrijven in een traditie van schilderende vrouwen?

Indien de twintigjarige dochter van een Antwerpse maniërist er in het midden van de zestiende eeuw voor kiest om de rode draad van de vrouwelijke traditie terug op te nemen, kan dit alleen maar mogelijk zijn geweest onder invloed van het 'moderne' humanistische gedachtegoed.

Juan Luis Vives kwam al eerder ter sprake als auteur van *De anima et vita* maar hij kan tevens worden aangezien als één van de meest vrouwvriendelijke auteurs van de zestiende eeuw. In 1523 schreef hij *De instructione feminae christianae*, waarvan even later verscheidene vertalingen verschenen.[33] Zijn werk was in de Zuidelijke Nederlanden verspreid hoewel de geschriften van Erasmus en Thomas More aan Jan van Hemessen als kunstenaar beter bekend moeten zijn geweest. Als 'navolger' van Metsijs' moraliserende genrestukken kunnen we gerust veronderstellen dat hij vertrouwd was met Erasmus' hekelende stijl, zijn appreciatie van het portretgenre kende en via Erasmus geïnformeerd was over de geleerde dochters van Thomas More. In september 1521 schreef Erasmus over de dochters van More aan Budé: '[...] Zoudt ge de dochters van More eens bezoeken, dan zult u hen niet in ledigheid aantreffen... De een vertaalt Titus Livius; zij zijn met de studiën reeds zover gevorderd, dat zij dergelijke schrijvers zonder moeite kunnen lezen, hoogstens bij een enkel woord aarzelend (een woord dat ook voor mensen als ik nog wel eens een probleem zou zijn)... Doorgaans zijn de mensen van mening, dat de wetenschappen voor de onschuld en de goede naam van het meisje niet erg bevorderlijk zijn. Hierin heeft More mij wel van het tegendeel overtuigd.'[34]

Uit een brief die More in het najaar van 1523 schrijft aan zijn oudste dochter Margaret (vóór oktober 1505–1544) blijkt eveneens dat hij haar intellectuele ambities ten zeerste stimuleerde. Verder wordt uit het citaat meteen duidelijk dat intellectueel bedreven vrouwen als curiosa werden aangezien en dat het wantrouwen ten opzichte van dit onbekende fenomeen groot was. Niettemin waardeerde hij haar als geleerde en als moeder: 'Mijn lieve Margaret, [...] toen ik je voortreffelijke brief las, had ik juist bezoek van een voorname, zeer geleerde heer. Hij liet zich slechts met veel moeite ervan overtuigen, dat je daarbij noch door een leraar noch door iemand anders geholpen was. En het is toch ook werkelijk zo, dat de anderen eerder jouw hulp konden gebruiken dan jij de hunne. Het werd mij nog weer eens te meer duidelijk, dat wat ik je vroeger schertsenderwijs gezegd heb, ook in alle ernst zo is: Nimmer zal men jouw geschriften als je eigen werk beschouwen, steeds zal men menen, dat je daarbij hulp van vreemden hebt gehad, ja, zelfs denken, dat je een en ander van een ander hebt overgeschreven. Lieve Margaret, hoewel je nimmer kunt hopen dat je naam beroemd zal zijn, toch zet je je studiën en je verdere vorming voort. Je houdt van je man en van mij en bent er geheel tevreden mee, dat wij je lezers vormen. Wij hopen en bidden, dat de aanstaande geboorte van je kind voorspoedig en gelukkig zal verlopen. Moge je ons een nakomeling schenken, die uitgezonderd de kunne zijn moeder in alles zal mogen evenaren. Er is tenminste één vrouw, die de achterstelling van haar geslacht door des te meer uitblinkende deugden en geleerdheid enigszins teniet doet. Aan één zo'n jonge vrouw zou ik uiteraard de voorkeur geven boven drie knapen. Het ga u goed, mijn lieve dochter.'[35] Zijn visie op de 'achterstelling van het vrouwelijk geslacht' klinkt 'modern' in de oren en getuigt tegelijk van een onverstoorbaar fatalisme.

Naast het antieke prototype waren er dus voor Catharina van Hemessen ook min of meer contemporaine inspiratiebronnen voorhanden. De dochter(s) van More waren geen artiesten maar ambieerden in geleerdheid wat hun mannelijke tijdgenoten probeerden te bereiken. Zij werkten echter niet voor de roem maar om het genoegen van de studie zelf. Ze stelden zich tevreden met een publiek bestaande uit vader en echtgenoot.

In een dergelijke culturele context met een voorzichtig ontluikende belangstelling voor de mogelijkheden van een handvol elitaire vrouwen moet ook Catharina van Hemessens activiteit worden gesitueerd. En al was Jan van Hemessen verantwoordelijk voor deze vormen van cultuuroverdracht, toch participeerden vader en dochter niet geheel aan eenzelfde traditie. Ook More maakt onderscheid tussen de openbare masculiene wereld van de geleerdheid en de binnenskamerse activiteiten van vrouwen. Het voorbeeld van Marcia of Iaia kan dan ook moeilijk een vergelijkbare relevantie hebben voor vader en dochter. De geheroïseerde antieke voorbeelden schitteren enkel aan het subculturele feminiene firmament omdat ook bij Plinius artistiek actieve vrouwen uitsluitend als uitzondering op de regel worden gepresenteerd. Het vrouwelijk zelfportret schrijft zich dankzij intertextuele en/of interpicturale linken in een andere traditie in. Het lijkt me dan ook onaanvaardbaar portretten van verleden vrouwelijke kunstenaars bij het ontstaan (of de heropleving) van een uitzonderlijke picturale traditie zonder meer naast werk van mannelijke tijdgenoten te plaatsen.

De vraag blijft natuurlijk wel op welke wijze zich beide genres tot elkaar verhouden. En al is het verlokkelijk te veronderstellen dat via het Marcia-spoor ook mannelijke kunstenaars de relevantie van het 'zelfthema' herontdekten, voorlopig ontbreken daarvoor voldoende argumenten. Uit recente publicaties aangaande vroege zelfportretten van Vlaamse Primitieven is anderzijds wel gebleken dat het genre langs mannelijke lijn eveneens effectief werd geïnspireerd vanuit de antieke literatuur.[36] Cicero, Valerius Maximus, Plutarchus en Dio Chrysostomus verhalen allen dat Phidias zichzelf zou hebben afgebeeld op het schild van Athena Parthenon. Deze indirecte, wat verdoken presentie, zou Jan van Eyck op het idee hebben gebracht een minuscuul zelfportret ten voeten uit aan te brengen op het schild van de Heilige Joris in zijn compositie met kanunnik Van der Paele (Brugge, Groeningemuseum; 1434–1436).[37] Zoals Justus Müller Hofstede terecht opmerkte, biedt de antieke bron geen verklaring voor het uiterst beperkte formaat van het zelfbeeld. Onsterfelijkheid zoeken in bescheidenheid ten opzichte van de meer belangrijke opdrachtgever uit wiens hand de kunstenaar eet, is dit een mogelijke topos?[38] Of is het kleine formaat van het zelfbeeld een laatste restant van een middeleeuwse traditie die de kunstenaar dwingt – op de drempel van de Renaissance – zichzelf als 'scheppend kunstenaar' te relativeren?[39] Het mag in ieder geval duidelijk zijn dat de interesse voor het genre van het zelfportret in de Nederlanden ontstaat in een milieu met duidelijke connecties naar miniaturisten toe. Slechts via de literaire overlevering en de beeldvormgeving van deze overlevering wordt de continuïteit inzichtelijk.[40]

Wellicht werden zowel mannelijke als vrouwelijke kunstenaars geïnspireerd door antieke prototypes met een seksespecifiek karakter. Men kan vervolgens veronderstellen dat tussen beide gehanteerde schema's een zekere vorm van migratie ontstond die het genre als zodanig een nieuw artistiek élan bezorgde. In dit verband kan er ook op worden gewezen dat een kunstenares als Clara Peeters (ca. 1589–na 1648), zowat tweehonderd jaar later, in haar stillevens graag een minuscuul zelfportret integreert dat 'iconografisch' aansluit bij Van Eycks 'disguised self-portraits'.[41]

Van een 'genre sui generis' tot boedelstaten

Zelfbeeld, zelfportret en alaam: concept, ontwerp en uitvoering anders bekeken. De drie partners van de driehoeksverhouding zijn in dit geval zo verweven dat het moeilijk is te spreken over het hoe en het waarom van de uitvoerende accessoires zonder eerst een 'psychologisch' statement te maken. Dit laatste belet evenwel niet dat abstracte bespiegelingen dienen getoetst te worden aan markante realia. Op zoek naar de toenmalige realiteit werden alle aspecten van de atelierpraktijk in Erik Duvergers achtdelige bronnenpublicatie van Antwerpse inboedels geverifieerd. Het materiaal was voorhanden (nog steeds zonder indices) maar het leek me nuttig met het oog op het kijken naar zelfafbeeldingen in ateliercontext na te gaan welke concrete gegevens er te vinden zijn.[42] Zoals eerder gezegd, stelde ook Raupp voor 'die Frage nach dem dokumentarischen Wert der Künstlerdarstellungen erneut aufzuwerfen.'[43] Het is pas na de afweging van de dosis fictie enerzijds en de dosis realiteit anderzijds dat men kan inschatten wat de inhoud en de vorm van het portret heeft bepaald. Zo kunnen we via een omweg opnieuw aansluiten bij de vraag naar de psychologische diepgang van het Zuid-Nederlandse zelfportret. De bronnen beslaan de periode 1600–1666 en hebben uitsluitend betrekking op:

1. Het atelier als ruimte (plaats van uitvoering en denkbeeldige handelingsruimte van het zelfportret).
2. Het alaam (materiaal van uitvoering).
3. De beroepsomschrijving (informatie over de uitvoerder).

Het atelier: van 'werckcamer' tot 'schilderhuys'

De ruimte die we nu atelier noemen, had begin zeventiende eeuw een minder specifieke naam.

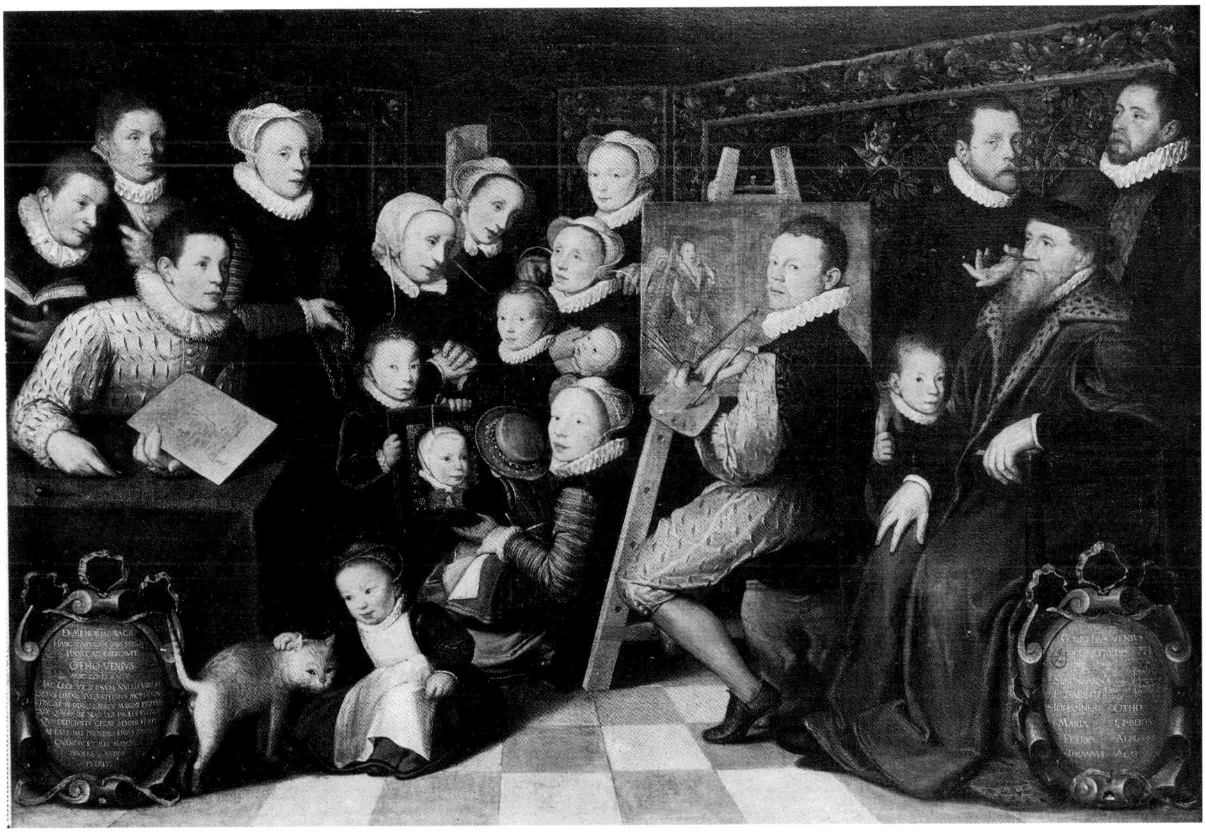

Afb. 4. Otto Vaenius, *Zelfportret met familie*. Parijs, Musée du Louvre, 1584

Op basis van het hele bestand van schildersboedels daterend uit de periode 1620–1666 zijn er slechts een viertal te noemen waarin uitdrukkelijk wordt gesproken over een 'schildershuijs', een werkplaats die duidelijk wordt onderscheiden van de eigenlijke woning. In de boedelstaat van Rubens wordt onrechtstreeks gerefereerd aan het atelier. De erfgenamen waren nog twee gulden schuldig 'aen eenen clatschilder voor het schilderhuys te grauwen'.[44] In april 1652 laat Cornelis Schut in zijn tuin een 'schilderhuys' optrekken van 32 bij 24 voet ten belope van 1500 gulden.[45] Nog geen jaar later maakt Jan Cossiers een overeenkomst met de welgekende Peter Stevens, zijn achterbuurman, om tegen de gemeenschappelijke tuinmuur een 'schilderhuys' te bouwen (13 februari 1653).[46] Bij het registreren van de goederen van Jan van Balen op 1 april 1654 treft men 'Int 't Schilderhuys achter den Hoff' een aantal ezels aan, hoewel men ook elders in de woning alaam aantreft.[47] Vrijstaande werkplaatsen waren blijkbaar uitzonderlijk en komen, voor zover duidelijk uit de boedels, niet vroeger voor dan vanaf zowat 1650.[48]

De overige schilders werkten op zeer verschillende plaatsen. Uit de inventarissen blijkt bovendien dat de activiteit niet strikt verbonden was aan een concrete ruimte. Op 21 boedels van schilders zijn er 13 inventarissen waarbij schildersalaam in de brede zin van het woord wordt gelokaliseerd in meerdere kamers van dezelfde woning. Als we kijken naar de gebruikte terminologie, dan blijkt dat bepalingen als 'schilderscamer' (Jan I Snellinck, Jeremias Wildens)[49] en 'werckcamer' (Victor Wolfvoet, Philips Fruytiers)[50] het meeste kans maken om te refereren aan wat nu 'een atelier' pleegt te heten. Het is tevens opvallend dat de schildersezels – alaam bij uitstek van schilderkunstige activiteit – veelal in deze ruimte worden vermeld. Een uitzondering vormt de inventaris van de goederen van De Momper uit 1635 waarbij zowel een ezel op de 'lange werckkamer' als verscheidene ezels op de 'Schildercamer' worden opgetekend.[51] Philips Fruytiers had in 1666 een 'Werckcamer' naast een 'wercksolder', waar ook zijn ezels waren geïnstalleerd.[52] Zolders bleken ook toen uiterst geschikte plaatsten om allerlei gerei onder te

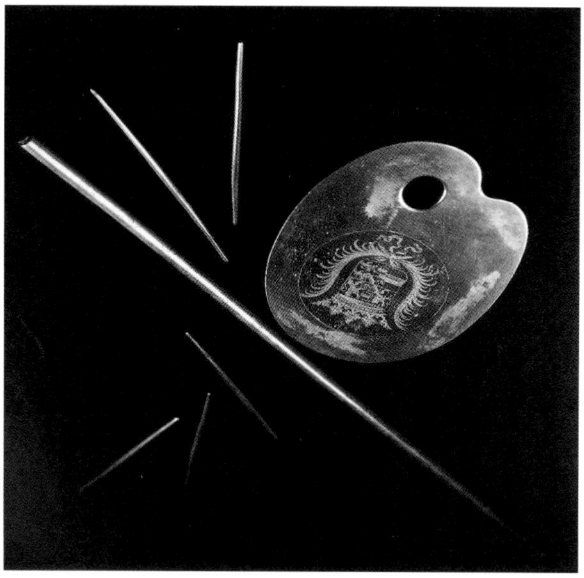

Afb. 5. *Palet van Pieter Pauwel Rubens* (?). Antwerpen, Rubenshuis

brengen. Ook ezels worden er soms teruggevonden, hoewel het hier mogelijk af en toe om afgedankte exemplaren gaat. Indien er geen afzonderlijke werkkamer wordt vermeld, ontmoet men schildersezels en ander alaam in zowat alle kamers van het huis. De boedel van Deodatus Delmonte van 1622 spreekt over alaam in 'syns testateurs comptoor ende elders'.[53] De term 'comptoir' wordt ook gebruikt bij de goederenregistratie van de weduwe van Philips III Liesaert in 1649[54] en ook Jan Wildens beschikte over een 'comptoir'.[55] In beide laatste gevallen is echter lang niet duidelijk of er in deze 'kantoorruimten' ook geschilderd werd. Abraham Matthys herbergde in 1649 enkel gerei in de 'constcamer'.[56] De schilder Jacques Sangelon exposeerde verscheidene ezels 'op den Zolder' (1623).[57] De kunstschilder Peter Wagen had zijn ezel staan 'op de bovenste Voorcamer' (1653),[58] werkte dus op de eerste verdieping. Bij de weduwe van Hendrik I van Balen werden in vier verschillende vertrekken ezels genoteerd, alle bewaard in kamers op de verdieping of 'Op de Solders van 't voorhuys'.[59]

De conclusie ligt voor de hand: veel uniformiteit lijkt er niet te zijn geweest; een riant schildershuis was uitzonderlijk en de meeste schilders stelden zich tevreden met een enkele werk- of schilderkamer als men dan het overige alaam kwijt kon in belendende vertrekken. De scheiding tussen werk- en woonruimten was blijkbaar minimaal. Een goede illustratie biedt het familie- en zelfportret van Otto Vaenius (afb. 4) uit het Louvre, 1584 gedateerd. Ook dit portret is vanzelfsprekend fictief maar het biedt wel een kleurrijke en goed georchestreerde visualisering van een dagelijkse leefsituatie. Het alaam is voor de gelegenheid ten dele opgeruimd.[60]

Het alaam: van 'pinceelstocken' tot 'blauwen vryffsteen'

Het bronnenonderzoek laat tevens uitschijnen dat schilders in het zeventiende-eeuwse Antwerpse kunstmilieu, voortgaande op de bronnenpublicatie van Erik Duverger, slechts over een beperkte voorraad materiaal beschikten. Een ezel had elke kunstenaar wel in huis; meestal waren er twee of drie exemplaren ter beschikking. Een enkele keer wordt in aansluiting bij de ezel een 'dryvoetstoel' of 'stoeltken' vermeld wat laat vermoeden dat dit het soort zitmeubel was waarop veelal werd gezeten tijdens de arbeid.[61] De boedel van de weduwe van Hendrik van Balen registreert zelfs 'vier dryvoetstoelen' en 'Dry Spaenssche schildersstoelen' in het atelier.[62]

Meerdere ezels waren noodzakelijk wanneer men leerlingen opleidde en konden ook dienst bewijzen bij het simultaan werken aan verschillende composities. Materiaal-technisch worden de ezels zelden geduid. Een enkele keer spreekt men over een 'weeckhouten ezel', vaker over een 'schildersesel'.[63] Voortgaande op de bekende iconografie, ging het vrijwel steeds om ezels van het drievoettype.[64] Grote uitzondering vormen de twee ezels die Frans Snijders in een testament van september 1627 aan zijn schoonbroers vermaakt. Paul de Vos zal 'den grooten schraefesel ontvangen' terwijl 'eenen schraefesel' wordt toegedacht aan Hendrik Rosiers.[65] Hier moet het duurdere voorbeelden betreffen waarbij de hoogte instelbaar was door het gebruik van schroefdraad op de verticale partijen. Een illustratie van dit type hebben we helaas niet kunnen terugvinden in de schilders- of 'schilderscamer'-iconografie.

Naast de ezel zijn er het palet en de penselen. Frans Snijders vermaakte naast zijn 'schraefesel' ook 'de peletten ende pinceelen' (1627).[66] Adriaen Brouwer had in 1632 'dry dosynen pinceelen' in gebruik. Daarnaast

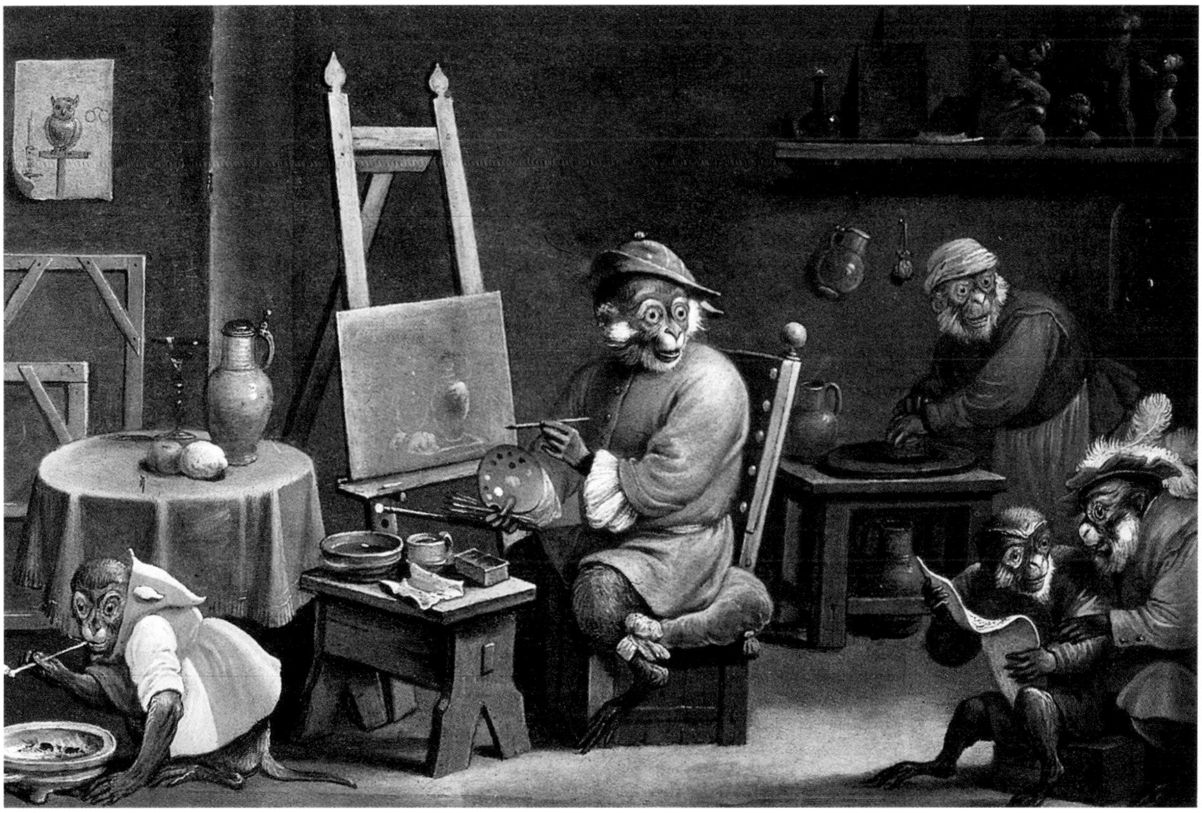

Afb. 6. Ferdinand van Kessel, *Apen in atelier*. Bewaarplaats onbekend

beschikte hij over 'achthien pinceelen mette stocken en Thien pinceelstocken' zonder meer.[67] Joos de Momper bewaarde drie jaar later op zijn schilderskamer 'vijff paletten, wat prondelingen van pinceelen, olie ende verwe van cleijnder importantie'.[68] Veelal wordt slechts gesproken over enkele penselen; uitzonderlijker is de vermelding van 'een partyken pinceelen' of '1 doosken met wat pinceelen daerinne'.[69] De schilder Jan van Balen had in 1654 een 'pinceelback' in zijn bezit terwijl Hendrik Bruiant zijn penselen opborg in laden: 'dry groen houte laeykens met vier pincheelen'.[70]

Zo goed als elke schilder beschikte over een dozijn of meer penselen. Dat blijkt tevens uit de schildersiconografie waarbij de schilder veelal een palet en een waaier van penselen in de hand houdt. Het beeld geeft in dit geval geen reden om niet geloofwaardig realistisch te zijn. De registratie van Brouwers set penselen met stokken en penseelstokken zonder penselen is interessant omdat blijkt dat penselen verwisseld werden van stok en men dus borstels van verschillende dikte kon koppelen aan stokken van verschillende lengte.[71]

Uit de inventaris van de jurist Maximiliaan I Martini is verder af te leiden dat sommige schilders ook penselen verkochten. Begin 1637 was 'Gillis Fijens, pinceelmaker ende schilder' nog iets meer dan één gulden schuldig aan het sterfhuis van de overledene.[72] Uit de staat van goederen van het sterfhuis van de schilder Peter I van Avont is af te leiden dat kort voor 24 juli 1654 iets meer dan veertien gulden werd betaald aan 'Geeraert Vinckbons, pinceelmaeker alhier, over soovele hy van den afflyvigen in desen hebben moeste over vercochte ende geleverdtde pinceelen'.[73] Het is dus verre van zeker dat schilders allen hun eigen penselen fabriceerden.

Paletten worden af en toe ook vermeld hoewel die vermoedelijk eveneens kunnen schuilgaan onder de meer algemene term 'schildersgereetschap' (1655) of 'prondelinge'.[74] Joos de Momper had in 1635 'vijff paletten' in zijn 'schilderscamer';[75] terwijl Jan I Snellinck in 1638 maar beschikte over '2 palletten'. De inventaris van Joannes Gompaerts vermeldt uitdrukkelijk 'een schilderspaillet'.[76]

De schilderstok wordt nergens met naam beschreven maar dat kan ook wijzen op de

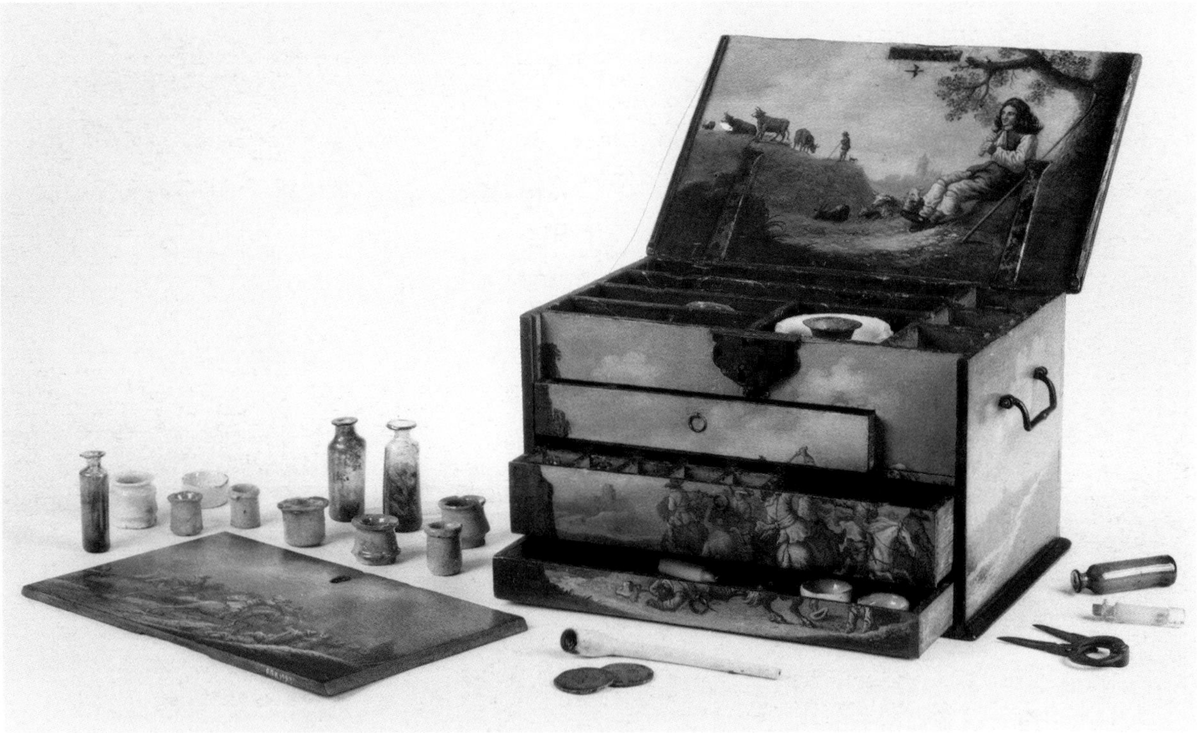

Afb. 7. Anthonie Jansz. Van der Croos (?) en Jan Martszens de Jonge (?), *Gedecoreerde schilderskist*, ca. 1650. Amsterdam, Rijksmuseum

geringe financiële implicatie van het voorwerp dat wellicht meestal tot de regionen van de eigen fabricatie behoorde. Veel belangrijker is alles wat met verf, verfbereiding en verfconservering te maken heeft.

Als we zoeken naar sporen van verf in de boedels, is het resultaat meestal beperkt. Men spreekt over 'noch wat verwe'[77] of '1 deel verffpotten',[78] of over 'prondelinghe van verwen'[79] of over 'diversche cleyne dooskens met verven'.[80] Een enkele keer gaat het over een bepaalde kleurstof, zoals in de inventaris van Jan van Balen, waar over 'wat pampieren met asure outermarin' wordt gesproken.[81] Interessant in dit verband is de inventaris van Margriet Briers, weduwe van Hendrik van Balen waar op 4–5 november 1638 'op de camer boven de groote ceucken' een partij verf wordt beschreven. Van Balens weduwe had vooral ultramarijn in huis en bewaarde een beetje in 'ronde gedraeyde dooskens', in '3 toubuskens', wat in een ivoren doosje en verder nog van dezelfde verf in '2 cleyn leire quicksilver saecxkens'. Er was nog wat 'smalte' te vinden, '1 doosken met medalikens van solffer', en nog een doosje met 'Florentijnse lack'.[82] Het materiaal moet er gevarieerd en wat rommelig hebben uitgezien, zoals het is afgebeeld op enkele uitzonderlijke portretten, zo bijvoorbeeld in het zelfportret van de scheelogende – en naar het voorbeeld van Zeuxis lachende – Arent de Gelder uit 1685 (Frankfurt, Städelsches Kunstinstitut),[83] of in de 'Apenateliers' van David Teniers de Jonge en Ferdinand van Kessel (afb. 6).[84] Nochtans beschikten een aantal kunstenaars over een specifiek bergmeubel dat 'in de wandeling' een 'weeckhoute vervecasse' heette te zijn (1637–1638).[85] De schilder Hans Daep (of Dape) vermaakte aan Michiel Dape op 26 oktober 1622 'sijns testateurs schildersgereetschap 't schilderen eenichssints raeckende, midtsgaders seker sijn schappraeijken met wttreckende laeijkens mette verwen, pincheelen ende anders daerinne berustende'.[86] Zulke ladenkast is niet vaak afgebeeld; een idee geeft mogelijk het zelfportret met vrouw en kind én kast van de Hongaarse schilder Johann Kupezky (ca. 1718).[87] Een nog beter idee geeft de schilderskist die wordt bewaard in het Amsterdamse Rijksmuseum (afb. 7). De ladenkist is aan binnen- en buitenzijde beschilderd met decoratieve landschapjes die worden toegeschreven aan Anthonie Jansz. van der Croos (ca. 1606–na

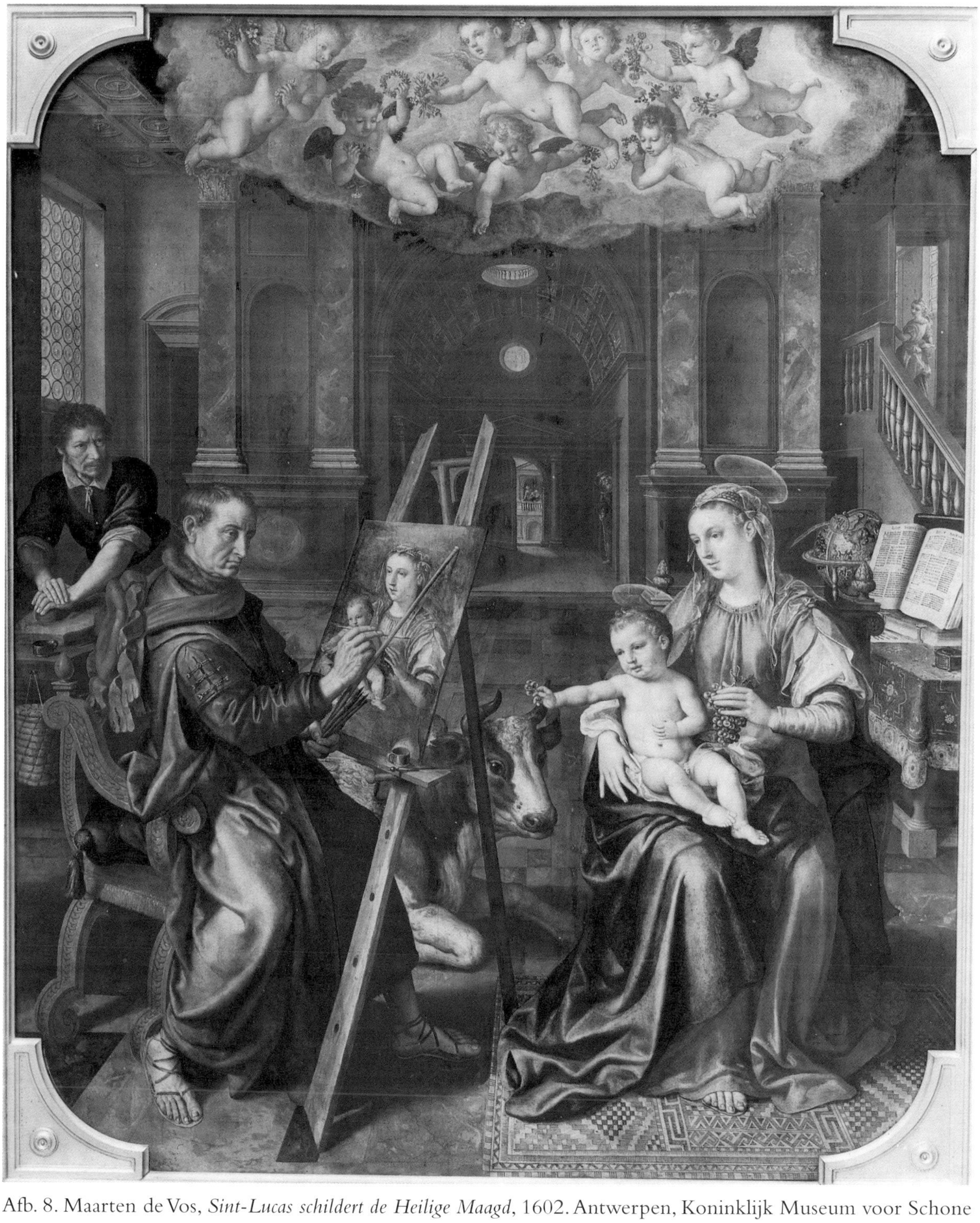

Afb. 8. Maarten de Vos, *Sint-Lucas schildert de Heilige Maagd*, 1602. Antwerpen, Koninklijk Museum voor Schone Kunsten

1662). De twee ruiterscènes zijn mogelijk van de hand van Jan Martszens de Jonge (ca. 1609–na 1647), neef van Isaïas van de Velde en geroutineerd in taferelen met vechtende ruiters.[88] Het exemplaar bleef wellicht bewaard omwille van de kleurrijke decoratie die zo goed als zeker ongewoon kan worden genoemd. Van der Croos was in 1656 medeoprichter van de confrerie Pictura in Den Haag, wat iets zegt over de manier waarop hij tegen zijn 'professie' aankeek. De stoffering van de schilderskist wijst allicht op de appreciatie van het alaam.

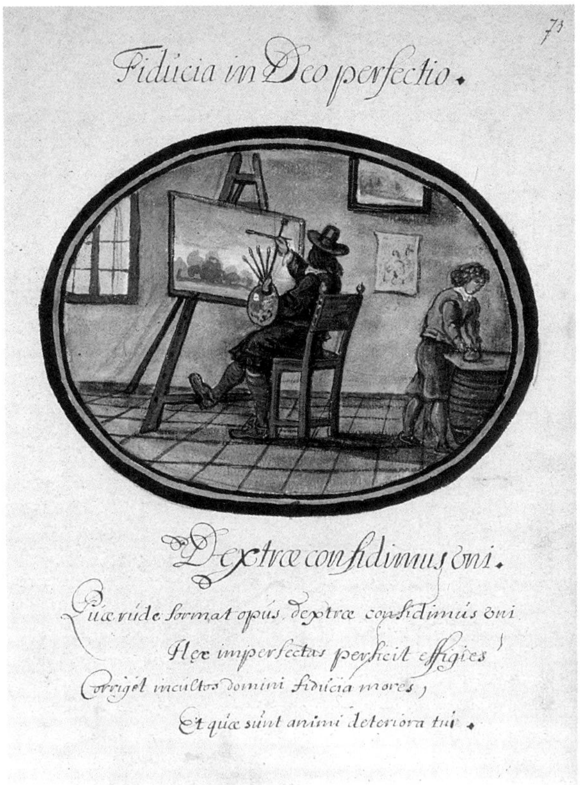

Afb. 9. Anoniem, *Een schilder in zijn atelier met verfwrijver,* Handschrift van de Brusselse jezuïeten. Brussel, Koninklijke Bibliotheek, inv. 20.306, fol. 73r

Aan de ladenkist werd energie besteed om deze tot een hoogwaardig recipiënt voor kunstenaarsgerei te maken. De stiel werd blijkbaar ernstig genomen.

Hoe de 'naerbeschreven verwen' in de winter van 1653–1654 werden bewaard op ''t Comptoir' van wijlen Jan Wildens, is moeilijk uit te maken. Uitzonderlijk is de omvang van het materiaal. In totaal worden 96 partijen verf en aanverwante beschreven, waarvan het gewicht nauwkeurig werd bepaald en geregistreerd. Voor wat de pigmenten en verf betreft, wordt er o.m. gesproken over azuur ('asur', 'heel fyn asur', 'fynen schonen asur' en 'heel schonen asur'), 'bruinen en lichten schytgeil', 'rooden mastico', 'Duytssche groen assche', 'Harlemsche altemarin', een 'casken met oker', 'acht pampieren met terra verde' en een 'casken met venetiaenschen serruys' (loodwit).[89] Alles wordt bewaard in doosjes, 'sacxkens' of in papier. Groot is tevens het aantal geregistreerde smaltpartijen, zowat dertig in getal. Smalt kan verwijzen naar smaltblauw, een specifiek pigment of naar vet dat als bindmiddel werd gebruikt.[90] Jeremias Wildens verhandelde die koopwaar, maar het document biedt ook een goed overzicht van ter beschikking zijnde verfsoorten in Antwerpen in het midden van de zeventiende eeuw.

In de *Thesaurus* van Plantin van 1573 komt reeds het gezegde voor 'van zijn vaders verwe sijn. Estre de la couleur de son pere. Colorem paternum referre', een uitspraak die ongetwijfeld zijn wortels moet hebben in het schildersmilieu van meesters en wijnmeesters.[91]

Rechtstreekse informatie over verfbereiding is niet aanwezig in de boedelstaten. Wel verneemt men een en ander over alaam dat gebruikt werd bij het maken van de verf. Dit aspect is niet relevant voor de zelfportreticonografie omdat dit soort objecten niet als attribuut wordt weergegeven. Verfwrijven was trouwens geen schilderswerk maar werd overgelaten aan leerlingen. Kunstenaars als Rubens hadden zelfs een 'professionele' wrijversknecht in dienst zoals blijkt uit de kostenstaat van Rubens' sterfhuis waar 'Franchois de vryver' wordt uitbetaald voor hulp bij de 'vuytroep' evenals voor de 'huere'.[92] Bekend is natuurlijk ook Maarten de Vos' voorstelling van Sint-Lucas die Maria schildert van 1602 waarbij de nog jonge Abraham Grapheus, die effectief meer knecht was dan schilder, als wrijver is afgebeeld (afb. 8).[93] In het werk van David III Rijckaert komen realistisch ogende ateliertaferelen voor.[94] In de al genoemde emblematabundels van de Brusselse jezuïeten is voor het jaar 1647 ook een voorstelling van een schilderende landschapschilder opgenomen waarbij op het zijplan een jonge man wrijvend verschijnt (afb. 9). 'Dextre confidimus uni' staat er onder.[95]

Via de boedelstaten leert men de toenmalige terminologie kennen en verkrijgt men inzicht in de typologie van het gebruikte materiaal. Er wordt onderscheid gemaakt tussen de verfsteen en de wrijfsteen of de 'lapis pigmentarius'.[96] De verfsteen of 'schildersvrijffsteen' is de steen waarmee de pigmenten worden verpulverd of tot 'asse' of 'cendre' worden gemaakt.[97] De verfsteen wordt ook een enkele keer 'purmuersteen' of 'lacksteen' geheten en was soms van marmer, een enkele keer niet meer dan een 'cleyn keyken'.[98] Het materiaal van de wrijfstenen werd slechts zelden geïdentificeerd. Steven II Wils beschikte in 1628 over een porfieren exemplaar;[99] François Geffels, jonkman en schilder, had in de zomer van 1650 'noch eenen blauwen vryffsteen'.[100]

De 'grooten schildersvryffsteen' van Hendrik van Balen stond in 1638 'op een schrage'[101] en de al genoemde Abraham Grapheus beschikte in 1655 over 'eenen vryfsteen mette kasse daer denselven inne staet'.[102] Slechts één keer wordt iets meegedeeld over de vorm van het object. Steven Wils had in 1628 een porfieren en een 'ronde' 'wrijffsteen', wat laat besluiten dat er ook rechthoekige of vierkante stenen moeten zijn geweest.[103] De kwaliteit van de steen bepaalde wellicht ook de prijs. De weduwe van Rombout van Avont verklaarde in 1637 dat zij was voldaan voor onder meer 'een schildersvrijfsteen tot vier guldens' die haar stiefzoon in gebruik had genomen.[104] Uit het atelier van Rubens verkocht men een 'vryfsteene' voor 24 gulden (1645).[105]

De uitvoerder: van 'schilder' over 'fijnschilder' tot 'kunstschilder'

En ten slotte iets over de uitvoerder. De man (vrouwen komen niet voor) achter de ezel laat via de boedelbeschrijvingen niet makkelijk in zijn kaarten kijken. Inventarissen bieden op dit vlak slechts schaarse informatie. Nochtans loont het de moeite even stil te staan bij de wijze waarop de kunstenaar-schilder omschreven wordt door de registrerende notaris of klerk. Op het ogenblik dat de boedelstaat werd opgemaakt, is de betrokken kunstenaar al overleden maar het ligt voor de hand dat de echtgenote of kinderen een beroepsomschrijving hanteerden die hen bekend in de oren klonk. Tussen 1611 en maart van 1637 werden er in Antwerpen een kleine twintig boedelstaten van schilders opgesteld. Beroepsmatig werden ze steevast 'schilder' genoemd. Er zijn geen uitzonderingen. In de zomer van 1637 trad er verandering op. Willem (alias Guilliam) van Haecht, eigenaar van een geschilderde 'constcamer' zoals we weten, wordt in de boedelstaat plots als 'kunstschilder' aangeduid en dit gold ook voor Jan Snellinck die iets meer dan een jaar later ten grave werd gedragen.[106] Zij gelden zowat als de 'avant-garde' van de nieuwe trend. Negen andere 'schilders' die worden vermeld tussen november 1638 en oktober 1652, houden het op één uitzondering na bij 'schilder'. De uitzondering geldt een in 1645 geregistreerde 'fijnschilder', Jan van Pelt, over wie nauwelijks iets bekend is.[107] In 1617–1618

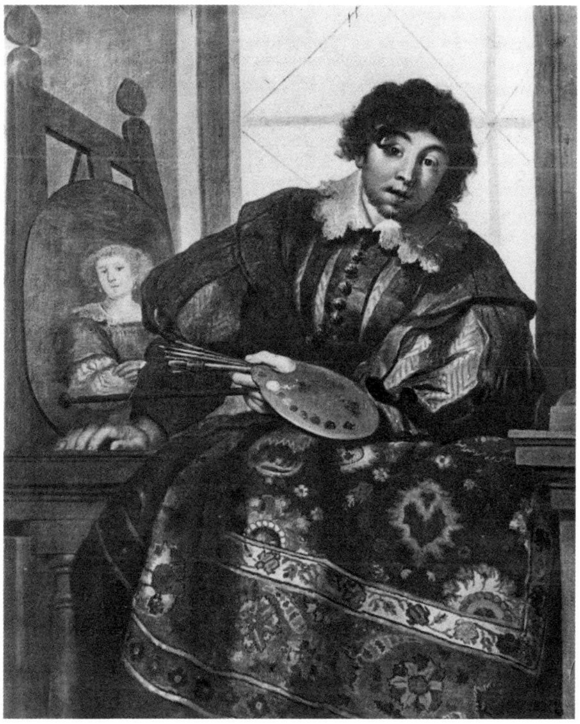

Afb. 10. Cornelis de Vos, *Portret van de jonge Jan Cossiers*. Bewaarplaats onbekend

werd hij als leerjongen opgetekend van de bloemstillevenschilder Jacob van Hulsdonck.[108] Hij stierf niet bepaald vermogend.

Vanaf 1652 tot 1663, of anders gezegd van Cornelis Schut tot David I Rijckaert, komen er nog uitsluitend 'konstschilders' voor.[109] Noch in het Antwerpse *Tetraglotton* van 1562, noch in de *Thesaurus* van Plantin van 1573 treft men de term 'konst-schilder' aan. Er is de rubriek 'schilder' en de rubriek 'kunstener' of 'konstenaer' en dit wordt vertaald of toegelicht als 'artifex', 'epifex' of 'hantwerckman'.[110] De nieuwe terminologie was duidelijk zeventiendeeeuws en was ongetwijfeld geïnspireerd door psychologische motieven. Het kan geen toeval zijn dat na 1637 in Antwerpen geen portretten meer ontstonden van kunstenaars met professioneel alaam in de handen.[111]

De grote drie hadden met anderen op sleeptouw het goede voorbeeld gegeven. Rubens, Van Dijck en Jordaens hebben – hoe verschillend ze ook zijn – de handen vrij voor andere dingen. Zo ook de burgerlijke Cornelis de Vos die tot tweemaal toe zichzelf en zijn gezin ten tonele voert zonder enige allusie op zijn broodwinning (Brussel, Koninklijke Musea voor Schone Kunsten en Sint Petersburg, Hermitage).[112] Al is er een uitzondering: hij portretteert zijn leerling opnieuw met schildersalaam. Het portret is niet gelokaliseerd (afb. 10) maar toont duidelijk – zij het met barokke bravouraccenten als balkon en draperie – een schildersezel, een palet en penselen.[113] Cossiers werd meester in 1628 en het portret werd iets vroeger of rond deze tijd gemaakt. Het model was dus jong en onervaren.[114] In 1653 wanneer hij in zijn tuin een schildershuis denkt op te richten, heet hij 'Sieur Jan Couchiers' en noemt hij zichzelf 'constschilder'.[115] Cornelis de Vos was dan al overleden maar mocht hij opnieuw met het idee hebben gespeeld zichzelf te portretteren of te laten 'uitschilderen' dan was het alaam achterwege gebleven. Van eervol accessoire werden ezel, palet en penseel tot onzichtbare attributen. De 'eigentijdse' decorumvoorschriften werden pas toegepast na een psychische interiorisering bij de man die van 'artisan' tot 'constschilder' werd.

Peter Gay schrijft in zijn baanbrekend werk *Freud for historians* van 1985 in aansluiting bij John Putnam Demos dat het persoonlijke domein steeds dient vermengd te worden met het publieke domein om zodoende de inwerking van de intieme neurose enerzijds en van maatschappelijke spanningen anderzijds te analyseren.[116] Honderden schilders maakten het proces van nabij mee maar slechts enkelen opteerden voor de zelfafbeelding waarvan nog minderen 'het zelf' associeerden met alaam of dit enkel kortstondig als de juiste keuze beschouwden. Heymans stelde in zijn *Inleiding tot de Speciale Psychologie* (1932) reeds dat autobiografen meestal te vinden zijn onder de 'gepassioneerden', de 'sentimentelen' en de 'nerveuzen', om even in psychologische categorieën te spreken.[117] Vraag blijft dan of één van de drie categorieën graag het zelfbeeld koppelde aan dagelijks gehanteerde materialen of ervan uitging dat de eigen identiteit onlosmakelijk was verbonden met de eigen professionaliteit.

Concluderend komen we geleidelijk tot enkele meer concrete vaststellingen:

1. Het atelier was bij de meeste kunstenaars veel meer een ruimte als alle andere dan algemeen werd vermoed; niet de kamer maakte de plek tot atelier, veeleer de activiteit van het schilderen-zelf.

2. Het materiaal van uitvoering dat voor de kunstenaar onmiddellijk ter beschikking was, bleek eveneens beperkter dan verwacht. Wat wordt afgebeeld als attribuut bij het portret zijn de duidelijke objecten met een accent op de ezel, het palet, de penselen. Het verfmateriaal zelf komt minder aan bod wat mogelijk ook had te maken met het weinig decoratieve uitzicht van allerlei zakjes, doosjes en stukjes papier.

3. Ten derde valt het op dat er een distantiëring ontstaat van de kunstenaar ten opzichte van schildersmaterialen naarmate de eeuw vordert en men zich eerder 'constschilder' dan 'schilder' laat noemen. Het accent verplaatst zich in het door een aristocratiseringstendens gekenmerkte Zuiden van hand naar hoofd.

Dat de dimensie van het persoonlijkheidsvervangende portret zelfs niet-schilderende Antwerpenaars aansprak, illustreer ik ten slotte met een citaat van de gepassioneerde briefschrijver Petrus Paulus Fourment, verwant aan de vrouw van de andere Pieter Paul.[118] Kort vóór 1650 schreef hij vanuit Frankrijk aan een verre geliefde een brief, waaruit volgend citaat: '[...] il me semble de vous avoir imprimée dans ma cervelle et il n'échappe pas un moment que je ne vous depeigne a mon imagination, mais dans ce souvenir j'experimente que je ne suis pas peintre expert, car il m'est impossible d'exprimer toutes les vivez couleurs dont est orné vostre visage. Mon pinceau est trop rude pour tirer ces traicts si delicats qui attraijent tous ceux qui les regardent et ma peinture auroit besoigne d'autre matiere plus subtile que l'huille pour donner le lustre a ces perfections dont vostre visage est enrichij. Je cognois mon incapacité et de peur de faillir en cet ouvrage j'aijme mieux finir que de dire autre chose si non que je suis votre serviteur.' Tot daar het woord van een onkundig schilder die de topos van de bescheidenheid hanteert. Het is goed mogelijk dat ook de kunstige schilders met het 'alaamzelfbeeld' tot de 'bescheiden gepassioneerden' behoorden.

Bijlagen

Atelier en alaam zoals vermeld in E. Duverger, *Antwerpse kunstinventarissen uit de zeventiende eeuw*, Fontes Historiae Artis Neerlandicae. Bronnen voor de kunstgeschiedenis van de Nederlanden I–VIII, Brussel, 1984–1995 (hierna afgekort als Duverger).

12 september 1611
Uittreksel uit de staat van goederen van het sterfhuis van Suzanna van Leemputte, echtgenote van Matthijs (van) Willenhoudt, schilder

Item alle ende yegelycke de meuble ghoeden des voors. sterffhuys metter coopmanschappe van schilderye, verwen ende ghereetschappe daertoe dienende, soe die corts voor date van d'aenghaen van synen tweeden houwelycke bevonden werden, syn op den voorschreven sevenentwintichsten meye anno sesthienhondert ende ses by Peeter ende Niclaes de Both, beyde geswoiren oudecleercoopers ende schatters deser stadt, geschat, geprisseert ende geëstimeert tsamen op de somme van tweehondert pondt drye schellinghen ende ses ghrooten Brabants eens, maeckende in guldens de somme van achthondert guldenen ende veerthien stuyvers naer luyt den schatboeck daeraff synde (...)

(Duverger, I, pp. 249–250)

15 maart 1612
Uittreksel uit het testament van Frans Francken, schilder, en van zijn echtgenote Elisabeth Mertens (Duverger, I, pp. 287–288)

Item Jeronimus Francken, hennen sone, oick de somme van eenhondert gulden eens ende sal blijven behouden allen tgene zy testateuren hem Jeronimusvan constwegen hebben gegeven met oick syn vaders conterfeytsel ende de Fortsen van Hercules als anderssints Ende Ambrosius Francken oick de somme van eenhondert gulden eens ende sal oick blijven behouden allen tgene zy testateuren hem van constwegen ende anderssints gegeven hebben

(Duverger, I, pp. 384–385)

26 maart 1616
Uittreksel uit de staat van goederen van het sterfhuis van Cornelis III Floris, schilder en echtgenoot van Anna van Baerne

Item voorts soe heeft men uuyter hant vercocht als beter gedaen dan gelaten tgene des naevolght te wetene
(...)
Item noch vercocht eenen vryffsteen met vier raemkens Fl. 9–00
Item noch eenen vrijffsteen van porfiel Fl. 1600

(Duverger, I, pp. 347–348)

13 januari 1617
Uittreksel uit de staat van goederen van het sterfhuis van Anna Coevoets, echtgenote van Andries van Baesrode, schilder

Item 't voors. achterhuys [de Seven Sterre gestaen ende gelegen in de Cammerstrate alhier] is bewoont geweest by Andriese Snellincx tot tnegentich guldens 't siaers, daervan hy ten tyde der voors. schattinge niet meer en schuldich en was dan een vierendeel jaers dwelck te verschynen stondt Kersse anno XVIc sesthien bedragende a raison des jaers als voren de somme van Fl. 2210

(Duverger, I, pp. 384–385)

15 februari 1617
Uittreksel uit de inventaris van de nagelaten goederen van François I Francken, schilder, echtgenoot van Elisabeth Mertens

Op de Solders
Twee vryffsteenen

(Duverger, I, pp. 389–394)

16 november 1620
Uittreksel uit de inventaris van de nagelaten goederen van Antonio I de Succa, schilder, echtgenoot van Magdalena de Cocquiel

Op't Gaelderyecamerken:
Een viercante houtten kiste met alderhande verwe
Twee verffsteenen ende sesse wryfsteenen
Een weeckhoutten esel
Eenentwintich weechoutten ramen om doecken op te spannen
Een mandeken met diverse prondelinghe ter schilderen dienende

In de Neercamer an 't Strate:
(...)
Een verffsteen

(Duverger II, pp. 143–144)

8 maart 1621
Uittreksel uit de staat van goederen van het sterfhuis van Anna Vrolijck, weduwe van Hendrik Leunis, schilder, en echtgenote van Hubrecht Diericxs. de Clee, ook schilder

Inden iersten alsoo de voorschreven afflijvighe op den derden december van den voorleden jaere sestienhondert ende twintich deser weerelt is overleden soo heeft den voorgenompden Huijbrecht Diericxs. de Clee op den thinden der voors. maent daernaer alle de meublen ende ruerende haeffelijcke goeden midtsgaders het winckelgoet van de verve ende allen tgene des dien aencleeft doen ende laeten inventariëren door den notaris
(...)
Item soo heeft den voorgenompden rendant op den tweeëntwintichsten dach der maent van december anno voors. alle ende iegelijcke de meublen ende ruerende haeffelijcke goeden des voors. sterffhuijs, midtsgaders het winckel-goet van pinceelen, van verven ende allen tgene des dien aencleeft, doen ende laeten schatten bij Gabriël Bonnecroij ende Symon de Graesse, beijde gesworen schatters
(...)
Item sterffhuys is schuldich aen Hans Snellincx de Jonge, verffvercooper, de somme van seventien guldens ses stuijvers eens ter saecken ende als reste van gecochte verve die alhier oock tot

gemeijnen laste worden gebrocht ende vuytgetrocken comt de voorschreven somme van Fl. 1706

(Duverger II, pp. 152, 154)

25 mei 1621
Uittreksel uit de staat van goederen van het sterfhuis van Margriet van Leemputte, weduwe van Gaspard I van den Hoecke, schilder

Schulden ende lasten die desen sterffhuyse jegens de goeden voorseyt schuldich is (...)

In den iersten den vyftienden may van den jegenwoordighen jaere XVIc XXI betaelt Michiel Vrindt de somme van vyftich guldens vyff stuyvers die sterffhuys hem ter zaecken van lysten ende panneelen schuldich was compt volgens de quitancie Fl. 50–05
Item van gelycken betaelt aen Jacques Verhaeght de somme van tweelff gulden tweelff stuyvers die desen sterffhuyse hem van lysten ende panneelen schuldich was compt Fl. 1212
Item desen sterffhuyse is noch schuldich aen Gomma van Oosterwyck, goutslager, ter saecken van geslagen gout tot vergulden gelevert de somme van Fl. 12408
Item aen Laurentius Gillemans, oick goutslager, ter saecken als voren de somme van Fl. 120–00
Item desen sterffhuyse is oock schuldich aen Michiel Claessens, tafereelmaecker, de somme van vierenvyftich gulden tweelff stuyvers ter zaecken van geleverde panneelen ende lysten compt Fl. 5412
Item aen Lambrecht Steens, oock tafereelmaker, ter saecken als voren de somme van F. 32512
(...)

(Duverger, II, pp. 167–168)

3 april 1622
Uittreksel uit het testament van Deodatus van der Mont (Del Monte), schilder, en van zijn echtgenote Geertruide van den Berge

Ende oft gebeurde dat hy testateur eerst afflyvich quaem te wordden, wilt ende begeert dat alles tgene der consten raeckende is van 't schilderen, te weten alle boecken, pampieren, gedructe oft geteeckende pampieren, oock geschilderde teeckeningen tsy van wat meester tselve soude mogen wesen, oft van syne testateurs eygen van plaester, rontwerch ende wassche ende alle tgene der const raeckende es, met noch alle sijns testateurs gereetschappen van 't voors. schilderen berustende ende bevonden wordden inne syns testateurs comptoor ende elders dat tselve by niemantden en sal mogen geruert ofte getoucheert wordden by iemanden, maer dat tselve sal volgen den bequaemsten van den kinderen oft sone oft wel verdeylt soe tselve by lieden hen des verstaende sullen bevinden te behoren

(Duverger, II, pp. 215–216)

26 oktober 1622
Uittreksel uit het testament van Hans Daep (Dape), schilder

Item aen Michiel Dape des voors. Gommaers broeder laet ende maeckt hij testateur eenen rinck wesende eenen agaet in 't goudt ende daertoe alle ende ijegelycke sijns testateurs schildersgereetschap 't schilderen eenichssints raeckende, midtsgaders seker sijn schappraeijken met wttreckende laeijkens mette verwen, pincheelen ende anders daerinne berustende

(Duverger, II, pp. 229–230)

16 februari 1623
Uittreksel uit de inventaris van de nagelaten goederen van Jacques Sangelon (Zangelon), schilder, en van zijn echtgenote Colette Kellens

Op den Zolder:
Een boeck met printen
Twee schildersesels
Een schraegsken
Eenen vryffsteen

(Duverger, II, pp. 272–273)

3–6 juni 1625
Uittreksel uit de inventaris van de nagelaten goederen van Catharina Andriessens, dochter van Godevaart Andriessens, weduwe van Daniël de Rijckere, schilder, en echtgenote van Gaspard I Tasse

Op de 2e Bovenvoorcamer:
(...)
Een weeck- met een herthoute kisten elck met eenen slote daerinne wat schilders printen ende ander gereetschap

Op de Solders aen de Strate wtcomende:
Wat schildersramen ende gereetschap

(Duverger, II, pp. 389–393)

20 september 1627
Uittreksel uit het testament van François Snijders, schilder, en van zijn echtgenote Margriet de Vos

Item Pauwels de Vos, syns testateurs swaghere, synen grooten vryffsteen ende den grooten schraefesel
Item aen Hendrick Rosiers den anderen vryffsteen, eenen schraefesel ende de peletten ende pinceelen (...)

(Duverger, III, p. 70)

6–8 juli 1628
Inventaris van de schilderijen, van het schildermateriaal, van het beeldhouwwerk, de tekeningen en de gravures nagelaten door Steven II Wils, schilder en echtgenoot van Clara Christoffels

Ander diversche Stucken:
(...)
Item eenen porphiere vryffsteen ende noch eenen ronden vryffsteen

(Duverger, III, pp. 103–111)

26 mei 1629
Uittreksel uit het testament van Suzanna Bernoille, weduwe van Filips Liesaert (Liesart), schilder

Item oock alle de gereetschap dienende totten schilderswinckel

(Duverger, III, p. 156)

5 oktober 1632
Inventaris van de meubilaire goederen uit het bezit van Adriaan (de) Brouwer, schilder, die procureur Anselmo de Cocquiel aan Jan van den Bossche overmaakt

Achthien pinceelen mette stocken
Thien pinceelstocken
Een houten Manneken met sijn pedestael
(...)
Een gelas met verwen daerinne
(...)
Dry dosynen pinceelen

(Duverger, III, pp. 313–314)

19–20 november 1632
Uitttreksel uit de inventaris van de nagelaten goederen van Arnout I de Bruijne, schilder en kapitein van de burgerlijke wacht, echtgenoot van Petronella Ijsenbout

Op de oostwaertse Voorcamer:
(...)
Een herthouten kiste met eenentwintich leesboecken daerinne ende wat prondelinghe van verwen

Schilderijen:
(...)
Eenen hoop schildersramen

(Duverger, III, pp. 315–319)

6 februari 1635:
Uitttreksel uit de inventaris van de nagelaten goederen van Joos de Momper (Mompere), schilder

Op de lange Werckcamer:
Eenen quaden schildersesel, tweelff ramen met doecken op ongeschildert aengaende deselve doecken den meestendeel vremde persoonen, eenen vrijffsteen(sic)
(...)
Eenen doeck met een swertte lijste

Op de Schildercamer:
Drij schildersesels
(...)
Vier groote doecken in swertte lijste onvolmaeckt: de drij begonst
(...)
Vier raemen met gepremuerde doecken, eenen grooten gepremuerden doeck, noch eenen gedootverwden doeck, vijff paletten, drij stoelen, een Spaensche vrouwenstoel, wat prondelingen van pinceelen, olie ende verwe van cleijnder importantie, een houten trap oft sitten, sesse tredekens toecomende Clara Heijmans tot Brussel

(Duverger, III, pp. 429–431)

10 november 1636
Op verzoek van Abraham van Avont getuigt Philippina Palludaen (Palladaen) (33 jaar), weduwe van Rombout van Avont, dat onmiddellijk na het overlijden van haar man diens voorzoon Peter van Avont enige meubilaire goederen uit haar huis heeft weggehaald

(...) Flippina Palladaen (...) heeft geseyt ende verclaert op haere vrouwe waerheyt (...), warachtich te wesen dat terstonts naer d'aflyvicheyt van den voors. Rombout van Avondt, haeren manne, desselfs voorsoon genaempt Peeter van Avondt wt haeren ende desselfs syns vaders sterfhuys tot hemwaerts heeft genomen ende aenveerdt: eerst een bedde, item een weeke voetbancke, item eenen schildersvryfsteen, item eene weecke houte winckelcasse, syn vaders ende moeders contrefeytsels, item eenige leesboecken, item en deel yserwercke, item een sweert lakenen accoutrement met eenen mantel van tselve, item ettelycke cruysefixen

(Duverger, IV, p. 49)

26 januari–17 maart 1637
Uittreksel uit de inventaris van de nagelaten goederen van Maximiliaan I Martini, licentiaat inde rechten en advocaat, echtgenoot van Johanna Kelckens

(...) Hiernaer volghen de schulden openstaende in de nageruerde salarisboecken in desen sterffhuyse bevonden (...)
Gillis Fijens, pinceel-maker ende schilder Fl. 110

(Duverger, IV, pp. 63–65)

28 februari 1637
Uittreksel uit de inventaris van de nagelaten goederen van Marie Lombaerts, weduwe van Artus I Vergouts

Op de Camer boven de Poorte van de wtganck van de huysinge van Sieur Jan de Letter:
(...)
Een vryfsteen

(Duverger, IV, p. 69)

26 maart 1637
Uittreksel uit de inventaris van de schilderijen, de prenten, het schildersgereedschap en andere goederen uit het bezit van Jaspar Becx

Een cleijn doecxken alleenlyck geplamurt
(...)
Twee swerte vilten hoeden elck met een valsch silver bandeken daeromme
(...)
Een panneel wesende een guldenmaet daerop geteeckent is met crijt
(...)
Een deel verwen
(...)
een olieraemken, II paletten, 1 deel verwen
Een panneel wesende een 8-stuyversmaete
(...)
een weeckhouten schilderscasken, I wecken oliebacxken
(...)
Twee doecken op een genaeijt geplamurt
Noch een doeck geplamurt
Eenen esel
(...)

Twee gelaese flessen met olie, 1 deel verffpotten
Een cleijn doecxken geplamurt
Noch eenen esel

(Duverger, IV, pp. 76–77)

27 juli 1637
Uittreksel uit de inventaris van de nagelaten goederen van Guilliam van Haecht, kunstschilder

Eenen wryffsteen, drye schildersesels, eenen deel schildersramen

(Duverger, IV, p. 91)

5 september 1637
Uittreksel uit de inventaris van de nagelaten goederen van Michiel Claessens, tafereelmaket (paneelmaker), weduwnaar van Elizabeth Baseliers en echtgenoot van Elizabeth Coenens

Op de Hangende Camerkens:
(...)
Sesthien guldenslysten met binnelysten
Tweentnegentich achtstuyverssmaten oick met binnelysten
Sevenenvyftich ordinarise achtstuyverslysten

(Duverger, IV, pp. 97–100)

15 oktober 1637
Philippine Palludaen (Paludaen), weduwe van Rombout van Avont, verklaart dat zij voldaan is vanwege haar stiefzoon Peter van Avont

Joffrouwe Philippyne Paludaen, weduwe van wijlen Rombault van Avont, ende vercleert dat sij van alles tot alles wel is vernuecht, gecontenteert ende betaelt (...) een bedde van oft ten pryse van acht guldens eens, eene weecke winckelcas tot twee guldens, eenen schildersvrijfsteen tot vier guldens (...) ende eenige andere vodderije

(Duverger, IV, p. 114)

29 augustus 1638
Uittreksel uit de inventaris van de nagelaten goederen van Jacob Gentius

Twee ongeschilderde panneeltkens
Eenen quaden kintscorff met een deel prondelingen ende verwe van cleynder weerde

(Duverger, IV, p. 170)

9–11 oktober 1638
Uittreksel uit de inventaris van de nagelaten goederen van Jan I Snellinck (Snellincx), kunstschilder en weduwnaar van Helena de Jode, en van zijn echtgenote Paulina Cuypers

Op de Schildercamer:
(...)
Eenen lacksteen met 1 vryffsteen, 1 schilderscraem, 2 schildersesels, 2 palletten, 3 quade stoelen
(...)
Een verffschapprayken, noch 1 vryffsteentken

Op de Camer boven den Vloer ende cleyn Camerkens daer neffens:
(...)
Seven binnenlystkens van 8-stuyversmaten

op de Solders:
(...)
Drie schildersraemen
(...)
Acht lysten met vier binnelystkens

(Duverger, IV, pp. 183–190)

4–5 november 1638
Inventaris van de nagelaten goederen van Margriet Briers, weduwe van Hendrik I van Balen, schilder

Op de Camer boven 't Comptoir aen den Hoff:
(...)
Vier weeckhoute lystkens

Op de Camer boven de groote Ceucken:
(...)
een sacxken met smalt van 6 1/4 lb.; 2 ronde gedraeyde dooskens daerinne in elckx synde wat outermarin; noch 3 toubuskens daerinne oock synde outermarin van ander sorte; 1 yvoiren doosken daerinne oock synde wat van de voors. verve; 2 cleyn leire quicksilver sacxkens daerinne oock wat van de voors. verve; 1 doosken Florentiensen lack; 1 doosken met medalikens van solffer; 1 doose met wat smalte

Op de Camer boven de groote Neercamer aen de Strate:
(...)
Een weeckhoute vervecasse
Een luypaersvelle
Drie schildersesels
Drie ebbenhoute lysten
Dry Spaensche schildersstoelen
Vier dryvoetstoelen
een lapken wit modellaecken van ontrent 3 1/2 ellen
(...)
Op de Camer neffens de voorscreven Camer synde boven den Vloer:
(...)
Een schilderesel; 1 dryvoetstoel; 1 cleyn stoelken

Op de Solders van 't Voorhuys:
Eenen grooten schildersvryffsteen op een schrage
(...)
Een ebbenhouten lyste met 4 andere binnenlysten
Een groote herthoute lyst
Drie schildersesels met 3 dryvoetstoeltkens
Twee gepromierde oultaerdeuren
(...)
Vyf lysten
(...)
Op de Camer boven de cleyn Ceucken:
(...)
Een houte busken daerinne wat outermarin (...)
Twee schildersesels

(Duverger, IV, pp. 200–211)

16 mei 1639
Uittreksel uit de inventaris van de meubilaire goederen in de woning de Vliegende Os op de Vaart van Jan de Heim

In den Hoff:
eenen houten esel

Op de groote Bovencamer:
Een caerte wesende de Stadt van Ceulen
Twee weecke raemen
Eenen doeck geplamuert met een groote raeme
Eenen schilderesel
Een panneel van een stuck
een partye oliepottekens

Op de Achtercamers:
Eenen schildersesel(...)
Een partije pinceelen

(Duverger, IV, pp. 249–250)

17 maart 1645
Uittreksel uit de inventaris van de nagelaten goederen van Jan van Pelt, fijnscilder en weduwnaar van Elizabeth Rommens

Op de Camer:
Twee schildersesels, eenen vrijffsteen met een cleyn keyken, een raem, noch wat verve

(Duverger, V, pp. 208–209)

25 april 1645
Uittreksel uit de inventaris van de nagelaten goederen van Zacharias Rem, schilder

Een houten figuerken wesende een Lemanneken
(...)
Sesse teekeningen waeroppe men geschreven vonde dese akodemannekens zyn aen Sieur Jacques Jordaens mynen meester

(Duverger, V, pp. 211–212)

7 augustus 1645
Overeenkomst tussen Gonzalo Coques, als echtgenoot en voogd van Catharina Ryckaert, enerzijds, en David II Ryckaert die eveneens optreedt in naam van zijn zuster Martine Ryckaert, anderzijds, betreffende de nagelaten goederen van David I Ryckaert

Ende [hij, David Ryckaert II] sal voorts oock behouden den vryffsteen ende andere meublen onder hem berustende.

(Duverger, V, pp. 233–234)

17 november 1645
Uittreksel uit de staat van goederen van het sterhuis van Pietro Paolo Rubens, heer van Steen, etc., weduwnaar van Isabella Brant (Brandt) en echtgenoot van Helena Fourment

Ende ierst aengaende den ontfanck:
24. Aen eenen clatschilder voor het schilderhuys te grauwen gl. 200
(...)
35. Van eenen vercochten vryfsteene ontfangen de somme van gl. 2400

Vuytgeven ende lasten tegens den ontfanck ende proffyten hiervore gestelt:
(...)
70. Aen de arbeyders ende Franchois de vryver voor dat sy in den vuytroep geholpen hadden gl. 1200
(...)
123. Aen Franchois de vryver soo van huere als aen synen backer betaelt tsaemen gl. 5300

(Duverger, V, pp. 263–284)

11 maart 1647
Inventaris van de nagelaten goederen van Joannes Gompaerts, schilder

(...) eenen schildersesel, een partyken pinceelen, (...) eenen swerten vilten hoet, een schilderspaillet (...)

(Duverger, V, p. 385)

18 september 1649
Uittreksel uit de inventaris van de nagelaten goederen van Suzanna Bernolie (Bernoille), weduwe van Philips III Liesaert, schilder

Op 't Comptoir:
(...)
Twee dooskens met 6 rondekens verlichterije, een coperen vergult kinneken op eenen pedestael, een Dornicx tafelcleet, dertich lysten van verscheyde sorten

Op den oppersten Solder:
Een deel oude lysten ende ander rommelingen van houtwerck ende anders

Op den Solder aen den Hoff:
(...)
Een partye lijsten groot ende cleijn
(...)
Noch een partije lijsten
(...)
Noch vier platte lijsten breedt

Op den oppersten Achtersolder:
Noch een partije oude lijsten, drije esels om op te schilderen

(Duverger, VI, pp. 34–44)

22 september 1649
Inventaris van de nagelaten goederen van Abraham Matthijs) (Matthys), schilder

In de Constcamer:
(...)
Een sacxken met smalt geteeckent littera M, noch een sacxken met smalt geteeckent littera N, noch een sacxken met smalt geteeckent littera O, noch een sacxken met smalt geteeckent littera P, noch een sacxken met smalt geteeckent littera Q, twee papieren met wat schilderskac of verw, twee paperen met wat indigo, een sacxken met groen asschen, een papier met blauw,

een papier met geel mastico, negen leire bundeltkens ende twee papierkens met oultremarin geteeckent respectiev A,B,C,D,F,G,H,I,K,L,M, alles gedaen by malcanderen in een doosken buyten geteeckent littera R

(Duverger, VI, pp. 44–55)

24 mei 1650:
Uittreksel uit het testament van Charles de Cauwer, schilder, en van zijn echtgenote Elizabeth Weckhamers

Ende omme alle onminne ende twist te schouden, soo sal de lancxtlevenste gehouden wesen een maent naer de doot van de eerst aflyvigen te laten vercoopen alle ende yegelyck henne meuble goederen (wtgenomen degene die de lancxtlevende noodelyck tot huyshouden van doene hebben sal, (...) ende den testateur lancxtlevenste zynde alle zyne schildergereetschap als ramen, patroonen, vryffsteenen ende alle andere mitsgaders oock zyne cleederen, lynen ende wullen, oock by behoorelycken inventaris daeraf te maken sonder deselve te mogen verminderen) (...)

(Duverger, VI, pp. 117–118)

30 augustus 1650
Inventaris van de goederen van François Geffels, jonkman ende schilder, die hij aan zijn zuster Margriet Geffels en haar echtgenoot Peter Stuyck heeft overgemaakt

(...)
Eene schalie in een houten kasse, noch eenen blauwen vryffsteen, eenige schildersgereetschap

(Duverger, VI, pp. 145–146)

24 november 1650
Uittreksel uit de inventaris van de nagelaten goederen van Hendrik Bruiant (Brinanat) en van Maria de la Croix (Crois)

(...)
dry groen houte laeykens met vier pincheelen
(...)
Vier kieckhorentkens, diversche cleyne dooskens met verven, een groen doose met diversche van was geboetseerde patroontkens
(...)
Een sack met blauw verve ende twee cleyn saxen, twee packen ende dry doosen met Duytsche asschen, een doos met schelpen van silver, een doosken met asschen, op den solder vyftich lysten soo groot als cleyne
(...)
Een pinneel 16-stuyversmaet

Op 't cleyn Camerken:
Eenen schildersesels [sic]

(Duverger, VI, pp. 157–158)

28 januari 1651
Uittreksel uit de staat van goederen van het sterfhuis van Abraham Matthys, schilder

Vuijtgeeff ende lasten tegens den ontfanck en de proffijten voorgemelt:
(...)
Aen Niclaes Vriendt... voor een rekeninge van doecken ende lijsten aen den afflijvigen gelevert Fl. 20–05

(Duverger, VI, pp. 170–171)

19 augustus 1651
Nicolaas Lamorlet (Lamorlette), schilder, heeft aan Jan Bordincx drie schilderijen verkocht, maar deze laatste weigert de gevraagde prijs daarvoor te betalen

(...) seggende den voorscreven comparant met de twee ducatons ende twee oorden met noch eenige partije smalt ten huijse des comparants gelaten daermede voldaen te hebben. (...)

(Duverger, VI, pp. 215–216)

18 maart 1652
Cornelis Schut, kunstschilder, en zijn echtgenote Anastasia Scelleir (Scelleirs) hebben van Jan Augustin du Jon, licentiaat in de rechten, het Huis met de Toren in Borgerhout gekocht. (zie verder bij 24 april 1652)

(Duverger, VI, pp. 283–284)

24 april 1652
Gommar Wouters, timmerman, verplicht er zich toe op het landgoed dat Cornelis Schut, kunstschilder, onlangs te Borgerhout heeft gekocht, een schilderatelier te bouwen (...)

Te weten dat d'eerste comparant heeft aenbesteedt aen de tweeden comparant, denwelcken heeft aengenomen te maecken op de erve gestaen tot Borgerhout by den eersten comparant nu onlancx gecocht van Joncker... Du Jon, een schilderhuijs lanck tweendertich voet ende breet vierentwintich in conformiteyt van de conditie daervan zijnde by beyde comparanten onderteeckent, waertoe zij hun om cortsheytswille zijn refererende, ende daertoe te leveren alle de materialen daertoe noodich, zoo van hout, kalck, steen, yserwerck, schaliën, gelaesen ende alles anders sonder eenige reserve wagenvracht ende den arbeyt. Ende dat voor de somme van vyfthienhondert guldenen permissiegelt te betaelen (...). Ende zal tselve werck moeten volbrocht zijn vier weken naer Sint-Jansmisse toecommende sonder langer vuijtstel. (...)

(Duverger, VI, pp. 289–290)

24 en 26 oktober 1652
Inventaris van de nagelaten goederen van Victor Wolfvoet, kunstschilder en weduwnaar van Elizabeth Merttens

Op de cleynste Bovencamer aen den Hoff:
(...)
Eenen schildersvryffsteen, (...)

Op de Werckcamer commende aen den Hoff:
(...)
Drye houte schildersesels, drye oude leere stoelen, een yseren stove

Op de Solders:
Eenen schildersvryffsteen, eenen grooten houten mansleenstoel

(Duverger, VI, pp. 343–361)

13 februari 1653
Akkoord tussen Peter Stevens, oud-aalmoezenier, en Jan Cosssiers, kunstschilder, betreffende de bouw van een schildersatelier

Decima tertia february 1653 compareerden Sieur Peeter Stevens, out-aelmoessenier deser stadt, proprietaris van den huijse het Cruijs genaemt gestaen in de Cortte Gasthuijsstraet alhier ter eenre, ende Sieur Jan Couchiers, constschilder, proprietaris van den huijse genaemt de Drij Vlammen gestaen op de Lombaerdeveste alhier, ter andere sijden. Ende bekenden tsamen aengegaen ende gemaect te hebben het naervolgende accoort, te weten dat alsoo den voorn. Sieur Couchiers in sijnen hoff achter synen voos. huijse geirne soude maecken een schilderhuijs ende tselve niet gevoechelyck en can geschieden tensij den voors. eersten comparant hem accordere te mettsen oft timmeren in de muer van synen voors. huyse het Cruijs, hem alleene toebehoirende, ende commende achter tegen den hoff des voors. tweede comparant. Soo is 't dat den voors. eersten comparant aen den tweeden comparant heeft vercocht de helft van synen voors. muer comende achter tegen den hoff des tweeden comparants ter lenghde van twintich voeten, sulcx dat den tweeden comparant daerinne sal mogen wercken ende anckeren gelijck in eenen gemeijnen muer vermach te doene met conditie dat den voors. tweeden comparant met sijnen bouwe sal moeten blijven onder de twee vensters die den eersten comparant in synen voors. muer is hebbende ontrent seventhien voeten hooch staende van der aerden sonder die te mogen becommeren oft het licht te benemen. Ende sal den tweeden comparant tusschen het dack van syn te maecken werck enede den voors. muer op synen coste gehouden sijn te leggen ende te onderhouden een loode gote, sulcx dat den voors. muer daerdoore niet en worde beschadicht maer ter contrariën geconserveert. (...)

(Duverger, VI, pp. 416–417).

2 september 1653
Uittreksel uit de inventaris van de nagelaten goederen van Peter Wagen (Wagge), kunstschilder en echtgenoot van Maria Matthijs (Mattijs)

Op de Bovenste Voorcamer:
Eenen swerthouten leyst
Eenen esel

Op den Solder:
Een marbelen purmuersteen met eenen vryfsteen
(...)

(Duverger, VI, pp. 455–457)

11 september 1653
Uittreksel uit de staat van goederen van het sterfhuis van Jan Goossens, lijstmaker, weduwnaar van Anneken Ghyssels en echtgenoot van Maria Racijmakers

Alvorens van de goeden ende proffyten:

Item... Peeter Antheunissen, schilder in de Vleminckstraete Fl. 106
Item David Ryckaert Fl. 8.00
Item Joannes Schoeff woonende tot Stabroeck... ter saecken van geleverde lijsten de somme van tweendertich guldens eens, (...)
Memorie

(Duverger, VI, p. 458)

30–31 december 1653 en 1 en 11 januari 1654
Inventaris van de nagelaten goederen van Jeremias Wildens, zoon van wijlen Jan Wildens, kunstschilder

Op de Schilderscamer:
Vijff schildersesels, een partije schildersgereetschap, een ijseren stene, twee ijsere geerden

Op den Solder aen de Straete:
(...)
Een partije raemen, een schijfftaefel, eenen gepremuerden doeck, een partije lijnwaetstocken(...)
Twee rouw panneelen met lijsten, twee schildersesels, twee raemen, een partije platte boonen

Op den oppersten Solder:
Hondert houte raemen sonder doecken, seventhien geprumeerde doecken, twee vrijfftaeffels, dry vrijff-steenen, vier maletten

Op't Comptoir van des Overledene Vader:
(...)
Ende syn alnoch op 't comptoir van des overeledene vader gevonden de naerbeschreven verwen die gewegen hebben ende genombreert syn als volgt:
N° 1. Dry dooskens met asur geteeckent n°1 met een sacxken wegende tsamen 3 1/2 oncen
N° 2. Een dooskens ende een sackxken met asur wegende tsamen 1 1/2 once
N° 3. Een doosken wegende 1 1/4 once asur
N° 4. Seven dooskens asur wegende 6 3/4 once
N° 5. Twee dooskens asur wegende 4 3/8 oncen
N° 6. Een doosken heel fyn asur wegende 7/16 van een once
N° 7. Een doosken heel fyn asur wegende een half once ende een half quaert
N° 8. Een doosken met een pampier met weynich cendres van asur
N° 9. Vier dooskens met fynen schoonen asur wegende 3 3/4 oncen
N° 10. Vier dooskens heel schonen asur wegende 4 1/8 oncen
N° 11. Een doosken asur wegende 1 1/8 once
N° 12. Een doosken asur wegende 3/4 once
N° 13. Een weynigh cendres van asur
N° 14. Een doosken cendres van asur wegende 1 1/4 once
N° 15. Twee ponden bruynen schytgeil in twee pampieren
N° 16. Een pont bruynen schytgeil in een pampier
N° 17. Twee ponden lichten schytgeil in twee pampieren
N° 18. Eenen sack asschens wegende drij pont
N° 19. Een sacxken asschen wegende 3/4 pont
N° 20. Een sacxken fyn Duytsche assens wegende dry oncen
N° 21. Een sacxken asschen wegende twee oncen
N° 22. Een pampier in een sacxken met Engelsche asschen
N° 23. Een pampier met 1 1/4 bruynen schytgeil
N° 24. Een pampier met rooden mastico wegende een half pont
N° 25. Een doos met schoonen lack wegende twee oncen
N° 26. Een papier indigo wegende een half pont

N° 27. Eene doosken met Venetiaenschen lack wesende twee ende een half oncen
N° 28. Een doosken met Venetiaenschen lack wegende twee ende een half oncen
N° 29. Een doos met lack wegende schaers een pont
N° 30. Vier pampieren met Florentinschen lack wegende 1 15/16 pont
N° 31. Een pampier met lack wegende seven oncen
N° 32. Eenen sack met smalt wegende een ende een half pont
N° 33. Een doos met smalt ongewegen
N° 34. Een doos met wat Engelsche assen ongewegen
N° 35. Een doosken met Duijtsche assen
N° 36. Een pampier assen wegende drij ende een half once
N° 37. Een sacxken met groen assen wegende drij oncen
N° 38. Een sacxken met diverse assens wegende seven oncen
N° 39. Een sacxken met diversche assens wegende seven oncen
N° 40. een sacxken met Duytsche assens wegende een half once
N° 41. Een sacxken met assens wegende 1 14/16 oncen
N° 42. Een sacxken met Duytsche assens wegens 2 3/16 oncen
N° 43. Een sacxken met groen assen wegende 1 10/16 pont
N° 44. Een sacxken met groen assen wegende een pont
N° 45. Een sacxken met schoon Duytse assens wegende vyfthien oncen
N° 46. Een sacxken met Duysche groen assens wegende derthien oncen
N° 47. Eenen sacxk assens wegende 2 7/16 pont
N° 48. Een sacxken assen wegende vijerthien oncen
N° 49. Een saecxken met groen Duytsche assens wegende tweentwintich oncen
N° 50. Een saecxken met groen Duytsche assens wegende 2 12/16 asen
N° 52. Een sacxken schoon assen wegende een ende een half pont
N° 53. Een sacxken blauw assen wegende elff oncen
N° 54. Een sacxken met Duytsche groen assen wegende tweelff oncen
N° 55. Een sacxken met blauw schoon assen wegende 2 2/16 oncen
N° 56. Een sacxken met assens wegende dry pont
N° 57. Een sacxken met slechte groen assen wegende vier pont
N° 58. Eenen sack met smalt wegende twee pont
N° 59. Een pampier met Harlemsche altemarin wegende een half pont
N° 60. Eenen sack met smalt wegende twee pont
N° 61. Een pampier met Engelsche assen wegende 1 12/16 pont
N° 62. Vierthien pampieren wegende vierthien pont Spaensche assen
N° 63. Een casken met oker
N° 64. Een doos ende een pampier met slechten lack wegende twee pont
N° 65. Acht pampieren met terra verde wegende vijfentwintich pont
N° 66. Een casken met Venetiaenschen serruys
N° 67. Eenen sack met smalt wegende twee ende een half pont
N. 68. Eenen sack met smalt wegende dry pont
N° 69. Eenen sack met smalt wegende drij ende een half pont
N° 70. Eenen sack met smalt wegende drij ende een half pont
N° 71. Eenen sack met smalt wegende vyf pont
N° 72. Eenen sack met smalt wegende vier ende een quaert pont
N° 73. Eenen sack met smalt wegende twee een quaert pont
N° 74. Eenen sack met smalt wegende dry pont
N° 75. Eenen sack met smalt wegende twee ende 1/4 pont
N° 76. Eenen sack met smalt wegende twee ende een half pont
N° 77. Eenen sack met smalt wegende seven pont
N° 78. Eenen sack met smalt wegende vier pont
N° 79. Eenen sack met smalt wegende drij ende een half pont
N° 80. Eenen sack met smalt wegende vier pont
N° 81. Eenen sack met smalt wegende drij ende een half pont
N° 82. Eenen sack met smalt wegende vier pont
N° 83. Eenen sack met smalt wegende twee ende een half pont
N° 84. Eenen sack met smalt wegende vier pont
N° 85. Eenen sack met smalt wegende vier ende een half pont
N° 86. Eenen sack met smalt wegende drij pont
N° 87. Eenen sack met smalt wegende drij ende een half pont
N° 88. Eenen sack met smalt wegende dry ende een half pont
N° 89. Eenen sack met smalt wegende dry pont
N° 90. Eenen sack met smalt wegende vier pont
N° 91. Eenen sack met smalt wegende dry pont
N° 92. Eenen sack met smalt wegende vyf pont
N° 93. Eenen sack met smalt wegende vier ende 3/4 pont
N° 94. Eenen sack met smalt wegende dry pont
N° 95. Eenen sack met smalt wegende dry ende 3/4 pont
N° 96. Eenen sack met smalt wegende dry ende 3/4 pont
(…)

(Duverger, VI, pp. 475–506)

1 april 1654

Inventaris van de nagelaten goederen van Jan van Balen (Baele), kunstschilder, weduwnaar van Joanna van Weerden

Int 't Schildershuys achter den Hoff:
Een kasken met wat gemeyne verven, 1 blecken olieback ende pinceelback, 1 schilderstoel, 2 paletten
(…)
Twee schilderesels met een porte folie, 2 herthoute schragen, 1 cleynen verffvryffsteen

Op de Camer aen de Strate:
Een groot rouw panneel ongeschildert
(…)
Een verkykerken van een gelaesken, 1 doosken met wat pinceelen daerinne, wat pampieren met asure outermarin, (…)

Op de Camer neffens de voors. Voorcamer aen de Straete:
(…)
Negen rouw panneeltkens gepromuert
(…)
Item is te wetene dan den afflyvige competeert het derde paert van sekeren grooten vryffsteen ten desen sterffhuyse bevonden
(…)

(Duverger, VII, pp. 27–32)

30 mei 1654

Uittreksel uit de staat van goederen van Jan Wildens, weduwnaar van Maria Stappaert, en van zijn zoon Jeremias Wildens, kunstschilder

Commeren ende lasten deses sterffhuys tegens de goederen ende proffyten voorseyt:

(...)
Item... aen de weduwe van Salomon Cock voor diversche verwen gelevert soo aen den voors. afflyvigen in desen alsmede aen synen vader saliger Fl. 6300

(Duverger, VII, pp. 50–53)

24 juli 1654
Uittreksel uit de staat van goedere van het sterfhuis van Peter I van (den) Avont, kunstschilder, weduwnaar van Catharina van Hersten en echtgenoot van Catharina Tkint

Commeren ende lasten tegens den ontfanck, baeten ende proffyten voorseyt:
Item soo compt ende pretendeert... Gabron, panneelmaker alhier... ter saecken van diversche panneelen aen den afflyvighen gelevert Fl. 40–00
Item soo compt ende pretendeert Isaac Wiltens, ebbenhoutwercker in 's Gravenhage...ter saecken van ebbenhouten lysten voor den afflyvigen in desen gemaeckt Fl. 40–14
Item soo compt ende pretendeert... perckementvercooper... ter saecken van vercochte ende gelevert parckement aen den afflyvigen gedaen Fl. 29–04
(...)
Item betaelt aen Geeraert Vinckbons, pinceelmaecker alhier...over soovele hy van den afflyvigen in desen hebben moeste over vercochte ende geleverde pinceelen Fl. 1405

(Duverger, VII, pp. 66–67)

31 oktober 1654
Uittreksel uit het testament van Johan Boeckhorst

Wat aengaet syne meubelen, die hy testateur verclaert tot Münster te hebben, raeckende de schilderconst als schilderijen, printen, teeckeningen, boecken ende anderssints, ordonneert den testateur dat binnnen dese stadt Antwerpen sullen worden gebrocht ende alhier beneffens syne cleederen ende gelycke meubelen van schilderconst als voorschreven is, (...)met publiecquen wtroep aen den meestbiedende vercocht sullen worden.

(Duverger, VII, pp. 83–84)

10 december 1655
Uittreksel uit de inventaris van de nagelaten goederen van Abraham I Grapheus, weduwnaar van Anna Volders, en echtgenote van Cecilia Claessens

Op de Voorcamer:
Eenen vryffsteen mette kasse daer denselven inne staet
(...)
Een partye schildersgereetschap

In den Winckel:
(...)
eenen grooten swerten lyst
(...)
Eeene sepulture met twee doren maer nyet beschildert
(...)

(Duverger, VII, pp. 184–185)

12 augustus 1658
Uittreksel uit het besloten testament van Philips Fruytiers, kunstschilder

Item soo maecke ick aen Francis Fruijtiers, Jacques sone, dese naervolgende const oft meubelen, als sijn: alle mijn plaesterconst met de berder ende scraghe dienende om de plaesterconst op te setten ende de tafel om de portefolliën op te leggen, alle de teeckeninghen, plaeten, schetsen, oock de Troniën die op pampier als andersins naer het leven geschetst sijn, alle de printen die in de grootsten geelen perquementen gebonden boeck liggen, met denselven boeck, van mij vergeerdert.

(Duverger, VIII, pp. 12–15)

31 maart 1661
Inventaris van de nagelaten goederen van Hendrik van Balen, kunstschilder en jonggezel

(...)
Twee groote lysten eensdeels vergult
(...)
Ende eenen vryffsteen daerinne den afflyvige een derde paert is competerende

(Duverger, VIII, pp. 199–200)

15 oktober en 7 november 1663
Uittreksel uit de staat van goederen van het sterfhuis van David I Ryckaert (Rijckaert), kunstschilder, echtgenoot van Jacobmijne Pallemans (Palmans)

(...)
Item in denselven roep is gemackt van blau verff Fl. 404

(Duverger, VIII, pp. 332–333)

3 juni 1664
Inventaris van de platen, prenten en tekeningen door Cornelis Schut, kunstschilder, in het huis van N.N. de Licht achtergelaten

(...)
Item een lessenaer ende teeckeningen van de soon van de aflyvigen N° 42

(Duverger, VIII, pp. 377–379)

15 juni 1666
Uittreksel uit een codicil van Philips Fruijtiers (Fruytiers), kunstschilder

(...)
Laetende ende maeckende in plaetse van dien aen Franciscus Fruytiers, synen sone ende syns testateurs neve, soo hy in eenich clooster gaet ende daerinne comt te professiën, dryehondert guldens eens ende synen grooten royen constboeck. Ende by sooverre denselven synen neve in de werelt blyft, laet ende maeckt aen hem dryehondert guldens eens ende alle de constboecken begrepen in syn voors. testament voor den voors. notaris Cleren gepasseert.(...)

(Duverger, VIII, pp. 484–485)

19 juni en 8 juli 1666
Uittreksel uit de inventaris van de nagelaten goederen van Philips Fruijtiers (Fruytiers), kunstschilder

(…)
Voor op de Werckcamer:
(…)Eenige gereetschap om te schilderen

Op den Wercksolder:
(…)
Dry esels met een houte tafelken

Op den hoochsten Solder:
Dry vry[f]steenen

(Duverger, VIII, pp. 486–488)

NOTEN

1. Joseph Leo Koerner, *The Moment of Self-Portraiture in German Renaissance Art'*, Chicago–Londen, 1993.

2. Hans Joachim Raupp, 'Untersuchungen zu Künstlerbildnis und Künstlerdarstellung in den Niederlanden im 17. Jahrhundert', *Studien zur Kunstgeschichte*, XXV, Hildesheim, 1984.

3. Raupp 1984 (zie noot 2), pp. 353–354.

4. Raupp 1984 (zie noot 2), p. 354 en pp. 10–11: 'Dem Selbstbildnis wurde und wird als einer Selbstbefragung und Selbstentäusserung des Künstlergeistes mehr Verehrung als wissenschaftliche Aufmerksamkeit gezollt. Dabei ist die Frage, ob und inwiefern ein Bildnis überhaupt etwas über den Charakter und das "Innerste" einer Persönlichkeit aussagen kann, schon längst zu Ungunsten der psychologisierenden Deutung entschieden'. Zie Hans Joachim Raupp, 'Selbstbildnisse und Künstlerporträts - ihre Funktion und Bedeutung', in [cat. tent.] *Selbstbildnisse und Künstlerporträts von Lucas van Leyden bis Anton Raphael Mengs*, Braunschweig, Herzog Anton Ulrich-Museum, 1980, pp. 7–35: ' (...) weil eine solche Absicht der Selbsterforschung und selbstbefragung ein Niveau psychologischer Erkenntnis vorausgesetzt hätte, das zu dieser zeit zwischen 1500 und 1800 nicht gegeben war'. (p. 7).

5. J.A. Emmens, 'Inleiding', in [cat. tent.] *De schilder in zijn wereld. Van Jan van Eyck tot Van Gogh en Ensor*, Delft, Stedelijk Museum 'Het Prinsenhof'; Koninklijk Museum voor Schone Kunsten, Antwerpen, 1965, p. 9.

6. Raupp 1984 (zie noot 2), p. 354 en cf. J.A. Emmens, recensie van 'Rudolf en Margot Wittkower, Born under Saturn. The Character and Conduct of Artists: A documented History from Antiquity to the French Revolution', *The Art Bulletin*, LIII, 1971, pp. 427–430.

7. Een gedachte die ook bij P. Spigt, *Het ontstaan van de autobiografie in Nederland*, Amsterdam, 1985, in zijn *Inleiding* (pp. 7–20) evenals in zijn 'uitleiding' (pp. 215–225) is terug te vinden.

8. Jacques Claes, *Psychologie, een dubbele geboorte. 1590 en 1850: bakens voor modern bewustzijn*, 2de druk, Kapellen, 1982, p. 60; Max Friedländer, *Landscape. Portrait. Still-life*, New York, 1952, p. 231. Zie in dit verband vooral: Joanna Woods-Marsden, *Renaissance Self-Portraiture. The Visual Construction of Identity and the Social Status of the Artist*, New Haven-Londen, 1998, pp. 13–40.

9. Claes 1982 (zie noot 8), p. 60.

10. Nicholas Mann, 'Petrarch and Portraits' in Nicholas Mann en Luke Syson, ed., *The Image of the Individual. Portraits in the Renaissance*, Londen, 1998, pp. 15–21; Ph. de Vries, 'Petrarca's brief over de bestijging van de Mont Ventoux', in *Ego-documenten*, Groningen, 1970; Spigt 1985 (zie noot 7), p. 17.

11. Claes 1982 (zie noot 8), pp. 54–55.

12. Claes 1982 (zie noot 8), pp. 83–85.

13. Claes 1982 (zie noot 8), pp. 80–82.

14. Raupp 1984 (zie noot 2), pp. 43–44.

15. Een tweede versie wordt bewaard in The Metropolitan Museum in New York, zie: Bodo Brinkmann, *Die Flämische Buchmalerei am Ende des Burgunderreichs. Der Meister des Dresdener Gebetbuchs und die Miniaturisten seiner Zeit* (*Ars Nova*, 1), Turnhout, 1997, p. 16, noot 36; Maurits Smeyers en Jan Van der Stock, ed., [cat. tent.] *Flemish Illuminated Manuscripts, 1475–1550*, Gent, 1996, p. 27.

16. Zie: Justus Müller Hofstede, in [cat. tent.] *Peter Paul Rubens 1577–1640. Katalog I: Rubens in Italien. Gemälde, Ölskizzen, Zeichnungen*, Keulen, Kunsthalle, 1977, p. 23, noot 52; Jacques Hendrick, *La peinture au pays de Liège. XVIe, XVIIe et XVIIIe siècles*, Luik, 1987, pp. 67–69, pl. 55.

17. Spigt 1985 (zie noot 7), pp. 79–80.

18. Spigt 1985 (zie noot 7), p. 80.

19. Spigt 1985 (zie noot 7), p. 75.

20. Spigt 1985 (zie noot 7), pp. 81, 83.

21. Spigt 1985 (zie noot 7), p. 20 en p. 16: 'Het is de tijd dat de spiegel veel gehanteerd wordt en het zelfportret als genre ontstaat'. De auteur situeert het ontstaan van het eerste zelfportret in 1447. Zie ook: *Oog in oog met de spiegel*, Amsterdam, 1988, passim en Jorgis Baltrusaitis, *Essai sur une légende scientifique, le miroir. Révélations, science-fiction et fallacies*, Parijs, 1978, pp. 181–212.

22. Spigt 1985 (zie noot 7), p. 221: '(...) Er is geen verlossing uit de onontkoombare subjectiviteit (...). In dit licht bezien, is de zelfbeschrijving een zeldzaam fenomeen, het zelfportret een toppunt van pogen en vermogen'.

23. Zie in dit verband ook Mieke Bal, 'Narcissus en zijn zelfportret', in *Het Rembrandt effect. Visies op kijken, Kwarto-reeks VIII*, Utrecht, 1987, pp. 31–38.

24. J. Claes 1982 (zie noot 8), pp. 25–26.

25. J. Claes 1982 (zie noot 8), pp. 114–115 en Spigt 1985 (zie noot 7), p. 15: 'Het meest geweldige ter wereld is te weten wie men is' (citaat Montaigne).

26. Zie *Basel. Oeffentliche Kunstsammlung. Katalog. I. Teil. Die Kunst bis 1800. Sämtliche ausgestellte Werke*, Bazel, 1957, p. 63 (inv. 6092). Er zijn drie versies mét signatuur bekend van hetzelfde portret (Kaapstad, Michaelisverzameling van het Stadhuis; inv. 30; Sint-Petersburg, Hermitage, inv. 10062). Zie hiervoor: Karolien De Clippel, *Catharina van Hemessen (1528–na 1581). Een monografische studie over een uytnemende wel geschichte vrouwe in de conste der schilderyen*, onuitg. licentieverhandeling, KU Leuven, 1997, pp. 75–79. Zie ook: Lola B. Gellman, 'Catharina van Hemessen', in Delia Gaze ed., *Dictionary of Women Artists*, 1, Londen–Chicago, 1997, pp. 661–664.

27. Günter Schweikhart, 'Boccaccios De claris mulieribus und die Selbstdarstellungen von Malerinnen im 16. Jahrhundert', in Matthias Winner ed., *Der Künstler über sich in seinem Werk. Internationales Symposium der Bibliotheca Hertziana Rom 1989*, Weinheim, 1992, pp. 113–136.

28. *Pliny, Natural History in Ten Volumes*, IX, *Libri XXXIII–XXXV*, The Loeb Classical Library, nr. 394, met een Engelse vertaling door H. Rackham, Cambridge–Londen, 1968, pp. 368–370 (boek XXXV, 147–148).

29. Zie Koerner 1993 (zie noot 1), pp. 109–111. Voor de relatie met het zelfportret van Sofonisba Anguissola, zie: Woods-Marsden 1998 (zie noot 8), p. 264: 'Was van Hemessen's invention known in Italy? Given the provincial centers in which

each young artist worked, it seems unlikely, and yet the Italian's identical pose raises questions of chronology that can probably never be satisfactorily answered.'

30. Schweikhart 1992 (zie noot 27), p. 119.

31. Karel Porteman, [cat. tent.] *Emblematic Exhibitions (affixiones) at the Brussels Jesuit College (1630–1685). A Study of the Commemorative Manuscripts* (Royal Library, Brussels), Turnhout, 1996, pp. 98–99.

32. Schweikhardt 1992 (zie noot 27), p. 119.

33. G. Tournoy, J. Roegiers en C. Coppens, ed., *Vives te Leuven. Catalogus van de tentoonstelling in de Centrale Bibliotheek te Leuven*, Leuven, 1993, nr. 33–35. Zie ook: M.A. Nauwelaerts, 'De meisjesopvoeding volgens Juan Luis Vives', in *Liber Amicorum Professor Dr. Victor D'Espallier*, Leuven, 1976, pp. 117–142: 'Vives drijft een herwaardering van de vrouw door: van de modieuze, praatzieke modepop wil hij overstappen naar de zedelijk hoogstaande, verstandige, geleerde en zelfbewuste vrouw. Het huwelijk beschouwt hij als een gemeenschap van twee gelijken' (citaat p. 142).

34. Thomas More, *Ter bemoediging*, vert. uit het Duits, Den Haag, 1979, pp. 34–36. Over de dochters van Thomas More, met name Margaret, zie ook: R. J. Schoeck, 'Elizabeth en Cecily More en Margaret More', in Peter G. Bietenholz en Thomas B. Deutscher, ed., *Contemporaries of Erasmus. A biographical register of the Renaissance and Reformation*, 2, Toronto–Buffalo–Londen, 1986, pp. 452–453 en pp. 455–456; [Madame] de Witt, *Marguerite More*, *Les femmes dans l'histoire*, Parijs, 1888.

35. More 1979 (zie noot 34), p. 36.

36. Zie in dit verband ook: Koerner 1993 (zie noot 1), p. 111: 'At this point its enough to say, that, within the visual culture of French illuminators around 1400 (a culture that exerted enormous influence on Jan van Eyck), the acheiropoetos has been humanized as a production of artisanal labor, and the self-portrait finds a place within the cultic images'.

37. Zie Justus Müller Hofstede, 'Der Künstler im Humilitas-Gestus. Altniederländische selbstporträts und ihre Signifikanz im Bildkontext. Jan van Eyck-Dieric Bouts-Hans Memling-Joos van Cleve', in *Autobiographie und Selbstporträt in der Renaissance, Atlas. Bonner Beiträge zur Renaissanceforschung. Band 2*, Keulen, 1998, pp. 49–53; met referentie aan Rudolf Preimesberger, 'Zu Jan van Eycks Diptychon der Sammlung Thyssen-Bornemisza', *Zeitschrift für Kunstgeschichte*, LX, 1991, pp. 459–489.

38. Müller Hofstede 1998 (zie noot 37), pp. 51–52.

39. Justus Müller Hofstede 1998 (zie noot 37), pp. 44–45, introduceert de term 'signifikative Selbstverkleinerung' en meent dat een vergelijkbare bescheidenheidstopos ook tot uiting komt in Van Eycks lijfspreuk 'Als ich can'. Een identificatie van het portret van de *Man met de rode tulband* uit 1433 (Londen, The National Gallery, inv. 222) als een zelfportret van Jan van Eyck, ziet de auteur niet meteen als een hinderpaal voor de verdere analyse van de 'humilitas-idee'. Persoonlijk vind ik het wel vreemd dat Van Eyck zou hebben geëxperimenteerd met het eigen gelaat op 'groter' formaat vooraleer hij tot een parafrase van de bescheidenheidstopos zou komen. Schuilt hierin een argument om de identificatie als zelfportret te herzien of ligt het experimenteel aspect in de registratie van het zelfbeeld ten voeten uit? Indien het Londense portret geen zelfportret is, dient men Rogier van der Weyden als oudste 'Nederlandse' verbeeldenaar van het zelf te aanzien. Al bleef het portret niet bewaard, de beschrijving van een zelfportret uit 1462 in de Venetiaanse collectie van Giovanni Ram, laat weinig twijfel bestaan: 'El retratto de Rugerio de Burselles pittore antico celebre in un quadretto de tavola a oglio, fin al petto, fu de mano de l'istesso Rugerio fatto al specchio nel 1462'. Zie John Pope-Hennessy, 'The Portrait in the Renaissance', *The A. W. Mellon Lectures in the Fine Arts, 1963 (Bollingen Series*, XXXV, 12), Princeton, 1966, p. 310, noot 80. Schildersalaam is – voor zover bekend – nergens aanwezig.

40. Deze relatie tussen antieke bronnen en beeldvorming gaat ook op voor Jean Fouquet van wie eveneens een kleinschalig zelfportret uit ca. 1470 bewaard bleef (Parijs, Musée du Louvre, inv. Objets d'art, AO56). Zie ook: Sean Kelly en Edward Lucie-Smith, *The Self-Portrait. A modern view*, Londen, 1987, pp. 9–10.

41. Frances Borzello, *Seeing Ourselves. Women's self-portraits*, Londen, 1998, pp. 59–65.

42. Zie Erik Duverger, *Antwerpse kunstinventarissen uit de zeventiende eeuw*, Fontes Historiae Artis Neerlandicae. Bronnen voor de kunstgeschiedenis van de Nederlanden, I–VIII, Brussel, 1984–1995 (hierna afgekort als Duverger). Als bijlage is een overzicht opgenomen van alle betreffende items.

43. Raupp 1984 (zie noot 2), p. 353.

44. Duverger, V, p. 277.

45. Duverger, VI, pp. 289–290.

46. Duverger, VI, pp. 416–417.

47. Duverger, VII, pp. 27–32.

48. Zie G.Th.M. Lemmens, 'De schilder in zijn atelier', in [cat. tent.] Delft–Antwerpen 1965 (zie noot 5), p. 19, stelt het volgende: 'Als atelierruimte gebruikte de schilder een normaal vertrek in zijn woning, dat in inventarissen meestal de "schildercamer" heet. Speciaal gebouwde ateliers, met bovenlicht en dergelijke, waren, onbekend'. Zie in dit verband ook: [cat. tent.] *Kunst-pro-thesen. Ateliergeheimnisse und Arbeitsweisen*, Düsseldorf, 1994, passim en Xesqui Castañer Lopez, 'Los gabinetes de pintura: talleres y academias a traves de los grabados del Rijksprentenkabinet de Amsterdam', *Goya, Revista de Arte*, nr. 253–254, 1996, pp. 18–24.

49. Duverger, IV, p. 183 en VI, p. 475.

50. Duverger, VI, pp. 343–361 en VIII, pp. 486–488.

51. Duverger, III, pp. 429–431.

52. Duverger, VIII, pp. 486–488.

53. Duverger, II, pp. 215–216.

54. Duverger, VI, pp. 34–44.

55. Duverger, VI, pp. 475–506: 'Op 't Comptoir van des Overledene Vader' (...)

56. Duverger, VI, pp. 44–55.

57. Duverger, II, pp. 272–273.

58. Duverger, VI, pp. 456–457.

59. Duverger, IV, pp. 200–211.

60. Zie Erik Larsen, *17th Century Flemish Painting*, Freren, 1985, pp. 59–60, pl. 9; Arnauld Brejon de Lavergnée, Jacques Foucart en Nicole Reynaud, *Ecoles flamande et hollandaise. Catalogue sommaire illustré des peintures du Musée du Louvre*, Parijs, 1979, p. 142, inv. 1911: de signatuur luidt 'D. Memoriae Sacr. Hanc tabulam sibi suisq. Pinxit ac dedicavit Otho Venius anno MDXXCIV'.

61. Duverger, IV, pp. 200–211: op de zolders van het voorhuis van Hendrik van Balen worden verder nog 'Drie schildersesels met 3 dryvoetstoeltkens' vermeld. De boedel van Jan van Balen bevat een 'schilderstoel' (1 april 1954), zie: Duverger, VII, pp. 27–32.

62. Duverger, IV, pp. 200–211. Het is dit type van stoel dat ook in de iconografie van het atelier geregeld aanwezig is, zoals

op het schilderij van Jan Miense Molenaer te Berlijn. Zie: *Staatliche Museen zu Berlin. Gemäldegalerie. Malerei 14.–18. Jahrhundert im Bode-Museum*, Berlijn, 1978, p. 58, nr. 124 (in.v 873).

63. Duverger, II, pp. 143–144 (boedel van Antonio I de Succa; 16 november 1620); zie hoger onder noot 56 en verder bij wijze van voorbeeld: Duverger, II, pp. 272–273: 'Twee schildersesels' (16 februari 1623, boedel van Jacques Sangelon); Duverger, III, pp. 429–431: 'Eenen quaden schildersesel' (6 februari 1635, boedel van Joos de Momper); Duverger, IV, pp. 183–190: '2 schildersesels' (911 oktober 1638, boedel van Jan I Snellinck; Duverger, VI, pp. 34–44: 'drije esels om op te schilderen' (18 september 1649, boedel van Philips III Liesaer).

64. Een goede illustratie van het drievoettype is te vinden in de *Painter's Studio* van Michiel Sweerts, zie: Rolf Kultzen, *Michael Sweerts Brussels 1618–Goa 1664*, vert. door Diane L. Webb, Doornspijk, 1996, pl. III, inv. A1957.

65. Duverger, III, p. 70.

66. Ibidem.

67. Duverger, III, pp. 313–314.

68. Duverger, III, pp. 429–431.

69. Duverger, V, p. 385 en VII, pp. 27–32.

70. Duverger, VI, pp. 157–158 en VII, pp. 27–32.

71. Uit het detail van het zelfportret van Joachim Wttewael uit 1601, afgebeeld op het omslag van de catalogus *De schilder in zijn wereld. Van Jan van Eyck tot Van Gogh en Ensor*, Delft–Antwerpen, 1964, cat. 120, blijkt dat één van de penselen met koord werd omwonden om op de stok gefixeerd te worden.

72. Duverger, IV, p. 65.

73. Duverger, VII, pp. 66–67.

74. Zoals hoger reeds ter sprake kwam met betrekking tot de boedel van Frans Snijders: 'peletten ende pinceelen' (Duverger, III, p. 70; 20 september 1627); in de inventaris van Abraham I Grapheus wordt in de voorkamer 'Een partye schildersgereetschap' geregistreerd. In het Rubenshuis te Antwerpen wordt een palet bewaard dat door Rubens zou zijn gebruikt (afb. 5).

75. Duverger, III, pp. 429–431.

76. Duverger, V, p. 385. In dit verband kan ook worden verwezen naar een weinig bekend anoniem portret van een jongen (Parijs, Musée du Louvre) met een paletje in de hand dat vroeger ten onrechte werd toegeschreven aan Michiel Sweerts, zie: Kultzen 1996 (zie noot 64), cat. R22, afb. 178.

77. Duverger, V, pp. 208–209.

78. Duverger, IV, pp. 76–77.

79. Duverger, III, pp. 315–319.

80. Duverger, VI, pp. 157–158.

81. Duverger, VII, pp. 27–32.

82. Duverger, IV, pp. 200–211.

83. Over het zelfportret van Arent de Gelder, zie: [cat. tent.] *Arent de Gelder [1645–1727]. Rembrandts laatste leerling* (Dordrecht, Dordrechts Museum; Keulen, Wallraf-Richartz-Museum), Gent, 1998, cat. 22B (detailopname op p. 123): *Zelfportret als Zeuxis* en zie ook Ekkehard Mai, 'Zeuxis, Rembrandt en De Gelder - Het zelfportret als statement in de beeldende kunst', in [cat. tent.] Dordrecht–Keulen 1998, pp. 99–110. Vergelijk tevens met *Het schildersatelier* mét verfwrijver van ca. 1710–1715; cat. 46.

84. Voor het apenatelier van Teniers, zie [cat. tent.] *Van Bruegel tot Rubens. De Antwerpse schilderschool 1550–1650*, Antwerpen, 1992, p. 209, nr. 93. De locatie van Van Kessels *Apenatelier* is onbekend. Het schilderij circuleerde rond 1995 in de Londense kunsthandel.

85. Duverger, IV, p. 200 211. Mogelijk wordt met de term 'winkelkas' een vergelijkbaar object aangeduid. Zie bijvoorbeeld 'eene weecke winckelcas tot twee guldens' vermeld in één adem met 'eenen schildersvrijfsteen' door Philippine Paludaen (Duverger, IV, p. 114; 15 oktober 1637). De betekenis van 'schilderscraem' is mogelijk eveneens vergelijkbaar, zie: Duverger, IV, pp. 183–190, 10–11 oktober 1638.

86. Duverger, II, pp. 229–230.

87. Voor een afbeelding, zie: [cat. tent.] *Rembrandt, Rubens, van Dyck... Italiensehnsucht nordischer Barockmaler. Meisterwerke aus dem Museum der Bildenden Künste Budapest*, Sinclair-Haus Bad Homburg v.d. Höhe en Von der Heydt-Museum Wuppertal, 1995, pp. 92–93.

88. *Alle schilderijen van het Rijksmuseum te Amsterdam. Volledig geïllustreerde catalogus*, Amsterdam–Haarlem, 1976, p. 182, inv. RBK 15234: de kist meet 21,2 x 30 x 23 cm.

89. Duverger, VI, pp. 475–506. Serruys is hetzelfde als loodwit; de term is afgeleid van het Latijnse 'cerusa', zie: Emil Ernst Ploss, *Ein Buch von alten Farben. Technologie der Textilfarben im Mittelalter mit einem Ausblick auf die festen Farben* ('mit zwei vorangestellten Beiträgen über die Geschichte der farben Rot und Blau'), 6de verb. uitg., München, 1989, p. 108.

90. Ibidem. Voor de betekenis van smalt, zie: Ashok Roy ed., *Artist's Pigments. A Handbook of their History and Characteristics*, 2, New York–Oxford, 1997, pp. 113–189: 'smalt'; J.A. van de Graaf, *Het de Mayerne manuscript als bron voor de schildertechniek van de barok*, Mijdrecht, 1958, p. 145 en passim; Ploss 1989 (zie noot 89), pp. 102–103: 'Valentin Boltz von Rufach, ein humanistisch gebildeter Kleinmaler nach 1500 schrieb in seinem bekannten Illuminierbüchlein: *Schmeltze. Ein edel köstlichs Blaw ist diss... Das braucht man auff liecht Blauw ferblin. es wirt gar selten in teutschen landen gefunden.* An einer anderen Stelle heisst es: *Esch blauw Schmeltzasch (...)*. Das heutige Schmalteblau entsteht durch Verschmelzen von Pottasche, Kieselsäure und geröstetem Speisekobalt'. Zie ook: Margarete Bruns, 'Von Azurit, Indigo und Anilin. Zur Geschichte der blauen Farbe', in Ploss 1989 (zie noot 89), pp. 15–20 en meer algemeen: Knut Nicolaus, *Het schilderij: materiaal, techniek, behoud*, vert. uit het Duits, Keulen, 1980, pp. 116–117, 128, 135, 137–138, 142.

91. *Thesaurvs Thevtonicae linguae. Schat der Neder-duytscher spraken. De Thesaurus van Plantijn van 1573, Oude Woordenboeken. Reeks II: 16de eeuw*, 2, Den Haag, 1972, s. pag., sub 'VE'.

92. Duverger, V, p. 279.

93. *Koninklijk Museum voor Schone Kunsten Antwerpen. Catalogus Schilderkunst Oude Meesters*, Antwerpen, 1988, p. 411, nr. 88. Voor zijn boedelstaat, zie: Duverger, VII, pp. 184–185. Hij beschikte bij zijn dood nog over een wrijfsteen in een kast en over een partij schildersgereedschap.

94. Zie Bernadette M.R. Van Haute, *David III Rijckaert. A seventeenth-century Flemish painter*, doctoraatsverhandeling, University of South Africa, 1996, cat. A1, A18 (met verfwrijver); A48 (met verfwrijver). De verhandeling verschijnt in 1999 als deel VI in de reeks Pictura Nova (Brepols Publishers).

95. Zie [cat. tent.] Brussel 1996 (zie noot 31), pp. 106–107 voor bredere context en referentie (evenwel zonder illustratie) aan de bundel in de Brusselse Koninklijke Bibliotheek. Een treffende illustratie van een atelier met schilder en wrijver [1652] is te vinden in het Poëzie-album van Gesina Ter Borch. Zie: Alison McNeil Kettering, *Drawings from the Ter Borch Studio Estate, Catalogus van de Nederlandse Tekeningen in het*

Rijksprentenkabinet, Rijksmuseum Amsterdam, V.2, 's-Gravenhage, 1988, p. 423, folio 1 recto; p. 482 (afb.).

96. Voor de terminologie, zie *Het tetraglotton van 1562*, 1, uitg. door F. Claes, F. De Tollenaere en J.B. Veerbeek, facsimile-editie van de Antwerpse uitgave van 1562, 's-Gravenhage, 1972, p. 309: 'vrijfsteen: Tophus, I, vel Tosus: und sorte de pierre qui aisseement se menuise en gravois. Tufsteen / Santsteen / Morselsteen / Rouwen vrijffsteen'. In E. Verwijs en J. Verdam, *Middelnederlandsch Woordenboek*, 9, 's-Gravenhage, 1929, kol. 2871: wrijfsteen of 'lapis pigmentarius' kan zowel een steen zijn waarop men iets fijn wrijft als een steen om te wrijven; een puimsteen (= een soort tufsteen).

97. Voor de terminologie, zie ook: Lydia De Pauw-De Veen, *De begrippen 'schilder', 'schilderij' en 'schilderen' in de zeventiende eeuw*, Verhandelingen van de Koninklijke Vlaamse Academie voor Wetenschappen, Letteren en Schone Kunsten van België. Klasse der Schone Kunsten, XXXI, nr. 22, Brussel, 1969. De termen 'wrijfsteen' of 'schilderhuis' komen echter niet voor in haar index. Zie ook de recensie van het gelijknamige boek door Wolfgang Stechow, in *The Art Bulletin*, LIII, 1971, pp. 260–261.

98. Voor 'eenen lacksteen met 1 vryffsteen', zie Duverger, IV, pp. 183–190; 'voor eenen marbelen purmuersteen met eenen vryfsteen', zie Duverger, VI, pp. 456–457; voor 'eenen vrijffsteen met een cleyn keyken', zie Duverger, V, pp. 208–209.

99. Duverger, III, pp. 103–111 en zie ook de boedel van Cornelis III Floris van 1616: 'Item noch eenen vrijffsteen van porfiel' (sic), zie Duverger, I, pp. 347–348. Naast een porfieren exemplaar beschikte hij ook over 'eenen ronden vrijfsteen'.

100. Duverger, VI, pp. 145–146: vermoedelijk wordt een wrijfsteen van arduin bedoeld.

101. Duverger, IV, pp. 200–211.

102. Duverger, VII, pp. 184–185.

103. Duverger, III, pp. 103–111.

104. Duverger, IV, p. 114.

105. Duverger, V, p. 277.

106. Duverger, IV, p. 91 en Duverger, IV, p. 183.

107. Duverger, V, p. 208.

108. P. Rombouts en T. Van Lerius, *De Liggeren van de Antwerpsche Sint-Lucasgilde*, I, Antwerpen, 1872, p. 542.

109. Dit geldt voor Cornelis Schut (18 maart 1652 en 24 april 1652 en cf. 3 juni 1664), Victor Wolfvoet (24–26 oktober 1652), Jan Cossiers (13 februari 1653), Peter Wagen (2 september 1653), Jeremias Wildens (30–31 december 1653; 11 januari 1654 en cf. 30 mei 1654), Jan van Balen (1 april 1654), Peter van den Avont (24 juli 1654), Philips Fruytiers (12 augustus 1658 en cf. 19 juni 1666 en 8 juli 1666), Hendrik van Balen de Jonge (31 maart 1661), David I Rijckaert (15 oktober 1663; 7 november 1663). Zie voor de betreffende boedels, de bijlage.

110. *Het tetraglotton van 1562*... (zie noot 96), p. 107b (Schilder) en p. 26b ('Konstenaer: Artifex; Qui scait faire quelque ouvrage; Hantwerckman; Konstenar'); *Thesaurus Thevtonicae linguae*, 1, s.p., sub 'KU': 'Een kunstener. Un artiste, artisan, Artifex, epifex'; *Thesaurus Thevtonicae linguae*, 2, s.p., sub 'SC': 'Schilder, maler, Peinctre; Pictor, zographus'.

111. Een late uitzondering biedt het zelfportret van ca. 1658 van Michiel Sweerts met het palet en penselen in handen, poserend voor een open landschap. Kultzen beweert dat het portret zeer waarschijnlijk in Amsterdam ontstond, wat op een andere invloedssfeer wijst (Kultzen 1996 [zie noot 64], p. 62, 116, cat. 89, pl. 88 met kleurafb. in frontispice).

112. Katlijne Van der Stighelen, *De portretten van Cornelis de Vos. Een kritische catalogus*, Verhandelingen van de Koninklijke Academie voor Wetenschappen, Letteren en Schone Kunsten van België, LI, Brussel, 1990, cat. 9 en 80; Katlijne Van der Stighelen, '"Op dat het recht gae": elf familieportretten van Cornelis de Vos (1584/5–1651)', *Leids Kunsthistorisch Jaarboek*, VIII, 1989, pp. 123, 131–132.

113. Met dank aan Arnout Balis die een afbeelding van het portret bezorgde. De foto is in The Witt Library, Londen (zonder herkomstgegevens) geklasseerd als een zelfportret van Jan Cossiers.

114. Over Jan Cossiers, zie: Jef Stoffels, Jan Cossiers (1600–1671). Een monografische benadering, onuitg. licentieverhandeling, Rijksuniversiteit Gent, 1986, p. 46.

115. Duverger, VI, pp. 416–417.

116. Peter Gay, *Freud voor historici*, vert. uit het Engels door Walter van Opzeeland, Amsterdam, 1987, pp. 174–175: 'Biografie, psychologie, sociologie, geschiedenis', zo besluit hij [Demos] zijn programmatische opmerkingen, 'vier streken van het kompas van en wetenschapsbeoefenaar, vier gezichtspunten van waaruit één enkel veld van ervaring uit het verleden kan worden overzien' (p. 175).

117. Zie Spigt 1985 (zie noot 7), pp. 219–220 en cf. G. Heymans, *Inleiding tot de speciale psychologie*, 1, Haarlem, 1932, p. 235.

118. De bundel met een vijftigtal brieven (bewaard als eigentijdse kopieën van verloren originelen) wordt bewaard op het Stadsarchief in Antwerpen. Een geannoteerde editie is in voorbereiding.

Entstehung und Veränderung von Rubens' Bildgedanken. Zum Beispiel die *Zwei Satyrn* in der Alten Pinakothek

Konrad Renger

Es ist bekannt, daß Planänderungen, Pentimenti und Erweiterungen Einblick in Rubens' Bildgedanken geben und das Verständnis nicht nur für die Komposition, sondern auch für den Bildinhalt schärfen. Ich hoffe, daß ich dies seinerzeit unter anderem an den beiden Münchner Bildern *Silen* und *Hirtenszene* zeigen konnte.[1]

In der Alten Pinakothek wurden seit ca. 1990 systematisch alle Holztafeln von Rubens im Hinblick auf Anstückungen untersucht und die Ergebnisse verstreut publiziert.[2] Inzwischen konnte auch das wenig bekannte Bild *Zwei Satyrn* (Inv. 873) geröntgt werden – mit überraschendem Ergebnis.

Das Gemälde zeigt in ungewöhnlicher Zusammenstellung zwei Satyrn. Der eine mit einem Löwenfell bekleidet und gehörnt, mit gesenktem, ganz leicht nach rechts gedrehtem Kopf von unten aus dem Bild schauend, mit seiner rechten Hand Trauben zerdrückend. Der andere links neben ihm ins Profil nach links gewendet, einen Tierkopf auf seinem Haupt, trinkt genüßlich mit geschlossenen Augen aus einer Weinschale.

Es war schon immer bekannt, daß die Tafel später um ca. 10 cm erweitert worden war und zwar nacheinander in zwei Stufen. Von dieser Ergänzung wurden 1910 unten 5 cm entfernt.[3] Die alte Bruckmann-Photographie zeigt den Zustand mit allen Ergänzungen, das neue Foto den jetzigen Zustand (Abb. 1, 2). Die ergänzten Ränder sind heute vom Rahmen abgedeckt, sie hätten der Komposition die Spannung genommen, die sie mit den Überschneidungen im engen Rahmen hat.

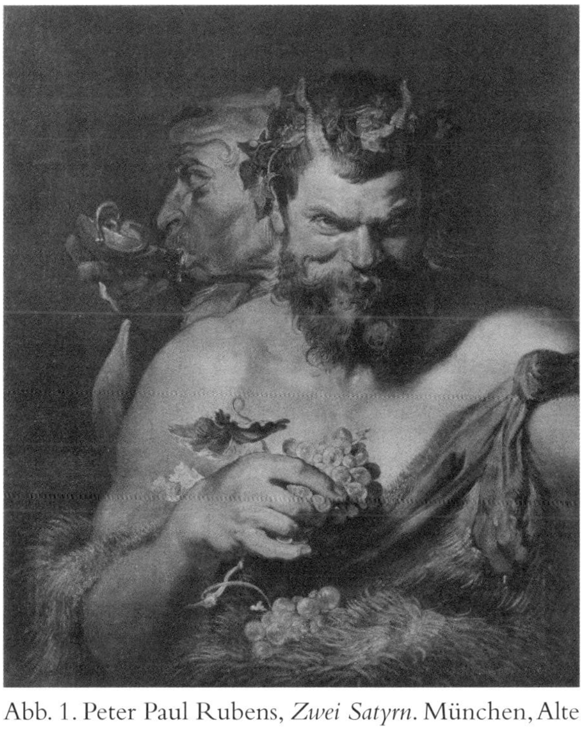

Abb. 1. Peter Paul Rubens, *Zwei Satyrn*. München, Alte Pinakothek, Zustand mit allen Ergänzungen, Foto Bruckmann um 1910

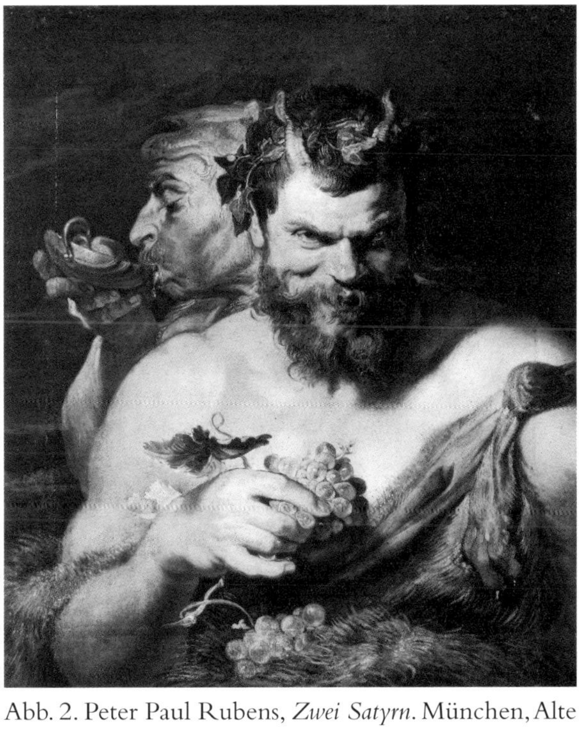

Abb. 2. Peter Paul Rubens, *Zwei Satyrn*. München, Alte Pinakothek, heutiger Zustand

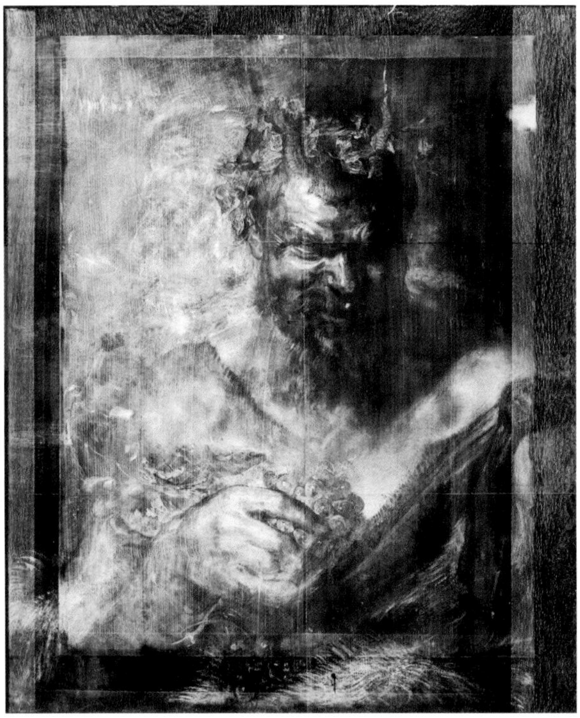

Abb. 3. Peter Paul Rubens, *Zwei Satyrn*. München, Alte Pinakothek, Röntgenfoto

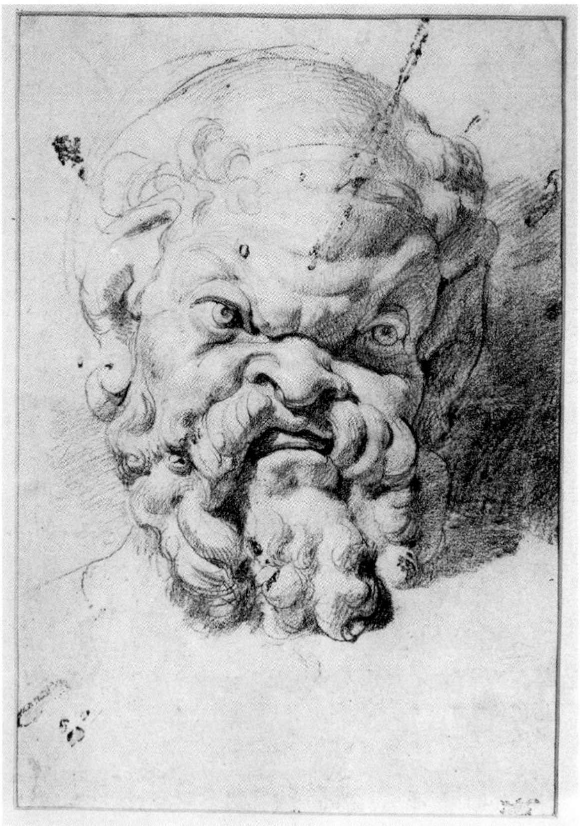

Abb. 4. Peter Paul Rubens, *Kopf des Silen*, Zeichnung. Moskau, Puschkin-Museum

Das Röntgenbild (Abb. 3) gibt einen erwähnenswerten Unterschied zur sichtbaren Ausführung wieder: die Rechte des vorderen Satyrn liegt nicht vor seiner Brust und zerdrückt Trauben, sondern hält eine Trinkschale, die er dem Betrachter entgegenstreckt. Über seiner rechten Schulter ist er mit einem Fell bekleidet

Im Röntgenbild sind aber auch Unterschiede im Aufbau des Gemäldes erkennbar. Der hintere Satyr ist nicht zusammen mit dem Vorderen entstanden. Das Bleiweißgerüst seines Kopfes weicht von dem des Vorderen ab, ist auf heller Grundierung und nicht auf der dunkleren Farbe des Hintergrundes wie der des Vorderen angelegt. Außerdem ist deutlich zu erkennen, daß der hintere an den vorderen Kopf herangemalt wurde.

Rubens hatte also zunächst nur einen Kopf vorgesehen, wie er sie gelegentlich dargestellt hatte, so beispielweise in der Moskauer Zeichnung (Abb. 4).[4] Er war möglicherweise auch Vorbild für die Komposition *Satyr und Mädchen*, die in zahlreichen Varianten und Kopien überliefert ist.[5]

Frappante Übereinstimmung zeigt das Bild mit der sog. Rubens-Vase. Nicht nur in dem Motiv der Hörner, sondern in der gesamten Physognomie, dem Blick von unten, dem halb geöffneten Mund – kurz insgesamt in dem lebendigen Ausdruck. Das Bild erscheint wie eine farbige Umsetzung der Vase, die Rubens in einer Zeichnung kopiert hatte (Abb. 5, 6).[6] Unklar ist, wann Rubens die Vase erwarb, die Peiresc 1619 auf dem Markt in St Germain gesehen und Rubens später erworben hatte.[7] Wenn das ein terminus post wäre, müßte man die Datierung der *Zwei Satyrn* auch neu bedenken. Auch eine Entstehung um 1620 wäre vorstellbar.[8]

Wie auch immer, das einzelne Satyrgesicht erschien Rubens auf einmal zu wenig, er fügte den Kopf des anderen in einer merkwürdigen Zusammenstellung in einem Winkel von 90° links hinzu.

Eine Erklärung für die Kombination der ungewöhnlich zueinander gestellten Köpfe wurde bisher nicht versucht. Sie erinnert an ein Detail im *Silen*, die Köpfe oben rechts, den Mohren und den links neben ihm im Profil erscheinenden Trinker mit der Schale.

Das Vorbild findet sich wiederum in der antiken Kleinkunst. Römische Gemmen standen

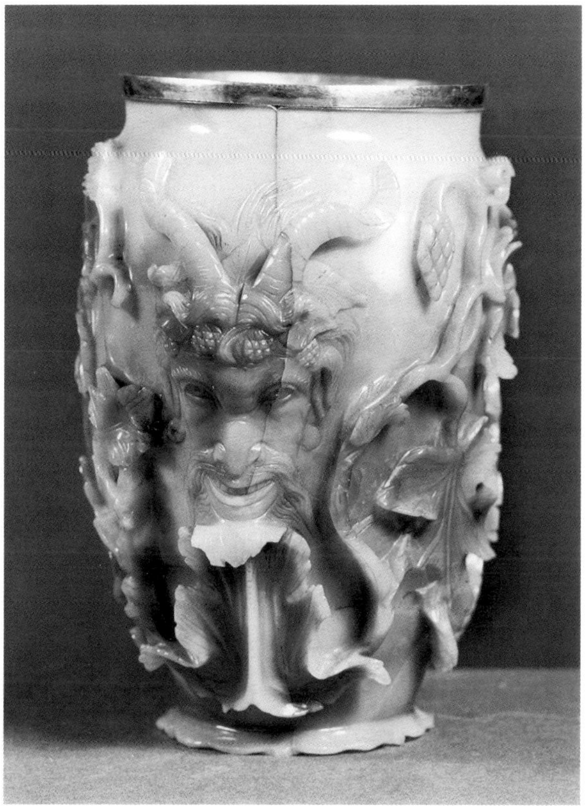

Abb. 5. *Rubens-Vase*. Baltimore, Walters Art Gallery

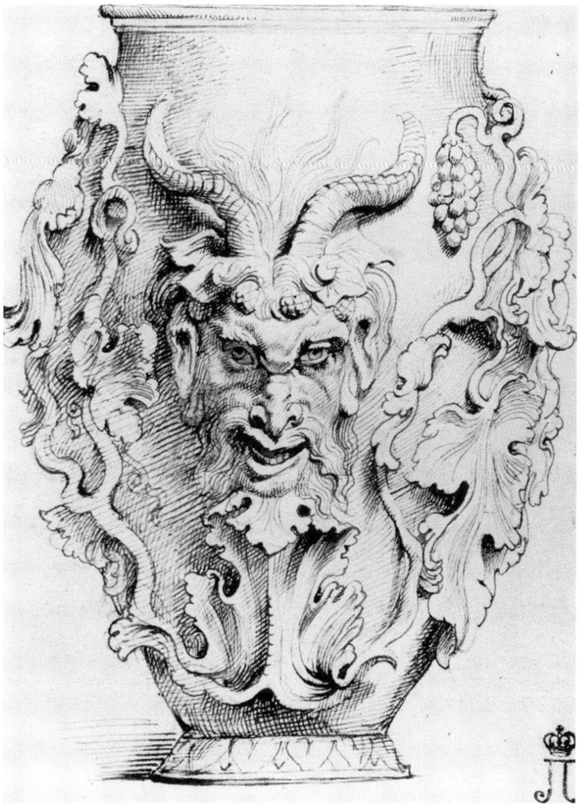

Abb. 6. Peter Paul Rubens, *Zeichnung nach der Rubens-Vase*. St Petersburg, Eremitage

Pate. Eine römische Glasgemme, 1. Jahrhundert v. Chr. (11,3 x 10,1; Abb. 7), zeigt einen efeubekränzten bärtigen Satyr mit wulstigem Gesicht frontal nach vorn gedreht, rechts neben ihm ein jüngeres Gesicht im Profil nach rechts gewendet.[9] Oder ein Karneol (11,5 x 10,3; Abb. 8) aus der gleichen Epoche zeigt die gleiche Konstellation, diesmal mit dem hinteren Profilgesicht wie bei Rubens auf der linken Seite.[10]

Rubens beschränkt sich nicht auf die einfache Zusammenstellung wie im spröden Vorbild, sondern er läßt den hinteren Satyr lebendig agieren und glaubwürdig aus der Schale schlürfen, mit halb geschlossenenen Augen und eingezogenen Backen, am Mund leicht sabbernd.

Eine ähnlich enge Kombination zweier Köpfe zeigt der Münchner Silen, dessen verschiedene Schritte der Erweiterung ich an anderer Stelle dargelegt habe.[11]

Die wichtigsten Beobachtungen seien hier noch einmal kurz wiederholt: Die Kerntafel A ist nach Aussage des Neffen Philipp Rubens und nach allgemeiner kunsthistorischer Meinung um 1618 entstanden. Die Erweiterung geschah ca.

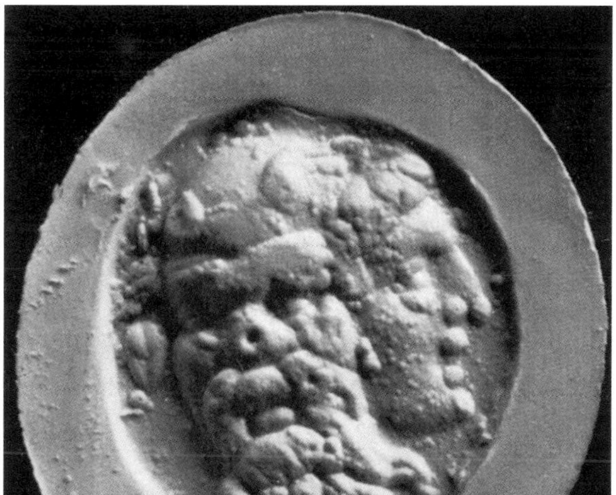

Abb. 7. *Glasgemme*, 1. Jahrhundert vor Chr.. Wien, Kunsthistorisches Museum

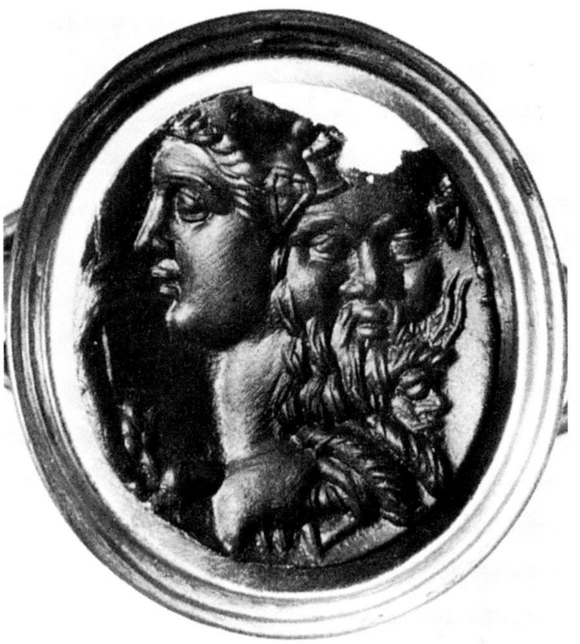

Abb. 8. *Karneol*, 1. Jahrhundert vor Chr. Wien, Kunsthistorisches Museum

1625 und zwar in zwei Stufen B und C. Die beiden äußeren Bretter, also Stufe C, wurden an diejenigen der Stufe B angesetzt, als diese schon begonnen aber noch nicht vollendet war. Soviel zur Rekapitulation.

Der Urzustand der Phase A ist in einer seitenverkehrten Radierung von Pieter Soutman und einer Gemälde-Kopie in Kassel mit geringen Abweichungen überliefert.[12] Zunächst stapfte der Silen mit behaartem Bauch und Schenkeln breitbeinig einher. Die Haare wurden übermalt und die Konturen der Oberschenkel zu einer deutlicheren Schrittstellung verändert, die Efeuranken an Kopf und Beinen reduziert (einzelne Blätter sind mit bloßem Auge noch sichtbar). Der efeubekränzte, ins Profil gewendete Satyr links neben dem Mohren, der aus einer Schale Wein schlürft, erscheint in der Kasseler Kopie nicht, wohl aber in der Radierung. Kieser glaubte daher, er sei erst in der erweiterten Münchner Fassung hinzugekommen.[13] Der Befund des Bildes widerspricht dem aber, der Hintergrund ist an den Kontur des Kopfes herangemalt, er muß also von Anfang an da gewesen sein.[14]

So wage ich zum Schluß die kühne Hypothese: die Kasseler Werkstattkopie könnte in statu nascendi des Silen entstanden sein als der hintere Trinker noch nicht gemalt war, gleichsam in einem simultanen Gedankengang mit dem kleinen Bild der *Zwei Satyrn*.

ANMERKUNGEN

1. Konrad Renger, 'Rubens-Stücke. Die Anstückungen von Münchner "Silen" und "Schäferszene"', *Wallraf-Richartz-Jahrbuch*, LV, 1994 (Festschrift Justus Müller Hofstede), S. 171–178.

2. Veronika Poll-Frommel, Konrad Renger und Jan Schmidt, 'Untersuchungen an Rubens-Bildern. Die Anstückungen', *Bayerische Staatsgemäldesammlungen, Jahresbericht*, 1993, S. 24–35. Konrad Renger, 'Anstückungen bei Rubens', in E. Mai, K. Schütz und H. Vlieghe, ed., *Die Malerei Antwerpens. Gattungen, Meister, Wirkungen. Internationales Kolloquium* (Wien, 1993), Köln, 1994, S. 157–167. Die Brettschemata zusammengestellt von Hubert von Sonnenburg, 'Rubens, Bildaufbau und Technik', in Hubert von Sonnenburg und Frank Preußer, *Rubens. Gesammelte Aufsätze zur Technik* (München) 1980 (Sonderdruck aus Maltechnik-Restauro 2, 3, 1979).

3. Zu dieser Maßnahme siehe: Paul Kaemmerer, *Tschudi's Eingriffe in zwei Bilder des Rubens*, München, 1910, S. 39–41.

4. Zeichnung, Moskau, Puschkin-Museum; Marjon van der Meulen, *Rubens. Copies after the Antique*, Corpus Rubenianum Ludwig Burchard, XXII, London, 1994, Nr. 33, Abb. 67. Ohne die Pariser Zeichnung (Lugt Nr. 1236) neuerdings gesehen zu haben, schließe ich mich Lugts Zweifel an der Eigenhändigkeit an. Die große Übereinstimmung spricht eher für eine Kopie nach, als für eine Zeichnung für das Gemälde.

5. Am bekanntesten die Fassungen der Gemäldegalerie Dresden (Inv. 957A) und der Sammlung Schönborn-Buchheim, Salzburg Residenzgalerie, Katalog 1975, S. 79, Abb. 38; Stich von Alexander Voet II: F.W.H. Hollstein, *Dutch and Flemish Etchings, Engravings and Woodcuts, ca. 1450–1700*, Nr. 10; Michael Jaffé, *Rubens. Catalogo completo*, Mailand, 1989, Nr. 427.

6. Baltimore, Walters Art Gallery; Van der Meulen 1994 (siehe Anm. 4), Abb. 358, 359. Zeichnung, St Petersburg, Eremitage; Van der Meulen 1994, Nr. 184, Abb. 360.

7. Van der Meulen 1994 (siehe Anm. 4), II, S. 212.

8. Rudolf Oldenbourg, in *P.P. Rubens. Des Meisters Gemälde, Klassiker der Kunst*, 4. Aufl., hrsg. von Rudolf Oldenbourg, Berlin–Leipzig, 1921, S. 135 [1616–1617]; Jaffé 1989 (siehe Anm. 5), Nr. 514 [1618–1619].

9. Erika Zwierlein-Diehl, *Die antiken Gemmen des Kunsthistorischen Museums in Wien*, II, München, 1979, Nr. 836. Siehe auch: Adolf Furtwängler, *Beschreibung der geschnittenen Steine im Antiquarium [Kgl. Museen Berlin]*, Berlin, 1896, Nrn. 5310 oder 5312

10. Zwierlein-Diehl (siehe Anm. 9), III, 1991, Nr. 2090; Furtwängler 1896 (siehe Anm. 9), Nr. 5312.

11. Siehe Anm. 1.

12. Emil Kieser, 'Rubens Münchner Silen und seine Vorstufen', *Münchner Jahrbuch der bildenden Kunst*, NF XIII, 1938–1939, Abb. 5; Bernhard Schnackenburg, *Flämische Meister in der Kasseler Gemäldegalerie*, Kassel, 1985, Abb. 49; Radierung: Frank van den Wijngaert, *Inventaris der Rubeniaansche Prentkunst*, Antwerpen, 1940, Nr. 641; Hollstein (siehe Anm. 5), XXVIII, Amsterdam, s.a., S. 204, Nr. 7 [Jonas Suyderhoef].

13. Kieser 1938–1939 (siehe Anm. 5), S. 195, Anm. 20. Ihm folgend: Reinhild Stephan-Maaser, *Mythos und Lebenswelt. Studien zum 'Trunkenen Silen' von Peter Paul Rubens*, Münster–Hamburg, 1992, S. 263.

14. Der Landschaftszipfel zwischen den Beinen des Silen, den Kieser ebenfalls der erweiterten Fassung zurechnet, ist an das Fell des Silen herangemalt, ist also im Zuge der Erweiterung gemalt, könnte aber auf einer ursprünglich vorhandene Landschaft liegen, die der Einheitlichkeit wegen überdeckt wurde.

The Construction and Development of Rubens's Landscapes: Reflections on the London Exhibition

Christopher Brown

There are about forty painted landscapes by Rubens. Landscape was not a major theme in Rubens's art and yet it was important to him. The landscapes were painted for the most part for himself and a number of close friends and relatives: they are the private art of a very public artist and no fewer than eighteen of them, nearly half, were still in his possession at the time of his death in 1640.

The precise dating of the landscapes is difficult because of the personal nature of these works but Gluck's chronology[1] has been widely accepted and although I have suggested slight modifications in the exhibition catalogue it seems to me basically correct. To simplify, Rubens painted landscapes at two particular moments in his career, between about 1612 and 1620 and between about 1636 and 1638. There were special personal circumstances which caused Rubens to turn to the depiction of landscape at these times in his life.[2]

One of the first paintings in the exhibition was the Prado *Landscape with Psyche* which traditionally has been said to be a collaboration between Rubens and Paul Bril (Fig. 1).[3] It is dated 1610 in the bottom left hand corner in the very characteristic calligraphy of Bril – he has a very particular open 6 – and the con-

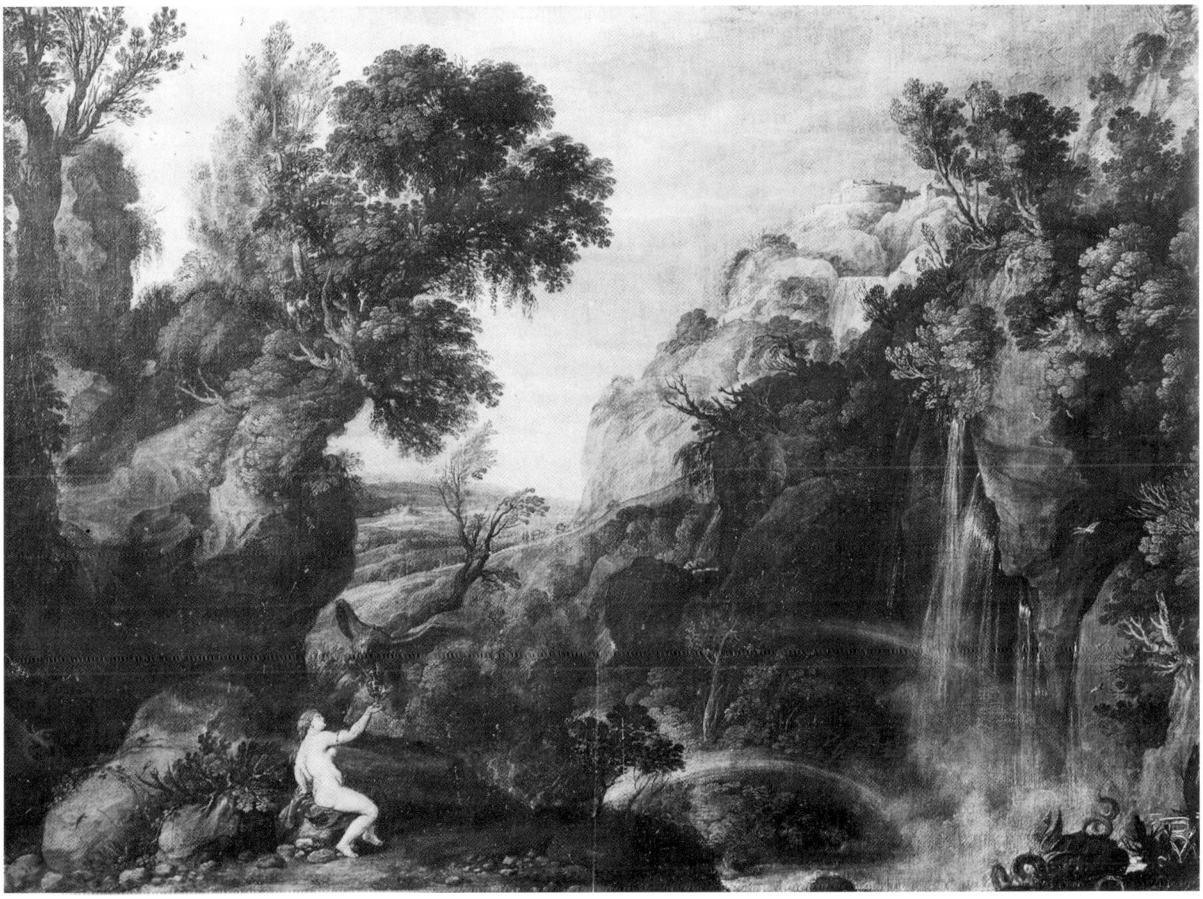

Fig. 1. Paul Bril, overpainted by Peter Paul Rubens, *Landscape*, 1610. Madrid, Museo del Prado

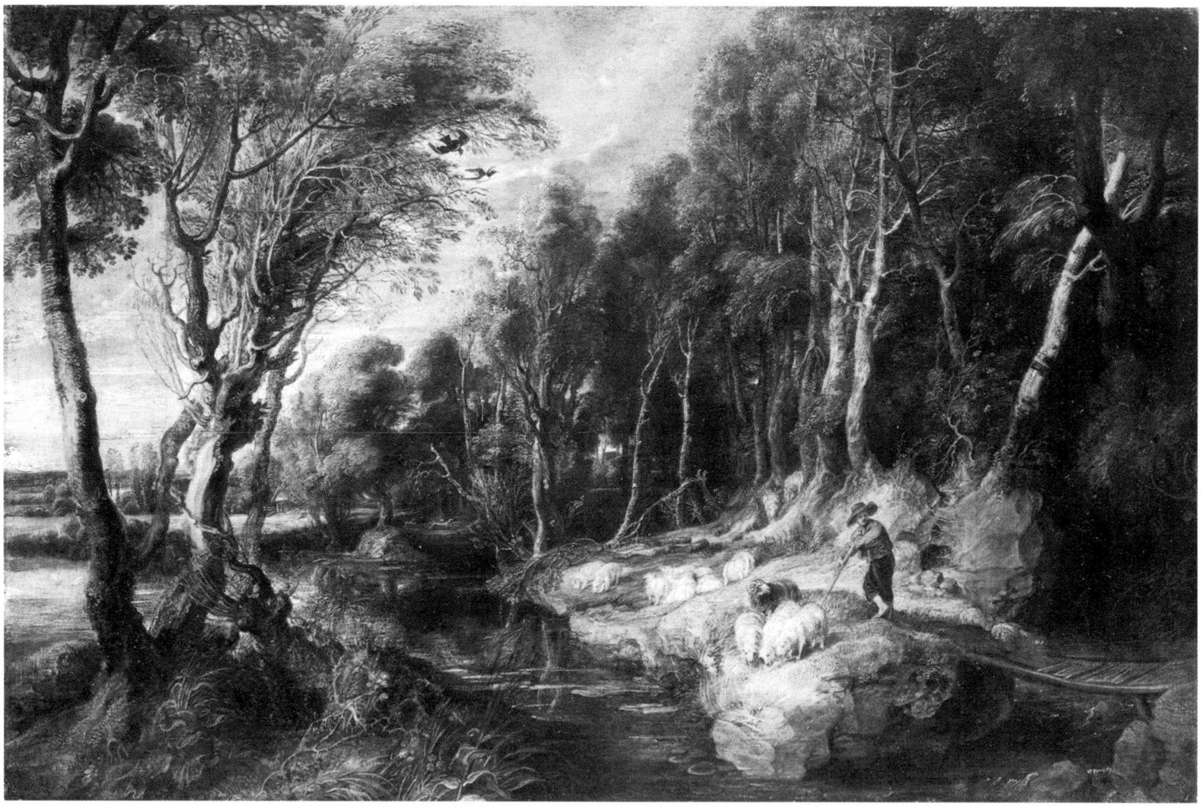

Fig. 2. Peter Paul Rubens, *A Shepherd with his Flock in a Woody Landscape*. London, National Gallery

ventional wisdom is that the landscape was painted in Rome by Bril and then sent to Antwerp for Rubens to add the figure of Psyche and Jupiter in the form of an eagle.

The painting was cleaned for the exhibition and inspection with the naked eye made it clear that the collaboration was a good deal more complicated than at first appears. The outlines of the eagle in its first position could be made out and Rubens must have realized that in this position the eagle would not show up against the dark of the rock. He therefore decided to move the outline of the rock in order to create a light space in which to place the eagle. This involved him in repainting the landscape passage and the entire rocky outcrop with the trees which cling to it. He also painted in the rainbows, part at least of the waterfall, the dragon guarding the Styx and, of course, the figure of Psyche (which has a significant pentimento).

Luuk Pijl has argued that the picture is in fact a finished painting by Bril which had been overpainted by Rubens. He has drawn our attention to a painting by Martin Rijckaert, known to have been a copyist of Bril, showing a very similar composition with a shepherd and a flock of sheep in the bottom left hand corner. Xrays have revealed not a shepherd and his flock but the figure of St Jerome with his hourglass beneath Psyche. So what in fact happened was that Rubens took a completed landscape by Bril, either sent to Rubens from Rome or bought by Rubens on the Antwerp art market, and remodelled it. He has changed it from a landscape with St Jerome to a treatment of the extremely rare subject of Psyche taking water from the Styx with the help of Jupiter. The only previous treatment of this subject of which I am aware is the quite different one by Giulio Romano at the Palazzo del Te in Mantua,[4] with which Rubens was naturally very familiar.

Bril had been enormously admired in Rome since the earliest years of the seventeenth century and in 1622 Mancini was to describe him as the leading landscape painter in the city.[5] To take a painting by Bril and recast it in this way is a remarkably self-confident act and while we know many examples of Rubens doing this to drawings it is very rare for him to treat paintings in this way. When did he do it? The date

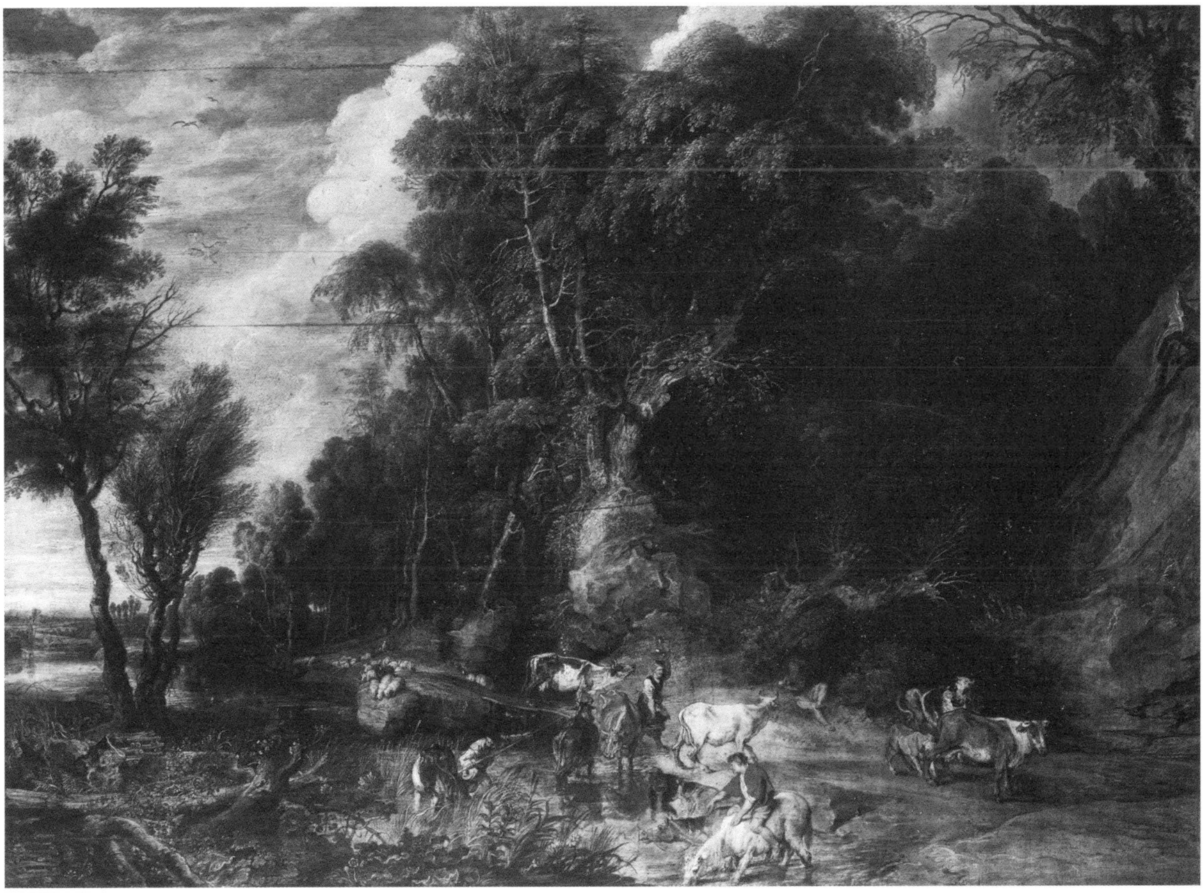

Fig. 3. Peter Paul Rubens, *The Watering Place*. London, National Gallery

of 1610 is original but there is no compelling reason why Rubens should have intervened very shortly after that. The figure of Psyche seems close to the female allegorical figures in the great series of the senses in the Prado, painted in collaboration with Jan Brueghel the Younger in about 1616. Justus Müller-Hofstede has recently suggested to me that Rubens's changes could have been made as late as the 1630s. I prefer, however, the earlier date. This Psyche has presumably been correctly identified with "Une paysage avec Psyche par Paulus Bril" in the inventory of Rubens's collection made after his death in 1640.[6]

The exhibition in London provided a welcome opportunity to reexamine the relationship between two landscapes in the National Gallery, the *Landscape with a Shepherd and his Flock* (Fig. 2) and the *Watering Place* (Fig. 3), painted during the earlier period of Rubens's landscape painting and probably in about 1618–1620. Gregory Martin established the essential elements of this relationship in his Flemish School catalogue of 1970,[7] but it was possible to add some further detail. Rubens began by painting the central composition of the *Landscape with a Shepherd and his Flock* on two oak panels butted together along a central join, an entirely conventional arrangement. He then decided to expand the composition on all four sides. This involved adding four pieces of oak. Whether this simple carpentry was done in Rubens's own studio or in a panelmaker's studio we do not know.

After the *Landscape with a Shepherd and his Flock* had been painted in two stages, a small copy of it was made in Rubens's studio. Rooses first suggested that Lucas van Uden was responsible for much of *The Watering Place*[8] and recently Arnout Balis has revived this idea by suggesting that it was Van Uden who made this copy.[9] This idea seems to me very attractive, particularly as it is so unlikely that Rubens would copy his own composition in this way. However, the argument is complicated by the fact that we have no evidence of Van Uden's

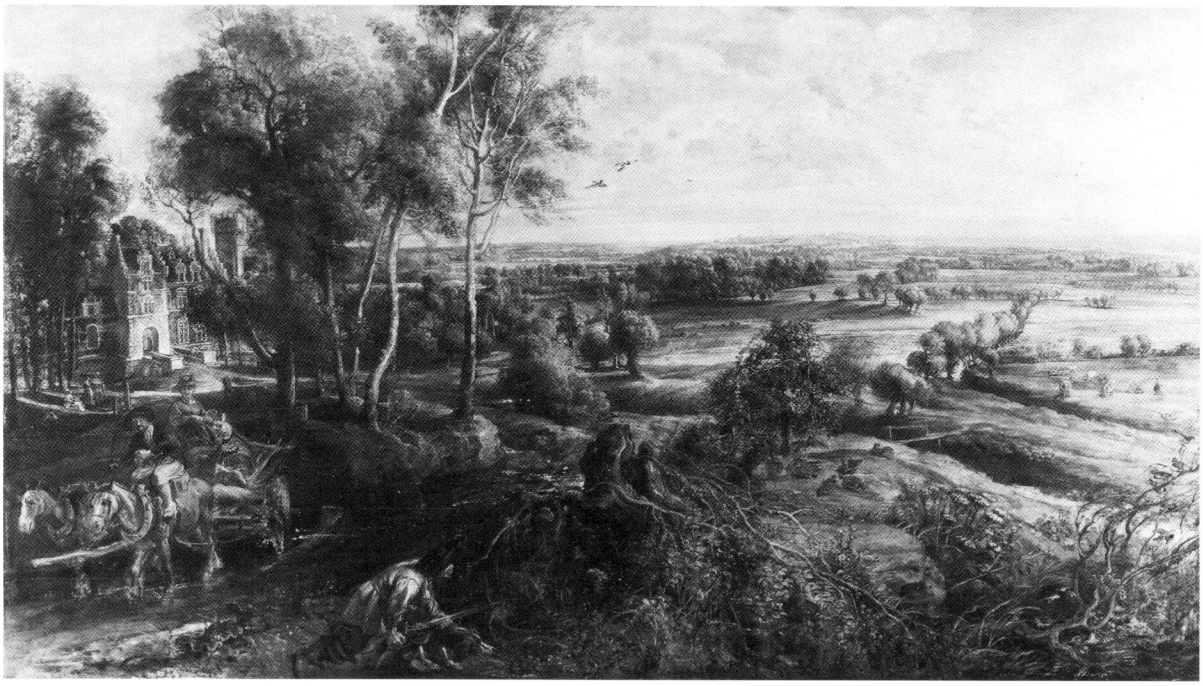

Fig. 4. Peter Paul Rubens, *An Autumn Landscape with a View of Het Steen*. London, National Gallery

activity in Rubens's studio at this date and this copy is of a higher quality than much of Van Uden's later, securely documented work. However, a copy was made – down to the figure of the shepherd which Rubens was later to paint out – and then the composition expanded in at least two further stages. This sequence of work can be established by a study of the technical photographs and a study of the paint layers on the edges of the individual panels under high magnification. The grain of the wood on the far right hand side runs vertically, while the grain of the other 9 pieces runs horizontally, a denial of one of the basic rules of carpentry which has caused *The Watering Place* to be the single most unstable panel in the National Gallery's entire collection, a constant headache to its Conservation Department.

Panelmaking was a highly developed skill in seventeenth-century Antwerp. The panelmakers were members of the St Luke's Guild and the quality of panels was strictly controlled by guild regulations.[10] According to these regulations – and it is never quite clear the degree to which guild regulations were adhered in the seventeenth century – panels had to be inspected by 'keurmeesters' and only then was the guild brand and the panelmaker's personal stamp applied to the back. What cannot be in any doubt is that panels made up of numerous, relatively small pieces of wood like the *Landscape with a Shepherd and his Flock* and *The Watering Place* – not to mention the even more complicated *Landscape with Het Steen* (Fig. 4) and *Landscape with a Rainbow* (Fig. 5) – would not have passed a rigorous guild inspection. These panels must have been made in the artist's studio or by Rubens's panelmaker as a personal favour to the artist.

The *Watering Place* (Fig. 3), painted in about 1620, is the culmination of Rubens's first period of landscape painting. He did not return to the subject in an intensive manner until the mid-1630s. There is, however, a group of stormy landscapes from the late 1620s: the *Landscape with a Shipwreck of St Paul*, *Philemon and Baucis* and a lost storm landscape, the composition of which survives in an engraving by Schelte a Bolswert and a copy in Rotterdam.[11] Associated with this group of stormy landscapes is what has been usually described as a sketch, which is in oil on paper.[12] This small painting had been seen by very few specialists before being included in the exhibition. I had only seen photographs of it, but on seeing it I was troubled, particularly by the broad brushwork of the torrent and the extraordinary stick figures of drowning people. I studied it again and

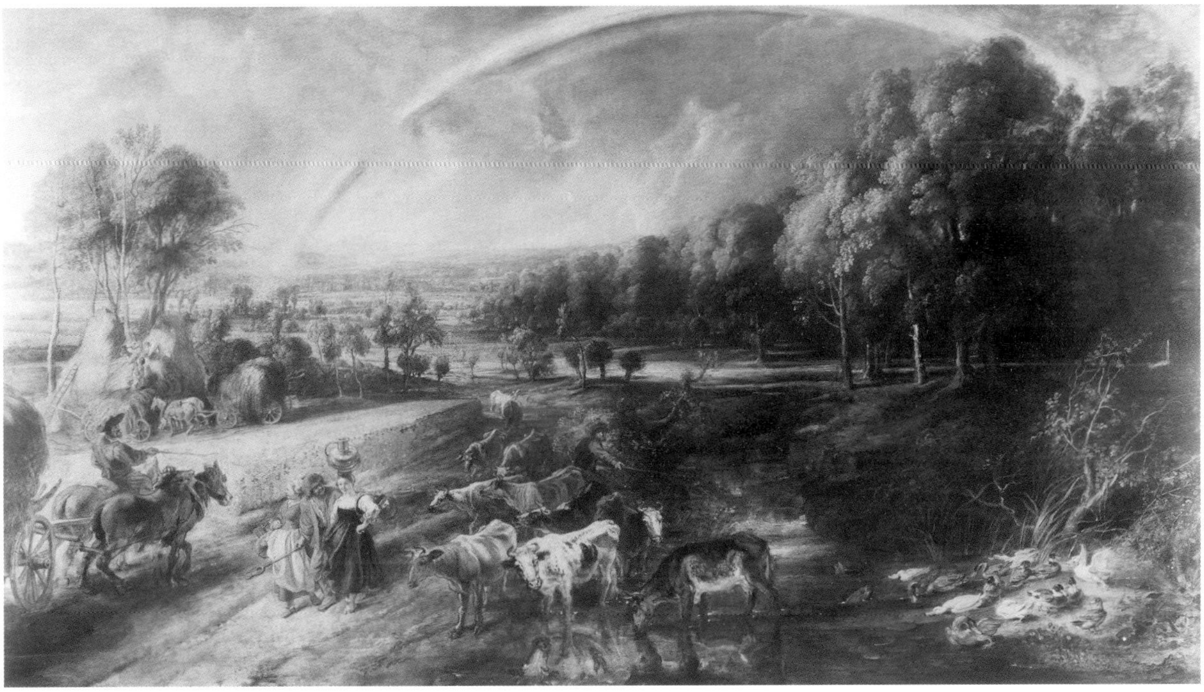

Fig. 5. Peter Paul Rubens, *Landscape with a Rainbow*. London, Wallace Collection

again and now consider that it has nothing to do with Rubens at all. It is one of those paintings which, having entered the literature, is very difficult to look at freshly: it is probably an Italian late seventeenth-century painting from the circle of Salvator Rosa. The pair of landscapes, *The Afternoon* and *The Evening*,[13] owned by Ludwig Burchard and still in the collection of his heirs, were dated by him to the late 1620s. Comparison with secure small landscapes by Rubens in the exhibition made it clear that they are not by Rubens but by a Flemish landscape painter of the subsequent generation.

At the heart of the exhibition hung the *Landscape with Het Steen* (Fig. 4) and *Landscape with a Rainbow* (Fig. 5),[14] Rubens's greatest achievements as a landscape painter. One hung in the original and the other in a same-size colour photograph, due to the conditions of Lady Wallace's will. This was intended to concentrate visitors' minds on the question of how these paintings were displayed. I believe that the two paintings formed a unified decorative scheme, hanging opposite one another in a north-facing room, probably at Het Steen. As with the earlier landscapes, Rubens painted this pair on panel and these particular panels have an extremely complex make-up, being composed of 19 and 20 pieces of oak respectively.

The first, and most basic question is why did Rubens go to all this trouble – creating complex panels which he knew to be unstable – in order to paint his landscapes on panel. It is a far simpler procedure to extend a canvas than to extend a panel. The answer must be that he painted most of his landscapes on panel because he wanted to achieve delicate and precise effects which he felt he could not achieve on canvas. He wanted to create a luminosity, with the underlying imprimatura layer shining through the paint glazes, which could only be done on panel. He wished to include details of flowers, bushes, trees and birds which were harder to realize on canvas: comparison in the exhibition between *Summer*,[15] painted on canvas, and *Landscape with a Rainbow*, painted on panel, made this clear. Rubens painted *Landscape with Het Steen* and *Landscape with a Rainbow* on panel in order to achieve the luminosity and the degree of detail he required. Both have similar constructions, with three relatively large central planks, one row of small planks on the left, two rows on the right and the whole held together by long planks at top and bottom.

Why should Rubens have painted these large pictures on a support made up of so many different elements and so inherently unstable? With our knowledge of the earlier cases, we

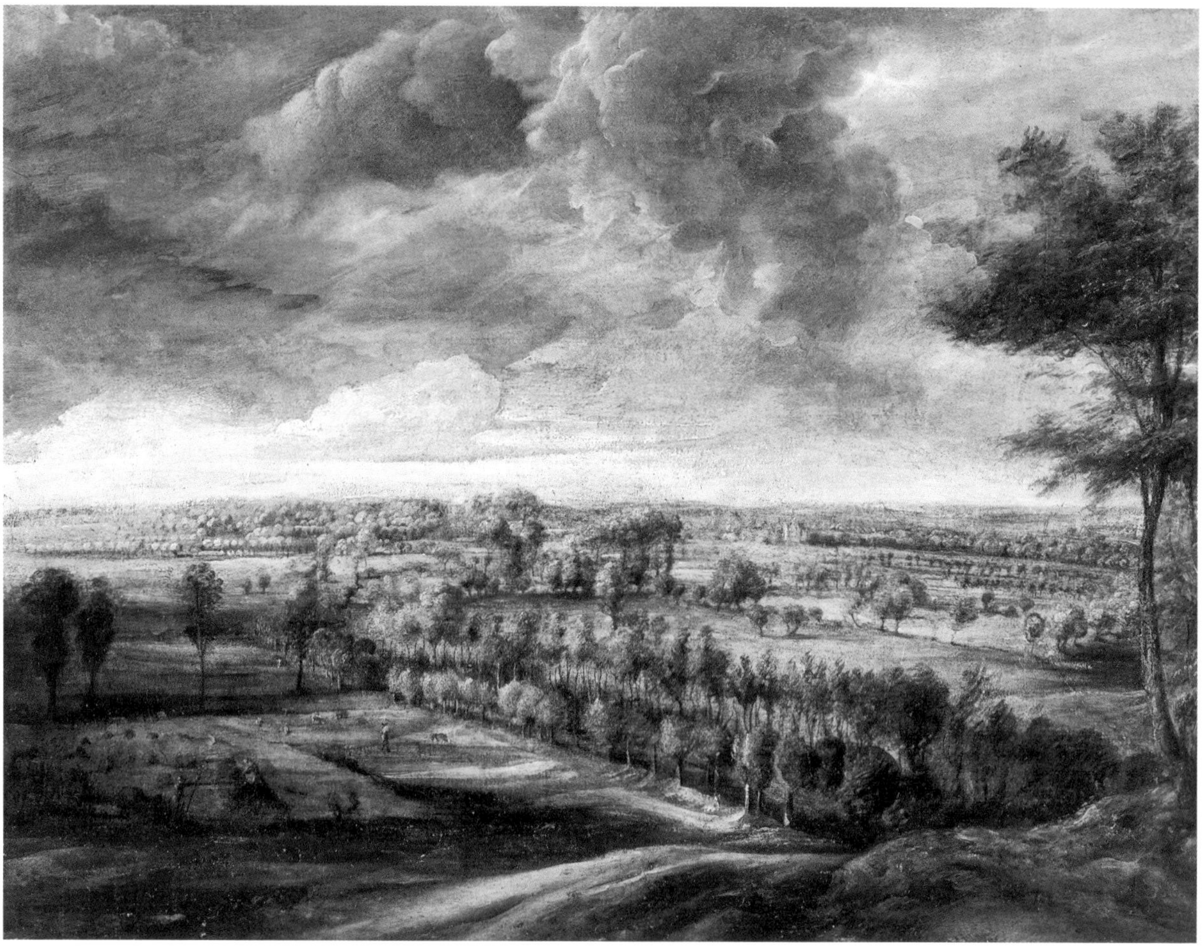

Fig. 6. Peter Paul Rubens, *Landscape with an Avenue of Trees*. Boston. Museum of Fine Arts

might at first imagine that Rubens began with a core composition which he then expanded in several stages and that he undertook this expansion as both paintings developed. The idea of both paintings being expanded in a very similar way seems complicated but it is possible, and this has been the presumption in the recent literature. However, when the joins of the individual panels are examined through the microscope, we do not find the overlapping layers of paint which are such a feature of these joins in *The Watering Place* (Fig. 3). Indeed, in examining the paint surface of both paintings, it is clear that both were painted in single campaigns. They are broadly, fluently painted in bold brushstrokes which go right across the joins in the panel. We must, therefore, find another explanation for the complex make-up of these panels. In my view the only reasonable explanation is the simplest. Because these paintings were to comprise a decorative scheme for his country house, Rubens did not think it necessary to invest in very expensive panels made up of a few individual pieces of wood, such as would be appropriate for an altarpiece or a major private commission like the *Samson and Delilah* painted for Nicolaes Rockox in 1609, a large painting which is made up of six equally sized planks butted jointed together.[16] As has been noted in the exhibition catalogue, following an observation by Jørgen Wadum, the fact that the *Landscape with Het Steen* is gessoed on the back follows a recommendation in technical treatises of the seventeenth century that multi-member panels be treated in this way in order to prevent damp entering and the joins cracking open.[17] There it is argued that these panels were prepared in their present size and gessoed at the back, providing Rubens with large supports which were inexpensive and relatively stable.

There have been two principal objections to this explanation. The first is that Rubens, having enjoyed immense success for many years

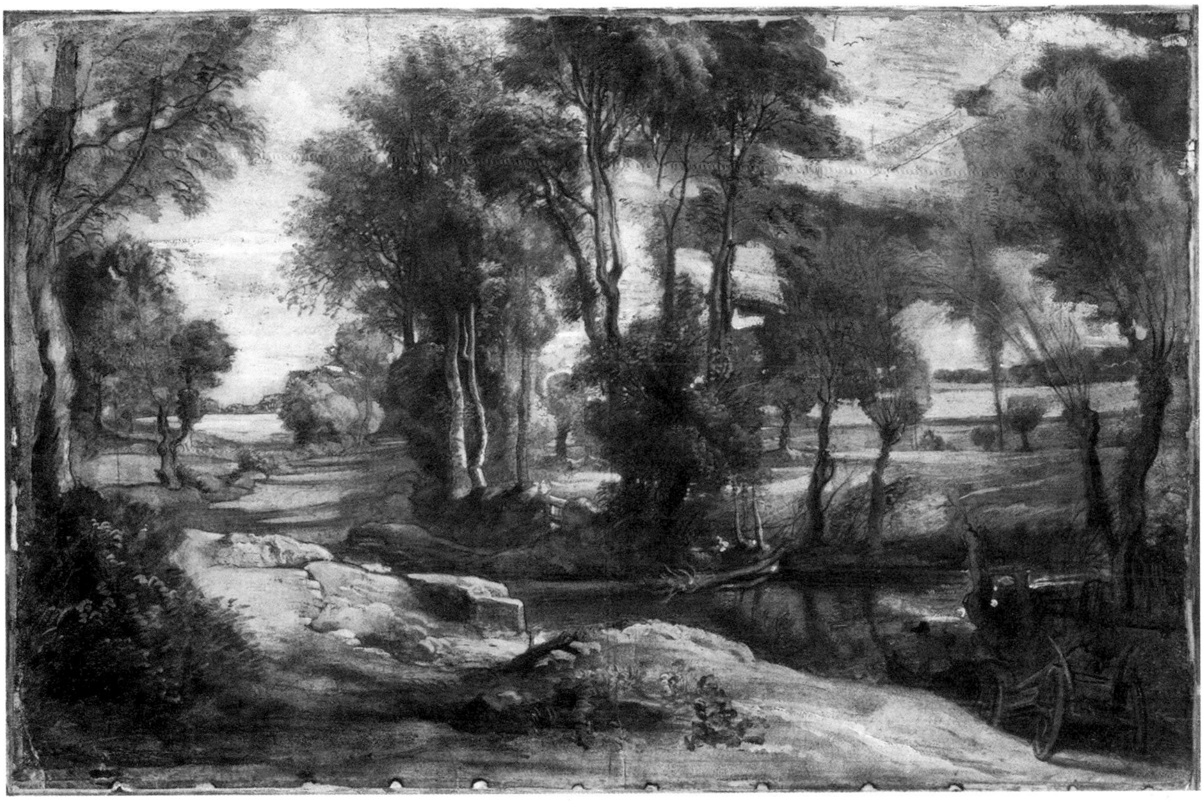

Fig. 7. Peter Paul Rubens, *A Wagon fording a Stream*. London, National Gallery

and having just spent a large sum of money on his estate, had no need to make savings of this kind. In fact, it is quite clear that Rubens was careful with his money. An extremely important element in Rubens's psychological make-up was his determination to build up the family wealth and position to an extent that what had happened to his father – the loss of property and status following his being forced into exile – could not happen again. Rubens considered that money spent on property was well spent but there was no unnecessary expenditure. A second objection has been that the construction of panels made of twenty pieces of wood would be far more expensive than the construction of panels made up of, say, six planks and any saving on wood would therefore be cancelled out. This cannot be true: the construction of these large multi-member panels was work which could be given to apprentices in his own or the panelmaker's workshop and so was inexpensive. The most significant cost was that of large planks of oak brought from the Baltic, a cost which rose substantially during periods of war in that region. A panel made from smaller pieces of wood, some of them off-cuts, must have been significantly cheaper.

There are no preparatory compositional drawings for Rubens's largest and most complex landscape compositions, the *Landscape with Het Steen* (Fig. 4) and the *Landscape with a Rainbow* (Fig. 5). Making compositional drawings for landscapes does not seem to have been part of Rubens's procedure when creating landscapes. This is one reason why I am inclined to reject the drawing in Hamburg which has been proposed as a preparatory study for the *Pond with Cows and Milkmaids* (Liechtenstein, Princely Collections).[18] It seems to be a free copy after the painting rather than a study for it. In his large compositions Rubens did not make a detailed underdrawing in charcoal or black chalk but blocked in the principal features on the imprimatura layer using a warm red-brown on a thick brush, sometimes stressing outlines or particular elements in a darker, blackish pigment.[19] This layer, known in the theoretical textbooks as 'dead colour', is often allowed to show through in the finished paintings to serve as shadows and half-tones under areas of flesh. Rubens then painted his main

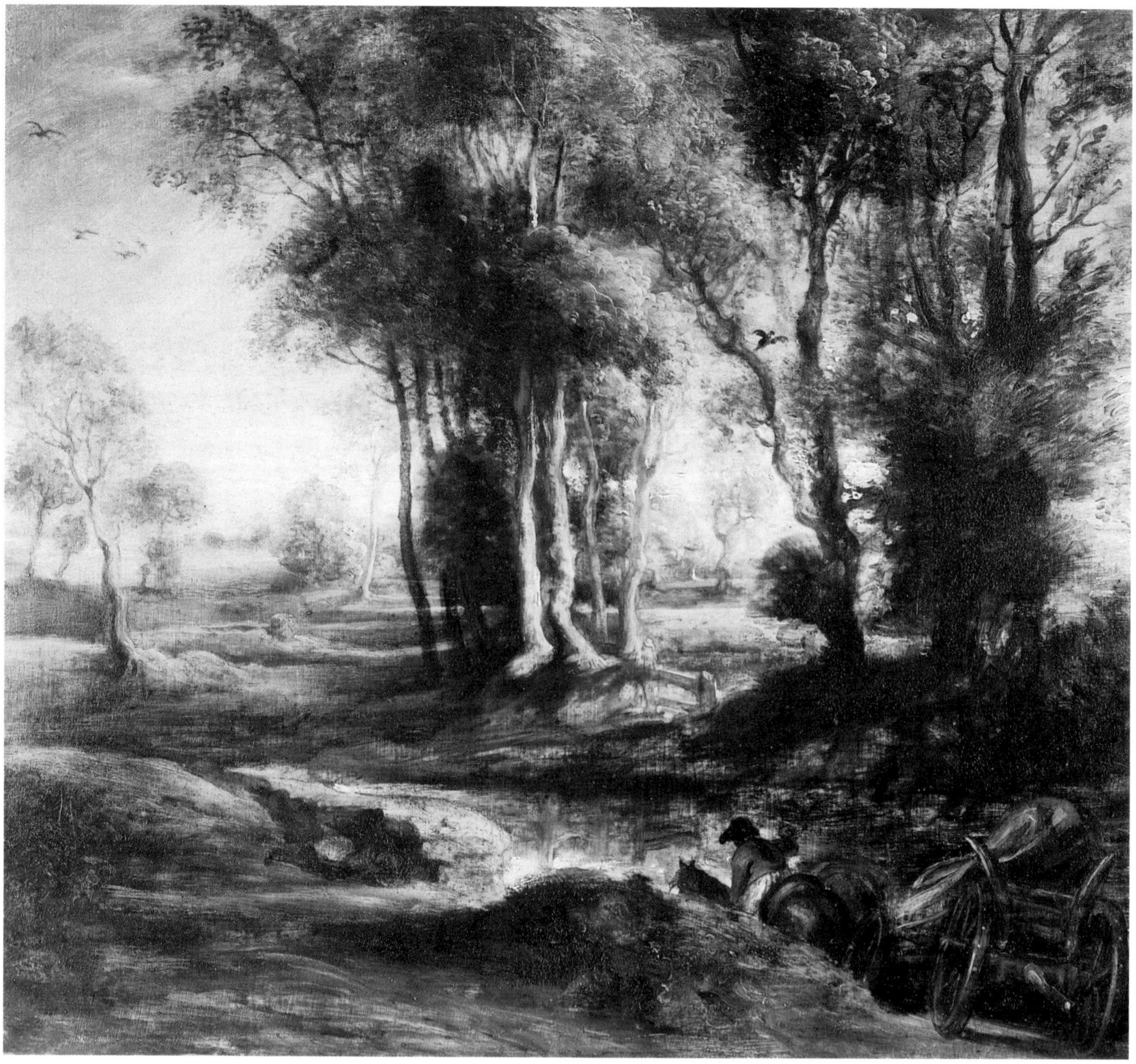

Fig. 8. Peter Paul Rubens, *Landscape with a Wagon at Sunset*. Rotterdam, Museum Boijmans-Van Beuningen

colour layers in broad and fluid brushstrokes. Rubens used drawings for particular details. For example, for the bushes in the foreground of *Landscape with Het Steen*, he would have used drawings made in black chalk with red and white chalk highlights and detailed colour notes such as the sheet at the Courtauld Institute Galleries.[20]

In the Museum of Fine Arts in Boston, hung for many years in the depot, is a painting in oil on paper showing an extensive view in Brabant (Fig. 6).[21] When it was requested for the exhibition in London, the Museum restored it and as a consequence its status has become far clearer. The painting was substantially added to at the top, bottom and on the right hand side, probably late in the seventeenth century. The central section, however, is a landscape by Rubens which is closely related to the *Landscape with a Rainbow*. It appears to show the same view of the landscape of Brabant as can be seen in the left middle distance of the *Landscape with a Rainbow*, with the same small *lusthof* or country house visible in the countryside. It is more difficult to define the nature of the relationship between the two paintings. Can it be thought of as preparatory to the larger painting in the sense that a head study is preparatory to a history painting? Or is it entirely independent of it?

Rubens did make oil sketches for landscape at this period of his career. There is, for exam-

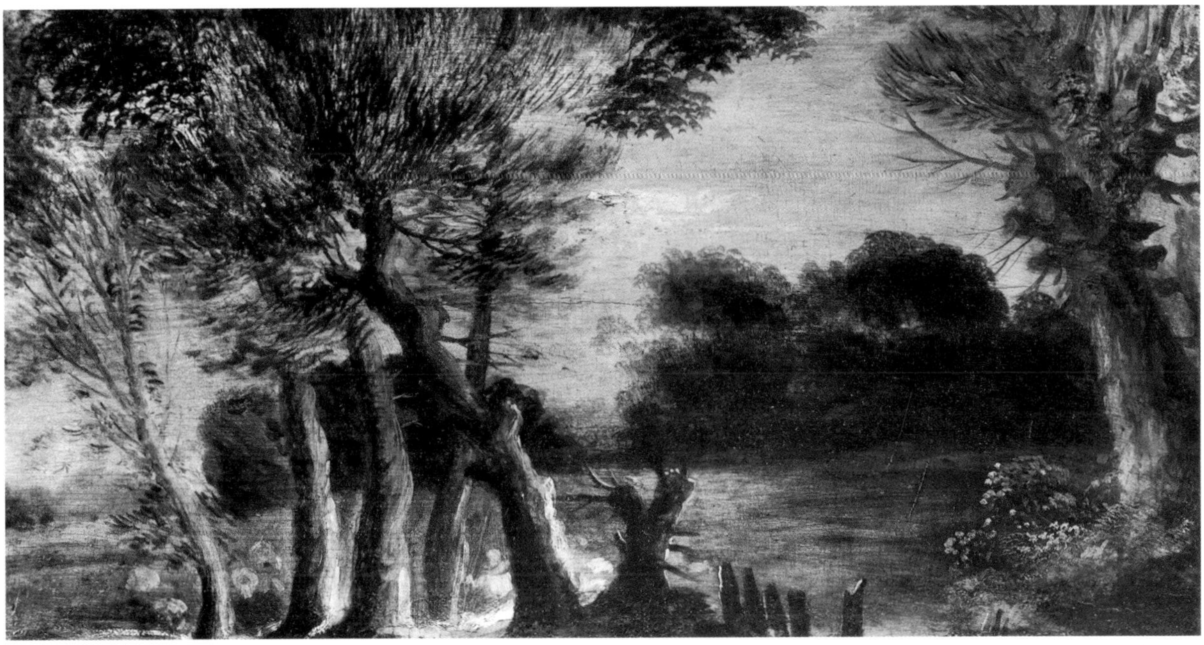

Fig. 9. Peter Paul Rubens, *Willows*. Private collection, on loan to the National Gallery of Art, Washington

ple, a sketch in oil on paper in the National Gallery (Fig. 7)[22] in which Rubens returned to the subject of *La Charette Embourbée*, which he had first tackled in about 1620 in the painting in the Hermitage.[23] However, unlike the richly fantastic rocks and streams of that painting, Rubens here shows us the willow-lined streams of Brabant. The sketch seems to be unfinished and gives us a valuable insight into Rubens's technique when making such sketches. The drawing and undermodelling can clearly be seen. The main landscape features such as the groups of trees and the structure of the foreground were then broadly painted in their intended colours and patches of sky painted around and between the trees. Rubens's next stage, not carried out in this sketch, would have been to develop the structure of the trees and other features of the landscape, adding details, highlights and shadows.

The National Gallery sketch is related to a small landscape on panel in the Museum Boijmans Van Beuningen (Fig. 8),[24] which was also cleaned for the exhibition and hung alongside the London sketch. The relationship is very close despite the fact that one is horizontal in format and the other vertical. Detailed comparison reveals that the configuration of the trees is very similar. This is not, of course, a sketch in the sense that the oil sketches for large history paintings are preparatory sketches, to be shown to patrons and given to members of the studio to be worked up on a large scale. It is a sketch in the sense of a first thought, which was then fully worked out.

The Rotterdam painting is a remarkable treatment of atmosphere: the sun shines through the trees to create an effect which is quite unlike that in any of Rubens's earlier landscapes. It belongs to a group of broadly painted landscapes from about 1636–1638 which are all suffused with a particularly vivid sense of atmosphere. At this moment Rubens was particularly interested in these natural effects which he created with the direct strokes of a heavily-laden brush. Two other examples of this remarkable group of late landscapes are *The Deer Hunt* in the Metropolitan Museum of Art[25] and, most extraordinary of all, the *Moonlit Landscape* in the Courtauld Institute Galleries.[26] In the catalogue of the exhibition I stressed the traditional aspects of Rubens's landscapes, their indebtedness to the formulae established by his Antwerp predecessors, particularly Pieter Bruegel the Elder. However, it seems to me – and this was an impression gained from living with these works for several months – that in fact in these late atmospheric landscapes Rubens is doing something quite new and breaking the mould of Flemish landscape. There

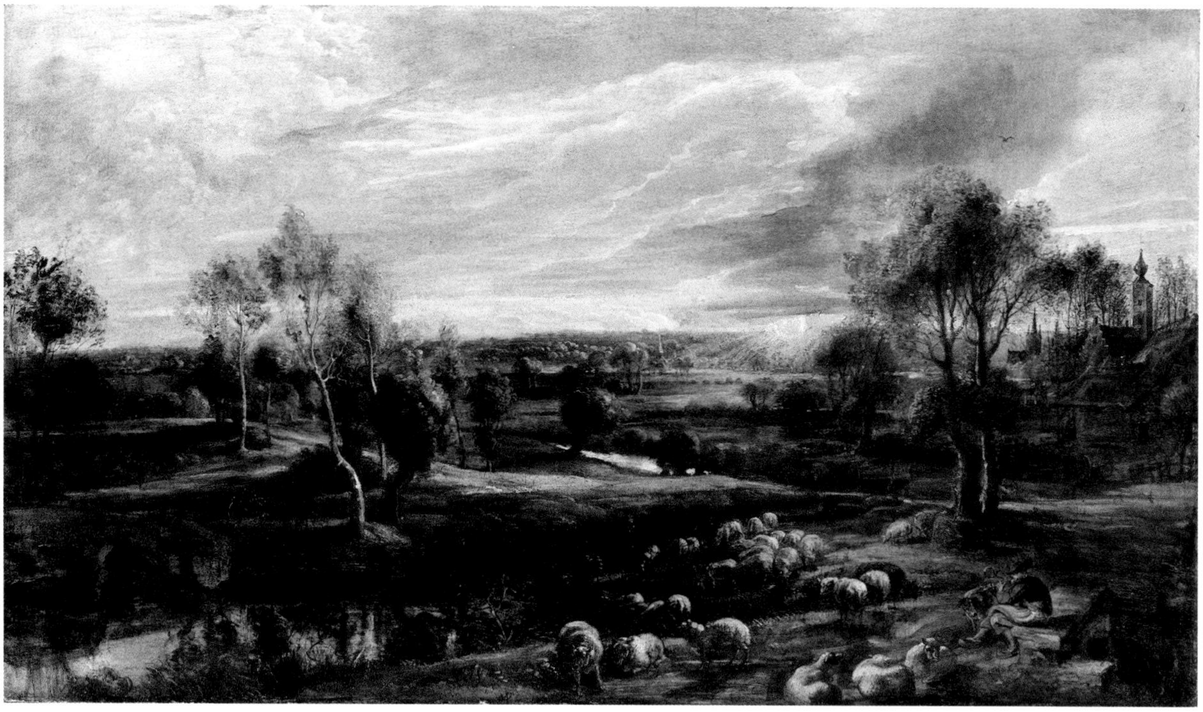

Fig. 10. Peter Paul Rubens: *Sunset Landscape with a Shepherd and his Flock*. London, National Gallery

is nothing like them in the earlier Flemish tradition, nor did his contemporaries attempt anything of this kind. It is only in the Northern Netherlands, in the landscapes of Cornelis Vroom and the young Jacob van Ruisdael, that similar effects of atmosphere are created.

The conventional wisdom is, of course, that paintings were all done in the studio in the seventeenth century and that painting in the open air is a nineteenth-century phenomenon. However, painters' travelling boxes survive[27] and could well have been used in the countryside. Roger de Piles says that Rubens 'se plaisoit a peindre des paisages d'apres le Naturel...'[28] In the exhibition was a very small oil sketch of willows (Fig. 9)[29] which seems to me to have the best claim of all Rubens's landscape paintings to have been made in front of the subject: it is a freshly observed study of a group of trees at the edge of a meadow, bathed in morning sunlight. Sitting between the trees with his back to the viewer is a shepherd whose sheep are grazing in the meadow. It was painted quickly and instinctually.

This type of intense observation and representation of natural phenomena is not limited to Rubens's paintings. He made a number of drawings in these years which show the same sharply observant sensibility. One morning, for example, he rode or walked out from Het Steen and saw a screen of trees along the bank of a stream. Their outlines were slightly obscured by the early morning mist and he noticed that the outlines as reflected in the water were sharper than the actual outlines. Having sketched them he made a note to this effect on the paper, a note which was later translated into English by Jonathan Richardson the elder, who owned the drawing in the eighteenth century.[30]

Rubens's last landscape, perhaps one of the last pictures he ever painted was the *Sunset Landscape with a Shepherd* in the National Gallery (Fig. 10).[31] In the Ashmolean Museum in Oxford there is a small painting with a similar composition which has been said to be a preparatory sketch for it[32] – and indeed that is what I wrote in the exhibition catalogue. However, after prolonged study of it, I have come to the view expressed by Gregory Martin in the National Gallery catalogue of 1970,[33] that it is a free copy or pastiche after the London painting by a slightly later imitator of Rubens. Infra-red radiography of the London picture has revealed an inscription in the top right hand corner. It is discussed in the catalogue but I read it incorrectly.[34] It is an instruction to the panelmaker and reads, as Carl van de Velde pointed out, 'So veel hier aen'.

In the *Sunset Landscape* Rubens drew together two previously independent strands which run through his depiction of landscape in the 1630s, the actual landscape of Brabant and the ideal convention of pastoral landscape. The setting is unmistakeably Brabant, the familiar meadow landscape dotted with trees and criss-crossed by streams. In the foreground is a shepherd who plays his pipe in the evening sunlight. Like other late landscapes, it is richly atmospheric, recreating a late afternoon landscape in summer. It is an image of great simplicity. At the end of his life landscape had a profound personal resonance for Rubens. It became synonymous with Het Steen, his retreat from his hectic life in Antwerp and the pleasures of his life there, the pleasures of country life and family. There he developed a new type of landscape art – the study of atmosphere and natural phenomena – which was based on an unmediated response to what he saw and drew as he walked and rode over his estate.

NOTES

This paper arises from the exhibition *Making and Meaning: Rubens's Landscapes* held at the National Gallery, London from 16th October 1996 to 19th January 1997. The catalogue of the exhibition is referred to as [cat. exh.] London 1996 throughout. There was a small symposium preceding the opening of the exhibition during which many of the ideas discussed here were first raised. I am especially grateful to Frans Baudouin, Justus Müller-Hofstede, Luuk Pijl and Hans Vlieghe for their observations.

1. G. Gluck, *Die Landschaften von Peter Paul Rubens*, Vienna, 1945.

2. Discussed in [cat. exh.] London 1996 (see preliminary note), especially chapters 3–6.

3. The evolution of this painting has now been discussed in full by Luuk Pijl in The Burlington Magazine, CXL, 1998, pp. 660–667.

4. For Giulio Romano's treatment of this subject, see E.H. Gombrich *et al.*, *Giulio Romano*, Mantua, Palazzo Te, 1989, pp. 343–346, 348.

5. For Mancini on Bril, see [cat. exh.] London 1996 (see preliminary note), pp. 27, 110 (note 30).

6. See J.M. Muller, *Rubens: The Artist as Collector*, Princeton, 1989, p. 100 (cat. 1, no. 26).

7. G. Martin, *The Flemish School 1600–1900, National Gallery Catalogues*, London, 1970, pp. 208ff.

8. M. Rooses, *L'Œuvre de P.P. Rubens*, Antwerp, 1890, IV, no. 1196.

9. A. Balis, '"Fatto da un mio discepolo": Rubens's Studio Practices Reviewed', in T. Nakamura ed., *Rubens and his Workshop: The Flight of Lot and his Family from Sodom*, National Museum of Western Art, Tokyo, 1994, pp. 97–127, esp. p. 117.

10. [cat. exh.] London 1996 (see preliminary note), chapter 8.

11. W. Adler, *Landscapes*, Corpus Rubenianum Ludwig Burchard, XVII, 1, London–Oxford–New York, 1982, nos. 36, 29 and 30.

12. Adler 1982 (see note 11), no. 34. This painting, formerly in the collection of Gottfried Neuerburg, was recently sold at Christie's as "Attributed to Rubens".

13. Adler 1982 (see note 11), nos. 32 and 33; [cat. exh.] London 1996 (see preliminary note), nos. 37 and 38.

14. Adler 1982 (see note 11), nos. 53 and 55; [cat. exh.] London 1996 (see preliminary note), no. 45.

15. Adler 1982 (see note 11), no. 22; [cat. exh.] London 1996 (see preliminary note), no. 42.

16. London, National Gallery. R.A. d'Hulst and M. Vandenven, *Rubens. The Old Testament*, Corpus Rubenianum Ludwig Burchard, III, London–New York, 1989, no. 31, pp. 107–113.

17. [cat. exh.] London 1996 (see preliminary note), pp. 100–101.

18. The attribution to Rubens of this drawing was argued for by Mattias Winner in 'Zu Rubens' Eberjagd in Dresden (Landschaft oder Historienbild)', in *Peter Paul Rubens: Werk und Nachruhm*, Munich 1981, pp. 16–65.

19. For an account of Rubens's technique in his landscapes, see [cat. exh.] London 1996 (see preliminary note), chapter 8.

20. Adler 1982 (see note 11), no. 71; [cat. exh.] London 1996 (see preliminary note), no. 27.

21. Adler 1982 (see note 11), no. 52; [cat. exh.] London 1996 (see preliminary note), no. 47.

22. Adler 1982 (see note 11), no. 57; [cat. exh.] London 1996 (see preliminary note), no. 21.

23. Adler 1982 (see note 11), no. 19; [cat. exh.] London 1996 (see preliminary note), no. 20.

24. Adler 1982 (see note 11), no. 58; [cat. exh.] London 1996 (see preliminary note), no. 22.

25. Adler 1982 (see note 11), no. 49; [cat. exh.] London 1996 (see preliminary note), no. 41.

26. Adler 1982 (see note 11), no. 63; [cat. exh.] London 1996 (see preliminary note), no. 43.

27. See, for example, the painter's travelling box displayed in the Rijksmuseum (here reproduced on p. 242, fig. 7).

28. See C. Ruelens, 'La Vie de Rubens par Roger de Piles', *Rubens-Bulletijn*, II, 1883, pp. 157–175.

29. Adler 1982 (see note 11), no. 50; [cat. exh.] London 1996 (see preliminary note), no. 34. Now on long loan to the National Gallery of Art, Washington. Its recent cleaning has made the spontaneity of this sketch even more apparent.

30. Adler 1982 (see note 11), no. 77; [cat. exh.] London 1996 (see preliminary note), no. 32.

31. Adler 1982 (see note 11), no. 68; [cat. exh.] London 1996 (see preliminary note), no. 51.

32. Adler 1982 (see note 11), no. 68a; [cat. exh.] London 1996 (see preliminary note), no. 50.

33. Martin 1970 (see note 7), op. cit., pp. 144ff.

34. [Cat. exh.] London 1996 (see preliminary note), p. 121.

Rubens and Dead Colouring: Some Remarks on Two Unfinished Paintings

Nico Van Hout

Rubens's complex painting practices and the large output of his studio have prevented generations of artists and art historians from giving a coherent technical survey. Frequently, the basic literature, on which our expectations are based, has been contradicted by new scientific evidence, which from time to time reveals one of Rubens's habits.

The way a painter superimposes paint layers provides us with an insight to his approach as he developes it. Throughout the history of European painting, successful strategies established themselves in specific traditions of execution. As an heir both to Flemish and Venetian painting, Rubens confronted, improved and merged these traditions as no one did before. In Rubens's unfinished works we can catch a glimpse of the artist at work. Moreover, in studying his underpainting, which is called 'doodverf' or 'dead colouring' in technical terms, we get an insight in his capability or incapability of overcoming compositional and technical problems.

This article focusses on two contemporary and unfinished projects: *A Battle Scene* from the Henry IV series at the Rubenshuis and *The Miracles of St Benedict* in the Brussels museum. The two paintings have been examined with the naked eye, with a stereo-microscope and have been studied in infrared.[1] Taking into consideration that the two pictures have never been X-rayed and that no sampling was carried out, the present research must remain incomplete. Nevertheless, I hope that the following results can be corroborated by these and other techniques in the future.

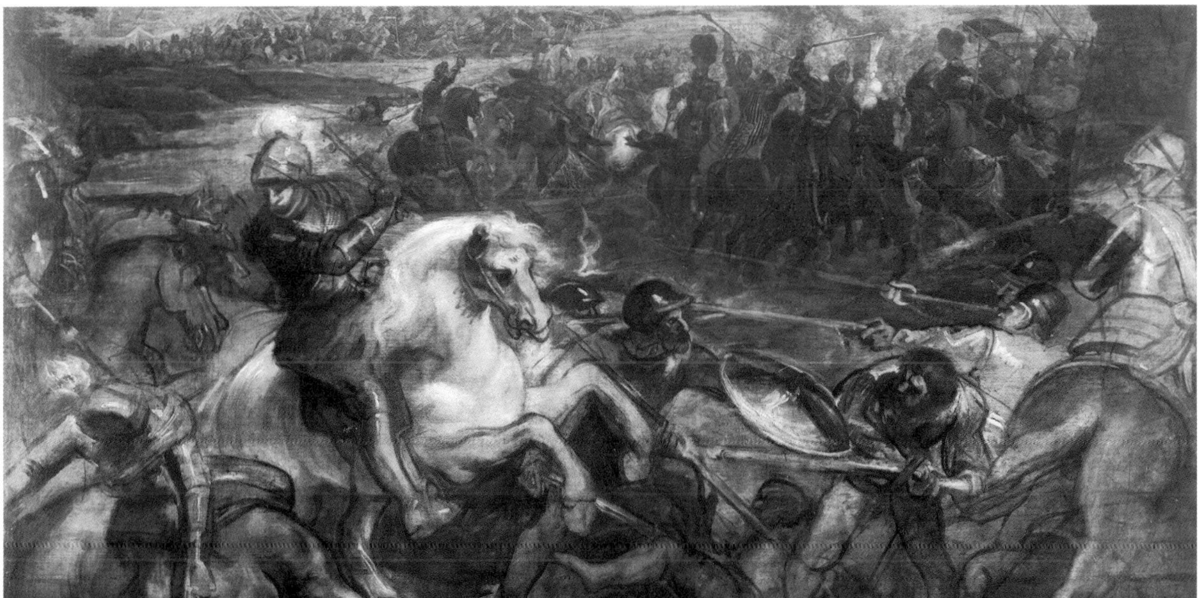

Fig. 1. Peter Paul Rubens, *A Battle of Henry IV of France*. Antwerp, Rubenshuis

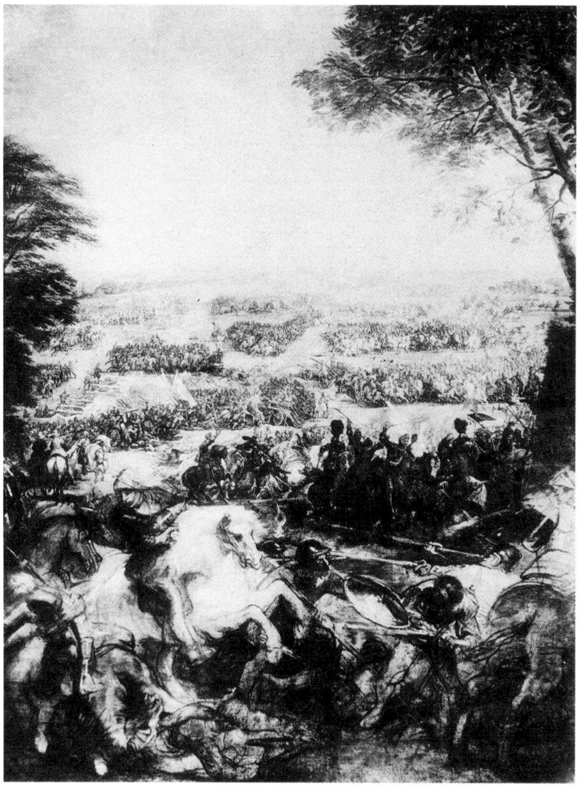

Fig. 2. Peter Paul Rubens, *A Battle of Henry IV of France* (before mutilation). Antwerp, Rubenshuis

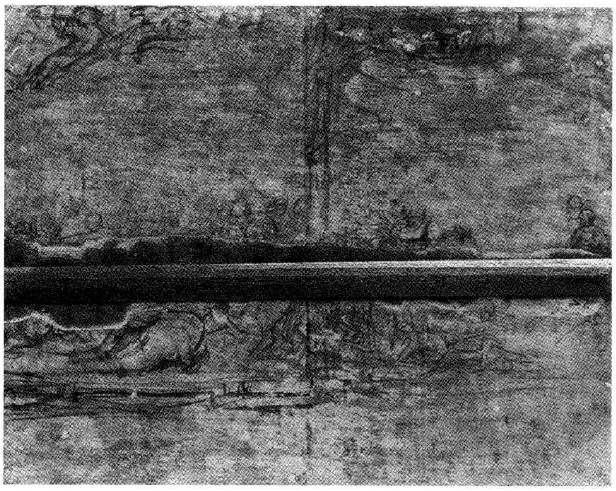

Fig. 3. Peter Paul Rubens, *Studies for a Battle of Horsemen*. Frankfurt, Städelsches Kunstinstitut

A Battle of Henry IV of France

Originally, the Antwerp canvas was twice as big as it is today (Figs. 1–2).[2] An old photograph, taken before it was cut down by the previous owner, shows that the original dimensions of the painting were equal to other battle scenes of the Henry cycle, now in Munich and Gothenburg.[3] The upper half of the canvas is still missing.

Like all paintings belonging to this cycle, the Rubenshuis fragment is painted on a canvas with a herring-bone weave, a textile pattern which is frequently found in Venetian painting, but also regularly appears North of the Alps.[4] Examination of the canvas with a stereo-microscope revealed a double structured ground, consisting of a smooth whitish ground layer, covered with a cool-grey imprimatura that includes larger white and red particles. The ground layers show fine-meshed crackle. This and the horizontal abrasions that show threads of the support, suggest frequent rolling and unrolling of the canvas. Besides damage to the upper paint layers, examination revealed many underlying scratches, which often permit the white ground layer to appear on the surface. Most likely, these marks resulted from spreading the grey imprimatura with a priming knife.[5]

Relatively few preparatory works for the Henry cycle are preserved and only one oil sketch has been connected with the Rubenshuis Battle Scene. Instead of using a new panel, Rubens began to work out the composition on the reverse of another sketch, namely, the Virgin adored by Saints, now in Frankfurt (Fig. 3)[6]

According to Held, the two compositions, which are dealt with side by side, probably show two alternatives for one painting, as they both prominently show the fallen horse.[7] Three features in the right scene recur in the Rubenshuis picture: the fallen horse in the left foreground, the monarch's bent arm and the horseman on the right. Obviously, Rubens was not pleased with the compositional solutions he had formulated in the Frankfurt sketches, for, as we will see, he entrusted the trial-and-error to the final support. We do not know why in this case Rubens postponed decisions, losing time in starting his canvas with a rudimentary concept, although it should be noted that this practice is very similar to the painting method employed by Titian, an artist in whom Rubens showed a renewed interest in the 1630's.

Before Rubens tried out some new ideas on the final supports, the Antwerp canvas (like the Munich and Gothenburg ones) was passed on

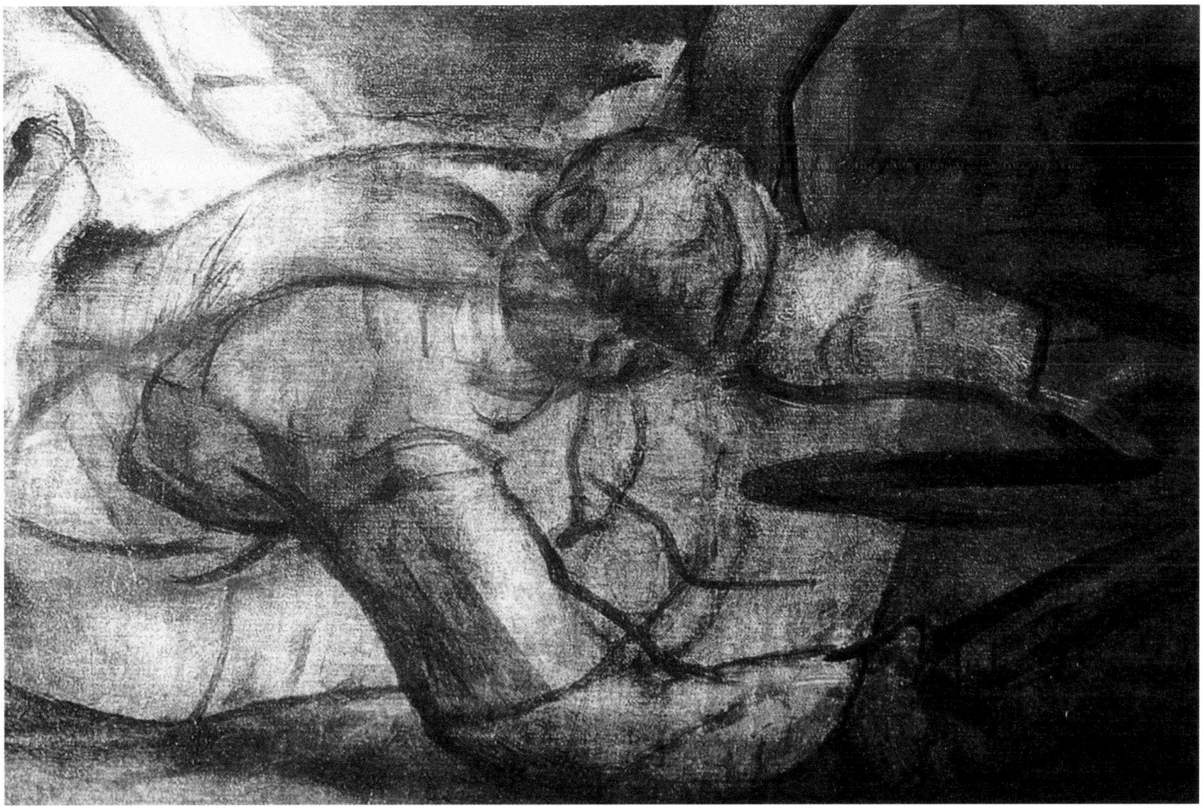

Fig. 4. Peter Paul Rubens, *A Battle of Henry IV of France* (detail). Antwerp, Rubenshuis

to the Brussels-based artist Pieter Snayers.[8] Snayers was hired to provide the background of each of Henry's battles with the right topography. Research with IRR confirms that in all three of the battle scenes Snayers's work preceded Rubens's 'dead colouring'. The sharp and irregular form of Snayers's part suggests that Rubens somehow defined his colleague's territory.

Long, curved lines in grey or black paint underly the brown contours of the fallen horse and the victim in the lower left of the Antwerp painting (Fig. 4). They belong to the artist's earliest lay out on the final canvas. Other dark lines, which play no part in the actual composition, run through the horse to the right. Bowed lines underneath the horse to the right partly seem to merge with superimposed strokes that outline the animal. The flowing curved lines with which Rubens began to indicate volumes, are not unlike the patterns shown in some of his drawings on paper, in which convincing shapes are strengthened and drawn over first ideas that became irrelevant.[9] Due to technical limitations, IRR did not yield better insight in Rubens's initial play with forms. Clearly, the readability of Rubens's earliest layout is hampered by the painting process itself, in that information is diluted by subsequent paint-layers.

Indeed, the artist continued the 'dead colouring' of his Battle scene by washing darker or more distant parts and by brushing-in some areas, opposite to his contours, with a lighter colour. This trick allowed him to give the scene more depth. On the other hand, several areas, like the second soldier to the right, the victim in the lower left and several horsetails, were kept in reserve. The shape to the right, which Snayers carefully avoided, was partly filled with a grey wash, blocking in a horseman. In some of the contours, traces of a blue-green wash have also been detected, as well as a few contour lines, such as the initial right outline of one of the soldier's legs, were painted in red colour.

The shadows and reflections of the men's armour were immediately brushed upon the earlier lay-out (Fig. 5). As such, the King's body is largely sketched over the background (some banners, painted by Snayers, still show through the monarch's helmet and armour). Rubens

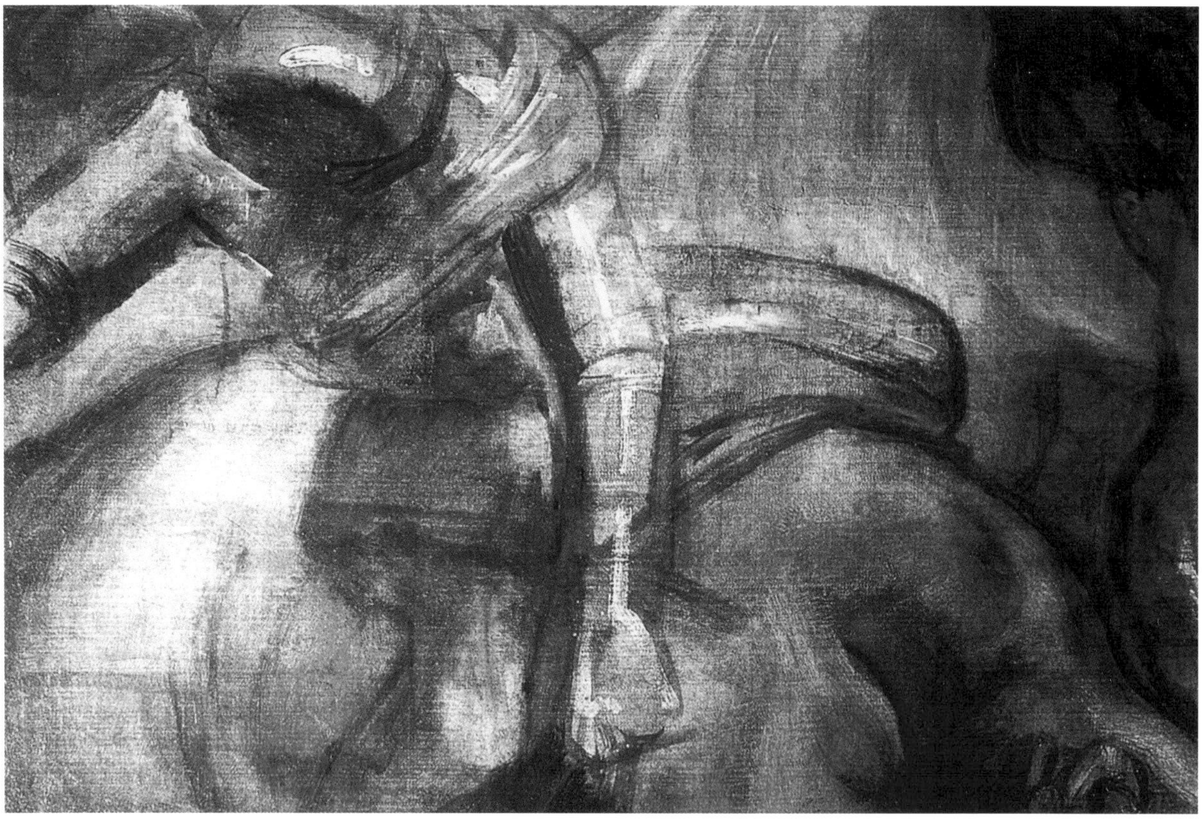

Fig. 5. Peter Paul Rubens, *A Battle of Henry IV of France* (detail). Antwerp, Rubenshuis

underpainted the faces and hands of his figures with vigorous brushstrokes. Some dark brown shadows were applied in a wet vermillion or ochre colour, while other faces consist of ochre highlights, brushed into a dark underlayer.

The King's horse consists of thick white brushwork, turning it into the focal-point of his composition. The filling up with white paint could not prevent the darker Snayers part from shining through in the horse's head, which results in a cooler tone (Fig. 6).

At the same time, Rubens unified the rest of Snayers's intervention with his own. The border zone was succesfully camouflaged with opaque greyish-ochre colours, suggesting smoke. Not all the overpainting, however, was done on Rubens's initiative. The overpainted horsemen to the left of the monarch's head turned out to be the result of unscrupulous retouching in recent times. Comparison of the canvas with the above mentioned old photograph, which was taken before the painting was cut down, shows that the group was still entirely uncovered at this time (Fig. 7).

We can only guess how some limbs were to fit into the battle scene when finished. Particularly problematic is the soldier in the middle foreground, bearing a shield in one hand, grabbing a sword with the other and holding a lance with a third hand (Fig. 6).

Apparently, Rubens had not yet decided which weapon he would provide the man with. The leg-like shape growing in the belly of the King's horse is another puzzling feature. This outline is not unlike a horse's leg and back. It is tempting to explain it by imagining that Rubens shifted the king's horse to the left. Nevertheless, close examination of the area to the right of the present horse did not yield any clue that could point in this direction.

In my opinion, work on the Rubenshuis Battle Scene was interrupted during a specific moment in the 'dead colouring', which Anthony Van Dyck called 'Maniera sbozzata' and explained as 'a forming process; because it is supposed to give the entire work its final form.'[10] The Munich and Gothenburg battle scenes do not share the monochrome character (nor the hesitating design) with the Antwerp

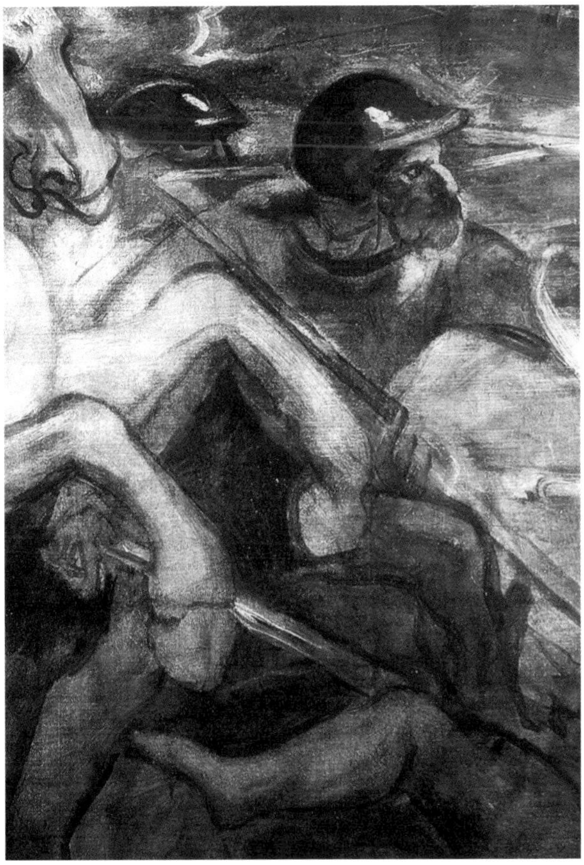

Fig. 6. Peter Paul Rubens, *A Battle of Henry IV of France* (detail). Antwerp, Rubenshuis

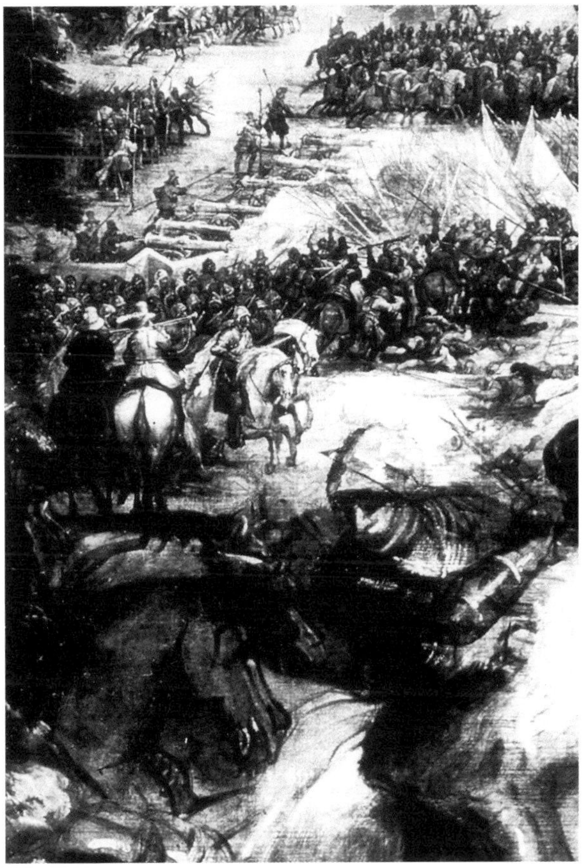

Fig. 7. Peter Paul Rubens, *A Battle of Henry IV of France* (detail; before mutilation). Antwerp, Rubenshuis

piece. On the contrary, the modelling of these paintings, in which Henry IV is more envolved in strategic planning than in dynamic action, was begun in bright colours, applied directly to the grey priming.

The Miracles of St Benedict

Despite the fact that it was copied by Eugène Delacroix and praised in letters by Paul Claudel, Rubens's unfinished *Miracles of St Benedict* in the Brussels Museum (Fig. 8) received surprisingly little attention up to the present, at least from the technical point of view.[11]

The way in which the painting's support was extended, gives reason to believe that *The Miracles of St Benedict* was not painted in one sequence (Fig. 9). The support consists of five strips of canvas, which can clearly be detected in raking light. Initially, Rubens began to paint on the largest piece of textile, measuring approximately 157 x 194 centimetres. This canvas (A) is tinted with a thin greyish imprimatura that allows the colour of the fabric to shine through.

In a second stage, Rubens added two more strips, one to the left (B), between nine and eleven centimetres wide, and one to the right (C), about thirty centimetres wide. Raking light makes clear that the threads of the textile in strip C run in a different direction than those in canvas A. Besides this feature, the right side of this strip shows pronounced cusping. Originally, a band several centimetres wide on the right side of strip C was not primed.

Strips B and C are covered with a thicker and cooler grey imprimatura, containing coarse white pigment particles. This priming clearly overlaps that of the initial canvas. The imprimatura of strip C partly covers a black chalk sketch of a column pediment, which Rubens drew in the lower right edge of canvas A (Fig. 14).

In the third stage, Rubens widened his composition by twenty-three to twenty-four centimetres on the right side. This enlargement was done with two strips of canvas, D and D'. Overlapping the imprimatura of strip C, the

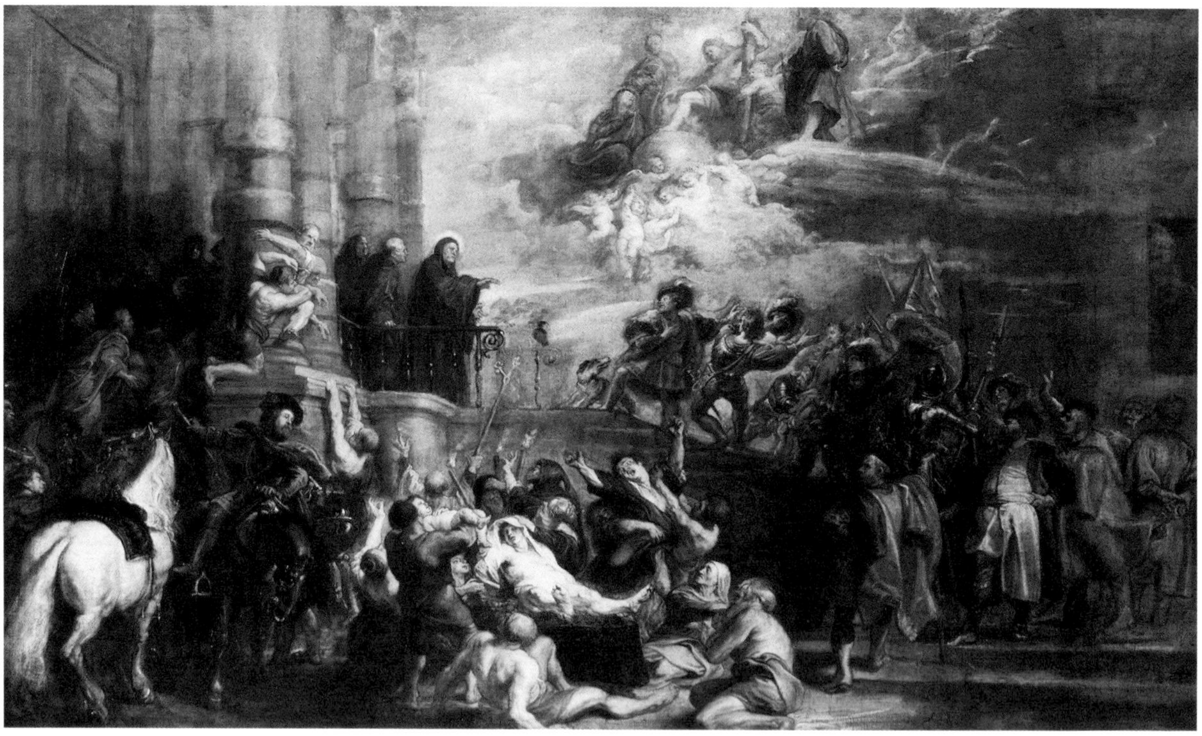

Fig. 8. Peter Paul Rubens, *The Miracles of St Benedict*. Brussels, Royal Museums of Fine Arts of Belgium

priming layer on D and D' is equally thick, but has a warmer and lighter tone. During the priming of strip D, a surplus of paint was scraped off onto strip C.

The part of the composition painted by Rubens upon canvas A seems to be heavily retouched by the master himself. At least some of this reworking came after the support was

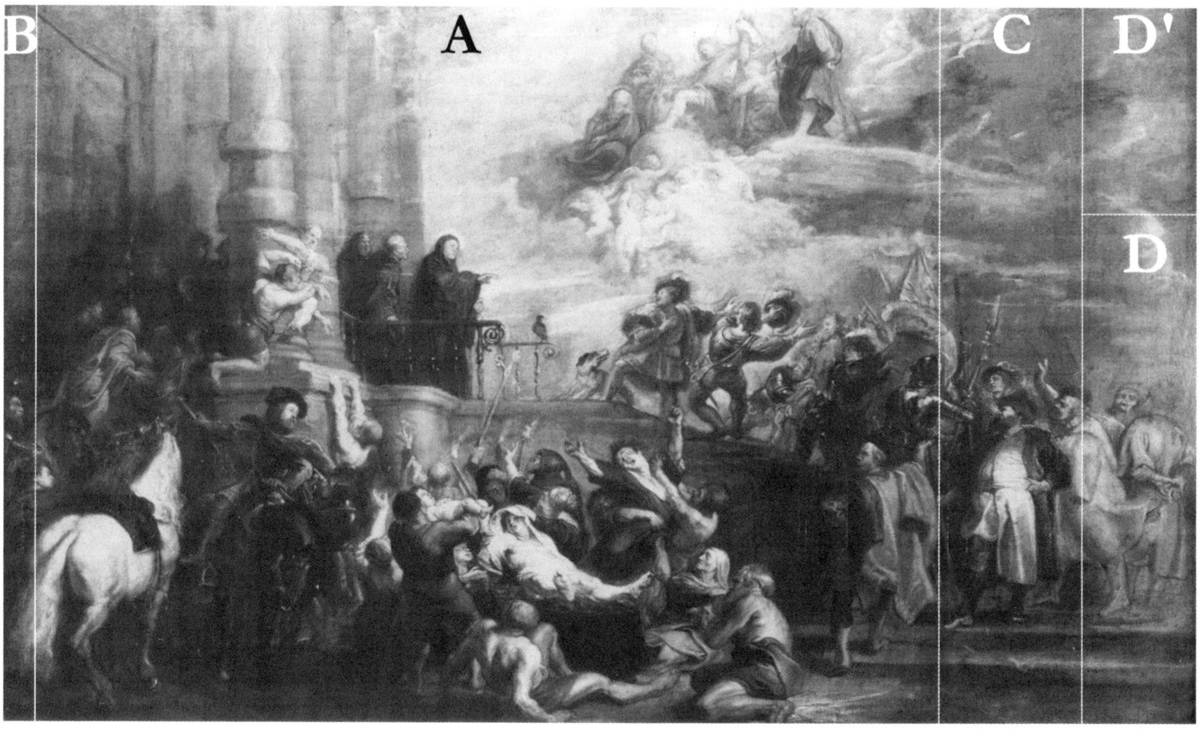

Fig. 9. Peter Paul Rubens, *The Miracles of St Benedict* (construction scheme), Brussels, Royal Museums of Fine Arts of Belgium

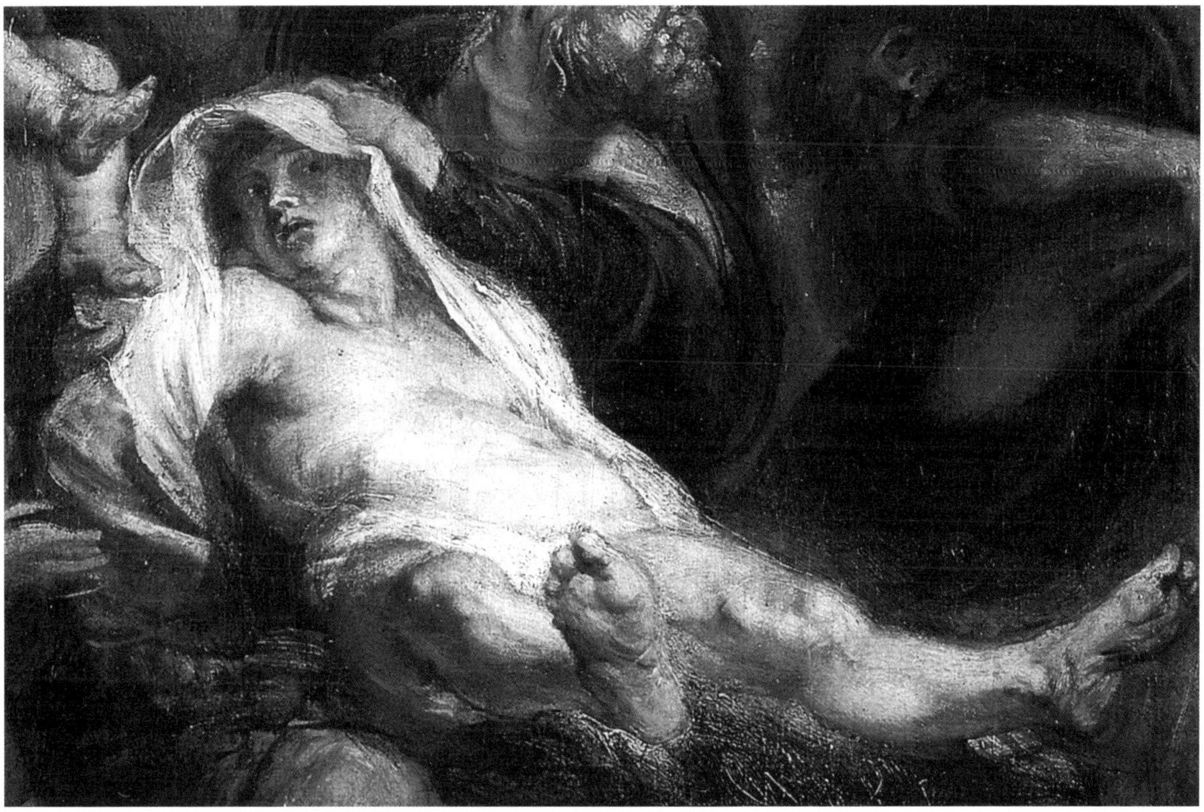

Fig. 10. Peter Paul Rubens, *The Miracles of St Benedict* (detail), Brussels, Royal Museums of Fine Arts of Belgium

extended with strips B and C, for a good deal of it runs over the seam between A and C.

Several areas of the original painted composition were painted out. This was done to some angels below Christ, to the flying bird at the right of the Saint, and to the cross pointed in its direction. While giving the sky its hazy appearance, Rubens repositioned the figure of St Paul and lowered the left arm of the deceiver.

The group of invalids on the foreground were retouched as well. The pale-coloured naked man received orange accents. Part of his white cloth was changed into shadowed carnation (Fig. 10). The lower part of this cloth and the crimson dress of the blond woman was overpainted with black. The area to the right of this central group was covered with a strong shadow, to create more space between the invalids and the Ostrogoths. Originally, this spot contained a man gesturing with his hand, as apparent in the infrared reflectogram (Fig. 11).

The infrared photograph of the white horse to the left shows that the position of the animal was changed during the execution of the

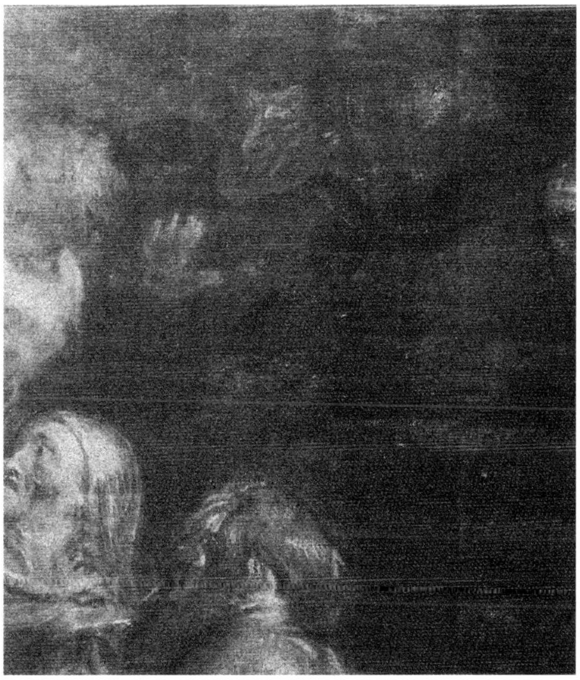

Fig. 11. Peter Paul Rubens, *The Miracles of St Benedict* (infrared reflectogram), Brussels, Royal Museums of Fine Arts of Belgium

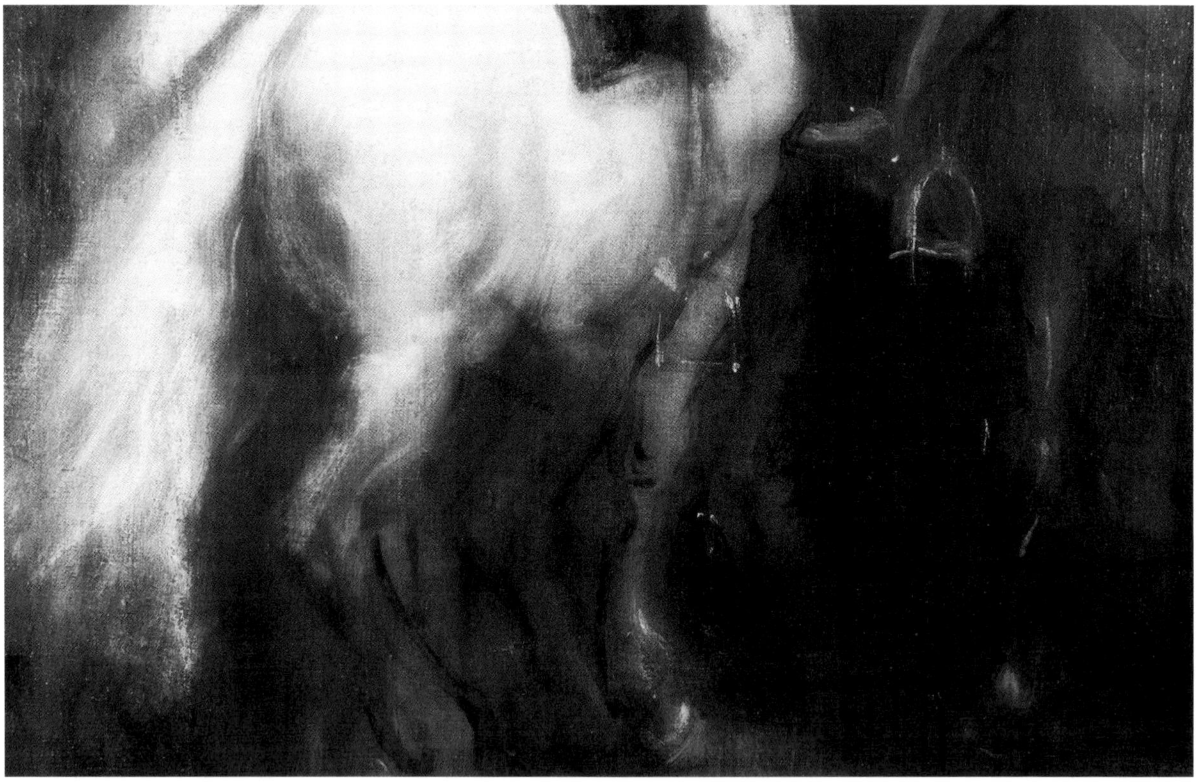

Fig. 12. Peter Paul Rubens, *The Miracles of St Benedict* (infrared photograph), Brussels, Royal Museums of Fine Arts of Belgium

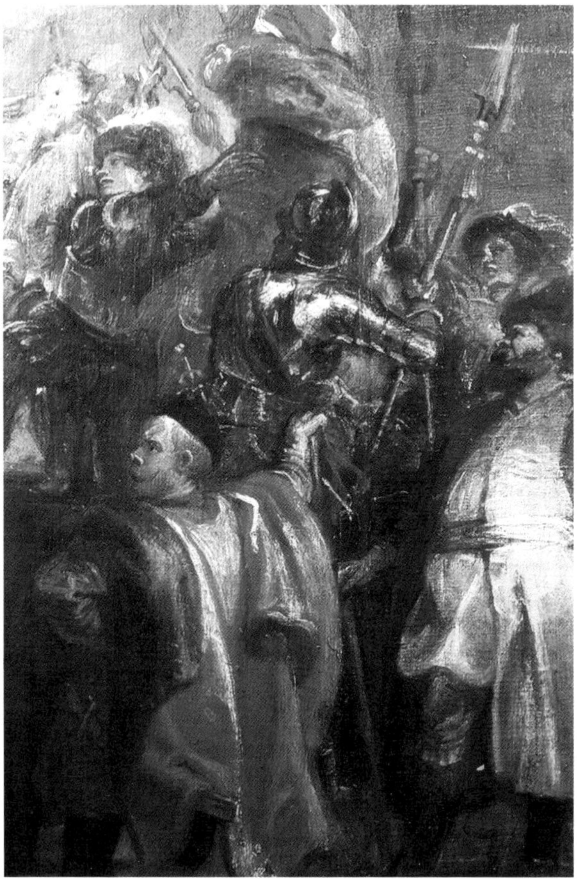

work. It was originally seen more from the back and was then turned two-quarters so as to occupy the extra space provided by strip B (Fig. 12).

The right side of Rubens's first composition was closed off with the man in a red garb, leaning on a large stick (Fig. 13). At first, this repoussoir-figure seems to have held a banner instead. His pose became less convincing, however, after Rubens had overpainted part of the red flag with an armoured knight.

It is hard to explain the presence of some black chalk sketches on the lower right edge of canvas A (Fig. 14), representing column pediments. The question is whether or not these sketches relate to the present composition, and if not, to which other project.

It has long been observed that parts of the painting are left unfinished.[12] These include the extensions to the right, the sacred group in

Fig. 13. Peter Paul Rubens, *The Miracles of St Benedict* (detail). Brussels, Royal Museums of Fine Arts of Belgium

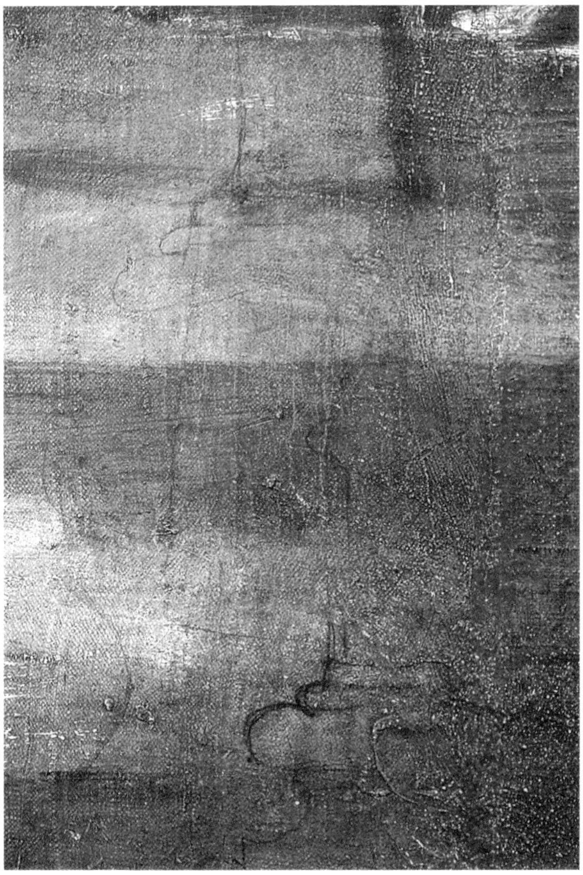

Fig. 14. Peter Paul Rubens, *The Miracles of St Benedict* (detail). Brussels, Royal Museums of Fine Arts of Belgium

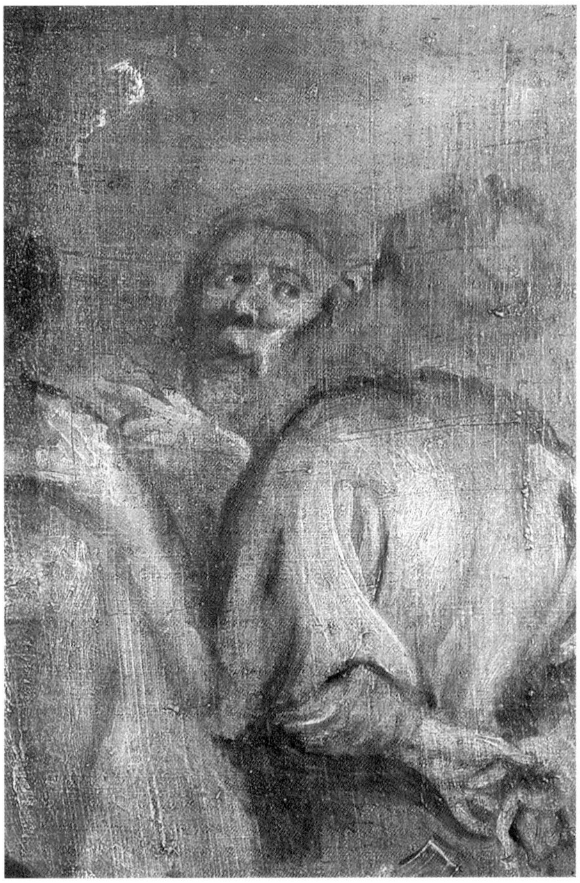

Fig. 15. Peter Paul Rubens, *The Miracles of St Benedict* (detail). Brussels, Royal Museums of Fine Arts of Belgium

the sky and, above all, the portico to the left. However, when closely examined, even more developed areas like the middle foreground appear less finished than expected (Fig. 10). Despite the fact that this part shows more saturated colours, it still lacks the joining of contours. Unlike the chiaroscuro *dead colouring* of the Rubenshuis canvas, the least finished areas on the Brussels painting are based on pale local colours, which fill very fine brown or black contour lines (Fig. 15). Forms are sparingly modelled in subdued tones and painted wet-in-wet. The *dead colouring* on the Brussels painting seems to form part of another tradition: it is more closely related to the underpainting of the Henry IV *Battle Scenes* in Munich and Gothenburg. Apparently, Rubens made use of two coexisting traditions in *dead colouring* at the same time.

We are all familiar with support-extensions in Rubens's landscapes or in some of his other works.[13] It is uncertain, however, whether enlargements of this kind are compatible with the commission of a religious painting in seventeenth-century Flanders. Therefore, I am convinced that the enlargements of the support and the retouching are the result of a more complex genesis than hitherto has been suggested for the Brussels picture. Canvas A, for example, might have been painted for another destination, before the composition was recycled, enlarged and retouched to match the demands of the new (Affligem) patrons.

For the time being, this must remain speculative. This article can only add some question marks to the discussion. At present, we can only guess why the artist wanted to change his square composition into a Venetian panorama.

NOTES

The author is indebted to Arnout Balis, Ben Van Beneden and Adri Verburg for their comments and suggestions.

1. Infrared research on the two paintings was carried out with a Silicium CCD focal array camera and a Nikon F3 Photo-camera, using Kodak infrared high speed film. In both systems, a Kodak Wratten 87C filter was used.

2. Antwerp, Rubenshuis, inv. S.30, canvas, mounted on hardboard, 174 x 260 cm. Until 1956, this canvas formed part of the Neuerburg collection, Hamburg. It passed through the Bührle collection, Zürich, before it was acquired for the Rubenshuis. The original measurements were 350 x 260 cm. The painting was studied with the naked eye, with a stereomicroscope and with infrared reflectography. The most comprehensive study on the Henry IV series has been published by Ingrid Jost ('Bemerkungen zur Heinrichsgalerie des P.P. Rubens', *Nederlands Kunsthistorisch Jaarboek*, 1964, pp. 175–219), mainly focussing on the painting of the King's *Triumph* in the Uffizi, Florence (inv. 1899, no. 729).

3. Munich, Bayerische Staatsgemäldesammlungen, inv. 952, canvas, 340 x 273 cm, and Gothenburg, Konstmuseum, inv. 1380, canvas, 354 x 273 cm.

4. Maarten De Vos, for examle, painted his *Adoration of the Magi* in Valenciennes on canvas with a herring-bone weave and the same textile-pattern can also be discerned in Otto Van Veen's *Last Supper* in Antwerp Cathedral.

5. A priming knife, measuring about thirty centimetres, is reproduced in De Mayerne's treatise: see J.A. Van de Graaf, *Het De Mayerne manuscript als bron voor de schilderkunst van de barok*, Mijdrecht, 1958, p. 138, no. 6, ill., pp. 16–17.

6. Frankfurt, Städelsches Kunstinstitut, inv. 464; Julius S. Held, *The Oil Sketches of Peter Paul Rubens*, Princeton, 1980, pp. 135–136, cat. 89, pl. 91.

7. J. Müller Hofstede ('Rubens' erste Entwürfe für den Heinrichs-Zyklus', *Pantheon*, XXVII, 1969, 1, pp. 459–463) related the left scene of the sketch to the Uffizi *Battle of Ivry*, although its proportion better suits the Rubenshuis picture than it suits the oblong battle scene in Florence.

8. We only can speculate on the reasons for this collaboration. One possible answer could be that during the moment of creation Rubens was deeply involved in diplomatic missions. In this case, distribution of work could simply have meant a time-saving factor. A more plausible answer could be that the artist may have been inclined to give the topographical part to a capable collaborator. Rubens may have been less interested in reproducing specific locations than in rendering the monarch's deeds.

9. See, for example, the *Battle Scene* drawing in the Courtauld Institute, London, reproduced in [A. Seilern], *Flemish Paintings and Drawings at 56 Princes gate, London SW7*, London, 1969, pp. 103–104, no. 65, pls. CXXV–CXXVI.

10. See the 'commonplace book' of Thomas Marshall (1621–1685) fol. 11r and 12v, Bodleian Library, Oxford, Summary Catalogue, no. 8661, published by Horst Vey in 'Anton Van Dijck über Maltechnik', *Bulletin des Musées Royaux des Beaux-Arts de Belgique*, X, 1960, pp. 193–201. Ernst Van de Wetering (in 'De jonge Rembrandt aan het werk. Materiaalgebruik en schildertechniek van Rembrandt in het begin van zijn Leidse periode', *Oud Holland*, XCI, 1977, pp. 27–60, p. 43) has put forward the idea that the 'maniera sbozzata' only applies to monochrome undermodelling. As Van de Wetering makes clear, this is the case within Rembrandt's system of layering. However, Rembrandt's dead colouring cannot be regarded as common practice. According to Van Dyck, the mode of underpainting depends upon the artist's ingenuity. Unlike Rembrandt's underpainting, Van Dyck's own 'maniera sbozzata' is based upon paint–layering, similar to watercolour technique, in which the application of local colours is undertaken before the rendering of 'rilievo'.

11. Brussels, Royal Museums of Fine Arts of Belgium, inv. 4063, canvas, 164 x 262 cm. The most thorough study on the picture has been published by H. Vlieghe, *Saints*, Corpus Rubenianum Ludwig Burchard, VIII, I, Brussels–London–New York, 1972–1973, pp. 110–115, no. 73, Fig. 125. It is very unlikely that Rubens painted this specific subject just for his own pleasure. As Vlieghe pointed out, the only possible commissioner or buyer is the Benedictine abbey of Affligem near Brussels, for the abbey's patron Saints, SS. Peter and Paul, are floating above the miraculous events. Unfortunately, the Affligem connection is problematic due to the fact that the painting was never sold during Rubens's life-time, as Hélène Fourment presented it to Gaspar De Crayer in 1641. The painting was later certainly acquired by the religious order, for its presence at Affligem is proved by two late eighteenth-century documents. Vlieghe dates the picture in the very early 1630's.

12. In a letter dated October 14th, 1777, Beda Regaus, provost of Affligem, described the painting as 'eene schetse'; six years earlier, J.F.M. Michel described the picture as 'esquisse' (Vlieghe, *Saints*, p. 113). In older documents, 'schetse' or 'esquisse' often seem to have been used to indicate both the preparatory work for a painting on a separate support, as well as the beginning of a painting itself ('doodverf' - 'ébauche'), although contemporary specialized dictionaries clearly make this distinction (see for instance A.L. Millin, *Dictionnaire des Beaux-Arts*, Paris, 1806, I, pp. 474–475).

13. For extensions in Rubens's landscapes, see G. Martin, 'Two closely related landscapes by Rubens', *The Burlington Magazine*, CVIII, 1966, pp. 180–184; R. Bruce-Gordon, 'Rubens's "Landscape by Moonlight": technical examination', *The Burlington Magazine*, CXXX, 1988, pp. 591–596. A good survey is provided by C. Brown and A. Reeves, 'The Structure of Rubens's Landscapes', in C. Brown, [cat. exh.] *Making and Meaning. Rubens's Landscapes*, London, 1997, pp. 116–121. For other cases of extensions, see K. Renger, 'Anstückungen bei Rubens', *Die Malerei Antwerpens: Gattungen - Meister - Wirkungen*, Vienna, 1993, pp. 157–160 and 'Rubens-stücke. Die Anstückungen von Münchner "Silen" und "Schäferszene"', *Wallraf-Richartz-Jahrbuch*, LV, Festschrift für Prof. Dr. Justus Müller Hofstede, Cologne, 1994, pp. 171–184.

ISBN 2-503-50731-X
9 782503 507316